Prehistoric Britain

BLACKWELL STUDIES IN GLOBAL ARCHAEOLOGY

Series Editors: Lynn Meskell and Rosemary A. Joyce

Blackwell Studies in Global Archaeology is a series of contemporary texts, each carefully designed to meet the needs of archaeology instructors and students seeking volumes that treat key regional and thematic areas of archaeological study. Each volume in the series, compiled by its own editor, includes 12–15 newly commissioned articles by top scholars within the volume's thematic, regional, or temporal area of focus.

What sets the *Blackwell Studies in Global Archaeology* apart from other available texts is that their approach is accessible, yet does not sacrifice theoretical sophistication. The series editors are committed to the idea that usable teaching texts need not lack ambition. To the contrary, the *Blackwell Studies in Global Archaeology* aim to immerse readers in fundamental archaeological ideas and concepts, but also to illuminate more advanced concepts, thereby exposing readers to some of the most exciting contemporary developments in the field. Inasmuch, these volumes are designed not only as classic texts, but as guides to the vital and exciting nature of archaeology as a discipline.

Prehistoric Britain

Edited by

Joshua Pollard

Blackwell
Publishing

BLACKWELL PUBLISHING
350 Main Street, Malden, MA 02148–5020, USA
9600 Garsington Road, Oxford OX4 2DQ, UK

The right of Joshua Pollard to be identified as the author of the editorial material in this work has been asserted in accordance with the UK Copyright, Designs, and Patents Act 1988.

Designations used by companies to distinguish their products are often claimed as trademarks. All brand names and product names used in this book are trade names, service marks, trademarks, or registered trademarks of their respective owners. The publisher is not associated with any product or vendor mentioned in this book.

This publication is designed to provide accurate and authoritative information in regard to the subject matter covered. It is sold on the understanding that the publisher is not engaged in rendering professional services. If professional advice or other expert assistance is required, the services of a competent professional should be sought.

First published 2008 by Blackwell Publishing Ltd

1   2008

Library of Congress Cataloging-in-Publication Data

Prehistoric Britain / edited by Joshua Pollard.
        p. cm — (Blackwell studies in global archaeology; 11)
    Includes bibliographical references and index.
    ISBN 978-1-4051-2545-1 (hardcover : alk. paper)—ISBN 978-1-4051-2546-8
(pbk. : alk. paper)   1. Antiquities, Prehistoric—Great Britain.   2. Prehistoric peoples—
Great Britain.   3. Great Britain—Antiquities.   I. Pollard, Joshua.

    GN805.P67 2008
    936.1—dc22

                                                                2008001977

A catalogue record for this title is available from the British Library.

Set in 10 on 12.5 pt Plantin
by SNP Best-set Typesetter Ltd., Hong Kong
Printed and bound in Singapore
by Utopia Press Pte Ltd

The publisher's policy is to use permanent paper from mills that operate a sustainable forestry policy, and which has been manufactured from pulp processed using acid-free and elementary chlorine-free practices. Furthermore, the publisher ensures that the text paper and cover board used have met acceptable environmental accreditation standards.

For further information on
Blackwell Publishing, visit our website at
www.blackwellpublishing.com

Contents

Figures

Tables

Notes on Contributors

Joanna Brück completed her PhD at the University of Cambridge and is a Senior Lecturer at University College Dublin. Her research focuses on British Bronze Age settlement and ritual practice, although she has also published on aspects of archaeological theory, including phenomenology. She is editor of *PAST*, the newsletter of the Prehistoric Society, and is also a director of the Discovery Programme in Dublin. She helps to run the Bronze Age Forum, which organizes biannual conferences on the Bronze Age of Britain and Ireland, and is co-director of the Shovel Down Project, a collaborative research project investigating the origins and social implications of prehistoric land enclosure on Dartmoor. Recent publications include papers on Bronze Age exchange in the *European Journal of Archaeology*, and on the links between archaeology, colonialism and travel writing in the *Journal of Social Archaeology*.

Chantal Conneller is a Lecturer in Archaeology at the School of Arts, Histories and Cultures, University of Manchester. She undertook her BA and PhD at the University of Cambridge and held a postdoctoral research fellowship at Queens' College, Cambridge. She has worked at various periods for the Cambridge Archaeological Unit, and as a lithic analyst, and was a Lecturer in Prehistoric Archaeology at the University of Wales, Bangor. She specializes in the European Upper Palaeolithic and Mesolithic. Ongoing projects include work on the now drowned North Sea Plain and the adjacent lands; and mortuary practices in the British Mesolithic. She is particularly interested in technology, human bodies, animals and stone. She is conducting excavations at the Final Palaeolithic site of Rookery Farm, Cambridgeshire, and on Mesolithic sites in the Vale of Pickering, North Yorkshire.

Vicki Cummings is a Lecturer in Archaeology at the University of Central Lancashire. Her research focuses on the Mesolithic and Neolithic of Britain and Ireland, with a particular focus on the monuments of the Irish Sea zone, landscapes and the transition period. Recent publications include *From Cairn to Cemetery*, on excavations in Scotland (with Chris Fowler, 2007); *Going Over* (coedited with Alasdair Whittle, 2007); and *Prehistoric Journeys* (coedited with Robert Johnston, 2007). She is currently running an excavation project with Gary Robinson looking at the prehistory of Kintyre.

David Field has worked for almost 20 years on the archaeological landscapes of central southern England including on many of the major chalkland sites of Wessex, first for the Royal Commission on the Historical Monuments of England, and more recently as an Archaeological Investigator for English Heritage. He has been involved in major multi-period landscape analyses of the Salisbury Plain Training Area and the Marlborough Downs and elsewhere, as well as in survey and investigation of Neolithic flint mines and stone quarries. He takes a special interest in Neolithic and Bronze Age landscapes, particularly the human impact that agriculture, "Celtic" fields, burial and ritual monuments and prehistoric raw material extraction sites had on the land.

Melanie Giles is a Lecturer in Archaeology at the School of Arts, Histories and Cultures, University of Manchester. Her main research interests are the Iron Age of Britain, focusing on themes of identity, funerary practice, material culture and Celtic art, as well as landscape studies. She is also Programme Director of the MA in Archaeological Field Practice, with a particular interest in the relationship between fieldwork and interpretation, and the creative representation of the past.

Robert Johnston completed a PhD at the University of Newcastle on the topic of land tenure and Bronze Age field systems in Britain. He has since taught at the University of Wales, Bangor, and is currently a Lecturer in Landscape Archaeology at the University of Sheffield. He has published articles and edited books on various aspects of landscape archaeology and the later prehistoric settlement of upland Britain. His current research involves field projects in north Wales and south-west England, and is focused upon the constitution of environmental knowledge, later prehistoric land enclosure in north-west Europe, and the cultural perception of upland landscapes.

Andrew Jones is a Lecturer in Archaeology at the University of Southampton. He has previously held a fellowship at the McDonald Institute for Archaeological Research, Cambridge, and a lectureship at University College Dublin. He is the author of *Archaeological Theory and Scientific Practice* (2002) and *Memory and Material Culture: tracing the past in prehistoric Europe* (2007), and editor of *Colouring the Past* (with G. Macgregor, 2002) and *Prehistoric Europe* (2008).

Lesley McFadyen is a Lecturer in Prehistory at the University of Leicester. In 2007 she became a Leverhulme Early Career Fellow on Archaeological Architectures, exploring the character of accounts of architecture within prehistory, historical archaeology and architectural history. She is currently writing a book entitled *Between Material Culture, Architecture and Landscape: issues of scale in prehistory*.

Jacqui Mulville is a senior Lecturer in Bioarchaeology at Cardiff University. She has undertaken extensive work on later prehistoric animal bone assemblages from sites across the British Isles, and fieldwork projects in the Western Isles of Scotland and the Isles of Scilly.

Stuart Needham recently retired as Curator of British Prehistory at the British Museum. He has published extensively on the Bronze Age metalwork of Britain and the Continent. Among other projects, he is currently preparing for publication the final reports on the important Neolithic and Late Bronze Age Thames-side settlement at Runnymede Bridge. Recent publications include *The Ringlemere Cup: precious cups and the beginning of the Channel Bronze Age* (with K. Parfitt and G. Varndell, 2006).

Paul Pettitt is a Senior Lecturer in Palaeolithic Archaeology at the University of Sheffield. After a spell as a field archaeologist he read Ancient History and Archaeology at the University of Birmingham and took an MA in Archaeology at the Institute of Archaeology, University College London. His doctoral research at Cambridge focused on the Middle Palaeolithic lithic technology of south-west France and what this revealed about Neanderthal behaviour. From 1995 to 2001 he was Senior Archaeologist at the Radiocarbon Accelerator Unit, University of Oxford, and was Douglas Price Junior Research Fellow and Research Fellow and Tutor in Archaeology and Anthropology at Keble College, Oxford. His research interests focus on Middle and Upper Palaeolithic Europe, the origin of modern humans and particularly Neanderthal mortuary activity, Palaeolithic art and the British Late Upper Palaeolithic.

Joshua Pollard is a Senior Lecturer in the Department of Archaeology and Anthropology, University of Bristol. He completed his PhD at the University of Wales, Cardiff, and has worked for the Cambridge Archaeological Unit and at the Universities of Newcastle, Queen's (Belfast) and Wales (Newport). Much of his research is focused on the British and north-west European Neolithic. The latter has included work on depositional practices, materiality, aspects of monumentality, cultural perceptions of the environment and approaches to the study of Neolithic settlement and routine. He is currently involved in fieldwork in the Avebury and Stonehenge landscapes.

Rick Schulting is a Lecturer in Scientific and Prehistoric Archaeology at the University of Oxford. Over the past decade, he has undertaken research into various aspects of the Mesolithic and Neolithic in western Europe. A major focus has been investigating the nature of coastal Mesolithic economies through stable isotope analysis, and assessing the evidence for dietary change at the transition to the Neolithic. Related to this is an interest in AMS-dating of human remains, with the goal of securely identifying Mesolithic individuals as a precursor to further dietary and mortuary analysis; acquiring a better understanding of the range of contemporary burial practices in the Neolithic; and refining the chronologies of the two periods. Another ongoing interest lies in understanding the role(s) of interpersonal violence in prehistoric societies. Various papers on these subjects have appeared in academic journals.

Julian Thomas is Professor of Archaeology at the University of Manchester. He was educated at the Universities of Bradford and Sheffield. His doctoral research was concerned with social and economic change in the Neolithic of Wessex and the Upper Thames Valley. He was a Lecturer in Archaeology at the University of Wales, Lampeter, and also taught at Southampton University. His main research interests are concerned with the Neolithic period in Britain and north-west Europe, and with the theory and philosophy of archaeology. Between 1994 and 2002 he directed excavations on a series of prehistoric monuments in Dumfries and Galloway, and he is currently a co-director of the Stonehenge Riverside Project. Publications include *Understanding the Neolithic* (1999), *Archaeology and Modernity* (2004) and *Place and Memory* (2007).

Ann Woodward (previously Ann Ellison) is a Senior Research Fellow at the University of Birmingham, a Fellow of the Society of Antiquaries of London and former chair of the Prehistoric Ceramics Research Group. An authority on British Bronze Age and Iron Age pottery, she is particularly interested in integrated landscape archaeology, settlement studies and ancient religion, on which she has published widely. Major publications relating to the holistic study of prehistoric ceramics include a monograph on the excavations carried out at Cadbury Castle, Somerset in the 1970s (Barrett, Freeman and Woodward, 2000) and a synthetic volume jointly edited with J. D. Hill, *Prehistoric Britain: the ceramic basis* (2002). She has also authored two books relating to ritual sites in the landscape, *Shrines and Sacrifice* (1992) and *British Barrows* (2000).

Acknowledgements

Lynn Meskell first suggested that I produce this volume, and both she and Rosemary Joyce have provided constructive support through the process of its production. Staff at Blackwell Publishing have provided much encouragement and support, and I would particularly like to thank Jane Huber and Emily Martin for their input in the early stages, and latterly Rosalie Robertson and Deirdre Ilkson. Helen Harvey and Jacqueline Harvey have guided the text through its final stages of production with great skill. The contributors are thanked for their patience in seeing this volume through. Mhairi Gibson and Philippa Moloney provided invaluable assistance in the final stages, and Anne Leaver stepped in to provide much needed illustration support.

Joshua Pollard

1

The Construction of Prehistoric Britain

Joshua Pollard

Introduction

The papers in this volume cover ca. 35,000 years of prehistory within the British Isles, from the first appearance of anatomically modern humans at the start of the Upper Palaeolithic to the early centuries of the first millennium A.D. when Britain and Ireland were brought within the orbit of Roman and early post-Roman Europe, and so history of sorts. The volume is not intended as a comprehensive overview of British prehistory, nor is it organised along the lines of a linear or period-based narrative (such accounts are available, notably Hunter and Ralston 1999; Bradley 2007). Rather, it provides a theoretically informed review of current research set within a thematic format. These themes include: the interpretation of major points of social, ideological and economic transition (during the Upper Palaeolithic, Meso-lithic–Neolithic and the Middle Bronze Age); landscape and inhabitation; domestic and ceremonial architecture; foodways; productive technology; exchange; identity; and mortuary practice.

While intended as a stand-alone work, the volume was conceived alongside that on *Prehistoric Europe*, edited by Andrew Jones for this series. A broad attempt was made to match themes, while at the same time acknowledging how differences in theoretical position (see Hodder 1991), fieldwork traditions and the character of the record between Britain, Ireland and Continental Europe have shaped the ways in which prehistory has been studied and written in these different regions.

The geographic scope of this volume covers the modern countries of England, Scotland and Wales, with reference to Ireland (both the Northern counties that form part of the United Kingdom and the Republic) (figs. 1.1 and 1.2). This does not constitute a large area: at 244,820 sq. km the United Kingdom is slightly smaller than the state of Michigan, for example. A volume on prehistoric Britain might appear myopic by comparison with others in this series which have dealt with archaeology on a continental or equivalent scale (e.g., Africa: Stahl 2005; Oceania:

Figure 1.1 Map of Britain and Ireland, showing major topography, countries, major island groups, seas and principal rivers. Drawing by Anne Leaver.

Lilley 2006). Nonetheless, there are good reasons for the inclusion of this volume within the *Global Archaeology* series, not least the quantity of archaeological information available, the strength of research traditions and the quality of that work, which make aspects of British prehistory of more than regional or national interest. In comparison with many areas of the world, there exists a level of detail of knowledge relating to the prehistoric sequence that is often difficult to match; a consequence of a long and sometimes intense history of investigation which goes back

Figure 1.2 Map of Britain and Ireland, showing principal regions mentioned in the text. Drawing by Anne Leaver.

to the antiquarianism of the seventeenth and early eighteenth centuries and the work of key figures such as William Camden, John Aubrey and William Stukeley (Piggott 1989). Over the last half century extensive use has been made of British prehistoric material in the exposition of new theoretical positions, within influential early functionalist (Clark 1952), processual (Clarke 1972; Renfrew 1973a) and post-processual (Hodder 1982; Barrett 1994; Tilley 1994) archaeologies. British post-Palaeolithic prehistory especially has become a testing ground of much Anglo-American theory.

Currently, there are over 90 full-time members of academic staff within United Kingdom universities alone that are actively engaged in research on British prehistory. When those in fixed-time academic posts, research students and archaeological professionals within the commercial sector are included, the number of active researchers within the field numbers several hundred. This is a healthy community and one that ensures reproduction of interest for the immediate future at least. Public interest in prehistory is also high, aided by media exposure and the production of high-selling popular works that play, if sometimes uncomfortably, upon themes of long-standing identity whose "heritage" can be traced back to prehistory (e.g., Pryor 2003; Miles 2005).

Time and Space

Sections of this chapter were prepared while in the Western Isles of Scotland and at Avebury, in Wiltshire, southern England. These are two very different landscapes, set several hundred kilometres apart, and their archaeology can be used to illustrate elements of theme and diversity that are explored in many of the volume's chapters.

The massive complex of megalithic, timber and earthen monuments at Avebury was one of several foci on the chalklands of southern England for community-level ceremonial activity during the fourth and third millennia B.C. The rolling landscape around Avebury is dotted with visible archaeological sites, many of prehistoric date (Pollard and Reynolds 2002). The landscape and its archaeology provide an archetypal image of Wessex, a region without any current political status, but defined to varying degree by Thomas Hardy's literary creation (appearing in his *Far from the Madding Crowd* of 1874), which was in turn inspired by a real Middle Saxon kingdom that extended across much of central southern and south-western England during the sixth to ninth centuries A.D. (Yorke 1995). The "archaeological Wessex" refers in large part to the chalk areas of the counties of Wiltshire, Dorset and Hampshire. A manifestation of archaeological landscape romanticism (Johnson 2007), the Wessex label was first used in O. G. S. Crawford and Alexander Keiller's 1928 *Wessex from the Air* (a publication detailing the results of pioneer aerial survey), and gained common currency during the 1930s, finding a lasting expression in Stuart Piggott's formulation of an Early Bronze Age "Wessex Culture" in 1938 (Piggott 1938). The setting of the great Neolithic and Early Bronze Age monument complexes of Avebury, Stonehenge, Knowlton and Dorchester, extensive later prehistoric agrarian landscapes and the spectacular and "iconic" Iron Age hill forts of Maiden Castle, Hambledon and Hod Hill in Dorset, the Wessex region, has attracted considerable archaeological attention since the seventeenth century. Such sustained research has been engendered by the highly visible and well-preserved nature of the region's archaeology, an early pulse of interest that established its position in works of synthesis, and the area's proximity to researchers and institutions in the urban centres of Oxford, London and Southampton. No doubt the area also carried a special status at certain points in prehistory, as evidenced by the scale of monument-building projects and fluctuating long-distance networks of exchange and alliance that, in one of the most audacious instances of lithic movement, facilitated the transport of bluestone megaliths over 250 km from the Preseli Hills of south-west Wales to Salisbury Plain and Stonehenge. Until recently Wessex has dominated accounts of British prehistory, even to the extent of being perceived as a model against which other regions are judged. But, as numerous regional and wider-scale studies show (e.g., Cooney and Grogan 1999; Harding and Johnston 2000; Lynch et al. 2000; Bradley 2007), the prehistory of this region never was "the norm", and the archaeological Wessex is as much that "partly real, partly dream-country" (Hardy 1902:vi) that characterised Hardy's literary landscape.

Facing the North Atlantic Ocean, and incorporating some dramatic mountain topography, the Western Isles can at first sight present the visitor with an image of a hard environment, cultural isolation, and marginality. Such a view is occasionally present within the popular imagination, especially that of the metropolitan centres of the United Kingdom, in which the Western Isles are perceived as remote and socially, politically, and economically peripheral. In the late 1930s the Sussex archaeologist E. C. Curwen (1938) thought the Hebrides to be a cultural backwater in which Iron Age lifestyles persisted. In fact, the image of marginality and cultural fossilisation is erroneous and coloured by a post-medieval economic downturn brought about by changes in tenure and the levy of heavy rents following the collapse of the Scottish chiefdom system (Parker Pearson 2004). The islands' prehistory and early history tells a different story, one of highly successful subsistence (especially along the machair sands of the west coast of South Uist and Harris), occasionally dense and long-lived settlement, and Atlantic connections stretching north to the Northern Isles of Orkney and Shetland, and beyond, and south into the Irish Sea (Armit 1996; Parker Pearson et al. 2004). There exists a rich prehistoric record within the Western Isles that includes the important and well-known complex of Neolithic stone circles at Callanish and the Iron Age broch (a tower-like, stone-built settlement) of Dun Carloway, both on Lewis. The Callanish complex is one of a number of ceremonial centres of late fourth and third millennia B.C. date that occur throughout Britain and Ireland, while Dun Carloway belongs to a distinctive tradition of monumental "Atlantic roundhouses" particular to western and northern Scotland and the Isles. Embodied in these sites is an illustration of our knowledge that there are certain periods in the prehistory of the Western Isles when events appear to reflect wider patterns of practice and change, and other points when a distinctly regional identity came to the fore.

Wherever you stand on the Western Isles the sea is never far away. You are conscious of the importance of the ocean as a means of livelihood, of the maritime connections that it affords and of the way in which coastal lives and the practice of "sea-craft" construct an identity that can transcend particular geographic localities. In a recent publication Barry Cunliffe (2001) has sought to define a *longue durée* perspective on the peoples of the Atlantic façade which places Britain within an "Atlantic zone" that includes Iberia, Brittany and the western North Sea. The flows of ideas and processes of long-distance exchange and alliance that he identifies create a prehistory of expansive networks, one that counters a certain insularity prevalent in British prehistoric studies over recent decades, itself a reaction against an earlier over-reliance on invasion or migration as a means of explaining cultural change (Clark 1966). As papers in this volume illustrate, writing prehistory is about tacking between scales: delineating "big processes" – early human colonisation, the spread of the Neolithic, the impact of the emergence of state societies in the Mediterranean world during the first millennium B.C. and so forth – yet seeking to interpret these through the local, lived conditions of routine life, through individual and group agency, and the structures and resources that characterised particular places at particular moments in time. As such, there can be as many and varied narratives of British prehistory as there were events, understandings and responses to the projects of living.

The prehistoric sequence: a brief overview

The earliest hominid occupation of Britain dates to ca. 700,000 B.P. and is associated with groups of *Homo heidelbergensis,* as represented by the fossil find from Boxgrove, Sussex (Roberts et al. 1994). Subsequent human presence during the Palaeolithic was periodic, being tied to phases of climatic amelioration. As Paul Pettitt details (see chapter 2), forays by groups of *Homo sapiens* into Britain during the early part of the Upper Palaeolithic may have been of short duration and executed by small groups; but from the very end of the terminal Upper Palaeolithic/ Younger Dryas onwards human presence looks to have been continuous. Evidence for Holocene (Mesolithic) hunter-gatherers is much more extensive, with the colonisation of new regions such as Ireland and northern and western Scotland by around the eighth millennium B.C. Steady population rise may be inferred from the incidence of dated sites and material culture (Smith 1992a). The signature of Mesolithic sites varies, from small scatters of lithics reflecting hunting forays or episodes of re-tooling to dense concentrations of material indicative of group aggregation and repeated return over many years – true "persistent places". Perhaps a product of greater diversity in subsistence strategies, but also in lifestyles and identities, shell middens appear during the later Mesolithic on coastal areas of western Britain, as they do in southern Scandinavia and the Atlantic coasts of Brittany and Iberia. This period sees the first evidence for monumental expression in the British Isles, both with shell midden accumulation ("incidental monuments") and the construction of large post settings such as the eighth millennium B.C. examples at Stonehenge and Hambledon Hill in southern England (Allen and Gardiner 2002).

Set against the available data is the knowledge that many important sites lie submerged under the present North Sea, a region that Bryony Coles has referred to as "Doggerland" (Coles 1998). Early Holocene sea-level rise progressively encroached upon the lowland areas of the North Sea basin and English Channel where human activity was likely to have been most intensive during the earlier part of the Mesolithic, the present land masses of Britain and Ireland effectively representing upland regions during this time. Preservation of many of the submerged sites and land surfaces of this period is known to be good because of anaerobic conditions (Fleming 2004), and future investigation of these has the potential to transform our knowledge of the north-west European Mesolithic. The final separation of Britain from Continental Europe – the severing of the erroneously termed "land bridge" – is estimated at ca. 7500 B.C., though it could have occurred as much as 2,000 years later (Coles 1998:67).

Major changes in the human story of Britain and Ireland took place around 4000 B.C. with the appearance of new material technologies such as ceramics and ground stone tools (although the latter are known from Late Mesolithic contexts in Ireland and Wales), and a shift from a hunter-fisher-gatherer subsistence base to one reliant to varying degrees on domesticated livestock and cereal cultivation. The Neolithic was, however, more than just a shift in economy and material technology, since these practices were inextricably implicated in wider transformations in person-hood, social relations and ideology (see Thomas, chapter 3). Components of the British and Irish Neolithic have their origins ultimately in that of central and south-east Europe (Whittle 1996), and indeed the Neolithic of the eastern Mediterranean and Near East. However, while components of new lifestyles, and certainly livestock and cereals, have to represent Continental "imports", population movement at the transition need not have been great and indigenous uptake perhaps best explains the distinctive features of the British and Irish Neolithic.

By the second quarter of the fourth millennium B.C. traditions of building megalithic, timber and earthen monuments were well established (see Cummings, chapter 6). Their creation served to mark time and place, honour ancestors and other spiritual agencies, provide contexts in which dispersed groups could come together and so generate and reproduce social networks, while some acted as foci for the deposition of the remains of the dead (see Jones, chapter 8). By the late fourth to third millennia B.C. insular forms of public monument – henges, stone and timber circles and large mounds – were being constructed on a scale previously unseen, many as elements within larger ceremonial centres (e.g., the Boyne valley, west Mainland on Orkney and around Stonehenge). By contrast with monumental architecture, the energies and resources invested in building houses and settlements was in many regions surprisingly slight, perhaps because mobility remained a feature of the lives of most communities. It is only from the second millennium B.C. onwards that "domestic" architecture as such becomes more visible in the archaeological record (see Brück, chapter 11), usually in the form of settlements of roundhouses. Rare in Continental Europe, the roundhouse was a persistent architectural form in Britain and Ireland, its longevity maintained perhaps because of the way in which, in varied contexts, it materialised key cosmological values and facilitated the reproduction of social order.

Alongside an emerging emphasis on the house during the early to mid second millennium B.C. were transformations in land tenure and agricultural practice (see Field, Johnston and Mulville: chapters 9, 12 and 10 respectively) that left their signature in new landscapes of field systems and major land boundaries. For Barrett (1994:147), the creation of agricultural landscapes during this period marks the development of a "place-bound sense of *being*", in which the communal identities

expressed by earlier public monuments gave way to more localised senses of belonging based around the household and settlement. However, by the Middle Iron Age
those settlements could themselves be substantial, particularly in the case of the
developed hill forts of southern Britain. Like the henge monuments of the later
Neolithic, hill forts – whether permanently or intermittently occupied – gave definition to new forms of communal identity within landscapes that were otherwise
dominated by small farmstead-scale settlements. Many sites of the first millennium
B.C. were defined by earthwork, stone wall or palisade enclosures. The purpose of
enclosure was not always defence or containment, it being a multivalent technology
that was also employed to provide a largely symbolic barrier, or as a means to define
a sense of household or corporate identity (Bowden and McOmish 1987).

The end of prehistory in England, southern Scotland and Wales is marked by
Roman political and military takeover during the first century A.D. In Ireland and
Highland and Island Scotland the break between prehistory and proto-history
occurs in the middle centuries of the first millennium A.D. with the coming of
Christianity and assimilation into the politics and networks of Late Antique and
early medieval Europe. In fact, if the absence or presence of documentary record
is taken to differentiate prehistoric from historic circumstance, then for the Atlantic
island of St Kilda, 60 km west of Harris, prehistory effectively ended in the mid
sixteenth century (Fleming 1995). Even within those areas brought under Roman
rule, the transition was complex and varied. Certain practices continued, such as
the use of roundhouses and "Iron Age" farmstead settlements in the militarised
zone of northern England and southern Scotland – active cultural defiance, perhaps.
Even in the heavily Romanised areas of southern and eastern England this was a
time of cultural hybridisation rather than outright replacement by a dominant
donor, and the history of change was long and complex. In response to the expanding sphere of influence of Rome, those communities closest to France and the Low
Countries were already beginning to restyle themselves from the first century B.C.
Coinage, Roman-style cremation burial, Roman and Gaulish luxury imports, new
consumption habits, proto-urbanism and perhaps even literacy marked the last
decades of prehistory in certain regions of southern England.

If general and long-lived themes are to be identified in British prehistory they
would include the curious scarcity of representational art; monumentality of various
forms (including in settlement architecture); traditions of votive deposition within
rivers, lakes and other natural places; and funerary traditions that with a few exceptions (e.g., during the earlier Neolithic and Early–Middle Bronze Age) left little
visible archaeological signature.

Periodisation and the division of research

Throughout this volume the classic period divisions of Palaeolithic, Mesolithic,
Neolithic, Bronze Age and Iron Age are employed (table 1.1). A legacy of the
"Three Age" system formulated during the nineteenth century, these period labels
are by no means unproblematic. Even from an empirical point of view, they have

Table 1.1 A simplified, period-based chronology for prehistoric Britain from the Upper Palaeolithic to the Iron Age*

Upper Palaeolithic	ca. 40,000/35,000–10,000 B.C.
Mesolithic	ca. 10,000–4000 B.C.
Earlier Neolithic	ca. 4000–3000 B.C.
Later Neolithic	ca. 3000–2200 B.C.
Early Bronze Age	ca. 2200–1500 B.C.
Middle Bronze Age	ca. 1500–1200 B.C.
Late Bronze Age	ca. 1200–800 B.C.
Earlier Iron Age	ca. 800–400 B.C.
Later Iron Age	ca. 400 B.C.–A.D. 43/ca. A.D. 500

*The end of the Iron Age in southern Britain is defined by the Roman conquest, but in those regions beyond Roman subjugation (i.e., Scotland and Ireland) it is taken as the middle of the first millennium A.D.

taken on a life that has dislocated them from the technological stages they were supposed to define. Thus, the start of the Iron Age in Britain is normally placed around 800 B.C., yet traces of ironworking – both smelting and forging – are known from ninth- and even tenth-millennia B.C. contexts, as at Hartshill Copse, Berkshire (Collard et al. 2006); and copper axes were in circulation during the later Neolithic (the end of the "Stone Age").

Periodisation should at best be a heuristic device, creating temporal blocks within which to hang the study of practices and processes – a categorisation that makes manageable the study of large and complex data. At worst, it is insidiously linked to models of social "progress" and unilinear evolution (Lucas 2005:50–1). It can also promote "layered thinking" in which homogeneity is arbitrarily defined within periods (e.g., Bronze Age economies) and differences sought between them, generating discrete blocks of time within which practices and styles of material culture are seen as self-contained. This in turn has led to a situation where different theoretical approaches are felt to be appropriate to different periods. The most obvious example is provided by the British Mesolithic and Neolithic. Until recently, the former was studied through functionalist perspectives which foregrounded the subsistence economy, rational foraging, adaptations to fluctuating environments and a universal human condition (e.g., Mithen 1990; Smith 1992b). By contrast, scholars engaged in studying the Neolithic adopted broadly post-processual agendas that stressed social relations and reproduction, agency, symbolism and historical contingency (e.g., Barrett 1994; Thomas 1999). Such was the disparity in theoretical approach to these contiguous periods that Richard Bradley was to write memorably that it almost seemed as though "successful [Neolithic] farmers have social relations with one another, while [Mesolithic] hunter-gatherers have ecological relations with hazelnuts" (Bradley 1984:11). That theoretical division is now being progressively eroded (see Conneller and Warren 2006; McFadyen, chapter 5).

Despite the problems they might induce, period divisions continue to be used, as reflected in the titles of recent, and theoretically-informed, volumes on the

Mesolithic (e.g., Conneller and Warren 2006), Neolithic (e.g., Thomas 1999; Noble 2006), Bronze Age (e.g., Brück 2001) and Iron Age (e.g., Haselgrove and Moore 2007; Haselgrove and Pope 2007). The majority of prehistorians recognise the somewhat arbitrary nature of periodisation and the issues raised above, therefore the retention of these time categories may have more to do with the desire on the part of scholars for intra-disciplinary identity and the creation of communities or "colleges" of researchers. These are maintained and reproduced by fora with annual meetings such as the Pal-Meso Discussion Group, Neolithic Studies Group, Bronze Age Forum and Iron Age Research Student Seminar.

A recent focus on memory, material biography and responses to the physical remains of the past in prehistory (e.g., Marshall and Gosden 1999; Bradley 2002; Jones 2007) has gone some way to countering the legacy of periodisation and acknowledging the multi-temporality of the archaeological record (Lucas 2005:56–59). John Barrett (1999) and Chris Gosden and Gary Lock (1998), for example, have talked about how the construction of the landscapes of Iron Age southern England drew upon the resources of an earlier prehistoric past in which relict monuments such as Early Bronze Age round barrows became mythic features that were appropriated to provide a source of legitimacy for new social orders. Adopting a similar perspective, Niall Sharples (2006) has argued that, within the context of an understanding of deep history of landscape occupancy, the remains of Neolithic chambered tombs on Orkney provided a model of permanence that was necessary to create the conditions in which long-lived Iron Age broch settlements could develop. Of course, being able to recognise how the physical legacy of the past structured the conditions of later inhabitation is the key to any multi-temporal archaeology, and in this respect impetus has come from the results of recent large-scale excavation projects in which the relationships between features and practices of different dates can be understood (Lucas 2005:40–3). A good example is provided by Framework Archaeology's (2006) work at Heathrow Airport's Terminal 5, to the west of London. The work was guided at the outset by a focus on the "archaeology of inhabitation" – understanding how knowledgeable human agents worked within the particular political and social conditions of their time and the physical legacy and resources of the landscape as produced by present and past generations. The extent to which these multi-temporal perspectives can be applied to broad-brush accounts of prehistory as opposed to the interpretation of individual landscapes or features (e.g., the tombs and brochs of Orkney) remains to be established, but their potential to erode the legacy of periodisation is already being felt.

The Practice of Prehistory

British prehistory is a construct of 400 years of research; a process that has always represented an interplay of developing fieldwork traditions and theoretical approaches, influenced by national and regional identities, academic structures, legislation, funding/sponsorship and the changing academic popularity of certain research themes. There exists a fortunate legacy in the long history of research, the early creation of national and county archaeological societies, a strong tradition of university-based work, amateur involvement (occasionally of an exceptionally high standard: e.g., Green 2000) and, in the post-Second World War period, state intervention in the face of rescue demands.

The objects of study themselves – the physical remains of prehistoric sites, landscapes and material culture – have had their own role in this process, since their insistent presence demanded explanation and positioning within narratives of human occupancy of the British Isles. It was after all the remains of megalithic tombs and stone circles and earthwork monuments such as barrows, hill forts and henges that first attracted antiquarian attention and provided the possibilities for creating first national, then ethnic, narratives of early history separate from those offered by the writings of classical authors (Piggott 1989; Trigger 1989).

It was during the second half of the nineteenth century that prehistory as a subject of enquiry was given definition, chronological framework and theoretical focus. The Scandinavian "Three Age" system was applied to British material in Daniel Wilson's *The Archaeology and Prehistoric Annals of Scotland* (1851), a work in which the term "prehistoric" was first coined (Chippindale 1988). Eight years later the authoritative acknowledgement by members of the Geological Society of London of the great age of stone tools found with the bones of extinct mammals in the Somme gravels at Abbeville, France finally provided recognition of "deep antiquity" to human presence in Europe. These and other developments (e.g., the publication of Charles Darwin's *On the Origin of Species*, also in 1859) marked the critical break from earlier reliance on biblical and classical texts as sources of information on pre-Roman Britain (Trigger 1989:93–94). Cultural evolution and comparative ethnography initially provided an interpretive framework, as in John Lubbock's influential *Prehistoric Times* (1865 and subsequent editions).

If the first legislation for the protection of ancient monuments in Britain (the 1882 Act for the Better Protection of Ancient Monuments) is treated as an index of archaeological significance at the time, then the clear majority of prehistoric over later sites on that list is telling. A bias towards certain types of monument, especially megaliths and hill forts, that were seen as representative of an early British past is also discernible (the first list includes Stonehenge, South Cadbury, Navan, Tara, Pentre Ifan, the Clava cairns and the stone circles of Brodgar and Stenness). Within the realms of national politics and identity, prehistory had come to matter. In the most explicit instance of geopolitical influence, it was national pride stirred by a period of increasing imperial tension that underpinned a willingness by the academic community to accept the authenticity of the infamous Piltdown skull, "discovered" in 1912. It would take over three decades for the forgery of this apparently archaic hominid to be revealed (Weiner 1955). Parity with Continental Europe and discoveries being made there was of concern. As an example, work undertaken between 1892 and 1907 on the Iron Age "lake village" at Glastonbury was heavily influenced by nineteenth-century European research on lake dwellings and an expectation that similar lacustrine settlements had to exist in Britain (Bullied and Gray 1911:1–5).

The middle decades of the twentieth century witnessed a "modernisation" of prehistory through improved fieldwork and scientific methods, interdisciplinary collaboration, critical synthesis, its inclusion in university curricula and, in 1935, the transformation of the Prehistoric Society of East Anglia into the Prehistoric Society. The Second World War and its aftermath had a notable impact on the practice of archaeology. Within a climate of "new world" social responsibility, the state began to take a more active role in funding rescue excavations; a process that had in fact begun during the war in response to the destruction of archaeological sites during the construction of airfields (Grimes 1960). In the form of agricultural intensification, housing and road-building, and aggregate extraction, the scale of post-war development took its toll on Britain's prehistory, even on those sites offered statutory protection as Scheduled Ancient Monuments (SAMs). A 1964 survey of the archaeology of Wiltshire, for instance, showed that 250 of 640 SAMs existing 10 years previously had been badly damaged or destroyed, largely through agricultural activity (Barker 1974:29). Many of those sites were Bronze Age round barrows. However, successful lobbying by the archaeological community brought about a rapid increase in central government funding for rescue archaeology during the early 1970s and led to the establishment of county Sites and Monuments Records, and the creation of county or regional units and county archaeological officers.

Ironically, it was the building of motorways in the 1960s and 1970s, especially rescue work on the M4 and M5 motorways, that alerted archaeologists to the density of prehistoric and later archaeology across the countryside (Fowler 1974); while work in advance of aggregate extraction on the gravels of lowland England and Scotland has seen a productive encounter with areas previously subject to little investigation, resulting in the discovery of different kinds of prehistoric landscape and different histories of activity to those represented in upland regions (Bradley 1992). The pessimistic prophecies of the early 1970s that, with ongoing development and destruction, there might only be "a few dozen sites left by A.D. 2000" (Rahtz 1974:1) have been firmly replaced by an understanding of the ubiquity of archaeological traces (while, of course, recognising what has gone).

While government funding of archaeology in England especially has significantly decreased since 1990, the requirement for developers to fund pre-construction archaeological investigation as outlined in Planning Policy Guideline 16 (PPG16) has led to a dramatic increase in the scale of excavation. This is seen most dramatically in gravel-rich and economically "super-charged" regions such as the Thames Valley and East Midlands where it has been possible for the first time to undertake excavation work on a true landscape scale. With publication, the results of this are slowly being felt, and projects such as those in the Middle Thames at Eton and Yarnton (Allen et al. 2004) and in the Great Ouse Valley/Fen-edge (Dawson 2000) are set to have a profound impact on future accounts of British prehistory. Without the same level of resource, university-led research excavations cannot compete with the scale of developer-funded work undertaken by commercial archaeological units. This might at first seem to exacerbate the gulf between what Richard Bradley has termed the "two cultures" – academic archaeologists on the one hand and professional field archaeologists on the other – but with growing links between the two, and a greater commitment to research rather than simply data recovery by contracting units, the opposite is true (Bradley 2006).

Current and Future Directions

A combination of willing engagement with archaeological theory and the momentum provided by active traditions of fieldwork have made British prehistory a vibrant and dynamic area of research. Over the last two decades British prehistorians have been at the forefront of interpretive developments in Anglo-American archaeology, creating a distinctive social archaeology that has drawn upon a variety of theoretical positions. Underpinning many of these are concerns with agency and a recognition of the active role played by material culture in structuring social relations and change. There currently exists a strong interest in exploring dimensions of social memory, material agency, materiality, cognition, the body and personhood; in critically reworking dualist paradigms such as the nature–culture distinction; and in exploring the dimensions of landscape encounter through phenomenological studies. Far from operating in abstraction, such an engagement with theory has been used to create challenging and exciting accounts of social life, as essays in this volume show.

To predict the future would be a foolhardy exercise, especially since wider social and political events and processes, new discoveries and analytical techniques can all impact on the directions that research might take. This acknowledged, certain currents of change are discernible. One is apparent in recent studies that have highlighted the scale of evidence for interpersonal violence during the Neolithic (Schulting and Wysocki 2005) and later periods (Mercer 2006). These illuminate the very real tensions that accompanied the transactions of life during prehistory, and stand in contrast to the rather comfortable images of prehistoric social life generated by many recent narratives of inhabitation and routine.

The second current takes the guise of a quiet scientific revolution represented by the impact of refined radiocarbon chronologies, and biochemical and geochemical analyses. The results of this work have been many and varied, and often unexpected. Thus, lipid analysis of pottery vessels has shown conclusively that dairying was a major component of farming practices in the Neolithic, Bronze Age and Iron Age of southern Britain (Copley et al. 2003; 2005); stable isotope analysis of human skeletal material has delineated changing consumption practices, including a dramatic shift away from marine resources at the onset of the Neolithic (see Schulting, chapter 4); and strontium and oxygen isotope signatures have provided evidence of regional and much longer distance lifetime movements of individuals (Montgomery et al. 2000). With reference to the latter, isotope analyses of mid- to late-third-millennium B.C. Beaker burials from the Stonehenge region have shown that certain individuals remained relatively sedentary during their lives, while others originated from areas with radiogenic geology such as Wales or Brittany, and another – the "Amesbury Archer" – came perhaps from central Europe (Fitzpatrick

2003; Evans et al. 2006). Knowing the possible extent of long-distance, lifetime movement during this important period, which is coeval with the widespread adoption of metallurgy, raises interesting issues about the transmission of geographical knowledge, the reception of "outsiders" and the introduction of new practices.

The first true "radiocarbon revolution" could be said to have come with calibration (Renfrew 1973b). This finally put paid to models of hyper-diffusion for phenomena such as megalithic tombs, demonstrating indigenous development within several areas from the Mediterranean to western Britain. Another is being heralded with the application of large-scale dating programmes on Neolithic long barrows, long cairns and causewayed enclosures in southern England, in which Bayesian statistical modelling is employed to interpret radiocarbon dates (Whittle and Bayliss 2007; Whittle et al. 2007). The results are much finer-grained chronologies, and so more refined histories, than we have been used to in British prehistoric studies: half centuries or generations suddenly become definable, and so too lived timescales rather than coarse periodisation.

Applied to individual contexts, even the remains of specific individuals, all of these techniques provide a level of resolution and detail on prehistoric lives that was previously unobtainable. Their development and application is timely, inasmuch as it coincides with current interpretive interests in agency, memory and personhood; with the specifics of routine and lived experience rather than abstracted process. Here science and archaeological theory come together to provide a sense of what life was like at certain times for certain people living within social and symbolic conditions that may be beyond immediate ethnographic analogy. The challenge of British prehistory is to further develop our knowledge of those different worlds.

REFERENCES

Allen, M., and J. Gardiner, 2002 A sense of time: cultural markers in the Mesolithic of southern England? In Inscribed Landscapes: marking and making places. B. David and M. Wilson, eds. pp. 139–153. Honolulu: University of Hawaii Press.

Allen, T., A. Barclay and H. Lamdin-Whymark, 2004 Opening the wood, making the land: the study of a Neolithic landscape in the Dorney area of the Middle Thames Valley. In Towards a New Stone Age: aspects of the Neolithic in south-east England. J. Cotton and D. Field, eds. pp. 82–98. London: Council for British Archaeology.

Armit, I., 1996 The Archaeology of Syke and the Western Isles. Edinburgh: Edinburgh University Press.

Barker, P., 1974 The scale of the problem. In Rescue Archaeology. P. A. Rahtz, ed. pp. 28–34. Harmondsworth: Penguin.

Barrett, J., 1994 Fragments from Antiquity: an archaeology of social life in Britain, 2900–1200 BC. Oxford: Blackwell.

——1999 The mythical landscapes of British Iron Age. In Archaeologies of Landscape. W. Ashmore and A. B. Knapp, eds. pp. 253–65. Oxford: Blackwell.

Bowden, M., and D. McOmish, 1987 The required barrier. Scottish Archaeological Review 4(2):76–84.

Bradley, R., 1984 The Social Foundations of Prehistoric Britain. London: Longman.
——1992 The gravels and British prehistory from the Neolithic to the Early Iron Age. *In* Developing Landscapes of Lowland Britain. The Archaeology of the British Gravels: a review. M. Fulford and E. Nichols, eds. pp. 15–22. London: Society of Antiquaries.
——2002 The Past in Prehistoric Societies. London: Routledge.
——2006 Bridging the two cultures: commercial archaeology and the study of prehistoric Britain. Antiquaries Journal 86:1–13.
——2007 The Prehistory of Britain and Ireland. Cambridge: Cambridge University Press.
Brück, J., eds., 2001 Bronze Age Landscapes: tradition and transformation. Oxford: Oxbow Books.
Bullied, A., and H. St. G. Gray, 1911 The Glastonbury Lake Village: a full description of the excavations and the relics discovered, 1892–1907. Glastonbury: Glastonbury Antiquarian Society.
Chippindale, C., 1988 The invention of words for the idea of "Prehistory". Proceedings of the Prehistoric Society 54:303–314.
Clark, J. G. D., 1952 Prehistoric Europe: the economic basis. London: Methuen.
——1966 The invasion hypothesis in British archaeology. Antiquity 40:172–189.
Clarke, D. L., ed., 1972 Models in Archaeology. London: Methuen.
Coles, B. J., 1998 Doggerland: a speculative survey. Proceedings of the Prehistoric Society 64:45–81.
Collard, M., T. Darvill and M. Watts, 2006 Ironworking in the Bronze Age? Evidence from a 10th century BC settlement at Hartshill Copse, Upper Bucklebury, West Berkshire. Proceedings of the Prehistoric Society 72:367–421.
Conneller, C., and G. Warren, eds., 2006 Mesolithic Britain and Ireland: new approaches. Stroud: Tempus.
Cooney, G., and E. Grogan, 1999 Irish Prehistory: a social perspective. 2nd edition. Bray: Wordwell.
Copley, M. S., R. Berstan, S. N. Dudd, S. Aillaud, A. J. Mukherjee, V. Straker, S. Payne and R. P. Evershed, 2005 Processing of milk products in pottery vessels through British prehistory. Antiquity 79:895–908.
—————, G. Docherty, A. J. Mukherjee, V. Straker, S. Payne and R. P. Evershed, 2003 Direct chemical evidence for widespread dairying in prehistoric Britain. Proceedings of the National Academy of Sciences 100:1524–1529.
Cunliffe, B., 2001 Facing the Ocean: the Atlantic and its peoples 8000 BC–AD 1500. Oxford: Oxford University Press.
Curwen, E. C., 1938 The Hebrides: a cultural backwater. Antiquity 12:261–289.
Dawson, M., ed., 2000 Prehistoric, Roman and Post-Roman Landscapes of the Great Ouse Valley. London: Council for British Archaeology.
Evans, J. A., C. A. Chenery and A. P. Fitzpatrick, 2006 Bronze Age childhood migration of individuals near Stonehenge, revealed by strontium and oxygen isotope tooth enamel analysis. Archaeometry 48(2):309–321.
Fitzpatrick, A. P., 2003 The Amesbury Archer. Current Archaeology 184:146–152.
Fleming, A., 1995 St. Kilda: stone tools, dolerite quarries and long-term survival. Antiquity 69:25–35.
Fleming, N. C., ed., 2004 Submarine Prehistoric Archaeology of the North Sea: research priorities and collaboration with industry. London: English Heritage/Council for British Archaeology.
Fowler, P., 1974 Motorways and archaeology. *In* Rescue Archaeology. P. A. Rahtz, ed. pp. 113–129. Harmondsworth: Penguin.

Framework Archaeology, 2006 Landscape Evolution in the Middle Thames Valley: Heath-row Terminal 5 excavations, vol. 1: Perry Oaks. Oxford and Salisbury: Framework Archaeology.

Gosden, C., and G. Lock, 1998 Prehistoric histories. World Archaeology 30(1):2–12.

Green, M., 2000 A Landscape Revealed: 10,000 years on a chalkland farm. Stroud: Tempus.

Grimes, W. F., 1960 Excavations on Defence Sites, 1939–1945. 1: Mainly Neolithic–Bronze Age. London: HMSO.

Harding, J., and R. Johnston, eds., 2000 Northern Pasts: interpretations of the later prehis-tory of northern England and southern Scotland. Oxford: British Archaeological Reports.

Hardy, T., 1902 Far from the Madding Crowd. New edition. London: Macmillan.

Haselgrove, C., and T. Moore, eds., 2007 The Later Iron Age in Britain and Beyond. Oxford: Oxbow Books.

——and R. Pope, eds., 2007 The Earlier Iron Age in Britain and the Near Continent. Oxford: Oxbow Books.

Hodder, I., ed., 1982 Symbolic and Structural Archaeology. Cambridge: Cambridge University Press.

——ed., 1991 Archaeological Theory in Europe: the last three decades. London: Routledge.

Hunter, J., and I. B. M. Ralston, eds., 1999 The Archaeology of Britain. London: Routledge.

Johnson, M., 2007 Ideas of Landscape. Oxford: Blackwell.

Jones, A., 2007 Memory and Material Culture. Cambridge: Cambridge University Press.

Lilley, I., ed., 2006 Archaeology of Oceania. Oxford: Blackwell.

Lucas, G., 2005 The Archaeology of Time. London: Routledge.

Lynch, F., S. Aldhouse-Green and J. L. Davies, 2000 Prehistoric Wales. Stroud: Sutton.

Marshall, Y., and C. Gosden, eds., 1999 The cultural biography of objects. World Archaeol-ogy 31(2).

Mercer, R. J., 2006 By other means? The development of warfare in the British Isles 3000–500 BC. Journal of Conflict Archaeology 2(1):119–151.

Miles, D., 2005 The Tribes of Britain: who are we? and where do we come from? London: Weidenfeld and Nicolson.

Mithen, S., 1990 Thoughtful Foragers: a study of prehistoric decision making. Cambridge: Cambridge University Press.

Montgomery, J., P. Budd and J. Evans, 2000 Reconstructing the lifetime movements of ancient people. European Journal of Archaeology 3(3):370–385.

Noble, G., 2006 Neolithic Scotland: timber, stone, earth and fire. Edinburgh: Edinburgh University Press.

Parker Pearson, M., 2004 Island prehistories: a view of Orkney from South Uist. In Explain-ing Social Change: studies in honour of Colin Renfrew. J. Cherry, C. Scarre and S. Shennan, eds. pp. 127–140. Cambridge: McDonald Institute Monographs.

——N. Sharples and J. Symonds, 2004 South Uist: archaeology and history of a Hebridean island. Stroud: Tempus.

Piggott, S., 1938 The Early Bronze Age in Wessex. Proceedings of the Prehistoric Society 4:52–106.

——1989 Ancient Britons and the Antiquarian Imagination. London: Thames and Hudson.

Pollard, J., and A. Reynolds, 2002 Avebury: the biography of a landscape. Stroud: Tempus.

Pryor, F., 2003 Britain BC: life in Britain and Ireland before the Romans. London: Harper Collins.

Rahtz, P. A., 1974 Part One: the background to the crisis. *In* Rescue Archaeology. P. A. Rahtz, ed. pp. 1–2. Harmondsworth: Penguin.

Renfrew, C., ed., 1973a The Explanation of Culture Change: models in prehistory. London: Duckworth.

——1973b Before Civilisation: the radiocarbon revolution and prehistoric Europe. London: Cape.

Roberts, M. B., C. B. Stringer and S. A. Parfitt, 1994 A hominid tibia from Middle Pleistocene sediments at Boxgrove, UK. Nature 369:311–313.

Schulting, R., and M. Wysocki, 2005 "In this chambered tumulus were found cleft skulls . . .": an assessment of the evidence for cranial trauma in the British Neolithic. Proceedings of the Prehistoric Society 71:107–138.

Sharples, N., 2006 The first (permanent) houses: an interpretation of the monumental domestic architecture of Iron Age Orkney. Journal of Iberian Archaeology 8:281–305.

Smith, C., 1992a Upper Palaeolithic and Mesolithic populations. Proceedings of the Prehistoric Society 58:37–40.

——1992b Late Stone Age Hunters of the British Isles. London: Routledge.

Stahl, A. B., ed., 2005 African Archaeology. Oxford: Blackwell.

Thomas, J., 1999 Understanding the Neolithic. London: Routledge.

Tilley, C., 1994 A Phenomenology of Landscape: places, paths and monuments. Oxford: Berg.

Trigger, B. G., 1989 A History of Archaeological Thought. Cambridge: Cambridge University Press.

Weiner, J. S., 1955 The Piltdown Forgery. London: Oxford University Press.

Whittle, A., 1996 Europe in the Neolithic: the creation of new worlds. Cambridge: Cambridge University Press.

——and A. Bayliss, 2007 The times of their lives: from chronological precision to kinds of history and change. Cambridge Archaeological Journal 17(1):21–28.

——A. Barclay, A. Bayliss, L. McFadyen, R. Schulting and M. Wysocki, 2007 Building for the dead: events, processes and changing worldviews from the thirty-eight to the thirty-fourth centuries cal BC in southern Britain. Cambridge Archaeological Journal 17:1 (suppl.):123–147.

Yorke, B., 1995 Wessex in the Early Middle Ages. London: Leicester University Press.

2

The British Upper Palaeolithic

Paul Pettitt

Introduction and Context

A considerable advance in our understanding of the Upper Palaeolithic has occurred since Dorothy Garrod's famous survey of 1926, and particularly since John Campbell published his in 1977. These still, however, remain the only two academic monographs on the period. Considerable advances have, in fact, occurred in our understanding of the entirety of the British Palaeolithic. These are particularly clear in the Lower and Middle Palaeolithic periods over the last two decades, which include the discovery, excavation and publication of the major sites of Boxgrove (yielding some of Europe's oldest hominid remains), High Lodge, Barnham, Elveden, Beeches Pit and Purfleet, and of the Middle Palaeolithic site of Lynford and Early Upper Palaeolithic site of Glaston. New discoveries at Happisburgh and Pakefield in East Anglia have pushed back the age of the earliest known human settlement of Britain to ca. 700,000 B.P., and ambitious analyses of the national dataset have done much to improve our understanding of the brief pulses of human occupation over Middle Pleistocene time (White and Schreve 2000; Ashton and Lewis 2002), human habitat preferences at the beginnings and ends of interglacials when *Homo heidelbergensis* populations inhabited the South and the Midlands (e.g., Ashton et al. 2006; Preece et al. 2006), and technological variability in the landscape (White and Pettitt 1995; White et al. 2006). The British Lower Palaeolithic record is truly international in quality.

In the light of these significant advances in Lower and Middle Palaeolithic archaeology one could be forgiven for thinking that the British Upper Palaeolithic has seen relatively modest change, but this view is illusory. While it has been dogmatic that much of the country's Upper Palaeolithic record has been excavated out of relatively few caves, and that little accessible archaeology can be found on open sites, there exist vast amounts of data which remain to be integrated into new syntheses. Roger Jacobi in particular has made considerable achievements in improving our understanding of the typology, chronology and phasing of the period, while the excavation of new sites and new analyses of old collections have taken us into a new dawn in our appreciation of Upper Palaeolithic life in the north-west extremity of Pleistocene Europe. In recent years this improved understanding has come about through impressive advances in the following areas:

- the development of a formal mammalian biostratigraphy for the Upper Pleistocene of Britain;
- work on the connectedness of Britain to the Continent during periods of lowered sea levels, reconstruction of the plains and hills of "Doggerland" under what is now the North Sea, and of the rivers of the English Channel, providing a detailed geographical context of changing landscapes for human settlement;
- major radiocarbon dating projects that have refined our knowledge of the timing of human occupation and, in particular, gaps in human settlement, of Britain;
- the discovery in 2003 of Britain's first known examples of Upper Palaeolithic cave art and subsequent contextualisation of the finds;
- ongoing comparisons of British archaeological materials to those of contemporary Continental sites;
- dietary reconstruction by stable isotope analysis of Upper Pleistocene human bone, e.g., Eel Point (Caldey Island), Kendrick's Cave (north Wales) and Gough's Cave and Sun Hole, Cheddar;
- major re-analyses and publications of key sites such as Coygan Cave (Dyfed), Goat's Hole (Paviland) on Gower, Gough's Cave (Cheddar) and Aveline's Hole (in Burrington Combe, North Mendip), Church Hole at Creswell Crags, Launde and Bradgate Park (Newtown Lynford) in Leicestershire, and Pontnewydd and Beedings (both forthcoming);
- major debates on the nature and timing of the Late Upper Palaeolithic human recolonisation of Britain after the Last Glacial Maximum in the context of wider issues in Late Pleistocene human demography of northern Europe;
- new excavations and analyses of Final Palaeolithic and Early Mesolithic period sites resulting in an improved understanding of human responses to the Pleistocene–Holocene transition;
- survey of the archaeological potential of caves and rock shelters of the Creswell Heritage Region which have demonstrated that a large number of sites with full sediments remain to be excavated, and the identification of a potentially large Late Upper Palaeolithic open site by fieldwalking (surface collection).

I shall try to convey in this chapter a feel for the new understanding of the British Upper Palaeolithic that has come about through these developments. My perspective is overtly Europeanist and I make no apologies for using Continental names for cultural groupings when I believe British materials can be identified with them. The degree of cultural connectedness of British Upper Palaeolithic societies to those of the Continent has been debated since Dorothy Garrod (1926) coined the term "Creswellian" to mark the distinct characteristics of the British material in contrast to the contemporary Late Magdalenian of the Continent. From a modern perspective it seems clear that sufficient similarities can be found between all British phases of the Upper Palaeolithic and the Continent to warrant abandonment of the term "Creswellian" and the adoption of Continental terminology. From a European perspective, then, I am unashamedly unificationist.

The topics current in British Upper Palaeolithic archaeology very much reflect the wider interests of the European Palaeolithic community, and include the nature of leafpoint assemblages and their relevance to Neanderthal extinction and/or modern human expansion; the Aurignacian and timing of the initial dispersal of *Homo sapiens* to Britain; occupational gaps when the country seems to have been devoid of human inhabitants, particularly during the Last Glacial Maximum; bio-stratigraphy and changing faunal communities and their relationship to human dispersals; the human recolonisation of the region during the climatic amelioration that followed the Last Glacial Maximum; the nature of Late Upper Palaeolithic art and enculturation of the landscape; the distribution and behaviour of Late Glacial hunter-gatherers and their degree of cultural connectedness with the Continent; and the transition to "Mesolithic" communities over the major environmental changes of the Pleistocene–Holocene transition. I shall discuss our current under-standing of the period in chronological order, which is the most logical approach to take as the region saw only intermittent occupation by culturally disparate groups separated, often, by thousands of years. I begin by discussing the environmental context of human occupation. Many aspects of the geography of later Upper Pleis-tocene Britain have considerable ramifications for the nature of its human occupa-tion, yet remain to be seriously incorporated into any consideration of human activity in Britain. I make here some tentative first steps in this light.

Peninsular Britain: Upper Pleistocene Landscapes and Resources

Publications addressing the physical nature of the connection of Britain to the Continent in the Pleistocene refer to a "land bridge" connecting the South-East to northern France during periods of lowered sea level (e.g., Barton and Roberts 1996:249). Such a description is highly misleading, evoking as it does something akin to a dry land equivalent of the Channel Tunnel connecting Kent to Picardy. In fact, a sizeable portion of what is now the eastern coast of England was con-nected to the vast plains of central and southern North Sea, an area which Coles (1998) has termed "Doggerland". A sea level drop of 100 m was sufficient to establish this connection, affecting the extension of a continuous Northern European Plain across to the North-West European Uplands of Wales and western Scotland. Faunal remains and artefacts dredged up from banks such as Leman and Ower, Dogger and Brown (the hills of Doggerland) have demonstrated that this was a vast area rich in herbivorous and avian resources, and from a settlement point of view we can regard England and Wales as being an upland periphery.

Research into the history of the English Channel has also stressed connectedness, although it may be that this was more of a significant barrier to settlement because of its major east–west flowing river systems. Geologically, the Pleistocene English

Channel can be described as a fluvial basin periodically invaded by the sea (Lagarde et al. 2003). The modern submarine relief of this basin is incised with a complex network of channels, which represent extensions of the river valleys of southern Britain such as the Solent and Arun, and those of northern France such as the Seine, Somme and Béthune (Gibbard and Lautridou 2003). During periods of lowered sea level the basin saw a system whereby these rivers drained into the vast Channel River, itself draining into the Atlantic around the −100 m contour located to the south of modern Penzance. The Channel basin would have been dominated by the massive valleys, typically 10–20 km wide, of the Channel River, a huge anastomosing system. As with northern France, a number of high-energy, multi-channelled or braided rivers flowed into this, many of which still exist although their lower reaches have been flooded by marine transgression but are recognised by submarine valley systems (Antoine et al. 2003). One such English tributary was the (now extinct) palaeo-Solent, which flowed south through the Hampshire basin receiving tributary waters from the Arun, Test, Stour and Ichen before flowing south-easterly to the east of the Isle of Wight and turning south to flow into the Channel River some 10 km south of Portsmouth. The Channel River system, and those of its English and French tributaries was established by the Early Middle Pleistocene "Cromerian Complex" of glacials and interglacials, and from the time of the formation of the Pas de Calais/Straights of Dover, the Channel River also drained the rivers of south central England (the Thames system), western Belgium (the Scheldt system) and the Rhine–Meuse system. The scale of the Channel River should therefore be readily apparent when one considers that from at least 250,000 B.P. it was carrying drainage from almost half of western Europe, which included meltwater from the Alpine and northern European ice-sheets (Bourillet et al. 2003). The whole basin was surrounded by high ground to south and north, typically an erosional coastline characterised by cliffs which in many areas stretched up to 80 m in height. Using the Hurd deep as a referent (which is today at −200 m OD) it can be seen that the scale of cliff and plateaux heights would have reached up to 800 m (this figure for the area of Dartmoor). The character of these southern uplands differed from west to east: Cornwall, like Brittany, was a rugged landscape of steep slopes and short southern-draining rivers incised into deep valleys, which contrasts with the east where gently rolling smooth slopes, dry valleys and long rivers gave way to the plains and hills of Doggerland.

For much of Pleistocene time, Britain can therefore be regarded as a peninsula, not an island. Like the Americas or Sahel-land (the joined continent of Australia, Tasmania and New Guinea), Britain was peripheral to the main human settlement of the Upper Pleistocene world. It follows that human occupation of the region was not continuous. Rather, it was restricted to those windows of opportunity when it was connected to the Continent, experienced climates that were not too severe, and supported a rich herbivorous fauna. It is not surprising in this context that much attention has been paid to the timing and extent of Upper Palaeolithic occupation. One should not, however, view the vast area across which Britain was connected to the Continent as a continuous area of potential population movement. While Doggerland probably provided a number of easy opportunities for movement, the Channel River and its tributaries may well have constituted a major impediment to movement. Overall, with the exception of the earliest demonstrably Upper Palaeolithic groups of Britain (which one might argue arrived by canoeing along the western coast), communities seem to have arrived from the east. Certainly the distribution and character of Upper Palaeolithic sites can be interpreted as reflecting this.

The severe conditions of the Last Glacial Maximum (centred upon ca. 20,000 B.P.[1]) persisted in Britain beyond 16,000 B.P., and the period is referred to as the Dimlington Stadial. Between 13,000 and 11,000 B.P. Britain experienced two warm periods separated by a cold stadial (the Older Dryas ca. 12,200–12,000 B.P.), referred to as a whole as the Late Glacial Interstadial. In the first half of this period (the Bölling), from ca. 13,000 B.P., temperatures rose rapidly some 8°C to reach a July maximum of 17°C (i.e., nearly as warm as today) but with open environments lagging behind the warming and dominated by juniper scrub. It is only with the latter part of the Late Glacial Interstadial (the Allerød) that pollen spectra indicate an expansion of birch woodland (Walker et al. 1993), although climate seems to have been relatively unstable in this 11,800–11,000 B.P. period and it occurs in the context of a marked cooling towards the cold conditions of the Younger Dryas stadial (12,000–10,000 B.P.) as revealed in the Greenland Ice Cores and beetle assemblages (Atkinson et al. 1987; Johnsen et al. 2001). During the earlier part of the Younger Dryas Britain experienced a major ice re-advance centred around the Loch Lomond glacier,[2] and palaeo-environmental indicators suggest a cold and arid environment (Jones and Keen 1993).

Given the marked climatic oscillations of the Upper Pleistocene, it is no surprise that faunal communities varied considerably. A useful baseline for such change is the mammalian biostratigraphy developed by Currant and Jacobi (2001). They recognise for the entire Upper Pleistocene five formal Mammalian Assemblage Zones (MAZs) each represented by an eponymous type-site, and one interzone, of which two MAZs and the interzone are relevant to the Upper Palaeolithic. The Pin Hole MAZ belongs to the oscillating climatic conditions of Oxygen Isotope Stage (OIS) 3[3] (ca. 71,000–25,00 B.P.) and is characterised by a rich mammoth steppe fauna which included spotted hyaena, fox, lion, mammoth, horse, woolly rhinoceros, bison, reindeer, arctic hare and, on occasion, Early Upper Palaeolithic humans. Following this, the Dimlington Stadial Interzone has yielded a comparative rarity of mammalian fossils in England, which reflects the severity of conditions. Some time after conditions ameliorated from ca. 16,000 B.P. the Late OIS2 Gough's Cave MAZ is established, which at the type-site can be dated to ca. 12,900–9,900 B.P. This was broadly similar to the preceding Pin Hole MAZ, although apparently lacking spotted hyaena, lion, bison and woolly rhino and in which horse and reindeer seem to have been particularly common. In addition there seems to have been relatively marked regional differentiation in the Gough's Cave MAZ, with, for example, mammoth and reindeer better represented in the north and red deer in the south-west (Housley 1991), to which I shall return below. One might also argue that, from a British perspective, it is only in part of the Gough's Cave MAZ that human hunter-gatherers appear to have been a major feature.

Table 2.1 Periodization of the British Upper Palaeolithic from a "splitting" perspective using Continental parallels. Such a perspective maximises cultural variability of Upper Palaeolithic groups in Britain, which are viewed as relatively discrete occupational pulses deriving from the Continent, separated by periods in which humans were not present. The table does not present an exhaustive list. Sites in bold indicate the absence of unambiguous type fossils and are assigned to these periods on the basis of absolute dates only. Data from Jacobi 1980; 1991; 2004; Barton and Roberts 1996; Barton and Dumont 2000

Period	Cultural group	Example sites
40,000–35,000 B.P.	**Leafpoints**	Kent's Cavern (Devon)
		Beedings (Sussex)
		Badger Hole, Wookey Hole (Somerset)
		Pin Hole and Robin Hood's Cave (Creswell)
		Ffynnon Beuno (Clywd)
31,000–30,000 B.P.	**Aurignacian II**	Nottle Tor (Pembrokeshire)
		Uphill Quarry cave 8 (Somerset)
		Hyaena Den (Somerset)
		Kent's Cavern (Devon)
		Goat's Hole, Paviland (Gower)
		Hoyle's Mouth (Dyfed)
		Cae Gwyn (Clwyd)
		Ffynnon Beuno (Clwyd)
29,000–27,000 B.P.	**Early Gravettian/**	Pin Hole, Creswell (Derbyshire)
	Perigordian Va	Peper Harrow Park, Godalming (Surrey)
	(Fonterobertian)	Mildenhall (Suffolk)
		Bramford Road, Ipswich (Suffolk)
		Barnwood (Gloucestershire)
		Kent's Cavern (Devon)
		Goat's Hole, Paviland, Gower (Glamorgan)
		Cat Hole, Swansea (Glamorgan)
12,600–12,200 B.P.	**Late Magdalenian**	Major sites include:
(first half of Late	**(Creswellian, *sensu***	Gough's Cave, Sun Hole, Soldier's Hole
Glacial	**Garrod 1926)**	(Somerset)
Interstadial		Kent's Cavern (Devon)
– Bölling)		Robin Hood Cave, Mother Grundy's Parlour, Church Hole, Pin Hole (Creswell)
12,200–12,000 B.P.	**Hamburgian/Late**	Hengistbury Head (Dorset)
(stadial in the middle	**Magdalenian with**	Fox Hole (Staffordshire)
of the Late Glacial	**Hamburgian**	Farndon Fields (Nottinghamshire)
Interstadial – Older	**influence**	Cranwich (Norfolk)
Dryas)		Long Island (Langstone Harbour, Portsmouth)
12,200–12,000 B.P.	**Curved-backed**	Mother Grundy's Parlour (Creswell)
(stadial in the middle	**points (Bipointes)**	Gough's Cave, Cheddar (Somerset)
of the Late Glacial		Aveline's Hole (Somerset)
Interstadial – Older		Hoyle's Mouth (Pembrokeshire)
Dryas)		Bob's Cave, Kitley (Devon)

Table 2.1 *Continued*

Period	Cultural group	Example sites
12,000–11,000 B.P. (second half of Late Glacial Interstadial – Allerød)	*Federmessergruppen* (Penknife points, Monopointes)	Three Holes Cave, Torbryan Valley (Devon)
		Pixie's Hole (Devon)
		Symonds Yat (Glocestershire)
		Mother Grundy's Parlour (Creswell)
		Pin Hole (Creswell)
		Robin Hood Cave (Creswell)
		Kendrick's Cave (north Wales)
		Dowel Cave (Derbyshire)
		Callow Hill, Cheddar (Somerset)
		Cotgrave (Nottinghamshire)
		Seamer Carr Site C, Vale of Pickering (Yorkshire)
		Risby Warren Lower Assemblage (Humberside)
		High Furlong, Poulton-le-Fylde (Lancashire)
11,000–10,000 B.P. (Younger Dryas)	Ahrensburgian	**Faunal accumulation at Chelm's Coombe Shelter, one flake possibly contemporary**
		Sproughton (Suffolk)
		Avington VI (Berkshire)
Pleistocene–Holocene transition	Long blade assemblages	Avington VI (Berkshire)
		Three Ways Wharf (Greater London)
		Sproughton (Suffolk)
		Riverdale (Kent)
		Swaffham Prior (Suffolk)
		Gatehampton Farm (Oxfordshire)
		Seamer Carr Site C, Vale of Pickering (Yorkshire)

It should be remembered that these are formal biostratigraphic zones, not attempts to reconstruct faunal communities which were presumably constantly remodelled as responses to the highly unstable climates of the period. Lack of faunal assemblages which can be confidently dated to, for example, the Older Dryas or Dimlington Stadial leave us fairly ignorant of the nature of British faunal communities at these times, even though it is known that human groups were operating in the former. Some indications of dramatic change in faunal communities, at least in OIS3, can be glimpsed in the well-dated collection of material from Paviland cave. Here, for example, a relatively impoverished fauna of woolly rhino, reindeer, aurochs and bear was replaced by a richer mammoth steppe community around 29,000 B.P. (Pettitt 2000). In the last 3,000 years of the Late Glacial, horse and

red deer appear to have been important resources to Late Upper Palaeolithic foragers, mammoth were still present and saiga antelope has been recorded on Mendip
(Jacobi et al. 2001).

In the context of the ca. 35,000 (^{14}C) years of the European Upper Palaeolithic,
Britain was devoid of human occupants for most of the time. Even a generous
interpretation of the chronological information available to us amounts to no more
than 5,000 years of time over five or more phases, but in reality actual human
presence was probably far briefer (see table 2.1 for a periodisation of Upper Palaeolithic human presence in Britain). From this point of view, animals such as bison,
aurochs and horse seem to have been far more successful in their exploitation of
the region. A similar pattern of human absence can, however, be observed for
neighbouring regions of the Continent, such as northern France, Belgium and the
Netherlands (Housley et al. 1997), and over the entire period one has to look as
far south as the Loire or Mittelgebirge to find essentially continuous human
presence.

The British Early Upper Palaeolithic: Brief Occupation of the Peninsula by Early European *Homo Sapiens*

The earliest indication of *Homo sapiens* in Britain may be the KC4 partial human
maxilla from Kent's Cavern (Oakley et al. 1971; Stringer 2006:197), which is
assumed to represent *Homo sapiens* although its taxonomic status is not clear. Similarly ambiguous are the enigmatic leafpoint assemblages which seem to date to the
period ca. 40,000 to ca. 35,000 B.P., but at present it is unknown whether these
were made by anatomically modern humans or Neanderthals. They are known from
36 findspots, usually as isolated examples but several sites have yielded multiple
examples such as Kent's Cavern (10), Robin Hood Cave at Creswell Crags (at least
10), fissure fillings at Beedings, near Pulborough in Sussex (43), and Badger Hole
at Wookey Hole, Somerset (fig. 2.1). Jacobi's (1990) survey of leafpoint assemblages showed how, with the exception of Ffynnon Beuno, their distribution falls
south of the limits of the glaciers of the Last Glacial Maximum, a pattern which is
characteristic of all British Early Upper Palaeolithic archaeology and which presumably reflects the destructive effects of this period rather than human distribution.
Leafpoints are known from both cave and open contexts, and seem to occur in the
context of rich Pin Hole MAZ faunas. They fall into two broad technological categories; minimally worked examples on blades where retouch – always restricted to
the ventral surface – was employed simply to reduce the natural curvature of the
object; and bifacially worked pieces showing far more intensive manufacture (see,
e.g., Jacobi 2000). These forms show clear parallels with the broadly contemporary
assemblages to the east such as Ranis and Mauern in Germany and especially the
Jerzmanovician of Poland. An accumulation of leafpoints and associated endscrapers and burins in a small fissure at Beedings in West Sussex is suggestive of a
hunting camp situated at a point in the landscape commanding extensive views
across the Sussex Weald (Jacobi 2007b).

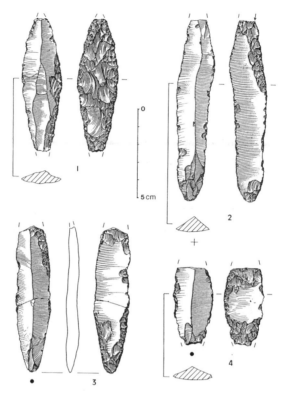

Figure 2.1 Bifacially worked leafpoints (or bladepoints) from Badger Hole at Wookey Hole, Somerset. Drawings by Joanna Richards. Courtesy of Roger Jacobi and Wells and Mendip Museum.

It is usually assumed that Continental leafpoint assemblages (the Ranisian–Jermanowician group) were produced by late Neanderthals, although if by extension the British examples were assumed to have been made by this species one would have to conclude that they had arrived at a clearly Upper Palaeolithic technology before their extinction. British leafpoints tend to be made on blades, and in situations where they are associated with other tool forms these are clearly Upper Palaeolithic (if culturally undiagnostic) in nature, such as endscrapers on blades, and burins. By contrast there is no evidence to associate them with Mousterian assemblages of Neanderthal manufacture (Jacobi 1999). Campbell (1977) suggested that leafpoints formed part of a wider technology of which the few British Aurignacian assemblages were part, but as Jacobi (1990) has noted there are no associations between the few British Aurignacian artefacts in Britain and leafpoints. Only three sites (Kent's Cavern, Paviland and Ffynnon Beuno) have yielded both assemblage types but this can probably be explained by the strategic position and thus importance of these caves rather than any meaningful connection between the assemblages (Jacobi 1980:17). At Kent's Cavern, the distribution of the two is significantly different. Furthermore, south of the limit of the Last Glaciation ice the distribution of leafpoints is strongly biased to central and eastern England, which contrasts strongly with the distribution of the seven known Aurignacian sites (see below). Thus if the two were related in a technological whole employed by the same groups of modern humans, one would have to conclude that these groups used weapons tipped with leafpoints in England, and then changed their toolkits radically when operating in Wales. Clearly the sensible interpretation is that the two assemblage type represented distinct human populations, but the issue as to whether these were biologically distinct (i.e., *Homo neanderthalensis* and *Homo sapiens*) remains to be resolved.

Recent re-dating of relevant sites has clarified the picture somewhat, and it now appears that leafpoint assemblages predated the few Aurignacian sites of Britain, thus reinforcing the notion that they were distinct entities. The few existing dates on fauna found in stratigraphic association with leafpoints at Badger Hole (Somerset), Bench Quarry (Devon) and Pin Hole (Creswell Crags, Derbyshire) suggest ages in excess of 35,000 B.P. (Jacobi et al. 2006). The only potential association between human remains and leafpoints is at Kent's Cavern, where the KC4 human maxilla was originally dated directly by AMS radiocarbon to ca. 31,000 B.P. The maxilla, however, was found in a separate area of the cave (the Vestibule) from the cluster of leafpoints, and a clear association is obviously lacking. Recent AMS radiocarbon dating of bones found in stratigraphic relation to the mandible suggest that its age is between 35,000 and 37,000 B.P. (Jacobi et al. 2006; Jacobi 2007b). The few lithics apparently associated with the maxilla are certainly Upper Palaeolithic but culturally undiagnostic. All one can do is assume that there is a very broad connection on the grounds of stratigraphic and technological parsimony. Recent dating of fauna stratigraphically related to the maxilla pre-treated using the new ultrafiltration technique at the Oxford Radiocarbon Accelerator Unit has demonstrated that the age of the maxilla is likely to be in the range of 37,000–35,000 B.P. (Jacobi et al. 2006). As such, the taxonomic identification of the fragmentary maxilla – previously assumed to be *Homo sapiens* but now open to question – has become of critical interest. Whatever the biological identity of leafpoint makers was (and one cannot rule out that it was a technology sufficiently generalised to have been used by both the last Neanderthals and the first modern humans on the Northern European Plain) the connection with the east is typologically apparent. This suggests that the rivers of the Channel were already impeding movement.

The first clear indicators of the presence of *Homo sapiens* in Britain are the Aurignacian assemblages from a total of eight sites[4] in the south-west of England and Wales. It has to be said that, while most scholars assume that the Aurignacian is the signature of modern humans, actual fossil associations of the two are remarkably rare, although on the grounds of the few fossil associations that do exist one can say that from 35,000 B.P. the Aurignacian was exclusive to modern humans. On the basis of the existing chronological information it can be hypothesised that at least 3,000 (radiocarbon) years separate the Aurignacian sites of Britain and the preceding leafpoint assemblages, which further suggests there is no meaningful relationship between the two. If this is correct the different geographical distribution of each presumably reflects an adaptation to plains and wide river valleys derived

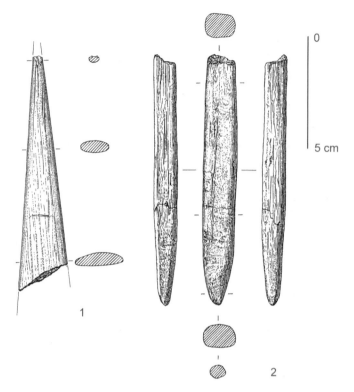

Figure 2.2 Aurignacian bone and antler points from the Axe Valley. (*Left*) Lozangic antler point from Uphill, North Somerset. Bristol City Museum and Art Gallery. (*Right*) Bone point from Hyaena Den at Wookey Hole, Somerset. Wells and Mendip Museum. Drawings by Julie Cross. Courtesy of Roger Jacobi.

from the east for leafpoint users, and an adaptation to upland ecotones derived from the Atlantic coast for the Aurignacian.

British Aurignacian sites are united by similar lithic assemblages in which nosed/shouldered endscrapers and *burins busqué* are the dominant culturally diagnostic items (Jacobi 1980; 1999; Swainston 1999; 2000; Jacobi and Pettitt 2000; Dinnis 2005). Two organic armatures are known (fig. 2.2): at Uphill Quarry Cave 8, Weston-super-Mare (Somerset), a broken lozangic antler point has been dated directly by AMS radiocarbon to 31,730 ± 250 B.P. (OxA-13716; Higham et al. 2006) which is in good agreement with the French Aurignacian II which contains typologically similar points. A bone/antler point from the Hyaena Den at Wookey (Somerset) – like Uphill associated with the Axe river – also bears similarities to those from Continental Aurignacian sites and has been dated to 31,550 ± 340 B.P. (OxA-13803; Higham et al. 2006), but otherwise the cave contained no identifiable Aurignacian artefacts. The similarities to the Continental Aurignacian II, lack of evidence of any typological subdivisions within the British material and the clustering of the eight sites in the western uplands of Britain (Jacobi 1999; Jacobi and

Pettitt 2000) suggest that Britain was visited by one or a small number of groups probably along the coast from France. While a major part of Aurignacian territories in north-west Europe could now be submerged (R. Dinnis, pers. comm.), the clustering of British sites in the west, which contrasts with the distribution of all subsequent British Upper Palaeolithic materials, probably has demographic significance. If so, it would represent the first example of the importance of the Atlantic coast for human movement in western Europe (Cunliffe 2001). In view of the complexities of the Channel River and its tributaries it could be argued that the most parsimonious route would be to follow the Atlantic coastline of the time, which assuming this was west of the −100 m contour would take populations from similar rugged landscapes of north-western France along a route west of Cornwall, with the plains of what is now the Bristol Channel and the Severn Valley being the first obvious area of incursion one would reach. As the Axe formed a tributary of the drowned reaches of the Severn at the time this would explain the presence of the organic points at both its source and lower reaches, and as the Gower Peninsula formed an impressively visible upland to the west of the plains this presumably explains the importance of the Goat's Hole (Paviland). The wider (and largely Welsh) distribution of the Aurignacian could furthermore reflect a simple northwards dispersal from this area. Culturally diagnostic Aurignacian material is remarkably limited (about 50 artefacts according to Dinnis 2005) and only the Goat's Hole (Paviland) has an assemblage to speak of. I suggest that the small number of sites, their geographical clustering and the small number and formal similarity of tools that links the sites indicates very strongly that these were discarded by one single forager group which was derived from western French Aurignacian II groups.

The Axe Valley finds suggest the re-tooling of weapons in the context of hunting whereas the sites further to the west and north are perhaps more suggestive of more general activities and/or hunting with bladelet-based armatures. Although it is clear that bladelets produced from cores previously described as endscrapers were used as armatures in the Aurignacian, the prevalence of organic armatures in the Axe Valley suggests that robust and reliable weapon systems were employed in the area, as opposed to the immediately lethal but fragile lithic-tipped weapons, which one might expect in exploratory situations where one cannot predict the availability of flint to replace broken weapons. By contrast, the presence of carinated endscrapers at Ffynnon Beuno, Paviland, Kent's Cavern and possibly Hoyle's Mouth might suggest that bladelet-tipped weapons were employed in these regions (R. Dinnis, pers. comm.). If one were to use abundance and variability of lithics as indicative of any "core" area then Paviland, with its panoramic views onto a vast plain and towards a homeland, would be it, but even this site cannot account for more than a few days' occupation. Perhaps the group entered Britain along the coastal route from France and established a temporary core area in the ecotonal boundary between the uplands of south Wales and the plain of the Bristol Channel and Severn river system, operating out of there to the north, east and south only occasionally. The whole Aurignacian record might account for little more than one seasonal trip some time around 31,000 B.P.

The poor radiocarbon database suggests that the next human visits to Britain occurred around 29,000 B.P., that is, after a gap of at least 2,000 (^{14}C) years. Between ca. 29,000 and 25,000 B.P. (probably only 29,000–28,000 B.P.) Britain seems to have been visited sporadically by groups of Gravettian cultural attribution. As with the preceding Aurignacian, the remarkably low number of sites for this period (eight: Jacobi 1980;1999) and absolutely low numbers of diagnostic artefacts indicates that Britain was infrequently occupied, although the distribution of sites, which now includes Pin Hole at Creswell (Derbyshire), Barnwood (Gloucestershire), Mildenhall[5] and Bramford Road (Ipswich) in East Anglia, Godalming (Surrey) and Kent's Cavern (Devon), in addition to Goat's Hole (Paviland) and possibly Cathole (Gower), indicates that the Gravettians at least had a wider distribution in the country. This might indicate either that they had wider and more mobile foraging patterns than the Aurignacians, although this would be surprising in the absence of any further diagnostic assemblages, or that they were here for a relatively longer period of time than the Aurignacians, although again this would be surprising given the remarkably low amounts of material. It could be that Britain was visited briefly at several different times by small Gravettian groups. The spread of ^{14}C dates from Paviland have been taken to support this notion (Pettitt 2000) although recent re-dating of these using ultrafiltration pre-treatment at Oxford is tending to reveal that diagnostic Gravettian archaeology clusters around 29,000–27,000 B.P. In fact, all British Gravettian sites are characterised by the presence of Font Robert points, which on the Continent are the type fossil of the early Gravettian (Perigordian Va or Fontirobertian). In France this is securely dated to 28,000–27,000 B.P., which is in accord with the available dating evidence from Paviland. Thus, a parsimonious interpretation of the Gravettian material of Britain would be a chronologically tight pulse of activity, perhaps even of a single group. If this were the case, the distribution of material – effectively English unlike the Aurignacian – might suggest a derivation of these groups from the east, and the parallels between the British lithic material and those from the Gravettian sites of Masières Canal, Belgium, and Cirque de la Patrie in the Paris Basin noted by Jacobi (1980:25) would support this notion. At Paviland it is interesting that the Gravettians appear in the context of a rich mammoth steppe fauna, which suggests they were an integral part of it and expanded with it prior to the Last Glacial Maximum.

With the exception of Paviland, British Gravettian sites reveal little about human behaviour except that they were discarding lithic armatures and knives.[6] Given their similarities with the Aurignacian sites (low in number, singular/very low numbers of diagnostic artefacts, typologically identical), it is interesting that they contrast with them quite markedly. With the exception of the bone/antler points of the Axe Valley, British Aurignacian sites are characterised by tools, not weapons, whereas the reverse is true for the Gravettian (although see Otte and Caspar 1987). Gravettian tools from Continental sites are typologically diagnostic, and the lack of these in Britain may suggest that Gravettians were here so infrequently that little maintenance activity was carried out. Perhaps it is significant also that the two known Aurignacian weapon tips derive from reliable but not immediately lethal weapons,

Figure 2.3 Plan and section drawing of Buckland's excavations at Goat's Hole, Paviland, showing the location of the burial of the "Red Lady" in a side alcove, and the associated mammoth skull (from Buckland 1823).

whereas one can probably assume that the Gravettian spears tipped with Font Robert points, while prone to breakage, were probably a far more effective killing technology. This may imply a greater confidence in the knowledge of the raw-material environment among the Gravettians, although given potential differences between the ecosystems in which both groups were operating it is probably best seen as reflecting distinct differences in hunting organisation.

The Goat's Hole at Paviland has yielded one diagnostic Gravettian lithic artefact – the broken tang of a Font Robert point (Swainston 2000) – and the totality of the cave's archaeology has been recently subject to a major re-analysis (Aldhouse-Green 2000). Most spectacular is the burial of the "Red Lady" (originally thought to be female and so named due to ochre staining) which was tucked into a small alcove to the left side of the cave (see fig. 2.3). Although the burial was excavated in the infancy of archaeology (Buckland 1823) enough information survives to reveal striking similarities with some 55 Continental burials of the Gravettian period (Pettitt 2006). All of the bones of the Red Lady are stained with ochre, which is far stronger on the bones of the lower body than the upper, which suggests that the Red Lady was buried in a two-piece set of clothing, perhaps in the form of a parka and leggings. A number of common periwinkle shells (*Littorina littorea*) pierced for suspension were recovered, according to Buckland (1823:88) in the waist or pubic area. One might argue on the basis of analogy with Gravettian and later Epigravettian burials elsewhere that these were sewn onto the clothing of the Red Lady (Aldhouse-Green 2000:115), perhaps to the base of a parka or to a loincloth. Buckland also found with the shells fragments of mammoth ivory rings (1823:88–89). He noted that the diameter of these thin rings was in the order of 100–125 mm, although the curvature of surviving ring fragments suggests that these at least were closer to 70 mm (personal observation). Assuming that one or two rings are now lost it is conceivable that the Red Lady wore bracelets/armlets of this polished material, although it is difficult to see how the surviving forms (probably two) could have been slid over the hands of a young adult male of the Red Lady's stature (over 1.8 m). Either they had been worn continuously from youth, derived from another, smaller, individual, or were worn suspended about the person. Whichever the case, it is easy to imagine how complex meaning was attached to such personal ornamentation. Around 40–50 fragments of mammoth ivory rods were recovered from the chest area of the Red Lady, suggesting that tapering elongated rods with bulbous ends similar to those from Aurignacian and Gravettian contexts on the Continent were deliberately broken before being laid over the burial. Ochre staining on these fragments indicates that they were polished, presumably to bring out a metallic sheen. The morphology of the pieces suggests that they were not blanks for the production of beads but instead finished items, either of adornment or of power.

A number of other items of personal adornment were recovered in proximity to the burial although it is impossible today to ascertain whether they formed part of it or were left at the time or during subsequent visits to the cave. These include the Sollas egg pendant made from an egg-shaped pathology of mammoth ivory (excavated by Buckland's successor, William Sollas), for which parallels are also known on the Continent (in Belgium and the Czech Republic – both to the east). A small oval bead of mammoth ivory, two perforated reindeer canines (now lost) and two heavily modified teeth of cervid or bear similar to Continental examples of perforated *croches de cerf*[7] may have joined this item as ornaments on the Red Lady's body. More enigmatically, three objects of horse metapodials usually referred to as knives or spatulae were recovered from the cave by collectors in the 1830s and have been dated to the Gravettian,[8] as with a number of enigmatic items of worked mammoth ivory. While the former may have had a physical function (daggers, butchery tools, tent pegs or weaving knives, for example) a decorative function cannot be ruled out, especially as "waists" on two of them could have taken line, perhaps for suspension. Parsimoniously one might regard all of these items as having adorned the burial, which in its relative richness would be in keeping with Continental examples spanning ca. 30,000–25,000 B.P. and distributed from Paviland and Lagar Velho (Portugal) in the west to Sungir' in Russia to the east. Previous interpretations of the Red Lady have suggested, for example, that it was an accidental death of a hunter, perhaps when the group was in the country during the summer procuring mammoth ivory, which does seem to have been worked in the cave. The nature of Gravettian burials, however, which are usually of pathological young men (Pettitt 2006), suggests that a deeper meaning can be attached to the burial, and certainly indicates that one of the more enigmatic characteristics of Gravettian behaviour was practised at their north-western periphery.

In a major discussion of the cave's Gravettian archaeology and of the burial itself, Aldhouse-Green (2000) has suggested that the cave was a sacred location, a place in which a powerful burial and powerful artefacts were deposited (see also Aldhouse-Green and Pettitt 1998; Aldhouse-Green and Aldhouse-Green 2005). If it is true that Paviland cave was of numinous significance as a special place rather than a prosaic camp, then it would appear that Gravettians, at least on this occasion, were enculturating the landscape. There is no evidence of this behaviour in the British Aurignacian; instead it suggests that the Gravettians were more similar to the Late Upper Palaeolithic Magdalenians who enculturated two caves in Creswell Crags with figurative engravings (see below).

It is probable that Gravettian activity in Britain was curtailed by the climatic downturn towards the severe conditions of the Last Glacial Maximum that centred on 20,000 (radiocarbon) years B.P. There are certainly no convincing indications of human activity in the country after ca. 24,000 B.P. Some leafpoints were originally identified with those of the Continental Solutrean, which although it spans the Last Glacial Maximum is not found elsewhere north of the Loire. Today, it is known that all British leafpoint finds belong to the Early Upper Palaeolithic as discussed above, and where notions of a British Solutrean unfortunately persist today (such as in Pryor 2003) they are erroneous. The next available dates on humanly modified materials appear around 13,000 B.P., indicating that a period of at least 8,000 years, probably more, passed during which humans were absent. This is part of a wider abandonment of the Northern European Plain.

Late Upper Palaeolithic Activity I: Recolonisation after the Last Glacial Maximum and the Late Magdalenian

The human recolonisation of the Northern European Plain as the conditions of the Last Glacial Maximum ameliorated has attracted considerable attention in recent years. Gamble et al. (2005) identify this with a Magdalenian expansion out of the Franco-Iberian refugium beginning ca. 16,000 B.P. Housley et al. (1997) suggested a two-phase recolonisation process, in which temporary pioneer colonists were operating in areas two to three centuries before year-round seasonal cycles could be established in them, although the robustness of this argument has been contested (Blockley et al. 2000; 2006; and see Housley et al. 2000). Although there has been debate regarding the phasing of the recolonisation of the Continent, specialists agree that Late Upper Palaeolithic societies had re-established themselves in Britain by ca. 12,600 B.P., and perhaps somewhat earlier with the pronounced warming at the start of the Late Glacial Interstadial (Jacobi 1980:36–44; Barton 1999; Barton and Dumont 2000).

In the Late Glacial, normal river flow was still occurring out in the Channel River system, where fluviatile erosion was removing sediments from even the Deeps up to the flooding of the Channel by marine transgression in the Holocene (Antoine et al. 2003). One can therefore still regard the Channel as a significant barrier. Culturally, the Late Upper Palaeolithic assemblages of Britain may be most closely compared to those in Belgium, the Netherlands and Germany, reflecting a derivation from the east, and Shackley (1981) drew attention to the proximity of the major Late Upper Palaeolithic sites of Bramford Road (Ipswich) and Hengistbury Head to the Continent.

Garrod (1926) coined the term "Creswellian" to refer to British Late Glacial assemblages which now seem clearly restricted to the first half of the Late Glacial Interstadial. The term was employed to distinguish between the British sites and those of the related, but typologically distinct, Late Magdalenian. Thus, to Garrod, while the British assemblages were certainly similar (and presumably therefore related) to the contemporary Magdalenian assemblages, enough differences warranted a taxonomic distinction. Since Garrod the nature of the connection between British and Continental Late Glacial assemblages has been debated (e.g., Jacobi 1980; 1991; 2007; Campbell 1977; Roberts and Barton 1996; Charles 1999; Pettitt 2007).

British Late Magdalenian assemblages are characterised by blade production on uni- and bipolar blade cores using the cresting technique and a degree of platform preparation, and the use of the *en eperon* technique for isolating the striking platform of blades; also by angle-backed points with one single oblique truncation (Creswell points) and trapezoidal-backed points with two opposed oblique truncations (Cheddar points); endscrapers on blades, burins (often dihedral but also on truncations) and a specific type of long-pointed borer made on a thick blank (*Zinken*). A small number of curved-backed points, penknife points (*Federmesser*) and shouldered points have been recovered from these assemblages but it is unclear whether they belong to the British Late Magdalenian as a whole or are restricted to its later phases or, more probably, post-date it (see below). Straight-backed blades, which are ubiquitous in contemporary Continental Late Magdalenian sites, appear to be entirely lacking (Jacobi 1991; Barton and Roberts 1996). The collection of 2,115 Late Magdalenian artefacts from Gough's Cave, Cheddar, forms the largest assemblage of this period in Britain, and has recently been subject to a magisterial study by Jacobi (2004). It is clear that this number is all that remains of potentially over 7,000 lithic artefacts recovered from the site, alongside a rich collection of human and animal bone. Over 99 per cent of the lithics are made on black upper Cretaceous chalk flint, the source of which is probably the northern part of Salisbury Plain (to which I shall return below). Although flakes are numerous the assemblage is dominated by blades. Cores are low in number, reflecting the transport to the site of finished blades and/or the transport of blade cores away from the site, although the cores that exist, as well as a number of complete and partial crested blades, core tablets and platform preparation flakes, indicate that unipolar blade cores were being worked on site. A total of 552 tools are dominated by abruptly modified (i.e., backed) pieces including Cheddar Points (fig. 2.4), Creswell Points and curved-backed pieces (79 per cent of which are broken), burins, endscrapers (of which 30 are on blades) and pieces with continuous lateral retouch including

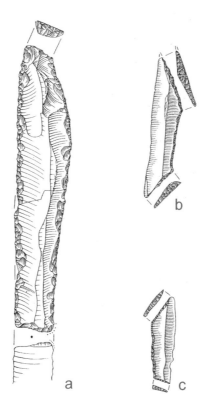

Figure 2.4 Late Magdalenian lithics from Gough's Cave, Cheddar Gorge, Somerset. (*a*) Blade with Magdalenian retouch. (*b*) and (*c*) Angle-backed Cheddar points. Drawings by Hazel Martingell. Courtesy of Roger Jacobi.

Magdalenian retouched blades as recognised on the Continent. Given the spread of radiocarbon dates on material from Gough's Cave into the second half of the Late Glacial Interstadial, it is conceivable that the 14 examples of curved-backed pieces belong to a later phase of occupation from which also derive the human remains (see below). The lack of Late Magdalenian/Hamburgian shouldered points (see below) is in keeping with radiocarbon dates on humanly modified material from the site, the majority of which cluster between ca. 12,600–12,300 B.P. (Jacobi 2004:fig. 46). Only a few dates exist to suggest human activity in the succeeding Allerød period, and re-dating of samples using the improved ultrafiltration method will probably push these back to the Late Magdalenian period.

Organic tools and weapons recovered from British Late Magdalenian contexts include eyed needles (Church Hole, Cat Hole, Gough's Cave and Kent's Cavern); awls made on the tibiae of arctic hare (Church Hole, Robin Hood Cave, Pin Hole and Gough's Cave) and on a hyoid bone (Kent's Cavern); four enigmatic *batons percés* of reindeer antler[9] (three from Gough's Cave, one from the Thames at Zion Reach: R. M. Jacobi, pers. comm.) *sagaies* of mammoth ivory (Gough's and Pin

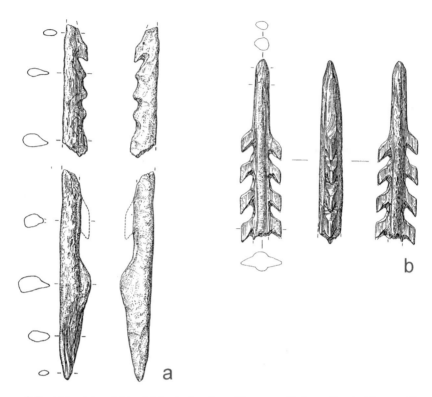

Figure 2.5 Uniserial and biserial barbed points ("harpoons") from Kent's Cavern, Torquay, Devon. Drawings by Julian Cross. Courtesy of Roger Jacobi.

Hole: fig. 2.6); and, conceivably, uniserial and biserial barbed points (Kent's Cavern:[10] fig. 2.5) (Armstrong 1925; Currant et al. 1989; Jacobi 2007; Pettitt 2007). Engravings on the mammoth ivory *sagaie* from Pin Hole have parallels in stylised fish on Continental Magdalenian sites, and the recovery of such designs on other *sagaies* suggests a wide currency for this weapon–symbol combination (Pettitt 2007). Numerous Continental parallels can be found for the horse's head engraved on bone from Robin Hood Cave (Pettitt 2007).

Stray finds of Late Magdalenian lithics, for example from several areas of Nottinghamshire (Garton 1993; Jacobi et al. 2001), suggest degrees of activity in the landscape, but it has to be said that densities are remarkably low despite intensive surface collection. The possibility remains that a sizeable camp site may eventually be found, and such a candidate may be from Farndon Fields near Newark (Garton 1993). An assemblage of ca. 450 Late Magdalenian lithics recovered from eroding deposits at Newtown Linford, Leicestershire, derive from a scatter around 5 m in extent, which suggests at least a small open-air camp (Cooper 2002).

Late Magdalenians in Britain, as on the Continent, were drawn to the parts of the landscape where uplands meet lowlands, which presumably offered both ecotonal resources as well as landscapes that could be used tactically in the procurement

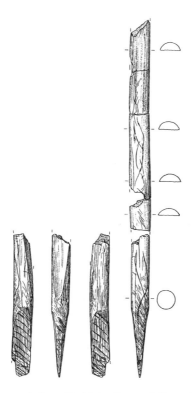

Figure 2.6 Mammoth ivory *sagaie* from Pin Hole, Creswell Crags. Note engraved design. Courtesy of Roger Jacobi.

of herbivores. Cooper (2002:79) has suggested that the location of the Newtown Lynford camp at the narrow mouth of a pronounced gorge perhaps indicates its importance in this light, and a parallel exists here with Cheddar Gorge (Jacobi 1997:501). Creswell Crags, another steep-walled gorge but without a narrow mouth, may have been important as it channelled migrating animals such as reindeer, possibly between winter grazing areas in the lowlands of Lincolnshire and Doggerland and spring calving grounds in the uplands of the Peak District, which were certainly in place by the second half of the Late Glacial Interstadial (Pettitt 2007).

Creswell Crags, a kilometre-long west–east trending gorge through limestone bordering Nottinghamshire and Derbyshire, was an important focus of Late Magdalenian activity. Archaeology of the period has been found in four of its caves: Pin Hole, Robin Hood Cave and Mother Grundy's Parlour on the northern (Derbyshire) side of the gorge, and Church Hole on the opposite (Nottinghamshire) side. If the number of backed points – the most dominant Late Magdalenian tool form in the crags – can be taken as a coarse estimate of occupation intensity, Mother Grundy's Parlour was the most used site (n = 57), followed by Robin Hood Cave (n = 40). Pin Hole cave yielded significantly less (n = 17), Church Hole hardly any (n = 4: Jacobi 2007:table 7.9). (I shall return to the relative lack of occupation at

Church Hole below.) Creswell contains the most abundant evidence of Late Magdalenian activity in Britain, although it seems to have attracted only brief, seasonal human visits.

In addition to typical Late Magdalenian lithics, several organic items are known from the Late Magdalenian at Creswell, including eyed needles, four awls on the tibiae of arctic (mountain) hare[11] and a serially notched horse vertebra erroneously described as a pendant in earlier publications but which may have been used as a line spindle, perhaps for storing line for hare traps or for sewing (Jacobi, pers. comm.) All of these come from Church Hole, and may represent a cached or lost sewing kit. If this interpretation is correct the removal of fur from arctic hare at Robin Hood Cave (and cutmarks on bones of this taxon from Church Hole) is of interest as it would indicate that the replenishment of clothing was one seasonal activity in the Crags. Two objects of *art mobilier* are known; the engraving of an enigmatic humanoid on a woolly rhino bone from Pin Hole and a typically Magdalenian style horse head engraved on a horse rib from Robin Hood Cave (see Pettitt and Bahn, in press).

At present, Creswell contains the only known examples of British Palaeolithic cave art (see papers in Pettitt et al. 2007). With the exception of one motif of converging lines (generally identified in cave art as a "vulva") in Robin Hood Cave, Church Hole cave on the south side of the gorge contains all of the engravings. These comprise a cervid (probably a young red deer with first year spikes), a bovid (probably aurochs), three (possibly four) vulvae, an incomplete horse, the head of an ibis, a group of images depicting either long-necked birds or stylised Magdalenian women, and an enigmatic image that may be a variant on the latter (figs. 2.7, 2.8 and 2.9). With the exception of the birds/women these all cluster in the daylight zone of the cave. I have elsewhere (2007) drawn attention to a number of Continental parallels to the Creswell art among the Continental Magdalenian, enough I hope to demonstrate an intimate connection between British Late Magdalenian groups and their contemporaries.

It is of interest that Church Hole, as noted above, seems to have contained less Late Magdalenian archaeology than the three caves of the north side of the gorge (Jacobi 2007). This could simply reflect the greater desirability of south-facing caves, but one wonders why in this case Church Hole contains almost all of the parietal art. This may indicate one way in which the landscape was imbued with meaning, as it is reminiscent of the Magdalenian caves of La Vache and Niaux, which face each other in a pronounced valley. In the former, parietal art is non-existent but a rich inventory of archaeology (including *art mobilier*) is known, and in the latter no archaeology to speak of has been found although its parietal art is some of the most spectacular known. Although it would be incorrect to draw too black-and-white a distinction this does suggest that some caves had more spiritual functions, others more prosaic. Jacobi (2007a) has noted that the use of Church Hole came to an end with the Late Magdalenian, whereas later Upper Palaeolithic groups seem to have made use of the other caves, and has suggested that the creation of the art may have marked it out as special from that point onwards, i.e., a place perhaps to be avoided.

Figure 2.7 Creswell cave art: engraving of cervid (probably red deer, facing left) in the main cave mouth area of Church Hole. Note how a natural erosional hole (vug) has been taken as an eye and a natural burrow as a mouth. Note also the incipient antler spike and graffiti from the 1940s. Late Magdalenian.

Abundant cutmarked bones of arctic hare indicate that their meat, fat and fur were important in the period, and the recovery of several awls made on their tibiae at Creswell and Gough's suggests an intimate connection between clothing manufacture and this species (Charles and Jacobi 1994; Jacobi 2007a). Horse seems also to have been an important resource (at Gough's Cave, Mother Grundy's Parlour, Kent's Cavern and several other sites), and modified bones of red deer, mammoth, saiga antelope, aurochs and reindeer indicate that these species were also exploited, in the latter case at least for antler (Barton and Roberts 1996; Barton and Dumont 2000; Jacobi 2004; 2007; Lister 1991; Pettitt 2007; Roberts 1996). Cutmarks on bones of whooper swan and ptarmigan from Gough's Cave remind us of the importance of avifaunal resources at the time, for which Continental parallels exist.

Seasonality data indicates that Gough's Cave was used during both summer and winter (Beasley 1987; Parkin et al. 1986), and the dominant herbivore among the fauna is horse (Currant 1986; 1991), which seems to have been hunted without regard for age, and from which cutmarks and smashes indicate that meat and marrow was used. Red deer seems also to have been an important resource, although as Currant (1986; 1991) has noted there is a marked absence of reindeer (excepting the three antler *bâtons*). A direct date of 12,480 ± 130 B.P. on a reindeer antler base (OxA-1122: Hedges et al. 1987) from Aveline's Hole (north Mendip,

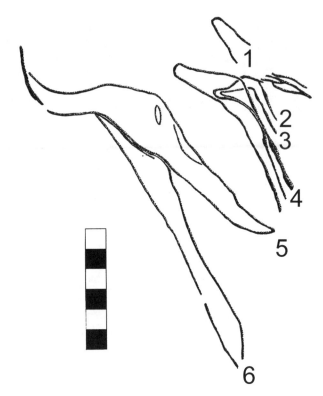

Figure 2.8 Creswell cave art: engraving of enigmatic figures in the back of Church Hole, Creswell, interpreted as either stylised Magdalenian females or long-necked birds. Flowstone overlying the birds has been dated to ca. 12,800 B.P. by Uranium-Series, which provides a minimum age for the engravings and thus verifies its Palaeolithic antiquity. Late Magdalenian.

where red deer dominates the fauna) indicates that the species was present in the region during the period, so its absence at Gough's presumably indicates that it was not a desired resource during these seasons. Jacobi (2004:76) has suggested that it may have been sparse due to high summer temperatures at the time and that its distribution may have been more northerly in the main.

At Creswell, horse seems also to have been important, although arctic hare seems to have been a particular focus of activity, and although the presence of reindeer in the region can only be attested towards the end of the first half of the Late Glacial Interstadial, the establishment of calving grounds in the Peak District may have formed an important seasonal focus of activity in the region, and the migrating reindeer may well have passed through the Crags. Although seasonality data are lacking, spring seems to be indicated on a variety of grounds, that is, concentration on calving (assuming that the reindeer calving established by the Younger Dryas in the Peak District extends back to the earlier part of the Late Glacial Interstadial), procurement of arctic hare and the depiction of a young cervid with first year spikes which appear in spring. If correct, this may indicate that Cheddar Gorge and the

Figure 2.9   Creswell Crags: 2006 excavation outside Church Hole, Nottinghamshire, into spoil heap from 1876 excavation, Holocene levels and *in situ* Pleistocene talus deposits. Note resemblance of the cave's entrance to a chancel arch – which may explain its name. Photograph: Paul Pettitt.

Creswell Crags gorge played complementary roles in an annual scheduled subsistence strategy. The similarity of specific items from the two sites, such as the awls made on arctic hare tibiae which bear the same modifications, supports the notion that the two are connected. One might hypothesise that Creswell represents the trapping of arctic hare in spring, perhaps geared to the replenishment of clothing (calfskin is particularly good for this, and arctic hare fur has many uses: see Owen 2005). This may have occurred en route to the reindeer calving grounds in the Peaks, although this remains to be tested. By contrast, Cheddar represents winter and summer hunting of horse and red deer. The two may be thus seen as critical nodes in an annual territory.

The differences in subsistence foci between Gough's Cave and the Creswell sites is interesting in the light of raw-material movement patterns and object typology, which in my opinion link the sites intimately. In Gough's Cave, high-quality flint was imported from sources at the northern edge of Salisbury Plain, Wiltshire, over a distance of ~70 km (Jacobi 1997; 2004; Barton and Dumont 2000). The raw-material source for Kent's Cavern flint is different and implies either the activities of a totally different group or another node in raw-material sources. Even more surprisingly, this material has also been identified using trace element analysis of lithics from Robin Hood Cave, Creswell, a distance of over 200 km (Rockman 2003). Currently, Late Magdalenian material from at least four sites can be linked to this source, which is specifically identified with the Vale of Pewsey. Two amber pebbles were recovered from Gough's Cave (Currant et al. 1989) and one from Creswell (probably Robin Hood Cave). In subsequent periods when Britain became an island, the source for such Baltic amber is the east coast, although during the Late Pleistocene the most obvious source must have been the northern coast of the North Sea over 200 km from the Creswell sites. These objects indicate that Late Magdalenian groups had access to this region, perhaps for coastal resources.

Figure 2.10 shows the location of Late Magdalenian sites and findspots relative to the physical geography of the Late Glacial Interstadial. There are about 35 in total. Barton et al. (2003:637) has stressed the importance of the upland margins to Late Magdalenian groups. This is clear from a number of findspots but more widely the distribution relates strongly to the Trent and Severn rivers (highlighted), which together fringe the upland margins and form a NE–SW communication axis through Britain at the time. Lithic raw-material movements have been superimposed on this, as have movements of amber from a presumed northern coastal source. The similarity of artefacts from Gough's Cave and the Cheddar sites, and subsistence strategies which are both similar and complementary, supports the notion of an interconnectedness of these critical sites, and the use of the Pewsey flint source further suggests that Kent's Cavern and Three Holes Cave belong to the same system.

On the Continent there is evidence of much change in lithic assemblages during the last few thousand years of the Late Pleistocene, and in the later part of the Bölling, as Jacobi (1980:44) has noted, shouldered points with oblique distal truncations seem also to have been part of Late Magdalenian lithic assemblages. Recent excavations at Le Tureau des Gardes 7 in the Paris Basin have shown how a particular lithic facies attributable to the Late Magdalenian contains a number of such points, probably due to interaction with Hamburgian groups to the east (Weber 2006). Such Magdalenian shouldered points are rare in Britain, but have been recovered in number (>20, mostly broken) at Hengistbury Head, Dorset (Barton 1992), and singularly at Fox Hole cave, Derbyshire, apparently in association with reindeer antler foreshafts, a hearth and remains of reindeer, horse and a large bovid (Bramwell 1971), also at one of the Kitley caves, Yealmpton, Devon, Farndon Fields near Newark (Garton 1993), Cranwich, Norfolk (Jacobi and Martingell 1980), and Long Island in Langstone Harbour, Portsmouth (Draper 1962). Fox Hole also yielded two reindeer antler rods apparently in association with the shouldered point and with one *Federmesser*. One of the rods can be clearly identified as a javelin foreshaft of a type known from Church Hole cave at Creswell and from the Hamburgian level at Stellmoor, Germany (Lund 1993), and the second rod, while incomplete, was conceivably a similar artefact. The rods have been dated directly to 11,970 ± 120 B.P. (First Chamber, OxA-1493) and 12,000 ± 120 B.P. (Bear Chamber, OxA-1494; Hedges et al. 1989:214), and the two similar artefacts from Church Hole, Creswell, have been dated to 12,020 ± 100 B.P. (OxA-3717)

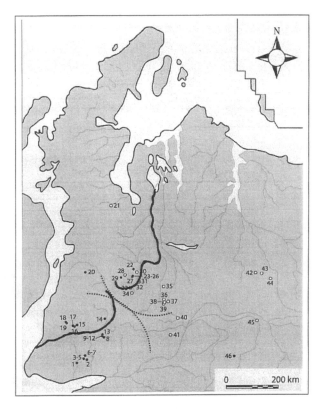

Figure 2.10 Map of Britain in the Late Glacial Interstadial showing Late Magdalenian sites and findspots. The Trent and Severn rivers have been highlighted to show how they form a communication axis between the main clusters of sites. The dotted arcs show the boundary between spring and summer activities on the upland borders of the Trent Valley (arctic hare trapping, clothing replenishment, possibly exploitation of reindeer calves) and winter activities on the borders of the Severn (red deer and horse hunting). *Key:* 1. Bob's Cave; 2. Kent's Cavern; 3. Three Holes; 4. Tornewton Cave; 5. The Old Grotto; 6. Cow Cave; 7. Pixies' Hole; 8. Badger Hole; 9. Gough's Cave; 10. Gough's Old Cave; 11. Soldier's Hole; 12. Sun Hole; 13. Aveline's Hole; 14. King Arthur's Cave; 15. Cathole; 16. Goat's Hole (Paviland); 17. Worm's Head Cave; 18. Hoyle's Mouth; 19. Nanna's Cave; 20. Kendrick's Cave; 21. Fairnington; 22. Edlington Wood; 23. Pin Hole; 24. Robin Hood Cave; 25. Mother Grundy's Parlour; 26. Church Hole; 27. Langwith Cave; 28. Little Spinney, Froggatt; 29. Fox Hole Cave; 30. Lound; 31. Farndon Fields; 32. East Stoke; 33. Lockington-Hemington; 34. Bradgate Park; 35. Gill's Smallholding, Heacham; 36. Feltwell; 37. Thetford; 38. Lakenheath Warren; 39. Mildenhall; 40. Walton-on-Naze; 41. Oare; 42. Zeijen; 43. Seigerswoude; 44. Emmerhout; 45. Op de Hees; 46. Presle. Base map and site locations courtesy of Roger Jacobi.

and 12,250 ± 90 B.P. (OxA-3718; Hedges et al. 1994:339). These dates, and comparison with dated Continental sites suggests that British shouldered points belong to the late Bölling or Older Dryas. Broad sequences are now well understood for the Continent (e.g. Street et al. 2002). In Germany, the Late Magdalenian is dominated by straight-backed bladelets, which may give way towards the end of the Magdalenian to end-retouched backed bladelets. In northern Germany the classic shouldered points of the Hamburgian give way to the long slender Havelt points after 12,200 B.P. In southern Germany sites with angle-backed and/or shouldered points appear around 12,500 B.P. and seem related to both classic Hamburgian sites and to the English/Dutch Creswellian. Although the lithic assemblage from Church Hole appears to be typologically earlier (i.e., Late Magdalenian), all of the direct dates noted above are in keeping with the Continental Hamburgian, and for this reason, and the typological similarity of shouldered points to those from Continental Hamburgian sites, I interpret these British sites as incursions of Hamburgians between 12,200 and 12,000 B.P. Once again, the main distribution of the Hamburgian is to the east of Britain.

The Late Upper Palaeolithic site at Hengistbury Head (Dorset) is the largest site that may be assigned to this period, with over 13,000 lithic artefacts, although the presence of straight-backed blades (which are absent on the Continent) suggests it may represent Hamburgian influence or contact rather than the Hamburgian *sensu stricto*. Technology was geared towards the production of blades and 649 formal tools have been identified from surface collections and three separate excavations. These are dominated by backed blades and bladelets, endscrapers and burins. The lack of organic material for radiocarbon dating and the coarse precision of thermoluminescence dates for the site render its true age unknown; it may be of Allerød age, although the existing dates and some of the lithic typology of the site are certainly consistent with a late Bölling or Older Dryas occupation. Thermally fractured stone slabs and burnt flints suggest the presence of hearths and the spatial distribution of a large amount of lithics suggests the use of one hearth as a focus of activity. The large number of backed blades and bladelets showing signs of burning probably reflect re-tooling and maintenance activities sitting around the fire. Fragments of worn ochre and pieces of flint cortex bearing engraved lines suggest other, more enigmatic activities.

Late Upper Palaeolithic Activity II: The Second Half of the Late Glacial Interstadial

In northern Germany the Havelt phase Hamburgian gives way to *Federmessergruppen* (Penknife Point Group) around 12,000 B.P. In some areas such as the Neuwied Basin the *Federmessergruppen* seem largely restricted to the later phases of the Allerød, i.e., to 11,400–11,100 B.P. In France, the Late Magdalenian gives way to assemblages characterised by large crescent backed points (Bipointes) after 12,300 B.P., which are succeeded (probably quite quickly, certainly by 12,000 B.P.) by those characterised by *Federmesser* (Monopointes) and less laminar technologies, and over the course of the second half of the Late Glacial Interstadial the regularity of these forms gives way to more variable examples which are dated to around 11,000 B.P. More broadly speaking these can be seen as increasingly regionalised northern European variants of a wider emphasis on curved-backed points, which in southwest Europe takes the form of the Azilian.

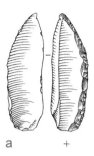

a   +

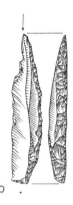

b   .

Figure 2.11   Curved-backed points (*Federmesser*) from Gough's Cave, Cheddar Gorge, Somerset. Drawings by Hazel Martingell. Courtesy of Roger Jacobi.

With the onset of the Allerød, Britain appears to have been occupied by groups using curved-backed points and *Federmesser* (penknife points), which are chronologically contemporary with better-understood bipointe sites in northern France and *Federmessergruppen* sites in France, Belgium, the Netherlands and Germany (fig. 2.11). Activity in the late second half of the Late Glacial Interstadial is indicated at Torbryan Six Cave in the Torbryan Valley by a cutmarked reindeer dentary (OxA-3894, 11,130 ± 100 B.P.; Hedges et al. 1996:398) which derived from a remnant hearth. Similarly, Late Glacial lithics, including a curved-backed point from Pixie's Hole, Devon (Barton and Roberts 1996), were found in a horizon containing a cutmarked aurochs bone and a partially burnt bone of the same species associated with an *in situ* hearth which indicate activity in the cave at 11,630 ± 120 B.P. (OxA-5794) and 11,910 ± 90 B.P. (OxA-5795) respectively (Hedges et al. 1998:228). Barton and Roberts (1996) have proposed the term "Final Palaeolithic" for these Allerød assemblages, a term which I reject as it bears no cultural information and as they are not the final British assemblages which can be assigned to the Palaeolithic (see below).

Penknife points are curved-backed points bearing a proximal oblique truncation which creates an offset tang. At present it is unclear whether they were an integral part of the Late Magdalenian or whether, as on the Continent, they are associated more with a discrete cultural (and chronological) group. At Mother Grundy's Parlour, Creswell, they were recovered mixed with Late Magdalenian and Mesolithic lithics (Armstrong 1925), which might indicate an origin in the Late Magdalenian, but this is hardly a convincing association. In some cases penknife points are stratigraphically younger than assemblages containing Cheddar points (Jacobi et al. 2001); thus, given the lack of convincing association with Magdalenian lithics, it seems likely that they reflect later human groups rather than items within Late Magdalenian toolkits. Although the size of penknife points varies, small and light examples from Kent's Cavern, King Arthur's Cave and Pin Hole bear impact damage consistent with use as weapon tips; larger forms may have served other purposes, although one might account for such differences simply as those between different weapon systems, e.g., arrows or light javelins and thrusting spears. A number of authors have stressed the lack of large, well-made blades among Allerød assemblages, as well as the use of locally available raw materials often of poor quality, which suggests that very different raw-material strategies were employed by the *Federmessergruppen*. It may well be that the abundant access to exposed sources of high-quality flint in cold periods contrasted with a lack of access in the vegetated Allerød, during which less desirable sources would have had to be employed.

A small number of organic tools date to the Allerød. The antler barbed point famously dredged up from the Leman and Ower Bank in the North Sea attests to Allerød period activity in Doggerland around 11,740 ± 150 B.P. (OxA-1950). Two incomplete uniserially barbed points of bone were found in association with an elk (*Alces alces*) skeleton in Allerød age deposits at High Furlong, Poulton-le-Fylde, Lancashire (Hallam et al. 1973). This site indicates that human groups achieved a considerable north–west distribution in the forested conditions of the period, yet despite this the points are of the same typological form as those from Dinslaken, Germany, 700 km to the east (Jacobi 1980:60). An antler barbed point from Porth-y-Waen (Shropshire), has been directly dated to 11,390 ± 120 B.P. (OxA-1946). A bone point from Lynx Cave (north Wales) dates to 11700 ± 90 B.P. (OxA-8164; Bronk Ramsey et al. 2002:21). As Jacobi (in Bronk Ramsey et al. 2002:21) notes, there is some question as to whether the point can be associated with Late Glacial lithics from the cave that include straight-backed and partially backed blades and bladelets, but it is interesting that these pieces are of a form that does not appear in Late Magdalenian assemblages from the first half of the Late Glacial Interstadial. It remains a possibility, therefore, that, if the lithics and bone point derive from the same assemblage, a novel artefact group appears in the second half of the Late Glacial Interstadial.

Organic objects dating to the later part of the Allerød include the broken tang of an antler artefact from Dowel Cave, Earl Sterndale, Derbyshire (OxA-1463, 11,200 ± 120 B.P.; Hedges et al. 1989:214); a broken artefact of reindeer antler from Kinsey Cave, North Yorkshire (OxA-2456, 11,270 ± 110 B.P.; Hedges et al. 1992:142); and a complete bone point from a fissure at Coniston Dib in the same area (OxA-2847, 11,210 ± 90 B.P., Hedges et al. 1992:142). Two barbed points from the flood plain of the River Gipping at Sproughton, Suffolk (Wymer et al. 1975), date to between ca. 11,300 and ca. 11,050 B.P. (antler point OxA-15219, 10,960 ± 50 B.P.; bone point OxA-14943, 11,485 ± 60 B.P.; Jacobi, pers. comm.[12]). An antler barbed point from Victoria Cave has been dated to the end of the period (OxA-14888, 10,930 ± 45 B.P.; Jacobi, pers. comm.). The chronological range of barbed bone/antler points (even a conservative estimate places them from ca. 11,600 B.P. to ca. 10,000 B.P.) indicates a long currency for these weapon tips, and Continental evidence indicates their persistence through the Younger Dryas into the Holocene (Cziesla and Pettitt 2003).

Several items of less obvious function belong to this period. One of five ochred and incised tallys of roe deer metapodia from Kendrick's Cave in north Wales, which may have functioned as personal ornamentation as well as for information storage, has been directly dated to 11,795 ± 65 B.P. (OxA-6116; Richards et al. 2005). Seven fragments of mammoth ivory bearing incisions, a rib fragment incised with several series of short lines along two lateral edges (akin to a modern ruler) and an arctic hare tibia awl bearing three registers of grouped incisions were recovered from Gough's Cave, and it is difficult to interpret these in any way other than as artificial memory systems (see Pettit and Bahn, in press). The three reindeer antler *bâtons percés* recovered from Gough's Cave, noted above, each bear incised markings in a spiral pattern, and one has been directly dated to 11870 ± 110 B.P. (OxA-2797; Hedges et al. 1991:283) which suggests that they may belong to this later period rather than the Magdalenian although it remains to be ascertained. A broken bevelled rod of reindeer antler from Victoria Cave (North Yorkshire) which has been dated to 11750 ± 120 B.P. (OxA-2455; Hedges et al. 1992:141) may have had a similar function to the earlier Magdalenian foreshafts discussed above.

The bones and teeth of between four and eight humans, including three adults and a child, were recovered from Gough's Cave, many of which display cutmarks indicative of defleshing and disarticulation of the cranium and mandible (Currant et al. 1989; Cook 1986). Although the distribution of radiocarbon measurements on these bones in some cases goes back into the Bölling, others do not and a parsimonious interpretation of the results, assuming they are broadly contemporary, suggests that they all belong to the early Allerød. These were found mixed with animal bones against the cave wall. Jacobi (2004:79) has suggested that the local disappearance of horse may have been responsible for the cessation of prosaic activity at Gough's Cave, and that the clustering of human remains in the Allerød, that is, after the Late Magdalenian horse and red deer hunting, might indicate that the cave subsequently became more important as a funerary (or ritual) site. He has similarly drawn attention to the cessation of Late Magdalenian activity in Church Hole, Creswell (which has no *Federmesser* or curved-backed points, or dates relating to the Allerød), whereas such visitations continued in the caves of the north side of the gorge. In the former case this could simply be changing roles of the gorge as resources change, but in the latter one may have a fascinating example of powerful enculturation of the landscape – a cave imbued with spiritual meaning (the cave art) being avoided for prosaic use.

Stable isotope analyses of the Gough's Cave and Sun Hole human bones indicates that dietary protein was mainly derived from meat, as perhaps one would expect, mainly from red deer, reindeer and aurochs (Richards et al. 2000). This would initially seem to be at odds with the dominance of horse in the fauna, although it should be remembered that the horse relates in the main to Late Magdalenian hunting whereas the human remains are generally younger. These are in good agreement with analyses of Allerød period human remains from Kendrick's Cave (Clwyd) which also indicate a high animal protein diet, although, interestingly, they also suggest that ca. 30 per cent of dietary protein was obtained from marine sources (Richards et al. 2005).

Late Upper Palaeolithic Archaeology III: The Younger Dryas and the Terminal Upper Palaeolithic

Direct dates on humanly modified bone/antler artefacts clearly establish human presence in Britain during the severe conditions of the Younger Dryas, although these are remarkably rare (e.g., OxA-811, 10,600 ± 110 B.P. on a cutmarked vertebra of *Cervus elaphus* from Elder Bush Cave, Staffordshire). A reindeer antler ("Lyngby axe") from Earl's Barton in Northamptonshire is often quoted as belonging to this period although new AMS radiocarbon dates indicate that it dates to the Pleistocene–Holocene transition (Jacobi, pers. comm.). In addition to the ochred and incised roe deer metapodia discussed above, Kendrick's Cave in north Wales yielded 11 pierced and incised teeth of red deer and bovid, one of the latter dating to 10,580 ± 100 B.P. (OxA-4573; Richards et al. 1995), and the famous horse mandible bearing chevron decoration dated to 10,000 ± 200 B.P. (OxA-111; although this is almost certainly a minimum age and the sample probably dates to earlier than the Younger Dryas). The nature of these objects is discussed in Pettitt and Bahn (in press). From the poor data noted here one can certainly infer that cave use vanished in the Younger Dryas, and one might actually question whether human presence amounted to anything more than a few visits.

The problem with these organic items is that they lack lithic associations and thus their specific cultural attribution is open to question. On the neighbouring parts of the Continent, the Ahrensburgian clearly corresponds to this period. Finds of Ahrensburgian points (small points with a clear tang), although rare, do indicate that groups of this cultural affiliation were operating in south-eastern Britain in this period, although it is interesting that these are lacking in sites further to the northwest in which there is unambiguous evidence of human activity at the time. At the very end of the Pleistocene some 28 sites are known in south-east England that are characterised by long blades accompanied by large cores and few retouched tools (Barton and Dumont 2000). At Avington VI in the Kennet Valley these were found in association with two Ahrensburgian points (Froom 2005), and there is no reason why long blade assemblages may not be late Ahrensburgian in cultural derivation. Barton (1991) has shown that these British assemblages of the latest Younger Dryas often include "bruised blades" (*lames mâchurées*), a phenomenon also observed on the Continent, for example, in the Ahrensburgian of Stellmoor (Rust 1943). A discrete cluster of flakes, blades and bladelets, cores, microlithic points, scrapers, burins and knapping waste at Launde in east Leicestershire probably represents hearth-related activities at an open camp site (Cooper 2006). At present, all one can say is that British Younger Dryas lithic and organic artefacts are not typologically inconsistent with the Continental Ahrensburgian.

One can say little about the subsistence strategies of Younger Dryas groups in Britain. The faunal accumulation at Chelm's Coombe, Cheddar, indicates that reindeer and wild horse were present in southern England at the time (Currant 1991). This is in keeping with the site at Three Ways Wharf Site C in the valley of the Colne river (Uxbridge, Greater London). Here, fluvial deposits contained a lithic scatter that was excavated over an area of 64 sq. m and contained ca. 700 lithic artefacts and ca. 100 fragments of bone (Lewis 1991). Blade production is well attested at the site, and the tools are dominated by obliquely truncated points. The fauna consists of horse and reindeer (perhaps one of each) and the relatively low density of finds can be best interpreted as a couple of episodes of butchery activity at the beginning of a phase of Terminal Pleistocene warming as indicated by two direct dates (OxA-1778 horse molar 10,270 ± 100 B.P.; OxA-1902 horse mandible 10,010 ± 120 B.P.). Lewis (1991:254) has suggested that Scatter A of Site C is of the Long Blade Assemblage tradition which Barton (1989) has placed in the latest Glacial and Preboreal period, and attributes the relatively small size of blades from the site to limitations of locally available flint. The little information available for Britain is in keeping with Continental evidence. Baales (1999) has shown how Younger Dryas Ahrensburgian groups were hunting reindeer (including calves) in the spring in the upland zone from the river Meuse in the west to the Oder in the east. In his model the reindeer spent the winter scattered widely in small groups on the Northern European Plain, aggregating at the start of spring to migrate as a large herd southwards to the upland areas of the Eifel, Ardennes and Westphalian highlands for calving. Traditional routes for this migration were probably broad river and stream beds, in which intercept strategies could be employed by Ahrensburgians with a knowledge of the position of valley bottlenecks along these routes. Certainly, the distribution of Ahrensburgian sites in this region testifies to the importance of such localities. Similar opportunities for intercepting large herds would present themselves when the herd migrated once more to the north in autumn, and in this way Ahrensburgians could provide for the summer and winter.

Intriguingly, a survey of the distribution of directly dated human remains from the British Late Glacial and Early Holocene has revealed a hiatus in known human remains that corresponds to the Younger Dryas (Barton et al. 2003). Given the rarity of dated archaeology in this period one would not want to overstress this. If this cannot be ascribed to human absence, it presumably relates to differences in the nature of occupation or in the methods of disposal of corpses in this period. Such a regional difference is of interest when set against the wider European context for this period. Gamble et al. (2005) have noted that the number of open camps relative to caves and rock shelters in western Europe rises for the first time in the

Younger Dryas, and have interpreted this as a response to the demand for larger camps in situations where human groups were aggregating in larger numbers than previously known. Although it would be premature to fit the British data into such a picture, it may suggest a relative lack of interest in enclosed sites corresponding to increased aggregations at open-air camps. This would certainly explain the rarity of archaeology from the period. Whatever the specific nature of late Younger Dryas groups, it seems that there was a continuity from these to the Early Mesolithic groups of the Preboreal. Barton (1991) has suggested that technological changes over the Pleistocene–Holocene transition lagged behind environmental change and thus adaptation to post-glacial woodlands occurred only gradually. The close resemblance between Terminal Pleistocene and earliest Holocene lithic assemblages certainly reinforces the view of a continuous cultural tradition across the transition (Barton 1989).

Conclusion: New Directions into the British Upper Palaeolithic

We are at an exciting period in British Upper Palaeolithic studies. After the great burst of activity from the 1870s to the 1920s we have now identified many caves and rock shelters, and perhaps some open sites, which should contain rich assemblages from the period, and which can be excavated with modern techniques. New fieldwork at Creswell – the first major investigations there since the 1920s – is beginning to overhaul our understanding of this important focus of activity. The ongoing analysis of lithic and organic items, and the discovery of our first examples of Palaeolithic cave art are showing that British Upper Palaeolithic communities were much more connected to the Continent than has perhaps been assumed. The phenomenal advances in our understanding of the physical nature of this north-western European peninsula allow us to put our changing views of humans into perspective, and suggest that the great defining feature of western Europe – the highway of the Atlantic (Cunliffe 2001) – was not important for much of the period. With the possible exception of a small group of French Aurignacians, British Upper Palaeolithic societies seem to have derived far more from the east, and in this sense Upper Palaeolithic Britain has more in keeping with the early medieval rather than high medieval period – mobile, Germanic, and focused on the North Sea.

ACKNOWLEDGEMENTS

I am especially grateful to Roger Jacobi for his critical comments on a draft of this chapter, for sharing with me his unpublished data and for allowing me to reproduce several illustrations from his previous publications. As ever, the work has benefited greatly from his help. I also owe a considerable debt to Robert Dinnis, who also took the time to go over the draft in detail and in doing so helped to improve it. Needless to say, where I diverge from their opinions this is either due to mistake (for which I apologise) or difference in opinion (in which case I resolutely stick to my guns!). Finally, I thank Joshua Pollard for inviting me to contribute to this volume – for giving me the opportunity to think about the British Upper Palaeolithic systematically and for being so patient.

NOTES

1 Due to the lack of agreed calibration beyond ca. 11,000 B.P. for northern Europe, and in the interests of consistency across the chapter, I use only uncalibrated ^{14}C dates B.P. here. Although CALPAL and INTCAL04 have been increasingly used to calibrate Late Glacial dates, the relevance of U-Series dated corals from the South Atlantic to northern European materials (on which INTCAL04 relies) is questionable. Suffice it to say, ^{14}C dates for the first half of the Late Glacial Interstadial (13–12,000 B.P.) would calibrate to ca. 14–16,000 cal B.P. using these calibration curves.

2 Thus the Younger Dryas is often referred to in Britain as the Loch Lomond Stadial.

3 Oxygen Isotope Stages (increasingly referred to as Marine Isotope Stages) are defined by the ratios of ^{16}O and ^{18}O preserved directly in ice cores from Greenland and Antarctica or in the shells of microscopic forams in deep sea cores. These are laid down annually and cores can thus be assigned a chronology in a way akin to dendrochronology and varve dating. The ratio of these two isotopes of oxygen informs about the relative size of the oceans, from which one can infer cold stadials and glacials (in which oceans are small as water is locked up as polar ice) and warm interstadials and interglacials (in which oceans are relatively large). Peaks and troughs of the resulting "saw toothed curves" are assigned numbers which refer to OIS(MIS) stages, with odd numbers referring to warm periods and even numbers to cold. Numbering proceeds backwards from OIS1 (The Holocene) through OIS2 (10,000–25,000 B.P.), OIS3 (25,000–60,000 B.P.), OIS4 (60,000–71,000 B.P.), OIS5 (The Last Interglacial *sensu lato* 71,000–125,000 B.P.) and back into the earlier part of the Middle Pleistocene.

4 England: Kent's Cavern (three shouldered scrapers and two nosed scrapers); Uphill Quarry (lozangic antler point); Aston Mills (one shouldered scraper and one nosed scraper). Wales: Goat's Hole, Paviland (27 nosed and/or shouldered scrapers, four carinated scrapers, four *burins busqués*, one *burin des Vachons* and one Aurignacian blade fragment); Hoyle's Mouth (one carinated scraper and one *burin busqué*); Ffynnon Beuno (one *burin busqué*); Nottle Tor (one shouldered scraper); Cae Gwyn (endscraper on Aurignacian blade, possible bladelet). Data from Dinnis 2005 and Jacobi 1980.

5 Roberts and Barton (2001) have interpreted the Mildenhall point as a Late Upper Palaeolithic Lyngby (Bromme) Point on the grounds that it does not correspond to the morphometrics of the majority of Font Robert points and as it does correspond to a (broad and vague) description of Lyngby points. This piece is certainly not inconsistent with an identification as a Font Robert point, and the vague definition of Bromme points is problematic. The piece is actually very similar to Font Robert points from Gravettian sites in Belgium (e.g., Maisieres Canal: Jacobi, pers. comm., and Otte 1979:fig. 235) and for this reason and the absolute rarity of Bromme points in Britain I ascribe it to the Gravettian.

6 It is generally assumed that Font Robert points were hafted as armatures on spears and javelins, although microwear analysis of 20 Belgian examples suggested a variety of functions amidst which projectile points was surprisingly absent (Otte and Caspar 1987).

7   Basket-shaped pendants made by a particular way of carving and piercing cervid teeth.

8   An AMS radiocarbon date of 22,780 ± 320 B.P. (OxA-7081) reported by Aldhouse-Green and Pettitt (1998) should be taken as a minimum age given indications of possible contamination of the piece, whereas a recent measurement on another spatula yielded an age of 26,170 ± 150 B.P. (OxA-13656). See discussion in Jacobi et al. 2006.

9   These are defined on the basis of a circular hole at the point the antler widens, the interior of which is often scored with incisions forming a screw shape like a bottle top. Because of this the function of these items is thought to have involved line, although early interpretations saw these *bâtons du commandement* as being of ritual significance.

10 Although in the absence of direct dating of these pieces they could belong to a later Upper Palaeolithic context.

11 The fragment of a fifth, bearing incisions that suggest notation rather than cut marks, was recovered from the spoil heap left by the excavation of Church Hole in 1876 during an excavation directed by myself in 2006.

12 These were originally thought to be Early Mesolithic on typological grounds, but as Jacobi (1980) noted, such comparisons ignored parallels from Continental sites of the same period. Original direct AMS radiocarbon dates suggested a Younger Dryas age for the points (see Gowlett et al. 1986a:120), but these measurements have been proven invalid by the new dates using ultrafiltration at Oxford I quote in the text, courtesy of Roger Jacobi.

REFERENCES

Aldhouse-Green, M., and S. Aldhouse-Green, 2005 The Quest for the Shaman: shape-shifters, sorcerors and spirit-healers of ancient Europe. London: Thames and Hudson.

Aldhouse-Green, S., ed., 2000 Paviland Cave and the "Red Lady": a definitive report. Bristol: Western Academic and Specialist Press.

——and P. B. Pettitt, 1998 Paviland Cave: contextualizing the Red Lady. Antiquity 72: 756–772.

Antoine, P., J.-P. Coutard, P. Gibbard, B. Hallegouet, J.-P. Lautridou and J.-C. Ozouf, 2003 The Pleistocene rivers of the English Channel region. Journal of Quaternary Science 18:227–243.

Armstrong, A. L. 1925 Excavations at Mother Grundy's Parlour, Creswell Crags, Derbyshire. Journal of the Royal Anthropological Institute 55:146–178.

Ashton, N., and S. G. Lewis, 2002 Deserted Britain: declining populations in the British late Middle Pleistocene. Antiquity 76:388–396.

——S. Parfitt and M. White, 2006 Riparian landscapes and human habitat preferences during the Hoxnian (LIS11) interglacial. Journal of Quaternary Science 21:497–506.

Atkinson, T. C., K. R. Briffa and G. R. Coope, 1987 Seasonal temperatures in Britain during the past 22,000 years, reconstructed using beetle remains. Nature 325:587–592.

Baales, M., 1999 Economy and seasonality in the Ahrensburgian. In Tanged Point Cultures in Europe. S. Kozlowski, J. Gurba and L. Zaliznak, eds. pp. 64–75. Lublin: Maria Curie-Skłodowska University Press.

Barton, R. N. E., 1989 Long Blade technology in southern Britain. In The Mesolithic in Europe. C. Bonsall, ed. pp. 264–271. Edinburgh: John Donald.

——1991 Technological innovation and continuity at the end of the Pleistocene in Britain. In The Late Glacial in North West Europe: human adaptation and environmental change at the end of the Pleistocene. R. N. E. Barton, A. Roberts, and D. A. Roe, eds. pp. 234–245. London: Council for British Archaeology.

——1992 Hengistbury Head, Dorset, vol. 2: The Late Upper Palaeolithic and Early Mesolithic Sites. Oxford: Oxford University Committee for Archaeology Monograph 34.

——1999 Colonisation and resettlement of Europe in the Late Glacial: a view from the western periphery. Folia Quaternaria 70:71–86.

——and S. Dumont, 2000 Recolonisation and settlement of Britain at the end of the Last Glaciation. Mémoires du Musée de Préhistoire d'Ile-de-France 7:151–162

——and A. J. Roberts, 1996 Reviewing the British Late Upper Palaeolithic: new evidence for chronological patterning in the Lateglacial record. Oxford Journal of Archaeology 15(3):245–265.

——R. M. Jacobi, D. Stapert and M. J. Street, 2003 The Late-Glacial reoccupation of the British Isles and the Creswellian. Journal of Quaternary Science 18:631–643.

Beasley, M. J., 1987 A preliminary report on incremental banding as an indicator of seasonality in mammal teeth from Gough's Cave, Cheddar, Somerset. Proceedings of the University of Bristol Spelaeological Society 18:116–128.

Blockley, S. P. E., R. Donahue and A. M. Pollard, 2000 Radiocarbon calibration and Late Glacial occupation in northwest Europe. Antiquity 74:112–121.

——S. M. Blockley, R. E. Donahue, C. S. Lane, J. J. Lowe and A. M. Pollard, 2006 The chronology of abrupt climate change and Late Upper Palaeolithic human adaptation in Europe. Journal of Quaternary Science 21:575–584.

Bourillet, J. F., J. Y. Reynaud, A. Baltzer and S. Zaragosi, 2003 The "Fleuve Manche": the submarine sedimentary features from the outer shelf to the deep-sea fans. Journal of Quaternary Science 18:261–282.

Bramwell, D., 1971 Excavations at Foxhole Cave, High Wheeldon, 1961–1970. Derbyshire Archaeological Journal 91:1–19.

Bronk Ramsey, C., T. Higham, D. C. Owen, A. Pike and R. E. M. Hedges, 2002 Radiocarbon dates from the Oxford AMS system: Archaeometry datelist 31. Archaeometry 44 (supplement 1):1–150.

Buckland, W., 1823 Reliquiae Diluvianae; or, Observations on the Organic Remains contained in Caves, Fissures and other Geological Phenomena Attesting the Action of an Universal Deluge. London: John Murray.

Campbell, J. B., 1977 The Upper Palaeolithic of Britain: a study of man and nature in the late Ice Age. Oxford: Clarendon Press.

Charles, R., 1999 Garrod and the Belgian Creswellian. In Dorothy Garrod and the Progress of the Palaeolithic. W. Davies and R. Charles, eds. pp. 57–76. Oxford: Oxbow Books.

——and R. Jacobi, 1994 Lateglacial faunal exploitation at the Robin Hood Cave, Creswell Crags. Oxford Journal of Archaeology 13:1–32.

Coles, B. J., 1998 Doggerland: a speculative survey. Proceedings of the Prehistoric Society 64:45–82.

Cook, J., 1986 Marked human bones from Gough's Cave, Somerset. Proceedings of the University of Bristol Spelaeological Society 17:275–285.

Cooper, L., 2002 A Creswellian campsite, Newtown Linford. Transactions of the Leicestershire Archaeology and History Society 76:78–80.

——2006 Launde: a Terminal Palaeolithic camp site in the English Midlands and its North European context. Proceedings of the Prehistoric Society 72:53–94.

Cunliffe, B., 2001 Facing the Ocean: the Atlantic and its peoples. Oxford: Oxford University Press.

Currant, A., 1986 The Late Glacial mammal fauna of Gough's Cave, Cheddar, Somerset. Proceedings of the University of Bristol Spelaeological Society 17:286–304.

——1991 A Late Glacial Interstadial mammal fauna from Gough's Cave, Somerset, England. In The Late Glacial in North West Europe: human adaptation and environmental change at the end of the Pleistocene. R. N. E. Barton, A. Roberts and D. A. Roe, eds. pp. 48–50. London: Council for British Archaeology.

——and R. Jacobi, 2001 A formal mammalian biostratigraphy for the Late Pleistocene of Britain. Quaternary Science Reviews 20:1707–1716.

————and C. B. Stringer, 1989 Excavations at Gough's Cave, Somerset 1986–7. Antiquity 63:131–136.

Cziesla, E., and P. B. Pettitt, 2003 AMS 14C datierungen von Spätpaläolithischen und Mesolithischen funden aus dem Bützee (Brandenburg). Archäologisches Korrespondenzblatt 33:21–38.

Dinnis, R., 2005 A Comprehensive Study of British Aurignacian Artefacts. MSc dissertation, University of Sheffield.

Draper, J. C., 1962 Upper Palaeolithic type flints from Long Island, Langstone Harbour, Portsmouth. Proceedings of the Hampshire Field Club and Archaeological Society 22:105–106.

Froom, R., 2005 Late Glacial Long Blade Sites in the Kennet Valley. London: British Museum.

Gamble, C., W. Davies, P. Pettitt, M. Richards and L. Hazelwood, 2005 The archaeological and genetic foundations of the European population during the Late Glacial: implications for "agricultural thinking". Cambridge Archaeological Journal 15(2): 193–223.

Garrod, D. A., 1926 The Upper Palaeolithic Age in Britain. Oxford: Clarendon Press.

Garton, D., 1993 A Late Upper Palaeolithic site near Newark, Nottinghamshire. Transactions of the Thoroton Society of Nottinghamshire 98:145.

Gibbard, P., and J. P. Lautridou, 2003 The Quaternary history of the English Channel: an introduction. Journal of Quaternary Science 18:195–199.

Gowlett, J. A. J., E. T. Hall, R. E. M. Hedges and C. Perry, 1986a Radiocarbon dates from the Oxford AMS system: Archaeometry datelist 3. Archaeometry 28:116–125.

——R. E. M. Hedges, I. A. Law and C. Perry, 1986b Radiocarbon dates from the Oxford AMS system: Archaeometry datelist 4. Archaeometry 28:206–221.

Hallam, J. S., B. J. N. Edwards, B. Barnes and A. J. Stuart, 1973 The remains of a Late Glacial elk associated with barbed points from High Furlong, near Blackpool, Lancashire. Proceedings of the Prehistoric Society 39:100–128.

Hedges, R. E. M., R. A. Housley, I. A. Law, C. Perry and J. A. J. Gowlett, 1987 Radiocarbon dates from the Oxford AMS system: Archaeometry datelist 6. Archaeometry 29:289–306.

————and C. R. Bronk, 1989 Radiocarbon dates from the Oxford AMS system: Archaeometry datelist 9. Archaeometry 31:207–234.

————C. R. Bronk and G. J. van Klinken, 1991 Radiocarbon dates from the Oxford AMS system: Archaeometry datelist 13. Archaeometry 33:279–296.

————C. Bronk Ramsey and G. J. van Klinken 1992. Radiocarbon dates from the Oxford AMS system: Archaeometry datelist 14. Archaeometry 34:141–159.

——————, 1994 Radiocarbon dates from the Oxford AMS system: Archaeometry datelist 18. Archaeometry 36:337–374.

——P. B. Pettitt, C. Bronk Ramsey and G. J. van Klinken, 1996 Radiocarbon dates from the Oxford AMS system: Archaeometry datelist 22. Archaeometry 38:391–415.

————————1998 Radiocarbon dates from the Oxford AMS system: Archaeometry datelist 25. Archaeometry 40:227–239.

Higham, T. F. G., R. M. Jacobi and C. Bronk Ramsey, 2006 AMS radiocarbon dating of ancient bone using ultrafiltration. Radiocarbon 48(2):179–195.

Housley, R. A., 1991 AMS dates from the Lateglacial and early Postglacial in north-west Europe: a review. *In* The Late Glacial in North West Europe: human adaptation and environmental change at the end of the Pleistocene. R. N. E. Barton, A. Roberts and D. A. Roe, eds. pp.25–39. London: Council for British Archaeology.

——C. Gamble, M. Street and P. Pettitt, 1997 Radiocarbon evidence for the Lateglacial human recolonisation of northern Europe. Proceedings of the Prehistoric Society 63:25–54.

————and P. Pettitt, 2000 Reply to Blockley, Donahue and Pollard. Antiquity 74:117–119.

Jacobi, R. M., 1980 The Upper Palaeolithic of Britain with special reference to Wales. *In* Culture and Environment in Prehistoric Wales. J. A. Taylor, ed. pp. 15–100. Oxford: British Archaeological Reports.

——1990 Leafpoints and the British Early Upper Palaeolithic. *In* Les Industries a Pointes Foliacées du Paléolithique Supérieur Européen. J. Kozlowski, ed. pp. 271–289. Liège: ERAUL 42.

——1991 The Creswellian, Creswell and Cheddar. *In* The Late Glacial in North West Europe: human adaptation and environmental change at the end of the Pleistocene. R. N. E. Barton, A. Roberts and D. A. Roe, eds. pp. 128–140. London: Council for British Archaeology.

——1997 The "Creswellian" in Britain. *In* Le Tardiglaciaire en Europe du Nord Ouest. J. P. Fagnart and A.Thévenin, eds. pp. 497–505. Paris: Éditions du Comité des Travaux Historiques et Scientifiques.

——1999 Some observations on the British Earlier Upper Palaeolithic. *In* Dorothy Garrod and the Progress of the Palaeolithic. W. Davies and R. Charles, eds. pp. 35–40. Oxford: Oxbow Books.

——2000 The Late Pleistocene archaeology of Somerset. *In* Somerset Archaeology: papers to mark 150 years of the Somerset Archaeological and Natural History Society. C. J. Webster, ed. pp. 45–52. Taunton: Somerset County Council.

——2004 The Late Upper Palaeolithic lithic collection from Gough's Cave, Cheddar, Somerset and human use of the cave. Proceedings of the Prehistoric Society 70:1–92.

——2007a The Stone Age archaeology of Church Hole, Creswell Crags, Nottinghamshire. *In* Palaeolithic Cave Art at Creswell Crags in European Context. P. Pettitt, P. Bahn and S. Ripoll, eds. pp. 71–111. Oxford: Oxford University Press.

——2007b A collection of Early Upper Palaeolithic Artefacts from Beedings, Near Pulborough, West Sussex, and the context of similar finds from the British Isles. Proceedings of the Prehistoric Society 73:229–325.

——and H. E. Martingell, 1980 A Late-Glacial shouldered point from Cranwich, Norfolk. Norfolk Archaeology 37:312–314.

——and P. B. Pettitt, 2000 An Aurignacian point from Uphill Quarry, Somerset, and the colonization of Britain by Homo sapiens. Antiquity 74:513–518.

——D. Garton and J. Brown, 2001 Field-walking and the Late Upper Palaeolithic of Nottinghamshire. Transactions of the Thoroton Society of Nottinghamshire 105:17–22.

——T. F. G. Higham and C. Bronk Ramsey, 2006 AMS radiocarbon dating of Middle and Upper Palaeolithic bone in the British Isles: improved reliability using ultrafiltration. Journal of Quaternary Science 21:557–573.

Johnsen, S., D. Dahl-Jensen, N. Gundestrup, J. Steffensen, H. Clausen, H. Miller, V. Masson-Demotte, A. Sveinbjornsdottir and J. White, 2001 Oxygen isotope and palaeotemperature records from six Greenland ice core stations: Camp Century, Dye-3, GRIP, GISP2, Reinland and NorthGRIP. Journal of Quaternary Science 16:299–307.

Jones, R. L., and D. H. Keen, 1993 Pleistocene Environments in the British Isles. London: Chapman and Hall.

Lagarde, J. L., D. Amorese, M. Font, E. Laville and O. Dugué, 2003 Structural evolution of the English Channel. Journal of Quaternary Science 18:201–213.

Lewis, J., 1991 A Late Glacial and early Postglacial site at Three Ways Wharf, Uxbridge, England: interim report. In The Late Glacial in North West Europe: human adaptation and environmental change at the end of the Pleistocene. R. N. E. Barton, A. Roberts and D. A. Roe, eds. pp. 246–255. London: Council for British Archaeology.

Lister, A., 1991 Late Glacial mammoths in Britain. In The Late Glacial in North West Europe: human adaptation and environmental change at the end of the Pleistocene. R. N. E. Barton, A. Roberts and D. A. Roe, eds. pp. 51–59. London: Council for British Archaeology.

Lund, M., 1993 Vorshäft für Kerbspitzen der Hamburger Kultur. Archäologisches Korrespondezblatt 23:405–411.

Oakley, K. P., B. G. Campbell and T. L. Molleson, 1971 Catalogue of Fossil Hominids, part II : Europe. London: British Museum (Natural History).

Otte, M., 1979. Le Paleolithique Superieur Ancien en Belgique. Brussels: Musees Rotaux d'Art et d'Histoire.

——and J.-P. Caspar, 1987 Les "pointes" de la Font-Robert: outils emmanchés? In Le Main et l'Outil: Manches et Emmanchements Préhistoriques. D. Stordeur, ed. pp. 75–88. Lyon: Travaux de la Maison de l'Orient 15.

Owen, L., 2005 Distorting the Past: gender and the division of labor in the European Upper Palaeolithic. Tübingen: Kerns Verlag.

Parkin, R. A., P. Rowley-Conwy and D. Serjeantson, 1986 Late Palaeolithic exploitation of horse and red deer at Gough's Cave, Cheddar, Somerset. Proceedings of the University of Bristol Spelaeological Society 17:311–330.

Pettitt, P. B., 2000 Radiocarbon chronology, faunal turnover and human occupation at the Goat's Hole, Paviland. In Paviland Cave and the "Red Lady": a definitive report. S. Aldhouse-Green, ed. pp. 63–71. Bristol: Western Academic and Specialist Press.

——2006 The living dead and the dead living: burials, figurines and social performance in the European Mid Upper Palaeolithic. In The Social Archaeology of Funerary Remains. C. Knüsel and R. Gowland, eds. pp. 292–308. Oxford: Oxbow Books.

——2007 Cultural form and context of the Creswell images: an interpretative model. In Palaeolithic Cave Art at Creswell Crags in European Context. P. B. Pettitt, P. Bahn and S. Ripoll, eds. pp. 112–139. Oxford: Oxford University Press.

——and P. Bahn, in press. Rock art and art mobilier of the British Upper Palaeolithic. In Art as Metaphor: the prehistoric rock-art of Britain. A. Mazel, G. H. Nash and C. Waddington, eds. Oxford: Archaeopress.

——and S. Ripoll, eds., 2007 Palaeolithic Cave Art at Creswell Crags in European Context. Oxford: Oxford University Press.

Preece, R. C., J. A. J. Gowlett, S. A. Parfitt, D. R. Bridgland and S. G. Lewis, 2006 Humans in the Hoxnian: habitat, context and fire use at Beeches Pit, west Stow, Suffolk, UK. Journal of Quaternary Science 21:485–496.

Pryor, F., 2003 Britain BC. London: Harper Collins.

Richards, M. P., R. E. M. Hedges, R. M. Jacobi, A. P. Currant and C. B. Stringer, 2000 Gough's Cave and Sun Hole Cave human stable isotope values indicate a high animal protein diet in the British Upper Palaeolithic. Journal of Archaeological Science 27:1–3.

——R. Jacobi, J. Cook, P. B. Pettitt and C. B. Stringer, 2005 Isotope evidence for the intensive use of marine foods by Late Upper Palaeolithic humans. Journal of Human Evolution 49:390–394.

Roberts, A., 1996 Evidence for Late Pleistocene and Early Holocene human activity and environmental change from the Torbryan Valley, south Devon. *In* The Quaternary of Devon and East Cornwall: Field Guide. D. J. Charman, R. M. Newnham and D. G. Croot, eds. pp. 168–204. London: Quaternary Research Association.

——and R. N. E. Barton, 2001 A Lyngby point from Mildenhall, Suffolk, and its implications for the British Late Upper Palaeolithic. *In* A Very Remote Period Indeed: papers on the Palaeolithic presented to Derek Roe. S. Milliken and J. Cook, eds. pp. 234–241. Oxford: Oxbow Books.

Rockman, M., 2003 Landscape Learning in the Late Glacial Recolonisation of Britain. PhD dissertation, University of Arizona.

Rust, A., 1943 Die Alt- und Mittelsteinzeitlichen Funde von Stellmoor. Neumünster: Karl Wachholz.

Shackley, M., 1981 On the Palaeolithic archaeology of Hampshire. *In* The Archaeology of Hampshire from the Palaeolithic to the Industrial Revolution. S. Shennan and T. Shadla-Hall, eds. pp. 4–9. Hampshire Field Club and Archaeological Society.

Stringer, C. B., 2006 Homo Britannicus: the incredible story of human life in Britain. London: Penguin/Allen Lane.

Swainston, S., 1999 Unlocking the inhospitable. *In* Dorothy Garrod and the Progress of the Palaeolithic: studies in the prehistoric archaeology of the Near East and Europe. W. Davies and R. Charles, eds. pp. 41–56. Oxford: Oxbow Books.

——2000 The lithic artifacts from Paviland. *In* Paviland Cave and the "Red Lady": a definitive report. S. Aldhouse-Green, ed. pp. 95–113. Bristol: Western Academic and Specialist Press.

Walker, M. J. C., G. R. Coope and J. J. Lowe, 1993 The Devensian (Weichselian) Lateglacial palaeoenvironmental record from Gransmoor, East Yorkshire, England. Quaternary Science Reviews 12:659–680.

Weber, M.-J., 2006 Typologische und technologische apekte des fundplatzes Le Tureau des Gardes 7 (Seine-et-Marne, Frankreich): ein zur erforschung des Magdalénien im Pariser Becken. Archäologisches Korrespondenzblatt 36:159–178.

White, M. J., and P. B. Pettitt, 1995 Technology of Early Palaeolithic Western Europe: innovation, variation and a unified framework. Lithics 16:27–40.

——and D. Schreve, 2000 Island Britain – Peninsular Britain: palaeogeography, colonization and the earlier Palaeolithic settlement of the British Isles. Proceedings of the Prehistoric Society 66:1–28.

——B. Scott and N. Ashton, 2006 The early Middle Palaeolithic in Britain: archaeology, settlement history and human behaviour. Journal of Quaternary Science 21:525–542.

Wymer, J. J., R. M. Jacobi and J. Rose, 1975 Late Devensian and early Flandrian barbed points from Sproughton, Suffolk. Proceedings of the Prehistoric Society 41:235–241.

3

The Mesolithic–Neolithic Transition in Britain

Julian Thomas

Introduction: Models of Transition

Toward the end of the fifth millennium B.C. or the beginning of the fourth, a series of significant changes took place in Britain. Domesticated animals were kept for the first time, and cereal crops began to be cultivated. Pottery vessels were introduced for the preparation and serving of food, a variety of forms of polished stone tools were adopted, and flint started to be mined from deep shafts with radial galleries. Finally, substantial structures were increasingly built from wood, earth and stone, ranging from huge timber halls to simple megalithic tombs. It is not in question that most of these novel cultural elements were in existence in Continental Europe at an earlier date than in Britain and Ireland. There was apparently no indigenous domestication of plants or animals, and the ceramics, polished axes and megalithic structures of Neolithic Britain were all inspired by Continental prototypes to some degree. However, the processes by which the phenomena became established in these islands, and the consequences of their use, are matters of continuing debate. Prehistorians remain divided over a series of aspects of the Mesolithic–Neolithic transition. For some, the period saw the arrival of Continental migrants, either in small groups or as a concerted wave, who brought the various aspects of a Neolithic way of life with them as a coherent "package". For others, Neolithic innovations were adopted by indigenous hunter-gatherer communities, whether as piecemeal additions to an existing way of life, or wholesale, in the process of conversion to a new religion, ideology, world-view or identity. And whether exogamous or endogenous, the change from Mesolithic to Neolithic is variously presented as abrupt or gradual, uniform or regionalised. Opinions on the fate of British Mesolithic groups vary considerably, and different authorities present the shift to the Neolithic as alternatively a matter of subsistence economics, or cosmology, or social relations.

Over the years, the intractable quality of the problem of Neolithic origins in Britain has often been attributed to the paucity of the evidence. However, in the past two decades there has been an unprecedented expansion both in the quantity of the material available, and in the forms of information that can be drawn on in studying the period. New and more reliable radiocarbon dates have facilitated a refinement of Early Neolithic chronology. Finds of rectangular timber buildings (numerous smaller ones in Ireland, and fewer, larger ones in Britain) and increasingly sophisticated artefact studies have started to identify specific material forms as characteristic of the earliest Neolithic. DNA studies of both humans and cattle have provided suggestive results, and the analysis of stable isotopes in human and animal bones has yielded direct information on diet. However, while each of these in turn has been hailed as providing a definitive answer, mature reflection reveals the ambiguities and complexities that attend all forms of archaeological evidence. We have increasing quantities of useful information, but it can all be read in a variety of different ways, and the range of interpretations has, if anything, tended to proliferate in recent years. This presumably demonstrates that as well as more and more evidence, our understanding of the period requires coherent and subtle theorisation. The evidence will not speak for itself.

One quite specific problem has been that of scale and contingency: how far can generalised, pan-European models of agricultural origins be applied to the British situation? As we have noted, the introduction of domesticates and new material technologies into Britain can ultimately be attributed to their expansion across Eurasia. Cereals, sheep and cattle had been domesticated in the Near East, while ceramic pyrotechnology spread westwards from East Asia. However, it is debatable whether a single set of causal motors can explain processes that were played out over millennia, or whether more localised factors must be invoked when we consider how innovations passed between social groups who occupied distinct material, historical and ecological conditions. This might be particularly the case with Britain and Ireland, offshore islands whose cultural development was distinctive, if not unconnected from that of the Continental mainland. Continental-scale interpretations have, of course, always informed our views of the British situation. Culture-historic archaeologists like Childe (1940:31–32) and Piggott (1954:15–16) understood agriculture, artefacts and monuments as aspects of the cultural assemblages of particular groups of people, and therefore identified the expansion of the Neolithic with that of a specific "folk". By implication, the arrival of the assemblage in Britain could be equated with that of a cultural or ethnic community.

The introduction of processual approaches to archaeology in the 1960s led to a rejection of "normative" views that presented all aspects of culture as manifestations of the shared customs and beliefs of human groups. In their place, new explanations of agricultural origins came to emphasise the dynamic interrelationships between population, resources, and technology (e.g., Binford 1968). In the context of temperate Europe, this perspective inspired the argument that the spread of agriculture had been a process driven by population dynamics. Ammerman and Cavalli-Sforza (1971:675) proposed that the continuous rise in population promoted by farming and sedentism led to a gradual expansion of agricultural communities across the

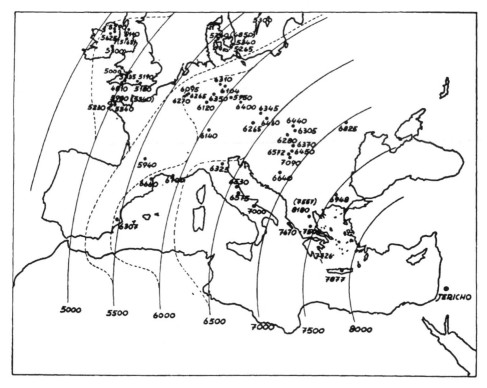

Figure 3.1 Ammerman and Cavalli-Sforza's "wave of advance" model for the introduction of agriculture into Europe. The crescentic lines across the map show the dates (B.P.) by which the Neolithic advance was considered to have penetrated into Europe (from Ammerman and Cavalli-Sforza 1971).

Continent, not by consciously directed migration but by "demic diffusion" (fig. 3.1). This meant that as each social group exceeded the carrying capacity of its immediate territory sub-groups would "bud off" and seek new land to cultivate, at a constant rate. In this scheme of things, "early farming and Neolithic are virtually equivalent" (Ammerman and Cavalli-Sforza 1971:674), and the material culture change of the period was understood to be epiphenomenal in relation to the development of subsistence practice. However, Ammerman and Cavalli-Sforza noted that although the spread of the Neolithic across Europe proceeded at a regular pace, the *Linearbandkeramik* of central Europe appeared to have expanded more rapidly. This anomaly was dismissed as an effect of poor evidence, but the subsequent contribution of Zvelebil and Rowley-Conwy (1984) was grounded in the proposition that the extension of the Neolithic into Europe had been characterised by periods of stasis as well as rapid change. This they explained in terms of a three-stage process, composed of phases of the availability, substitution, and consolidation of dependence on domesticated resources. In some areas, such as Scandinavia and the North European Plain, local foraging groups may have had contact with farming communities – and consequentially access to domesticates – for prolonged periods before they finally adopted a fully Neolithic way of life. This consolidation might have been promoted by a crisis in the availability of wild resources, and might have been virtually impossible to reverse. More subtle than Ammerman and Cavalli-Sforza's argument, this account retains the view that subsistence economics were the determinant of other developments during the Neolithic.

In some more recent discussions, Zvelebil and Rowley-Conwy's distinction between periods of stasis and rapid expansion has been placed in a more deterministic framework. Bonsall et al. (2002:18) suggest that the introduction of domesticates into the north-western fringes of Europe in the period between 4100 and 3800 B.C. can be attributed to the development of a Continental climate, which enhanced the agricultural potential of the area. At the same time, in various parts of Europe increasingly detailed evidence has demonstrated the complexities of the social and cultural processes involved in the transfer of innovations between regions. Esther Bánffy (2004:66), for instance, has described the development of a "central European agro-ecological border" during the sixth millennium B.C., a process in which local conditions made it impossible for the south-east European tell-based food production system to expand into temperate Europe. The consequent slowing of the Neolithic advance rendered Transdanubia as a "cultural frontier zone", in which Starčevo agriculturalists came into protracted contact with local hunter-fisher-gatherer groups. It was this period of interaction that allowed the reformulation of the Neolithic in a form appropriate for temperate conditions, in the form of the *Linearbandkeramik*, around 5500 B.C. The earliest manifestation of the LBK, as at Szentgyörgyvölgy-Pityerdomb in Hungary, saw the combination of Starčevo-style pottery with central European-style longhouses, in areas outwith the distribution of Starčevo sites. The implication of this study is that Neolithic did not take an invariant form across Europe, but had to be adapted to localised circumstances.

Situations comparable with those in Transdanubia have prompted a number of authors to question the notion that the Neolithic represented a fixed set of traits (e.g., Armit and Finlayson 1992; Pluciennik 1998). This suggests that distinct, regionalised forms of a Neolithic way of life could be identified, and in some cases these owed their character to a specific and contingent set of relations and interactions between different communities, which might include both "Neolithic" and "Mesolithic" groups. Consider, for instance, the complicated circumstances that preceded the beginning of the Neolithic in southern Scandinavia, in which Ertebølle hunter-gatherers had begun to make their own pottery (perhaps acquiring the skills involved from foraging groups in the east Baltic), and were involved in exchange relations with agriculturalists further south, perhaps trading furs for shafthole adzes and exotic foodstuffs (Jennbert 1985:197; Tilley 1996:30; Hallgren 2004:123). The specific form taken by the earliest Neolithic in Denmark and southern Sweden owed much of its character to this history (Koch 1998: 175; Fischer 2002: 379). That these kinds of exchanges and interactions could take place should lead us to question the conventional wisdom that hunting and farming are entirely incompatible ways of life. Indeed, it seems that in the Netherlands crop cultivation and animal husbandry were successfully integrated into the broad spectrum economy of the Swifterbant, and that the labour demands of these different practices were reconciled (Raemaekers 1999:182). What is unclear is whether such a "hybrid" system could have been sustained in other areas, or whether the Swifterbant combination of wild and domesticated resources was a passing anomaly, conditioned by the inhabitation of wetlands in proximity to Rössen and Michelsberg Neolithic communities.

Models of Transition in Britain

These considerations demonstrate that we cannot necessarily assume that precisely similar processes were at work in the Mesolithic–Neolithic transitions of areas as distinct as Britain, Ireland and Denmark (as seems to be the case argued by Rowley-Conwy 2004:84). Commonalities between regions need to be demonstrated through fine-grained analysis, or accounts of the past will be developed that are over-generalised and insensitive to regional variation. What is at stake here is the question of whether the indigenous population of Britain was overwhelmed by an incoming Continental economic system (and/or population) of which it had hitherto been largely unaware, or whether the shift to a Neolithic way of life resolved or elaborated processes that had already been present in Mesolithic society. Prior to the 1970s, archaeologists had been in little doubt about the nature of this process. When Grahame Clark questioned the prevailing orthodoxy that attributed all significant cultural changes in prehistoric Britain to Continental incursions, the Neolithic transition was the one major episode that survived his critique. If, as he put it, "the whole complex of technology, practices and ideas that make up our Neolithic culture must have been introduced from overseas" then "no one can doubt that the invasion hypothesis is here essential and justified" (Clark 1966:176). Yet any argument involving the arrival in Britain of a Continental Neolithic population has to explain what became of the native hunter-gatherers. For the culture-historic archaeologists of the inter-war years this issue was resolved by suggesting that Mesolithic elements re-emerged within "secondary Neolithic" cultural formations in the later Neolithic (Fox 1932:10; Childe 1940:81; Piggott 1954:277). Thus elements such as *petit tranchet* arrowheads, mace-heads, bone pins and cord-decorated pottery (which was compared to that of the "Forest Neolithic" of the eastern Baltic) were presented as the outcome of a fusion of Mesolithic and Neolithic folk. However, when these authors were writing the entire duration of the British Neolithic was held to be only half a millennium. Radiocarbon calibration now demonstrates that the period lasted for three or four times that length of time. This means that we must reconsider the ways in which we imagine processes of social change being played out in prehistory. It is simply unimaginable that Mesolithic people can have lain dormant for 1,000 years or so, creating no discernible archaeological record, and awaiting their incorporation into Secondary Neolithic cultures.

Another problem for the invasion hypothesis lay in the practicalities involved in transporting a pioneer agricultural community and their paraphernalia across the

English Channel, and establishing viable settlements. This issue was discussed in some detail by Case (1969:177), who hypothesised trussed cattle and seed corn being loaded into skin boats, interactions with hunter-gatherers and a period of relative instability prior to the construction of monuments by mature Neolithic communities. Yet the picture of colonists slowly developing a foothold in Britain, and gradually incorporating indigenous people into their societies, is at odds with the apparent swiftness of the change from Mesolithic to Neolithic material culture (if not necessarily of all aspects of economic practice). There are no closed assemblages in Britain that contain both pottery and microliths, and the Neolithic presence is not appreciably earlier or later in any particular part of the country (Schulting 2000:32). Despite this, the picture of small groups of migrants arriving from the Atlantic seaboard of Europe is one that continues to have its supporters. In a series of recent articles, Alison Sheridan has drawn attention to the similarities between the bipartite pottery bowl from the west Scottish chambered tomb of Achnacreebeag and Late Castellic vessels from Brittany, and has compared the tomb itself to early passage tombs in Armorica (Sheridan 2000; 2003a; 2003b; 2004). Her argument is that these cultural markers document the arrival of a small group of agriculturalists from north-west France in western Scotland at the beginning of the Neolithic. This migration up the Irish Sea was paralleled by contemporary movements from Normandy and Belgium into south and east England.

Sheridan's (2004:10) argument focuses on "the lack of evidence for contact between Late Mesolithic communities around the Irish Sea or between this area and north-west France at this time". This point demands some consideration, for it is fundamental to our understanding of British and Irish societies in the period immediately before the beginning of the Neolithic. The notion of the "cultural isolation" of Britain and Ireland in the later Mesolithic ultimately springs from the work of Roger Jacobi (1976:78), who claimed that in the period following the postglacial flooding of the land bridge between Britain and France social contact between the two sides was severed. His argument was based on the stylistic attributes of stone tools. In southern British assemblages after 7500 B.C., there is a preponderance of narrow rod microliths, and microtriangles. These can be distinguished from the laterally truncated broad-blade trapezoids and rhomboids and *Feuilles de Gui* found in some Continental collections of the same date (Jacobi 1976:75). In practice, the chronological correlation between the emergence of these mutually exclusive assemblages and the flooding of the English Channel is less secure than Jacobi implied: it may date to 7000 B.C., or even later (Barton and Roberts 2004:345). More seriously, the proposition that the similarity or difference between stone tool assemblages is an index of the degree of contact or communication between human groups should be viewed with a degree of scepticism. In the 1960s and 1970s a number of New Archaeologists working in the south-west United States argued that the sharing of stylistic traits of pottery vessels directly reflected the extent of interaction between different pueblo communities (Plog 1978:145–146). However, later ethnoarchaeological work demonstrated the fallacy of this view. Material culture may be used knowingly and strategically by human groups to enhance their identities and maintain boundaries, irrespective of the degree of contact between those groups (Hodder 1982:21). That two societies have different kinds of flint projectile points is no indication that they lack contact. Our problem with the later Mesolithic is that there is so little evidence that does not take the form of chipped stone implements. None the less, within Continental Europe Peter Gendel (1984:125) has demonstrated that the period saw a general process by which lithic assemblages became more regionally distinctive. The "insular" character of southern British microliths was perhaps no more than an aspect of a development that encompassed much of north-west Europe. There is no suggestion that Late Mesolithic groups in north-east France, Belgium, the Netherlands and western Germany were isolated from one another.

Similar arguments apply to the relationship between Ireland and the wider world during the later Mesolithic. The absence of large mammals (other than pig) in post-glacial Ireland resulted in a very different Mesolithic sequence from that in Britain, in which marine and riverine resources figured centrally (Woodman 2000:247). Ultimately, a material assemblage developed that was unique in Europe, based on large and characteristic "Bann flakes", and lacking both microliths and the burins and scrapers associated with the processing of animal hides (Finlay 2003:88). The very particularity of the Irish later Mesolithic has often been attributed to its insularity (e.g., Cooney 2000:13), but it may be that this is to fail to distinguish the function of stone tools from their stylistic attributes. The flake-based assemblage developed as part of a distinctive way of life, without the emphasis on encounter hunting found in mainland Britain. The usefulness of such a technology in the insular setting might be unrelated to the degree of contact between Ireland and Britain or the Continent (although some examples of these artefacts are now known from south-west Scotland: Hannah Cobb, pers. comm.). Indeed, exactly the same assemblage is found on the Isle of Man (McCartan 2003:338), and the notion that that island might have cultural contacts with Ireland but not with south-west Scotland or the Lake District seems inconceivable.

These points are dramatically underlined by the presence of pre-Neolithic domesticated animal bones from a number of sites in Ireland, most notably Ferriter's Cove. At this site, cattle bones were found in the same general area as a cache of polished axes of local manufacture (Woodman and O'Brien 1993:28; Woodman et al. 1999:124). This would appear to document some kind of interaction between Mesolithic Ireland and Continental Europe (Tresset 2003). Whether this involved the exchange of calves, or merely of joints of beef, it demonstrates that Ireland was not cut off from contact in the later Mesolithic, irrespective of whatever stone tools might have been in use (Woodman and McCarthy 2003:36). It is also worth questioning who was responsible for transporting these animals – Continental farmers who evidently eschewed any food from the sea, or hunter-fisher-gatherers whose way of life would have involved a deep familiarity with the ocean, and probably routine marine travel?

In both Britain and Ireland, the hypothesis of Late Mesolithic cultural isolation does not hold up to scrutiny. If Mesolithic people in Ireland had access to domesticated cattle, the probability is that communities in both Ireland and Britain had a general familiarity with the Continental Neolithic. For whatever reason, the economic and social practices associated with the Neolithic were resisted until around 4000 B.C. Such resistance might be attributed to the emphasis on sharing, reciprocity and non-accumulation often encountered in hunting and gathering societies (Ingold 2000:44). In this respect, the situation in Britain and Ireland during the terminal Mesolithic was broadly comparable with that in southern Scandinavia: something like a weakly developed form of Zvelebil and Rowley-Conwy's "availability phase". This being the case, it is hard to see how the arrival of small groups of agricultural colonists on the island coasts could have brought about a sudden and synchronous adoption of Neolithic culture. Their mere proximity would not have been enough to persuade the indigenous population to adopt a new economic system, if they had already been aware of its potentials and pitfalls for some centuries. Nor, on the other hand, is it likely that such small groups could have slaughtered the entire Mesolithic population quickly enough for them to have vanished entirely from the archaeological record. For while the sudden ubiquity of Neolithic material culture in Britain after 4000 B.C. is remarkable enough, the total disappearance of Mesolithic assemblages is in even greater need of explanation. One further possibility is that Continental migrants brought with them new diseases which decimated the native people. However, any period of biological isolation experienced by British and Irish Mesolithic groups cannot have approached that which rendered pre-Columbian Native Americans susceptible to European infections – and even they were not exterminated to the extent that they ceased to leave any archaeological signature. Overall, the hypothesis that the British Neolithic was established by small colonising communities does not seem to explain the existing evidence adequately. The principal alternatives are a massive, coordinated seaborne invasion, or the adoption of a Neolithic way of life by Mesolithic hunter-gatherers. The author considers the latter to be more likely.

Mesolithic Antecedents

If we accept the possibility that Mesolithic people had some role in the formation of the British Neolithic, it is clearly important to consider the forces that were at work within Mesolithic societies. In recent years, debate on social change in the Mesolithic has been dominated by the "complex hunter-gatherer" model, in which incipient inequalities and cultural elaboration are attributed to the intensification of subsistence practices and increasing sedentaryness (Rowley-Conwy 1983:117). The model is ultimately derived from examples such as the Pacific north-west coast of the Americas, where the exploitation of migratory fish facilitated the development of sedentary village-based communities (Rosman and Rubel 1971). It might, with some justification be applied to later Mesolithic Scandinavia, where very large shell middens may document semi-sedentary groups, although even this is disputed (Rowley-Conwy 1981a:52; Nielsen 1986; Andersen 2004; Johansen 2006). However, in Britain later Mesolithic developments are better described in terms of diversification than of intensification. The enhanced use of shoreline resources doubtless represents a part of this pattern, although the western Scottish and south-west English middens do not approach the scale of those in Denmark (Mellars 2004). With the post-glacial rise in sea level, a more extensive and productive coastline developed, and in some areas it is probable that sporadic movements between coast and inland enabled people to take fish, shellfish and seals at critical points during the year when other foods were scarce (Jacobi 1980:191; Finlayson 2004:225). At the same time, the declining intensity of the seasonal variation in climate and the growing density of woodland appear to have promoted a change in the pattern of hunting large mammals, away from planned interception and toward opportunistic encounter strategies (Myers 1989). With thicker forest cover the management of woodland by burning off undergrowth may have been partly a means of creating clearings in which animals would gather to eat sprouting plants, presenting a relatively easy target for hunters (Innes and Simmons 2000:162). But it seems likely that such controlled burning would also have removed dead vegetation and reduced pests, while speeding up the recycling of nutrients into the soil and in the process promoting the growth of plant foods such as berries, acorns and hazelnuts (Moore 1996:67; Mason 2000:140).

While mobility appears to have been important throughout the British Mesolithic, the picture of a seasonal alternation between dispersal in the uplands and aggregation at lowland base camps which has been debated since the excavation of Star Carr (Clark 1954; 1972) has been questioned in recent years. New work in the Vale of Pickering has stressed the dispersal of activities across the landscape, rather than a simple division between base camps and task camps (Conneller and Schadla-Hall 2003:104), and a similar pattern has been reported in the southern Hebrides, where all sites appear to have been specialised to some degree (Finlayson 2004:226). However, within this Mesolithic taskscape there appear to have been "persistent places", which were not so much locations where many different activities were concentrated as ones that maintained a quite specific significance over a considerable period of time. Some of these were simply repeatedly visited for economic reasons (Barton et al. 1995:104), but in other cases the specialness may relate to a place having been set apart or culturally sanctioned for specific practices (Pollard 2000a:128). In the case of Star Carr, Conneller (2004:45) suggests that the site was distinguished by the transformation of animal bodies into artefacts to be used by humans (barbed bone points and antler frontlets), which were also deposited there at the end of their use-life. Some at least of the shell middens of western Scotland may have been visited intermittently for the gathering of shoreline foods and to conduct a series of transformative activities (Pollard 1996). For instance, it seems that the mammal bones recovered from these sites may not have been hunted locally, and could have been brought there with the aim of working them into bone tools (Kitchener et al. 2004: 80). Similarly, at midden sites such as Cnoc Coig and Carding Mill Bay, fragments of human bone were encountered, particularly the small bones of the hands and feet (T. Pollard 1996:204; J. Pollard 2000a:131). This has sometimes been interpreted as evidence that the dead were exposed at such places. If only such extremities remained it is possible that other body parts were removed and distributed elsewhere, in which case the midden would represent a critical location in the post-mortem dispersal of the human body.

If these practices could be read as precursors for certain aspects of Neolithic mortuary activity, the possibility that monumental architecture may also have had Mesolithic precedent has also been raised recently. A series of large post-holes located in the course of the construction of the car-park at Stonehenge produced radiocarbon dates in the eighth millennium B.C. (Cleal et al. 1995:47) and a land snail assemblage indicating a mature Boreal woodland. Similar post-holes have also been identified at Boscombe Down and Hambledon Hill (Allen and Gardiner 2002:145). These instances provide the definitive refutation of the notion that monument-building can take place only where an agricultural economy exists to sustain it (see Legge 1989:224; Rowley-Conwy 2004:84–85). But what is remarkable about them is not simply that colossal timber uprights were being raised during the Mesolithic, but that in each case these structures have been found on sites that would much later be the locations of Neolithic ceremonial activity. As with the "persistent places" noted above, this appears to demonstrate the longevity of meaning in the landscape, in this case clearly spanning the Mesolithic–Neolithic boundary.

Britain and Ireland: Contrasting Trajectories?

This mention of continuity in the landscape brings to mind some of the differences between the Neolithic archaeology of Britain and that of Ireland. For this kind of continuity is much more apparent in the former than the latter. In Ireland, there is little or no overlap between the findspots of Mesolithic flintwork and those of the carinated pottery bowls of the earliest Neolithic (Sheridan 2004:12), yet in Britain it is comparatively common to find leaf-shaped arrowheads among Meso-lithic flint-scatters, indicating at least that the same places continued to be fre-quented into the Neolithic (Edmonds 1995:35). Similarly, Neolithic funerary monuments were often constructed in places that had been occupied during the Mesolithic. At Hazleton North, Gloucestershire (Saville 1990:14), and Ascott-under-Wychwood, Oxfordshire (Case 1986:24), long cairns were built over scatters of Mesolithic artefacts, while at the Scottish sites of Crarae (Scott 1961:7) and Glecknabae (Bryce 1903:42) (fig. 3.2), chambered tombs were constructed on top of shell middens. It is also notable that the large natural shaft at Fir Tree Field on Cranborne Chase in north Dorset contained a deposit of microliths and one of Early Neolithic bowl pottery which may have been separated from each other by a matter of decades (Allen and Green 1998) (fig. 3.3). Such examples are difficult to parallel in Ireland. It is arguable that these differences can be traced back to the contrasting Late Mesolithic ways of life that have already been mentioned. Lacking aurochs, elk, red deer and roe deer, the Irish Mesolithic was both less economically diverse and perhaps less mobile, and more focused on coastal, lacustrine and riv-erine areas (Woodman 2000:237). I have argued elsewhere that in parts of Britain, the beginning of the Neolithic saw a "substitution" of domesticated cattle for wild ungulates, with the result that communities remained semi-mobile and maintained an attachment to particular landmarks (Thomas 2004a). In Ireland this kind of

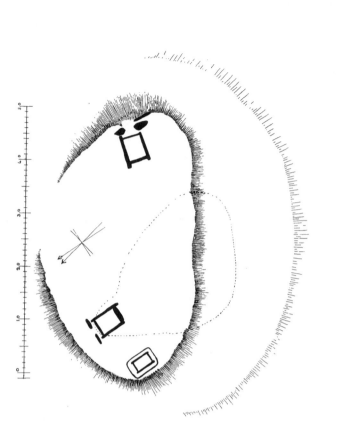

Figure 3.2 The chambered tomb at Glecknabae, Bute, located on top of a Mesolithic shell midden (from Bryce 1903).

Figure 3.3 The natural shaft at Fir Tree Field, Down Farm, Dorset, which contained deposits of Mesolithic microliths and Neolithic pottery stratified in proximity to one another. Photograph: Martin Green.

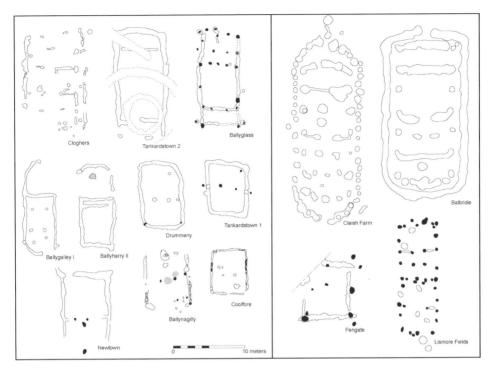

Figure 3.4 Early Neolithic timber buildings in Ireland (*left*) and in Britain (*right*).

substitution could not be undertaken by communities who had invested so thoroughly in the use of the seashore. Here the start of the Neolithic involved greater disruption and dislocation, with a swift change to a dependence on domesticated resources. This dependence, however, may not have been maintained throughout the Neolithic period (Bradley 2007:44).

In the Irish context, Cooney (2003:51) has presented cogent arguments for the development of "house societies" during the Early Neolithic. However, while the numbers of modestly sized rectangular buildings of Early Neolithic date have mushroomed in recent years (Armit et al. 2003:146), the same is not true of Britain (fig. 3.4). Despite Rowley-Conwy's (2004:93) efforts to present the evidence for domestic buildings in Britain, Ireland and Scandinavia as homogeneous, the British examples remain a mixture of large "halls", structures associated with monuments in some manner (and potentially representing part of the constructional history of the monument itself), and amorphous combinations of post-holes, stake-holes, hearths and floors (Darvill 1996:85–90). These latter may certainly be representative of episodes of domestic dwelling, but not necessarily of sedentism. In the case of Scotland, where several of the large halls are concentrated, Barclay (2003:71) has discussed possible reasons for the relative paucity of domestic structures, compared with Ireland. These include the masking of Neolithic deposits by colluvium, damage by intensive agriculture and more thorough archaeological monitoring of recent development in Ireland. These are all serious arguments, but it can be countered that recent archaeological evaluation and monitoring in Britain (particularly in the wake of Planning Policy Guidance 16: Archaeology and Planning, which promoted developer-funded evaluation and investigation in advance of construction work) has produced numerous Neolithic pits but few dwellings, and that numerous house structures of Bronze and Iron Age date have also been uncovered over the same period in England, Scotland and Wales. If the scarcity of Neolithic houses is to be attributed to post-Roman colluviation and post-medieval agriculture, later prehistoric buildings which leave no more robust an archaeological signature might be expected to have been equally affected.

This suggests that the inception of the Neolithic took different forms in Britain and Ireland. A variety of other forms of evidence underline this conclusion. A decade ago, two examples of Neolithic field systems were regularly cited in the literature: Fengate in East Anglia and Céide Fields in Co. Mayo (Pryor 1978; Caulfield 1978). Now, other examples of Neolithic fields have been suggested in western Ireland (Cooney 2000:47), while the Grooved Ware from Fengate has been identified as residual and the field ditches reassigned to the Middle Bronze Age (Cleal 1999:6; Evans and Pollard 2001). A definitive statement would be premature, but it may be that Neolithic fields are very scarce on the British mainland, and rather more common in parts of Ireland. Similarly, while pits containing deposits of Neolithic pottery which have sometimes been filled with a degree of formality are common in Britain (Thomas 1999:64; Garrow 2006), they are far rarer in Ireland. In some cases, such pits arguably relate to "clearing up" activities following episodes of inhabitation, or discrete events of consumption (Pollard 1999; 2000b:365). They may thus relate in an indirect way to a transient way of life. Something similar might be said of causewayed enclosures, which are numerous in southern Britain, but scarce in Ireland (Sheridan 2001; Cooney 2002). Such enclosures often seem to have been frequented seasonally by groups of people who spent much of their time elsewhere (Healy 2004:22). This does not make them a signature of a mobile society, but it does evoke a pattern distinct from Cooney's "house societies", among whom social action may have been structured at a different level.

Humans, Animals and Diet

Despite these differences, there is little doubt that cattle were of great social value in both Britain and Ireland from the start of the Neolithic. Recent DNA studies have demonstrated that the domesticated cattle of Europe were ultimately of Anatolian origin, and there is little likelihood that wild cattle were domesticated locally in Britain (Tresset 2000:21; Troy et al. 2001:1089). Cattle generally dominate Early Neolithic faunal assemblages in Britain, with pig and sheep in the minority (Tresset 2003:21). While sheep might not be expected to thrive until extensive areas of grassland had been established, there is an evident contradiction between this emphasis on cattle and the traditional model of small, dispersed farmsteads. A single cow can provide 200–300 kg of meat, fat and offal (Whittle 2003:31; Healy

2004:22). In recent Greece, Halstead (2004:156–157) reports that a family group might consume a chicken or a small lamb, while a whole sheep might be eaten at a wedding. Cattle would be eaten only at a village-wide festival. In the absence of advanced food storage technologies, the consumption of beef might have to be reserved for special occasions, although ethnographic evidence demonstrates that such special occasions can be quite frequent in non-state societies (Stenning 1963:111; Kottak 1980). Of course, causewayed enclosure sites have provided a series of large faunal assemblages, which indicate that very large quantities of cattle meat were being consumed at sites that were occupied seasonally or sporadically (e.g., Whittle et al. 1999). The argument has been proposed that the predominantly female cattle at these sites were the surplus from a dairying economy (Healy 2004:22), and this appears to be supported by the presence of milk lipids in contemporary pottery (Copley et al. 2003). However, it should be remembered that causewayed enclosures are a phenomenon of the mature Early Neolithic, predominantly dating to the thirty-seventh century B.C. and later (Oswald et al. 2001). We therefore have very little direct evidence for cattle husbandry practices during the first three or four centuries of the British Neolithic, although it may be safe to assume that herds provided milk and/or milk products, and that cows were slaughtered episodically, at times when larger groups of people were gathered together. Over time, it is probable that cattle became an important form of mobile wealth for particular communities, and that their slaughter and consumption took on a central role in the formation of alliances, funerals, marriages and the construction and maintenance of social obligations (Schulting 2004:26; Ray and Thomas 2003). It is entirely possible that a reconfiguration of society which put cattle at the heart of a variety of transactions was a critical element in the Mesolithic–Neolithic transition, and was precisely the change that Mesolithic communities had been resisting up to this point.

While there is a level of agreement that cattle were important from the start of the Neolithic, even if their calorific contribution to everyday diet is open to debate, there is much less harmony over the role of domesticated plants, and in particular cereals. At one end of the argument, Moffett et al. (1989:252) point out the contrast between the carbonised plant assemblages of the Neolithic and those of later prehistory. While the former are commonly dominated by hazelnut shells, crab apple pips and other wild plant remains, the latter are much more likely to be made up almost exclusively of cereals and associated processing waste. At the other pole, Jones (2000:83) points to the assemblage from Lismore Fields in Derbyshire, and suggests that it is characteristic of "permanent cereal-based settlements". So, while there is a general acceptance that both cereals and wild plants were consumed during the early stages of the Neolithic, it is the relative importance of the two that is at question. The group of authors who defend a "horticultural" Neolithic base their arguments on taphonomy and middle range theory, in considering the processes which contribute to the formation of the archaeological deposits that are available for study. There is a strong case that cereals may be systematically under-represented in carbonised assemblages. The by-product of eating hazelnuts is nut-shell, which is likely to be used as fuel, and preserves well under these circumstances. By contrast, the by-products of processing and consuming cereals are chaff and straw, which may be used for animal fodder or building, and if burned are less likely to be preserved, as well as small weed seeds (Jones 2000:80; Monk 2000:75; Rowley-Conwy 2000:51; 2004:90). It is further argued that a more representative sample of plant remains is likely to be recovered from burnt houses, which are the products of domestic accidents rather than the disposal of waste products (Jones 2000:81).

While these arguments show commendable rigor in addressing the formation of the archaeological record, they are weaker when the representativeness of the samples concerned is considered. Robinson (2000:86) distinguishes between a normal Neolithic assemblage, with a preponderance of wild plants and a minority of cereal remains, and exceptional sites with rich finds of cereals, including the causewayed enclosure at Hambledon Hill and the burnt timber structures at Balbridie and Lismore Fields. While causewayed enclosures are self-evidently sites of unusual character, Jones, Rowley-Conwy and Monk would clearly like to portray the large timber buildings as typical dwellings, characteristic of sedentary agricultural societies, and burned down as a result of everyday carelessness. As we have seen, it is more probable that these structures were held in common by larger social groups and were deliberately destroyed, and that their contents amount to "gifts" or "sacrifices" rather than representative snapshots of an arable economy. To reiterate the point: if Neolithic societies in Britain were as fully reliant on cereal agriculture as Iron Age ones were, why would the archaeology of the two periods be so different? Rowley-Conwy (2004:90) argues that the preponderance of wild plants on British Neolithic sites can be attributed to the "vegetational mantle" of nut and berry plants that would naturally form around the edges of woodland clearances made for cereal plots. But wild plants are virtually absent from botanical assemblages attributable to the *Linearbandkeramik*, communities who were certainly conducting fixed-plot cereal agriculture in wooded landscapes, demonstrating that is not the case (Bakels and Zeiler 2005:313). The taphonomic factors attending the survival of charred plant remains would have been the same in later prehistory as in the Neolithic, yet the relative proportions of wild to cultivated plants appears to decline over time, while field systems, storage facilities and permanent settlements become more established. There is little doubt that some people in Early Neolithic Britain cultivated cereals, and that these would have been grown in small garden plots that might have been quite long-lived (Rowley-Conwy 1981b; Fairbairn 2000). But it is likely that such cultivation was not engaged in by all Early Neolithic communities, and that for many cereals were a special food, acquired through exchange or eaten only at special occasions. As with cattle meat, cereals might not be an everyday staple, even if both made an occasional if significant contribution to diet. This is *not* to claim, as Rowley-Conwy (2004:90) implies, that such foods were restricted to a separate sphere of ritual activity. Rather, it means that Early Neolithic diets will have been diverse, with particular persons, kin groups or communities having access to varied combinations of domesticated and wild resources according to location, time of year, social status and position in networks of exchange and alliance. This kind of diversity is hinted at by the stable isotope evidence for human diet (Richards 2000:312), although this technique remains a rather blunt instrument when considered in the context of the likely complexity of diets.

The study of diet through the stable isotopes of carbon and nitrogen contained in human bone collagen has been one of the most important developments in the study of the Mesolithic–Neolithic transition in Europe during the past decade. The method can distinguish the relative proportions of animal versus plant and marine versus terrestrial protein habitually consumed by a person during roughly their last 10 years of life (Ambrose 1993). In areas as diverse as Portugal, Brittany, Scandinavia and Britain, claims have been made for a rapid change from a dependence on marine resources to entirely terrestrial diets coincident with the opening of the Neolithic (Tauber 1981; Lubell et al. 1994; Schulting 1998; Richards and Hedges 1999; Schulting and Richards 2001; Richards et al. 2003). Problems have been raised in relation to this evidence: in some areas the pattern may be less clear-cut than originally suggested (Lidén et al. 2004), while the continuing archaeological evidence for marine subsistence activities into the Neolithic sits uneasily with the apparently total rejection of foods from the sea (Milner et al. 2004). This may tell us no more than that whatever amounts of sea fish, seals and shellfish Neolithic people continued to eat, they were not great enough to affect the overall composition of isotopes in their bones. Perhaps more problematic is the point that most of the Neolithic skeletons studied in Britain are derived from long barrows and causewayed enclosures dating from 200 or 300 years after the beginning of the period, so that the results do not reflect the initial generations of Neolithic activity. This makes the speed of any change in diet difficult to assess.

If, however, we accept the argument that a fundamental transformation overtook culinary practices in north-west Europe during the late fifth and early fourth millennia B.C., problems of interpretation still remain. The most obvious explanation would be that the abandonment of marine foods simply reflects the universal adoption of mixed farming, reliant upon domesticated plants and animals (as implied by Richards and Hedges 1999). There are some problems with such an account, however. We have addressed above the objections that can be raised against any model of large-scale population movement: these are even stronger when we consider processes that operate on a pan-European scale. The alternative would be that indigenous people abruptly adopted domesticates and forswore any appreciable consumption of marine foods. This might be because the tending of crops and livestock cattle made it impossible to gain access to the shoreline, or that eating the meat of domesticated mammals made fish unpalatable to them, or that a new social network based on the circulation and consumption of cattle rendered other foods redundant (Schulting 2004:23). Equally, the categorical nature of the change implies an outright avoidance of food from the sea, and one suggestion that has been made is that its speed and ubiquity implies the involvement of some new cultural phenomenon, such as a religion (Richards 2003:34). One point that is often missed is that while stable isotope measurements can discriminate between land and sea, and between animal and plant foods, they cannot distinguish between tame and wild. The process that has been identified might thus also involve the introduction of a new series of food taboos, without requiring an absolute reliance on domesticates (Thomas 2003). There might be little direct evidence to support this,

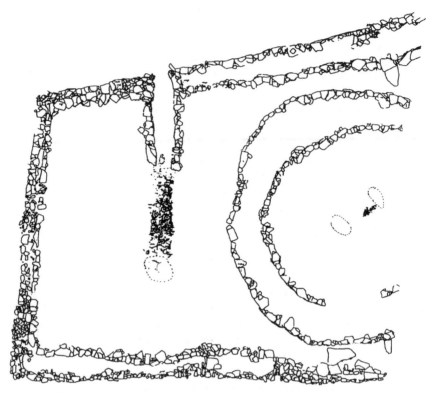

Figure 3.5 The chambered cairn at Whitwell Quarry, Derbyshire (from Schulting 2000).

but it does demonstrate that the case for a universal adoption of a way of life based exclusively on domesticated plants and animals is far from proven (*contra* Rowley-Conwy 2004:91). Furthermore, if cattle rather than plants were the critical economic innovation of the Early Neolithic, herding might make access to coastal resources more difficult without precluding terrestrial hunting and gathering. The probable complexity of the emergent pattern is hinted at by the human skeletal remains from the chambered tomb at Whitwell Quarry in Derbyshire (fig. 3.5), a relatively early mortuary structure (dating to the thirty-eighth century B.C.), whose stable isotopes show an exclusively terrestrial diet (itself unremarkable, given an inland location) (Schulting 2000:30; Whittle et al. 2007:127), yet whose occlusal wear patterns and lack of dental caries are indicative of a diet dominated by wild plants (Chamberlain and Witkin 2003:55).

Portable Artefacts

The most archaeologically visible aspect of the Mesolithic–Neolithic transition in Britain is the disappearance of microlithic stone tools, and the introduction of pottery and a range of new lithic artefacts, including leaf-shaped arrowheads and

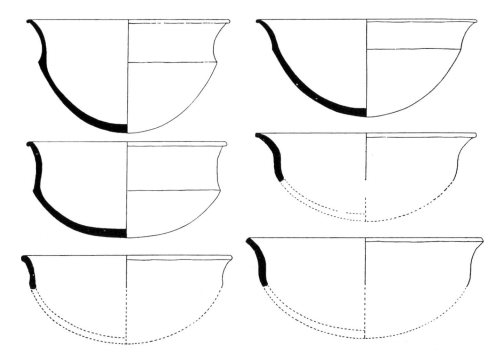

Figure 3.6 Classic "Grimston"-style carinated bowls and s-profiled vessels from Hanging Grimston, Kemp Howe and Heslerton (from Newbiggin 1937).

polished flint and stone axes. Traditionally, it has been normal to identify this change in material culture as a reflection of the arrival of a new population, and this view still has its adherents. Thus Sheridan argues that "the earliest communities whom we identify as 'Neolithic' shared the same continental ancestry and so brought the same basic traditions to Britain and Ireland" (2004:9). Alternatively, we might consider the active role of material things in bringing about social transformation. Through their manufacture, circulation and use, both pottery vessels and stone tools might affect the tempo and structure of social interaction, rather than simply standing as the markers of a particular ethnic identity. It has been recognised for some while that fine carinated "Grimston" bowls represent a fundamental aspect of the earliest ceramic assemblages in both Britain and Ireland (Herne 1988) (fig. 3.6). In a recent review of this material, Cleal (2004:165) points out that these early assemblages can also contain a variety of other vessel forms, including s-profiled bowls, deep carinated bowls, simple neutral bowls and inflected round-bodied bowls. None the less, the carinated bowl remains the core element of the earliest pottery in Britain and Ireland (Cleal 2004:180).

Carinated round-bottomed bowls clearly have Continental origins, but the picture of a European ceramic assemblage being transported wholesale to Britain with a migrant population is not supported by the evidence. There are decorated shouldered and bipartite bowls in Rössen and Castellic contexts, but the true plain carinated bowl is not evident anywhere in Europe long before 4000 B.C. (Whittle

1977:125; Boujot and Cassen 1992:204). Interestingly, at this point the vessel form emerged in a variety of different cultural contexts across north-west Europe. Yet in all cases it formed part of a much broader repertoire. Michelsberg assemblages in Belgium and Holland have carinated bowls, but they are generally dominated by wide-mouthed bowls, ranging from tulip beakers to open inflected vessels, and there are also wide dishes, large storage jars, lugged flasks, clay disks (baking plates or jar covers), vessels with perforated lugs and pottery spoons (Schollar 1959:56; Whittle 1977:131; Louwe Kooijmans 1980:203; Raemaekers 1999:142). Assemblages from the Low Countries which have been cited as especially close parallels for the classic "Grimston" bowls, such as at Het Vormer and Hazendonk 2, again have a wider range of forms, including tulip beakers, closed jars, shouldered bowls and deep storage vessels. Indeed, it is an overall heterogeneity that characterises these assemblages (Louwe Kooijmans 1976:263). Further west, Michelsberg and Chasséo-Michelsberg assemblages may be dominated by globular vessels with open necks and no clear carination, while flasks, hemispherical lugged bowls, globular jars and spoons are also present (Dubouloz 1998:11; Jeunesse 1998:35; Mordant and Mordant 1988:242). In north-west France, Chasséen sites again have small numbers of carinated bowls, alongside "pseudo-carinated" pottery, inflected and open bowls, bag-shaped lugged vessels, pottery disks and vase supports (Boujot and Cassen 1992:205; Whittle 1977:170).

Now, it may be that at some time in the future a Belgian Michelsberg site will emerge with a pottery assemblage dominated by carinated bowls, and may then be able to claim to be the progenitor of the entire British Early Neolithic. However, we should remember that such a discovery has been anticipated for a considerable while (Piggott 1954:99; 1955:99). It may be more realistic to suggest that rather than representing the straightforward transportation of a particular ceramic inventory from one place to another, the foundation of the insular Grimston tradition involved the active selection of a very specific element from Continental assemblages, precisely because it was held in common by a range of diverse and geographically dispersed communities. The earliest pottery in Britain is restricted in its range of vessel forms. The first potters in Britain were doing a limited range of things, but they were doing them well – although Peterson (2003:152) points out that the fabrics that they were using involved recipes that were experimental and over-complex. It is interesting to speculate who these early potters might have been. Potting involves both the selection of materials from the landscape and transformative pyrotechnology. These are skills that would have had to be learned over a protracted period of time, by people who lived within communities that practised potting. We have argued already that there was probably contact between Britain and the Continent throughout the later Mesolithic, but at a certain point the circulation of personnel between social groups will have taken on a greater urgency. For it is more likely that, rather than whole communities migrating to Britain, ceramic technology reached these islands through the transfer of particular people between social groups. This might have involved prolonged visiting or apprenticeship relationships, or the exchange of marriage partners. If the number of people who could make and fire pots was initially limited, it is probable that their skills would have been perceived as magical and highly valued. It is by no means universal that ceramic vessels are produced by women in non-state societies lacking a developed division of labour (Arnold 1985; 1993); but if these first potters *were* women it is conceivable that they might have occupied positions of considerable authority in the society of the earliest Neolithic.

While potting represented an entirely new technology in Britain at the start of the Neolithic, the new stone tools that began to be made and used deployed an existing technology in the creation of new products. This would mean that the acquisition of the skills required to manufacture these two forms of material culture would have been fundamentally different in character. The use of single-platform flint cores to produce narrow flakes and blades was common to both later Mesolithic and Early Neolithic (Edmonds 1995:37), and it is to be presumed that a person who had the necessary skills to produce microliths could learn to make leaf-shaped arrowheads quite quickly. Similarly, while Neolithic polished axes are of very distinctive form, the practice of grinding stone tools was already established in Mesolithic Britain and Ireland (David and Walker 2004:327). Where stone tools were concerned, existing skills were applied to the making of unfamiliar objects at the start of the Neolithic. Again, these artefact types have Continental precedent. Leaf-shaped arrowheads are present in Michelsberg assemblages – but they occur alongside triangular and transverse forms (Raemaekers 1999:142). So as with pottery there seems to have been a degree of selection involved in the formation of the British Neolithic cultural repertoire: one form of arrowhead was being adopted, to the exclusion of other possibilities. This pattern of selection and recombination applies in other areas, and indicates that no one Continental community provided all of the elements of the British Neolithic. For while the Belgian Michelsberg inventory included ceramics and arrowheads that are comparable with those in Britain, it lacked funerary monuments (Whittle 1996:293), and the closest parallels for the earthen long barrows that began to be built within two centuries of the start of the period have to be found further east (Madsen 1979). The "small migrant groups" hypothesis would demand that a variety of communities from an area which spanned Denmark to Armorica all simultaneously decided to colonise Britain, bringing some elements of their material culture with them while leaving others at home, and then pooling the various bits once they had arrived!

Public Architecture

Perhaps unusually for the culture-historic era, Stuart Piggott chose field monuments as the defining elements of the primary Neolithic in Britain, his "Windmill Hill Culture" (1954:18). Yet it now appears that both earthen long barrows and causewayed enclosures were characteristic of more or less mature stages of the period (Cleal 2004:169; Scarre et al. 2003; Schulting 2000; Whittle et al. 2007). This information might easily encourage us to return to the view that monuments are a kind of "luxury good", which require the establishment of an economy with a recurrent surplus before their construction can be supported. Yet "surplus" is a

concept closely linked with contemporary capitalist economics, and may be anachronistic when applied to the Neolithic. An alternative view is that monuments were
not a passive product of Neolithic societies, but were instrumental in the formation
of such communities (as argued in different ways by Barrett 1994; Sherratt 1995).
While it is clear that major monumental complexes such as the Hambledon Hill
causewayed enclosure and the Dorset Cursus were constructed some centuries after
the start of the Neolithic, other non-domestic structures were much earlier, and
can be argued to have been integral to the social and economic developments of
the time. These early structures were not distinguished by their colossal scale and
the conspicuous investment of labour to the same degree as those of the mid fourth
millennium B.C., so that it may be more appropriate to speak of them in terms of
"public architecture" than "monumentality".

In both Britain and Ireland, one form of architecture which may date back to
the earliest decades of the Neolithic is the megalithic chambered tomb, although
this has yet to be satisfactorily demonstrated (Whittle et al. 2007:126–127). Candidates for early dates include portal dolmens and simple passage tombs. In both
cases the structure consists of little more than a capstone raised on supporting
orthostats, with perhaps a small surrounding mound. This is rather different from
later, more elaborate tombs with chambers hidden deep under an extensive mound
(Whittle 2004:86). None the less, the distinction between a "closed" dolmen and
an accessible passage tomb implies different relationships between the living community and the tomb contents, including, potentially, the dead. In western Ireland,
some of the radiocarbon dates from Carrowmore, which appear to recede back into
the fifth millennium B.C., have been regarded with a degree of scepticism (Woodman
2000:234; Scarre et al. 2003:67). Yet there is little to indicate that the simple
passage tombs within this group do not date to 4000 B.C. or shortly afterwards.
Other chambered tombs that have produced dates in the same chronological bracket
include Coldrum, Kent (Whittle et al. 2007:127), although the early dates from
Whitwell, Derbyshire, have been replaced by new determinations on fresh material,
suggesting construction after 3800 B.C. (Schulting 2000:30).

Where radiocarbon dates are lacking, there are other indications that particular
tombs may fit into the earliest part of the Neolithic sequence. In Ireland, portal
dolmens at Ballykeel, Kilclooney More, Ballyrenan and Agnaskeagh are associated
with carinated bowl pottery (ApSimon 1986:6). More often, relatively simple structures have been identified as the primary element in multi-phase monuments. In
Wales, portal dolmens at Pentre Ifan and Dyffryn Ardudwy were incorporated into
later long cairns (Whittle 2004:87), while in Ireland similar chambers were envel-
oped by long cairns at Ballyrennan and Ballywholan (Corcoran 1960:110). In
south-west Scotland, Noble (2005:29) has recently suggested that the small, "pro-
tomegalithic" tombs already identified by Corcoran (1970) at Mid Gleniron may
also have been present within the Cairnholy long cairns. Furthermore, among the
Cotswold-Severn tombs of south-west Britain, Darvill has described a variety of
structures that were later enclosed by long cairns. These include passage tombs, as
at Ty Isaf, and "rotunda graves" with closed cists, as at Notgrove (Darvill 2004:57).
Significantly, while Grimes (1939:138) argued that the Ty Isaf structure was

integral to the build of the main cairn, Peterson (2003:104) has demonstrated that it contained pottery of quite a different type from that found in the long mound. Yet it is not clear in any case that such primary structures predated the later monuments by a great length of time (Smith and Brickley 2006:350–351). It is clear that the adequate dating of the earliest phases of multi-stage megalithic structures should now be a major research objective.

Like the long cairns of the west, earthen long barrows in southern and eastern Britain appear to broadly date to a horizon after 3800 B.C. (Schulting 2000:28; Scarre et al. 2003:76; Whittle et al. 2007). Yet very often the long mounds were constructed over timber mortuary structures which had been the scene of protracted activities involving the deposition and reorganisation of human remains (Thomas 2000:660). Such linear chambers, structured around two or three large wooden uprights, had a broader geographical distribution than earthen long mounds, and formed the initial stage in the histories of a variety of kinds of monuments. At Slewcairn and Lochill in south-west Scotland they were incorporated into trapezoidal long cairns (Masters 1973; 1981); at Pitnacree in Perthshire and Callis Wold 275 in Yorkshire they were covered by round barrows (Coles and Simpson 1965; Coombs 1976), and at Dooey's Cairn, Ballymacaldrack, in Antrim a linear structure eventually formed part of a horned cairn (Collins 1976:5). At Dooey's Cairn the chamber had been burned, and produced a radiocarbon date of close to 4000 B.C. (Cooney 2000:99). Conceivably, a number of these linear mortuary structures may have been built at the very start of the Neolithic, with their eventual monumental setting being decided upon only at a later date.

A further form of public architecture which undoubtedly dates to the earliest Neolithic is the large timber halls already mentioned above. In the south of Britain examples at Yarnton and White Horse Stone are known only from post-hole arrangements, and neither produced any carbonised plant remains (Hey et al. 2003:81). Those in the north, Balbridie, Craithes, Claish and Lismore Fields, had apparently all been burned, Claish apparently on more than one occasion (Ralston 1982:244; Garton 1991:13; Barclay et al. 2002:102; Fraser and Murray 2005:1). All were associated with deposits of charred cereals, and those at Balbridie had been cleaned elsewhere, to judge from the scarcity of spikelet fragments and weed seeds (Fairweather and Ralston 1993:4). It is notable that a suite of other large, rectilinear timber structures, all made of oak and all deliberately burned, also forms a distinctive element of the earliest Neolithic of southern Scotland. These include the fenced "mortuary enclosure" at Inchtuthil (Barclay and Maxwell 1991), post-defined cursus-type enclosures at Holm, Dunragit, Castle Menzies and Doulasmuir (Kendrik 1995; Barclay et al. 2002:121; Thomas 2004b) (fig. 3.7), and the pit-defined enclosure at Bannockburn (Rideout 1997). It is arguable that both roofed halls and rectilinear post enclosures drew on the theme of the "great house", and provided spaces intended for the temporary gatherings of dispersed populations. In both cases, the life history of the structure was brought to an end in deliberate destruction by fire (Thomas 2006). Elsewhere such gatherings were marked less by the traces of burnt architecture than by substantial pits containing the evidence of communal feasting in the form of animal bones and carinated bowl-dominated

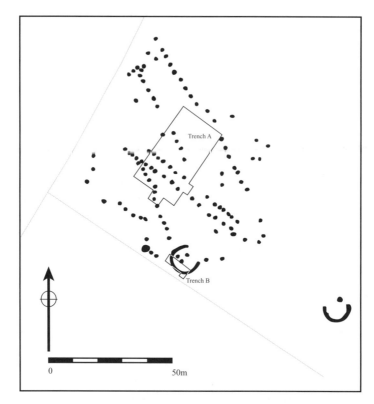

Figure 3.7   The timber post alignment/cursus at Holm Farm, Dumfries and Galloway, which has produced a series of radiocarbon dates in the 4000–3900 B.C. interval. Image: Julian Thomas.

ceramic assemblages, as at Roughridge Hill and Coneybury in Wiltshire, and Cannon Hill, Berkshire (Cleal 2004:176).

In Conclusion

The enigma of the Mesolithic–Neolithic transition in Britain is the combination of very swift and more gradual processes of change that appear nevertheless to be linked to one another. While the development of a fully agricultural landscape took many generations, domesticated plants and animals appeared abruptly in Britain, alongside pottery, timber architecture and polished stone tools. One way of rationalising this process would be to suggest that a new kind of identity was widely adopted, a new means of self-identification. This involved a set of practices that were not restricted to either a sphere of "subsistence" activities or "ritual" acts. Several of the innovations of the Neolithic might initially have been used under special, non-utilitarian conditions, and their adoption might in time have led to the transformation of the everyday. In these terms it is important to recognise that the change from the Mesolithic to the Neolithic was not simply a matter of changes in diet and the acquisition of sustenance, or of symbolic and ideational activities, but of the practices of inhabitation through which people made themselves at home in the world.

REFERENCES

Allen, M., and J. Gardiner, 2002 A sense of time: cultural markers in the Mesolithic of southern England. *In* Inscribed Landscapes: marking and making place. B. David and M. Wilson, eds. pp. 139–153. Honolulu: University of Hawai'i Press.

——and M. Green, 1998 The Fir Tree Field Shaft: the date and archaeological and palaeoenvironmental potential of a chalk swallowhole feature. Proceedings of the Dorset Natural History and Archaeology Society 120:25–37.

Ambrose, S. H., 1993 Isotopic analysis of paleodiets: methodological and interpretive considerations. *In* Investigations of Ancient Human Tissue: chemical analysis in anthropology. M. K. Sandford, ed. pp. 59–129. Langhorne, PA: Gordon and Breach Science Publishers.

Ammerman, A. J., and L. L. Cavalli-Sforza, 1971 Measuring the rate of spread of early farming in Europe. Man 6:674–688.

Andersen, S. H., 2004 Danish shell middens reviewed. *In* Mesolithic Scotland and its Neighbours. A. Saville, ed. pp. 393–412. Edinburgh: Society of Antiquaries of Scotland.

ApSimon, A., 1986 Chronological contexts for Irish megalithic tombs. Journal of Irish Archaeology 3:5–15.

Armit, I., and B. Finlayson, 1992 Hunter-gatherers transformed: the transition to agriculture in northern and western Europe. Antiquity 66:664–676.

——E. Murphy, E. Nelis and D. Simpson, 2003 Irish Neolithic houses. *In* Neolithic Settlement in Ireland and Western Britain. I. Armit, E. Murphy, E. Nelis and D. Simpson, eds. pp. 146–148. Oxford: Oxbow Books.

Arnold, D., 1985 Ceramic Theory and Cultural Process. Cambridge: Cambridge University Press.

——1993 Ecology and Ceramic Production in an Andean Community. Cambridge: Cambridge University Press.

Bakels, C., and J. Zeiler, 2005 The fruits of the land: Neolithic subsistence. *In* The Prehistory of the Netherlands, vol. 1. L. Louwe Kooimans, P. van den Broeke, H. Fokkens and A. van Gijn, eds. pp. 311–336. Amsterdam: Amsterdam University Press.

Bánffy, E., 2004 Advances in the research of the Neolithic transition in the Carpathian Basin. *In* LBK Dialogues: studies in the formation of the linear pottery culture. A. Lukes and M. Zvelebil, eds. pp. 49–70. Oxford: British Archaeological Reports.

Barclay, G. J., 2003 Neolithic settlement in the lowlands of Scotland: a preliminary survey. *In* Neolithic Settlement in Ireland and Western Britain. I. Armit, E. Murphy, E. Nelis and D. Simpson, eds. pp. 71–83. Oxford: Oxbow Books.

——and G. J. Maxwell, 1991 Excavation of a Neolithic long mortuary enclosure within the Roman legionary fortress at Inchthuthill, Perthshire. Proceedings of the Society of Antiquaries of Scotland 121:27–44.

——K. Brophy and G. McGregor, 2002 Claish, Stirling: an early Neolithic structure in its context. Proceedings of the Society of Antiquaries of Scotland 132:65–137.

Barrett, J. C., 1994 Fragments from Antiquity. Oxford: Blackwell.

Barton, R. N. E., and A. Roberts, 2004 The Mesolithic period in England: current perspectives and new research. *In* Mesolithic Scotland and its Neighbours. A. Saville, ed. pp. 339–359. Edinburgh: Society of Antiquaries of Scotland.

——P. J. Berridge, R. E. Bevins and M. J. Walker, 1995 Persistent places in the Mesolithic landscape: an example from the Black Mountain uplands of South Wales. Proceedings of the Prehistoric Society 61:81–116.

Binford, L. R., 1968 Post-Pleistocene adaptations. *In* New Perspectives in Archaeology. S. R. Binford and L. R. Binford, eds. pp. 313–42. Chicago: Aldine.

Bonsall, C., M. G. Macklin, D. E. Anderson and R. W. Payton, 2002 Climate change and the adoption of farming in north-west Europe. European Journal of Archaeology 5:9–23.

Boujot, C., and S. Cassen, 1992 Le development des premieres architectures funeraires monumentales en France occidentale. *In* Paysans et Bâtisseurs: l'emergence du Néolithique Atlantique et les origines du Mégalithisme. C.-T. Le Roux, ed. pp. 195–211. Vannes: Revue Archéologique de l'Ouest, Supplément 5.

Bradley, R. J. 2007 The Prehistory of Britain and Ireland. Cambridge: Cambridge University Press.

Bryce, T. H., 1903 On the cairns and tumuli on the island of Bute: a record of explorations during the season of 1903. Proceedings of the Society of Antiquaries of Scotland 38:17–81.

Case, H. J., 1969 Neolithic explanations. Antiquity 43:176–186.

——1986 The Mesolithic and Neolithic in the Oxford region. *In* The Archaeology of the Oxford Region. G. Briggs, J. Cook and T. Rowley, eds. pp. 18–37. Oxford: Oxford University Department of External Studies.

Caulfield, S., 1978 Neolithic fields: the Irish evidence. *In* Early Land Allotment in the British Isles. H. C. Bowen and P. J. Fowler, eds. pp. 137–143. Oxford: British Archaeological Reports.

Chamberlain, A., and A. Witken, 2003 Early Neolithic diets: evidence from pathology and dental wear. *In* Food, Culture and Identity in the Neolithic and Early Bronze Age. M. Parker Pearson, ed. pp. 53–58. Oxford: British Archaeological Reports.

Childe, V. G., 1940 Prehistoric Communities of the British Isles. London: Chambers.

Clark, J. G. D., 1954 Excavations at Star Carr. Cambridge: Cambridge University Press.

——1966 The invasion hypothesis in British archaeology. Antiquity 40:172–189.

——1972 Star Carr: A Case Study in Bioarchaeology. Reading, MA: Addison-Wesley Modules in Anthropology.

Cleal, R. M. J., 1999 Introduction: the what, where and when of Grooved Ware. *In* Grooved Ware in Britain and Ireland. R. Cleal and A. MacSween, eds. pp. 1–8. Oxford: Oxbow Books.

——2004 The dating and diversity of the earliest ceramics in Wessex and south-west England. *In* Monuments and Material Culture: papers on Neolithic and Bronze Age Britain in honour of Isobel Smith. R. Cleal and J. Pollard, eds. pp. 164–192. East Knoyle: Hobnob Press.

——K. E. Walker and R. Montague, 1995 Stonehenge in its Landscape: twentieth-century excavations. London: English Heritage.

Coles, J., and D. Simpson, 1965 The excavation of a Neolithic round barrow at Pitnacree, Perthshire, Scotland. Proceedings of the Prehistoric Society 31:34–57.

Collins, A. E. P., 1976 Dooey's Cairn, Ballymacaldrack, Co. Antrim. Ulster Journal of Archaeology 39:1–7.

Conneller, C., 2004 Becoming deer: corporeal transformations at Star Carr. Archaeological Dialogues 11:37–56.

——and T. Schadla-Hall, 2003 Beyond Star Carr: the Vale of Pickering in the 10th millennium BP. Proceedings of the Prehistoric Society 69:85–106.

Coombs, D., 1976 Callis Wold round barrow Humberside. Antiquity 50:130–131.

Cooney, G., 2000 Landscapes of Neolithic Ireland. London: Routledge.

——2002 From Lilliput to Brobdignag: the traditions of enclosure in the Irish Neolithic. In Enclosures in Neolithic Europe. G. Varndell and P. Topping, eds. pp. 69–82. Oxford: Oxbow Books.

——2003 Rooted or routed? Landscapes of Neolithic settlement in Ireland. In Neolithic Settlement in Ireland and Western Britain. I. Armit, E. Murphy, E. Nelis and D. Simpson, eds. pp. 47–55. Oxford: Oxbow Books.

Copley, M. S., R. Berstan, S. N. Dudd, G. Docherty, A. J. Mukherjee, V. Straker, S. Payne and R. P. Evershed, 2003 Direct chemical evidence for widespread dairying in prehistoric Britain. Proceedings of the National Academy of Sciences 100:1524–1529.

Corcoran, J. W. X. P., 1960 The Carlingford culture. Proceedings of the Prehistoric Society 26:98–148.

——1970 Excavation of two chambered cairns at Mid Gleniron Farm, Glenluce, Wigtownshire. Transactions of the Dumfriesshire and Galloway Natural History and Antiquarian Society 41:29–90.

Darvill, T., 1996 Neolithic buildings in England, Wales and the Isle of Man. In Neolithic Houses in Northwest Europe and Beyond. T. Darvill and J. Thomas, eds. pp. 77–112. Oxford: Oxbow Books.

——2004 Long Barrows of the Cotswolds and Surrounding Areas. Stroud: Tempus.

David, A., and E. A. Walker, 2004 Wales during the Mesolithic period. In Mesolithic Scotland and its Neighbours. A. Saville, ed. pp. 299–338. Edinburgh: Society of Antiquaries of Scotland.

Dubouloz, J., 1998 Réflexions sur le Michelsberg ancien en Bassin Parisien. In Die Michelsberger Kultur und ihre Randgebiete: Probleme der Entstehung, Chronologie und des Siedlungswesens. J. Biel, H. Schlichtherle, M. Strobel and A. Zee, eds. pp. 9–20. Stuttgart: Theiss.

Edmonds, M., 1995 Stone Tools and Society: working stone in Neolithic and Bronze Age Britain. London: Batsford.

Evans, C., and J. Pollard, 2001 The dating of the Storey's Bar Road fields reconsidered. In The Flag Fen Basin: archaeology and environment of a Fenland landscape. F. Pryor, pp. 25–26. London: English Heritage.

Fairbairn, A. S., 2000 On the spread of plant crops across Neolithic Britain, with special reference to southern England. In Plants in Neolithic Britain and Beyond. A. S. Fairbairn, ed. pp. 107–122. Oxford: Oxbow Books.

Fairweather, A. D., and I. B. M. Ralston, 1993 The Neolithic timber hall at Balbridie, Grampian Region, Scotland: the building, the date, the plant macrofossils. Antiquity 67:313–324.

Finlay, N., 2003 Cache and carry: defining moments in the Irish later Mesolithic. In Peopling the Mesolithic in a Northern Environment. L. Bevan and J. Moore, eds. pp. 87–94. Oxford: British Archaeological Reports.

Finlayson, B., 2004 The use of stone tools in Mesolithic Scotland: function, vale, decision-making and landscapes. In Mesolithic Scotland and its Neighbours. A. Saville, ed. pp. 221–228. Edinburgh: Society of Antiquaries of Scotland.

Fischer, A., 2002 Food for feasting? An evaluation of interpretations of the neolithization of Denmark and southern Sweden. *In* The Neolithization of Denmark: 150 years of debate. A. Fischer and K. Kristiansen, eds. pp. 343–393. Sheffield: J. R. Collis.

Fox, C., 1932 The Personality of Britain. Cardiff: National Museum of Wales.

Fraser, S., and H. Murray, 2005 New light on the earliest Neolithic in the Dee Valley, Aberdeenshire. Past 50:1.

Garrow, D. 2006 Pits, Settlement and Deposition during the Neolithic and Early Bronze Age in East Anglia. Oxford: British Archaeological Reports.

Garton, D., 1991 Neolithic settlement in the Peak District: perspective and prospects. *In* Recent Developments in the Archaeology of the Peak District. R. Hodges and K. Smith, eds. pp. 3–22. Sheffield: J. R. Collis.

Gendel, P. A., 1984 Mesolithic Social Territories in Northwestern Europe. Oxford: British Archaeological Reports.

Grimes, W. F., 1939 The excavation of Ty-Isaf long cairn Brecknockshire. Proceedings of the Prehistoric Society 6:119–142.

Hallgren, F., 2004 The introduction of ceramic technology around the Baltic Sea in the 6th millennium. *In* Coast to Coast – Arrival: results and reflections. H. Knutsson, ed. pp. 123–142. Uppsala: Uppsala University.

Halstead, P., 2004 Farming and feasting in the Neolithic of Greece: the ecological context of fighting with food. Documenta Praehistorica 31:151–162.

Healy, F., 2004 Hambledon Hill and its implications. *In* Monuments and Material Culture: papers on Neolithic and Bronze Age Britain in honour of Isobel Smith. R. Cleal and J. Pollard, eds. pp. 15–38. East Knoyle: Hobnob Press.

Herne, A., 1988 A time and a place for the Grimston bowl. *In* The Archaeology of Context in the Neolithic and Bronze Age: recent trends. J. C. Barrett and I. A. Kinnes, eds. pp. 2–29. Sheffield: Department of Archaeology and Prehistory.

Hey, G., J. Mulville and M. Robinson, 2003 Diet and culture in southern Britain: the evidence from Yarnton. *In* Food, Culture and Identity in the Neolithic and Early Bronze Age. M. Parker Pearson, ed. pp. 79–88. Oxford: British Archaeological Reports.

Hodder, I., 1982 Symbols in Action. Cambridge: Cambridge University Press.

Ingold, T., 2000 The Perception of the Environment: essays in livelihood, dwelling and skill. London: Routledge.

Innes, J. B., and I. Simmons, 2000 Mid Holocene charcoal stratigraphy, fire history and palaeoecology at North Gill, North York Moors, UK. Palaeogeography, Palaeoclimatology, Palaeoecology 164:151–161.

Jacobi, R. M., 1976 Britain inside and outside Mesolithic Europe. Proceedings of the Prehistoric Society 42:67–84.

——1980 The early Holocene settlement of Wales. *In* Culture and Environment in Prehistoric Wales. J. A. Taylor, ed. pp. 131–206. Oxford: British Archaeological Reports.

Jennbert, K., 1985 Neolithization: a Scanian perspective. Journal of Danish Archaeoology 4:196–197.

Jeunesse, C., 1998 Pour une origine occidentale de la culture de Michelsberg? *In* Die Michelsberger Kultur und ihre Randgebiete: Probleme der Entstehung, Chronologie und des Siedlungswesens. J. Biel, H. Schlichtherle, M. Strobel and A. Zee, eds. pp. 29–46. Stuttgart: Theiss.

Johansen, K. L., 2006 Settlement and land use at the mesolithic–neolithic transition in southern Scandinavia. Journal of Danish Archaeology 14:201–223.

Jones, G., 2000 Evaluating the importance of cultivation and collecting in Neolithic Britain. *In* Plants in Neolithic Britain and Beyond. A. S. Fairbairn, ed. pp. 79–84. Oxford: Oxbow Books.

Kendrik, J., 1995 Excavation of a Neolithic enclosure and an Iron Age settlement at Douglasmuir, Angus. Proceeding of the Society of Antiquaries of Scotland 125:29–67.

Kitchener, A. C., C. Bonsall and L. Bartosievicz, 2004 Missing mammals from Mesolithic middens: a comparison of the fossil and archaeological records from Scotland. In Mesolithic Scotland and its Neighbours. A. Saville, ed. pp. 73–82. Edinburgh: Society of Antiquaries of Scotland.

Koch, E., 1998 Neolithic Bog Pots from Zealand, Møn, Lolland and Falster. Copenhagen: Nordiske Fortidsminder.

Kottak, C. P., 1980 The Past in the Present: history, ecology and cultural variation in Highland Madagascar. Ann Arbor: University of Michigan.

Legge, A. J., 1989 Milking the evidence: a reply to Entwistle and Grant. In The Beginnings of Agriculture. A. Milles, D. Williams and N. Gardner, eds. pp. 217–242. Oxford: British Archaeological Reports.

Lidén, K., G. Eriksson, B. Nordqvist, A. Götherstöm and E. Bendixen, 2004 "The wet and the wild followed by the dry and the tame" – or did they occur at the same time? Diet in Mesolithic–Neolithic southern Sweden. Antiquity 78:23–33.

Louwe Kooijmans, L. P., 1976 Local developments within a borderland. Oudheidkundige Mededelingen 57:226–297.

—— 1980 De midden-Neolitische vondstgroep van Het Vormer bij Wijchen en het cultuurpatroon rond de zuidelijke Noordzee circa 3000 v, Chr. Oudheidkundinge Mededelingen 61:116–208.

Lubell, D., M. Jackes, H. Schwarcz, M. Knyf and C. Meiklejohn, 1994 The Mesolithic–Neolithic transition in Portugal: isotopic and dental evidence of diet. Journal of Archaeological Science 21:201–216.

Madsen, T., 1979 Earthen long barrows and timber structures: aspects of the early Neolithic mortuary practice in Denmark. Proceedings of the Prehistoric Society 45:301–320.

Mason, S. L. R., 2000 Fire and Mesolithic subsistence: managing oaks for acorns in northwest Europe? Palaeogeography, Palaeoclimatology, Palaeoecology 164:139–150.

Masters, L., 1973 The Lochhill long cairn. Antiquity 47:96–100.

—— 1981 Chambered tombs and non-megalithic barrows in Britain. In The Megalithic Monuments of Western Europe. C. Renfrew, ed. pp. 97–112. London: Thames and Hudson.

McCartan, S., 2003 Mesolithic hunter-gatherers in the Isle of Man: adaptations to an island environment? In Mesolithic on the Move: papers presented at the Sixth International Conference on the Mesolithic in Europe. L. Larsson, H. Kindgren, K. Knutsson, D. Leoffler and A. Åkerlund, eds. pp. 331–339. Oxford: Oxbow Books.

Mellars, P., 2004 Mesolithic Scotland, coastal occupation, and the role of the Oronsay middens. In Mesolithic Scotland and its Neighbours. A. Saville, ed. pp. 167–184. Edinburgh: Society of Antiquaries of Scotland.

Milner, N., O. Craig, G. Bailey, K. Pedersen and S. Andersen, 2004 Something fishy in the Neolithic? A re-evaluation of stable isotope analysis of Mesolithic and Neolithic coastal populations. Antiquity 78:9–23.

Moffett, L., M. Robinson and V. Straker, 1989 Cereals, fruit and nuts: charred plant remains from Neolithic sites in England and Wales and the Neolithic economy. In The Beginnings of Agriculture. A. Milles, D. Williams and N. Gardner, eds. pp. 243–261. Oxford: British Archaeological Reports.

Monk, M., 2000 Seeds and soils of discontent: an environmental archaeological contribution to the nature of the Early Neolithic. In New Agendas in Irish Prehistory. A. Desmond, G. Johnson, M. McCarthy, J. Sheehan and E. Shee Twohig, eds. pp. 67–88. Dublin: Wordwell.

Moore, J., 1996 Damp squib: how to fire a major deciduous forest in an inclement climate. *In* The Early Prehistory of Scotland. T. Pollard and A. Morrison, eds. pp. 62–73. Edinburgh: Edinburgh University Press.

Mordant, C., and D. Mordant, 1988 Les enceintes Néolithiques de la haute-vallée de la Seine. *In* Enclosures and Defences in the Neolithic of Western Europe. C. Burgess, P. Topping, C. Mordant and M. Maddison, eds. pp. 231–254. Oxford: British Archaeological Reports.

Myers, A. M., 1989 Reliable and maintainable technological strategies in the Mesolithic of mainland Britain. *In* Time, Energy and Stone Tools. R. Torrence, ed. pp. 78–91. Cambridge: Cambridge University Press.

Newbiggin, N. 1937 The Neolithic pottery of Yorkshire. Proceedings of the Prehistoric Society 3:189–216.

Nielsen, P. O., 1986 The beginning of the Neolithic: assimilation or complex change. Journal of Danish Archaeology 5:240–243.

Noble, G., 2005 Ancestry, farming and the changing architecture of the Clyde cairns of south-west Scotland. *In* Set in Stone: new approaches to Neolithic monuments in Scotland. V. Cummings and A. Pannett, eds. pp. 25–36. Oxford: Oxbow Books.

Oswald, A., C. Dyer and M. Barber, 2001 The Creation of Monuments: Neolithic causewayed enclosures in the British Isles. London: English Heritage.

Peterson, R., 2003 Neolithic Pottery from Wales: traditions of construction and use. Oxford: British Archaeological Reports.

Piggott, S., 1954 The Neolithic Cultures of the British Isles. Cambridge: Cambridge University Press.

——1955 Windmill Hill: east or west? Proceedings of the Prehistoric Society 21:96–101.

Plog, S., 1978 Social interaction and stylistic similarity: a reanalysis. *In* Advances in Archaeological Method and Theory, vol. 1. M. B. Schiffer, ed. pp. 143–182. New York: Academic Press.

Pluciennuk, M., 1998 Deconstructing "the Neolithic" in the Mesolithic–Neolithic transition. *In* Understanding the Neolithic of North-West Europe. M. Edmonds and C. Richards, eds. pp. 61–83. Glasgow: Cruithne Press.

Pollard, J., 1999 "These places have their moments": thoughts on settlement practices in the British Neolithic. *In* Making Places in the Prehistoric World. J. Brück and M. Goodman, eds. pp. 76–93. London: University College London Press.

——2000a Ancestral places in the Mesolithic landscape. Archaeological Review from Cambridge 17:123–138.

——2000b Neolithic occupation practices and social ecologies from Rinyo to Clacton. *In* Neolithic Orkney in its European Context. A. Ritchie, ed. pp. 363–370. Cambridge: McDonald Institute.

Pollard, T., 1996 Time and tide: coastal environments, cosmology and ritual. *In* The Early Prehistory of Scotland. T. Pollard and A. Morrison, eds. pp. 198–210. Edinburgh: Edinburgh University Press.

Pryor, F., 1978 Excavation at Fengate, Peterborough, England: the second report. Toronto: Royal Ontario Museum.

Raemaekers, D. C. M., 1999 The Articulation of a "New Neolithic". Leiden: University of Leiden.

Ralston, I. M. B., 1982 A timber hall at Balbridie Farm. Aberdeen University Review 168:238–249.

Ray, K., and J. Thomas, 2003 In the kinship of cows: the social centrality of cattle in the earlier Neolithic of southern Britain. *In* Food, Culture and Identity in the Neolithic and

Early Bronze Age. M. Parker Pearson, ed. pp. 37–44. Oxford: British Archaeological Reports.

Richards, M. P., 2000 Human consumption of plant foods in the British Neolithic: direct evidence from bone stable isotopes. *In* Plants in Neolithic Britain and Beyond. A. S. Fairbairn, ed. pp. 123–135. Oxford: Oxbow Books.

——2003 Explaining the dietary isotope evidence for the rapid adoption of the Neolithic in Britain. *In* Food, Culture and Identity in the Neolithic and Early Bronze Age. M. Parker Pearson, ed. pp. 31–36. Oxford: British Archaeological Reports.

——and R. E. M. Hedges, 1999 A Neolithic revolution? New evidence of diet in the British Neolithic. Antiquity 73:891–897.

——T. D. Price and E. Koch, 2003 Mesolithic and Neolithic subsistence in Denmark: new stable isotope data. Current Anthropology 44:288–294.

Rideout, J., 1997 Excavation of Neolithic enclosures at Cowie Road, Bannockburn, Stirling, 1984–5. Proceedings of the Society of Antiquaries of Scotland 127:29–68.

Robinson, M. A., 2000 Further consideration of Neolithic charred cereals, fruit and nuts. *In* Plants in Neolithic Britain and Beyond. A. S. Fairbairn, ed. pp. 85–90. Oxford: Oxbow Books.

Rosman, A., and P. G. Rubel, 1971 Feasting with Mine Enemy: rank and exchange among Northwest Coast societies. Prospect Heights: Waveland Press.

Rowley-Conwy, P., 1981a Mesolithic Danish bacon: permanent and temporary sites in the Danish Mesolithic. *In* Economic Archaeology. A. Sheridan and G. Bailey, eds. pp. 51–55. Oxford: British Archaeological Reports.

——1981b Slash and burn in the temperate European Neolithic. *In* Farming Practice in British Prehistory. R. Mercer, ed. pp. 85–96. Edinburgh: Edinburgh University Press.

——1983 Sedentary hunters: the Ertebølle example. *In* Hunter-Gatherer Economy in Prehistory: a European perspective. G. Bailey, ed. pp. 111–126. Cambridge: Cambridge University Press.

——2000 Through a taphonomic glass, darkly: the importance of cereal cultivation in prehistoric Britain. *In* Taphonomy and Interpretation. S. Stallibrass and J. Huntley, eds. pp. 43–53. Oxford: Oxbow Books.

——2004 How the west was lost: a reconsideration of agricultural origins in Britain, Ireland, and southern Scandinavia. Current Anthropology 45:83–113.

Saville, A., 1990 Hazleton North: the excavation of a Neolithic long cairn of the Cotswold-Severn group. London: English Heritage.

Scarre, C., P. Arias, G. Burenhult, M. Fano, L. Oosterbeek, R. J. Schulting, A. Sheridan and A. Whittle, 2003 Megalithic chronologies. *In* Stone and Bones: formal disposal of the dead in Atlantic Europe during the Mesolithic–Neolithic interface 6000–3000 BC. G. Burenhult and S. Westergaard, eds. pp. 65–111. Oxford: British Archaeological Reports.

Schollar, I., 1959 Regional groups in the Michelsberg Culture: a study in the middle Neolithic of central Europe. Proceedings of the Prehistoric Society 25:52–134.

Schulting, R. J., 1998 Slighting the sea: the transition to farming in northwest Europe. Documenta Praehistorica 25:203–218.

——2000 New AMS dates from the Lambourn long barrow and the question of the earliest Neolithic in southern England: repacking the Neolithic package? Oxford Journal of Archaeology 19:25–35.

——2004 An Irish Sea change: some implications for the Mesolithic–Neolithic transition. *In* The Neolithic of the Irish Sea: materiality and traditions of practice. V. Cummings and C. Fowler, eds. pp. 22–28. Oxford: Oxbow Books.

——and M. P. Richards, 2001 New palaeodietary and AMS dating evidence from the Breton Mesolithic cemeteries of Téviec and Höedic. Journal of Anthropological Archaeology 20:314–344.

Scott, J. G. 1961 The excavation of the chambered cairn at Crarae, Loch Fyneside, Mid Argyll. Proceedings of the Society of Antiquaries of Scotland 94:1–27.

Sheridan, A., 2000 Achnacreebeag and its French connections: vive the "auld alliance". In The Prehistory and Early History of Atlantic Europe. J. C. Henderson, ed. pp. 1–16. Oxford: British Archaeological Reports.

——2001 Donegore Hill and other Irish Neolithic enclosures: a view from outside. In Neolithic Enclosures in Atlantic Northwest Europe. T. Darvill and J. Thomas, eds. pp. 171–189. Oxford: Oxbow Books.

——2003a French connections I: spreading the marmites thinly. In Neolithic Settlement in Ireland and Western Britain. I. Armit, E. Murphy, E. Nelis and D. Simpson, eds. pp. 3–17. Oxford: Oxbow Books.

——2003b Ireland's earliest "passage" tombs: a French connection? In Stone and Bones: formal disposal of the dead in Atlantic Europe during the Mesolithic–Neolithic interface 6000–3000 BC. G. Burenhult and S. Westergaard, eds. pp. 9–26. Oxford: British Archaeological Reports.

——2004 Neolithic connections along and across the Irish Sea. In The Neolithic of the Irish Sea: materiality and traditions of practice. V. Cummings and C. Fowler, eds. pp. 9–21. Oxford: Oxbow Books.

Sherratt, A., 1995 Instruments of conversion? The role of megaliths in the Mesolithic/Neolithic transition in north-west Europe. Oxford Journal of Archaeology 14:245–260.

Smith, M., and M. Brickley, 2006 The date and sequence of Neolithic funerary monuments: new AMS dating from the Cotswold–Severn region. Oxford Journal of Archaeology 25:335–355.

Stenning, D. J., 1963 Africa: the social background. In Man and Cattle: proceedings of a symposium on domestication. A. E. Mourant and F. E. Zeuner, eds. pp. 111–118. London: Royal Anthropological Institute.

Tauber, H., 1981 13C evidence for dietary habits of prehistoric man in Denmark. Nature 292:332–333.

Thomas, J. S., 1999 Understanding the Neolithic. London: Routledge.

——2000 Death, identity and the body in Neolithic Britain. Journal of the Royal Anthropological Institute 6:653–668.

——2003 Thoughts on the "repacked" Neolithic revolution. Antiquity 77:67–74.

——2004a Recent debates on the Mesolithic–Neolithic transition in Britain and Ireland. Documenta Praehistorica 31:113–130.

——2004b Materiality and traditions of practice in Neolithic south-west Scotland. In The Neolithic of the Irish Sea: materiality and traditions of practice. V. Cummings and C. Fowler, eds. pp. 174–184. Oxford: Oxbow Books.

——2006 On the origins and development of cursus monuments in Britain. Proceedings of the Prehistoric Society 72:229–241.

Tilley, C., 1996 An Ethnography of the Neolithic. Cambridge: Cambridge University Press.

Tresset, A., 2000 Early husbandry in Atlantic areas: animal introductions, diffusions of techniques and native acculturation at the north-western fringe of Europe. In The Prehistory and Early History of Atlantic Europe. J. C. Henderson, ed. pp. 17–32. Oxford: British Archaeological Reports.

——2003 French connections II: of cows and men. *In* Neolithic Settlement in Ireland and Western Britain. I. Armit, E. Murphy, E. Nelis and D. Simpson, eds. pp. 18–30. Oxford: Oxbow Books.

Troy, C. S., D. E. MacHugh, J. F. Bailey, D. A. Magee, R. T. Loftus, P. Cunningham, A. T. Chamberlain, B. C. Sykes and D. G. Bradley, 2001 Genetic evidence for Near-Eastern origins of European cattle. Nature 410:1088–1091.

Whittle, A., 1977 The Earlier Neolithic of Southern England and its Continental Background. Oxford: British Archaeological Reports.

——1996 Europe in the Neolithic: the creation of new worlds. Cambridge: Cambridge University Press.

——2003 The Archaeology of People: dimensions of Neolithic life. London: Routledge.

——2004 Stones that float in the sky: portal dolmens and their landscapes of memory and myth. *In* The Neolithic of the Irish Sea: materiality and traditions of practice. V. Cummings and C. Fowler, eds. pp. 81–90. Oxford: Oxbow Books.

——J. Pollard and C. Grigson, 1999 The Harmony of Symbols: the Windmill Hill causewayed enclosure. Oxford: Oxbow Books.

——A. Barclay, A. Bayliss, L. McFadyen, R. Schulting and M. Wysocki, 2007 Building for the dead: events, processes and changing worldviews from the thirty-eighth to the thirty-fourth centuries cal. B. C. in southern Britain. Cambridge Archaeological Journal 17 (suppl.):123–147.

Woodman, P. C., 2000 Getting back to basics: transitions to farming in Ireland and Britain. *In* Europe's First Farmers. T. D. Price, ed. pp. 219–259. Cambridge: Cambridge University Press.

——and M. McCarthy, 2003 Contemplating some awful(ly interesting) vistas: importing cattle and red deer into prehistoric Ireland. *In* Neolithic Settlement in Ireland and Western Britain. I. Armit, E. Murphy, E. Nelis and D. Simpson, eds. pp. 31–39. Oxford: Oxbow Books.

——and M. O'Brien, 1993 Excavations at Ferriter's Cove, Co. Kerry: an interim statement. *In* Past Perceptions: The Prehistoric Archaeology of South-West Ireland. E. Shee Twohig and M. Ronayne, eds. pp. 25–34. Cork: Cork University Press.

——E. Anderson and N. Finlay, 1999 Excavations at Ferriter's Cove, 1983–95: last foragers, first farmers in the Dingle Peninsula. Bray: Wordwell.

Zvelebil, M., and P. Rowley-Conwy, 1984 Transition to farming in northern Europe: a gatherer-hunter perspective. Norwegian Archaeological Review 17:104–127.

4

Foodways and Social Ecologies from the Early Mesolithic to the Early Bronze Age

Rick Schulting

Food, moreover, has a good claim to be considered the world's most important subject. It is what matters most to most people for most of the time. (Fernández-Armesto 2002:xiii)

Introduction

The period under consideration here saw the advent of great changes in how people obtained their sustenance, from hunting and gathering in the Mesolithic to a degree of mixed farming in the Neolithic and Early Bronze Age.[1] What did not change, however, is the underlying principle that foodways are inextricably bound up with wider social and cultural issues: concerns of social relations, status, gender and identity. The term "foodways" is being used here to denote the entire complex of food procurement, preparation, consumption and disposal that are at once practical activities and socially and culturally embedded. Each stage has the potential to inform on far more than calories and protein yields, though of course these are also very important. Procurement, preparation, serving, consumption and disposal all provide endless opportunities for the marking out of different identities and the creation, maintenance and challenging of the social order. The forms that these relations took, and the new opportunities presented by the appearance of domestic plants and animals, form the main focus of this chapter.

Procurement and Production

A wild harvest

There is a clear distinction to be made between the food procurement activities of hunter-gatherers, and the food production of cultivators and herders. Yet the gap is perhaps not as great as once thought. Ethnographically, there are many cases of hunter-gatherers modifying their landscape on a large scale through controlled burning to improve new growth and attract game, and to encourage desirable plants. Widespread evidence for anthropogenic burning has been claimed for the British Mesolithic, though not all accept this (Mellars 1975; Caseldine and Hatton 1993; Tipping 1996). Hunting and gathering activities can also be structured, whether by design or incidentally, in ways that approach something akin to husbandry (see Zvelebil 1995). For example, the Early Mesolithic site of Faraday Road in the Kennet valley, Berkshire (fig. 4.1), shows a concentration on wild pig, which make up 80 per cent of the fauna by number of identified specimens (or NISP), and of these some 90 per cent were juvenile and immature animals (Ellis et al. 2003). As will be seen below, this is in some respects reminiscent of the kill-off patterns observed with domestic pigs in the Neolithic.

And, as with farming and herding societies, subsistence activities for hunter-gatherers are highly structured by the changing seasons. Some communities would move from lowland to upland, or from inland to the coast. These movements might in many cases also entail shifting group composition, with alternating periods of aggregation and dispersal, that would strongly influence the rhythms of social life. Other communities may have been far less mobile. Much work on the important Early Mesolithic faunal assemblage from Star Carr, Yorkshire, has been directed towards seasonality. The site seems to have been used mainly in the summer (Legge and Rowley-Conwy 1988; though Carter 1998 presents a case for a late winter–early spring presence as well), possibly as a favourably located and so repeatedly visited hunting camp, with fauna dominated by large game animals – elk, red deer, aurochs, roe deer and wild boar. The main meat-bearing bones are missing, and have presumably been taken to a base camp elsewhere. Despite Star Carr's location on a lake shore, fish and fowl do not appear to have played a major role, though they may have been a focus at other sites yet to be found.

The Late Mesolithic shell middens of Oronsay present a very different kind of procurement site, though no doubt one biased by their location on a small island off the west coast of Scotland. The sites contain relatively few red deer and wild pig bones, and even these are mainly antler and distal limbs, with few meat-bearing elements. The mammalian fauna is instead dominated by seals, which, unlike the terrestrial fauna, are represented by all parts of the skeleton (Grigson and Mellars 1987). The sites themselves comprise massive accumulations of marine shells, mainly limpets. It has been suggested that these may have been used primarily for bait for the inshore saithe that make up most of the fish assemblage (Mellars and Wilkinson 1980).

The middens suggest a certain degree of permanence to the Oronsay sites, or at least repeated visits to the same locations. Studies of fish otoliths have suggested that a structured seasonal cycle of use may have existed even on this small island, with different middens apparently used predominantly at different seasons (Mellars and Wilkinson 1980). Superimposed hearths at Cnoc Coig indicate a degree of spatial structuring at these sites (Mellars 1987:237). The economic activities on Oronsay led to the creation of very visible markers on the landscape, a sense of

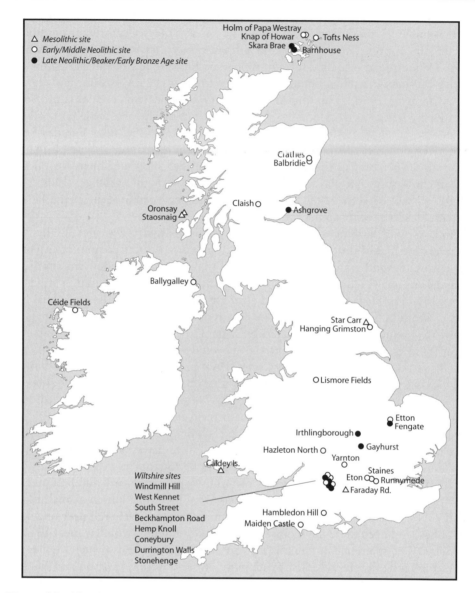

Δ Mesolithic site
○ Early/Middle Neolithic site
● Late Neolithic/Beaker/Early Bronze Age site

Holm of Papa Westray
Knap of Howar
Tofts Ness
Skara Brae
Barnhouse

Crathes
Balbridie

Claish
Ashgrove

Oronsay
Staosnaig

Ballygalley

Céide Fields

Star Carr
Hanging Grimston

Lismore Fields

Etton
Fengate
Irthlingborough
Hazleton North
Gayhurst
Yarnton
Caldey Is.
Staines
Eton
Runnymede
Faraday Rd.

Wiltshire sites
Windmill Hill
West Kennet
South Street
Beckhampton Road
Hemp Knoll
Coneybury
Durrington Walls
Stonehenge

Hambledon Hill
Maiden Castle

Figure 4.1   Map showing locations of Mesolithic, Neolithic and Early Bronze Age sites mentioned in the text.

place. This may have been in part intentional, and over time could have come to represent the social activities that went along with the collection of shells, the preparation of bait, fishing and the hunting of seals. The gathering of food would have been an opportunity to play out gender roles, and to define other social relationships in the community. If the limpets were used for bait, who collected them, and who fished? Perhaps there was a strong element of gender complementarity in the division of these tasks, which would have in turn helped to create and define (and perhaps challenge) social roles. And how were the larger packages of food, such as the seals, shared out? All of this raises far more questions than it answers, for the evidence is frustratingly incomplete. Nevertheless, posing the questions is a useful exercise in itself, if only to acknowledge the potential complexity of past foodways.

The importance of marine foods at Oronsay (ca. 4600–3900 B.C.) and also at Caldey Island, Pembrokeshire (ca. 7500–6500 B.C.), is confirmed by stable carbon and nitrogen isotope analysis of human bone collagen. The few isolated and fragmentary human bones from these sites show a strong reliance on marine protein, approaching 80 per cent or more in some cases (Schulting and Richards 2002a; 2002b). Since the results reflect the averaged diet over the last decade or so of an individual's life, they weigh against the possibility of only seasonal exploitation of marine resources (with, for example, inland hunting and gathering over the remainder of the year), and suggest instead a year-round focus on coastal settlement and subsistence for at least some individuals. The mere fact that there were communities specialising to a considerable extent on coastal resources provides a picture of far greater complexity for the Mesolithic than has usually been assumed, and raises the question of the relationship between such groups and those with a more inland focus. This is particularly germane here since food is so often used to define a common identity, in contrast to the foodways of other groups. Exchanges of food are likely to have played an important role in the creation and maintenance of these relationships. Indeed, possible evidence for the interaction of island and mainland communities is seen in the two sizes of red deer bones from Cnoc Coig on Oronsay, representing two distinct populations of animals, with the smaller animals presumably reflecting island dwarfism, and the larger animals originating on a larger island or the mainland (Grigson and Mellars 1987).

The site of Staosnaig on the adjacent island of Colonsay presents another aspect of Mesolithic foodways that can often be overlooked – the contribution of plant foods. A large pit dating to the seventh millennium B.C. was found to contain the remains of tens of thousands of charred hazelnut shells (Mithen et al. 2001). Dating to ca. 7800 B.C., Howick on the north-east coast of England presents similar evidence of hazelnut shells discarded into what is interpreted as an abandoned hut structure (Waddington et al. 2003). While hazelnut shells are ubiquitous on Mesolithic sites throughout north-west Europe (Zvelebil 1994), Staosnaig and Howick present an indication of the scale at which the resource may have been exploited, at least in certain places and at certain times. Hazelnuts, though seasonal, would be eminently storable, and have implications for the degree of settlement permanence and for ownership of the stored resource, since different factors often come into play when dealing with delayed versus immediate consumption (Woodburn 1982). The overall importance of hazelnuts in the Mesolithic is still unknown but, at least at Staosnaig and Howick, it can be proposed that their collection and preparation was likely to be a highly social, and perhaps gendered, group activity.

Procurement to production

One of the ongoing debates among British prehistorians involves the extent to which hunting and gathering continued to play an important role after the appearance of domesticated plants and animals in the Neolithic, from about 4000 B.C.[2] The evidence for the continued importance of wild plant foods consists of the presence of charred hazelnut shells on many Neolithic sites, at least as many sites as have yielded cereal remains (Moffet et al. 1989; Robinson 2000a; Hey et al. 2003). But, as Glynis Jones (2000) has succinctly argued, the taphonomic factors that can be expected to preserve cereals are very different from those that preserve hazelnut shells. What remains noteworthy is that later prehistoric sites seem to have far fewer hazelnut shells, which does suggest a greater role for them in the Neolithic than subsequently. But an indication of their contribution relative to cereals does not follow from this. Also, it might be questioned to what extent hazelnut itself should be considered as a fully "wild" food, since there is good evidence from early in the Neolithic for woodland management, including coppicing (Coles and Coles 1986; Pryor 1998). The distinctions drawn between wild and domestic foods, whether plant or animal, may not always be so straightforward (Zvelebil 1995; Whittle 2003:90–91).

A number of Early Neolithic sites have yielded substantial amounts of charred grain, the most important being Hambledon Hill, Balbridie and Lismore Fields (Jones 2000), with smaller assemblages from the recently excavated sites of Claish (Barclay et al. 2002) and Crathes (Fraser and Murray 2005). A large amount of charred grain has also been recovered at Ballygalley, Co. Antrim (Simpson 1996). Emmer and einkorn wheat generally dominate over barley, though there is some latitudinal variation present, with many sites in northern Scotland dominated by barley (Dickson and Dickson 2000). While this may have a straightforward ecological explanation – barley being hardier and needing a shorter growing season to ripen – it is worth reflecting on whether it could have at the same time marked a cultural division recognised by Neolithic communities (see Hastorf 1998). Bread wheat, with its higher gluten content, was also present from the Neolithic, and was grown and processed as a separate crop apart from emmer and einkorn (Fairweather and Ralston 1993).

The debate concerning wild and domestic animals is somewhat different. None deny the overwhelming dominance of domestic fauna from Neolithic and Early Bronze Age sites. The question is how representative these assemblages are, since the majority derive from what are seen as "special" contexts – causewayed enclosures, mortuary sites, henges – that might very well emphasise the slaughter of domestic animals, marking their cultural importance (Legge 1981; Kinnes 1988). Day-to-day subsistence could, it is argued, include a far higher proportion of wild game. Others would argue that the dominance of domestic animals is so great that this scenario seems increasingly implausible (Tresset 2003; Rowley-Conwy 2004; Schulting 2004). Moreover, faunal assemblages from the small number of available non-monumental contexts show the same prevalence of domestic animals; from southern Britain this includes the pre-monument phases of Windmill Hill and Hemp Knoll, and occupation sites at Runnymede, Yarnton and Eton Rowing Course, and from the far north the settlements of Knap of Howar, Tofts Ness and Skara Brae, Orkney (Watson 1931; Robertson-Mackay 1980; Ritchie 1983; Noddle 1989; Dockrill et al. 1994; Serjeantson 1996; Grigson 1999; Hey et al. 2003; Allen et al. 2004; see fig. 4.2). It is clear that cattle are by far the most numerous species on sites of the fourth millennium B.C. Their importance is even greater when one considers their actual contribution in meat, fat and offal, compared to the much smaller sheep/goat and pig (i.e., one cow is the equivalent of 10 to 20 sheep). One site, Coneybury Anomaly, is unusual in having a high proportion of roe deer (NISP 38 per cent), and is often cited as support for the importance of wild game away from ceremonial sites, but even here it is cattle that dominate numerically (57 per cent) (Maltby 1990), and the contribution of the roe deer becomes even less significant when meat-weight is considered.

Stable isotope data have also been used to argue for a very sudden and relatively comprehensive shift away from wild resources, and towards domestic resources, at least in coastal areas where the technique is able to make this distinction (Schulting and Richards 2002a; 2002b; Richards et al. 2003). But there is no reason to expect things to be otherwise in most inland contexts (though see Thomas 2003 for a different view), particularly since this is where the majority of the large domestic faunal assemblages mentioned above come from.

Another point of debate involves the relative importance of domesticated plants and animals, and this is a difficult issue. There are simply too many differences in preparation and consumption; most importantly, the preservational properties of bone, and its likelihood of recovery, far outweigh those of cereal remains in most circumstances. Thus, while there is currently something of an emphasis on animals in the Neolithic and Early Bronze Age, the role of cereals, at least at certain times and in some parts of Britain, may be far greater than currently envisaged by many researchers (see Jones 2000; Rowley-Conwy 2004). Much more work could be done with the cereal remains themselves; one recent study has identified the presence of immature cereal grains from Neolithic contexts, pointing to potential difficulties in ripening the crop in the British climate (McLaren 2000).

Stable isotopes again have something to contribute. Stable nitrogen isotope values reflect the trophic level of an organism, so that it should be possible to gain some indication of the extent to which humans were consuming plant versus animal protein.[3] There is considerable variability even within the comparatively limited area of southern Britain, with individuals from different Early Neolithic chambered tombs – Parc le Breos Cwm, Hazleton North and West Kennet – appearing to show greater isotopic homogeneity within each site than between the sites (Richards 2000). The same applies to individuals from the Hambledon Hill long barrow. In other words, those buried in each tomb appear to have shared a similar diet, one differing slightly from the diets of those in other tombs. Most intriguingly, humans from the Hambledon Hill causewayed enclosure show a greater range of stable nitrogen isotope values than has been seen in any individual chambered tomb or long barrow. These results are consistent with the view that causewayed enclosures

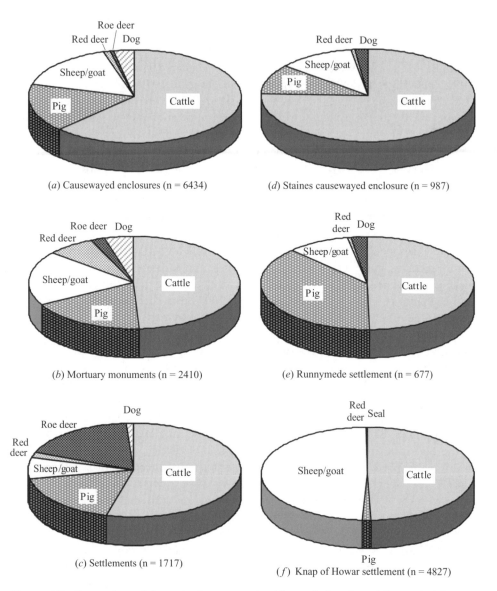

Figure 4.2 Proportions of the main domestic and wild animals found on different Early/Middle Neolithic site types (after Schulting 1998, with additions). Calculations are based on NISP (n = sample size) and exclude antler unless specified as unshed. Aurochs and wild pig are excluded from domestic counts when explicitly identified, but are so infrequent as to barely register on the graphs.

witnessed the coming together of a number of different communities from the wider region (Richards 2000:135; see Sharples 1991:39; Pryor 1998:64; Whittle and Pollard 1998). The isotopic data suggest that different local communities may have emphasized a slightly different balance of plants and animals in their subsistence economies. This idea of local variations on a theme is supported by variability in the prevalence of dental pathologies, such as caries (which are generally indicative of carbohydrate consumption), seen in human skeletons from contemporary Neolithic mortuary monuments in the same general area (Wysocki and Whittle 2000).

New ways of doing things: growing plants and keeping animals

Because of their high visibility, and presumed social importance, the investigation of monuments of one form or another has long dominated Neolithic and Early Bronze Age archaeology in Britain. Yet, as is being increasingly recognized, it is the more mundane activities, such as the keeping of plants and animals, that would have been of the most concern in the daily lives of prehistoric farmers, defining much of the daily, seasonal and yearly cycle (Pryor 1996; Whittle 2003:93).[4] While there is abundant evidence for some aspects of the economy, there is still little understanding of both the broad scope and of the detail of how crops were raised and how animals were managed.

The needs of domestic animals greatly influence the settlement patterns and social structure of societies dependent on them. Across much of southern Britain, the climate permits the year-round keeping of animals outdoors, without the need for foddering. This may not have been the case for the uplands of northern England and Scotland, and implies that communities there would have practised a degree of transhumance and/or winter foddering. And there are other considerations. Cattle adapt well to a wider range of habitats than sheep, which are essentially grazers and need grassland, though they are better suited than cattle to harsher climates. Pigs are forest animals, and are not easily herded; communities that keep pigs in any numbers do not tend to be very mobile (Grigson 1982). Crops need to be protected against the depredations of animals (and other people), which again present restrictions on the mobility of at least some members of the community. One way to deal with the varied needs of plants and animals would be to have age or gender sub-groups undertake different tasks, in some cases requiring their absence from the remainder of the group for weeks or months at a time (Whittle 1997).

If over-wintering is an issue, a significant portion of the year's animals are often slaughtered in the autumn. There may be some evidence for this in the high proportion of young cattle at sites situated as far apart as Hambledon Hill and Skara Brae (Legge 1981), and the large number of pigs killed within their first year at Durrington Walls (Albarella and Payne 2005). This presupposes either some kind of preservation technology or a massive glut of consumption. That large numbers of animals were brought together at least periodically receives excellent corroborative evidence from the ditches of the Etton causewayed enclosure, where the high concentration of dung beetles and high phosphate levels must indicate corralling (Pryor 1998; Robinson 2000b). The bringing together of animals and people from the wider region was probably the main function of causewayed enclosures, and would have provided the opportunity to exchange animals for breeding stock. No doubt it would have been the scene of intense social interaction, at times formal, as seen in the placed deposits often found in ditch terminals and interior pits, but at other times far less formal (Pryor 1998; Whittle et al. 1999).

A very few sites provide some sense of the potential scale of animal keeping. Foremost among these for earlier prehistory are the Céide Fields of Co. Mayo, Ireland, with its extensive system of stone field walls preserved under blanket peat, dating to before 3500 B.C. (Caulfield et al. 1998). Caulfield (1983) has argued that the size and layout of the fields are best suited to the keeping of considerable numbers of cattle, though ard furrows also indicate some arable farming. The most closely comparable sites from Britain are the Bronze Age landscapes of Dartmoor (Fleming 1988) and Fengate, the latter seen by Frances Pryor (1996; 1998) as evidence of the coordinated management of large numbers of livestock, especially sheep. Further insight into the sophistication of Neolithic animal management practices has recently come from the marine stable isotope values associated with AMS dates on neonatal sheep from Holm of Papa Westray, Orkney, strongly suggesting seaweed foddering of pregnant ewes in the months prior to lambing (Balasse et al. 2005). Year-round seaweed foddering of sheep is practised today on Ronaldsay, but this is the first prehistoric evidence for the practice anywhere in Europe. In addition, new research is investigating the possibility of detecting the manuring of fields in the Neolithic (Bogaard et al. 2007).

It should not be thought that a system of mixed farming, once established, remained static over time. One of the most notable changes is the increased importance of pigs on many Late Neolithic sites in southern Britain (Grigson 1982). It is uncertain whether the explanation is ecological, since many pollen diagrams from this time show widespread regeneration of woodland – and pigs are predominantly forest animals – or to do with the suitability of pigs for feasting (Grigson 1982; Thomas 1991; Albarella and Serjeantson 2002). In any case, this increase invariably refers to numbers of identified bones, and not to meat-weight. Thus, while pigs do increase significantly, cattle usually still provide more meat. The West Kennet palisades are an exception, with 87 per cent pig remains at enclosure 1, and 76 per cent at enclosure 2 (Edwards and Horne 1997). There is also regional variability: pigs never appear to attain much importance in Scotland (fig. 4.2(f)), though this may be biased by the fact that the available data are almost exclusively from Orkney.

Of course, there are economic uses of animals other than for their meat, as encapsulated in Andrew Sherratt's (1983) notion of a "secondary products revolution". There has been much debate about when the use of these secondary products – milk, wool, traction – began, and how they can be recognised archaeologically. The question of whether cattle and sheep were milked has been especially controversial, given low milk yields of primitive breeds and the possibility of lactose intolerance (Legge 1981, 1989; Entwistle and Grant 1989). However, recent analysis of lipid residues in pottery has confirmed the presence of milk from the Early Neolithic onwards (Jones 1999; Copley et al. 2003; 2005). Indeed, although there are other factors to consider, the proportion of sherds with milk fat residues was highest in Neolithic samples. This is a very important finding, with implications for the size and structure of herds (Legge 1981).

As for traction, the use of the plough, or, more properly, the ard, is documented by the criss-cross furrows underlying the mid fourth millennium B.C. South Street long barrow, Wiltshire (Ashbee et al. 1979). In addition, the molluscan evidence shows complex land use well before the construction of this monument, including clearance, ploughing (presumably for cultivation) and the creation of a grazed grassland. Additional evidence for the ard comes from arthritic changes noted on the bones of cattle from the Etton causewayed enclosure, suggesting the use of the animals for traction (Armour-Chelu and Clutton-Brock 1985), though comparable pathologies have not been found at other sites (Grigson 1999). Cattle – and in the case of Etton the animals showing bony changes were mainly cows, which may have been easier to handle than bulls – would need to be trained to pull the ard, and so would take on additional value, and another role in animal–human relations. The question of whether castration was practised in the Neolithic is still debated, though bullocks may be present at Skara Brae (Watson 1931).

Just as stone and often pottery (e.g., gabbroic wares) would be recognised as coming from, and perhaps standing for, different parts of the landscape – some local, some exotic – so too it is possible that animals would be recognisable in this way (see Jones and Richards 2003), particularly in the Neolithic and Early Bronze Age, when the movement and exchange of living animals would feature more prominently than in the Mesolithic. People living in close proximity with animals, and dependent on them for their livelihood, and often social standing, become very familiar with them, and can easily identify specific individuals (Abbink 2003). Distinct breeds can appear without intentional selective breeding programmes. Animals introduced into a new environment would initially be under strong selection pressure, and this could be expected to lead to variation at least at the regional level. As an obvious example, animals kept further north in Britain, particularly in the uplands, would need to be hardier than those in the lowland south. Even today, animals brought from one part of Britain to another often have problems adjusting (Webley 1976). There are also probable founder effects to consider, as initially relatively few animals would have been brought across from the Continent. The differences being invoked here need not all be apparent in the skeleton (though this possibility has been little explored), and would more likely involve such traits as coloration and other characteristics of the animals' coats, and the shape and size of their horns (the latter seen on the skeleton in the form of horn cores) (Volkman 1985:70; Parker Pearson 2000).[5] At the same time, we should not dismiss out of hand the idea that selective breeding would have been practised, perhaps for some of these very traits (specific coloration, size, etc.). These varied qualities of animals, and, by extension, those of their owners, would be noted and discussed, praised or depreciated.

Lambs to the slaughter

An aspect of foodways that has received little attention is the actual slaughter of domestic animals. How was this done, and how did it vary by species, occasion, location? Archaeology is not alone in this, as the topic is rarely mentioned in the otherwise vast anthropological literature on subsistence farmers and pastoralists (see Abbink 2003). Where animal sacrifice is considered, it is usually in a very sanitised way (Hoskins 1993:159). But when the killing and butchery is done in a ritualised context, which is arguably the case for a good portion of the available evidence, it is unlikely to be done inconspicuously. On the contrary, there is a strongly performative and often emphatically violent aspect to the slaughter of animals on ceremonial occasions in many societies (fig. 4.3). At the extreme, this can take the form of a long drawn-out affair, in which the animal may be subject to repeated cuts and blows (Bloch 1985; Hoskins 1993:159; Abbink 2003). The kind of death may be imbued with meaning (Parker Pearson 2000:225). For the Merina of Madagascar, there is a need to overcome the inherent vitality of cattle by means of a violent death (Bloch 1985). Similarly, in central Flores and highland Sulawesi, the killing of buffalo is deliberately protracted, "so that the earth will be 'drenched with blood' and the final human victory will be vividly remembered" (Hoskins 1993:160). This is high drama, and will be remembered and discussed, which is of course the point, as recognition of social rank and prestige in small-scale societies relies largely on word of mouth. Memories of these events are created in part by the scale and "quality" of animal sacrifice. These acts become points of reference with which to evoke the event marked by the slaughter – whether a stage in an individual's life cycle, a new alliance, a harvest celebration, etc.

Figure 4.3 Killing of water buffalo at a large feast among the Akha of northern Thailand. The surrounding spectator galleries have been constructed especially for the event. Photograph courtesy of Brian Hayden.

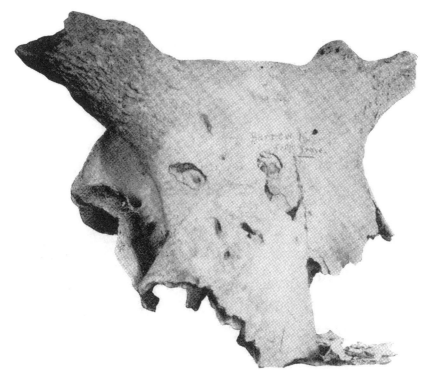

Figure 4.4 Cattle skull with peri-mortem injuries to the frontal bone resulting from two blows to the head (from Mortimer 1905:fig. 947).

For the periods under consideration here, skeletal evidence (and of course this need not be present at all) for slaughter is often hindered by fragmentation and by the erosion of bone surfaces (Grigson 1999). The few accounts that do exist emphasise the pole-axing of cattle from Early Bronze Age round barrows (Mortimer 1905:318; Mereweather, cited in Davis and Payne 1993) (fig. 4.4), though Watson (1931) reports similar trauma from Skara Brae. Evidence for a rather unexpected practice comes from the Late Neolithic site of Durrington Walls, where stone fragments – at least one of which can be identified as the tip of a flint projectile point – were found embedded in three pig bones and one cow bone (Albarella and Serjeantson 2003) (fig. 4.5). While it may not be particularly unusual for farmers to kill or bleed domestic animals by bow and arrow at close range, the expected target would be the jugular vein or a vital organ. But these stone fragments were embedded in limb bones. Though the wounds would not in themselves be fatal, the absence of healing indicates that other injuries must have been received at the same time. This could evoke a more complex and drawn-out means of slaughter for the animals. Alternatively, and perhaps more likely, it may be that some ostensibly "domestic" animals were feral and did need to be hunted (U. Albarella, pers. comm.).

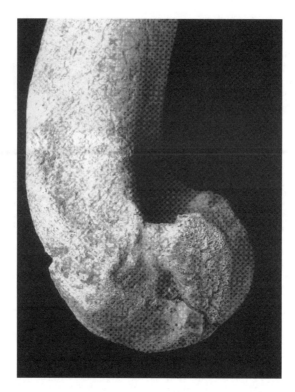

Figure 4.5 Pig humerus with embedded flint projectile point, from Late Neolithic site of Durrington Walls. Photograph courtesy of Umberto Albarella and Dale Serjeantson.

Preparation: Earlier Prehistoric "Cuisines"[6]

It is through their preparation and serving, be it simple or elaborate, that foods come into their own in terms of their ability to make social and cultural distinctions, and this they do very well indeed. In addition to conferring regional and/or ethnic identity, distinctive ways of cooking might serve as markers of various other identities, such as age, gender, group affiliation and status (Goody 1982; Hastorf 1991; Caplan 1994; Wiessner and Schiefenhövel 1996; Parker Pearson 2003). Food is also highly seasonal, an obvious fact that, nevertheless, few of us fully appreciate today, serving to mark the passage of time (Sutton 2001), and even of the life course: from the soft foods used to wean a child to the hard foods of adulthood, and back to the soft foods of old age, when tooth loss has greatly reduced an individual's ability to chew. Given the centrality of food in people's daily lives, then, it is surprising that issues surrounding the preparation and serving of food in prehistoric Britain have received very little attention. Admittedly, while we may very reasonably suppose that food was used in all of these ways, the difficulty lies in specifying the detail.

None the less, a number of lines of enquiry do seem to hold promise. From the Neolithic onwards, pottery presents the possibility of a new cooking technology, that of boiling. Jones (1996) suggests that the use of ceramics facilitates the recombination of foods that would previously have been both seasonally and temporally separated. This may be underestimating the ingenuity of Mesolithic communities; wooden bowls, tightly woven baskets or clay-lined pits can be filled with water and heated with hot rocks, or, with care, an animal skin can simmer water over a fire. Indeed, small pits containing fire-cracked rock found adjacent to hearths at the Cnoc Coig midden on Oronsay may reflect boiling with hot stones (Mellars 1987:238). Foods can also be combined in earth ovens, and it now seems that at least some of the thousands of burnt mounds known from across Britain and Ireland can be traced back to the Neolithic, though most are Bronze Age in date (Anthony et al. 2001; Ó Néill 2005). But pottery may be more convenient, and more visible (and so perhaps more performative), than other methods, and may thus have facilitated changes in the preparation and serving of food. Early pottery may have been more about the serving of food than its cooking, and there remains much potential for research here (e.g., Cleal 1992). Variability is to be expected: the pattern of charring and the presence of ketones in organic residues indicate direct contact with fire for Peterborough vessels at Upper Ninepence, Powys, while Grooved Ware vessels from the same site did not show evidence for such close association with flames (Dudd et al. 1999).

Another, and possibly more important, innovation facilitated by pottery is fermentation. Experiments by Dineley and Dineley (2000) have demonstrated the suitability of Late Neolithic Grooved Ware vessels for making ale. It has long been suggested that Beakers (ca. 2500–2000 B.C.) served as drinking vessels (Sherratt 1987), with supporting evidence deriving from a Beaker burial at Ashgrove, Fife. Pollen analysis of organic residues in and around the Beaker proved them to be rich with meadowsweet and lime (Dickson and Dickson 2000:78–84). The best explanation for the presence of these species is that the vessel contained a honey-based drink, the most likely candidate being mead. The presence of lime pollen is particularly interesting, since lime is not thought to have grown this far north at the time. Far-reaching exchange in earlier prehistory is well known through the movement of pottery and stone axes, but Ashgrove provides a rare glimpse of the exchange of organic food items. Honey would no doubt have been highly prized, as it was around the world, as a rare sweet food; further evidence for its use comes from Runnymede, where the analysis of food residues on Middle Neolithic pottery has demonstrated the presence of beeswax, presumably from honey, as well as of pork fat and fish (Needham and Evans 1987).

An exciting recent development involves the extraction and analysis of lipids and proteins absorbed into the very fabric of unglazed pottery. As noted above, the analysis of lipid residues has now demonstrated the presence of milk fats in pottery beginning in the Early Neolithic (Copley et al. 2003; 2005). Although insufficient work has as yet been undertaken to comment on regional variation, there is the possibility that some groups milked their animals while others did not. It is not yet possible to demonstrate whether living animals were bled for food, as done in many

African pastoral societies, but future advances in biochemical analysis may make this feasible. Lipid analysis of sherds from the site of Upper Ninepence revealed differences between pottery types, with Peterborough Ware (ca. 3000 B.C.) providing evidence for only ruminant fats (cattle and/or sheep), while slightly later Grooved Ware (ca. 2700 B.C.) had evidence for both ruminant and porcine fats (Dudd et al. 1999), supporting a cultural division in subsistence emphasis frequently noted on the basis of faunal associations elsewhere in southern Britain. Jones (1999) has identified different lipid residue signatures in different-sized Grooved Ware vessels at Barnhouse, Orkney. Lipids indicating cattle milk and meat were found to be confined to medium-sized vessels, with meat restricted to one house, while residues indicating barley were ubiquitous in small vessels, again raising the prospect of an alcoholic beverage. For that matter, fermented milk is another possibility to be considered, and is a practice known historically from Orkney (Fenton 1978). On occasion more direct evidence for food preparation is found, such as the loaf or cake of charred bread including partly crushed barley grains from Yarnton, directly dated to 3640–3350 B.C. (Hey et al. 2003).

Stable isotope analysis deals with the diet of individuals over a significant portion of their lives, and thus might be expected to detect, for example, gender-based differences in diet. The problem here is that the technique is able to distinguish only very broad food groups, while, for example, food taboos more often deal with very specific foods. It has not been possible as yet to suggest any consistent differences in earlier prehistoric male and female diets in Britain. On the other hand, few samples of adequate size and known sex have been analysed with this question in mind. Given the paucity of isotopic – and faunal, with a few exceptions in Scotland – evidence for the consumption for marine protein (Richards et al. 2003), Thomas (2003) suggests the possibility of a taboo against seafoods in the Neolithic.[7] While intriguing, there are other possible interpretations, such as the decision to focus on a more productive mixed farming economy. Malainey et al. (2001) offer a possible physiological mechanism for the avoidance of fish by pastoralists. Farmers' concerns with maintaining their newly established status and identity as farmers may also be relevant.

More abundant evidence for food preparation comes in the form of faunal assemblages, but the main focus here has been on quantifying the species represented and on their demographic profiles. Montón Subías (2002) makes an appropriate call for experimental studies to distinguish different cooking practices by their affects on bone, such as boiling or roasting, whole or jointed. While the proportion of burnt bone is often reported (Levitan 1990; Edwards and Horne 1997; Armour-Chelu 1998), this typically seems to relate to disposal rather than to cooking. In one study that explicitly addressed the issue, Grigson (1999:227) found no sign of burning on the ends of bones that would indicate roasting in the Windmill Hill faunal assemblage, leading her to propose that boiling was the main method of preparation.[8] Given the size of Early Neolithic pots, it would have been difficult to cook very large portions of meat, which could suggest that, whatever the scale of slaughter and butchery, the actual (and more intimate) preparation and consumption of meat remained at the level of the smaller social group. This could imply that while groups came together at causewayed enclosures, they also remained separate. This has resonance with Pryor's (1998:367) view that much of the deposition taking place inside the Etton causewayed enclosure was by family groups, as well as with the long-held view that the ditch segments themselves might represent the work of small social units (e.g., Sharples 1991; Whittle et al. 1999).

By contrast, at Durrington Walls, Albarella and Serjeantson (2002) note a pattern of butchery and burning on bones that points to a fairly standardised way of cooking pork, emphasising the roasting of large pieces of meat or possibly even complete carcasses. This could argue for a larger, more inclusive scale of commensality at Late Neolithic henges. Cattle appear to have been butchered differently, and their remains disposed of in different ways on the site. While cattle bones were often cracked open for their rich marrow, many pig bones were not; a similar pattern is seen at the West Kennet palisades (Edwards and Horne 1997). Wasteful consumption is a feature often associated with large-scale feasting. This is not unexpected at a site like Durrington Walls, and pigs have generally been seen as the feasting animal *par excellence*, since they reproduce and grow very quickly and, unlike cattle and sheep, have no other uses. What is interesting here is that cattle, despite presenting a much larger "package" of meat, were apparently *not* treated in the same way.

We know essentially nothing about the food preservation technologies that might have been employed throughout the periods under consideration here. This is an important point, as the killing of large animals such as aurochs or domestic cattle would have provided hundreds of kilograms of meat, fat and offal. Mature red deer and wild or domestic pig present smaller, though still not inconsiderable, packages. In a heavily meat-based society, an adult might consume from one to as much as four kilograms of meat and fat per day (Malainey et al. 2001), so there are clear implications for the numbers of people that would be involved if meat had to be consumed quickly. Drying with or without smoke presents the simplest preservation option, and it is likely that it was practised on some scale. Meat would be first removed from the bone by filleting, and there is evidence for this from the location of cutmarks at many sites (Armour-Chelu 1991; 1998; Grigson 1999), though of course this could also reflect immediate consumption. Salting greatly increases the effectiveness of all other forms of preservation, but evidence for its use is rare until the later Bronze Age – the single earlier reference to its possible presence comes from analysis of residues on Neolithic pottery at Runnymede (Needham and Evans 1987). Meat is not the only animal food that can be preserved: charring on vessels holding lipid evidence of milk residues may indicate pasteurisation or processing to make yoghurt or cheese (Dudd et al. 1999:1480).

Consumption

Consumption represents the culmination of the preceding stages of procurement and preparation. The act of consumption entails the most explicit and intimate expression of commensality. In a very real sense, social bonds, including even those of kinship, are often determined by who habitually share food. Food can also be involved in more antagonistic relationships. Mauss's (1969) influential concept of "the gift" refers to the idea that prestations of material culture are used to create, maintain and manipulate social relationships not only of reciprocity, but also of debt and obligation. Food operates in this system in a unique way in that once consumed the debt is internalised (Dietler 2001:73–74). Being directly incorporated into the body, it cannot be passed further along in a cycle of exchange – so creating another debt in turn – in the same way as other material culture, such as a valued polished stone axe. While consumption is important at all levels, it tends to be more archaeologically visible at the larger scale, and in special contexts, in a word, at the feast.

The social and political roles of feasting have received much attention of late, and offer a fruitful avenue for exploration (Dietler 1996; Hayden 1996; see also papers in Dietler and Hayden 2001). Feasting can be minimally defined as the communal consumption of food and drink in a special context (Dietler 2001; Hayden 2001). In Hayden's formulation, the food itself is special (i.e., not generally served at daily meals), but it may be the quantities involved that mark the occasion as special, and this is particularly likely to be the case in small-scale, classless societies that lack elaborate cuisines (Goody 1982). An exception to this might be the consumption of alcoholic or other psychoactive substances, which probably occurred mainly on special occasions (witness the funerary context of the Ashgrove Beaker). Feasts can serve a variety of purposes, and various analytical categories have been proposed (Hayden 1996, 2001), of which the two most important here can be summed up as solidarity and economic/competitive feasts. These serve to show some of the ways in which food can be mobilised socially to various ends, some consciously held by at least some of the participants, others perhaps constitutive but without the participants being explicitly aware of them.

Feasts held predominantly within the community usually promote a sense of solidarity. The sharing of food at this level serves to define and knit the group in the same way that daily sharing of food effectively defines smaller social units. Of course there may be competitive and political aspects to feasting even within the community, as individuals, families or lineages vie for pre-eminence. Similarly, feasting at the larger socio-political level can include strong elements of alliance and solidarity (who participates in food sharing may define the regional group, or create temporarily allied groups), but is more likely also to incorporate overtly competitive features (Dietler 1996; Hayden 1996; Dietler and Hayden 2001). This can take such extreme forms that feasting and fighting can be seen as two sides of the same coin (Codere 1950; Rosman and Rubel 1971; Young 1971). Feasts are times of much tension as well as celebration and conviviality; among the meat feasts of the Toraja of Sulawesi, Indonesia, "someone invariably is being shamed" (Volkman 1985:76). This applied equally in medieval Irish society, through perceived slights in the size of distributed portions or in the seating order (Patterson 1994:166).

Animal foods were probably a daily component of the diet for Mesolithic hunter-gatherers in Britain. If preservation was minimal (and this is uncertain), meat would need to be consumed within a relatively short time before it spoiled, and a large number of people must have gathered together. It is not clear to what extent this could be termed "feasting". However, in addition to providing an occasion for socialising, the division of meat may have presented an opportunity to reinforce the egalitarian ethos often seen in what Woodburn (1982) has called immediate-return hunter-gatherers. Ethnographically, this takes the form of demand sharing, in which the more or less equal sharing of meat to the group is expected as a matter of course, and the hunter receives no prestige, and indeed may even be belittled (Wiessner 1996). At the other extreme, the distribution of meat may be very unequal, and may be used to create social debts and obligations in the way referred to above. We do not know where on the continuum between these two extremes the British Mesolithic lay, though in the absence of convincing evidence for social differentiation, it seems more likely to have been towards the "sharing" end. This should emphatically not be seen as simply the absence of the socio-political use of food, since what Wiessner (1996) refers to as "levelling mechanisms" themselves represent an active strategy aimed at maintaining an egalitarian society. In either case, the division of meat may have still been subject to rules or conventions regarding who would receive which cuts, offering an avenue for the pursuit of social and political goals.

For the Neolithic and Early Bronze Age, considerably more and richer evidence for consumption is available. Still, given the paucity of earlier prehistoric domestic architecture in Britain, and the scarcity of plant and particularly animal remains (through poor preservation on mainly acid soils) on the sites that are known, it is difficult to deal with the small-scale, intimate contexts that would define the smallest social units (e.g., the "family"). This leads to a greater focus on the larger-scale events that are more likely to involve feasting. The available evidence emphasizes consumption, or at least deposition, at two broad classes of sites: mortuary monuments (long barrows and chambered tombs in the earlier Neolithic, and round barrows in the Beaker period and Early Bronze Age) and ceremonial enclosures (causewayed enclosures in the earlier Neolithic, and henges and timber circles in the Late Neolithic). At both, a good case can be made for at least some of the consumption taking the form of feasting events; at mortuary monuments this would perhaps tend to be at the community level, whereas enclosure sites would see broader participation.

Funerary feasting is a very widespread phenomenon, as the death of an individual provides an eminently appropriate occasion for the reinforcement or challenging of social roles. At another level, death is answered with death, in the form of animal sacrifice, and so perhaps in a way can be seen to be controlled. Unfortunately, many mortuary monuments in Britain were excavated long ago, and the quality of the surviving information is highly variable, particularly for the animal bone. But it is clear that domestic animals completely dominate the assemblages (fig. 4.2(b)). In some cases, the deposition of faunal remains clearly precedes the construction of the monument (Levitan 1990), and could potentially relate to work party feasts. Indeed, Dietler (1996) has argued that that work party feasts were the organisational force behind the monumental constructions of the European Neolithic.

Occasionally, the deposits are sufficiently discrete to indicate single depositional events. One of the most striking of these is the Early Neolithic long barrow at Hanging Grimston, Yorkshire, where a façade pit contained a minimum of 20 pig jaws, mainly of young animals (Mortimer 1905:102–103). If all of these animals were slaughtered at one time (and this is uncertain), the associated feast would have provided many hundreds of kilograms of meat and fat, possibly as much as 1,000 kg, depending on the age of the animals. It may be more likely that the jaws represent a curated record of past feasts, perhaps those hosted by the deceased; ethnographically, mandibles, horns or entire skulls of animals sacrificed at feasts are often kept for display (see Clarke 2001). In any case, faunal remains from Early Neolithic mortuary monuments are usually more modest, often representing a small number of animals, or perhaps only token deposits for much larger feasting events. At Hazleton North, Gloucestershire, the distribution of cattle and pig cranial fragments and teeth in the forecourt area suggests that the heads of one or two animals of each species had been placed on the cairn's revetment (Levitan 1990:213; see also Ashbee et al. 1979).

Finds from Beaker and Early Bronze Age round barrows can be more impressive. A deposit of 185 cattle skulls in a barrow overlay a rich adult male burial at Irthlingborough, Northamptonshire (Davis and Payne 1993). Many of the skulls had apparently been curated for some time before being placed on the mound, so it is unlikely that the animals were killed in a single event (see Parker Pearson 2000 for a parallel from Madagascar). There are partial post-crania from about 40 cattle of prime beef age (under two years), which would still represent over eight tonnes of meat, enough to feed thousands of people. One aurochs skull is represented, and, intriguingly, radiocarbon dating suggests that it may slightly predate the main deposit, raising the possibility that the skull was a valued heirloom passed down some generations (Davis and Payne 1993). Its significance would no doubt be heightened by the fact that aurochs were becoming quite rare in Britain by this time (Grigson 1999:231). Curation of cattle remains is also suggested at Stonehenge, where a skull and two mandibles dating to ca. 3300–3000 B.C. were intentionally placed in ditch terminals at the southern entrance (Serjeantson 1995:449).

At Gayhurst, Buckinghamshire, some 100 cattle were represented in test excavations of the ditches surrounding a round barrow. Extrapolating from this, the ditches may hold the remains of 300 or more cattle in total (Chapman 2004; Chapman et al. 2005). Unlike Irthlingborough, there is an abundance of high meat-yielding elements of the skeleton. If it was all consumed – and there is some question over this – then it represents a staggering amount of meat and indicates feasting on a massive scale, which becomes even more impressive when it is realised that all of this seems to be associated with only the first of the five successive burials in a large central grave. It speaks of the importance of the funerary event, with animals possibly being contributed from a number of different communities over a wide area (Chapman et al. 2005). Their slaughter and consumption would at once serve to commemorate the deceased and to provide closure, allowing the social space occupied by the deceased to be reopened and filled by a successor (Munn 1986). Slaughter and feasting on this scale would also almost certainly be bound up with cycles of debt, obligation and repayment, perhaps through generations (Mauss 1969; Adams 2004). The level of consumption seems even greater at the large enclosures, especially the Late Neolithic henge and timber circle monuments; if the remainder of the palisade trenches at West Kennet have the same density of faunal remains as the small excavated sample, thousands of animals are represented (Edwards and Horne 1997).

The idea of wasteful consumption referred to above as a typical characteristic of feasting is seen at a number of sites (Albarella and Serjeantson 2002). This practice probably comes to the fore primarily when a strong competitive element is involved. In some extreme cases, it may be more accurately described as conspicuous *non-*consumption, such as with the complete, articulated skeleton of a pig and a goat and the articulated joints of cattle found at Windmill Hill (Grigson 1999), articulated joints at Hambledon Hill and Maiden Castle (Legge 1981; Armour-Chelu 1991), and the complete, articulated cow skeleton in a pit at Yarnton (Hey et al. 2003). The contexts for these acts are unclear; they may involve competitive and ostentatious display, but another possibility is that of sacrifice to atone for a serious wrong (and hence not celebrated by consuming the flesh). As the term "scapegoat" itself indicates, animals may take on the burden of expiating human misdeeds. It seems to be invariably domestic animals that are used for this purpose, because of their intimate relationships with people (and, of course, the efforts and expense required to raise them) (Abbink 2003).

Deposition: Conceptualisation

Although it is not usually considered as an aspect of foodways, there is much to be learned from the ways in which the remains of animals are disposed of, usually though not always, after being consumed. Though rare, there is evidence for the special treatment of animal remains in the British Mesolithic (there is far more abundant evidence from the Continent). Some insight into the potential complexity of animal–human relationships at Star Carr is provided by the 21 red deer antler frontlets found at the site (Conneller and Schadla-Hall 2003). The antlers had been worked down to reduce their size and weight, and two holes drilled into the frontal bone, presumably to facilitate wearing the frontlet on the head. The most likely reason for this may involve some form of celebration, perhaps in dance, of the close links between people and animals that almost invariably feature in the world-views of hunter-gatherers (Ingold et al. 1988).

A key starting point for the Neolithic is Richards and Thomas's (1984) discussion of "structured deposition" as the archaeological signature of ritual action. Using as a case study the large Late Neolithic henge of Durrington Walls, they argue that patterning in the deposition of various categories of material culture provide insights into how these materials were conceptualised. The fauna from the original excavations (Wainwright and Longworth 1971) played a major role in their analysis, which indicates the separate deposition on different parts of the site of wild and domestic fauna, and of pig and cattle. This was interpreted as reflecting the different ways in which these animals were perceived and the culturally specific meanings they held. The distinction between wild and domestic animal bone was seen as particularly informative, denoting a conceptual division between "nature" and "culture". The bones of wild animals at Durrington Walls were said to be concentrated in the outer ditch, a pattern repeated to some extent in other Late Neolithic monuments in the area, including Mount Pleasant and the Sanctuary (Richards and Thomas 1984; Thomas 1991; Pollard 1995), though not at the West Kennet palisades (Edwards and Horne 1997). Much has since been made of this opposition, the origins of which have been pushed back to near the very beginnings of the Neolithic in Britain, at the Windmill Hill causewayed enclosure, where the outermost ditch is seen as marking a boundary between the inner domestic and the wild lying beyond (Whittle and Pollard 1998; Whittle et al. 1999).[9]

Recently, however, some of Richards and Thomas's findings have been called into question by Albarella and Serjeantson (2002) in their re-analysis of the Durrington Walls faunal assemblage. Given the state of the surviving archive, they cast doubt on the possibility of attributing bones to specific contexts. Any meaningful division between wild and domestic fauna is also problematic given the extreme rarity of the former at the site. Regarding the other sites where this distinction has been put forward, they need to be considered on a case-by-case basis, but what can be said is that caution needs to be exercised, particularly when dealing with material from older excavations. And even if some spatial separation can be found in the deposition of wild and domestic animals, it remains to be demonstrated exactly what this means. There are alternative explanations to a deep conceptual division between nature and culture (e.g., Pollard 2004); as has often been remarked, such universal interpretations may tell us more about our own society and ways of thinking than about people in the past.

Taking a slightly different approach, Thorpe (1984; see also Thomas 1988) has proposed a ranking of animals, with, in descending order, cattle, pig and sheep/goat. Cattle would be killed at the funeral of the most important individuals, since a large animal represents a far greater loss of investment than a small animal, and is capable of feeding more people, while at a symbolic level, cattle could have been perceived as the most important and culturally valued animal (Ray and Thomas 2003). While the idea is intriguing and makes sense theoretically, it is difficult to address it in any detail, since the fauna at most sites represent a palimpsest of activities that may have occurred over centuries, so that it is not usually possible to distinguish individual events, and certainly not to relate them to specific individuals. But what is clear is that cattle often do receive special treatment; perhaps the best-known example of this involves the placement of three complete cattle skulls along the central axis of the Beckhampton long barrow, which notably lacks human remains (Ashbee et al. 1979). Similarly, cattle skulls mark the layout of the Ascott-under-Wychwood long cairn (Benson and Whittle 2007). Also suggesting a special place for cattle are the "head and hooves" burials known from the Neolithic (Fussell's Lodge) and Early Bronze Age (Hemp Knoll). These indicate the placement of the animal's head and hide in the barrow, suggesting its sacrifice, and presumably consumption, at the funeral (Ashbee 1970; Robertson-Mackay 1980). A more

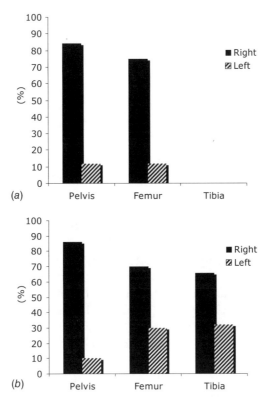

Figure 4.6 Distribution of selected right- and left-side animal bones at West Kennet palisade (a) enclosure 1 and (b) enclosure 2 (after Edwards and Horne 1997:figs. 75 and 76).

intimate association is seen at a Wiltshire round barrow, where an early account claims that the skulls of two oxen each "formed the resting place for the body of an infant" (Colt Hoare, cited in Thurnam 1869:539). More ambiguous is the human infant's femur found inserted into the broken shaft of a cattle humerus at Windmill Hill (Grigson 1999:fig. 161). The remains of other animals are rarely treated in this formalised way, though an exception would be the dog skulls placed in Late Neolithic Orcadian tombs (Jones and Richards 2003). One possible consequence of the converging economic, social and symbolic importance of cattle that has received little attention is the likelihood that they would make prime targets for raiding (Schulting 2004).

A striking pattern is seen in the distribution of pig remains at the West Kennet palisade enclosures, where there is a far greater representation of bones from the right side of the body, well beyond what could be explained by chance (Edwards and Horne 1997:120, figs. 75 and 76) (fig. 4.6). As remarked by Edwards and Horne (1997:125), this might imply the attribution of a certain propitiousness to the right side of the body that made it more appropriate for intentional deposition at the site. Given Parker Pearson and Ramilisonina's (1998) recent equation of timber circles with the living, and stone circles with the dead, it is interesting to speculate on the location of the missing left body parts: were these placed with the dead (the question is not easily answered, since few contemporary burials are known from this area), or were they taken away by the living to be consumed elsewhere, perhaps in a more mundane setting?

Conclusions

Much of the evidence discussed here is based on the preliminary findings of new kinds of analyses and approaches, and the interpretations drawn are necessarily speculative. Nevertheless, it does provide a sense of the kinds of questions that we should be exploring in order to understand prehistoric foodways more fully. Much remains to be discovered concerning the "materiality" of food, how plants and animals were managed, how animals were slaughtered and how foods were prepared. One of the most exciting prospects for future research is the ability to bring together all the various strands of evidence for foodways, from large-scale field systems, floral and faunal remains, bio-chemical analyses of human and animal tissues and residues on pottery, and archaeological context, within a theoretical framework that acknowledges both the practicalities of making a living, and the social and cultural meanings with which they are inextricably intertwined.

ACKNOWLEDGEMENTS

I would like to thank Umberto Albarella, Brian Hayden, Finbar McCormick, Joanna Ostapkowicz and Josh Pollard for their constructive comments on an earlier draft of this chapter.

NOTES

1   The Early Mesolithic refers to the period 9500–8000/7500 B.C.; Late Mesolithic, 7500–4000 B.C.; Early and Middle Neolithic, 4000–3200 B.C.; Late Neolithic and Beaker, 3200–2200 B.C.; and Early Bronze Age, 2200–1700 B.C.
2   There is little doubt that the first domesticates were introduced from the Continent. There is no issue with cereals, since the progenitors of the wheats and barleys that make up the earliest cereals throughout north-west Europe are not native to the area, but derive from the Near East. Nor, in the case of Britain, is there any question as regards sheep and goats, since there are no wild equivalents here. The situation becomes more complex with cattle and pig, since aurochs and boar were present. However, as has long been recognised, there is no support for local domestication of cattle at least (Noddle 1989; Grigson 1999). Cattle bones from the earliest Neolithic sites in Britain, as throughout north-west Europe, derive from a much smaller animal than the local aurochs populations, and do not show the gradual diminution in size that would be expected with local domestication. The question of some more limited genetic input from wild stock into

the domestic herds is more complex. Extensive DNA analyses of modern European cattle, together with some preliminary analysis of ancient mtDNA of British aurochs and domestic cattle bones, have been undertaken to address this question, and so far the results indicate little or no impact of wild female mitochondrial lineages on domestic stock (Troy et al. 2001; Edwards et al. 2004). By contrast, new mtDNA evidence for pigs shows multiple centres of domestication – including a European centre – supporting either "local" (though not necessarily in Britain) domestication or much interbreeding with female wild boar (Larson et al. 2005).

3 Stable isotope analysis is complicated by the fact that plants and animals do not contain the same amounts or kinds of protein, and so the former tends to be under-represented; nevertheless, some indication of their relative importance in different human groups can be gained.

4 A recent example comes from nineteenth-century rural Ireland, where meat was eaten almost exclusively in winter, when excess animals were butchered and preserved to minimise the need for feeding them over the winter, while butter and milk were mainstays of the summer diet (Evans 1942).

5 Some indication of the possibilities is given by the complex classification system of water buffalo among the Toraja of highland Sulawesi, Indonesia: "Different shapes and curvatures of horns are named, and a set of terms based on the human arm describes horn length. Other sets of terms distinguish the color of the coat and tail, spots and patterns, kinds of eyes, and types and locations of swirls of hair. All of these factors and their permutations, combined with size, strength, and general good looks, are considered in the animals' evaluation" (Volkman 1985:70).

6 While "cuisine" as used by Goody (1982) in its formal sense is not entirely appropriate to earlier prehistoric foodways in Britain, it provides a convenient term when discussing the culturally specific ways of preparing, serving, consuming and disposing of food.

7 It is also important to recognise that the isotope results from a few Neolithic individuals do suggest some low-level consumption of marine protein (Schulting 2004).

8 Earth ovens present another possibility, but evidence for these at causewayed enclosures appears to be lacking.

9 The structural opposition of nature (*agrios*) and culture (*domus*) receives its fullest exposition in Hodder's (1990) account, where it forms the cornerstone for understanding the entire process of neolithisation across Europe and the Near East. More recently, despite the continued widespread use of this scheme, some misgivings have been expressed (e.g., Whittle et al. 1999; Whittle 2003). The scheme is seen by some as too general to account for the construction of belief systems in more local situations, as well as failing to take account of how people constitute and understand their world on a daily basis (Bourdieu 1977).

REFERENCES

Abbink, J., 2003 Love and death of cattle: the paradox in Suri attitudes towards livestock. Ethos 68:341–364.

Adams, R. L., 2004 An ethnoarchaeological study of feasting in Sulawesi, Indonesia. Journal of Anthropological Archaeology 23:56–78.

Albarella, U., and S. Payne, 2005 Neolithic pigs from Durrington Walls, Wiltshire, England: a biometrical database. Journal of Archaeological Science 32:589–599.

——and D. Serjeantson, 2002 A passion for pork: meat consumption at the British Late Neolithic site of Durrington Walls. *In* Consuming Passions and Patterns of Consumption. P. Miracle and N. Milner, eds. pp. 33–49. Cambridge: McDonald Institute.

Allen T., A. Barclay and H. Lamdin-Whymark, 2004 Opening the wood, making the land: the study of a Neolithic landscape in the Dorney area of the Middle Thames Valley. *In* Towards a New Stone Age: aspects of the Neolithic in south-east England. J. Cotton and D. Field, ed. pp. 82–98. York: Council for British Archaeology.

Anthony, I. M. C., D. C. W. Sanderson, G. T. Cook, D. Abernethy and R. A. Housley, 2001 Dating a burnt mound from Kilmartin, Argyll, Scotland. Quaternary Science Reviews 20:921–926.

Armour-Chelu, M., 1991 The faunal remains. *In* Maiden Castle: excavations and field survey 1985–6. N. M. Sharples. pp. 139–151. London: English Heritage.

——1998 The animal bone. *In* Etton: excavations at a Neolithic causewayed enclosure near Maxey, Cambridgeshire, 1982–7. F. Pryor. pp. 273–288. London: English Heritage.

——and J. Clutton-Brock, 1985 Notes on the evidence for the use of cattle as draught animals at Etton. *In* An interim report on excavations at Etton, Maxey, Cambridgeshire, 1982–1984. F. Pryor, C. French and M. Taylor. Antiquaries Journal 65:297–302.

Ashbee, P., 1970 The Earthen Long Barrow in Britain. London: Dent.

——I. F. Smith and J. G. Evans, 1979 Excavation of three long barrows near Avebury, Wiltshire. Proceedings of the Prehistoric Society 45:207–300.

Balasse, M., A. Tresset, K. Dobney and S. H. Ambrose, 2005 The use of isotope ratios to test for seaweed eating in sheep. Journal of the Zoological Society of London 266:283–291.

Barclay, G. J., K. Brophy and G. MacGregor, 2002 Claish, Stirling: an Early Neolithic structure in its context. Proceedings of the Society of Antiquaries of Scotland 132:65–137.

Benson, D., and A. Whittle, eds., 2007 Building Memories: the Neolithic Cotswold long barrow at Ascott-under-Wychwood, Oxfordshire. Oxford: Oxbow Books.

Bloch, M., 1985. Almost eating the ancestors. Man 20:631–646.

Bogaard, A., T. H. E. Heaton, P. Poulton and I. Merbach, 2007 The impact of manuring on nitrogen isotope ratios in cereals: archaeological implications for reconstruction of diet and crop management practices. Journal of Archaeological Science 34:335–343.

Bourdieu, P., 1977 Outline of a Theory of Practice. Cambridge: Cambridge University Press.

Caplan, P., 1994 Feasts, Fasts, Famine: food for thought. Oxford: Berg.

Carter, R. J., 1998 Reassessment of seasonality at the Early Mesolithic site of Star Carr, Yorkshire, based on radiographs of mandibular tooth development in red deer (*Cervus elaphus*). Journal of Archaeological Science 25:851–856.

Caseldine, C., and J. Hatton, 1993 The development of high moorland on Dartmoor: fire and the influence of Mesolithic activity on vegetation change. *In* Climatic Change and Human Impact of the Landscape. F. M. Chambers, ed. pp. 119–131. London: Chapman and Hall.

Caulfield, S., 1983 The Neolithic settlement of North Connaught. *In* Landscape Archaeology in Ireland. T. Reeves-Smyth and F. Hammond, eds. pp. 195–216. Oxford: British Archaeological Reports.

——R. G. O'Donnell and P. I. Mitchell, 1998 Radiocarbon dating of a Neolithic field system at Céide Fields, County Mayo, Ireland. Radiocarbon 40:629–640.

Chapman, A., 2004 Gayhurst barrow cemetery. Current Archaeology 191:510–511.

——K. Deighton and P. Halstead, 2005 Gayhurst: reconstructing the burial of an Early Bronze Age lord. Current Archaeology 195:114–118.

Clarke, M. J., 2001 Akha feasting: an ethnoarchaeological perspective. *In* Feasts: archaeological and ethnographic perspectives on food, politics, and Power. M. Dietler and
B. Hayden, eds. pp. 144–167. Washington: Smithsonian Institution Press.

Cleal, R. M. J., 1992 Significant form: ceramic styles in the earlier Neolithic of southern
England. *In* Vessels for the Ancestors: essays on the Neolithic of Britain and Ireland. N.
Sharples and A. Sheridan, eds. pp. 286–304. Edinburgh: Edinburgh University Press.

Codere, H., 1950 Fighting with Property. Seattle: University of Washington Press.

Coles, B., and J. Coles, 1986 Sweet Track to Glastonbury. London: Thames and Hudson.

Conneller, C., and T. Schadla-Hall, 2003 Beyond Star Carr: the Vale of Pickering in the
10th millennium BP. Proceedings of the Prehistoric Society 69:85–105.

Copley, M. S., R. Berstan, S. N. Dudd, G. Docherty, A. J. Mukherjee, V. Straker, S. Payne
and R. P. Evershed, 2003 Direct chemical evidence for widespread dairying in prehistoric
Britain. Proceedings of the National Academy of Sciences 100:1524–1529.

——————, A. J. Mukherjee, S. N. Dudd, V. Straker, S. Payne and R. P. Evershed, 2005
Dairying in antiquity III: evidence from absorbed lipid residues dating to the British Neolithic. Journal of Archaeological Science 32:523–546.

Davis, S., and S. Payne, 1993 A barrow full of cattle skulls. Antiquity 67:12–22.

Dickson, C., and J. Dickson, 2000 Plants and People in Ancient Scotland. Stroud: Tempus.

Dietler, M., 1996 Feasts and commensal politics in the political economy: food, power,
and status in prehistoric Europe. *In* Food and the Status Quest: an interdisciplinary perspective. P. Wiessner and W. Schiefenhövel, eds. pp. 87–125. Providence: Berghahn.

——2001 Theorizing the feast: rituals of consumption, commensal politics, and power in
African societies. *In* Feasts: archaeological and ethnographic perspectives on food, politics,
and power. M. Dietler and B. Hayden, eds. pp. 65–114. Washington: Smithsonian Institution Press.

——and B. Hayden, eds., 2001 Feasts: archaeological and ethnographic perspectives on
food, politics, and power. Washington: Smithsonian Institution Press.

Dineley, M., and G. Dineley, 2000 Neolithic ale: barley as a source of malt sugars for fermentation. *In* Plants in Neolithic Britain and Beyond. A. S. Fairbairn, ed. pp. 137–153.
Oxford: Oxbow Books.

Dockrill, S. J., J. Bond, A. Milles, I. A. Simpson and J. Ambers, 1994 Tofts Ness, Sanday,
Orkney. An integrated study of a buried Orcadian landscape. *In* Whither Environmental
Archaeology? R. Luff and P. Rowley-Conwy, eds. pp. 115–132. Oxford: Oxbow Books.

Dudd, S. N., R. P. Evershed and A. M. Gibson, 1999 Evidence for varying patterns of
exploitation of animal products in different prehistoric pottery traditions based on lipids
preserved in surface and absorbed residues. Journal of Archaeological Science 26:1473–
1482.

Edwards, A., and M. Horne, 1997 Animal bones. *In* Sacred Mounds, Holy Rings: Silbury
Hill and the West Kennet palisade enclosures. A. Whittle. pp. 117–129. Oxford: Oxbow
Books.

Edwards, C. J., D. E. MacHugh, K. M. Dobney, L. Martin, N. Russell, L. K. Horwitz,
S. K. McIntosh, K. C. MacDonald, D. Helmer, A. Tresset, J.-D. Vigne and D. G. Bradley,
2004 Ancient DNA analysis of 101 cattle remains: limits and prospects. Journal of
Archaeological Science 31:695–710.

Ellis, C. J., M. J. Allen, J. Gardiner, P. Harding, C. Ingrem, A. Powell and R. G. Scaife,
2003 An Early Mesolithic seasonal hunting site in the Kennet Valley, southern England.
Proceedings of the Prehistoric Society 69:107–135.

Entwistle, R., and A. Grant, 1989 The evidence for cereal cultivation and animal husbandry
in the southern British Neolithic and Bronze Age. *In* The Beginnings of Agriculture.

A. Milles, D. Williams and N. Gardner, eds. pp. 203–215. Oxford: British Archaeological Reports.

Evans, E. E., 1942 Irish Heritage: the landscape, the people, and their work. Dundalk: Dundalgan Press.

Fairweather, A. D., and I. B. M. Ralston, 1993 The Neolithic timber hall at Balbridie, Grampion region, Scotland: the building, the date, the plant macrofossils. Antiquity 67:313–323.

Fenton, A., 1978 The Northern Isles: Orkney and Shetland. Edinburgh: John Donald.

Fernández-Armesto, F., 2002 Food: a history. London: Pan Macmillan.

Fleming, A., 1988 The Dartmoor Reaves: investigating prehistoric land divisions. London: Batsford.

Fraser, S., and H. Murray, 2005 New light on the earliest Neolithic in the Dee Valley, Aberdeenshire. PAST 50:1–2.

Goody, J., 1982 Cooking, Cuisine and Class: a study in comparative sociology. Cambridge: Cambridge University Press.

Grigson, C., 1982 Porridge and pannage: pig husbandry in Neolithic England. In Archaeological Aspects of Woodland Ecology. S. Limbrey and M. Bell, eds. pp. 297–313. Oxford: British Archaeological Reports.

——1999 The mammalian remains. In The Harmony of Symbols: the Windmill Hill causewayed enclosure, Wiltshire. A. Whittle, J. Pollard and C. Grigson. pp. 164–252. Oxford: Oxbow Books.

——and P. A. Mellars, 1987 The mammalian remains from the middens. In Excavations on Oronsay: prehistoric human ecology on a small island. P. A. Mellars, ed. pp. 243–289. Edinburgh: Edinburgh University Press.

Hastorf, C. A., 1991 Gender, space, and food in prehistory. In Engendering Archaeology: women and prehistory. J. M. Gero and M. W. Conkey, eds. pp. 132–162. Oxford: Blackwell.

——1998. The cultural life of early domestic plant use. Antiquity 72:773–782.

Hayden, B., 1996 Feasting in prehistoric and traditional societies. In Food and the Status Quest: an interdisciplinary perspective. P. Wiessner and W. Schiefenhövel, eds. pp. 127–147. Providence: Berghahn.

——2001 A prolegmenon to the importance of feasting. In Feasts: archaeological and ethnographic perspectives on food, politics, and power. M. Dietler and B. Hayden, eds. pp. 23–64. Washington: Smithsonian Institution Press.

Hey, G., J. Mulville and M. Robinson, 2003 Diet and culture in southern Britain: the evidence from Yarnton. In Food, Culture and Identity in the Neolithic and Early Bronze Age. M. Parker Pearson, ed. pp. 79–88. Oxford: British Archaeological Reports.

Hodder, I., 1990 The Domestication of Europe. Oxford: Blackwell.

Hoskins, J., 1993 Violence, sacrifice, and divination: giving and taking life in eastern Indonesia. American Ethnologist 20:159–178.

Ingold, T., D. Riches and J. Woodburn, eds., 1988 Hunters and Gatherers, vol. 2: Property, Power and Ideology. Oxford: Berg.

Jones, A., 1996 Food for thought: material culture and the transformation in food use from the Mesolithic to Neolithic. In The Early Prehistory of Scotland. T. Pollard and A. Morrison, eds. pp. 291–300. Edinburgh: Edinburgh University Press.

——1999 The world on a plate: ceramics, food technology and cosmology in Neolithic Orkney. World Archaeology 31:55–77.

——and C. Richards, 2003 Animals into ancestors: domestication, food and identity in Late Neolithic Orkney. In Food, Culture and Identity in the Neolithic and Early Bronze Age. M. Parker Pearson, ed. pp. 45–51. Oxford: British Archaeological Reports.

Jones, G., 2000 Evaluating the importance of cultivation and collecting in Neolithic Britain. *In* Plants in Neolithic Britain and Beyond. A. S. Fairbairn, ed. pp. 79–84. Oxford: Oxbow Books.

Kinnes, I., 1988 The cattleship Potemkin: the first Neolithic in Britain. *In* The Archaeology of Context in the Neolithic and Bronze Age: recent trends. J. Barrett and I. Kinnes, eds. pp. 2–8. Sheffield: Department of Archaeology and Prehistory.

Larson, G., K. Dobney, U. Albarella, M. Fang, E. Matisoo-Smith, J. Robins, S. Lowden, H. Finlayson, T. Brand, E. Willerslev, P. Rowley-Conwy, L. Andersson and A. Cooper, 2005 Worldwide phylogeography of wild boar reveals multiple centers of pig domestication. Science 207:1618–1621.

Legge, A. J., 1981 Aspects of cattle husbandry. *In* Farming Practice in British Prehistory. R. Mercer, ed. pp. 169–181. Edinburgh: Edinburgh University Press.

——1989. Milking the evidence: a reply to Entwistle and Grant. *In* The Beginnings of Agriculture. A. Milles, D. Williams and N. Gardner, eds. pp. 217–242. Oxford: British Archaeological Reports.

——and P. A. Rowley-Conwy, 1988 Star Carr Revisited. London: Birkbeck College, University of London.

Levitan, B., 1990 The non-human vertebrate remains. *In* Hazleton North: the excavation of a Neolithic long cairn of the Cotswold-Severn group. A. Saville. pp. 199–213. London: English Heritage.

Malainey, M. E., R. Przybylski and Sherriff, B. L., 2001 One person's food: how and why fish avoidance may affect the settlement and subsistence patterns of hunter-gatherers. American Antiquity 66:141–161.

Maltby, M., 1990 Animal bones. *In* The Stonehenge Environs Project. J. Richards. pp. 57–61. London: English Heritage.

Mauss, M., 1969 The Gift. London: Routledge and Kegan Paul.

McLaren, F. S., 2000 Revising the wheat crops of Neolithic Britain. *In* Plants in Neolithic Britain and Beyond. A. S. Fairbairn, ed. pp. 91–100. Oxford: Oxbow Books.

Mellars, P., 1975 Ungulate populations, economic patterns, and the Mesolithic landscape. *In* The Effect of Man on the Landscape: the Highland Zone. J. G. Evans, S. Limbrey and H. Cleere, eds. pp. 49–56. London: Council for British Archaeology.

——1987 Excavations on Oronsay: prehistoric human ecology on a small island. Edinburgh: Edinburgh University Press.

——and M. R. Wilkinson, 1980 Fish otoliths as evidence of seasonality in prehistoric shell middens: the evidence from Oronsay (Inner Hebrides). Proceedings of the Prehistoric Society 46:19–44.

Mithen, S., N. Finlay, W. Carruthers, S. Carter and P. Ashmore, 2001 Plant use in the Mesolithic: evidence from Staosnaig, Isle of Colonsay, Scotland. Journal of Archaeological Science 28:223–234.

Moffet, L., M. A. Robinson and V. Straker, 1989 Cereals, fruits and nuts: charred plant remains from Neolithic sites in England and Wales and the Neolithic economy. *In* The Beginnings of Agriculture. A. Milles, D. Williams and N. Gardner, eds. pp. 246–261. Oxford: British Archaeological Reports.

Montón Subías, S., 2002 Cooking in zooarchaeology: is this issue still raw? *In* Consuming Passions and Patterns of Consumption. P. Miracle and N. Milner, eds. pp. 7–15. Cambridge: McDonald Institute.

Mortimer, J. R., 1905 Forty Years' Researches in British and Saxon Burial-Mounds of East Yorkshire. London: A. Brown and Sons.

Munn, N., 1986 The Fame of Gawa: a symbolic study of value transformation in a Massim (Papua New Guinea) society. Cambridge: Cambridge University Press.

Needham, S., and J. Evans, 1987 Honey and dripping: Neolithic food residues from Runnymede Bridge. Oxford Journal of Archaeology 6:21–28.

Noddle, B., 1989 Cattle and sheep in Britain and northern Europe up to the Atlantic Period: a personal viewpoint. *In* The Beginnings of Agriculture. A. Milles, D. Williams and N. Gardner, eds. pp. 179–202. Oxford: British Archaeological Reports.

Ó Néill, J., 2005 Burnt Mounds in Northern and Western Europe. PhD thesis, School of Archaeology and Palaeoecology, Queen's University Belfast.

Parker Pearson, M., 2000 Eating money: a study in the ethnoarchaeology of food. Archaeological Dialogues 7:217–232.

——2003 Food, culture and identity: an introduction and overview. *In* Food, Culture and Identity in the Neolithic and Early Bronze Age. M. Parker Pearson, ed. pp. 1–30. Oxford: British Archaeological Reports.

——and Ramilisonina, 1998 Stonehenge for the ancestors: the stones pass on the message. Antiquity 72:308–326.

Patterson, N., 1994 Cattle Lords and Clansmen. Notre Dame, IN: University of Notre Dame Press.

Pollard, J., 1995 Inscribing space: formal deposition at the Later Neolithic monument of Woodhenge, Wiltshire. Proceedings of the Prehistoric Society 61:137–156.

——2004 A "movement of becoming": realms of existence in the early Neolithic of southern Britain. *In* Stories from the Landscape: archaeologies of inhabitation. A. Chadwick, ed. pp. 55–69. Oxford: British Archaeological Reports.

Pryor, F., 1996 Sheep, stockyards and field systems: Bronze Age livestock populations in the fenland of eastern England. Antiquity 70:313–324.

——1998 Etton: excavations at a Neolithic causewayed enclosure near Maxey, Cambridgeshire, 1982–7. London: English Heritage.

Ray, K., and J. Thomas, 2003 In the kinship of cows: the social centrality of cattle in the earlier Neolithic of southern Britain. *In* Food, Culture and Identity in the Neolithic and Early Bronze Age. M. Parker Pearson, ed. pp. 37–44. Oxford: British Archaeological Reports.

Richards, C., and J. Thomas, 1984 Ritual activity and structured deposition in later Neolithic Wessex. *In* Neolithic Studies: a review of some current research. R. Bradley and J. Gardiner, eds. pp. 189–218. Oxford: British Archaeological Reports.

Richards, M. P., 2000 Human consumption of plant foods in the British Neolithic: direct evidence from bone stable isotopes. *In* Plants in Neolithic Britain and Beyond. A. S. Fairbairn, ed. pp. 123–135. Oxford: Oxbow Books.

——R. J. Schulting and R. E. M. Hedges, 2003 Sharp shift in diet at onset of Neolithic. Nature 425:366.

Ritchie, A., 1983 Excavation of a Neolithic farmstead at Knap of Howar, Papa Westray, Orkney. Proceedings of the Society of Antiquaries of Scotland 113:40–121.

Robertson-Mackay, M. E., 1980 A "head and hooves" burial beneath a round barrow, with other Neolithic and Bronze Age sites, on Hemp Knoll, near Avebury, Wiltshire. Proceedings of the Prehistoric Society 46:123–176.

Robinson, M. A., 2000a Further considerations of Neolithic charred cereals, fruit and nuts. *In* Plants in Neolithic Britain and Beyond. A. S. Fairbairn, ed. pp. 85–90. Oxford: Oxbow Books.

——2000b Coleopteran evidence for the elm decline, Neolithic activity in woodland, clearance and the use of the landscape. *In* Plants in Neolithic Britain and Beyond. A. S. Fairbairn, ed. pp. 27–36. Oxford: Oxbow Books.

Rosman, A., and P. Rubel, 1971 Feasting with Mine Enemy. New York: Columbia University Press.

Rowley-Conwy, P., 2004 How the West was lost: a reconsideration of agricultural origins in Britain, Ireland, and southern Scandinavia. Current Anthropology 45 (suppl.): S83–S113.

Schulting, R. J., 1998 Slighting the Sea: the Mesolithic–Neolithic transition in Northwest Europe. PhD thesis, Department of Archaeology, University of Reading.

——2004 An Irish Sea change: some implications for the Mesolithic–Neolithic transition. In The Neolithic of the Irish Sea: Materiality and Traditions of Practice. V. Cummings and C. Fowler, eds. pp. 22–28. Oxford: Oxbow Books.

——and M. P. Richards, 2002a The wet, the wild and the domesticated: the Mesolithic–Neolithic transition on the west coast of Scotland. European Journal of Archaeology 5:147–189.

——and ——2002b Finding the coastal Mesolithic in southwest Britain: AMS dates and stable isotope results on human remains from Caldey Island, Pembrokeshire, South Wales. Antiquity 76:1011–1025.

Serjeantson, D., 1995 Animal bones. In Stonehenge in its Landscape. R. M. J. Cleal, K. E. Walker and R. Montague. pp. 437–451. London: English Heritage.

——1996 The animal bones. In Refuse and Disposal at Area 16 East, Runnymede. S. P. Needham and T. Spence. pp. 194–223. London: British Museum Press.

Sharples, N. M., 1991 Maiden Castle: excavations and field survey 1985–6. London: English Heritage.

Sherratt, A., 1983 The secondary exploitation of animals in the Old World. World Archaeology 15:90–104.

——1987 Cups that cheered: the introduction of alcohol to prehistoric Europe. In Bell Beakers of the Western Mediterranean. W. Waldren and R. Kennard, eds. pp. 81–106. Oxford: British Archaeological Reports.

Simpson, D. D. A., 1996 The Ballygalley houses, Co. Antrim, Ireland. In Neolithic Houses in Europe and Beyond. T. Darvill and J. Thomas, eds. pp. 123–132. Oxford: Oxbow Books.

Sutton, D. E., 2001 Remembrance of Repasts: an anthropology of food and memory. Oxford: Berg.

Thomas, J., 1988 The social significance of Cotswold-Severn burial practices. Man 23: 540–559.

——1991 Rethinking the Neolithic. Cambridge: Cambridge University Press.

——2003 Thoughts on the "repacked" Neolithic revolution. Antiquity 77:67–74.

Thorpe, I. J., 1984 Ritual, power and ideology: a reconstruction of earlier Neolithic rituals in Wessex. In Neolithic Studies: a review of some current research. R. Bradley and J. Gardiner, eds. pp. 41–60. Oxford: British Archaeological Reports.

Thurnam, J., 1869 On ancient British barrows, especially those of Wiltshire and the adjoining counties. Part II: Round barrows. Archaeologia 43:285–544.

Tipping, R., 1996 Microscopic charcoal records, inferred human activity and climate change in the Mesolithic of northernmost Scotland. In The Early Prehistory of Scotland. T. Pollard and A. Morrison, eds. pp. 39–61. Edinburgh: Edinburgh University Press.

Tresset, A., 2003 French connections II: of cows and men. In Neolithic Settlement in Ireland and Western Britain. I. Armit, E. Murphy, E. Nelis and D. Simpson, eds. pp. 18–30. Oxford: Oxbow Books.

Troy, C. S., D. E. McHugh, J. F. Bailey, D. A. Magee, R. T. Loftus, P. Cunningham, A. T. Chamberlain, B. C. Sykes and D. G. Bradley, 2001 Genetic evidence for Near-Eastern origins of European cattle. Nature 410:1088–1091.

Volkman, T. A., 1985 Feasts of Honor: ritual and changes in the Toraja Highlands. Urbana: University of Illinois Press.

Waddington, C., G. Bailey, I. Boomer, N. Milner, K. Pederson, R. Shiel and T. Stevenson, 2003 A Mesolithic settlement at Howick, Northumberland. Antiquity 77. Available at http://antiquity.ac.uk/projgall/waddington/waddington.html.

Wainwright, G., and I. Longworth, 1971 Durrington Walls: excavations 1966–1968. London: Society of Antiquaries.

Watson, D. M. S., 1931 The animal bones from Skara Brae. In Skara Brae, a Pictish Village in Orkney. V. G. Childe, ed. pp. 198–204. London: Kegan Paul, Trench, Trubner and Co.

Webley, D. P., 1976 How the west was won: prehistoric land-use in the southern Marches. In Welsh Antiquity. G. C. Boon and J. M. Lewis, eds. pp. 19–35. Cardiff: National Museum of Wales.

Whittle, A., 1997 Moving on and moving around: Neolithic settlement mobility. In Neolithic Landscapes. P. Topping, ed. pp. 15–22. Oxford: Oxbow Books.

——2003 The Archaeology of People: dimensions of Neolithic life. London: Routledge.

——and J. Pollard, 1998 Windmill Hill causewayed enclosure: the harmony of symbols. In Understanding the Neolithic of North-Western Europe. M. Edmonds and C. Richards, eds. pp. 231–247. Glasgow: Cruithne Press.

——, and C. Grigson, 1999 The Harmony of Symbols: the Windmill Hill causewayed enclosure, Wiltshire. Oxford: Oxbow Books.

Wiessner, P., 1996 Levelling the hunter: constraints on the status quest in foraging societies. In Food and the Status Quest: an interdisciplinary perspective. P. Wiessner and W. Schiefenhövel, eds. pp. 171–191. Providence: Berghahn.

——and W. Schiefenhövel, eds., 1996 Food and the Status Quest: an interdisciplinary perspective. Providence: Berghahn.

Woodburn, J., 1982 Egalitarian societies. Man 17:431–451.

Wysocki, M., and A. Whittle, 2000 Diversity, lifestyles and rites: new biological and archaeological evidence from British earlier Neolithic mortuary assemblages. Antiquity 74:591–601.

Young, M. W., 1971 Fighting with Food: leadership, values and social control in a Massim society. Cambridge: Cambridge University Press.

Zvelebil, M., 1994 Plant use in the Mesolithic and its role in the transition to farming. Proceedings of the Prehistoric Society 60:35–74.

——1995 Hunting, gathering, or husbandry? Management of food resources by the Late Mesolithic communities of temperate Europe. In Before Farming: hunter-gatherer society and subsistence. D. V. Campana, ed. pp. 79–104. Philadelphia: Museum of Applied Science Center for Archaeology (MASCA).

5

Temporary Spaces in the Mesolithic and Neolithic: Understanding Landscapes

Lesley McFadyen

Introduction

This chapter is not intended as an extensive review of Mesolithic and Neolithic landscape studies. Instead, through reference to the recent work of a number of prehistorians and anthropologists who have engaged with the topic, it discusses several key approaches that range from the "ecological" to the "social". Rather than playing these approaches off one against the other, and arguing that either represents inherently "good" or "bad" practice, this chapter explores how relationships between people and their worlds have been constituted in each domain. In particular, it offers a critique of approaches that fail to deal with the temporal conditions of past worlds, and argues that temporality is about process and not palimpsest (i.e., the superimposition of events). It is also argued that in our archaeological studies of the construction of landscape, the concept of location (i.e., of identified places) in the past has to be argued for rather than assumed. The chapter examines why in Mesolithic studies research has focused on the relationship between material culture and landscape, while in Neolithic studies the relationship has been between architecture and landscape. It highlights a recent move in archaeology to take a Neolithic approach to Mesolithic evidence and asks the question, what would happen if we did the opposite?

Landscapes Made from Environments

There exists within prehistoric archaeology a tradition of regional survey that attempts to characterise distributions of artefacts – especially worked flint – over geographical areas in terms of a variety of activities (e.g., Foley 1981; Haselgrove et al. 1985; Schofield 1991: see Hind 2004a for critique). Often these artefacts are understood to give us uncomplicated access to prehistoric technical practice

(e.g., settlement and subsistence). In this case the geographic distribution of techniques is understood to reflect a basic social process in terms of adaptation to surroundings or the management of resources. The conceptual understanding of
landscape is that of an environmental backdrop or setting in which activities take
place, a physical entity that is peppered with various natural features or resources.

The relative proportion of artefact types within lithic scatters, once identified
and carefully mapped, is used by archaeologists to infer different types of activity,
which are then set *in* the landscape by reference to the surrounding environment.
For example the scale and character of the finds at the Early Mesolithic (ninth
millennium B.C.) site of Star Carr, North Yorkshire, suggested to Graham Clark
that he was dealing with a settlement that had been occupied by a community group
(Clark 1954:10). He went on in his report to describe the ecological setting of this
occupation, claiming the presence of a living platform resting directly on the reed
swamp bordering the lake, with a water-lily zone between it and open water. On
the other side, the platform was enclosed by higher ground, and this was made up
of closed birchwood (Clark 1954:12–13). Clark saw the site as a semi-persistent
settlement or base camp situated between different zones, from which people would
then go out into other parts of the landscape in order to carry out a range of sub-
sistence-related activities. It is important to make clear that in Clark's work there
is a conceptual understanding of landscape as a setting in which activities took
place, and that Clark was most concerned with understanding this as an ecological
relationship (see Clark 1972). This is a particular understanding of ecology, where
humans are distinct from other organisms, and the world is described in terms of
the cultural exploitation of natural resources. Although he was dealing with evidence of hunter-gatherer life, Clark regarded these people as living between a series
of different fixed locations in the landscape rather than being placeless nomads.
Approaches such as this lead to a place-bound understanding of how past people
understood the landscape to be constituted. They also imply that to understand
mobility it is necessary only to track people's movements between a series of fixed
locations – where they have come from and where they are heading to – and to
establish when that activity occurs. Temporality is reduced to a description in terms
of seasonality, rather than a complex historical condition. The problem with work
such as that presented by Clark on Star Carr is not that it is solely an ecological
understanding of landscape, but that it is a two-dimensional or surface perception
of landscape. The notion of the site as a fixed location, a location from which
the larger landscape emerges, is prevalent in much spatial-modelling within
archaeology.

Landscapes Made from Sites

Two approaches that are famous for dealing with sites as fixed locations are site
catchment analysis and central place theory. The first originated with the British
School of Palaeoeconomy (Higgs 1972), and drew on a model of relationships
between spatial distributions of activities and land use around a fixed location: an

expression of the law of diminishing returns with distance. Danny Hind neatly summarises this approach:

> Typically it might assess the different types of land (forest, arable or pasture) within easy walking distance of an archaeological site. Circles are drawn around sites representing this distance, and potential resources available are identified. (2004a:37)

A more dynamic version of this approach has recently been proposed for the Neolithic site of Great Wilbraham causewayed enclosure, Cambridgeshire (Evans et al. 2006). David Clarke, a key exponent of the New Archaeology in Britain, co-directed excavations at the site in 1975 and 1976. Evans et al.'s report gives an account of how Clarke approached the site's interpretation, and also puts forward ideas about how he might have continued with this work had he not died prematurely. At first Evans et al. state that 1970s-style landscape modelling was all about establishing the type of site that the archaeologist was dealing with and then its location. In this case, Clarke's interpretation was of the causewayed enclosure as a settlement, and a settlement established in relation to specific patterns of landscape occupation that were situated between the fen and the chalk downland (Evans et al. 2006:153). It is interesting to note that this way of working is very similar to that set out in Graham Clark's work in the 1950s where activities were set *in* the landscape. However, the authors go on to suggest that "Clarke would have appreciated the greater level of *dynamic landscape modelling* this perspective affords (as opposed to the more stasis-based models of the Higgsian school . . .)" (Evans et al. 2006:159). What the authors are claiming is that David Clarke would have taken into consideration the duration and effort involved in different tasks, and made more of the dynamic or process of exchange between task and environment. In short, the authors are arguing that temporal conditions are a part of how people experience landscape, and one example they offer to illustrate this is to highlight the difference between canoeing down a river and walking towards the chalk downland (2006:157). Although a speculative exercise, the results are important and I will come back in my discussion of taskscapes to the concept of experiencing the world through the way in which you are involved in activities. Here it is important to note that complex dynamics can be involved in site catchment analysis and these do not always produce uniform zones of exploitation around a site. It is also important, and this is where this chapter differs from other reviews and critiques of landscape approaches (e.g., Thomas 2001; Fleming 2006), that we develop our understanding of ecological relationships in terms of how people engaged with different temporal conditions in the process of that relationship. It is in this way that we get near to the relationship of those others to the past that we study. Simply saying that certain forms of archaeology take an environmental approach and others a social approach will not take us very far: it is how those relationships are determined that is critical and this can be just as much a problem for the so-called "social" archaeology as the "ecological".

The second important approach is central place theory (Chorley and Haggett 1967; Christaller 1972). Adopted in the New Archaeology of Ian Hodder (1972),

David Clarke (1972) and Colin Renfrew (1973), this work emphasised levels of interaction between sites and involved the study of hierarchies of interaction. This is defined as a social rather than an ecological imposition on the landscape. It also marked a move away from the study of distributions of artefacts at the level of material culture to consider artefacts as architecture. What was being conveyed here was an architecture that was assumed to have existed as a preconceived idea that was then translated into a physical object or end-product. This was a concept of architecture which existed as one object: it was built for a reason, and it was assumed that it would be used or occupied in that way. To be more precise, architecture was considered as a non-portable object; portable artefacts could be divorced from their social contexts but not architecture (it was understood as being grounded in a context, rooted to the spot). So built forms were directly cor-related with social forms. Cultures were compared to each other in terms of the social and technical complexity of their architectural forms, making architecture the single most significant artefact (Buchli 2002). This has implications for a split in the study of prehistory between a distinctive Mesolithic archaeology which involves a relationship between material culture and landscape, and a separate Neolithic archaeology which involves a relationship between architecture and landscape. Central place theory proposes that any site that provides services for other sites will be determined by convenience so it can be reached with the least amount of effort. On this basis, a hexagon is the most economical geometric form for the equal division of an area between a number of points. In theory, central places that provide similar services will be spaced equidistantly from each other. In Renfrew's work (1973) he argued that there were clusters of Neolithic long barrows in the Wessex landscape, each associated with a causewayed enclosure, and that this distribution of monuments established a social landscape. Drawing Thiessen polygons between the long barrows, he postulated that this analysis indicated that each long barrow was the territorial focus for a small group of Neolithic farmers. Once again the site, in this case a monument, is understood as providing a focal point for activities and a landscape emerges from, or is delimited by, a series of fixed locations. The conceptual understanding of landscape is that of static backdrop in which architecture is set: a neutral space that is then filled with contents such as architecture. Temporal conditions are not a focus of this study, with human labour reduced to numbers of worker hours, and all of the sites are assumed to have existed in the same time frame like a large-scale photographic snapshot (see Buchli 1999).

   In all of the examples that I have drawn upon so far there is an understanding that archaeological sites, whether a concentration of artefacts or a monument, are to be considered in some way as focal points. Each site is treated as a fixed location and it is from these locations that a landscape is constructed. But what if archaeological sites did not lie at the centre of areas of land, but were instead understood as points along a route? Here we are addressing landscape studies within Mesolithic and Neolithic archaeology, periods of time when many people were living essentially mobile lives (albeit to differing degrees). Yet implicit within all of the work that I have outlined so far is the assumption of a place-bound sense of understanding the world. At this point it is instructive to move on to consider archaeological accounts that involve a discussion of how past landscapes were created through mobility.

Landscapes Made Through Movement

In a 1994 paper John Barrett wrote about the spatial distribution of early Neolithic long barrows in a very different way to Colin Renfrew. Rather than becoming fixated with staying fixed, he considered how a site operated as an assemblage of different tasks and activities that came from, and then extended elsewhere into, other things:

> The non-megalithic and megalithic long mounds and the causewayed enclosures did not lie at the centres of areas of land surface, but were instead places at the ends and at the beginnings of paths. (1994a:93)

This offers a profoundly different conceptual understanding of landscape, as in Barrett's account space does not precede the material and historical conditions of past people's lives; it is instead created through that engagement. Rather than focusing on where things mark a landscape surface, he remarks on the constructed quality of things and the different temporal conditions that are negotiated in the processes of doing. Put simply, architectures are created and keep changing through time; they are not simply translated from a design, into an architectural object, into the artefact that the archaeologist then deals with. Similarly, different parts or features of different sites materialise at different times, and so we have to understand architectures and landscape in the process of their construction in order to approach an understanding of the relationship past people had with the material we study. The other crucial aspect of the past relationship is that it is an ecological relationship of sorts, but one framed in a very different way to that envisaged by Clark for Star Carr (Ingold 1986; and referenced in Barrett 1994a). Humans are not necessarily considered as distinct from other organisms, and the world is understood as something that is constructed through a mutual process of exchange from the different qualities that animals, plants and people offer.

The anthropologist Tim Ingold, rather than engaging with a concept of landscape that has objects and understandings imposed upon it by people, instead encounters landscape through its inhabitation. A study of nomadic movement allowed Ingold to make more of the dynamic or "process of exchange" between task and environment, and it is this understanding of the ecological that Barrett (1994a) has drawn upon. Interestingly, Barrett's archaeology has always explored time-depth or different temporal conditions; he did not read Ingold to escape an understanding of landscape as surface. However in his paper "The temporality of the landscape", Ingold (1993) also set out a way of studying that took into consideration the duration and effort involved in different tasks. Space was given dimension through the ways in which things were done or from the doing of things, and this created a conceptual understanding of landscape constituted from the ways in which labour was framed as a taskscape. In this conceptualisation landscape is produced through the interrelationships of tasks in daily life (see Conneller, chapter 7). It is this structure of the taskscape that has been developed in later archaeological accounts, in particular in the work of Mark Edmonds (1997).

Edmonds refers to a series of sites in his work, but "site" here refers to a flint scatter rather than a location. This kind of study is reliant on two elements: first, that the archaeologist has a knowledge of worked flint; and second, that they can produce an account that successfully integrates technology and landscape. It is the first of these that I wish to explore here, asking whether this kind of knowledge provides a different kind of outlook. For example, information on the total number of pieces, and a breakdown of the assemblage in terms of tool types, is generated in order to define the character of flint scatters (see Mellars 1976; Foley 1981). Assemblages of worked flint are taken as evidence for past practice (e.g., working flint, hunting and butchering animals, the processing of plants, cutting wood, the preparation of food). Assemblages of worked flint are therefore about process and they connect to other things: animals (microliths as arrows and knives, scrapers, burins, awls, flakes), trees (axes, scrapers) and plants (microliths, serrated blades, flakes). Assemblages of worked flint are taken as evidence for tasks and the ways in which these actions connected to, or interlocked with, other activities in an extended network of structured action. A knowledge of how flint is worked has inscribed into it a spatial dimension (although see Conneller 2000 for a critique of the more traditional *chaînes opératoire* approach): the act of working is the object of discourse rather than a physical location. In his writing, Edmonds gives these different connections, or intersections between things and people, changing scales, rhythms and tempos, suggesting that the material remains of past actions were actively maintained by Mesolithic people (1997:101). In this, landscape is not a neutral space that exists behind activities, but on the contrary is produced through action. Landscapes are active and brought into being; they do not exist outside of practice.

Phenomenology of the Landscape

Another key thinker in the development of social understandings of Mesolithic and Neolithic landscapes is Christopher Tilley. Tilley's (1994) research shifted the focus from accounts of people's responses to a physically formed or environmentally defined land mass, to a consideration of the ways in which place comes into being through social practice. Rather than describing an environment as a space that is behind action, Tilley (1994:35) concentrates on the ways in which people interacted with, understood and related to their worlds through place. This relationship operates dialectically. In the first part of his *Phenomenology of Landscape*, Tilley foregrounded the ways in which hunter-gatherer worlds can be known, and the processes through which components of the landscape such as rivers, hills and rock outcrops are perceived. He understands place to be a conceptual space as much as a physical one, arguing that knowledge and perceptions of worlds are created through time, memory and movement. At first glance this would seem very similar to the space described by Barrett, or the taskscapes created in Edmonds's work (1997). However, Tilley is advocating a different kind of encounter between the archaeologist and the places and monuments that they study. The notion of place is once again very much in the foreground, seen in terms of his tautologous statement that "most significant places are located or positioned in space", or in the context of Mesolithic landscapes constructed around fixed locations (Tilley 1994:18, 145).

If Mesolithic flint scatters are exclusively singled out for what they mark, or where they are located, one learns very little. There is a problem with the archaeologist knowing place only as a location because it fixes material culture in a landscape and prevents a consideration of archaeological evidence as a medium for action. Rather than a scatter of flint being evidence for various activities connected to other things and actions elsewhere, it has instead to match something that is visible as a natural point of interest within the physical geography of the area – a river or woodland clearing, for example. Instead of engaging with how space is made through action, and tracing how it connects to other dynamic activities, the focus would seem to be on the kinds of natural feature that worked flint objects point to or mark. Tilley does not move through the spaces that were created from different practices of making in the past. He does not consider how space was articulated through people's relationships with things, or how such dynamics connected to other things and other activities elsewhere.

Within *Phenomenology of Landscape* Tilley (1994) is concerned with understanding the processes of experience and encounter as Mesolithic and Neolithic people moved through landscapes. In one section he produces a sense of movement between places as he walks down the monumental late-fourth-millennium B.C. Dorset Cursus. Here he creates an important concept of landscape as a medium of action. There is no binary opposition between nature and culture in terms of the places that Tilley has connected for us on his journey; the problem is that in his account all of these places exist at the same time. This archaeological account ignores the constructed quality of things: the landscape may be created in Tilley's work, but the architectures that are a part of it are to be negotiated around or through, rather than actively built along, the way. Pits, cliffs, long barrows and the cursus are all imagined to exist at the same time. The key question is at what point in time did people experience them in this way? At what point in the Neolithic would you experience this kind of landscape? What of its different temporal textures (Knight 2002), with earlier backfilled pits barely perceptible as bare patches in the grass, long barrows where the chalk has dirtied through exposure and is beginning to grass over, and parts of the line of the cursus that have been recently constructed with fresh chalk banks and other areas in the process of construction? Landscapes and architectures are created and keep changing through time. Landscapes are made up of past structures in varying states of disrepair, structures in present use, with others in the process of construction. Similarly different parts or features of different places materialise at different times, and so we have to understand architectures and landscape in the process of their construction in order to get near to the relationship past people had with the material we study. In Tilley's account there is no attentiveness to temporality, or inhabitation of these areas through the labour of construction. The landscapes and architectures are treated as archaic objects to move between.

Mesolithic Landscapes and Neolithic Landscapes

I described earlier a move away from the study of distributions of artefacts at the level of material culture, to consider instead artefacts as architecture. There are few references to an integrated technology and landscape approach to Neolithic evidence (e.g., Pollard 1999). Neolithic studies do not seem to explore the relationship between material culture and landscape particularly well (it often being worked through the notion of "structured deposition": Richards and Thomas 1984). In contrast, there is no difficulty in citing work that explores connections between architecture and the landscape (e.g., Barrett et al. 1991; Richards 1996; Bradley 1998; Brück 2001; Barclay et al. 2003; Cummings and Whittle 2003).

It is at this point that I want to stress how difficult it is in practice to take a landscape approach within archaeologies of the Mesolithic. This requires the long-term commitment to working in a particular region (e.g., the projects undertaken in the southern Hebrides (Mithen 2000a; 2000b), or in North or West Yorkshire (Schadla-Hall 1987; 1988; 1989; Mellars and Dark 1998; Conneller and Schadla-Hall 2003; Spikins 2003)), through multiple micro-excavations that are connected together over vast areas. There is great skill and understanding involved in constructing landscapes from small things over large areas. In contrast, there is the macro-scale work and substantial Neolithic and Bronze Age archaeology with landscapes composed of monuments, field systems and settlement, for example, work carried at Fengate, Etton and Maxey (Pryor 1998; 2001), and in the Ouse Valley and at Haddenham, all in Cambridgshire (Evans and Knight 2000; Evans and Hodder 2006). There is the Neolithic and Bronze Age landscape that has been revealed at Yarnton, Oxfordshire, and the landscape of the Middle Thames Valley (Lewis et al. 2006). Contract archaeologists are no longer excavating sites but instead are working at a landscape scale (Mark Knight, pers. comm.). There are also the research excavations on a larger scale around Avebury (Pollard and Reynolds 2002; Gillings and Pollard 2004; Brown et al. 2005), Stonehenge (Richards 1990; Cleal et al. 1995) and Cranborne Chase in Wessex (Barrett et al. 1991; Green 2000). Between Mesolithic and Neolithic archaeology there are two meanings of the word "site". For Neolithic and Bronze Age studies it is time we faced the challenge of excavations that are carried out at a landscape scale within contract archaeology and write historical accounts of lived experience that have a different dimension, a dimension that does not emerge from fixed locations (Andrews et al. 2000; Bradley 2007). Archaeologists must think about how different scales cross-cut, and how this is done in complex and changing ways, in order to develop approaches that have some sort of measure integral with how people lived their lives. Our prehistories must change; they can no longer work at the level of simply connecting architecture and landscape together; there must be more to our engagement. We need to rethink material culture, architecture and landscape relationships and attempt to articulate different understandings of the ways in which people and things could be caught up in materialness and each other.

Mesolithic landscapes on Neolithic terms

Mesolithic archaeology is at a point where it is in danger of simply repeating the social archaeologies developed for the Neolithic in the 1990s, rather than moving on from these works and dealing with what is unique about the challenge of engaging with kinds of archaeological evidence that often do not have a "solid" landscape signature (e.g., ditches, pits and other subsoil features).

Vicki Cummings (2000; 2003) has considered the significance of place during the Mesolithic, and has even brought in issues of monumentality. She effectively demonstrates how subtle differences in the landscape played a significant role in the location of Mesolithic activity. For example, she describes the impact of the colour of an exposed rocky outcrop and also gives dimension to the sound of the sea within Mesolithic life. But, like Tilley, she fixes place through a particular location. Although Cummings's work on the Mesolithic is of great interest, and very important as a social account, she explicitly emphasises the issue of place as a location in her research without questioning whether this was the only way in which landscapes were made in the past. She wants to know *why* one site location was chosen over another in the past, without first questioning whether the concept of "locatedness" was even an issue within Mesolithic hunter-gatherer life. Cummings mentions that Mesolithic people were building their worlds (2003:74), but this is construction only in the form of place becoming sedimented *within* landscape. Both Tilley and Cummings really consider histories to have marked place rather than to have made space in the Mesolithic. They do not move through the spaces that were created from different practices of making in the past. They do not consider how landscape was articulated through people's relationships with things (materials, animals, woodlands and so forth), or how such dynamics connected to other things and other activities elsewhere. Surely, different practices of making did not punctuate the landscape as isolated marks of activity but were mobile? Similarly, in temporal terms, different practices of making were not isolated events but connected to previous acts, other things elsewhere, and extended into future activities. It is by engaging with evidence for the spatial and temporal conditions of Mesolithic life that we can attempt to understand the ways in which landscape was mobile and actively made. There is the problem of a lack of discussion of how "locatedness" was an issue in Mesolithic lives. The archaeological account of this period offered by Tilley and Cummings seems to have jumped from environment to place, while both have been constructed as locations.

Neolithic landscapes on Mesolithic terms

I find a mobile understanding of landscape at its most active or evident in work that deals with technical practice. Nyree Finlay (2000) has written about the spatial dimensions of people's participation in the act of microlith manufacture. She has literally figured flint working as a constructive event by demonstrating the ways in which a person's body moves, turns and extends while working. She also gives dimension to task sharing. Through flint working she explores the ways in which several people would have been involved in the making of a microlith. If we think of landscapes in terms of mobility, then we can make more of these intimate connections between people and things, and attempt to trace the ways in which such relationships intersect with other people and so extend into further activities (see also Finlay 2003). In another successful account, Graeme Warren (2000; 2005; 2006) has written a spatial study of bloodstone. Here mobile space extends out to create a seascape, not a landscape. What is crucial about this work is the way in which Warren gives emphasis to what people made of the sea. Here, the sea is not a feature that is simply experienced, nor is it a bridge between masses of land (neither is it a sea mass). Instead it is understood through the ways in which it is caught up in dispersed and fluid workings of bloodstone. Technology has dimension, it is an important medium through which people make something of their lives. Acts of making are forceful and are a part of the dynamics through which the landscape is mobilised. The spatial dimension of technology or technical practice also figures prominently in the work of Danny Hind (2004a; 2004b) and Chantal Conneller (2000; 2004). By taking an integrated technological and landscape approach, these archaeologists explore the way in which material culture and landscape intersect in an attempt to understand the diverse scales at which past people themselves operated. The temporality of the landscape is generated by the interlocking and the partial, the temporary connecting of a whole range of practices and agencies. It is perhaps the research of Chantal Conneller (2006:45) that demonstrates best of all how these practices are also generated through a sense of future possibilities when she writes: "it is the interlocking of these different tasks which carry time forward and produce the more intricate temporalities of social life."

We can also explore the notion of architectures *as* landscape. To take an example, earlier Neolithic long barrows, often treated as simple covering mounds for timber mortuary chambers, can instead be understood as made from fragments of distributed practice with evidence for several different kinds of disjunction impressed upon the site of their construction (McFadyen, in press). The excavation of these sites repeatedly produces worked flint, animal bones, charcoal, turf, fence lines and other materials from within and around these mounds. Here, dispersed space is made through a series of tasks that range from the making and using of flint tools, the setting of fires, the working of wood into posts, the cutting of quarry pits, the butchery of animals, and the ways in which these things were also entwined with "recognised" building materials such as turf and chalk. In this account, there is no end-point to what we perceive architecture or indeed landscape to be, for architecture extended outwards and so is caught up in other parts of the landscape. Areas of flint working were needed for tools; areas of tree-fall and woodland clearance were needed for stakes; pathways and pasture were required for people to manage their herds; and so these features were also part of these distributed sites. One aspect to our study of these sites should focus on how these practices generated time gaps between events of construction. If disjunction is also a part of architecture, then building activities always have a disconnection and an elsewhere, and these time gaps are the materialisation of that absence (see also Garrow et al. 2005). What we need to start doing in our research is exploring what these conditions might be saying about mobility and how people went about living their lives.

In summary, if architecture is considered as practice rather than object, with disjunction as a vital part of that practice, then it is necessary to take a different landscape approach. This is an approach created through points of departure and dispersal rather than being about the nested quality of a location and "staying put".

Conclusion

This chapter has discussed how landscapes have almost come about second-hand, since they were seen to emerge from a series of fixed locations. Interestingly, it was a reinvestigation into the nature of ecological relationships by scholars such as Barrett and Ingold in the mid 1990s that led to a consideration of how sites operate as an assemblage of different tasks and activities that come from, and then extend elsewhere into, other things. However, more recently, landscapes that are understood as fragments of distributed practice seem to have been forgotten rather than developed in place-bound and architecture-fixated studies of the Neolithic.

In contrast, there are recent studies of the Mesolithic which have taken an integrated technological and landscape approach. These archaeologies explore the way in which material culture and landscape intersect in an attempt to understand the diverse scales at which past people themselves operated. The approach has broader implications for British prehistory in that it emphasises that productive space lies in between. Perhaps it is not simply that landscapes did not emerge from fixed locations, but that they did not have centres at all. A bright prospect for British prehistory will be when archaeologists start to give more account of decentred prehistoric landscapes.

REFERENCES

Andrews, G., J. Barrett and J. Lewis, 2000 Interpretation not record: the practice of archaeology. Antiquity 74:525–530.

Barclay, A., G. Lambrick, J. Moore and M. Robinson, 2003 Lines in the Landscape: Cursus monuments in the Upper Thames Valley. Oxford: Oxford Archaeology.

Barrett, J. C., 1994a Defining domestic space in the Bronze Age of southern Britain. In Architecture and Order: approaches to social space. M. Parker Pearson and C. Richards, eds. pp. 87–97. London: Routledge.

——1994b Fragments from Antiquity: an archaeology of social life in Britain 2900–1200 BC. Oxford: Blackwell.

——R. Bradley and M. Green, 1991 Landscape, Monuments and Society: the prehistory of Cranborne Chase. Cambridge: Cambridge University Press.

Bradley, R., 1998 The Significance of Monuments: on the shaping of human experience in Neolithic and Bronze Age Europe. London: Routledge.

——2007. The Prehistory of Britain and Ireland. Cambridge: Cambridge University Press.

Brown, G., D. Field and D. McOmish, eds., 2005 The Avebury Landscape: aspects of the field archaeology of the Marlborough Downs. Oxford: Oxbow Books.

Brück, J., 2001 Monuments, power and personhood in the British Neolithic. Journal of the Royal Anthropological Institute 7:649–667.

Buchli, V., 1999 An Archaeology of Socialism. Oxford: Berg.

——2002 Architecture and the domestic sphere. In The Material Culture Reader. V. Buchli, ed. pp. 207–214. Oxford and New York: Berg.

Chorley, R. J., and P. Haggett, eds., 1967 Socio-Economic Models in Geography. London: Methuen.

Christaller, W., 1972 How I discovered the theory of Central Places: a report about the origin of central places. In Man, Space and Environment. P. W. English and R. C. Mayfield, eds. pp. 601–610. Oxford: Oxford University Press.

Clark, J. G. D., 1954 Excavations at Star Carr: an early Mesolithic site at Seamer near Scarborough, Yorkshire. Cambridge: Cambridge University Press.

——1972 Star Carr: a case study in bioarchaeology. New York: Addison-Wesley

Clarke, D. L., 1972 A provisional model of an Iron Age society and its settlement system. In Models in Archaeology. D. L. Clarke, ed. pp. 801–869. London: Methuen.

Cleal, R. M. J., K. E. Walker and R. Montague, 1995 Stonehenge in its Landscape: twentieth-century excavations. London: English Heritage.

Conneller, C. J., 2000 Fragmented space? Hunter-gather landscapes of the Vale of Pickering. Archaeological Review from Cambridge 17(1):139–150.

——2004 Becoming deer: corporeal transformations at Star Carr. Archaeological Dialogues 10(2):37–56.

——2006 The space and time of the châine opératoire: technological approaches to past landscapes. Archaeological Review from Cambridge 21(1):38–49.

——and T. Scadla-Hall, 2003 Beyond Star Carr: the Vale of Pickering in the 10th millennium BP. Proceedings of the Prehistoric Society 69:85–106.

Cummings, V., 2000 Myth, memory and metaphor: the significance of place, space and the landscape in Mesolithic Pembrokeshire. In Mesolithic Lifeways: current research from Britain and Ireland. R. Young, ed. pp. 87–96. Leicester: Leicester Archaeology Monographs.

——2003 The origins of monumentality? Mesolithic world-views of the landscape in western Britain. In Mesolithic on the Move: papers presented at the Sixth International Conference on the Mesolithic in Europe, Stockholm 2000. L. Larsson, H. Kindgren, K. Knutsson, D. Loeffler and A. Åkerlund, eds. pp. 82–95. Oxford: Oxbow Books.

——and A. Whittle, 2003 Places of Special Virtue: megaliths in the Neolithic landscapes of Wales. Oxford: Oxbow Books.

Edmonds, M., 1997 Taskscape, technology and tradition. Analecta Praehistorica Leidensia 29:99–110.

Evans, C., and I. Hodder, 2006 A Woodland Archaeology: the Haddenham project, vol. 1. Cambridge: McDonald Institute.

——and M. Knight, 2000 A Fenland delta: later prehistoric land-use in the lower Ouse reaches. In Prehistoric, Roman and post-Roman landscapes of the Great Ouse Valley. M. Dawson, ed. pp. 89–106. London: Council for British Archaeology.

——M. Edmonds and S. Boreham, 2006 "Total archaeology" and model landscapes: excavation of the Great Wilbraham causewayed enclosure, Cambridgeshire 1975–6. Proceedings of the Prehistoric Society 72:113–162.

Finlay, N., 2000 Microliths in the making. *In Mesolithic Lifeways: current research from Britain and Ireland.* R. Young, ed. pp. 23–32. Leicester: Leicester Archaeology Monographs.

——2003 Microliths and multiple authorship. *In* Mesolithic on the Move: papers presented at the Sixth International Conference on the Mesolithic in Europe, Stockholm 2000. L. Larsson, H. Kindgren, K. Knutsson, D. Leoffler and A. Åkerlund, eds. pp. 169–178. Oxford: Oxbow Books.

Fleming, A., 2006 Post-processual landscape archaeology: a critique. Cambridge Archaeological Journal 16(3):267–280.

Foley, R., 1981 A model of regional archaeological structure. Proceedings of the Prehistoric Society 47:1–17.

Garrow, D., E. Beadsmoore and M. Knight, 2005 Pit clusters and the temporality of occupation: an earlier Neolithic site at Kilverstone, Thetford, Norfolk. Proceedings of the Prehistoric Society 71:139–157.

Gillings, M., and J. Pollard, 2004 Avebury. London: Duckworth.

Green, M., 2000 A Landscape Revealed: 10,000 years on a chalkland farm. Stroud: Tempus.

Haselgrove, C., M. Millett and I. Smith, eds., 1985 Archaeology from the Ploughsoil: studies in the collection and interpretation of field survey data. Sheffield: Sheffield University Press

Higgs, E. S., ed., 1972 Papers in Economic Prehistory: studies by members and associates of the British Academy Major Research Project in the Early History of Agriculture. Cambridge: Cambridge University Press.

——and C. Vita-Finzi, 1972 Prehistoric economies: a territorial approach. *In* Papers in Economic Prehistory. E. S. Higgs, ed. pp. 27–36. Cambridge: Cambridge University Press.

Hind, D. 2004a Where many paths meet: towards an integrated theory of landscape and technology. *In* Stories from the Landscape: archaeologies of inhabitation. A. M. Chadwick, ed. pp. 35–51. Oxford: British Archaeological Reports.

——2004b Picking up the trail: people, landscapes and technology in the Peak District of Derbyshire during the fifth and fourth millennia BC. *In* Stories from the Landscape: archaeologies of inhabitation. A. M. Chadwick, ed. pp. 130–176. Oxford: British Archaeological Reports.

Hodder, I., 1972 Locational models and the study of Romano-British settlement. *In* Models in Archaeology. D. L. Clarke, ed. pp. 887–909. London: Methuen.

Ingold, T., 1986 The Appropriation of Nature: essays on human ecology and social relations. Manchester: Manchester University Press.

——1993 The temporality of the landscape. World Archaeology 25:152–174.

Knight, M., 2002 Finding it Different. Paper given at the Theoretical Archaeology Group, University of Manchester.

Lewis, J., L. Brown and A. Smith, eds., 2006 Landscape Evolution in the Middle Thames Valley: Heathrow Terminal 5 Excavations, vol. 1: Perry Oaks. Oxford: Framework Archaeology.

McFadyen, L., in press Building and architecture as landscape practice. *In* The Handbook of Landscape Archaeology. B. David and J. Thomas, eds. Walnut Creek, CA: Left Coast Press.

Mellars, P. A., 1976 Settlement patterns and industrial variability in the British Mesolithic. *In* Problems in Economic and Social Archaeology. G. Sieveking, I. H. Longworth and K. E. Wilson, eds. pp. 375–99. London: Duckworth.

——and P. Dark, 1998 Star Carr in Context: new archaeological and palaeoecological investigations at the Early Mesolithic site of Star Carr, North Yorkshire. Cambridge: McDonald Institute.

Mithen, S., ed., 2000a Hunter-Gatherer Landscape Archaeology: the southern Hebrides Mesolithic Project 1988–98, vol. 1: Project Development, Palaeoenironmental Studies and Archaeological Fieldwork on Islay. Cambridge: McDonald Institute.

——ed., 2000b Hunter-Gatherer Landscape Archaeology: the southern Hebrides Mesolithic Project 1988–98, vol. 2: Archaeological Fieldwork on Colonsay, Computer Modelling, Experimental Archaeology, and Final Interpretations. Cambridge: McDonald Institute.

Pollard, J., 1999 These places have their moments: thoughts on settlement practices in the British Neolithic. In Making Places in the Prehistoric World: themes in settlement archaeology, J. Brück and M. Goodman, eds. pp. 76–93. London: UCL Press.

——and A. Reynolds, 2002 Avebury: the biography of a landscape. Stroud: Tempus.

Pryor, F., 1998 Etton: excavations of a Neolithic causewayed enclosure near Maxey, Cambridgeshire 1982–7. London: English Heritage.

——2001 The Flag Fen Basin: archaeology and environment of a fenland landscape. London: English Heritage.

Renfrew, A. C., 1973 Monuments, mobilisation and social organisation in Neolithic Wessex. In The Explanation of Culture Change. C. Renfrew, ed. pp. 539–558. London: Duckworth.

Richards, C., 1996 Henges and water: towards an elemental understanding of monumentality and landscape in late Neolithic Britain. Journal of Material Culture 1(3):313–336.

——and J. Thomas, 1984 Ritual activity and structured deposition in Later Neolithic Wessex. In Neolithic Studies: a review of some current research. R. Bradley and J. Gardiner, eds. pp. 189–218. Oxford: British Archaeological Reports.

Richards, J., 1990 The Stonehenge Environs Project. London: English Heritage.

Schadla-Hall, R. T., 1987 Recent investigation of the Early Mesolithic landscape in the Vale of Pickering, East Yorkshire. In Mesolithic Northwest Europe: recent trends. P. Rowley-Conwy, M. Zvelebil and H. Blankholm, eds. pp. 46–54. Sheffield: Department of Archaeology and Prehistory.

——1988 The early post-glacial in eastern Yorkshire. In Archaeology in Eastern Yorkshire: essays presented to T. C. M. Brewster. T. Manby, ed. pp. 25–34. Sheffield: Department of Archaeology and Prehistory.

——1989 The Vale of Pickering in the Early Mesolithic in context. In The Mesolithic in Europe: papers presented at the Third International Symposium in Europe, 1985. C. Bonsall, ed. pp. 218–224. Edinburgh: John Donald.

Schofield, J., ed., 1991 Interpreting Artefact Scatters. Oxford: Oxbow Books.

Spikins, P. A., 2003 Nomadic People of the Pennines: reconstructing the lifestyles of Mesolithic people on Marsden Moor. Leeds: West Yorkshire Archaeological Services.

Thomas, J., 2001 Archaeologies of place and landscape. In Archaeological Theory Today. I. Hodder, ed. pp. 165–186. Cambridge: Polity Press.

Tilley, C., 1994 A Phenomenology of Landscape. Oxford: Berg.

Vita-Finzi, C., 1978 Archaeological Sites in their Setting. London: Thames and Hudson.

Warren, G. 2000 Seascapes: people, boats and inhabiting the later Mesolithic in western Scotland. In Mesolithic Lifeways: current research from Britain and Ireland. R. Young, ed. pp. 97–104. Leicester: Leicester University Monographs.

——2005 Mesolithic Lives in Scotland. Stroud: Tempus.

——2006 Technology. In Mesolithic Britain and Ireland: new approaches. C. Conneller and G. Warren, eds. pp. 13–34. Stroud: Tempus.

6

The Architecture of Monuments

Vicki Cummings

Introduction

The Neolithic period in Britain is marked by the first widespread use of domesticated plants and animals, pottery and polished stone tools, as well as the beginning of the construction of monuments. Over the course of the next two millennia, people built a diverse range of monument forms, from small chambered tombs to massive stone circles. For many years the construction of monuments was primarily understood as an important part of the beginning and establishment of agriculture. However, more recently the idea that settled farming communities were found in this period has been challenged, and our understanding of monuments has broadened. Monuments are no longer regarded as a simple adjunct to farming, but are considered significant in their own right. Archaeologists have suggested that multiple meanings are embedded in monumental architecture which relate to how people understood the world around them. Older interpretations tended to see the meaning of monuments as static and fixed, but more recent approaches emphasise that the meaning of monuments was constantly changing. This chapter seeks to review and summarise some of the most up-to-date and innovative approaches to how archaeologists think about and understand the architecture of monuments. Examples will be drawn from across the British Isles and include sites dating from the Early Neolithic through to the Early Bronze Age.

To begin, it is important to note that monument construction was not found among all early agricultural societies. Monuments were therefore not a prerequisite for people adopting other aspects of Neolithic lifestyles. For example, the Neolithic of south-east and central Europe did not involve the construction of monuments at all (Whittle 1996). In these areas people did create architecture, but in the form of houses. It was only north-west Europe, including Britain and Ireland, that saw the widespread construction of monumental forms from the Early Neolithic onwards. This leads us directly to another important question. What exactly *is* a monument? Traditionally, monuments were considered as constructions that were not used primarily for domestic or subsistence activities. Therefore, houses, like those found in the Neolithic of south-east and central Europe, were not considered to be monuments. Instead, monuments are frequently (although not exclusively) places connected with the burial of the dead. They are also seen as permanent places for people to visit and to remember the dead, and conduct ritual or ceremonial (i.e., non-domestic) activities. The archaeological record of Britain is filled with places that fit this description, and include sites such as stone circles, long barrows and round cairns. However, as we shall see, some monuments share many similarities with houses and "domestic" architecture, while some "houses" have very little evidence of domestic use, so a simple division between domestic (houses) and ritual (monuments) is no longer adequate (see Bradley 2005). Nevertheless, for the purpose of this chapter we shall consider only those sites traditionally described and understood as monuments.

There is insufficient space here to run through all the different types of monument found in Britain in the Neolithic and Early Bronze Age, and good summaries exist elsewhere (Powell et al. 1969; Bradley 1993; Burl 1993; Parker Pearson 1993; Bradley 1998a; Edmonds 1999; Thomas 1999; Cooney 2000; Woodward 2000; Oswald et al. 2001; Harding 2003). However, the monumental evidence from Britain can be divided very roughly into three periods:

- Early Neolithic (ca. 4000–3200 B.C.): chambered tombs; wooden mortuary structures; long barrows; causewayed and tor enclosures; cursus monuments.
- Late Neolithic (ca. 3200–2500 B.C.): henges; stone circles; timber circles; palisades.
- Early Bronze Age (ca. 2500–1500 B.C.): henges and stone circles; timber circles; standing stones; round barrows; round cairns; stone rows.

This is a very simplified classification of monuments, and it is worth noting that there are many other atypical forms of monument found across the British Isles. I will now go on to detail some of the ways in which monumental architecture has been considered.

Monumental Architecture and the Dead

Monuments in Britain are frequently connected with the burial of the dead. The architecture of some monuments such as cairns and mounds containing chambers (known as "chambered tombs") seems to have been specifically designed so that remains of the dead could be housed, while at other monuments such as stone circles remains of the dead have been found associated with these sites. This has led to an enduring connection between monumental architecture and the dead.

Chambered tombs are found in many parts of the British Isles, with concentrations in Wessex, along the shores of the Irish Sea and in northern Scotland (fig. 6.1). These monuments date to the Early Neolithic, with the earliest examples

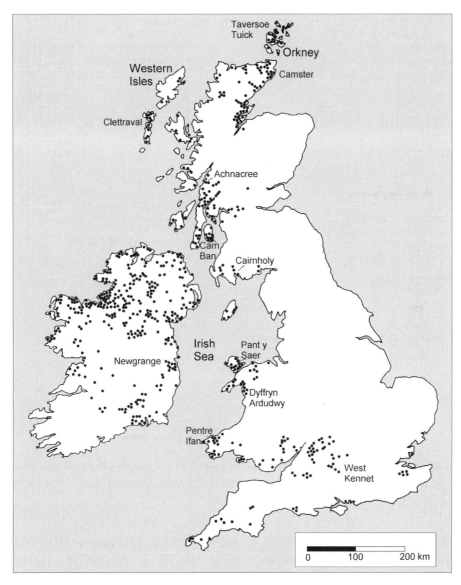

Figure 6.1 The distribution of Early Neolithic stone-built chambered tombs in Britain, with key sites named. This is a schematic representation, to show the overall density and distribution. Ireland alone has more than 700 Early Neolithic chambered tombs.

probably built around 3800 B.C., and were constructed using large stones (megaliths) to create a chamber area (Henshall 1963; 1972; Ashmore 1996; Cummings and Whittle 2004; Darvill 2004). The chamber or chambers were typically, although not always, placed in a long mound or cairn (fig. 6.2). Some sites were built quite quickly, while others were rebuilt and altered many times over hundreds of years. Many of these chambered tombs have been excavated and were found to contain

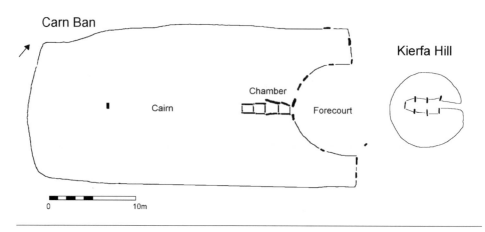

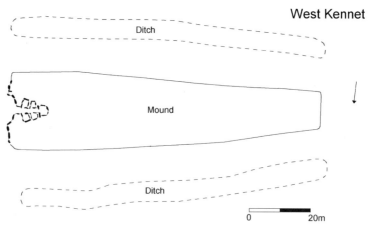

Figure 6.2 Three examples of Early Neolithic stone-built chambered tombs: Carn Ban (Clyde); West Kennet, Wiltshire (Cotswold-Severn); Kierfa Hill (Orkney-Cromarty) (after Henshall 1963; 1972; Pollard and Reynolds 2002).

the remains of the dead, both cremated and unburnt (inhumations). The number of people buried in each of these chambered tombs varies. At Carn Ban on Arran and Taversoe Tuick in Orkney the remains of only a few individuals were found. At other sites such as Hazleton North in Gloucestershire and Pant y Saer in north Wales larger numbers of people were represented, with 41 at Hazleton and 54 at Pant y Saer (Scott 1933; Saville 1990). Interestingly, at some sites no human remains have been found in the chamber: this may relate to poor preservation conditions at some monuments, but it is not the case at all sites and suggests that, although the monuments may have been designed for the burial of the dead, not all were used in this way.

The burial of the dead in the chambered tombs suggests that people built monuments to create places in the landscape for the formal deposition of the dead. The chambered architecture of the monuments not only creates an enclosed space for

the storage of the bones of the dead, but also allows the ancestral relics to be repeatedly accessed over time (see Barrett 1994). Because a number of sites contain
communal burials, it has been argued that the monuments were built to house the
remains of the entire community. In many of the chambers the remains of the dead
were mixed together, which could be understood as emphasising the communality
of the living population, where everyone was considered an equally important part
of society. At others sites such as West Kennet in Wiltshire, however, the monument was divided into compartments (Piggott 1962; see fig. 6.2). At West Kennet,
at least 45 people were buried in the five compartments and each section contained
the remains of different-aged and mixed sex groups. It seems that it was principally
men that were buried in the western, back, chamber. The opposing south-western
and north-western chambers have a mixture of men and women as well as some
children. The south-eastern chamber contained mostly juvenile bones, while the
opposing north-eastern chamber held the bones of older people (Thomas and
Whittle 1986; Pollard and Reynolds 2002). This suggests that architecture could
also be employed to create divisions in the community of the dead.

Architecture, then, may have been designed to reflect the social position of
people in life or in death. This could suggest simple differences between male and
female and the old and the young in Neolithic society. However, many sites contain
only the remains of a few individuals, which demonstrates that the entire community was not always interred. It does show that people thought it necessary and
important for there to be a place for the burial of some of the dead, illustrating the
potential importance of *ancestors* to people in the Early Neolithic (but see Whitley
2002). It remains unresolved as to why some people were buried and others were
not. However, chambered tombs were not the only places used for the deposition
of the dead in the Early Neolithic. Human remains have also been found at causewayed enclosures, in pits (Thomas 1999:68), on shell middens and even in rivers
(Bradley 2000).

From the later Neolithic into the Early Bronze Age, people began to construct
new kinds of enclosures throughout the British Isles – henges, palisades, timber and
stone circles (fig. 6.3). Henges are a diverse form of monument, but usually consist
of a bank and ditch with an internal arrangement of stones or timbers (Harding and
Lee 1987; Gibson 1999; Harding 2003; see fig. 6.4). Stone circles and timber circles
are also a varied form of monument, ranging in size from the massive circle of stones
at Avebury and Stanton Drew to the more modestly sized circles such as those at
Gors Fawr in Pembrokeshire and Sarn-y-bryn-caled in Powys (Barnatt 1989; Gibson
1994; Burl 1995). These monuments are usually not seen as creating places specifically designed for burial. However, some stone circles and henges did receive burials,
often as secondary deposits. At Woodhenge in Wiltshire, the skeleton of a 3-year-
old child was found in a small pit, another skeleton of a young man was found in
a grave in the ditch and cremated human bone was found in one of the post-holes
of the wooden circles (Pollard 1995). At Arbour Low in Derbyshire, the skeleton
of a man was found to the eastern corner of the cove (the central feature), and a
deep pit nearby contained a human arm-bone (Edmonds and Seaborne 2001).
Cremations have also been found at a number of sites such as Llandegai in north

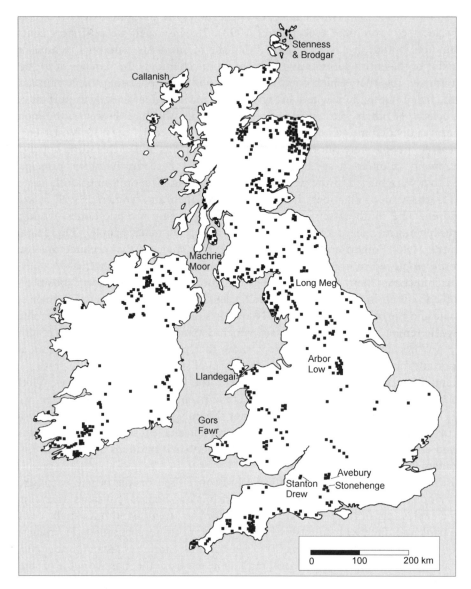

Figure 6.3 The distribution of henges and stone circles in Britain, with key sites named (after Harding and Lee 1987; Burl 1993).

Wales (Houlder 1968), and in exceptional numbers at Stonehenge (Cleal et al. 1995) and Dorchester on Thames (Atkinson et al. 1951).

Parker Pearson and Ramilisonina (1998) have recently reconsidered the burial evidence at these sites and noted that burials are very rarely found associated with wooden circles and henges, but more commonly found at stone monuments. Furthermore, they note that there is plenty of evidence for feasting activity at wooden monuments, but very little evidence for feasting at the stone monuments. They

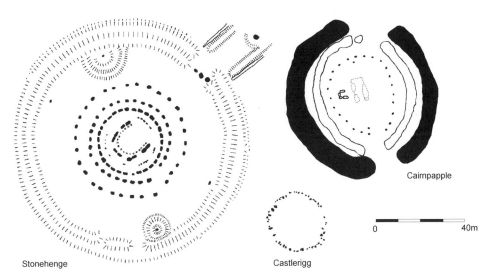

Figure 6.4 Three examples of stone circles and henges: Cairnpapple, Stonehenge and Castlerigg (after Burl 1979; Waterhouse 1985; Cleal et al. 1995).

have suggested therefore that wooden henges and circles were monuments designed to be used by the *living* while stone-built monuments were built exclusively for the dead or ancestors. A good example of this is the complex around Stonehenge. The large wooden monument at Durrington Walls has produced vast quantities of animal bones and pottery (Wainwright and Longworth 1971), while Stonehenge just a short distance away is virtually devoid of similar evidence (Cleal et al. 1995). Parker Pearson and Ramilisonina argue that Durrington Walls was a monument for the living, used for gatherings and feasting, while Stonehenge was reserved as a realm for the ancestral dead. In addition to this, it has been implied that burials found at these monuments represent the growth of important individuals in complete contrast to the earlier communal monuments (e.g., Renfrew 1973).

The implied growth in the importance of the individual at the very end of the Neolithic is reinforced by the appearance of single burials associated with Beaker pottery during this time. The classic example of a Beaker burial is Hemp Knoll in Wiltshire. A coffin containing a male aged 35–45 was found with a bell beaker, an archer's wristguard and a bone toggle. Outside the coffin were an antler tine, the head and hooves of ox plus a child burial. A small round barrow was built over the grave (Robertson-Mackay 1980; Barrett 1994). This monument seems to represent the final resting place for an important person as does the "Amesbury Archer" Beaker burial recently found near Stonehenge (Fitzpatrick 2002).

The importance of the individual seems to have continued into the Early Bronze Age. This period is notable for the widespread construction of round barrows and cairns in large numbers across Britain (about 30,000 are recorded). There are many different forms of barrow, and their different shapes and sizes are due to complex histories of use and construction (Ashbee 1960; Woodward 2000). One feature of the Early Bronze Age burial tradition that has been emphasised in the past, however, is the presence of a single inhumation under a number of round barrows. Bush Barrow in Wiltshire (Kinnes et al. 1988) contained a single male grave with a rich assemblage of material culture including a bronze axe, three daggers, a stone mace-head and gold belt-hook and two lozenges of gold. Again, just like with Beaker burials, these Early Bronze Age monuments can be seen as points in the landscape for the burial of important individuals.

Although the connection between Early Bronze Age barrows and cairns and the dead seems to be clear, the implication that these monuments represent the growth of the individual is problematic. To begin with, barrows frequently contain more than one body. For example, at Barrow 62, Rudston, a multiple grave containing elderly males, three adult men, two adult women, two children and two infants was found (Dymond 1966). Similarly at Winterborne St Martin G46, Dorset, the central grave contained four complete skeletons and disarticulated remains of several others. Furthermore, some barrows have no burials at all. Barrows such as Clandon Barrow, Dorchester, and Lockington, Leicestershire, were found to contain rich artefacts but no burials (Woodward 2000). These mounds have been called "cenotaph barrows" but this assumes that all barrows were designed for burials: it may not have been that simple. Finally, monuments associated with individual burials do not suddenly appear in the Late Neolithic and Early Bronze Age. Single graves and round barrows were actually found from the Early Neolithic onwards (see Thomas 1999).

Monuments, Ritual and Social Practice

Monuments were not simply places for the burial of the dead but also places for various types of social interaction within and between communities. Social gatherings may have been concerned with the deceased, or rites of passage for the dead, but monuments may also have been designed for other forms of ritual and social practice. Many monuments were built to last and therefore provided permanent places in the landscape for people to come together (Bradley 1993). The architecture of different forms of monument seem to have been designed to create a defined arena for social gatherings. For example, chambered tombs and long mounds usually have a forecourt area, a delineated zone in front of the chambers which could accommodate a sizeable group of people. Only a few people would be able to enter the chamber itself, however. Causewayed enclosures also created a central area for the gatherings of people. Dating to the Early Neolithic (built from about 3650 B.C.), these monuments were created by cutting sections of ditch around a central area (fig. 6.5). The Windmill Hill enclosure, for example, is a series of three rings of ditch with causeways between (Whittle et al. 1999). These sites could enclose considerable areas, as with the circuit of ditches at Hambledon Hill, Dorset, which surrounds 65 ha on a hill summit (Mercer 1980; see fig. 6.6); though overall there is much variation in the number of circuits and the size of the areas enclosed (Oswald et al. 2001). These enclosure sites were sometimes in use for hundreds of

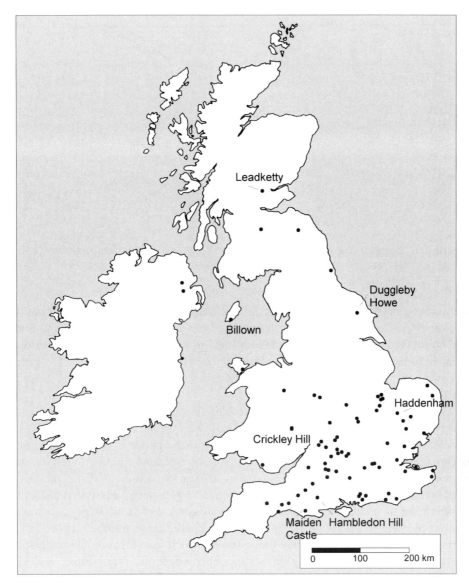

Figure 6.5 The distribution of causewayed enclosures in Britain (after Oswald et al. 2001).

years, and it has been suggested that they were designed as a central locale for the gatherings of a number of dispersed communities. To begin with, they are positioned on the edge of inhabited areas and away from other monuments. There is also evidence of a wide range of practices occurring within these sites. The ditches contain deposits which show that people were dealing with the remains of the dead and also feasting. Deposition seems to have been an important part of rituals, with different forms of material culture found in the ditches. There is also evidence that

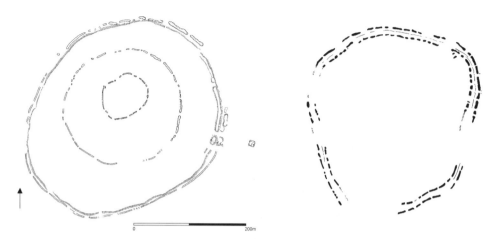

Figure 6.6 Examples of causewayed enclosures: Windmill Hill and Freston (after Oswald et al. 2001).

causewayed enclosures were arenas for exchange. At Windmill Hill, excavations uncovered a number of polished stone axes from as far away as Cornwall, Wales and Cumbria and a large amount of non-local pottery was also found. Enclosures, then, may have been designed as places set away from the everyday, for people to come together, to conduct rituals, for social gatherings and exchange (Oswald et al. 2001).

The architecture of many of the Late Neolithic and Early Bronze Age henges and circles created even larger spaces that could be used for periodic gatherings of people. The largest of these monuments, such as the henge at Avebury (fig. 6.7), enclosed a very sizeable part of the landscape. Superficially, we might imagine such large monuments to have been designed so that many hundreds if not thousands of people could be involved in ritual practices and gatherings. However, a detailed examination of a site like Avebury actually suggests that these large monuments may have been more about *exclusion* than to enable large numbers of people to participate. At Avebury, there are two avenues which lead towards the main stone circle (Pollard and Reynolds 2002). It has been suggested that people processed along these avenues in order to reach the main site. Both avenues, however, are not that wide, and so people would have been forced to walk in a particular order, perhaps with the most important people leading. Once inside the main circle, many thousands of people would have been able to fit inside. However, it seems that the main rituals at Avebury may have been conducted within the Northern or Southern Circles, two smaller yet still massive stone circles set within the main circle (fig. 6.7). Considerably fewer people would have fitted into these smaller circles, perhaps only a select group, and views into these circles from outside is very limited. Within the two smaller circles there are central features: a "cove" (a small rectangular setting of stones) and the Obelisk, a large central stone and an associated stone row). These smaller features may well have been the focus for ritual activity, and

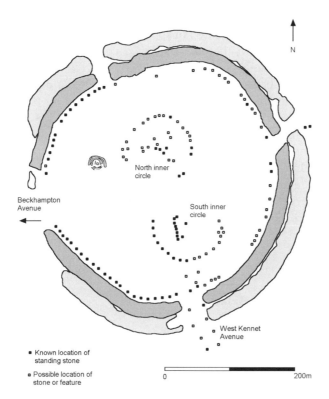

N

Beckhampton
Avenue

North inner
circle

South inner
circle

West Kennet
Avenue

■ Known location of
  standing stone

□ Possible location of
  stone or feature

0   200m

Figure 6.7 The henge monument of Avebury (after Pollard and Reynolds 2002).

in both cases only a few people would have been able to be involved in the rituals. Thus, a site like Avebury contains a series of "nested spaces", which increasingly exclude people, so that only a few individuals could actually be involved in any ceremonies or rituals taking place at the very centre of the site (Barrett 1994; Watson 2001a; Pollard and Reynolds 2002). Other monuments, including Stonehenge, have similar features, which means that only a few people could be present at the centre of the monument and at the heart of ritual activity.

While monuments were clearly used for ritual activities and special gatherings, there is a danger of seeing them as somehow separate from everyday or "domestic" life. As noted at the beginning of the chapter, it is not always that simple. The architecture of monuments may suggest that they were designed to accommodate people for rituals, but in some cases monumental architecture actually reflects house layouts. This is most noticeable in Orkney, where there is an exceptionally well-preserved range of domestic architecture available for study. A series of Early and Late Neolithic settlements and houses are known from across the islands, such as Barnhouse, Knap of Howar and Skara Brae (Childe 1931; Ritchie 1984; Richards 2004a). Colin Richards has demonstrated the existence of a series of connections between Orcadian houses and Late Neolithic henges and passage graves, including the location and orientation of the central hearth, the location of the entrance and the overall organisation of space (Parker Pearson and Richards 1994; Richards 1996). This is not the only suggested connection between monuments and houses. Bradley (1996) and Hodder (1990) suggest that there are so many similarities between fourth-millennium B.C. long mounds in Britain and late sixth- to early fifth-millennium B.C. longhouses on mainland Europe that monument construction must have been inspired by the form of earlier houses. They suggest that the houses of the living (longhouses) became houses of the dead (long mounds). Therefore, in some cases there may have been a direct link between monumental and domestic architecture. Further links exist between ritual and domestic. It seems likely that ritual activity did not occur just at monuments, but was inextricably bound up with everyday life in the same way that aspects of the domestic world were incorporated into monuments. This has prompted the suggestion that the terms "ritual" and "domestic" are not useful when referring to the Neolithic (Bradley 2005).

Monuments and Social Relations

It has already been shown that monumental architecture can be used to understand particular aspects of society. We have seen how the communal deposits in cham- bered tombs may have reflected how societies perceived themselves and how simple divisions in the deposits may reflect basic divisions within society. We have also seen how the discovery of individual burials in round mounds and henges has been interpreted as the growth of important individuals. The idea that architecture is a direct reflection of social relations originates with an important processual paper by Renfrew (1973). Here it was suggested that the social organisation of past com- munities could be determined by studying the architecture of monuments. Renfrew looked at how much effort was invested in the construction of different monuments found in Neolithic Britain. He worked out that each long barrow took about 10,000 hours to build, therefore each one was probably built by a single family. Cause- wayed enclosures, on the other hand, were bigger monuments, each taking about 100,000 hours to construct. This was too much for a single family, so he suggested that causewayed enclosures were the centre of emerging chiefdoms which com- manded a wide territory incorporating a number of family groups. Later Neolithic monuments took much longer to build, with henge monuments requiring around 1 million hours of labour. He argued that these represented full-scale chiefdom societies, with each henge representing the centre of a chiefdom's territory. The only monuments which did not seem to fit in with this pattern were Silbury Hill and Stonehenge. Silbury Hill is a massive mound not far from Avebury that would have taken 10 million hours to build. Stonehenge was an even bigger investment of labour, taking about 30 million hours to construct. He argued that these two monuments must therefore represent a "confederation" of local chiefdoms, where different chiefdom groups worked together on these projects. Therefore, by study- ing the amount of effort needed to build these monuments we can literally "read off" the underlying social system. In this way, monumental architecture was a direct reflection of society.

Recent approaches have explored the relationship between architecture and social order in greater depth. We have already seen how the architecture of the large and complex henge monuments such as Avebury and Stonehenge may have been designed around principles of exclusion. The argument has been taken further by Barrett (1994) who suggests that these were places where power relations are played out: only the privileged or initiated few were allowed access into the centres of monuments. These were the people who held detailed knowledge about ritual practices, which gave them power within society. Monumental architecture thus served to reproduce power relations and maybe even facilitated the growth of important individuals within society.

Although it is extremely attractive to follow suggestions that monumental architecture can be read as reflecting social organisation, others have suggested that it might not be that simple. Shanks and Tilley (1982) have argued that monumental architecture was constructed to mask or hide the nature of society. They discuss the evidence of communal burials from Early Neolithic long barrows. As we have seen, these have been interpreted as having been built to house a community of the dead, perhaps a family or parts of a larger social group. Although not everyone was buried in these monuments, all parts of society are represented: old and young, men and women, and children, which has led many archaeologists to suggest that society was essentially egalitarian. Shanks and Tilley (1982) suggest a different possibility. What if people in the Early Neolithic were anything but equal, and actually lived in a ranked society? Building monuments that gave the *appearance* that everyone (at least in death) was equal effectively hid the inequalities in society. This may have been a clever ploy by those with power and influence to keep themselves in a position of authority. This approach comes from a neo-Marxist theoretical background that suggests that we cannot read social relationships in the archaeological record in a simplistic way.

These arguments do not just apply to Early Neolithic chambered tombs. We have already seen how other monuments have been interpreted. It has been suggested that the large circular spaces of Late Neolithic henge monuments are all about exclusion: essentially the manifestation of a ranked society, or the means of creating one. But there is increasing evidence to suggest that these monuments were not necessarily the result of a ranked society. For example, at Avebury it appears that the massive bank and ditch may have been built in small sections, much like the ditches at earlier causewayed enclosures (Pollard and Reynolds 2002). Instead of these henges being conceived and realised in one massive operation, overseen by big men or chiefs, the monuments may have been built piecemeal over many years. Large sites like Avebury may have been the result of groups of people coming together to work on a communal project. We can see this again at Stonehenge where we know that people came together again and again to rearrange and rework the stones in the circle. The monuments may have been about including as many people as possible and about communicating social identity to other communities.

Monuments as Process

This brings us to another key aspect of how we understand monumental architecture: that it is the construction process itself that was significant, not the finished product. We can see monuments not as static and unchanging points in the landscape, but as places for people to come together and take part in a social event or series of events. Richards (2004b) has discussed the different elements involved in the construction of a monument. In order to construct a chambered tomb, for example, people needed to find an appropriate source of stone, make ropes to move the stones around and store enough food to feed people during the building work. This required a considerable investment of time, labour and negotiation before the construction event or events. Richards (2004b) also suggests that building a monument involved a considerable amount of risk, risk not only in terms of the investment of time, but what if things went wrong? What if a stone that was being dragged across the landscape broke en route? What would this mean to people in terms of their social standing or the auspiciousness of a construction project? We see only successful attempts at monument construction in the archaeological record, but we must also consider the possibility that there were a considerable number of failed attempts as well.

Interesting work has also been undertaken on the construction of long barrows and cairns. We have known for many years that some chambered tombs were built over earlier occupations, as either Late Mesolithic or Early Neolithic activity has been found underneath many such sites (examples include Hazleton North, Gloucestershire (Saville 1990), Gwernvale, Powys (Britnell and Savory 1984), Trefignath, Anglesey (Smith and Lynch 1987) and Glecknabae, Isle of Bute (Henshall 1972)). This suggests people were building monuments in locales that were already known and used and that were significant in the landscape. McFadyen (2003) has also studied the composition of these Early Neolithic monuments and discovered that many seem to have been built from a series of very carefully selected materials. She has argued that monuments were construction sites where people came together at different times to add to the monument. Long cairns were often constructed in small sections or bays where particular sets of material were brought together to make up one particular part of the monument. All the materials selected and used in each monument were significant to the people building the site, perhaps coming from a significant place or incorporating material that belonged to particular people. In this way, chambered tombs were carefully composed, constructed and reworked, with the materials and biographies of people and places interwoven into the fabric of the monument.

The construction process may also have been a crucial part of the meaning of other architectural forms. We have seen how causewayed enclosures consisted of a number of ditch segments. It may be that these monuments were also about communities coming together, perhaps at regular intervals, to add another ditch to the monument (Whittle et al. 1999). In relation to henges, which may also have been community projects essentially, it has been suggested that the sites were continually

in the process of being built (Barrett 1994). At henges and stone circles, the final
stage of the monument may never have been planned, but instead there were simply
a series of construction phases where stones and timbers were added and moved
around. Stonehenge would be the ultimate example of this, where the arrangements
of sarsen and bluestones were constantly being changed over several hundred years
(Cleal et al. 1995).

Although it is appealing to think that people were constantly revisiting and
reworking monuments, and that there was no set blueprint for the finished form of
the site, it should also be remembered that monuments are remarkably similar
across wide areas of Britain. For example, stone circles are found from Orkney to
Cornwall, and there are many characteristics which are common to all these monuments. It would be remarkable if people throughout Britain all managed to build
circular monuments independently. It is a similar situation in the Early Neolithic
where architecturally very similar chambered tombs were constructed throughout
the British Isles. This hints at the possibility of far-reaching contacts between people
in the period and a desire to do things in similar ways throughout the British
Isles.

Monuments and Landscape

Monuments were not isolated points in the landscape, but were intimately connected with their wider settings and environments. Over the past 15 years there has
been a growing interest in the significance of the landscape, particular in relation
to monuments (see Bender 1993; 1998a; 1998b; Cummings and Whittle 2004;
Tilley 1994). Before this the landscape was seen as a kind of backdrop to human
activity or an economic resource (Thomas 1993). People undertook projects such
as building monuments in the landscape, but the landscape itself had little impact
on these activities. However, recent work has emphasized that the landscape surrounding many monuments was an important part of the architecture of the site.

Early Neolithic chambered tombs have been the focus of a number of studies
which have shown that they were very carefully positioned in the landscape in relation to a range of natural features (Tilley 1994; Cummings and Fowler 2004;
Cummings and Whittle 2004). For example, chambered tombs found throughout
western Britain were built in coastal areas, although not on the shore itself. Monuments also seem to have been consistently built so that there were views of mountains as well as the sea. The careful positioning of chambered tombs may have been
an attempt to position the sites in relation to a perceived wider Neolithic community. For example, monuments in western Britain all have views of mountains, and
these mountains are widely inter-visible between areas around the Irish Sea. The
sites also have views of the sea, which connected together different parts of the
country (Cummings 2004). Views of the sea from chambered tombs may also be
a deliberate reference to the origins of the Neolithic, which must ultimately be
sought in Continental Europe. In other cases, monuments seem to have been
carefully positioned close to significant natural features such as rock outcrops. It

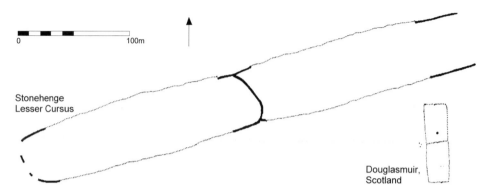

0   100m

Stonehenge
Lesser Cursus

Douglasmuir,
Scotland

Figure 6.8 Examples of cursus monuments (after Barclay and Harding 1999).

has been suggested that the form of some chambered tombs actually mirrored or replicated natural forms like outcrops (Bradley 1998b; Tilley and Bennett 2001; Cummings 2002a), and Neolithic people may not always have been able to tell the difference between a humanly constructed monument and a natural formation. Therefore, it can be suggested that people did not have a conception of "cultural" and "natural" worlds like we do.

By their very scale cursus monuments force us to consider their connection to landscape features. These linear monuments date to the later part of the Early Neolithic, and so were constructed after most chambered tombs and causewayed enclosures. Many cursus monuments are formed by banks and ditches (fig. 6.8), although the sides can also be defined by pits or posts. They vary in size, typically from 200 m to 4 km, although the massive Dorset Cursus is 10 km long (Barclay and Harding 1999). The very nature of these monuments means that they orchestrate the way in which one walks through the landscape. One of their most distinctive characteristics is their position in relation to earlier sites. They often incorporate long barrows into their banks, or are placed alongside long barrows. Cursus monuments also seem to be about viewing other monuments: sites were carefully built so that long barrows are sky-lined as one walks towards them. Chris Tilley has detailed how a person encounters a whole series of important landscape features including earlier barrows when one walks along the Dorset cursus (Tilley 1994). Cursus monuments are also connected to the wider landscape in other ways. It has been noted that they are often associated with rivers (Barclay and Harding 1999; Brophy 2000). A number of them have rivers at their terminal ends. In other instances, people would have to cross water when moving along a cursus, such as along the path of the Dorset cursus (Tilley 1994). At other sites, such as Holm in south-west Scotland, the cursus runs parallel to a river (Thomas 1998). This has led to suggestions that the flow of the river was analogous to the movement of people along the cursus. Water is also repeatedly visible at monuments, which may be related to its importance in ritual activity (Richards 1996).

Figure 6.9 The setting of Swinside stone circle, Cumbria.

Later Neolithic monuments also seem to have been fitted into the landscape very carefully. In the case of stone circles and henges, the circular architecture of these monuments is frequently reflected in their wider setting. For example, sites such as Long Meg and her Daughters and Castlerigg in Cumbria, and Avebury and Stonehenge in Wiltshire, are all circular monuments that are encircled by the surrounding landscape (Richards 1996; Bradley 1998a; Watson 2001a; see fig. 6.9). From these sites the monument sits as if at the very centre of the surrounding landscape, with wide views in all directions, which creates the sense of being inside another circular space. In this way, the circular space of the henge or stone circle reflects the wider circular landscape. This has led to the idea that monuments represent the surrounding landscape in miniature and are therefore a *microcosm* of the wider world (Richards 1996; Bradley 1998a). The concept has been explored at the two henge sites on mainland Orkney, the Stones of Stenness and the Ring of Brodgar. These sites are positioned between two lochs so that they both appear to be surrounded by water. Beyond the lochs are a ring of hills which encircle the site. The ditch and bank at each of the henges seem to mirror the local topography, the outer bank as the outer ring of hills and the ditch as the surrounding water. We know that the ditches were actually waterlogged for much of the year, so the stone circles were literally surrounded by water (ditch) and hills (bank) (Richards 1996).

Early Bronze Age barrows and cairns were also carefully positioned in the landscape. Due to differential preservation, many of the best-known sites are found in prominent locations so there is a tendency to think of barrows as being located on top of hills and ridges. However, many barrows actually cluster in valley locations, frequently near springs and streams (Woodward and Woodward 1996). Many Early

Bronze Age barrows seem to have been positioned so that they were visible in certain ways from particular places. This is very clear with the siting of barrows around Stonehenge which seem to be positioned so that they encircle the henge when one stands at its centre and are clearly visible on the horizon (Woodward and Woodward 1996; Watson 2001b).

Like earlier sites, Early Bronze Age barrows are not isolated points in the landscape, but may have been designed to be viewed and approached in particular ways. There are sometimes connecting ditches between barrows, which may have been built in order to channel movement between sites in a prescribed manner (Woodward 2000). The specific setting of individual sites in the landscape may also be important. Many barrows are positioned in relation to pre-existing sites such as henges. At Stanton Harcourt in Oxfordshire, for example, there was a long sequence of activity from the Middle Neolithic through into the Bronze Age. Middle Neolithic burials were followed by the construction henge and rich Beaker graves, then a series of Early Bronze Age graves and barrows (Lambrick and Allen 2004).

Monuments as Places for Experience

One of the characteristics of monumental architecture is its ability to create a wide range of experiences for people engaging with these sites. We could even go as far as to suggest that monuments were specifically designed to create distinctive experiences for people engaging with them, experiences which may have taken them to other worlds.

As we have already seen, Early Neolithic chambered tombs typically consist of stone-built chambers which frequently contained the remains of the dead. The chamber was sometimes entered along a passage or directly from the forecourt. However the chambers were entered, the architecture was designed so that there was room for only one person, or at the very most a few people, to enter the chamber at any time. Once inside there would be little room to move around. The interior of the monument, closed off from daylight, would be dark or illuminated only by fire. It may have been smoky or damp, and once burials were placed in the chamber, the interior of the monument would also smell of bones and decay and death. To enter one of these dark and enclosed spaces would have been a distinctive and emotive experience. It may have felt like entering another world, entering the earth and the world of the dead.

Other aspects of chambered tombs may have added to the supernatural or otherworldly experience of these places. The kind of rituals we might envisage going on would have produced sound, and there is even evidence of the production of music at chambered tombs: a bone flute was recovered from one of the chambers at Penyrwyrlod, south-east Wales (Britnell and Savory 1984). Acoustic tests have been conducted at a series of chambered tombs in Britain which showed that the use of sound in these sites would have created remarkable effects (Watson and Keating 1999; Watson 2001c). When sounds are produced inside a monument, their source is often unclear, and can appear to be inside the listener's head. They also often get louder instead of quieter the further away the listener is from the source. It is possible that Neolithic people may have attributed such effects to the dead or to supernatural forces. It has also been found that it is possible to create Helmholtz resonance through drumming in monuments. This is basically the reverberation of sound waves, but it has very distinctive effects on people. It can lead to feelings of nausea, speaking difficulties and headaches. This may ultimately have led to people entering altered states of consciousness, which may have been an important part of the ritual experience of the monuments.

There is further evidence for people attempting to attain altered states of consciousness in chambered tombs. Pottery deposited at these monuments may well have been used for the consumption of alcohol, and there is also limited evidence for the use of narcotics in Neolithic Britain (Sherratt 1991). There is thus the possibility that people took mind-altering substances at these sites. Furthermore, in Ireland a number of passage graves have been inscribed with rock art which, it has been suggested, was associated with altered states of consciousness (Dronfield 1995a; 1995b). The rock art on monuments such as Newgrange is very similar to art produced in a state of hallucination, and it has been suggested that rock art on passage graves could well have been produced by people using hallucinogenic substances. Altered states did not necessarily require narcotics, but could be induced by other means such as dancing, fasting or sound effects. It has been noted that many chambered tombs are constructed from stones of different colours and textures (Jones 1999; Cummings 2002b) which may also have added to the distinctive and surreal quality of these monuments.

The architecture of chambered tombs may thus have been specifically designed to create a range of very distinctive experiences for people. They may have been considered liminal places, locales for journeying between the worlds of the living and the dead. Furthermore, they can be considered special places built to create extraordinary experiences for the people encountering them. The acoustics, colours, textures and rock art would all have heightened the mystery and other-worldly experience offered by the monument.

It was not just chambered tombs which created distinctive experiences for people encountering them. The builders of stone circles, henges and Early Bronze Age cairns also incorporated distinctive coloured and textured materials into their monuments (Bradley 1989; Whittle 1997). Sound may also have produced interesting and confusing effects at henges and stone circles (Watson 2001c). A number of the later sites also have lunar and solar alignments, which added another element to the experience. The most famous example of a monument incorporating a solar alignment into its architecture is Stonehenge. At this site, a narrow beam of direct sunlight from the midsummer sunrise illuminates the very centre of the monument (Ruggles 1998). Very few people would have been able to stand at the heart of Stonehenge and observe the shaft of light entering this central point. It should be noted that the midwinter sunset may also have been significant at this site (Ruggles 1998). In a similar way, the architecture of recumbent stone circles in Aberdeenshire references the rising of the moon. Recumbent stone circles consist of a ring of standing stones that typically rise in height towards the south-west, where a recumbent block (a stone lying on its side) is flanked by the tallest monoliths. The recumbent stone in these stone circles is aligned on moonrise, so that the moon appears between the tallest uprights over the recumbent. At these sites the builders of the circles also included quartz which reflects light and shines white just like the moon (Burl 1993; Bradley 2004). Just as at chambered tombs, then, people may have encountered a whole range of distinctive and other-worldly experiences which, without scientific explanation, may have been interpreted in spiritual ways.

The Changing Role of Monuments over Time

Monuments endure (Bradley 1993). Stone-built architecture in particular created permanent places in the landscape to which people could repeatedly return. There is substantial evidence for many of these monuments being in use for long periods of time, although this is not ubiquitous. Some monuments fell out of use quite quickly, while other sites were visited and used over long periods of time. What is crucial is that at the sites which were used for hundreds, and in some cases thousands, of years, their meaning changed over time. Some chambered tombs, for example, seem to have started out as simple clearings where people gathered and dwelt. Some of the clearings were then subsequently chosen as a suitable location for the construction of a monument. Once constructed, the monument became a place for rituals involving both the living and placement of the dead. In some cases, deposition seems to have occurred over many hundreds of years, but at some sites human remains were placed in the chambers for only a few decades. At this stage, some sites fell out of use. Perhaps they were no longer considered important, or their meaning or purpose in society was forgotten or lost. At many other chambered tombs people sealed the chambers and blocked the forecourts so that deposits could no longer be made. Here we can see a shift in the meaning and use of the monuments. They change from being places which were actively used for deposition to places closed off and no longer accessible. This has led to the suggestion that chambered tombs now became realms of the long-dead ancestors.

Some sites, however, were subsequently reused. At West Kennet the chambers of the long barrow were reopened and fresh deposits placed within them on several occasions during the earlier and later Neolithic (Thomas and Whittle 1986). At a number of Clyde and Bargrennan chambered tombs in western Scotland, Early Neolithic monuments had their contents removed or pushed to one side and Early Bronze Age deposits added, such as at Cairnholy in Dumfries and Galloway. At Cairnderry, also in south-west Scotland, a series of Early Bronze Age cremations were placed around the edge of the chambered tomb. This suggests that the meaning of the monument had changed; earlier deposits no longer seem to be valued. However, the monuments themselves were obviously still considered important places and suitable for the burial of the dead. The meaning of chambered tombs, then, may have changed many times over the course of a few lifetimes, from being a place of dwelling, to being a construction site, a monument used for the burial of the dead and for gatherings, feasting and other-worldly experiences, to a location sealed off from the living.

Henges and stone circles also had complex histories of use and their meanings almost certainly changed over time. The location of these sites had frequently been used prior to the construction of the monument, so they began as known locales in the landscape. At Avebury, it has been suggested that the sarsen stones that were used in the stone circles were important places in the surrounding landscape *before* they were used in the henge (Gillings and Pollard 1999). At this site, then, people brought together bits of other places so that the monument was a combination of other locales and other meanings. At other sites we see evidence of a complex sequence of reworkings, such as at Stonehenge where the sarsens and bluestones were moved around into different configurations. And as we have seen, henges were subsequently the focus for burials, as well as for the placing of Bronze Age barrows, which suggests that monuments that were initially constructed for use by the living changed into places for the burial of the dead. Eventually, as these sites became less and less meaningful to the living, all monuments fell out of use. Some sites were reused or altered in the Middle Bronze Age, but most Neolithic sites were abandoned well before the Late Bronze Age.

Conclusions

In this chapter it has been suggested that monuments were not just empty spaces for people to use, but places where communities could create multiple meanings through architectural form. In the past, many interpretations of monumental architecture focused on classification and typology, with a strong interest in finding the origins of the British Neolithic in Europe. More recently, however, post-processual archaeology has emphasised the importance of how monumental architecture was perceived, experienced and used. Monuments are now seen as providing arenas for the gathering of people, the treatment of the dead and the exchange of material culture, and marking out special places and events. These were not isolated locales, but connected to the wider landscape. Through the detailed study of many different aspects and elements of a monument, from the biography of the stones used to build a monument to the depositional practices undertaken at sites, we can begin to think about the meaning that these places had in people's lives. It is critical that we do not assign a single meaning or interpretation to any one site, as meanings would have changed over time. Furthermore, monuments were not exclusively about ritual activity and there were considerable overlaps with everyday practices. In this way monuments were not isolated from broader society, but were embedded within social worlds, social identity and a broad understanding of the world.

ACKNOWLEDGEMENTS

Thanks are due to the Leverhulme Trust who currently support my research into megalithic architecture through an Early Career Fellowship. I would also like to thank Josh for giving me the opportunity to write this chapter, and for his useful comments on an earlier draft.

REFERENCES

Ashbee, P., 1960 The Bronze Age Round Barrow in Britain. London: Phoenix.

Ashmore, P., 1996 Neolithic and Bronze Age Scotland. Edinburgh: Historic Scotland.

Atkinson, R., C. Piggott and N. Sandars, 1951 Excavations at Dorchester, Oxon. Oxford: Ashmolean Museum.

Barclay, A., and J. Harding, eds., 1999 Pathways and Ceremonies: the cursus monuments of Britain and Ireland. Oxford: Oxbow Books.

Barnatt, J., 1989 Stone Circles of Britain. Oxford: British Archaeological Reports.

Barrett, J. C., 1994 Fragments from Antiquity. Oxford: Blackwell.

Bender, B., ed., 1993 Landscape: politics and perspectives. Oxford: Berg. – 1998 Stonehenge: making space. Oxford: Berg.

Bradley, R., 1989 Darkness and light in the design of megalithic tombs. Oxford Journal of Archaeology 8:251–259.

——1993 Altering the Earth. Edinburgh: Society of Antiquaries of Scotland Monograph.

——1996 Long houses, long mounds and Neolithic enclosures. Journal of Material Culture 1:239–256.

——1998a The Significance of Monuments: on the shaping of human experience in Neolithic and Bronze Age Europe. London: Routledge.

——1998b Ruined buildings, ruined stones: enclosures, tombs and natural places in the Neolithic of south-west England. World Archaeology 30:13–22.

——2000 The Archaeology of Natural Places. London: Routledge.

——2004 The Moon and the Bonfire: an investigation of three stone circles in NE Scotland. Edinburgh: Society of Antiquaries of Scotland Monograph.

——2005 Ritual and Domestic Life in Prehistoric Europe. London: Routledge.

Britnell, W., and H. Savory, 1984 Gwernvale and Penywyrlod: two Neolithic long cairns in the Black Mountains of Brecknock. Bangor: Cambrian Archaeological Association.

Brophy, K., 2000 Water coincidence? Cursus monuments and rivers. In Neolithic Orkney in its European Context. A Ritchie, ed. pp. 59–70. Oxford: Oxbow.

Burl, A., 1979 Prehistoric Avebury. Yale: Yale University Press.

——1993 From Carnac to Callanish: the prehistoric stone rows and avenues of Britain, Ireland and Brittany. Yale: Yale University Press.

——1995 A Guide to the Stone Circles of Britain, Ireland and Brittany. Yale: Yale University Press.

Childe, V.G., 1931 Skara Brae. London: Keagan Paul.

Cleal, R.M.J, K. Walker and R. Montague, 1995 Stonehenge in its Landscape: twentieth-century excavations. London: English Heritage.

Cooney, G., 2000 Landscapes of Neolithic Ireland. London: Routledge.

Cummings, V., 2002a All cultural things: actual and conceptual monuments in the Neolithic of Western Britain. In Monuments and Landscape in Atlantic Europe. C. Scarre, ed. pp. 107–121. London: Routledge.

——2002b Texturing the past: experiencing texture and transformation in the British Neolithic. Oxford Journal of Archaeology 21:249–261.

——2004 Connecting the mountains and sea: the monuments of the eastern Irish Sea zone. *In* The Neolithic of the Irish Sea: materiality and traditions of practice. V. Cummings and C. Fowler, eds. pp. 29–36. Oxford: Oxbow Books.

Cummings, V., and C. Fowler, eds., 2004 The Neolithic of the Irish Sea: materiality and traditions of practice. Oxford: Oxbow Books.

Cummings, V., and A. Whittle, 2004 Places of Special Virtue: megaliths in the Neolithic landscapes of Wales. Oxford: Oxbow Books.

Darvill, T., 2004 Long Barrows of the Cotswolds and Surrounding Areas. Stroud: Tempus.

Dronfield, J., 1995a Migraine, light and hallucinogens: the neurocognitive basis of Irish megalithic art. Oxford Journal of Archaeology 14:261–275.

——1995b Subjective vision and the source of Irish megalithic art. Antiquity 69:539–549.

Dymond, D., 1966 Ritual monuments at Rudston, East Yorkshire, England. Proceedings of the Prehistoric Society 32:86–95.

Edmonds, M., 1999 Ancestral Geographies of the Neolithic: landscape, monuments and memory. London: Routledge.

——and T. Seaborne, 2001 Prehistory in the Peak. Stroud: Tempus.

Fitzpatrick, A., 2002 "The Amesbury Archer": a well furnished Early Bronze Age burial in southern England. Antiquity 76:629–630.

Gibson, A., 1994 Excavations at the Sarn-y-bryn-caled cursus complex, Welshpool, Powys, and the timber circles of Great Britain and Ireland. Proceedings of the Prehistoric Society 60:143–224.

——1999 The Walton Basin Project: excavation and survey in a prehistoric landscape 1993–7. York: Council for British Archaeology.

Gillings, M., and J. Pollard, 1999 Non-portable stone artefacts and contexts of meaning: the tale of Grey Wether. World Archaeology 31:179–193.

Harding, A., and G. Lee, 1987 Henge Monuments and Related Sites of Great Britain. Oxford: British Archaeological Reports.

Harding, J., 2003 The Henge Monuments of the British Isles. Stroud: Tempus.

Henshall, A., 1963 The Chambered Tombs of Scotland, vol. 1. Edinburgh: Edinburgh University Press.

——1972 The Chambered Tombs of Scotland, vol. 2. Edinburgh: Edinburgh University Press.

Hodder, I., 1990 The Domestication of Europe. Oxford: Blackwell.

Houlder, C., 1968 The henge monuments at Llandegai. Antiquity 43:216–221.

Jones, A., 1999 Local colour: megalithic architecture and colour symbolism in Neolithic Arran. Oxford Journal of Archaeology 18:339–350.

Kinnes, I., I. Longworth, I. M. Mcintyre, S. Needham and W. A. Oddy, 1988 Bush Barrow gold. Antiquity 62:24–39.

Lambrick, G., and T. Allen, 2004 Gravelly Guy, Stanton Harcourt: the development of a prehistoric and Romano-British community. Oxford: Oxford Archaeology.

McFadyen, L., 2003 A Revision of the Materiality of Architecture: the significance of Neolithic long mound and chambered monument building practice, with particular reference to the Cotswold-Severn group. PhD thesis, University of Wales, Newport.

Mercer, R., 1980 Hambledon Hill: a Neolithic landscape. Edinburgh: Edinburgh University Press.

Oswald, A., C. Dyer and M. Barber, 2001 The Creation of Monuments: Neolithic causewayed enclosures in the British Isles. London: English Heritage.

Parker Pearson, M., 1993 Bronze Age Britain. London: English Heritage.

——and Ramilisonina, 1998 Stonehenge for the ancestors: the stones pass on the message. Antiquity 72:308–326.

——and C. Richards, 1994 Architecture and order: spatial representation and archaeology. *In* Architecture and Order. M. Parker Pearson and C. Richards, eds. pp. 38–72. London: Routledge.

Piggott, S., 1962 The West Kennet Long Barrow: excavations 1955–6. London: Her Majesty's Stationery Office.

Pollard, J., 1995 Inscribing space: formal deposition at the later Neolithic monument of Woodhenge, Wiltshire. Proceedings of the Prehistoric Society 61:137–156.

——and A. Reynolds, 2002 Avebury: the biography of a landscape. Stroud: Tempus.

Powell, T., J. X. W. P. Corcoran, F. Lynch and J. G. Scott, eds., 1969 Megalithic Enquiries in the West of Britain. Liverpool: Liverpool University Press.

Renfrew, C., 1973 Monuments, mobilisation and social organisation in Neolithic Wessex. *In* The Explanation of Culture Change. C. Renfrew, ed. pp. 539–558. London: Duckworth.

Richards, C., 1996 Henges and water: towards an elemental understanding of monumentality and landscape in late Neolithic Britain. Journal of Material Culture 1:313–336.

——2004a Dwelling among the Monuments: an examination of the Neolithic village of Barnhouse. Cambridge: Macdonald Institute.

——2004b Labouring with monuments: constructing the dolmen at Carreg Samson, southwest Wales. *In* The Neolithic of the Irish Sea: materiality and traditions of practice. V. Cummings and C. Fowler, eds. pp. 72–80. Oxford: Oxbow Books.

Ritchie, A., 1984 Excavation of a Neolithic farmstead at Knap of Howar, Papa Westray, Orkney. Proceedings of the Society of Antiquaries of Scotland 113:40–121.

Robertson-Mackay, M., 1980 A "head and hoofs" burial beneath a round barrow on Hemp Knoll, near Avebury. Proceedings of the Prehistoric Society 46:123–176.

Ruggles, C., 1998 Ritual astronomy in the Neolithic and Bronze Age British Isles: patterns of continuity and change. *In* Prehistoric Ritual and Religion. A. Gibson and D. Simpson, eds. pp. 203–208. Stroud: Sutton.

Saville, A., 1990 Hazleton North: the excavation of a Neolithic long cairn of the Cotswold-Severn group. London: English Heritage.

Scott, W., 1933 The chambered tomb of Pant y Saer, Anglesey. Archaeologia Cambrensis 38:185–228.

Shanks, M., and C. Tilley, 1982 Ideology, symbolic power and ritual communication: a reinterpretation of Neolithic mortuary practices. *In* Symbolic and Structural Archaeology. I. Hodder, ed. pp. 129–154. Cambridge: Cambridge University Press.

Sherratt, A., 1991 Sacred and profane substances: the ritual use of narcotics in Later Neolithic Europe. *In* Sacred and Profane. P. Garwood, D. Jennings, R. Skeates and J. Toms, eds. pp. 50–64. Oxford: Oxford University Committee for Archaeology.

Smith, C., and F. Lynch, 1987 Trefignath and Din Dryfol: the excavation of two megalithic tombs in Anglesey. Bangor: Cambrian Archaeological Association.

Thomas, J., 1993 The politics of vision and the archaeologies of landscape. *In* Landscape: politics and perspectives. B. Bender, ed. pp. 19–48. Oxford: Berg.

——1998 Holm, Dumfries: excavations 1998. Interim report. Available at http://www.arch. soton.ac.uk/Research/Dunragit/Holm98.htm.

——1999 Understanding the Neolithic. London: Routledge.

——and A. Whittle, 1986 Anatomy of a tomb: West Kennet revisited. Oxford Journal of Archaeology 5:129–156.

Tilley, C., 1994 A Phenomenology of Landscape. Oxford: Berg.

——and W. Bennett, 2001 An archaeology of supernatural places: the case of West Penwith. Journal of the Royal Anthropological Institute 7:335–362.

Wainwright, G., and I. Longworth, 1971 Durrington Walls: excavations 1966–1968. London: Society of Antiquaries.

Waterhouse, J., 1985 The Stone Circles of Cumbria. Chichester: Phillimore.

Watson, A., 2001a Composing Avebury. World Archaeology 33:296–314.

——2001b Round barrows in a circular world: monumentalising landscapes in early Bronze Age Wessex. In Bronze Age Landscapes. J. Brück, ed. pp. 207–216. Oxford: Oxbow Books.

——2001c The sounds of transformation: acoustics, monuments and ritual in the British Neolithic. In The Archaeology of Shamanism. N. Price, ed. pp. 178–192. London: Routledge.

——and D. Keating, 1999 Architecture and sound: an acoustic analysis of megalithic monuments in prehistoric Britain. Antiquity 73:325–336.

Whitley, J., 2002 Too many ancestors. Antiquity 76:119–126.

Whittle, A., 1996 Europe in the Neolithic: the creation of new worlds. Cambridge: Cambridge University Press.

——1997 Remembered and imagined belongings: Stonehenge in its traditions and structures of meaning. In Science and Stonehenge. B. Cunliffe and C. Renfrew, eds. pp. 145–166. Oxford: Oxford University Press.

——J. Pollard and C. Grigson, 1999 The Harmony of Symbols: the Windmill Hill causewayed enclosure, Wiltshire. Oxford: Oxbow Books.

Woodward, A., 2000 British Barrows: a matter of life and death. Stroud: Tempus.

——and P. Woodward, 1996 The topography of some barrow cemeteries in Bronze Age Wessex. Proceedings of the Prehistoric Society 62:275–291.

7

Lithic Technology and the *Chaîne Opératoire*

Chantal Conneller

Lithic Studies and British Prehistory

The manufacture and use of stone tools spans the earliest appearance of hominids in Britain to the historic period (Martingel 2003), though most archaeological studies of lithic material concentrate on the earlier periods of prehistory, particularly before the use of metal. The focus of these studies differs throughout early prehistory, conditioned in part by the research history of each period, but also by the nature of the evidence. Palaeolithic researchers have access, on the one hand, to individual artefacts representing the work of a single moment in time and, on the other, to palimpsests representing repeated actions spanning hundreds of thousands of years. With a few notable exceptions, such as the site of Boxgrove in Sussex (Roberts and Parfitt 1999), their data is unsuitable for interrogating intermediate time scales, which provide information on the role of technology in daily life. Palaeolithic data is difficult and the response has been ingenious studies, which by necessity focus on such issues as the use of raw materials, mobility in the landscape and technological change over long time scales. Approaches to lithic technology in the Palaeolithic are beyond the scope of this chapter, though some of the more important studies from this period are briefly touched on.

More contextual information is available for the Neolithic and often also the Mesolithic to help understand the role of technology in social life. Researchers in these periods also deal with palimpsests, but these can more easily be picked apart and interpreted in terms of generational or even more intimate scales of action. It is probably no coincidence that it is through the study of the Neolithic that Mark Edmonds (Bradley and Edmonds 1993; Edmonds 1995; 1997) has introduced social approaches to lithic technology into British prehistory. However, despite Edmonds's work and the rich datasets that exist, there has been a relative paucity of lithic studies (beyond basic reporting) in the British Neolithic; instead work on monuments has dominated much research. This contrasts with recent approaches to Mesolithic archaeology, where, following a period when lithic material was undervalued, artefact studies and technological approaches are flourishing and have become the mainstay of interpretation. Because the Mesolithic lacks the large monuments that have dominated Neolithic studies, recent research has been characterised by exhaustive studies of the artefactual evidence, which has produced a very detailed understanding of the intricacies of Mesolithic life.

New Approaches to Technology

In 1987 Peter Rowley-Conwy suggested that Mesolithic sites where organic materials were not preserved should not be excavated, since lithic (mostly flint) artefacts by themselves did not provide sufficiently interesting information to make this worth while (Rowley-Conwy 1987). This statement reflects the perception of lithic studies at the time. Much of the dynamism and creativity of early accounts had become stagnated in culture–function debates, typified by the dispute between Bordes and Binford over Mousterian industries in south-west France, where the former argued that lithic variability was the product of five distinct tribes and the latter that it represented the presence of distinct functional toolkits (Binford 1973). Such debates were replayed on a smaller scale in British prehistory, with reference to the Mesolithic (Mellars 1976), or in the context of the Lower Palaeolithic Clactonian debate, with the Clatonian either considered a culture or a functional component of the Acheulean (see White 2000).

A related problem for lithic studies has been the ascendancy of processual archaeology, which placed significant weight on faunal remains as economic indicators (Finlay 2000), and on the economy and environment as driving forces of social change. Attempts were made to use lithic material as a proxy gauge of the economy and the scheduling of resources. Myers (1987; 1989), for example, has argued that a switch to arrowheads incorporating a larger number of microlithic components during the late Mesolithic was part of an economic strategy designed to maximise available time and minimise risk through the adoption of a maintainable technology. This, he argues, became advantageous as encroaching forests favoured more solitary animals over the herds that had characterised open landscapes. This meant hunting was not concentrated during seasonal herd migrations, but took place all year round, resulting in a decrease in quiet periods in which to gear up by manufacturing and repairing hunting tools. In this context, tools with greater numbers of microlithic components would be more efficient, since if they were damaged they could still be used until the hunter had spare time to repair the tool.

Despite Myers's efforts, while economic concerns were primary, lithic studies could only ever be second best to faunal studies, which are, after all, a much better indicator of what people ate and how they procured it. However, in recent years, with the introduction of symbolic and subsequent interpretative approaches to archaeology, the potential of lithic studies for understanding past societies has begun to be recognised. This stems from a more complex understanding of technology and its role in both modern and prehistoric societies. Technology in past societies is increasingly being seen as inseparable from other aspects of social life.

Technology and Techniques

The impetus for new approaches to technology stems from the realisation of just how specific Western understandings of technology are. Technology is equated with rationality and objectivity and viewed as the means of our increasing mastery over nature. Dobres (2000) has traced the meaning of the concept "technology" from its Enlightenment origins to its modern usage, as a body of rational knowledge capable of practical application. She points out that archaeological usage of the term has been central to evolutionary views of man's progressive control of nature. In a similar vein, Ingold (1990:8; 1993a) has contrasted "technology" and "techniques", viewing the former as an objectified, discursive body of knowledge, capable of being imposed on material. Such concepts, he suggests, are closely linked to the marginalisation of the technician from the centre of the productive process in modern Western society and his/her replacement with a machine. By contrast, he uses the term "techniques" to describe situations in which the skilled individual is at the heart of a manufacturing process that is embedded in social relations. Ingold suggests that this is a more realistic representation of technology in small-scale societies.

However, a number of social theorists question the extent to which such a distinction between Western and non-Western societies is helpful. The philosopher of science Bruno Latour, for example, argues that Western representations of technology (both academic and folk) as something opposed to society misrepresent the ways in which people and things are always in practice intermingled and conjoined (Latour 1996). Technology for Latour is the product of imagining a domain of "things" as though it were separate from the domain of people or society. In fact, he suggests, this is never the case even in the West. Rather than there being a qualitative difference between Western and non-Western societies, Western networks are simply longer, composed of more things and people. In other words, the difference between Western and non-Western technologies is quantitative rather than qualitative and therefore a matter of degree not kind.

In a somewhat different vein, others have attempted to deconstruct a Western–non-Western opposition by demonstrating the extent to which non-functional social logic also plays its part in modern technologies (Lemmonier 1993). So despite Western self-representations in which technological efficacy is imagined in purely functional terms, these writers emphasise that social and subjective factors are in fact central in understanding how technologies do or do not work. Both anthropologists and philosophers of science have noted that it is not functional efficiency but social mores that can lead to the acceptance or rejection of particular technological innovations, in industrial and small-scale societies alike. Understandings derived from these anthropological and sociological studies have led archaeologists to think in new ways about technology. For example, they have led to questions concerning the ways in which technologies are socially determined and accepted, and the role of technology in extending and mediating relations between people. In addition a more specifically archaeological approach, the concept of the *chaîne opératoire*, has been an important theoretical and methodological influence on work on prehistoric Britain.

The *Chaîne Opératoire*

The *chaîne opératoire* refers to the entire sequence of technological actions: from the procurement of raw material, through manufacturing, use, resharpening and recycling to discard. As such it is very similar to the American concept of "reduction sequences", and there has been considerable debate about whether the two concepts are equivalent. The *chaîne opératoire* is increasingly used as a methodology to trace sequences of technological action, and in this sense it is equivalent to the concept of the reduction sequence. However the *chaîne opératoire* as a theoretical approach incorporates an additional element in that technology is conceived as a socially transmitted body of knowledge, as a socialised suite of gestures on matter. So the gestures used in any technological sequence will be socially specific, dependent on the particular way each society has of proceeding, but also on other factors, such as personal skill and individual or group identity. This conception of techniques as socially determined derives from the work of Mauss (1979) who described how seemingly universal techniques of the body, such as walking and swimming, were actually socially specific and varied over time. Though Mauss's work demonstrates that techniques need not necessarily incorporate physical objects, archaeological studies, as might be expected, have focused on the interplay between techniques and materials. The *chaîne opératoire* has been a concept that has informed the study of both bone tools and pottery; however, the majority of archaeologically based studies of the *chaîne opératoire* have focused on lithic material, since such artefacts represent technology which is both ubiquitous and subtractive.[1]

Technical action, in studies of the *chaîne opératoire*, has generally been seen as the product of a balance between a learned body of knowledge and individual experience or skill; between routine mechanical action and conscious decisions and choices (Leroi-Gourhan 1993[1964]). Recent applications of the *chaîne opératoire* in archaeology tend to take two forms: the techno-psychological, and the techno-sociological (Karlin and Julien 1994). Techno-psychological approaches focus on the cognitive aspect of technology and attempt to reconstruct the types of knowledge employed in technical sequences. Pelegrin (1990), for example, has distinguished conceptual knowledge (*connaissances*), which corresponds to mental representations of ideal forms and sequences, from know-how (*savoir-faire*), which is the product of memory and bodily practice. The cognitive approach has been important in exploring the abilities of pre-modern humans. Schlanger (1996) has examined the cognitive abilities of Neanderthals through the study of two Levallois sequences from the site of Maastricht-Belvedere in the Netherlands. He has argued that the Neanderthals who occupied the site, rather than behaving like automata and imposing an inflexible manufacturing sequence on the raw material, had the ability to act creatively and flexibly. They were able to modify their work when needed if problems – or new potentials – arose due to the nature of the raw material.

Techno-sociological approaches, in contrast, attempt a palaeo-ethnography of technology. This involves an understanding of the role of technology in daily life. Archaeologists have explored spatial organisation of technological sequences: where knapping took place, how tools and blades were moved around a site and into the broader landscape. Such studies have also focused on the social aspects of technology. Pigeot (1990), for example, has examined the skill displayed by knapping sequences found at habitation U5 on the French Upper Palaeolithic site of Etiolles in the Paris Basin. She interprets the material as representing children or apprentices learning to work flint through observation and imitation of a skilled, specialist flintknapper.

Two main methods are used to elucidate the study of lithic *chaînes opératoires*: experimental flintknapping and refitting. Refitting exploits the fact that flintknapping is a reductive technology. All the waste flakes involved in the knapping process, along with tools, blanks and cores, can be joined back together, like a giant jigsaw puzzle, in order to reconstruct the operational sequence employed. Refitting in conjunction with spatial analysis will provide information about how lithic material was used across a site, for example the relationship between knapping stations and areas of tool use or of middening. Refitting also reveals "phantom tools", gaps in the refit sequence caused by the removal of a tool or blank from site for use in the broader landscape. So Conneller and Schadla-Hall (2003) have suggested that cores, blades and tools missing from later Palaeolithic and Mesolithic refit sequences on sites in the Vale of Pickering, North Yorkshire, represent a dynamic technical economy based on the curation and transportation of lithic material, in particular blades, for future use. Because refitting reveals how people moved round sites and the landscape, it has been the mainstay of techno-sociological approaches to the *chaîne opératoire* (though see Schlanger 1996 for a techno-psychological approach based on refitting). Experimental flintknapping focuses attention on decision-making and the balance between learned ways of proceeding and individual knowledge and skill, and so has been important to techno-psychological approaches.

Problems with the *Chaîne Opératoire*

As Edmonds (1990) has pointed out, the concept of the *chaîne opératoire* is rooted in structuralism, the legacy of Leroi-Gourhan (1993[1964]), who coined the term. Hence many technologists have been concerned to uncover ancient *schema opératoire* – or socially or cognitively particular templates for technological action. For the same reason much research on the *chaîne opératoire* is predicated on dualisms: between mind and body (i.e., between *schema operatoire* and bodily practice) and between society and the individual (i.e., between a learned way of proceeding and individual skill and experience). As Ingold (1993a) has emphasised, these dualisms do not make sense to the knowledgeable agent acting in the world; they simply recapitulate the modern view of technology which separates and privileges abstract technological knowledge over technical (bodily) practice.

Dobres (2000) has also criticised the structuralism of the *chaîne opératoire*, favouring instead the use of practice theory as an alternative approach to the study of technology. In this understanding the relationship between people and society is mediated by practice, so an agent's way of proceeding is socially determined, but through the act of manufacture the agent can alter society. In Dobres's words "technology is an engendered, meaningful, social and corporeal experience of making and remaking the world and oneself through material means" (2000:179). However, in her study of Magdalenian bone tools, she recapitulates many of the structuralists' concerns as she seeks to explore the relationship between procedural templates and individual variation in terms of the relationship between structure (given cultural resources and rules) and agency (the ability to effect change).[2] Though the dialectic between structure and agency introduces a dynamism and flexibility lacking in structuralist approaches, it leads to a focus on a very particular type of relationship. Dobres's use of practice theory has the effect of drawing attention away from the specific articulation of relationships between people, places and things, as these simply become individual instances of the relationship between structure and agency.

An alternative approach comes from recent work in British Mesolithic archaeology, which explores technological relations through a focus on networks (Conneller 2000; Finlay 2000; 2003; Hind 2004a; 2004b; Warren 2006). In the view of practice theorists, technology is regarded as a point of articulation between society on the one hand, and agents on the other. By contrast, a focus on technical networks dissolves this dichotomy, enabling an exploration of the way in which agency is distributed across particular associations of people and things. Rather than imagining technology as a discrete domain of action, the focus is on how connections and disconnections are established between different entities. Networks encompass a series of less stable relationships than that between structure and agency, being produced through connections between people, places and things. Networks are contingent relationships; tracing these makes it possible to explore the fluidity of identity, meaning and things.

In the remainder of this chapter I shall discuss three different aspects of technical networks. First, I will outline how a focus on networks reveals the inherent sociality of technology, through the connection of different people in technological acts. Secondly, I want to explore the "exploding of technology across the landscape" (Warren 2006) and the influence of the concept of the "taskscape" (Ingold 1993b) on British prehistory. Finally, I will examine understandings of raw materials and their properties and how these materials connect peoples, animals and things in technological networks.

Networks of People and Technology

Very few technological acts are solitary. However, this is not the impression gained from representations of prehistoric technology (see Dobres 2000 for a selection of examples). Dobres (2000:175) has rightly criticised such studies of the *châine operatoire*, which usually focus on a single operational sequence. The image of the lone technologist or hunter, almost always male, has been soundly critiqued (Dobres 2000; Finlay 2000). Finlay (2000:74) has emphasised that this image of the solitary hunter/maker is impossible to sustain if even a single act of microlith manufacture is considered. For microlith manufacture involves a number of different actions, processes, components – manufacture of different microliths, mastic collection and preparation, working a haft, etc. – not all of which may have been undertaken by the same individual. She suggests that sharing of work would have engendered obligations and that different elements of the same task may have been apportioned on the basis of age, gender or kinship.

Some of the issues raised by Finlay can be explored at the Scottish Mesolithic site of the Sands of Forvie in Aberdeenshire, where detailed analysis of the lithic material recovered has revealed the presence of a number of different flintknappers (Warren and Conneller, in press). It has been suggested that both right-handed and left-handed individuals seem to have been present from a study of cortical location and microburin lateralisation.[3] At Scatter 3 at the Sands of Forvie, blades retaining cortex on their right-hand side suggests the presence of a left-handed individual undertaking the early stages of core reduction. However the microburins at the same location have a left-sided notch, suggesting they may have been made by a right-handed individual or individuals. This indicates the presence of at least two individuals in the production process working together, with one person modifying blanks made by the other into tools. Such patterns have important implications for understanding whether ownership of knapping products in Mesolithic societies was communal or personal, the sharing of labour and objects and the interrelationship of different individuals in the undertaking of different tasks.

Technological artefacts and gestures connect people and draw them into social networks. Pigeot's (1990) work on the French Magdalenian site of Etiolles identifies the presence of children in the archaeological record. She emphasises the importance of non-verbal instruction at the site, where children learned by watching a skilled knapper at work and copying the particular gestures they observed. Through attention to the work of others, children learned the appropriate techniques to undertake when working flint. There are also examples from British prehistory where the work of children or novices has been inferred archaeologically from knapping mistakes and unskilled operational sequences (Edmonds 1999; Edmonds et al. 1999; Mithen 2000). Again it is important not to view these novices in isolation, but to see that through their involvement in technical acts, through attention, imitation and play and through learning the socially appropriate gestures, children became incorporated as social beings.

Finlay (2003) has recently returned to her study of composite microlithic technologies through an exploration of the concept of multiple authorship (Strathern 1988). Microlith manufacture in Mesolithic studies has traditionally been seen as associated with men, arrow manufacture and hunting. However, microliths actually seem to have been part of more varied and complex technologies. Finlay considers these composite technologies of the Mesolithic and outlines different strategies of microlith production. Use-wear reveals that microliths were not simply arrows (Finlayson 1990; Grace 1992; Finlayson and Mithen 1997) but had other functions. Some composite tools appear to have been particularly elaborate: an example found by Francis Buckley at Readycon Dene, West Yorkshire, consisted of a linear arrangement of 35 microliths spaced over a length of two metres. Finlay suggests that "because of its reliance and emphasis on multiple components, microlithic technology can be seen as a forum for group participation and expression rather than individual action" (2003:175). She describes how the concept of multiple authorship allows us to subvert established notions of the gendered attribution of artefacts. The concept of multiple authorship is derived from ethnographic studies of artefacts, which reveal the involvement of both male and female action in the biographies of certain artefacts without privileging either. The connection of different people through the production of a composite artefact draws out the way in which identities are relational, with particular identities and persons produced in certain contexts through the different articulations of people and things.

Networks of People and Places

The network of relationships between tasks, people and the broader landscape has been explored by Ingold (1993b) through his concept of the taskscape. This approach has been extremely influential in prehistoric archaeology (Edmonds 1997; Conneller 2000; Warren 2000). The taskscape is the entire assemblage of tasks and their mutual interrelationship that constitute our lives. Ingold argues, furthermore, that the landscape is the "congealed" taskscape, produced through the interrelationships of tasks in daily life. The examination of even a single technical act can illustrate this point: tracing the actions that resulted in the production of a single microlith recovered from the site of VPD in the Vale of Pickering, North Yorkshire, reveals how tasks and people are caught up in the production of the landscape. This single episode of manufacture would draw together the previous actions of different individuals working in different parts of the landscape. The act of microlith manufacture would retain traces of the past actions of those involved in the procurement of the beach pebble from which it was made, in the manufacture of containers or means of transport to carry the raw material, and in the hunting or gathering activities which procured a bone or antler soft hammer or punch. Microlith manufacture would also anticipate the tasks involved in composite tool or arrow manufacture and in hunting or cutting, or piercing activities. The rhythm of microlith manufacture would respond to these other tasks and also to the actions of the people working in the immediate vicinity. Importantly this episode of microlith manufacture would create spatial relations: links between the beach (which was the source of the raw material), routes of transport to and from site VPD, the place where the tasks involving the use of the composite tool would occur, and the place of its deposition. So even a single task of microlith manufacture is caught up with other tasks and these involve not just other people, but different places, different seasons and different rhythms. Similarly, Warren (2006) considers bevel-ended tools of bone and antler recovered from the Oronsay middens. In addition to the different people drawn in to these networks through the manufacture and use of these tools, Warren emphasises the links to different places and the temporal and seasonal components of these networks. In this way the interlocking of a whole range of different tasks would produce the landscape itself as a temporal network of tasks, paths, actions and movements.

Edmonds (1997) argues that this focus on the taskscape allows an examination of how patterns of routine material engagement produced the rhythms of social life and social change. He explores social change though daily engagement in the world in the context of the Mesolithic–Neolithic transition, discussing how daily tasks, such as flint working, were caught up with both change and continuity over the transition. In the Early Neolithic, new tasks such as cattle herding produced new temporalities of social life and new engagements with the landscape. Herding created pastoral seasonal rounds: sometimes these involved mass movements of people in step with the cattle, at other times the movement of smaller groups. Herding also involved the consolidation of particular pathways and the persistence of pastures. The exchange of cattle produced new relations that stretched between communities and cattle themselves appear to have served as rich sources of metaphor, with their bones sometimes recovered from tombs. Finally, cattle, like other domesticates, helped redefine perceptions of culture and nature and the relationship between people and animals. However, at the same time, these movements were interwoven with more traditional tasks: people followed long-standing patterns of stone procurement that took them back, again and again, to the same outcrops, rivers and beaches. Edmonds focuses on the minutiae of everyday tasks, and their interrelationship, emphasising how meaning is drawn up from tasks like cattle herding and flintknapping and how the interrelationships of these and other daily tasks structure the rhythms of social life. Tasks make not only the landscape, but also time itself. Edmonds's work is particularly concerned with the temporality of the landscape, not just with these rhythms of daily life, but also with history and people's reading of past traces in the landscape (see also Hind 2004a; 2004b).

Material Matters

Finally, I want to return to raw materials and to how they have figured in technical networks. Raw materials are central to most approaches to technology. Processual accounts have tended to stress the role of raw material procurement in time budgeting, risk avoidance, overall mobility and technological strategies (see papers in Torrence 1989). Other studies have emphasised the constraints raw materials make on technological action (White 1998), or have focused on understanding the level of skill displayed by prehistoric stoneworkers in relation to certain material types (Inizan et al. 1992). However, this section will explore how raw materials have figured within technical networks. Recent work in this area has tended to focus on raw material sources rather than the actual physical properties of stone though, as discussed below, these are intimately linked.

The location of raw material sources has always been an important part of pre-historic studies, because of the information it has been seen to provide about mobility (for hunter-gatherers) or trade and exchange (for settled peoples). However, raw material is important not just as an indicator of trade or mobility; it also embodies a place, and many of the places from which material was procured appear to have been especially important to prehistoric people. Paul Taçon's (1991) study of stone procurement among Aboriginal groups in Western Arnhem Land has been particularly influential in encouraging prehistorians to think of stone sources in terms of the significance accorded to particular locations, rather than the functional demands of embedded procurement. Taçon discussed how the procurement and use of raw materials is intimately bound up with ideas about the activities of ancestral beings in particular places in the landscape (with quartz pebbles being seen as fossilised bones of these beings), and how materials are classified according to their aesthetic and spiritual qualities. Cooney (2002; 2005) has elucidated similar concerns in the Irish Neolithic. Drawing on a variety of evidence, he suggests that the white inclusions in the porphyry axes from Lambay Island were perceived as representations of ancestral bones. It was the very act of axe manufacture, the polishing of these inclusions, that would bring out the presence of the ancestors.

Some of the best evidence for the importance accorded to particular sources of stone in prehistoric Britain also comes from the study of Neolithic polished axes (Edmonds 1995). In the second quarter of the third millennium B.C., certain stone quarries were placed in deliberately dramatic and inaccessible places. At the Langdale Fells in Cumbria, workable stone occurs along an exposure that runs for 19 km. Though some easily accessible parts of this were worked, the quarries that were most intensively exploited were those on narrow ledges that were very difficult to reach (Bradley 2000). The quality of stone at these sources was no better than at more accessible locations, which may indicate that particular isolated or dangerous places were imbued with special significance. The importance attached to the location of the stone sources was echoed by many other aspects of the life histories of axes: they often circulated long distance from their sources and are discovered in unusual depositionary contexts. Edmonds argues that the exotic origins of the axes was seen as important, and that their circulation through exchange became a means of producing networks of relations through which political authority was established and expressed. So both the isolation and danger associated with the procurement of the raw material, and the distance between the sources and the areas where the axes circulated, were important in the ways these implements were perceived and valued. In a similar fashion, flint mines also appear to have been significant places. Flint could be obtained from surface exposures, but instead shafts were dug into the earth and nodules recovered in a process that would have been both time-consuming and dangerous. Formal deposits of Grooved Ware and other deliberate "offerings" have also been recovered from some of the shafts at Grimes Graves, Norfolk (Edmonds 1995; Barber et al. 1999:61–66).

The importance attached to particular types of stone through association with a place has also been explored in relation to pottery technology. Jones (2002) has discussed the use of different types of stone inclusions in Neolithic pots on Orkney, noting that at the site of Barnhouse different households used different sources of stone inclusion. Two of these sources are adjacent to the chambered tomb at Unstan, while another is located near the likely contemporary Late Neolithic settlement at Bookan. Jones suggests that different family groups were deliberately referencing particular parts of the landscape through their manufacture of pottery. Households emphasised connections with their ancestors by selecting stone adjacent to a chambered tomb and/or made connections with living individuals, with kin or exchange partners, at the Bookan settlement.

These studies emphasise the importance of the source of the raw material for the way the finished artefact was perceived. In both cases the raw material involved was stone, but other kinds of material may have been similarly important. Bone and antler were also routinely drawn upon for the manufacture of tools in early prehistory. Rather than representing a connection with a *place*, these tools were once part of animals' *bodies*, and in a similar way to stone, animal raw materials may have embodied, or retained, their origins in the ways they were perceived.[4] Rather than simply being a source of food, animals are important social and/or spiritual entities in most societies, including our own. Animals are also indispensable media for thinking about and categorising human societies. The following case study considers whether this potential significance of animals as social beings is evident in the ways in which their body parts were transformed in networks of technological action.

Animal Technologies at Star Carr

At Star Carr in North Yorkshire antler working seems to have been a particularly important task. The faunal assemblage is dominated by red deer antler: shed and unshed antlers, antler working debris and 192 barbed points (fig. 7.1) – all but two manufactured from red deer antler – were recovered (Clark 1954). The quantity of barbed points recovered from the site is extremely noteworthy: 30 years of excavations around the ancient lake Flixton on which Star Carr was situated have yielded only one additional example of this tool type. Furthermore, only the initial stages of barbed point manufacture are present on the site; the points appear to have been finished elsewhere, but especially returned to Star Carr for deposition.

The question remains as to why people were treating this seemingly mundane artefact – the barbed point, used as the tip of arrows, fish spears or hunting spears, or as a harpoon – in this unusual way. It seems that part of the answer may be found in their connection with another rare artefact type found at Star Carr – the perforated antler frontlets (fig. 7.2), which Clark, the original excavator of the site, had considered as potential ritual headgear. Again, none of these objects were found during the recent excavations of the Vale of Pickering – in fact the Star Carr frontlets are the only ones known from Britain, though examples have been found at three German sites (Chatterton 2003). Comparison of the Star Carr antler headgear with the German examples reveals that the Star Carr frontlets had been exploited as a source of raw material, probably for the manufacture of barbed points (Street

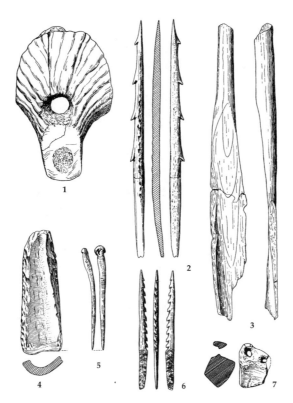

Figure 7.1 Bone (4, 5), antler (1, 2, 6) and wooden (3) tools, and amber bead (7), from Star Carr, North Yorkshire. Scales various. Reproduced with kind permission of Paul Mellars.

1991). So the barbed points seem intimately linked with the life histories of these potential ritual objects.

What links the two artefacts is their connections with red deer. I have argued elsewhere (Conneller 2004) that the antler frontlets can be viewed in terms of the effects they had on the human body, that they were part of an understanding of the world that encompassed ideas of bodily transformation. Ideas of bodily transformation appear to have focused on the relationship between people and red deer, rather than any of the other species represented at the site. Red deer seem to have been so important that tools made from their antler also needed to be disposed of in a particular way: Chatterton (2003) has argued that the waterlogged area of Star Carr represents the formal deposition of stone tools, debris and animal bones. So not only the barbed points, but also the burins and scrapers used in the manufacture of the points and frontlets, the microliths used in killing and processing animals, and even the debris produced in the manufacture of these tools which were used on the animal products, may have been caught up in these important acts of deposition, based on their technical relationship in the transformation of animal bodies into tools and food.

Figure 7.2 Red deer antler frontlet from Star Carr. Reproduced with kind permission of the Cambridge Museum of Archaeology and Anthropology.

If so, perhaps the *chaîne opératoire* of tool manufacture can be turned on its head. Animals are normally seen as lying at the end of stone tool *chaînes opératoires,* as the object on which the projectile point, scraper or knife is used. However, perhaps it is not the killing or the butchery of an animal that is the final outcome of the manufacture of tools, rather the animal lies at the beginning of *chaîne opératoire.* Perhaps it is the social position of the animal within hunter-gatherer ontologies that guides the *chaîne opératoire* of tools involved in their processing, from the manufacture, to the use and final deposition of these tools.

Conclusions

The studies of stone sources and the use of animal materials discussed in this chapter reveal the social understandings that are central to technical networks. The origins of a material have been shown to be extremely important, whether this origin embodies a place in the landscape or a once living creature. However it is noteworthy that the approaches that do pay attention to the importance of stone as a material all focus on objects that are perceived to be socially significant, such as Neolithic axes. The meanings and significance of the lithic material that was used in mundane, daily flint working has been ignored. However, the symbolic dimensions of materials are inseparable from their purely mechanical properties and we need to understand these in order to generate an understanding of prehistoric stone working. Unlocking the meaning of stone is a challenge for the future.

ACKNOWLEDGEMENTS

Many thanks to Thomas Yarrow and Graeme Warren for their comments on early drafts of this chapter.

NOTES

1 Waste flakes are removed in preparation of the finished product, so that technological sequences can be reconstructed; thus lithic technology differs from pottery, where the pot is built up through additions, rather than subtractions, making the exact sequences employed in pottery production much more difficult to reconstruct.
2 Though individual variation and divergence from procedural templates is explained by Dobres in terms of non-discursive social strategies, rather than the usual technological focus on "skill".
3 Experimental flintknapping suggests that right-handed and left-handed knappers work the core in different directions, meaning that the location of the cortext (the chalky outer surface of a flint nodule) on flakes and blades produced will differ. Similarly the lateralisation of the microburin notch in the production of a microlith can also depend on the handedness of the flintknapper.
4 Though animals themselves may also embody particular places in the landscape (Fowler 2004) through the places that they tend to inhabit (i.e., pigs in lowland forests, beavers in lakes, chamois in mountains, etc.).

REFERENCES

Barber, M., D. Field and P. Topping, 1999 The Neolithic Flint Mines of England. Swindon: English Heritage.

Binford, L., 1973 Interassemblage variability: the Mousterian and the "functional" argument. *In* The Explanation of Culture Change. C. Renfrew, ed. pp. 227–254. London: Duckworth.

Bradley, R., 1984 The Social Foundations of Prehistoric Britain. London: Longman.

——2000 An Archaeology of Natural Places. London: Routledge.

——and M. Edmonds, 1993 Interpreting the Axe Trade. Cambridge: Cambridge University Press.

Chatterton, R., 2003 Star Carr reanalysed. *In* Peopling the Mesolithic in a Northern Environment. L. Bevan and J. Moore, eds. pp. 69–80. Oxford: British Archaeological Reports.

Clark, J. G. D., 1954 Excavations at Star Carr. Cambridge: Cambridge University Press.

Conneller, C., 2000 Fragmented Space? Hunter-gatherer landscapes of the Vale of Pickering, North Yorkshire. Archaeological Review from Cambridge 17(1):139–150.

——2004 Becoming deer: corporeal transformations at Star Carr. Archaeological Dialogues 11(1):37–56.

——and T. Schadla-Hall, 2003 Beyond Star Carr: the Vale of Pickering in the 10th millennium BP. Proceedings of the Prehistoric Society 69:85–106.

Cooney, G., 2002 So many shades of rock: colour symbolism in Irish stone axe heads. *In* Colouring the Past. A. Jones and G. McGregor, eds. pp. 93–107. Oxford: Berg.

——2005 Stereo porphyry: quarrying and deposition on Lambay Island, Ireland. *In* The Cultural Landscape of Prehistoric Mines. P. Topping and M. Lynott, eds. pp. 14–29. Oxford: Oxbow Books.

Dobres, M.-A., 1999 Technology's links and *chaînes*: the processual unfolding of techniques and technician. *In* The Social Dynamics of Technology: practice, politics and world-view. M.-A. Dobres and C. Hoffman, eds. pp. 124–164. Washington: Smithsonian Institution Press.

——2000 Technology and Social Agency. Oxford: Blackwell.

Edmonds, M., 1990 Description, understanding and the *chaîne opératoire*. Archaeological Review from Cambridge 9(1):55–69.

——1995 Stone Tools and Society: working stone in Neolithic and Bronze Age Britain. London: Batsford.

——1997 Taskscape, technology and tradition. Analecta Praehistorica Leidensis 29:99–110.

——1999 Ancestral Geographies of the Neolithic: landscape, monuments and memory. London: Routledge.

——C. Evans and D. Gibson, 1999 Assembly and collection: lithic complexes in the Cambridgeshire Fenlands. Proceedings of the Prehistoric Society 65:47–82.

Finlay, N., 2000 Deer prudence. Archaeological Review from Cambridge 17(1):67–79.

——2003 Microliths and multiple authorship. *In* Mesolithic on the Move: papers presented at the Sixth International Conference on the Mesolithic in Europe. L. Larsson, H. Kindgren, K. Knutsson, D. Leoffler and A. Åkerlund, eds. pp. 169–178. Oxford: Oxbow Books.

Finlayson, B., 1990 Lithic exploitation during the Mesolithic in Scotland. Scottish Archaeological Review 7:41–57.

——and S. Mithen, 1997 The microwear and morphology of microliths from Gleann Mor. *In* Projectile Technology. H. Knecht, ed. pp. 107–129. New York: Plenum Press.

Fowler, C., 2004 The Archaeology of Personhood. London: Routledge.

Grace, R., 1992 Microwear analysis. *In* Excavations at a Mesolithic site at Thatcham, Berkshire. F. Healy, M. Heaton and S. J. Lobb. Proceedings of the Prehistoric Society 58:41–76.

Hind, D., 2004a Where many paths meet: an integrated theory of landscape and technology. *In* Stories from the Landscape: archaeologies of inhabitation. A. Chadwick, ed. pp. 114–129. Oxford: British Archaeological Reports.

——2004b Picking up the trail: people, landscapes and technology in the Peak District of Derbyshire during the fifth and forth millennia BC. *In* Stories from the Landscape: archaeologies of inhabitation. A. Chadwick, ed. pp. 130–176. Oxford: British Archaeological Reports.

Ingold, T., 1990 Society, nature and the concept of technology. Archaeological Review from Cambridge 9(1):5–18.

——1993a Technology, language and intelligence: A reconsideration of basic concepts. *In* Tools, Language and Cognition in Human Evolution. K. Gibson and T. Ingold, eds. pp. 449–472. Cambridge: Cambridge University Press.

—— 1993b The temporality of the landscape. World Archaeology 25:152–174.

Inizan, M.-L., H. Roche and J. Tixier, 1992 Technology of Knapped Stone. Prehistoire de la Pierre Taillee, 3. Meudon: CREP.

Jones, A., 2002 Archaeological Theory and Scientific Practice. Cambridge: Cambridge University Press.

Jordan, P., 2006. Analogy. *In* Mesolithic Britain and Ireland. C. Conneller and G. Warren, eds. pp. 83–100. Stroud: Tempus.

Karlin, C., and M. Julien, 1994 Prehistoric technology: a cognitive science? *In* The Ancient Mind: elements of cognitive archaeology. C. Renfrew and E. Zubrow, eds. pp. 152–164. Cambridge: Cambridge University Press

Latour, B., 1996 Aramis; or, The Love of Technology. Cambridge, MA: Harvard University Press.

Lemonnier, P., 1993 Introduction. *In* Technological Choices: transformation in material cultures since the Neolithic. P. Lemonnier, ed. pp. 36–76. London: Routledge.

Leroi-Gourhan, A., 1993 [1964] Gesture and Speech. A. Bostock Berger, trans. Cambridge, MA: MIT Press.

Martingel, H., 2003 Late prehistoric and historic use of flint in England. *In* Lithic Analysis at the Millennium. N. Moloney and M. Shott, eds. pp. 91–97. London: Institute of Archaeology.

Mauss, M., 1979 Body techniques. *In* Sociology and Psychology: essays. pp. 95–123. London: Routledge and Kegan Paul.

Mellars, P., 1976 Settlement patterns and industrial variability in the British Mesolithic. *In* Problems in Economic and Social Archaeology. G. Sieveking, I. Longworth and K. E. Wilson, eds. pp. 357–399. London: Duckworth.

Mithen, S., 2000 Hunter-gatherer Landscape Archaeology: the Southern Hebrides Mesolithic Project 1988–1998. Cambridge: McDonald Institute.

Myers, A., 1987 All shot to pieces? Inter-assemblage variability, lithic analysis and Mesolithic assemblage types. *In* Lithic Analysis and Later British Prehistory. A. Brown and M. Edmonds, eds. pp. 137–154. Oxford: British Archaeological Reports.

—— 1989 Reliable and maintainable technological strategies. *In* Time, Energy and Stone Tools. R. Torrence, ed. pp. 78–91. Cambridge: Cambridge University Press.

Pelegrin, J., 1990 Prehistoric lithic technology: some aspects of research. Archaeological Review from Cambridge 9(1):116–125.

Pigeot, N., 1990 Technical and social actors: Flintknapping specialists and apprentices at Magdelenian Etoilles. Archaeological Review from Cambridge 9(1):126–141.

Roberts, M., and S. Parfitt, 1999 Boxgrove: a Middle Pleistocene hominid site at Eartham Quarry, Boxgrove, West Sussex. London: English Heritage.

Roe, D., 1968 British Lower and Middle Palaeolithic handaxe groups. Proceedings of the Prehistoric Society 34:1–82.

Rowley-Conwy, P., 1987 Animal bones in Mesolithic studies: recent progress and hope for the future. *In* Mesolithic Northwest Europe: recent trends. P. Rowley-Conwy, M. Zvelebil and H.-P. Blankholm, eds. pp. 71–84. Sheffield: Sheffield University Press.

Schlanger, N., 1994 Mindful technology: unleashing the *chaîne opératoire* for an archaeology of mind. *In* The Ancient Mind: elements of cognitive archaeology. C. Renfrew and E. Zubrow, eds. pp. 143–151. Cambridge: Cambridge University Press.

—— 1996 Understanding Levallois: lithic technology and cognitive archaeology. Cambridge Archaeological Journal 6(2):231–254.

Strathern, M., 1988 The Gender of the Gift. Berkeley: University of California Press.

Street, M., 1991 Bedburg Konigshoven: a Pre-Boreal Mesolithic site in the Lower Rhine-land, Germany. *In* The Late Glacial in Europe: human adaptation and environmental change at the end of the Pleistocene. N. Barton, A. Roberts and D. Roe, eds. pp. 256–270. London: Council for British Archaeology.

Taçon, P., 1991 The power of stone: symbolic aspects of stone use and tool development in Western Arnhem Land, Australia. Antiquity 65:192–207.

Torrence, R., ed., 1989 Time, Energy and Stone Tools. Cambridge: Cambridge University Press.

Warren, G., 2000 Seascapes: people, boats and inhabiting the later Mesolithic in western Scotland. *In* Mesolithic Lifeways: current research in Britain and Ireland. R. Young, ed. pp. 97–104. Leicester: Leicester University Press.

——2006. Technology. *In* Mesolithic Britain and Ireland. C. Conneller and G. Warren, eds. pp. 13–34. Stroud: Tempus.

——and C. Conneller, in press. Analyses of Mesolithic assemblages from the Sands of Forvie, Aberdeenshire. *In* Lithic Technology, Manufacture and Replication Studies Reconsidered. C. Bond, ed. Lithic Studies Society Occasional Paper. Oxford: British Archaeological Reports.

White, M., 1998 On the significance of Acheulean Biface variability in Southern Britain. Proceedings of the Prehistoric Society 64:15–44.

——2000 The Clactonian question: on the interpretation of core and flake assemblages in the British Lower Palaeolithic. Journal of World Prehistory 14:1–63.

8

How the Dead Live: Mortuary Practices, Memory and the Ancestors in Neolithic and Early Bronze Age Britain and Ireland

Andrew Jones

Introduction: Tales from the Dead

How do the dead live? This question, and the title for this chapter, comes from a satirical novel by the British journalist and novelist Will Self. In the novel – on death – people simply change their addresses and shuffle off to reside in less fashionable parts of London (a state presumed to be akin to death by the fashionistas of contemporary London). The question is paradoxical. How can the dead *live*? Surely the dead are dead, inert and immobile?

Self parodies the mundane character of life and death in contemporary Britain. In doing so, he questions the contemporary rational belief that the body simply rots away after death. The dead may be dead and gone, but they continue to have an effect upon the living. The alternative world he presents resonates with innumerable non-Western belief systems in which – on death – the dead shift from one domain to another: from the world of the living to a world of the dead. The dead might be physically removed from the domain of the living, but they are accessible in the form of skeletal elements, effigies or other material forms. In some cases they may be consulted and venerated, in others they are feared for the spirits of the dead are often hard to control. The dead may be imbued with agency in a number of ways; they have the ability to shape the world by their continued influence on the living.

Traditionally the nature and scale of the assemblages associated with mortuary rites have been used by archaeologists to interpret social organisation, especially status, rank and social identity. Here the dead and the artefacts associated with them stand in for a range of social facts, which are considered to lie behind the patterns of deposition that archaeologists observe. I wish to take an alternative proach in this chapter. Rather than treating the dead and the assemblages associated with them as simple reflections of social norms, I want to analyse artefacts and the bones of the dead as mediums by which social relations are created and maintained (see Walter et al. 2004). I argue that artefacts and the bones of the dead should be treated as active components of the mortuary rituals that serve to form social ties between the living.

The Traditional View of Neolithic and Bronze Age Mortuary Practices

The mortuary archaeology of the British Neolithic and Early Bronze Age has been traditionally defined according to a series of oppositions. During the Early Neolithic people were interred in either megalithic tombs or earthen long barrows. The numbers of individuals buried in these contexts is large. The bones of individual burials were often fragmented and bodies exhibit evidence of deliberate disarticulation. In some cases composite bodies are composed from the remains of a number of individuals or rearranged according to sex, age or body parts. These aspects of Early Neolithic mortuary practice have led commentators to suggest that the deposition of human remains during the Early Neolithic were corporate or communal in nature (Shanks and Tilley 1982; Thomas and Whittle 1986; Bradley 1998). The apparently active manipulation of body parts in chambered tombs and the weathered and fragmented nature of bone assemblages beneath long barrows has led some to suggest that human remains were circulated amongst the living (Bradley 1984:23).

The communal nature of these deposits and their evident manipulation suggests that the bones of the dead were being treated as ancestral relics (Barrett 1988). This interpretation has been influenced by the work of the anthropologist Claude Meillassoux (1972). Meillassoux suggests that the conception of time amongst hunter-gatherers and farmers is quite different. Because they gather food from the land, hunter-gatherers do not invest in specific regions of land and their future subsistence does not depend upon the fortune of their forebears. Farming, by contrast, involves a long-term commitment to a specific territory and the fortune of present populations may depend upon the outcome of decisions made by their forebears. As a subsistence strategy farming produces a different conception of time and space. Farmers have a stronger sense of genealogy than hunter-gatherers. It is due to this altered sense of time and space that the shift to farming and agriculture during the Neolithic runs parallel with the novel construction of monuments to the dead (Bradley 1993).

The remains of the dead are considered to be ancestral for a number of reasons: the assumed shift in the conception of time and space with the arrival of farming; the construction of monuments to the dead; and the evidence for the manipulation of the bones of the dead. The characterisation of the dead during the Neolithic as "ancestors" has been criticised by some as an unexamined orthodoxy (Whitley 2001). I will critically examine this "orthodoxy" in more detail below. Here it is sufficient to note that the remains of the dead within Neolithic chambered tombs and long barrows have been characterised as communal and ancestral.

The mortuary traditions of the Early Neolithic stand in marked contrast to those of the Early Bronze Age. During the Early Bronze Age we observe instead the burial of single individuals beneath round barrows; individual burials accompanied by grave goods are interred on the ground surface, in a grave pit or occasionally in a container such as a wooden coffin. The inception of single grave burial in Britain has often been seen as the result of the arrival of the "Beaker folk" (Harrison 1980) in the mid third millennium B.C., who were interred with a characteristic assemblage of a decorated pottery Beaker, a stone archer's wrist-guard and barbed and tanged arrowheads of flint. The wholesale change of mortuary practice traditionally assumed to be the influence of Beaker burial has been questioned and the presence of an indigenous tradition of single grave burial has been emphasised (Burgess and Shennan 1976; Kinnes 1992b; Thomas 1999:151–156).

Whether we treat single grave burial as the product of external contact or indigenous change, the important point here is that single grave burial persists throughout the Early Bronze Age. The shift from the communal burial traditions of the Early Neolithic to the single grave burial of the Early Bronze Age has been traditionally taken to signify a fundamental change in society. Burials of individuals beneath round barrows have been taken to indicate either the existence of an elite, such as chiefs (Piggott 1938; Eogan 1994), or even ritual specialists, such as shamans (Piggott 1962; Woodward 2000). The emergence of this burial practice has also been viewed as evidence for centralising tendencies in society, such as chiefdoms (Renfrew 1973), or as ideological in nature (Shennan 1982) with a specific emphasis placed upon the advent of the individual (Renfrew 1974; Shennan 1975). Over the course of the second millennium B.C. we observe a shift from inhumation burials of individuals accompanied by grave goods to the deposition of one or more cremation burials. Cremations are either accompanied by grave goods or buried deposited within a burial urn, typically a Food Vessel, Collared Urn or Cordoned Urn.

The burial of single individuals within graves and beneath barrows is critically important since the grave offered a fixed placed in the landscape where the deceased was deposited (Barrett 1994:112). The burial of successive individuals made reference to previous acts of burials: individuals were either inhumed or cremated; burials were inserted within barrows, barrows were remodelled or fresh barrows were constructed. The series of choices open to people performing burial rituals during the Early Bronze Age led to the production of round barrow cemeteries (Woodward 2000:73–99). The spatial referencing of the dead, either by re-cutting barrows or constructing new monuments, meant that effectively the history of particular social groups was written upon the landscape: barrow cemeteries are therefore a form of genealogical map (Garwood 1991; Barrett 1994:123–129). It is likely that barrow cemeteries define the burials of specific lineages (Garwood 1991).

In sum, the communal burials of the Early Neolithic are opposed to the individualising single grave burials of the Early Bronze Age. The change in mortuary practices is traditionally seen to lie some time in the third millennium B.C. While "Beaker folk" are no longer held responsible for this change, the search for the origin of the change has in practice largely been deferred to the later periods of the Neolithic (Thomas 1999:151–156). As Barrett (1988:32) observes, the traditional perception of the dramatic shift in mortuary practice was partly the product of the short radiocarbon chronology of the 1950s (Piggott 1954). In fact there is considerable diversity in mortuary practice in the period from 4000 to 1500 B.C. I will provide an overview of this regional and chronological diversity below.

Mortuary Contexts in Early Neolithic Britain and Ireland

During the Early Neolithic, in the period 4000–3000 B.C., two major classes of monuments with mortuary functions were constructed: chambered tombs and long barrows (fig. 8.1). The former consisted of a mound constructed of stone which contained one or more chambers built of stone with a passage to the exterior. The latter was built of earth and wood, and often consisted of wooden structures sealed beneath a long earthen mound. Broadly speaking, the distribution of these monuments is divided between eastern and western halves of Britain, with the major distribution of earthen long barrows in south-eastern Britain, and the major concentration of chambered tombs in the north and west (see Cummings, chapter 6). The mortuary rites associated with both monuments have a series of similarities

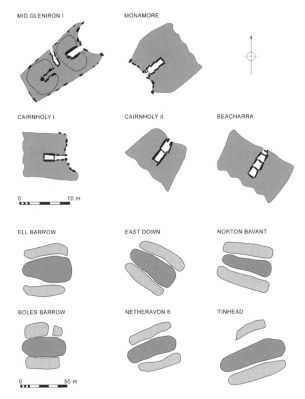

Figure 8.1 Comparison of chambered tombs and long barrows (after Henshall 1963 and Lynch 1969; drawing by Aaron Watson).

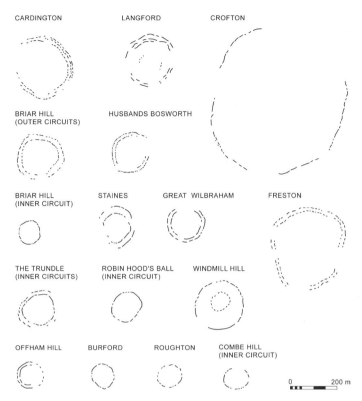

Figure 8.2 Southern English causewayed enclosures (after Oswald et al. 2001; drawing by Aaron Watson).

and differences. Both articulated and disarticulated individuals are deposited beneath earthen long barrows. The individuals within chambered tomb assemblages are generally disarticulated, although there are instances in which entire individuals are deposited. The major difference is one of access: once the bones of the dead are placed beneath the earthen long barrow they are inaccessible, whereas the open nature of chambered tombs offers continual access to the bones of the dead (Bradley 1998:62). It is possible that human bones were removed from chambered tombs and circulated as relics (Bradley 1984:23). Indeed the state of many human bone deposits beneath long barrows – often deposited as bundles of human bone as if they had been placed in bags or containers – speaks of the lengthy period of time the bones of the dead were circulated prior to deposition.

Another major context for the deposition of the dead in the Early Neolithic is in causewayed enclosures (fig. 8.2). Composed of interrupted ditches and banks, roughly circular or sub-circular in plan, the concentric circuits of causewayed enclosures delimit an interior space which might provide the frame for the hierarchic ordering of people, animals and artefacts (Evans 1988; Whittle et al. 1999); in this sense ditches are both boundaries and thresholds. Causewayed enclosures are a major context for the deposition of the debris of feasting in the form of large deposits of domestic animals, typically cattle and pig. In addition, causewayed enclosures also act as foci for the deposition of large numbers of artefacts, including stone axes and pottery. Some of these artefacts – such as the Gabbroic pottery deposited in a series of causewayed enclosures in south-western England and Wessex – demonstrate long-distance contacts as the origin of the pottery lay in the Lizard Peninsula in Cornwall (Peacock 1969). Similar long-distance links are evinced by the petrological analysis of stone axes from causewayed enclosures.

Mortuary deposits are a feature of a number of causewayed enclosures. At Hambledon Hill the dead were apparently defleshed and exposed within the ditches. The deposition of fragments of human remains, and in particular skulls, at sites such as Abingdon (Oxfordshire), Offham and Whitehawk (Sussex), Staines (Surrey) and Etton and Haddenham (Cambridgeshire), suggest similar practices. Child burials notably predominate, and there is a marked distinction in the frequency of child burials at causewayed enclosures and long barrows. The same goes for certain elements of the adult skeleton, as skulls predominate in causewayed enclosures, against the predominance of long bones in barrows (Thorpe 1984). Both of these observations suggest deliberate and patterned deposition. Coupled with the realisation that the bone deposits in both long barrows and chambered tombs may have been circulated for considerable periods of time, it seems feasible that mortuary rituals during the Early Neolithic involved a series of stages during which important decisions were made about the correct place and procedure for the burial of certain members of the community, such as children, and for specific skeletal elements, such as the skull.

The major distribution of causewayed enclosures is in southern Britain, with 66 monuments in total (Oswald et al. 2001). Scotland has three possible sites, Wales two, and Ireland two (Oswald et al. 2001). This variability in regional distribution serves to emphasise that there are regional distinctions in the monument traditions and mortuary practices of Britain and Ireland. Just as causewayed enclosures appear to be a distinctive regional tradition, albeit with connections to the European continent, so do the traditions of megalithic monument.

The construction traditions of chambered tombs differ regionally (fig. 8.3). In the north of Scotland we find Orkney-Cromarty tombs: long linear monuments with a series of chambers defined by upright monoliths (Davidson and Henshall 1989; 1990; Henshall and Ritchie 1995). In the extreme north of Scotland – in Shetland – so-called heeled cairns are constructed with immense crescent-shaped façades of stone with entrance into small internally divided chambers (Henshall 1963). In the west of Scotland Clyde tombs predominate (Henshall 1972). Clyde tombs often have impressive façades of megaliths, which enter a restricted chamber area with a series of internal divisions (Henshall 1972).

In the southern Midlands and Wales the Cotswold-Severn group of monuments often have impressive megalithic façades too. They contain stone chambers entered laterally at the side of the monument, or consist of stone chambers entered from the front of the monument, which can be either simple or complex transepted monuments with a number of chambers leading off a central passage (Darvill 1982; 2004). Those in the west of Britain – in Cornwall and west Wales – have portal

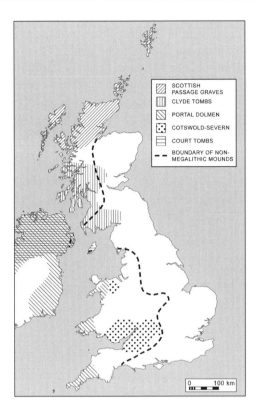

Figure 8.3 Regional traditions of chambered tombs (after Kinnes 1975). The dotted line running north–south denotes the approximate distribution of chambered tombs and earthen long barrows, with chambered tombs to the west, long barrows to the east. Drawing by Aaron Watson.

dolmens. These have substantial capstones many tonnes in weight propped up by smaller stones, creating a small but impressive chamber for the deposition of the dead (Whittle 2005). Regions such as Wales are diverse, with a series of different monument traditions utilised contemporaneously (Whittle and Cummings 2004). Such complexity is also observed in Ireland where there are three coeval chambered tomb traditions (de Valera and O'Nualláin 1961). Court tombs have an exaggerated megalithic façade often surrounding a courtyard arrangement off which one or more restricted chambers may exit. Portal tombs are comparable in form to the portal dolmens of Cornwall and Wales and passage tombs consisting of round stone-built mounds containing a small chamber with a long passage exiting the mound.

Earthen monuments also differ regionally. As Kinnes (1979) has demonstrated, round barrows are a feature of the Early Neolithic in a number of regions. In Scotland a series of round barrows are found (Kinnes 1992a). Pitnacree, Perthshire, contained a linear stone-lined trench enclosed by a stone mound and then sealed by an earth mound. The stone-lined trench contained evidence for an earlier wooden mortuary structure constructed of two massive posts. Similar structures are found under Scottish long barrows such as Lochhill and Slewcairn (Scott 1992) suggesting variability in the sequence of mortuary practice (Kinnes 1992a). Other round barrows in Scotland include Boghead (Burl 1984) and Midtown of Pitglassie (Shepherd 1996), both in the north-east of Scotland. The former may also have a wooden mortuary enclosure beneath a series of stone cairns and an earthen mound, the latter a series of pits sealed by a stone and earthen ring-shaped mound. All of these sites have evidence for cremation as the dominant mortuary rite, although other sites in Scotland – such as Gullane, Perthshire, and Sumburgh, Shetland – have evidence for multiple inhumations (Hedges and Parry 1980; Kinnes 1992a).

Cremations are a feature of the Irish Neolithic and cremation trenches similar to Pitnacree are found under Early Neolithic monuments such as Dooey's Cairn, Co. Antrim, and Fourknocks II, Co. Meath (Cooney 1999:99–112). Burial beneath round cairns is also a feature of the period 3500–3300 B.C., during the Middle Neolithic in Ireland (see table 8.1 for Irish Neolithic chronology). Linkardstown burials are characterised by the burial of one or more individuals in an articulated or disarticulated state accompanied by a highly decorated bipartite bowl. Individuals are deposited in a central cist beneath a round cairn. Only 15 of these monuments have been excavated, but on the basis of the data from these excavations most individuals buried within these monuments are adult males (Cooney 1999:97).

Table 8.1   A Comparison of Irish and British Neolithic chronologies (based on Sheridan 1995, Barclay and Bayliss 1999 and Woodward 2000)

4000 B.C.	3750 B.C.	3500 B.C.	3250 B.C.	3000 B.C.	2750 B.C.	2500 B.C.

Irish Neolithic

Early Neolithic (4000–3600 B.C.)
(court tombs; portal tombs; ?early passage tombs)

Middle Neolithic (3600–3100 B.C.)
(court tombs still in use; passage tombs; Linkardstown-type burials)

Late Neolithic (3100–2500 B.C.)
(final use of passage tombs; timber circles; emergence of Beaker pottery ca. 2500 B.C.)

British Neolithic

Early Neolithic (4000–3300 B.C.)
(chambered tombs, long barrows, causewayed enclosures, earliest round barrows)

Middle Neolithic (3300–2750 B.C)
(Cursus monuments, round barrow burials, passage tombs and henges in Orkney)

Late Neolithic (to 2000 B.C.)
(henges in southern England; emergence of Beaker burials)

Round barrows are also a major feature of the Early Neolithic of the Yorkshire Wolds and the Peak District in the north of England (Kinnes 1979; Harding 1997). Both cremations and inhumations are found beneath round barrows, and Kinnes (1979) establishes a sequence for Yorkshire beginning with crematoria and ending in the later Neolithic with the burial of one or more individuals beneath round barrows. The artefacts deposited in burials range from leaf-shaped flint arrowheads and Early Neolithic Grimston Ware and later Towthorpe bowls. By the end of the sequence transverse flint arrowheads, polished edge knives, Mortlake bowls and unusual items such as jet belt sliders, beaver incisors and boars tusks are deposited. The sequence culminates in cremation burials, as typified at Duggleby Howe, Yorkshire (Kinnes et al. 1983).

The shift towards single burials beneath round barrows is mirrored by a comparable shift towards single burials beneath long or oval barrows in other regions of Britain (Drewett 1975; Thorpe 1984; Kinnes 1992b). These are mainly restricted to southern England, and there is a concentration of U-shaped ditched monuments with single burials in the Cranbourne Chase region of Dorset (Barrett et al. 1991). As Harding (1997:285) notes for North Yorkshire, single burials may constitute a "strategy whereby the authority and power of specific groups and individuals became embedded in the landscape".

Mortuary Contexts in Later Neolithic Britain and Ireland

The contexts for mortuary practices during the later Neolithic are complex and regionally variable. In many regions we observe the continued use of sites constructed during the Early Neolithic. A good example of this is the chambered tomb at West Kennet, Wiltshire (Thomas and Whittle 1986). In other regions novel monuments were constructed. For example in Orkney passage graves, similar in form to those in Ireland, were constructed from around 3300 B.C. and continue in use down to around 1900 B.C. Although the tradition of inhumation burial persisted from the Early Neolithic the character of these monuments differs dramatically (Richards 1988). While earlier monuments are linear spaces, later passage graves are circular spaces entered by an exaggerated passage, which serves to mark the distinction between the domain of the living and that of the dead.

While passage tombs are a feature of an earlier phase of the Irish Neolithic it is during the later Neolithic that passage tombs of an immense scale began to be constructed (Sheridan 1986). It was during the later Neolithic that passage tomb cemeteries like those at the Boyne Valley and Loughcrew, Co. Meath, reached their apogee. The most famous of the later passage tombs are Newgrange, Knowth and Dowth in the Boyne Valley. These are associated with curvilinear and geometric megalithic art executed both in the interior of the monuments and on the exterior kerbstones. The mortuary practice predominantly associated with Irish passage tombs is cremation.

Passage tombs are a feature of the later phases of the Irish and Orcadian Neolithic and suggest contact between these two regions (Bradley 1984; Bradley and

Chapman 1986); indeed passage tombs are also found outside these regions, in places such as Anglesey, north Wales. The sites of Bryn Celli Ddu and Barclodiad Y Gawres, Anglesey, are both decorated with megalithic art motifs comparable to those in the great Boyne Valley tombs.

Another important feature of the later Neolithic is the continued significance of burials beneath round or oval barrows. As noted above, towards the end of the Early Neolithic sequence we begin to observe the burial of single individuals, often accompanied by a suite of grave goods including jet belt sliders, antler mace-heads, polished flint knives and transverse arrowheads. The burials in the Thames Valley region provide a good example of this later Neolithic burial tradition. At Radley, Oxfordshire, an oval barrow dating to just before 3000 B.C. covered the remains of two primary articulated inhumations. One of these was accompanied with a polished flint blade and a jet belt slider (Bradley 1992). A region of the Beaker-period cemetery adjacent to this site contained a mortuary trench with three individuals in various stages of articulation and disarticulation. In addition there were three flat graves and two ring ditches (Barclay and Halpin 2001). These monuments formed the focus for the later elaboration of the cemetery. A similar situation occurred at Dorchester, Oxfordshire, where it is likely that Sites I and XI were oval barrows containing inhumations (Atkinson et al. 1951; Bradley and Holgate 1984:118).

The practice of cremation also occurs late in the sequence of round barrows (Kinnes 1979). Cremation deposits occur in a number of Late Neolithic contexts most especially as secondary activity in Late Neolithic henges such as Stonehenge, Woodhenge and Coneybury (Wiltshire), Barford (Essex), Llandegai (north Wales), and Dorchester on Thames (Oxfordshire).

Cremation rites are not widespread, but as a practice cremation does appear to conjoin a series of distinct regions including Irish passage tombs, Yorkshire round barrows and the secondary deposits within henges. Thomas (1999:153) suggests that cremation rites may be one component of new networks of contact between different regions. In this regard it is worth noting the formal resemblance between the deposits within henges and the ring of cremation deposits around the passage tomb at the Mound of the Hostages, Tara, Co. Meath (O'Sullivan 2006).

Beakers and Beyond: Mortuary Contexts in Early Bronze Age Britain and Ireland

The continued significance of single burials accompanied by grave goods is important since it seems to presage Early Bronze Age mortuary practices. Beaker burials (fig. 8.4) emerged in southern Britain no earlier than 2600 B.C., and more likely around 2500 or 2400 B.C. (Garwood 1999:161). Beaker burials are often relatively standardised with a single burial accompanied by a pottery Beaker and possibly including a stone archer's wrist-guard, a copper or bronze dagger, bronze awl, a set of flint barbed and tanged arrowheads and jet buttons.

As Thomas (1991) cogently argues, the ordering of material culture around the corpse provides a means for categorising the person. The deposition of the Beaker

HEMP KNOLL   KEENOGE

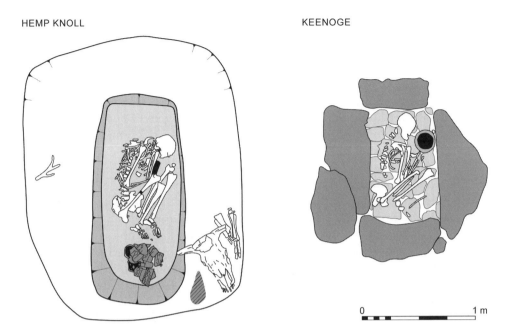

Figure 8.4 Comparison of British Beaker burial (Hemp Knoll) and Irish food vessel burial (Keenoge) (after Thomas 1991 and Waddell 1998). Drawing by Aaron Watson.

was key to how the burial was to be interpreted. As he notes, almost all Beaker burials contain Beakers; other items deposited around the corpse were in addition to, rather than replacements for, the Beaker. Beakers themselves are likely to be connected with some aspect of personal identity – Thomas (1999:159) proposes that they had connotations of eating, drinking and communality. The deposition of other objects alongside the Beaker served to qualify or add to the identity signalled by the deposition of the vessel (Thomas 1999:159).

The orientation of the corpse and the position of the Beaker is also a means of defining identity, particularly gender (Clarke 1970). Shepherd (in Greig et al. 1989) has analysed orientation for Beaker burials from north-eastern Scotland, and Tuckwell (1975) has analysed orientations for East Yorkshire. In both cases males are oriented with their heads to the east, females with their heads to the west. In Wessex a different pattern emerges as males are oriented with their heads to the north and females with their heads to the south.

Beaker burials are concentrated in regional groups that include Wessex, the Upper Thames Valley, Yorkshire and Aberdeenshire (Clarke 1970; Shepherd 1986). Notably those areas that contained substantial clusters of Neolithic round barrows, such as Yorkshire, the Upper Thames and Aberdeenshire, very often have early Beaker burials (Thorpe and Richards 1984; Shepherd 1986; Thomas 1999:161). The practice of Beaker burial is not regionally uniform and Beakers are found very late in the sequence in those areas where passage graves are constructed, such as Orkney and Ireland (Jones 2007).

A key difference lies between the use of Beakers in Britain and in Ireland. Although Beakers are a component of the final Neolithic–Early Bronze Age (around 2500–2400 B.C.), in Ireland they are rarely deposited in burial contexts, except in the megalithic tombs known as wedge tombs (Case 1995:25; Walsh 1995; O'Brien 1998).

In Ireland, Food Vessel burials, dating to 2500–2000 B.C., are comparable to those of Beakers in Britain (fig. 8.4). Like Beaker burials, Food Vessel burials consist of one or more flexed inhumations in a stone cist accompanied by Food Vessels of either vase or bowl form. Again the presence of the vessel acts as a material signifier of identity.

Food Vessels, Collared Urns and Cordoned Urns are a feature of Early Bronze Age burials throughout the British Isles. This is not to suggest there is uniformity in burial across Britain and Ireland during the period, for there are regional groupings of Food Vessels and urns. Two obvious examples are the highly decorated "Irish bowl" Food Vessels, whose distribution extends to western Scotland and the "Yorkshire vase" forms whose distribution extends from northern Britain to eastern Scotland (Cowie 1978). Collared urns are a feature of much of the British Isles (Longworth 1984), while Enlarged Food Vessels and cordoned urns tend to be found in northern Britain and Ireland (Kavanagh 1976). Towards the end of our period a series of regional pottery traditions associated with burial emerge. These include Deverel-Rimbury vessels in the south, Trevisker urns in the south-west, variants of the Deverel-Rimbury tradition in the north, and flat-rimmed vessels in Scotland.

There are also regional differences in mortuary practices during the Early Bronze Age. At a basic level, in the north and west we generally observe burials placed in stone-built cists (or stone boxes) beneath stone cairns, while in the south burials are likely to be in dug graves, wooden coffins or placed directly on the ground. These are beneath earthen barrows of a variety of forms, either inverted forms with shafts dug into the subsoil such as pond barrows, or a series of different barrow forms mounded up over the grave. In the north and west (especially in Scotland and Wales) burials may also be deposited in stone circles and ring cairns of a variety of forms (Lynch 1972; Bradley 1998:132–146).

Despite the model of single burial for the Early Bronze Age, closer analysis of the excavated material from Yorkshire and Derbyshire by Petersen (1972) suggests that barrows might be best considered as cemeteries covering a series of primary burials (see Mount 1995 for a similar argument for the Irish Bronze Age). Many deposits consisted of multiple burials of up to seven individuals. In this case Petersen argued that the primary burials in barrows should be seen as the beginning of a long sequence of burial, a sequence that was intended from the outset.

Analysis of burials in other parts of the country, including the barrow at Amesbury G71, Wiltshire (Barrett 1988), Long Crichel, Dorset (Barrett et al. 1991), Deeping St Nicholas, Lincolnshire (French 1994), and Barnack, Cambridgeshire (Donaldson 1977; Last 1998), indicate long mortuary sequences. Similar multiple burials have been excavated in Scotland at Sand Field, Orkney (Dalland 1999), and Horsburgh Castle Farm in the Scottish Borders (Petersen et al. 1974), while the burials in cairns in Kilmartin, Argyll, are likely to be the result of long sequences of development (Jones 2001). Cemetery barrows proper – containing up to 40 burials – are also an important feature of the Irish Early Bronze Age as at Grange, Co. Roscommon (O'Riordain 1997), and the Mound of the Hostages, Tara, Co. Meath (Kavanagh 1976; O'Sullivan 2006).

The Wessex Culture and the Problem of Individual Identity

In some regions of the country, especially in Wessex and the south coast as far west as Cornwall and as far east as Kent, a series of burials are accompanied by a suite of spectacular grave goods. Grave goods are produced in exotic substances including gold, amber, jet and the artificial glassy substance, faience. Many of these substances came from specific sources. Jet was procured from Whitby, Yorkshire, and Purbeck, Dorset; amber from the Baltic region; gold from either Wales or Ireland; while the production of faience was highly specialised and the earliest star- and quoit-shaped beads are likely to be Scottish (see Jones 2002; Taylor 1980 for a detailed discussion of the provenance and manufacture of these objects).

Piggott (1938) classically described the burials in southern England as the "Wessex culture", divided into a Wessex I and Wessex II phase. The Wessex I phase is dated from ca. 1900 to 1700 B.C. (Gerloff 1975; Needham 2000:171, fig. 11) and is composed mainly of male inhumations deposited with daggers, goldwork and other regalia; these burials contrast with female inhumations which are deposited with pendants of gold, bronze and amber. During the Wessex II phase, dated from ca. 1700 to 1500 B.C. (Gerloff 1975; Needham 2000:171, fig. 11), cremation became the dominant mortuary rite, and cremation burials are again distinguished by gender with males being buried with daggers, bronze pins and whetstones and females with necklaces composed of mixed beads (Woodward 2000:103–104). The Wessex phenomenon is not isolated and exotic substances had been deposited with the dead from the Beaker period onwards (Woodward 2000). Moreover, a series of burials in northern England and Scotland were also accompanied by beads and necklaces of jet, and occasional objects of gold and amber (Jones 2002; 2005a).

The presence of substantial quantities of exotic substances with these burials immediately leads us to consider questions of status and personhood. Piggott (1938) attributed the appearance of the Wessex culture to the rise of a wealthy chieftain-led society with long-distance contacts to regions on the Continent. Some of the more unusual grave goods accompanying the burial in the Upton Lovell G2a barrow included over 60 bone points graded in size, three polished flint axes, two stone battle axes, stone rubbers and polishers, perforated boars tusks and two cups of marcasite. By comparison with similar finds from Russia, these grave goods led Piggott (1962) to attribute a shamanic persona to the inhumation burial, with the bone points as decoration on a fringed garment similar to those worn by Eurasian shamans. Woodward (2000) follows this interpretation and suggests that shamans or ritual specialists may be a better description of the individuals in the Wessex culture burials. The deposition of grave goods in these Early Bronze Age burials are therefore taken to signify fairly fixed notions of identity; grave goods are read as signifiers of status.

After this detailed account of the chronological and regional differences in mortuary practices in Britain and Ireland from 4000 to 1500 B.C. we are faced with a series of problems which I now want to critically address. Many of the problems stem from the basic opposition between communal burial in the Neolithic and individual burial in the Early Bronze Age. The idea of a simple shift from communal burial in chambered tombs and long barrows to individual burials in round barrows is confounded by the presence of burials beneath round barrows from the beginning of the Neolithic and the evidence of multiple burials in Early Bronze Age contexts across Britain.

Equally the notion of inhumation as a feature of the Early Neolithic and cremation as a major characteristic of the later phases of the Early Bronze Age is problematised by a series of issues: the presence of cremation deposits in round barrows from the earliest phases of the Neolithic; the presence of cremations in a number of Late Neolithic contexts; and, of course, the abiding practice of cremation throughout the Irish Neolithic sequence. If we can no longer sustain a simple division between Neolithic and Bronze Age mortuary practice how are we to re-conceptualise the role of the dead during the Neolithic and Bronze Age?

Regarding Mortuary Process

One of the key points to emerge from my account of mortuary archaeology is the strong degree of diversity in practices. This diversity is particularly difficult to deal with if we simply define mortuary sites according to rigid typological schemes or if we bracket mortuary practices chronologically. It is in order to address this diversity that Barrett (1988) proposes that we instead focus upon mortuary ritual as a *process*. To begin with he draws on the anthropological literature on ritual to note that rituals consist of rites of passage (Turner 1967). These often have a tripartite form consisting of rites of separation, rites of liminality, and finally rites of incorporation (Van Gennep 1960). In taking this three-part structure mortuary rituals are involved in constructing the passage between life and death. The corpse is removed from the community of mourners, enters an often temporally protracted liminal stage between life and death and is then finally incorporated amongst the community of the dead. The inauspicious nature of death typically leads to the formal and solemn marking of each of these stages.

Barrett (1988:31) distinguishes between ancestor rituals and funerary rituals. The first are concerned with establishing the presence of the ancestors in the rites concerned with the living. Barrett (1988:31) suggests that both architecture and the bones of the dead may be significant components of ancestral rituals. Funerary rituals, on the other hand, are more specifically concerned with human burial. Here he notes that inhumations, cremations and secondary burials (re-interments some time after the initial burial of the corpse) might be components of funerary rituals depending upon the specific course that rites of passage take.

Importantly, he notes that inhumations, cremations and secondary burials structure the topographical relationship between the living and the dead. Inhumations
fix the place and moment at which the transition to death is socially achieved.
Cremations often occur at one place, while the cremated remains may be buried
at another. Similarly secondary burials often involve the transferral of remains from
one place to another. This is significant since the place of death and the final resting
place of the corpse are distinct: "The place of transition is separate from the final
place in which the ritual sequence is brought to a close" (Barrett 1988:32). Barrett
argues that by attending to the place and sequence of mortuary rituals along with
the architectural framework of ritual we can begin to comprehend how the relationship between the living and the dead are constructed, how certain modes of authority are either preserved or challenged.

This approach to understanding mortuary practices remains of signal importance. If we adopt this approach we can begin to discern that mortuary practices
are ritual processes which employ a diversity of different elements in sequence in
order to construct the relationship between the living and the dead. Rather than
viewing the different mortuary traditions discussed above as bound up with the
rigid expression of cultural identities (as would be expected with a culture-historical
approach) we can instead see each element of the mortuary process as a series of
flexible but interrelated choices (Mizoguchi 1993), each of which will have a consequence for the construction of the relationship between the mourners and the
deceased.

A series of critically important decisions must be made: whether to cremate or
to inhume the dead; whether to build a crematorium or a wooden mortuary structure; whether to bury earlier structures beneath a circular or a long mound; whether
to build a monument with an impressive façade, a passage or a chamber; whether
to inter the dead with grave goods or not; whether to elaborate an existing monument or to build a new monument. None of these are necessarily exclusive to one
period or another, and several coexist regionally. The material resources of architecture, mortuary rite and objects accompanying the corpse are all important and
each serves to emphasise different aspects of the mortuary process. I will illustrate
this point with a few examples.

The interchangeable nature of certain aspects of mortuary ritual can be observed
in the case of a series of Scottish Early Neolithic monuments. For example, the
monument at Pitnacree, Perthshire (Coles and Simpson 1965), began with a timber
structure enclosed by a linear stone-lined trench associated with a series of cremations. This was then covered by a stone mound and then sealed by an earth mound.
Similar structures to the stone-lined trench and timber structure are found beneath
barrows at Lochhill, Kirkcudbrightshire (Masters 1973), and Slewcairn, Kirkcudbrightshire (Kinnes 1992a). In these latter cases, however, the earlier mortuary
structures were covered not by a round barrow, but by long barrows of stone. This
example suggests that, while the mortuary ritual commences with similar structures,
this may follow quite a different route or trajectory in different regions, depending
upon how the relationships between living and deceased are structured.

Another example will be useful to demonstrate the interchangeability of different
elements of mortuary ritual. In a pioneering study Kinnes (1975) defines three ways

in which the monuments around the Irish Sea region could combine the same basic box-like structure to orchestrate different experiences of megalithic space. These three combinations were linear, agglomerated and dispersed. Thomas (1993) suggests that these different combinations may be indicative of the changing use and significance of different types of tomb architecture.

In Ireland during the Early Neolithic three major classes of tomb predominate: portal tombs, court tombs and passage tombs. There is a tendency to treat them as evidence for distinct cultural groupings, on the prevailing culture-historical model. However, as Cooney (1999:92–94) notes, they are often found in similar regions and their distribution does not suggest distinct cultural groupings. Similarly the available radiocarbon determinations suggest considerable chronological overlap. If we treat the monuments less as rigidly defined in terms of morphology, and more as architectural constructions each of which is meant to emphasise different aspects of the mortuary process, their distinctive architecture becomes more comprehensible. Court tombs with their large façades are evidently meant to emphasise the activity in the façade or court, which takes place prior to the deposition of the remains of the dead (Thomas 1993:86). Portal tombs, which often contain token deposits of human bone in the chamber, are greatly emphasised by the massive stones used in their construction. Passage tombs, on the other hand, mark out the distinction between the living and the dead by the construction of a long passage. This serves to emphasise the liminal space travelled by the living and the dead as they pass from the realm of the living (the monument's exterior) to the place of the dead (the monument's interior). Rather than treating each monument as the manifestation of distinct and bounded cultural identities, we can instead see that each invokes a different strategy for emphasising key aspects of the mortuary process.

Questioning the Ancestors

The next key point to consider is the characterisation of Neolithic mortuary practices as ancestral in character. As noted at the beginning of the chapter this relates partly to the view that the practice of monument construction began at the onset of the Neolithic (Bradley 1993; 1998). As we saw, John Barrett distinguished ancestral rites from funerary rites: ancestral rites could be distinguished architecturally by continued access to the dead and the use of human bone to establish the presence of the ancestors.

The notion of the ancestors has recently been criticised, partly because it has become something of an unexamined orthodoxy. One of the central arguments against the notion of ancestors during the Neolithic for Whitley (2001) is the difficulty of demonstrating real genealogical relationships. The term is too vague. I agree with Whitley's point that the term "ancestors" has a loose currency in Neolithic studies. However, he is mistaken in seeking to question the notion by recourse to a strictly genealogical argument. In discussing the notion of ancestry and its use by the United Nations to define indigenous relationships with the land, Ingold (2000:132–151) distinguishes between two models: genealogical and relational.

The genealogical model, usually adopted by officialdom, deals strictly with physical descent as a means of establishing people's rights to land (this is the definition adhered to by Whitley). The relational model favoured by Ingold more closely reflects people's perceived relationships with the landscape and each other. Rather than dealing very precisely with descent as a means of defining relationships to land, relational modes of ancestry foreground the continued engagement between people and landscape. Ingold notes that, rather than treating descent in a strictly linear fashion, a relational approach views descent as a multiple interconnected network. By engaging with the landscape and the people, creatures and things that inhabit it, ancestry may be traced to multiple points of origin. Ingold lists just four of a multitude of possibilities: "ancestors can be ordinary humans who lived in the past, or spirit inhabitants of the landscape, or mythic-other-than-human characters, or original creator beings" (Ingold 2000:140). Ancestry need not involve the physical transmission of substance – as we would expect if we treat ancestors purely as the genealogical predecessors of Neolithic populations – rather relations of ancestry are produced through continued engagement with the ancestors. Ancestry is manufactured, not just passively transmitted.

Ancestors may therefore take multiple forms and we need not place too much emphasis on physical genealogical lines of descent to argue for ancestry in the Neolithic. For example, it is perfectly plausible to consider animals as possible mythical ancestors for Neolithic populations (Whittle 2000; 2003; Jones and Richards 2003). But if we loosen the strict definition of ancestors are we in danger of simply glossing all relationships between the dead and the living as ancestral? I will argue below that the notion of ancestry may be equally helpful to understanding Neolithic and Early Bronze Age mortuary practices alike. We need to worry less about the notion of ancestors and to be more careful in distinguishing between *different forms of ancestral relationship*.

Ancestry and Personhood

Julian Thomas (1999:162) notes that towards the end of the Early Neolithic there may have been

> a decline in bounded, mutually exclusive, corporate social units. Instead of seeing themselves as members of a community, composed of relations with others in the present (including the dead), people might increasingly have placed themselves socially according to the principle of descent from named ancestors in the past.

What Thomas sketches out here is a shift from one kind of ancestor to another, from a concept of ancestry based on membership of a group based on multiple ties – possibly to multiple ancestors – to a notion of ancestry more closely based on a defined relationship with a single named ancestor. If we adopt the relational view of ancestry I advocate above then we can see that both the mortuary practices of the Neolithic and the Early Bronze Age can be viewed as ancestral. A lineage-based system, as supposed for the Late Neolithic and Early Bronze Age, is no less ancestral. It simply offers a different way of relating to past antecedents.

Crucially Thomas relates the generation of new notions of ancestry to the character of personhood. There has been considerable debate on the character of personhood in the Neolithic (Thomas 2001; 2002; Fowler 2001; 2004; 2005; Jones 2005a; 2005b; Pollard 2005). The past is assumed to have been inhabited by versions of the Western individual; and so the shift to single grave burial in the Bronze Age has been characterised as the emergence of individuality. Rather than simply assuming the existence of persons whose identity is defined by an indivisible and fixed notion of the self, a series of anthropological case studies indicate that other societies often conceive of the person in quite different ways. Persons are often conceived relationally: they are composed out of the multiple social relations in which they are engaged, and the boundaries of the person may be permeable (e.g. Strathern 1988; Wagner 1991).

The fragmented and communal nature of Neolithic mortuary deposits has been viewed as one possible example of relational personhood (Thomas 1999; 2001; 2002; Fowler 2001; 2004; 2005). While this is accepted, are we to simply read the mortuary rites of the Late Neolithic and Early Bronze Age as evidence for a new form of personhood: the rise of the individual? A number of authors have questioned this view (Thomas 1999:156; Jones 2002; 2005a Brück 2004). It may be best if we view persons as relationally constructed during the Late Neolithic and Early Bronze Age, simply in different ways from those of the Early Neolithic.

One of the key ways in which the person is constructed in different ways is through the treatment of the corpse and in the relationship between artefacts and the dead. Joshua Pollard (2005) has recently discussed the significance of processes of fragmentation and transformation in a range of Neolithic contexts, including chambered tombs, long barrows and causewayed enclosures. The fragmentation, dispersal and transformation of human bone offers a means by which personhood was both perpetuated and reworked. This is particularly highlighted by the process of re-assembly evident in chambered tomb contexts such as Pipton and Penywyrlod, Wales (Wysocki and Whittle 2000:598), where individual "skeletons" were composed of bones from several people. Through the transformative reworking of human bone new ways of relating to the ancestral dead presented themselves, and the dead and the living were equally transformed in this process. For Pollard, decay and disarticulation may have been part of the means of transforming people from corporeal entities into the material embodiment of ancestor spirits.

While human bone was used as a resource for the circulation and perpetuation of identity during the Neolithic, artefacts played a similar role in the Late Neolithic and Early Bronze Age (Jones 2005a). As noted above, many of the more spectacular artefacts associated with Late Neolithic and Early Bronze Age graves had considerable biographies, being procured from substances whose origins were distant and exotic. In some instances – as with the jet necklaces of Scotland and Wales – analysis using X-ray fluorescence has indicated that the objects had been curated and repaired a number of times; parts were often replaced with inferior materials such as cannel coal (Sheridan and Davis 2002). Artefacts such as these were involved in complex exchange histories.

Artefacts were deposited in funerary contexts in a number of ways. They could be arranged around the corpse as with Beaker burials (Thomas 1991); they might be deliberately destroyed at the graveside as with the deposition of fragments of jet or amber necklaces (Jones 2002); or fragments of artefacts or token objects might be deposited, such as the token deposits of jet beads in the north of Britain (Jones 2002). The deposition of artefacts in this way provided a means of fixing the image of the person in memory; it also offered a transaction between the living and the dead. As Jo Brück (2004) says, objects placed in the grave allowed mourners to comment metaphorically on the links between the living and the dead.

By contrast with the Neolithic, artefacts become foci of remembrance, the site of transactions between the living and the dead. The dead literally come to be represented by artefacts. This is most apparent during the later periods of the Early Bronze Age, from 2000 to 1500 B.C., where we increasingly find the bones of the dead contained in pots with varying levels of decorative complexity. Indeed in the large cinerary urns the bones of the dead are encompassed and contained by the pot – artefacts literally come to stand for the body of the dead.

Another way in which the image of the person was retained in memory was through the drama of mortuary display. During the Late Neolithic and Early Bronze Age funerary ritual would have been both a singular event and multi-stage. Cremation would have involved multiple stages, with the dressing of the corpse, its spectacular destruction on the funeral pyre and then the collecting and cleaning of the bones prior to burial, often in a ceramic container. Inhumation, on the other hand, is likely to have involved fewer stages. A good example of the dramatic nature of Early Bronze Age mortuary ritual is the burial at Irthlingborough, Northamptonshire, where a mound of over 180 cattle skulls was constructed over a wooden chamber containing a man buried with a Beaker and flint dagger, and a grave pit containing a second adult (Davis and Payne 1993).

Time and Memory in Mortuary Practices

We observe two different ways of treating the dead. In the first instance the bones of the dead were accessible and could be circulated and transformed. In the second instance the dead were sited in fixed locales in the landscape (in earthen barrows or stone cairns), and instead artefacts were dispersed. At first sight it seems feasible to say that these are chronologically distinct ways of treating the dead. In fact, during the Early Neolithic mortuary practices in which the dead remained fixed beneath round barrows, or were placed permanently beneath long barrows after having been circulated for some time, coexist chronologically with mortuary rituals in which the dead were continually accessible. Just as during the Early Bronze Age the dead may either have remained fixed in place beneath round barrows or may have been continually accessible.

Rather than thinking of these as two discrete modes of relating to the dead, it is best to think of them as complementary ways of reckoning time and organising remembrance. In those cases where the bones of the dead were accessible there is a degree of *temporal fluidity*; the bones of the dead were open to continual reworking.

Where the dead remained in a fixed situation between earthen barrows, time was treated as *punctuated*, modelled according to a series of discontinuous relationships.

In the first instance the relationship between the living and the dead occurred as a series of "material citations" (Jones 2005b; Jones 2007) – or references to the past – enacted using the medium of the bones of the dead themselves. In the second instance, where mortuary practices were punctuated, rituals were concerned with presenting a fixed memory of the corpse. One means of fixing memory is through the dramatic display of quantities of artefacts displayed around the corpse (Thomas 1991; Jones 2002); another way of producing fixed mnemonic images is through the spectacular immolation of the corpse by fire (see Williams 2005 for a related argument for Anglo-Saxon cremation practices). This may be one of the reasons that cremation deposits tend to be associated with burial beneath earthen barrows throughout the Early Neolithic to Early Bronze Age in Britain.

In the first instance the ancestors intercede in the lives of the living since their bones act as a continual reminder of their presence and influence. In the second, artefacts keep the memory of the dead alive; the continued circulation of material culture signifies not only the social ties created by the dead but the power of the dead person to influence people by continuing to engage the living population in exchange relations. In both cases rituals are concerned with processes of transformation. In the first scenario the corpse undergoes transformation through decay and disarticulation and the spirit of the dead is contained in the tomb: the bones of the dead instantiate the presence of the ancestors. In the second case the transformation of the person from living to dead occurs either at the graveside or through the cremation. The drama of mortuary ritual is a vehicle for the transformation of the person and the spirit of the dead is captured in the material form of the artefact either deposited in the grave or removed by the mourners. The ancestors are instead "presenced" by artefacts. In both cases the memory of the person persists in material form: this is how the dead live.

REFERENCES

Atkinson, R., C. M. Piggott and N. K. Sanders, 1951 Excavations at Dorchester, Oxon. Oxford: Ashmolean Museum.

Barclay, A., and A. Bayliss, 1999 Cursus monuments and the radiocarbon problem. *In* Pathways and Ceremonies: the cursus monuments of Britain and Ireland. A. Barclay and J. Harding, eds. pp. 10–29. Oxford: Oxbow Books.

——and C. Halpin, 2001 Excavations at Barrow Hills, Radley, Oxfordshire, vol. 1: The Neolithic and Bronze Age Monument Complex. Oxford: Oxford University Committee for Archaeology.

Barrett, J. C., 1988 The living, the dead and the ancestors: Neolithic and early Bronze Age mortuary practices. *In* The Archaeology of Context in the Neolithic and Bronze Age: recent trends. J. C. Barrett and I. A. Kinnes, eds. pp. 30–41. Sheffield: Department of Archaeology and Prehistory, University of Sheffield.

——1994 Fragments from Antiquity: an archaeology of social life in Britain, 2900–1200 BC. Oxford: Blackwell.

———R. Bradley and M. Green, 1991 Landscape, Monuments and Society: the prehistory of Cranborne Chase. Cambridge: Cambridge University Press.
Bradley, R., 1984 The Social Foundations of Prehistoric Britain. Harlow: Longman.
———1992 The excavation of an oval barrow beside the Abingdon causewayed enclosure, Oxfordshire. Proceedings of the Prehistoric Society 58:127–142.
———1993 Altering the Earth. Edinburgh: Society of Antiquaries of Scotland.
———1998 The Significance of Monuments: on the shaping of human experience in Neolithic and Bronze Age Europe. London: Routledge.
———and R. Chapman, 1986 The nature and development of long distance relations in later Neolithic Britain and Ireland. In Peer Polity Interaction and Socio-Political Change. C. Renfrew and J. Cherry, eds. pp. 127–158. Cambridge: Cambridge University Press.
———and R. Holgate, 1984 The Neolithic sequence in the upper Thames valley. In Neolithic Studies: a review of some current research. R. Bradley and J. Gardiner, eds. pp. 107–134. Oxford: British Archaeological Reports.
Brück, J., 2004 Material metaphors: the relational construction of identity in Early Bronze Age burials in Ireland and Britain. Journal of Social Archaeology 4:307–331.
Burgess, C., and S. Shennan, 1976 The beaker phenomenon: some suggestions. In Settlement and Economy in the Third and Second Millennia BC. C. Burgess and R. Miket, eds. pp. 309–331. Oxford: British Archaeological Reports.
Burl, H. A. W., 1984 Report on excavation of a Neolithic mound at Boghead, Speymouth Forest, Fochabers, Moray 1972 and 1974. Proceedings of the Society of Antiquaries of Scotland 114:35–73.
Case, H., 1995 Irish Beakers in their European Context. In Ireland in the Bronze Age. J. Waddell and E. Shee Twohig, eds. pp. 14–29. Dublin: Stationery Office.
Clarke, D. L., 1970 Beaker Pottery of Great Britain and Ireland. Cambridge: Cambridge University Press.
Coles, J., and D. D. A. Simpson, 1965 The excavation of a Neolithic round barrow at Pitnacree, Perthshire, Scotland. Proceedings of the Society of Antiquaries of Scotland 31:34–57.
Cooney, G., 1999 Landscapes of Neolithic Ireland. London: Routledge.
Cowie, T., 1978 Bronze Age Food Vessel Urns in Northern Britain. Oxford: British Archaeological Reports.
Dalland, M., 1999 Sand Field: the excavation of an exceptional cist in Orkney. Proceedings of the Society of Antiquaries of Scotland 65:373–415.
Darvill, T. C., 1982 The Neolithic Chambered Tombs of the Cotswold-Severn Region. Highworth: Vorda.
———2004 Long Barrows of the Cotswolds and Surrounding Areas. Stroud: Tempus.
Davidson, J. L., and A. S. Henshall, 1989. The Chambered Cairns of Orkney. Edinburgh: Edinburgh University Press.
———and——1990 The Chambered Cairns of Caithness. Edinburgh: Edinburgh University Press.
Davis, S., and S. Payne, 1993 A barrow full of cattle skulls. Antiquity 67:12–22.
de Valera, R., and S. O'Nualláin, 1961 Survey of the Megalithic Tombs of Ireland, vol. 1. Dublin: Stationery Office.
Donaldson, P., 1977 The excavation of a multiple round barrow at Barnack, Cambridgeshire 1974–1976. Antiquaries Journal 57:77–96.
Drewett, P., 1975 The excavation of an oval barrow mound of the third millennium BC at Alfriston, East Sussex. Proceedings of the Prehistoric Society 41:119–152.
Eogan, G., 1994 The Accomplished Art. Oxford: Oxbow Books.

Evans, C., 1988 Acts of enclosure: a consideration of concentrically-organised causewayed enclosures. *In* The Archaeology of Context in the Neolithic and Bronze Age: recent trends. J. C. Barrett and I. A. Kinnes, eds. pp. 85–96. Sheffield: Department of Archaeology and Prehistory, University of Sheffield.

Fowler, C., 2001 Personhood and social relations in the British Neolithic, with a study from the Isle of Man. Journal of Material Culture 6(2):137–163.

——2004 The Archaeology of Personhood: an anthropological approach. London: Routledge.

——2005 Identity politics: personhood, kinship, gender and power in Neolithic and early Bronze Age Britain. *In* The Archaeology of Plural and Changing Identities: beyond identification. E. C. Casella and C. Fowler, eds. pp. 109–129. New York: Kluwer/Plenum.

French, C., 1994 Excavation of the Deeping St. Nicholas Barrow Complex, South Lincoln-shire. Lincoln: Lincolnshire Archaeological Heritage Report Series.

Garwood, P., 1991 Ritual tradition and the reconstruction of society. *In* Sacred and Profane. P. Garwood, D. Jennings, R. Skeates and J. Toms, eds. pp. 10–32. Oxford: Oxford University Committee for Archaeology.

——1999 Grooved Ware in Southern Britain: chronology and interpretation. *In* Grooved Ware in Britain and Ireland. R. Cleal and A. MacSween, eds. pp. 145–176. Oxford: Oxbow Books.

Gerloff, S., 1975 The Early Bronze Age Daggers in Great Britain, and a reconsideration of the Wessex Culture. Munich: Beck.

Greig, M. K., C. Greig, A. N. Shepherd and I. A. G. Shepherd, 1989 A beaker cist from Chapelden, Tore of Troup, Aberdour, Banff and Buchan District, with a note on the orientation of beaker burials in Northeast Scotland. Proceedings of the Society of Antiquaries of Scotland 119:79–81.

Harding, J., 1997 Interpreting the Neolithic: the monuments of North Yorkshire. Oxford Journal of Archaeology 16(3):279–295.

Harrison, R., 1980 The Beaker Folk. London: Thames and Hudson.

Hedges, J., and G. W. Parry, 1980 A Neolithic multiple burial at Sumburgh Airport, Shetland. Glasgow Archaeological Journal 7:15–26.

Henshall, A. S., 1963 The Chambered Tombs of Scotland, vol. 1. Edinburgh: Edinburgh University Press.

——1972 The Chambered Tombs of Scotland, vol. 2. Edinburgh: Edinburgh University Press.

——and J. N. G. Ritchie, 1995 The Chambered Cairns of Sutherland. Edinburgh: Edinburgh University Press.

Ingold, T., 2000 The Perception of the Environment. London: Routledge.

Jones, A., 2001 Enduring images? Image production and memory in Earlier Bronze Age Scotland. *In* Bronze Age Landscapes: tradition and transformation. J. Brück, ed. pp. 217–228. Oxford: Oxbow Books.

——2002 A biography of colour: colour, material histories and personhood in the Early Bronze Age of Britain and Ireland. *In* Colouring the Past. A. Jones and G. MacGregor, eds. pp. 159–174. Oxford: Berg.

——2005a Matter and memory: colour, remembrance and the Neolithic/Bronze Age Transition. *In* Rethinking Materiality: the engagement of mind with the material world. E. De Marrais, C. Gosden and C. Renfrew, eds. pp. 167–178. Cambridge: McDonald Institute.

——2005b Lives in fragments? Personhood and the European Neolithic. Journal of Social Archaeology 5(2):193–224.

———2007 Memory and Material Culture: tracing the past in prehistoric Europe. Cambridge: Cambridge University Press.

———and C. Richards, 2003 Animals into ancestors: domestication, food and identity in late Neolithic Orkney. *In* Food and Identity in the Neolithic and Early Bronze Age. M. Parker Pearson, ed. pp. 45–51. Oxford: British Archaeological Reports.

Kavanagh, R., 1976 Collared and cordoned cinerary urns in Ireland. Proceedings of the Royal Irish Academy 76:293–403.

Kinnes, I. A., 1975 Monumental function in British Neolithic burial practices. World Archaeology 7:16–29.

———1979 Round Barrows and Ring-Ditches in the British Neolithic. London: British Museum Press.

———1992a Balnagowan and after: the context of non-megalithic mortuary sites in Scotland. *In* Vessels for the Ancestors. N. Sharples and A. Sheridan, eds. pp. 83–103. Edinburgh: Edinburgh University Press.

———1992b Non-Megalithic Long Barrows and Related Monuments in Britain. London: British Museum Press.

———T. Schadla-Hall, P. Chadwick and P. Dean, 1983 Duggleby Howe reconsidered. Archaeological Journal 140:83–108.

Last, J., 1998 Books of life: biography and memory in a Bronze Age barrow. Oxford Journal of Archaeology 17(1):43–53.

Longworth, I. H., 1984 Collared Urns of the Bronze Age in Great Britain and Ireland. Cambridge: Cambridge University Press.

Lynch, F., 1969 Megalithic tombs of North Wales. In Megalithic Enquiries in the West of Britain. T. G. E. Powell, J. X. W. P. Corcoran, F. Lynch and J. G. Scott, eds. pp. 107–174. Liverpool: Liverpool University Press.

———1972 Ring cairns and related monuments in Wales. Scottish Archaeological Forum 4:61–80.

Masters, L., 1973 The Lochill long cairn. Antiquity 47:96–100.

Meillassoux, C., 1972 From reproduction to production. Economy and Society 1:93–105.

Mizoguchi, K., 1993 Time in the reproduction of mortuary practices. World Archaeology 25(2):223–235.

Mount, C., 1995 New research on Irish early Bronze Age cemeteries. *In* Ireland in the Bronze Age. J. Waddell and E. Shee Twohig, eds. pp. 97–111. Dublin: Stationery Office.

Needham, S. P., 2000 Power pulses across a cultural divide: cosmologically driven acquisition between Armorica and Wessex. Proceedings of the Prehistoric Society 66: 151–208.

O'Brien, W., 1998 Sacred Ground: megalithic tombs in coastal south-west Ireland. Galway: Department of Archaeology, National University of Ireland, Galway.

O'Riordain, B., 1997 A Bronze Age cemetery mound at Grange. Co. Roscommon. Journal of Irish Archaeology 8:43–72.

O'Sullivan, M., 2006 Duma na nGiall: the Mound of the Hostages, Tara. Bray: Wordwell.

Oswald, A., C. Dyer and M. Barber, 2001 The Creation of Monuments: Neolithic causewayed enclosures in the British Isles. Swindon: English Heritage.

Peacock, D. P., 1969 Neolithic pottery production in Cornwall. Antiquity 139:145–149.

Petersen, F., 1972 Traditions of multiple burial in later Neolithic and Early Bronze Age England. Archaeological Journal 129:22–55.

———I. A. G. Shepherd and A. N. Tuckwell, 1974 A short cist at Horsburgh Farm, Peebleshire. Proceedings of the Society of Antiquaries of Scotland 105:43–62.

Piggott, S., 1938 The early bronze age in Wessex. Proceedings of the Prehistoric Society 4:52–106.

——1954 The Neolithic Cultures of the British Isles. Cambridge: Cambridge University Press.

——1962 From Salisbury Plain to south Siberia. Wiltshire Archaeological and Natural History Magazine 58:93–97.

Pollard, J., 2005 The art of decay and the transformation of substance. *In* Substance, Memory and Display: archaeology and art. C. Renfrew, C. Gosden and E. DeMarrais, eds. pp. 47–62. Cambridge: McDonald Institute.

Renfrew, A. C., 1973 Monuments, mobilisation and social organisation in Neolithic Wessex. *In* The Explanation of Culture Change: models in prehistory. A. C. Renfrew, ed. pp. 539–558. London: Duckworth.

——1974 Beyond a subsistence economy: the evolution of prehistoric Europe. *In* Reconstructing Complex Societies. C. B. Moore, ed. pp. 69–95. Cambridge, MA: Bulletin of the American Schools of Oriental Research.

Richards, C., 1988 Altered images: a re-examination of Neolithic mortuary practices in Orkney. *In* The Archaeology of Context in the Neolithic and Bronze Age: recent trends. J. C. Barrett and I. A. Kinnes, eds. pp. 42–56. Sheffield: Department of Archaeology and Prehistory, University of Sheffield.

Scott, J., 1992 Mortuary structures and megaliths. *In* Vessels for the Ancestors. N. Sharples and A. Sheridan, eds. pp. 104–119 Edinburgh: Edinburgh University Press.

Shanks, M., and C. Tilley, 1982 Ideology, symbolic power and ritual communication: a reinterpretation of Neolithic mortuary practices. *In* Symbolic and Structural Archaeology. I. Hodder, ed. pp. 129–154. Cambridge: Cambridge University Press.

Shennan, S., 1975 The social organisation at Branc. Antiquity 49:279–288.

——1982 Ideology, change and the European Early Bronze Age. *In* Symbolic and Structural Archaeology. I. Hodder, ed. pp. 155–161. Cambridge: Cambridge University Press.

Shepherd, A. N., 1996 A Neolithic ring-mound at Midtown of Pitglassie, Auchterless, Aberdeenshire. Proceedings of the Society of Antiquaries of Scotland 126:17–52.

Shepherd, I. A. G., 1986 Powerful Pots: beakers in north-east prehistory. Aberdeen: Marischal College.

Sheridan, A., 1986 Megaliths and megalomania: an account, and interpretation, of the development of passage graves in Ireland. Journal of Irish Archaeology 3:17–30.

——1995 Irish Neolithic pottery: the story in 1995. *In* Unbaked Urns of Rudely Shape. I. A. Kinnes and G. Varndell, eds. pp. 3–22. Oxford: Oxbow Monographs.

——and M. Davis, 2002 Investigating jet and jet-like artefacts from prehistoric Scotland: the National Museums of Scotland project. Antiquity 76:812–825.

Strathern, M., 1988 The Gender of the Gift. Berkeley: University of California Press.

Taylor, J., 1980 Bronze Age Goldwork of the British Isles. Cambridge: Cambridge University Press.

Thomas, J., 1991 Reading the body: beaker funerary practice in Britain. *In* Sacred and Profane. P. Garwood, D. Jennings, R. Skeates and J. Toms, eds. pp. 33–43. Oxford: Oxford University Committee for Archaeology.

——1993 The hermeneutics of megalithic space. *In* Interpretative Archaeology. C. Tilley, ed. pp. 73–97. Oxford: Berg.

——1999 Understanding the Neolithic. London: Routledge.

——2001 Death, identity and the body in Neolithic Britain. Journal of the Royal Anthropological Institute 6:603–617.

——2002 Archaeology's humanism and the materiality of the body. *In* Thinking through the Body: archaeologies of corporeality. Y. Hamilakis, M. Pluciennik and S. Tarlow, eds. pp. 29–46. New York: Kluwer/Plenum.

——and A. Whittle, 1986 Anatomy of a tomb: West Kennet revisited. Oxford Journal of Archaeology 5:129–156.

Thorpe, N., 1984 Ritual, power and ideology: a reconsideration of earlier Neolithic rituals in Wessex. *In* Neolithic Studies: a review of some current research. R. Bradley and J. Gardiner, eds. pp. 41–60. Oxford: British Archaeological Reports.

——and C. Richards 1984 The decline of ritual authority and the introduction of Beakers into Britain. *In* Neolithic Studies: a review of some current research. R. Bradley and J. Gardiner, eds. pp. 67–84. Oxford: British Archaeological Reports.

Tuckwell, A., 1975 Patterns of burial orientation in the round barrows of east Yorkshire. Bulletin of the Institute of Archaeology University of London 12:95–123.

Turner, V., 1967 The Forest of Symbols: aspects of Ndembu ritual. London: Cornell University Press.

Van Gennep, A., 1960 The Rites of Passage: structure and anti-structure. London: Routledge and Kegan Paul.

Waddell, J., 1998 The Prehistoric Archaeology of Ireland. Galway: Galway University Press.

Wagner, R., 1991 The fractal person. *In* Big Men and Great Men: personifications of power in Melanesia. M. Strathern and M. Godelier, eds. pp. 159–173. Cambridge: Cambridge University Press.

Walsh, P., 1995 Structure and deposition in Irish Wedge Tombs: an open and shut case? *In* Ireland in the Bronze Age. J. Waddell and E. Shee Twohig, eds. pp. 113–127. Dublin: Stationery Office.

Walter, R., T. Thomas and P. Sheppard, 2004 Cult assemblages and ritual practice in Roviana Lagoon, Solomon Islands. World Archaeology 36(1):142–157.

Whitley, J., 2001 Too many ancestors. Antiquity 76:119–126.

Whittle, A., 2000 Very like a whale: menhirs, motifs and myths in the Mesolithic–Neolithic transition of northwest Europe. Cambridge Archaeological Journal 10:243–259.

——2003 The Archaeology of People: dimensions of Neolithic life. London: Routledge.

——2005 Stones that float to the sky: portal dolmens and their landscapes of memory and myth. *In* The Neolithic of the Irish Sea: materiality and traditions of practice. V. Cummings and C. Fowler, eds. pp. 81–90. Oxford: Oxbow Books.

——and V. Cummings, 2004 Places of Special Virtue: megaliths in the Neolithic landscapes of Wales. Oxford: Oxbow Books.

——J. Pollard and C. Grigson, 1999 The Harmony of Symbols: the Windmill Hill causewayed enclosure, Wiltshire. Oxford: Oxbow Books.

Williams, H., 2005 Keeping the dead at arm's length: memory, weaponry and early medieval mortuary technologies. Journal of Social Archaeology 5(2):253–275.

Woodward, A., 2000 British Barrows: a matter of life and death. Stroud: Tempus.

Wysocki, M., and A. Whittle, 2000 Diversity, lifestyles and rites: new biological and archaeological evidence from British earlier Neolithic assemblages. Antiquity 74:591–601.

9

The Development of an Agricultural Countryside

David Field

Introduction

Change in the countryside has proceeded at a hectic pace during our own lifetimes and with the grubbing up of hedgerows taking place almost everywhere, the scale of that change has been immense. Often this has resulted in larger, "prairie" fields that can be ploughed, harrowed, manured, sprayed and harvested faster than ever by using bigger and more reliable machinery. Whether it was technology, that is, the availability of massive combine harvesters, that dictated the size of these fields, or an economic system designed to provide food for a metropolitan population that drove the move, is open to debate. The point is made for it is important to ask a similar question of Britain in the second millennium B.C. so that we can begin to identify and focus on the agents driving such change.

Two relevant "events" can be detected in the archaeological record, chiefly from the remains still visible on the land surface, but also from buried traces revealed by excavations. The first of these is the widespread layout of "Celtic" field complexes, increasingly dated to around the middle of the second millennium B.C., which mark the end of a process of intuitive response and an acknowledgement of contemporary and future needs, and which also imply that use of the land may have reached an intensity formerly unimagined. The second is, in part, represented by an extensive layout of larger, tithing or ranch-like land units that were in use during the first half of the first millennium B.C. and which, perhaps in response to shifting climatic and social conditions, announced a further change in agricultural practice.

Pioneers and prehistoric entrepreneurs there may have been, whose remains stand out as being dissimilar from others within their contemporary surroundings, but it is also likely that some differentiation in land use might be expected across the country as a whole, reflecting the nature of local topography and climate, just as it does today. Unfortunately, while environmental factors dictate that cultivation is likely to be more successfully carried out on the lower-lying, warmer south-eastern ground, it is precisely that area that has proved favourable to historic farmers too, and as a consequence much of it falls into Chris Taylor's (1972) "zone of destruction". It is this tract of productive and easily cultivated soils in favourable agricultural locations that often corresponds with the artefact distributions noted by others (e.g., Clark 1929; Grimes 1931) and, all things being equal, it is in such areas that we might expect to uncover the main foci of prehistoric activity. In recent times, Planning Policy Guidance-induced archaeological responses have reported the widespread presence of ditches containing Middle or Late Bronze Age pottery in many of these areas (Yates 1999; 2001), but the windows are generally quite restricted and it is often difficult to fully assess the nature of fields and systems of agriculture as a whole.

Landscape with Hazelnuts

The popular perception of terrain as landscape may have served to obscure interpretation, landscape being a modern concept derived from a school of painting (e.g., Hirsh 1995:2; Ingold 2000:202) that implies a traveller's perspective of terrain as aesthetic. However, such perspectives can be used in different ways. Ingold (2000:197), for example, used painting as a device for landscape analysis, notably, in examining Bruegel's *The Harvesters* in great depth in order to isolate perceptual relationships. When scrutinised, of course, landscape is more than scenery, for perception by those working in it is very different. Farmers, for example, consider that they work *on*, or *with*, the land rather than *in* the landscape, while women working on farms during the Second World War were referred to as *land* girls rather than *landscape* workers. In contrast to the scenic implications of the "-scape", land is sheer hard work. Its qualities include factors and values inherent in the soils as well as the presence and influences of other living creatures, but also the seemingly inexplicable elements – sun, wind, rain, warmth, shelter, drainage, micro-climate. Land implies intimate knowledge, rather more than the appreciative observations of a bystander. Such values along with the events inherent in the chronicle and scenery of work, might perhaps be incorporated in the concept of taskscape (Ingold 2000:194–198). Here, however, the country term is used.

Ingold's choice of artwork is apt, for the whole aim of those working on the land is successful harvest. It is a process of caring and nurturing, lest insect, disease or herbivores get more than their share and the investment is neutralised. The harvesting of hazelnuts, for example, figures large in the activities of pre-agricultural groups. Jacobi suggests that such food was being exploited to its capacity and that the amount of land needed to cater for the apparent importance of the hazelnut in pre-fourth-millennium diet left little of the countryside unexploited (Jacobi 1978:82–83; 1981). Jacobi wrote in terms of "cropping", "artificial control" and "nucleation", perhaps utilising fire to manipulate growth, all of which leaves a picture of countryside that was far from predominantly wildscape. For communities so heavily reliant on this resource, such assets will no doubt have been carefully curated and jealously safeguarded in order to be confident of a dependable crop and continued extensive use. This was a well-understood and cared-for land, with components incrementally utilised and where the enterprise, accomplishments and influences of inhabitants in one generation, or indeed millennium, were reaped and utilised by those in another (Ingold 2000:204; Barrett 1999). The harvest has a long pedigree.

Intervention in this delicate balance of well-established resource utilisation might be made only by creating suitable alternatives, but there is no indication in the record of dramatic early fourth-millennium change and, given the numbers of hazelnuts found at White Sheet Hill causewayed enclosure, similar practices may have continued well into the fourth millennium B.C. (Hinton in Rawlings et al. 2004:179) and perhaps much later. Rather the process appears to have been a slow but steady increase in the incidence of cereal use and of domestic animals, with greater emphasis on one or the other according to soils and micro-climate.

Terrain of Ancestral Memory

By the end of the third millennium B.C., the land so crafted – a patchwork of local resource units marked by ritual and funerary monuments and defined by managed woodland, grazing and cultivated areas around settlements, with important access to river frontage in order to water herds and flocks – was the product of millennia of accumulated animal and human activity. Such incremental use of the terrain by local communities will undoubtedly have resulted, in part, from intuitive responses, but also accrued knowledge that ultimately concluded in satisfactory levels of fecundity. Much as today, the land around settlements would be intimately known, and botanical and archaeological traces, if not local memory and legend, provided a trigger for understanding past inhabitation. Such "stacked up" genealogies in, for example, evidence of ancestral clearance still present in the piles of turf, stones and earth of local barrows, or traces of early gardens, provided relevance and rights, even though such places may still be inhabited by supernatural elements and considered taboo places. Where unhindered by old usage, or supernatural veto, new areas for cultivation could be carved out of the "waste" as and when they were needed.

The process of clearance can be observed in the uplands, whereby stone, turf and other surface vegetation was piled into mounds leaving unobstructed areas free for cultivation (Feachem 1973). In such places cairnfields – generally, though not universally, accepted as the product of such activity – are ubiquitous, for example, in Cornwall (Johnson and Rose 1994:41–42), Wales (Leighton 1997:91), the Peak District (Hart 1981; 1985; Barnatt 1986, 1999, 2000, 2004; Ainsworth 2001; Ainsworth and Pearson 2002), Northumberland (e.g., Jobey 1968) and Scotland (Ritchie and Ritchie 1981:86; Hunt 1987). Often the process is enhanced by clearance banks, linear accumulations of stony material with no architectural structure (Ainsworth 2001:30–31). In places of greater population density, however, such traces will have been reworked, enhanced, adapted and subdivided by generations, leaving little or no built evidence.

Prepared Terrain

In such places evidence of new agricultural intake survives in the presence of ard marks. At Hopton Street, Southwark, adjacent to the river Thames, where the well-drained soils, periodically refreshed by minerals from overbank floods, provided productive farmland, such ard marks are thought to be associated with Beaker pottery (Ridgeway 1999:74). Stake and post-holes immediately alongside may imply that general domestic or farmyard functions were taking place close by – evidently a compressed use of space.

Similar evidence has come from other sites in a liminal environment. On the west coast a series of ard and spade marks were found sealed in machair beneath a midden deposit at Rosinish, Outer Hebrides (Shepherd 1976; Shepherd and Tuckwell 1977). Radiocarbon dates of 2500–2270 cal B.C. (GU 1065) for the plough soil and 2600–2000 cal B.C. (GU 1064) for the lower level of the midden at 95 per cent confidence imply a late third-millennium focus for this episode of activity. While a series of ard marks discovered in a coastal location further south, at Gwithian, in Cornwall, were assigned a later, Middle Bronze Age date, two phases of Beaker house construction found immediately adjacent were associated with saddle querns and a post-hole structure thought to represent a drying rack, and may have been instrumental in establishing the original field layout there (Simpson 1971; Megaw 1976).

On the fringes of the Wessex drainage pattern are further traces of cultivation attributed to this period. A phase of Beaker-associated cultivation, evidently associated with clearance of sarsen, was present at Hambledon Hill, Dorset (Mercer 1988:97), while at South Street, Avebury, Wiltshire, ard marks were recorded in association with a plough soil containing Beaker potsherds, crossing (and disrespecting) the ditch of a long barrow (Fowler and Evans 1967:290–1; Ashbee et al. 1979:294; also Evans 1972:fig. 89). Traces of transient Beaker activity at Dean Bottom on the Marlborough Downs were associated with a clearance episode and evidence for a mixed farming economy (Gingell 1992:152), while the enigmatic Beaker site at Easton Down, Wiltshire (Stone 1931), lies immediately adjacent to an embryo field system (fig. 9.1). Visible activity in these less favourable agricultural areas might be held to imply a degree of intensification and pressure on land elsewhere.

Significant quantities of carbonised grain were recovered from the Rosinish excavations (Shepherd 1976:214) and Case (1977:76) pointed out that there are good numbers of grain impressions on Beakers generally, including the sherds from Belle Tout on the south coast (Arthur in Bradley 1970:373). At Bestwall Quarry, Wareham, Beaker pottery has been found in association with querns and carbonised grain (Ladle 1997) and Beaker pottery was also recovered from a field ditch there. As Case (1977:76) pointed out, Beaker evidence for archers and warriors, although undoubtedly of signal importance, may have been over-emphasised at the expense of farming initiatives.

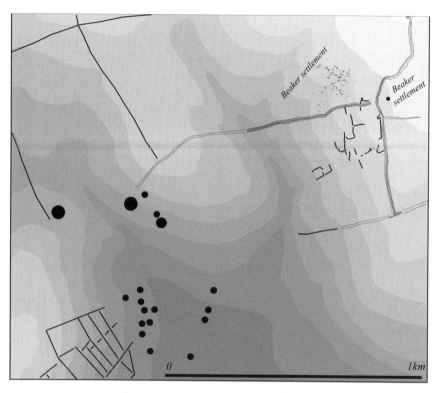

Figure 9.1 Intensification of land use on the Higher Chalk at East Winterslow, Wiltshire, with the Easton Down flint mines bounded by two areas of Beaker settlement at upper right. Two large bell barrows flank a western bifurcation of the valley, while the focus of the cemetery, perhaps a winterbourne spring, lay around the valley floor to the south of them. Whether the embryo fields on Easton Down relate to the adjacent Beaker settlement or represent a later phase of activity is not clear. They are extremely shallow earthworks and may focus on a sub-rectangular enclosure, but represent entrepreneurial cultivation of the Higher Downs. In contrast, the "Celtic" field system in the south-west (Palmer 1984) is well defined and, although a small area, it is composed of larger fields and probably represents an individual homestead. Formal division of the area by a system of linear ditches, probably at the beginning of the Late Bronze Age, then occurs. In at least two cases these are aligned on barrows. On Easton Down (upper right) the north-to-south linear makes an angled curve to avoid an existing feature, perhaps a still extant area of Beaker settlement, while the west-to-east linear curves slightly to the north to partly avoid the area of embryo fields.

Rarely can we observe how fields were laid out. Initial sod busting with an ard might encourage a tendency to angularity but no more, for subsequent cultivation with mattock, spade and hoe would not require straight edges and, given the preoccupation with circularity during the third and second millennia, there is in principle no reason why cultivation units should be square. Close proximity to neighbouring plots, however, may result in aggregating differences and squaring off tangents. In places, systems of irregular layout can be detected. Apparently organically created, they adhere to no overall framework with no requirement for fields to have four sides. They appear to relate to single farmsteads and often, given the assart-like shape of some, of pioneering settlements. They simply appear to have been carved out of the "waste" and "aggregate" around the settlement to form a system. There are early examples at Baldberg Beg, on the Atlantic coast of Co. Mayo, where they are dated to about 2600–2000 cal B.C. at 95 per cent, or on Shetland at the Scord of Brouster where fields were similarly subsumed by peat (Whittle et al. 1986:4). It seems likely that scores of these once existed on the agriculturally more favourable ground and, where crowding occurred, no doubt coalesced into a continuous patchwork.

Encouraged by a favourable climate, cultivation during the second millennium appears to have been increasingly widespread, taking in river edges and coastal environments, as well as the uplands. Four new plots found in an area of sandy islands, braided channels and marshes alongside the Thames join that already identified at Hopton St, Southwark (Drummond-Murray et al. 1994:254; Bates and Minkin 1999:326–327; Yates 2001). Preliminary micro-morphological analysis at one of these, Phoenix Wharf, indicates that the plough soil was manured (Macphail et al. 1990:53–69). None of these can be linked to large field complexes, but they do indicate that cultivation was taking place extensively relatively close to the river edge.

Structured Terrain

Along with recognition of the geographically widespread presence of "Celtic" fields (e.g., essays in Bowen and Fowler 1978), from Clwyd, Wales, to Lanarkshire, Scotland (essays in Spratt and Burgess 1985), traces of coaxial format have been found countrywide, from Dartmoor to the Thames Valley and from Wessex to the Yorkshire Dales (Bradley 1978; Fowler 1983; Fleming 1987; Horne and MacLeod 1995; 2001; Yates 2001; McOmish et al. 2002) as well as in Ireland (Herity 1971). With genesis, at least in the case of Behy/Glenulra, in the second half of the third millennium (Caulfield 1978; 1983), these systems became, if not ubiquitous, certainly widespread around the middle of the second millennium B.C. (Yates 2001). Over 40 such systems have been recorded in the Yorkshire Dales alone (Horne and MacLeod 1995; fig. 9.2), at least 11 on Dartmoor (Simon Probert, pers. comm.) and over 20 on Salisbury Plain (McOmish et al. 2002). These are extraordinary numbers and, given the areas covered, they can only relate to local communities. In their developed guise, these complexes or "management blocks" (Bowen 1978:117; Fowler 2000:23–25) comprise straight and parallel-sided land units subdivided by cross-boundaries into square or rectangular fields, all laid out across the countryside oblivious of obstacles. It is becoming clear from sites such as Perry Oaks in West London that it was a cumulative process, the longitudinal boundaries being laid out first and the linear units subdivided by cross-division only later.

Dating of such systems, however, as one might expect, with features re-scoured and adapted over generations, is notoriously imprecise and there are reports of some being laid out or used in the Iron Age and Romano-British period, for example, at

Figure 9.2 Multi-phase coaxial strips south of Kettlewell in upper Wharfedale, Yorkshire. The system here covers the middle zone of the west-facing slopes and depicts several phases of use on a common alignment. Coaxial walls can be traced as far the prominent limestone scar (near top). The lower terminal is in most cases untraceable, but probably lay within the zone of intense medieval cultivation. There is little evidence for cross-divisions within the fields, but several sub-circular platforms and other features indicate the presence of structures associated with one or more phases of the system (English Heritage NMR (Riley Collection), SE 0067 DNR1029/11).

Grassington, Yorkshire (Horne and MacLeod 1995), or in places on the Berkshire Downs (Bowden et al. 1991–1993) and it remains a priority to provide a secure chronological framework. The reuse of the whole, or part, of complexes such as those at Orcheston Down (fig. 9.3) or Charlton Down on Salisbury Plain, Wiltshire (McOmish et al. 2002), may be quite widespread, particularly where lynchet accumulation is present. Dating in Wessex comes almost entirely from the field evidence of earthworks where, consistently, the fields predate a series of linear ditches which themselves predate the construction of hill forts. Usually in these cases round barrows are respected, as at Orcheston Down, where lynchet accumulation overlies a barrow ditch, although there are one or two cases where the opposite sequence occurs. Excavated dating evidence is increasing, though invariably refers to lynchet accumulation or an isolated portion of ditch rather than field or system as a whole. While Middle Bronze Age dates have increasingly been obtained from excavated boundary ditches (Yates 2001), Perry Oaks in West London may provide the best indication of chronology and use. The earliest elements here were laid out early in the second millennium B.C. (Barrett et al. 2001; Pitts 2004) and the system modi-

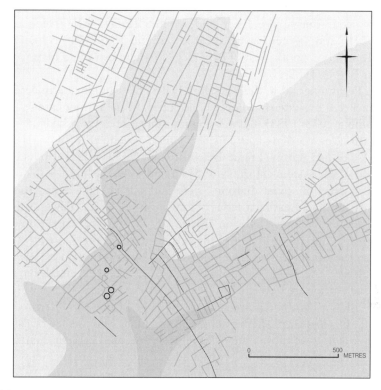

Figure 9.3   The junction of two coaxial systems on Orcheston Down, Wiltshire, one of which incorporates a small round barrow cemetery. A field lynchet spills over into and partly obscures one of the barrow ditches, indicating a period of considerable cultivation. In turn, the fields are cut by a linear ditch, probably of later Bronze Age date, which is aligned on, though curves to avoid, the still prominent barrow. The fields were brought back into use during the Romano-British period, a settlement of this period (not depicted) being present on the spur right of centre (English Heritage NMR).

fied at various points in time, until finally being obliterated during the Roman period.

Little evidence survives to indicate that efforts were made to cultivate the clays (Moffat 1988) or sandy heaths (Smith 1999), although a few enclosures are present in Purbeck, Dorset, where Bronze Age fields have been recorded on Arne Heath and New Mills Heath (Cox and Hearne 1991:28–31) and in Surrey, where a system of fields on Whitmoor Common could be of this period (Dolan et al., in press). Given the presence of well-preserved coaxial systems on the acidic and sandy heaths of the Netherlands and Germany (Brongers 1976; Bradley 1978; Harsema 1992) this absence comes as a surprise. Bradley (1978) raised the possibility that the substantial field banks of the Dutch examples may have helped to retain soil, and recent work has indicated that artificially created soils, plaggen soils, similar to those identified in the Outer Hebrides (Barber 1997; 2003), may have been contained within them (David McOmish, pers. comm.). No such systems have been discovered here, however, dramatic increases in podsolisation on the Dorset heaths appears to occur during the Early and Middle Bronze Age (Allen and Scaife 1991:216–218) and an increase in cereals at around 1320–1210 cal B.C. was registered at Rimsmoor, south-west of Bere Regis (date interpolated between samples: Waton and Barber 1987).

Both on Dartmoor and in the Yorkshire Dales, field systems terminated against, or were bracketed by, extensive linear boundaries, in the former case referred to as reaves (Fleming 1978; 1983). Often using interfluves and watersheds, these divided the land into large portions and coherent units. Seventeen of the systems in the Yorkshire Dales had terminal boundaries, at least five of which also had terminals at either end of the system (Horne and MacLeod 1995). Although the chronology is unclear, a series of spinal divisions were laid out at right angles to them and parallel to each other, creating a series of long strip-like units. Towards the western end of the Holme Moor system, on Dartmoor, incomplete strips evidently at an early stage of layout are visible, and there is an implication that new strips could be added to the others if it became necessary. Thus the system as a whole could easily be enlarged. Across the chalk and river gravels where terminals have not been recorded, such strips are nevertheless present. At Perry Oaks, spines were laid out, perhaps utilising a natural feature such as the edge of the gravel terrace on which to terminate. It is less clear whether terminals originally bounded coaxials in Wessex as the nether regions of most systems have been obscured by later cultivation. Parallel strips at right angles to the valley were identified as an early element of a coaxial system adjacent to Nettlecombe Tout hill fort in Dorset (Bradley 1978:270, fig. 3), and Fowler's (1971:176–177; 1983) brickwork-pattern field system is essentially part of the same process. At Orcheston Down (fig. 9.2), the strips dovetail with a second system at one end, but begin to fade out after several kilometres as they approach the higher ground. The individual strips have simply been extended according to need. However, by no means all land appears to have been subject to such parallel division and some strips at, for example, Windmill Hill, near Crawley, Hampshire (Crawford 1924; Crawford and Keiller 1928), were constructed at right angles to others. Even so, they appear to conform to the axes, measurements and principles of the rest of the complex. The width of strips differs considerably between complexes, from the enormous 150 m at Behy/Glenulra, in Ireland, to the quite narrow 30 m or so in Purbeck (Cox and Hearne 1991), although these extremes mask a curious consistency of just over 60 m at Bathampton Down (Crawford and Keiller 1928), many sites on Dartmoor, and Imperial Sports Ground and Perry Oaks in west London (Barrett et al. 2001; Crockett 2001:299, fig. 5). The number of similar units on the Marlborough Downs units has led Fowler (2000:24) to suspect that a 10 m basic unit of measurement may have been used. Being the major drainage features at the latter site, they were evidently periodically scoured out and were recorded as being repeatedly recut, these boundaries being considered to have been more meaningful in terms of land division, tenure and agricultural practice. The longitudinal divisions were traced for a considerable distance, at least 320 m, as far as the 20 ha excavated area permitted. It is not clear how far across the West London gravel terrace the system extended, but a coaxial field system with units of similar proportions and taking the same alignment has been reported at Cranford Lane some 3 km to the north-east (Elsden 1997:fig. 1). Such extensive coverage might not be unusual given the complexes on Salisbury Plain that can be traced for 4–5 km (McOmish et al. 2002). However, there is clearly much local variation. Systems in the Yorkshire Dales average around 350 to 400 m in length, the maximum being about 600 m (Horne and MacLeod 1995), while those in the Manton/Clatford and Preschute areas of the Marlborough Downs reach some 2 km (Fowler 2000:25; Gingell 1992:fig. 96).

The spacing of cross-divisions within each complex is reasonably consistent, but, although there appears to be much amendment and adaptation, there is also considerable difference between systems. Adjacent systems at Perry Oaks and Imperial Sports Ground both had transverse divisions placed every 90 m or so (Barrett et al. 2001; Crockett 2001:299, fig. 5) and here they appear to have served a more temporary and ephemeral role, perhaps not unlike an unploughed baulk in medieval systems. Thirteen of the systems recorded in the Yorkshire Dales had no cross-divisions visible from the air (Horne and MacLeod 1995). As a result, the size of fields varies quite considerably, from small garden-like plots at, for example, Orcheston Down or Beckhampton Down, Wiltshire, to more usual 0.25 ha, up to 0.8 ha paddock-like areas at Middle Brow and Buckland Bank, Sussex (Curwen and Curwen 1923). Bowen considered that long rectangular fields may be the product of Romano-British enlargement (Bowen 1978:117); however, the opposite may be the case and the small square patchwork the result of subdivision of larger units. Retention of long thin fields may have served a regional farming requirement. Such fields are extensive around Bath, along the escarpment overlooking the Severn Valley, onto the plateau on Charmy Down (Grimes 1960) and Bathhampton (Crawford and Keiller 1928).

The location of settlements associated with these complexes remains to be established. Buildings are often found in association with aggregate systems as at Gwithian (Megaw 1976) and Black Patch (Drewett 1980:381), but the link between huts and coaxial systems is less clear-cut. Huts occurring within such fields close to reave terminals on Dartmoor, if indeed houses, imply that some people at least were living amongst their holdings. Similarly, there are huts within some fields that may mark later adaptation of the system. At Bestwall, one circular structure was located on a field boundary, while two others all associated with pits containing Deverel-Rimbury associated debris, were built within fields (Ladle 1997; Ladle and Woodward 2003). It may be unwise to automatically assume that these are houses for some may be field barns, lambing pens or other agricultural buildings. There is a historic tradition of placing barns in fields at a distance from settlements in the south (e.g., on Salisbury Plain; McOmish et al. 2002) and the Cotswolds, as well as in the Dales of Yorkshire, where many are still visible. Generally, contemporary settlement is not visible within the field layout and the straight lines only occasionally deviate to incorporate awkward bits of contemporary or earlier building. A curving lynchet at Knook in Wiltshire appears to avoid an earlier feature, and similarly at Perry Oaks the excavators noted that the field system respected an earlier enclosure (Barrett et al. 2001:223), but these may be earlier ceremonial centres or similar features and do not cater for the great numbers of individuals hinted at by the field construction. For the most part, it appears likely that major settlements lay on the sites that they always occupied, close to the watercourses upon which many of these complexes focus.

Communities

There is a strong sense of community inherent in the coaxial field complexes. It might be claimed that each strip represents some kind of rotation, of different crop type or stock, but it could also be argued that such elaborate division is not necessary merely to serve such a function. Instead, they may represent family units – an interpretation first suggested for the system at Behy/Glenulra in Co. Mayo, Ireland (Herity 1971) – with each strip subdivided by the holders for their own purposes. If so, the 13 units at Semer Water, Wensleydale, in Yorkshire (Horne and MacLeod 1995), or the 11 at Sharp Tor, Dartmoor (plan in Butler 1991), will indicate the size of the local community. Most such communities on Dartmoor appear to number between seven and 11 strips, although some such as Horridge Common and Holne Moor reach above 18 and 24 respectively (plans in Butler 1991; 1993). The conformable manner in which new strips could be added implies that while individual choice might be permitted when it came to agriculture, such matters as tenure, organisation, enclosure and allocation were determined by the community.

Such consistent layout implies at the very least some overall, perhaps tacit, understanding and agreement and that the principle appears to have been only rarely transgressed might be taken to imply the presence of a significant and enterprising model, rooted in ancestral knowledge and supported by an overarching belief system, that impressed sufficiently to encourage wide-scale replication.

Links with earlier, traditional, use of the land are widespread. The connection between fields and barrows has often been made (e.g., Bowen 1978:117; Fowler 2000:27; McOmish et al. 2002), and links with chambered cairns (Ashbee 1976), stone rows (Fleming 1978:109) and the Heathrow cursus all discussed (Barrett et al. 2001). In the south, the intensity of round barrow cemeteries that are depicted in river valleys on aerial photographs (e.g., Green 1975; Woodward 1978) indicates that use of these places was too intensive to allow long-distance nomadism or transhumance. Instead cemeteries might mark the presence of stable communities and well-ordered domains. Thus while common elements of layout can be recognised in many of the coaxial systems, each will have incorporated a pre-existing domain, and the land presumably continued to be used by the local occupants. There are sometimes hints, but no more, of an underlying Beaker or Early Bronze Age framework, although as at Flag Fen (Pryor 2001:399, 409–412) there can be considerable chronological variation between one part of a system and another. However, the invisibility of earlier activity implies a system of land use that was easily modified and therefore likely to represent a series of open or unbounded plots, common pasture and meadow. Any firm former land use patterns would provide a template that might influence any subsequent reorganisation.

Recent investigation of land division on Dartmoor has also provided evidence of earlier activity (Brück et al. 2003) with analysis that has questioned the view of a planned moorland use (Fleming 1978; 1983) and instead argued for a piecemeal development of boundary accrual (Johnston 2005). The relevant question concerns time scale and the extent to which the fields are essentially a Middle Bronze Age phenomenon, or the latest in a series of piecemeal adaptations overlying an earlier (coaxial) template.

Whether land use reorganisation proved a satisfactory solution for the moment remains uncertain, but the system certainly endured. The visible systems represent the end of a lengthy process of increasingly intensive use of land, during which occupants were confirmed in their relationship with local surroundings and their right to make use of them.

Applied Cosmology

The occurrence of parallel boundaries on persistently straight orientations across landforms indicates that the chosen or dominant axis may have been of some significance. As Fleming first noted (1987), in many cases they have been laid out oblivious of, and sometimes despite, the terrain. Perhaps the easiest and expected option would be to establish fields according to the lie of the land with respect to the drainage pattern. In some cases this occurs, but even where it does, such as in the area of the fields to the south of the River Kennet near Avebury, Wiltshire (Crutchley 2005:fig. 3.9), it is almost incidental to the broader plan. With slight variations, orientations predominantly respect the north-east–south-west axis and this is a widespread phenomenon. The variations on Salisbury Plain, for example, cluster around 26–30° east of north (McOmish et al. 2000:fig. 3.4). In the Yorkshire Dales, 13 out of 32 systems follow this alignment; nine are at right angles to it, while only eight are oriented on the cardinal points (data in Horne and MacLeod 1995). The fields on Dartmoor and coaxials at Middle Brow and Buckland Bank in Sussex (Curwen and Curwen 1923) follow a similar pattern. The general orientation is constant and there appears to be an underlying principle that land division should be carried out in accordance with some rule and with respect to an underlying cosmology. This occurs even on the Continent: fields at Baroosterveld in the Netherlands, for example, follow a similar alignment (Harsema 1992:62–65). Whether it was the north-eastern direction that was important or the reverse cannot be deduced from the field evidence and, as noted above, there are some systems where the right angle appears to take prominence.

It is always possible that such orientations reflect that of the prevailing wind, which over much of the country takes a north-eastern course. It is easy to imagine how this invisible force, a formerly inexplicable phenomenon, may have been put down to the supernatural, and even in the medieval period it was considered to be the "breath of god". This could not be the case in the Dales, however, where the prevailing wind is from the east (Horne and MacLeod 1995). In greater probability, it is the celestial alignments that were significant, in this case the sun, the importance of which may have been practical as much as symbolic, for sunlight and warmth are crucial to successful cultivation. This is particularly so for those farming in areas of deeply dissected countryside, the deep coombes of the Higher Chalk, or the Yorkshire Dales, for example, which might be in shadow for much of the day, and where frost or snow in winter may not melt until late afternoon. Indeed the sun and its warmth has been responsible for the very morphology of much of the terrain. The asymmetrically profiled valleys of the chalk, are a product of differentially weathered slopes during the immediate post-glacial, where a greater degree of sun received on one flank has encouraged more solifluction.

Such practical implications will no doubt have been important in the laying out and apportioning of land in any new system and the advantages of south- or south-east-facing plots will have figured high. It may be that a form of *Solskifte* or sun-division, a system of land apportionment used in early medieval Scandinavia (Göransson 1961) and also noted in parts of Britain (Homans 1942:90–106; Baker and Butlin 1973; Sheppard 1973:175–185; Dodgshon 1975; Britnell 2004:30–32), was in operation. The origins of that system appear lost in tradition, but the principle regarding agrarian matters, that all members of the community are allocated a reasonable share of the sun and shadow agricultural land, may not have been lost on prehistoric communities.

Land Use beyond the Fields

When it is considered, land use beyond the fields is invariably thought of as an invisible component of the archaeological landscape. On Salisbury Plain it was presumed that some of the areas devoid of "Celtic" fields harboured woodland, but even with the possibility of intensively managed grazing catered for by the field systems, there would still be a role for "waste", the land that in historic times has become referred to as "common land", wherein turf digging, quarrying, grazing during summer while crops were ripening, leisure and a variety of other activities took place.

The reave systems on Dartmoor survive up to about 500 m OD and, in most cases, open ground lies beyond. Here for the first time we catch a glimpse of land beyond the fields, though its use remains archaeologically invisible, at least on the surface. However, gates and at least one access way through the fields on Holme Moor lead to it and there is an implication of use as summer grazing (Fleming 1978). The area, however, is by no means devoid of archaeology, for there are not only monuments of an earlier period, but also large groups of Bronze Age houses; whole villages set about 0.75 km apart consisting of, in one case, over 100 buildings. These houses are smaller than those associated with the field systems and may be later in date. However, assuming the fields were still operational, they represent either a great degree of transhumance, or perhaps shanty towns or squatter settlements of those unable for whatever reason to participate in use of the field system, similar to those that evolved on the edge of many historic "commons" (Ward 2002).

Enclosure or Reorganisation

It is not clear whether the coaxial systems represent wholesale or partial enclosure, or simply reorganisation of the agricultural land. While walls capable of containing stock were constructed in Co. Mayo (Caulfield 1978; 1983) and in some places on Dartmoor (Fleming 1978), elsewhere boundaries were mere linear heaps of rubble. There is no clear evidence of physical enclosure in Wessex (Bowen 1978:117), and little evidence for walls or hedges, although low walls of sarsen are certainly present at Fyfield (Fowler and Evans 1967). Field banks are generally low, shallow and broad, perhaps in part the result of 3,000 years of weathering, although when excavated their counterparts on Dartmoor revealed buried fence lines and stake-holes (Brück et al. 2003; Johnston 2005). However, much, if not most, of the system may have been quite open and accessed in a similar way to medieval open fields, with the banks merely delineating unploughed baulks between cultivated areas. In this scenario the arrangement is not enclosure in the sense that it would keep things in or out. Instead, it represents a re-demarcation of land. It is difficult to be certain of how far each system was laid out as a unified whole, but placing even a single boundary or rectangular enclosure across a piece of land formerly used in a different way would have significant effects for a local community that was reliant on the whole of that local terrain for subsistence. Indeed there are so few irregularities visible within the systems that the ability to impose such an ordered pattern across such large areas, even if it were done in an incremental manner, may mean that it represented the reorganisation of former areas of open pasture and ignored the complex of traditionally cultivated areas that must have lain close by each village.

However this is viewed, whether as re-demarcation, reorganisation or enclosure, it implies an inadequacy of the former arrangement and also signals a response to the problem. The new plots denote an understanding of the land and an appreciation of how improvements might be made, but they will also have resulted from addressing pressing social issues, including rights of tenure and inheritance and the division of land between families. There is an implication of a desire for order and it is likely to mark the end of a period of friction and problems in the countryside, and with it a perception of how the future might be. In order to fully comprehend the new proposals there must have been a resolution that allowed discussion, objection and amendment of the scheme. All this, both the laying out and discussion, implies intricate knowledge acquired from the experiences of daily life (Ingold 2000:192–195) with profound practical meaning for those working the land.

Impact on the Land

New plots were evidently set out locally. The evidence from Salisbury Plain appears to indicate areas of anything up to 15 sq. km being laid out by each community. Strip division produced almost regular equal-sized parcels as though laid out for impartial distribution of land, while enclosure would allow animals to be pastured in individual fields without disturbing crops in others. The reorganisation of land into ordered coaxial systems, however, is not necessary for this to apply, and it could be done by simply enclosing one or more of the pre-existing fields or paddocks. Construction of boundaries is, after all, expensive in terms of time and effort, and there is no need to enclose if the aim is one of collective purpose. As with historical enclosures, the advantage of a new system would be to allow individuals greater freedom over cultivation and husbandry practices, to dispense with any restrictions of a common open-field cropping regime with its periods of fallow and to allow cultivators to drain poor land, etc. – in other words, it allowed individual enterprise. Use and planning are, however, different issues and ultimately the organisation – the spacing of spines, the survey and planning, the straight axis and not least the ability to sweep away the pre-existing land uses – bespeaks a corporate arrangement or imposition.

Coaxial field division cut across and rearranged the area. Divided in this way, important places of the past will have been bisected and fragmented. While the barrow cemeteries on Orcheston Down and Beckhampton Down were respected, they were isolated and cut off by field boundaries, and contemporary methods of working meant that pieces of land would have enrolled new meanings. In contrast, far from representing meaningless space, the open area beyond was a tangible reminder of intimate locales, with good or bad grazing, places with names and a history derived from personal experience, coupled with visible traces of previous interventions, inherited traditions and legends of the past. The coaxial fields may have allowed individuals more control over their own chosen methods of subsistence within the context of a maturing political structure, but they also tell of a society engaging with new ideas and providing a shared stability.

Sheep Walks

A second major reorganisation occurred, at least in Wessex, from about 1000 B.C. This comprised the creation of a series of major ditched and banked boundaries that often stretched for kilometres and enclosed large tithing or ranch-like units (Bowen 1975; 1978; Bradley et al. 1994; McOmish et al. 2002). In terms of grand land division there are certain similarities with some of the contour reaves on Dartmoor that demarcate upland grazing, and which are thought to be later than those associated with the coaxials (Fleming 1978:106–107). In Wessex, these "linear ditches" consistently cut through blocks of "Celtic" fields and effectively put at least part of them out of use and the implication remains that the system as a whole, which must have functioned with difficulty without its constituent parts, was shelved. There is no evidence for the layout of new fields within these larger units and the assumption is that the new arrangement reflects pastoral activity (Bowen 1978:120). The new boundaries, some of which may have been recut and subdivided later in the first millennium B.C. (Bradley et al. 1994), appear to form landholdings invariably based on river frontage or some other water source.

The framework hinges on lengthy spinal banks and ditches, often of up to 8 km or more, and in the case of Grims Ditch in Berkshire almost 17 km in length (Bradley and Richards 1978), that invariably follow the contours of the upper valley slopes or interfluves, sometimes along the lip or false crest. Subsidiary linear ditches abut them at right angles, invariably descending to the valley below and forming an interlocking system of strip parish-like holdings, each of about 500 m in width. Given the fragmentary nature of many complexes, precision is impracticable, but there may be as many as 50 or more units on Salisbury Plain alone (e.g., McOmish et al. 2002:fig. 3:1). Similar land units were also cut elsewhere. In north-east Yorkshire, Spratt (1989:16) has identified some 27 political territories defined by such boundaries, each of which forms a "viable mixed farming estate".

While the land units generally utilise the valleys and watersheds, many appear to focus upon, or were perhaps laid out from, certain elevated positions where they appear to be integrated with large enclosures, for example Martinsell, Casterley, the earliest and outer phase at Sidbury, all in Wiltshire (McOmish et al. 2002), the outer element at Danebury, Hampshire (Palmer 1984) and the palisade at Quarley, Hampshire (Hawkes 1939); others such as Battlesbury and Oldbury (Bowden 2004) were later crowned by hill forts.

While the fields might be considered to be monumental in their extent and the way in which they fill the gap in visible communal effort, the linear ditches are monumental as constructions. Most banks and ditches, although not a serious deterrent, are rampart-like and pose a definite obstacle. There is no indication that they were surmounted with a hedge or palisade-like feature and while they are too massive to have been used for most pastoral purposes, without a fence they would not have prevented stock from wandering on to a neighbouring property.

Use of fields may have continued on the lower ground or closer to major settlements, although on the chalk such places are likely to be precisely those favoured by historic villages whose archaeology is therefore obscured. The fields at Perry Oaks may have been subdivided as a result of soil degeneration (Barrett et al. 2001:224) and new trackways constructed or placed alongside the major spinal divisions, curtailing the size of each field (Barrett et al. 2001:223). These are more than an unploughed baulk, for the bank and ditch imply a need to separate the activities of the trackway from those of the field. It seems likely, therefore, that they were constructed as stockways to get cattle to and from milking or watering places, without trampling crops. Similar fields with associated trackways have been observed in the fens, where Pryor (1996:321) has convincingly set out a case for large-scale livestock farming, complete with arrangements of stock pens. The massive midden at East Chisenbury, Wiltshire, itself the focus of five linear boundaries (McOmish et al. 2002:74), and which comprised ashed sheep dung as a major component of the matrix, is also estimated to have contained butchered bones from ca. 350,000 sheep. This implies a massive sheep population on the Downs. At what point these changes occurred is not clear, but they appear to herald a greater degree of the use of stock than hitherto and may be a response to a gradually changing climate that increasingly encouraged rich grass growth. If there was indeed a move towards stock, hedgerows may have been of greater importance and may even have been planted and laid at this time.

While these changes may be driven by climatic imperatives, the fate of those individuals who possessed interest in the "Celtic" fields is far from clear. In his *Utopia*, Thomas More bemoaned the widespread turning over of downland to sheep walks and the enclosing of great areas within a single fence with its adverse effect on the peasant population in the sixteenth century (Turner 1965:47). Similar processes took place in the Highlands during the late eighteenth and early nineteenth centuries (e.g., Cole and Postgate 1971[1938]:123) and, as on these occasions, there may have been similar casualties in prehistory. The time scale of the process, perhaps 400 years, may have allowed adjustments, though many boundaries were being recut soon after construction (Bradley et al. 1994). These were massive enclosures and must have been a statement of ownership rather than simply a defining of new methods of subsistence. The role of the individual can no longer be recognised; instead it is subsumed within ditch construction. However, the slighting of fields, that is, cutting off portions of the field complex, also indicates a degree of social reorganisation by a non-benevolent political regime, for essentially the same communities will have been involved.

Conclusion

Minor fluctuations aside, the temperature during the second millennium B.C. is thought to have been over a degree warmer than it is today and, assuming reasonable amounts of moisture, it would have allowed good crop yields in southern England with the prospect of successful cultivation of much higher ground (Tinsley and Grigson 1981:211). However, coupled with this is the possibility that grain-loving pests might have extended their range, as is currently predicted should the temperature rise by a similar amount in the near future (www.defra.gov.uk). The temperature appears to have cooled during the first half of the first millennium B.C., worsening earlier in the west (Tinsley and Grigson 1981:211–216), which would have had a dramatic impact on agricultural communities, not least making cultivation above ca. 300 m extremely difficult.

The fossilised field complexes are observed as they appeared after a millennium of experimentation, adaptation and use, when they were at their most developed. It is with a foreshortened time scale that we study such events and, while this perspective of the past can conflate and constrain incidents, elements of these activities may have been taking place in various parts of the country across half a millennium. That is not to say that these proceedings were not dramatic. To local people they must have been every bit as noteworthy as similar historic events. From these land divisions we can observe the social network at local village level as well as the larger polity, but we can also glimpse the accomplishments of individual families and their place within the community.

Only as the changing climate brought new social pressures were further alterations enforced on people. On the lower ground fields may have been adapted to cope with differing circumstances, but in the hills they were often abandoned altogether. These changes alone may have had a direct impact on methods of agriculture and, coupled with new technologies (for example, the use of vehicles), may have enabled the adoption of different work routines. It might be argued that the necessary stimulus to embark on new directions came entirely as a result of social imperatives, one of which was the need to feed ever increasing numbers of people, or economic drivers that included the import of desirable products, coupled with the need to pay for them, but it must also have been a matter of political will. Inevitably, as new systems of land use were introduced in some areas, as with any reorganisation there will have been a social price. In particular, reorganisation is likely to have reduced the pieces of open waste ground where goats and fowl might be kept and free grazing tolerated, leaving little free movement to individuals practising transhumant or nomadic lifestyles. However, we should not assume an opposition to change, for the ease in which it appears that new plots could be added to existing ones might be held to suggest that those within the mainstream of the community were served by it. As in the historic enclosures, it may be that the poorer elements within society and those on the fringes of the institutions were worst off (Cole and Postgate 1971[1938]:122; Trevelyan 1942:144–153; Thompson 1963:237–241).

The decisive demarcation, coaxial arrangement and extensive coverage of "Celtic" field systems was the product of a new social energy that betrayed a bold conviction concerning the future. Inhabitants were fully conversant with the land and how subsistence could profitably be obtained from it. The fields signify productivity, hard work and a newly realised efficiency, but also observed among them are social niceties and understandings, respect for neighbours and their labours, all presumably drawn from an appreciation that there was fairness in allocation and security of tenure. Inhabitants had an investment in the land.

The reorganisation of the middle centuries of the second millennium B.C. marks stability, a boldness, a new confidence – confidence in land ownership and local organisation, conviction in terms of farming practice and not least in being able to survey, lay out and construct such extensive systems. The web of places is linked by a common arrangement of ditches and hedges into something that encapsulates and defines the local community. Most importantly, each complex of fields, coupled with the common experience of laying them out, would have bound people together and provided a familiar framework within which to live.

ACKNOWLEDGEMENTS

My thanks to my colleague Judie English and to fellow "Celtic" fields explorers, Dave McOmish and Dave Yates, who all helpfully commented on an earlier draft of this chapter.

REFERENCES

Ainsworth, S., 2001 Prehistoric settlement remains on the Derbyshire Gritstone Moors. Derbyshire Archaeological Journal 121:91–169.

——and T. Pearson, 2002 Stanton Moor, Derbyshire. Archaeological Investigation Report Series AI/6/2002. Swindon: English Heritage.

Allen, M. J., and R. G. Scaife, 1991 The exploitation of the flora and fauna and its impact on the natural and derived landscape. *In* Redeemed from the Heath: the archaeology of the Wytch Farm Oilfield (1987–90). P. W. Cox and A. Hearne. Dorchester: Dorset Natural History and Archaeological Society.

Ashbee, P., 1976 Bant's Carn, St Mary's, Isles of Scilly: an entrance grave restored and reconsidered. Cornish Archaeology 15:11–26.

——I. F. Smith and J. G. Evans, 1979 Excavation of three long barrows near Avebury, Wiltshire. Proceedings of the Prehistoric Society 45:207–300.

Baker, A. R. H., and R. A. Butlin, eds., 1973 Studies of Field Systems in the British Isles. Cambridge: Cambridge University Press.

Barber, J., ed., 1997 The Archaeological Investigation of a Prehistoric Landscape: excavations on Arran 1978–81. Edinburgh: Scottish Trust for Archaeological Research.

——2003 Bronze Age Farms and Iron Age Mounds of the Outer Hebrides. Scottish Archaeological Internet Report 3. Available at www.sair.org.uk.

Barnatt, J., 1986 Bronze Age remains on the east moors of the Peak District. Derbyshire Archaeological Journal 106:18–99.

——1999 Taming the lands: Peak District farming and ritual in the Bronze Age. Derbyshire Archaeological Journal 119:19–78.

——2000 To each their own: later prehistoric farming communities and their monuments in the Peak. Derbyshire Archaeological Journal 120:1–86.

——2004 Excavation of a prehistoric clearance cairn and ritual pits on Sir William Hill, Eyam Moor, Derbyshire, 2000. Derbyshire Archaeological Journal 124:13–63.

Barrett, J. C., 1999 The mythical landscape of the British Iron Age. In Archaeologies of Landscape: contemporary perspectives. W. Ashmore and A. B. Knapp, eds. pp. 253–268. Oxford: Blackwell.

——J. S. C. Lewis and K. Welsh, 2001 Perry Oaks: a history of inhabitation, part 2. London Archaeologist 9(8):221–227.

Bates, J., and J. Minkin, 1999 Lafone Street, Southwark: prehistoric farming and a medieval bridge. London Archaeologist 8(12):325–330.

Bowden, M., 2004 Oldbury Castle Hillfort. Archaeological Investigation Reports AI/31/2004. Swindon: English Heritage.

——S. Ford and G. Mees, 1991–1993 The date of the ancient fields on the Berkshire Downs. Berkshire Archaeological Journal 74:109–133.

Bowen, H. C., 1975 Pattern and interpretation: a view of the Wessex landscape. *In* Recent Work in Rural Archaeology. P. J. Fowler, ed. pp. 44–56. Bradford on Avon: Moonraker Press.

——1978 "Celtic" fields and "ranch" boundaries in Wessex. *In* The Effect of Man on the Landscape: the lowland zone. S. Limbrey, and J. G. Evans, eds. pp. 115–123. London: Council for British Archaeology.

——and P. J. Fowler, eds., 1978 Early Land Allotment. Oxford: British Archaeological Reports.

Bradley, R., 1970 The excavation of a Beaker settlement at Belle Tout, East Sussex, England. Proceedings of the Prehistoric Society 36:312–379.

——1978 Prehistoric field systems in Britain and northwest Europe: a review of some recent work. World Archaeology 9:265–280.

——and J. Richards, 1978 Prehistoric fields and boundaries in the Berkshire Downs. *In* Early Land Allotment. H. C. Bowen and P. Fowler, eds. pp. 53–60. Oxford: British Archaeological Reports.

——R. Entwistle and F. Raymond, 1994 Prehistoric Land Division on Salisbury Plain: the work of the Wessex Linear Ditches Project. London: English Heritage.

Britnell, R., 2004 Fields, farms and sun-division in a moorland region, 1100–1400. Agricultural History Review 52:20–37.

Brongers, J. A., 1976 Air Photography and Celtic Field Research in the Netherlands Amersfoot: ROB.

Brück, J., R. Johnston and H. Wickstead, 2003 Excavations of Bronze Age field systems on Shovel Down, Dartmoor, 2003. Past 45:10–12.

Butler, J., 1991 Dartmoor Atlas of Antiquities, vol. 1: The East. Exeter: Devon Books.

——1993 Dartmoor Atlas of Antiquities, vol. 4: The South-East. Exeter: Devon Books.

Case, H. J., 1977 The Beaker culture in Britain and Ireland. *In* Beakers in Britain and Europe. R. Mercer, ed. pp. 71–102. Oxford: British Archaeological Reports.

Caulfield, S., 1978 Neolithic fields: the Irish evidence. *In* Early Land Allotment. H. C. Bowen and P. Fowler, eds. pp. 137–143. Oxford: British Archaeological Reports.

——1983 Neolithic settlement of North Connaught. *In* Landscape Archaeology in Ireland. T. Reeves-Smith and F. Hammond, eds. pp. 195–221. Oxford: British Archaeological Reports.

Clark, J. G. D., 1929 Discoidal polished flint knives: their typology and distribution. Proceedings of the Prehistoric Society of East Anglia 6:41–54.

Cole, G. D. H., and R. Postgate, 1971[1938] The Common People. London: Methuen.

Cox, P. W., and C. M. Hearne, 1991 Redeemed from the Heath: the archaeology of the Wytch Farm Oilfield (1987–90). Dorchester: Dorset Natural History and Archaeological Society.

Crawford, O. G. S., 1924 Air Survey and Archaeology. Southampton: Ordnance Survey/HMSO.

——1928 Air Photography for Archaeologists. Southampton: Ordnance Survey/HMSO.

——and A. Keiller, 1928 Wessex from the Air. Oxford: Clarendon Press.

Crockett, A., 2001 The archaeological landscape of Imperial College Sports Ground, part 1: Prehistoric. London Archaeologist 9(11):295–299.

Crutchley, S., 2005 Recent aerial survey work in the Marlborough Downs region. *In* Aspects of the Field Archaeology of the Marlborough Downs. G. Brown, D. Field and D. McOmish., eds. pp. 34–42. Oxford: Oxbow Books.

Curwen, E., and E. C. Curwen, 1923 Sussex lynchets and their associated fieldways. Sussex Archaeological Collections 64:1–65.

Dodgshon, R. A., 1975 Scandinavian "Solskifte" and the sunwise division of land in eastern Scotland. Scottish Studies 19:3–6.

Dolan, C., J. A. Entwistle and J. English, in press The use of multi-elemental analysis of acid-heathland and buried podzolic soils to investigate former land-use activity at Whitmoor Common, Worplesdon, Surrey. Seeoil.

Drewett, P., 1980 Black Patch and the Later Bronze Age in Sussex. *In* The British Later Bronze Age. J. Barrett and R. Bradley, eds. pp. 377–396. Oxford: British Archaeological Reports.

Drummond-Murray, J., D. Saxby and B. Watson, 1994 Recent archaeological work in the Bermondsey district of Southwark. London Archaeologist 7(10):251–254.

Elsden, N. J., 1997 Excavations at Nobel Drive, Harlington, and six sites to the north of Heathrow Airport, Hillingdon. Transactions of the London and Middlesex Archaeological Society 48:1–14.

Evans, J. G., 1972 Landsnails in Archaeology London: Seminar Press.

Feachem, D., 1973 Ancient agriculture in the highland of Britain. Proceedings of the Prehistoric Society 39:332–353.

Fleming, A., 1978 The prehistoric landscape of Dartmoor, part 1: South Dartmoor. Proceedings of the Prehistoric Society 44:97–123.

——1983 The prehistoric landscape of Dartmoor, part 2: North and East Dartmoor. Proceedings of the Prehistoric Society 49:195–241.

——1987 Coaxial field systems: some questions of time and space. Antiquity 61:188–202.

Fowler, P. J., 1971 Early prehistoric agriculture in Western Europe: some archaeological evidence. In Economy and Settlement in Neolithic and Early Bronze Age Britain and Europe. D. D. A. Simpson, ed. pp. 153–182. Leicester: Leicester University Press.

——1983 The Farming of Prehistoric Britain. Cambridge: Cambridge University Press.

——2000 Landscape Plotted and Pieced: landscape history and local archaeology in Fyfield and Overton, Wiltshire. London: Society of Antiquaries.

——and J. G. Evans, 1967 Plough-marks, lynchets and early fields. Antiquity 41:289–301.

Gingell, C., 1992 The Marlborough Downs: a later Bronze Age landscape and its origins. Devizes: Wiltshire Archaeological and Natural History Society/Wessex Archaeology.

Göransson, S., 1961 Regular open-field pattern in England and Scandinavian Solskift. Geografisker Annaler 43B:80–104.

Green, H. S., 1975 Early Bronze Age burial, territory, and population in Milton Keynes, Buckinghamshire and the Great Ouse Valley. Archaeological Journal 131:75–139

Grimes, W. F., 1931 The Early Bronze Age flint dagger in England and Wales. Proceedings of the Prehistoric Society of East Anglia 6:340–355.

——1960 Excavations of Defence Sites, 1939–1945, vol. 1: Mainly Neolithic–Bronze Age. London: HMSO.

Harsema, O. H., 1992 Geschiedenis in het landscap. Drenthe: Drenthe Museum.

Hart, C. R., 1981 The North Derbyshire Archaeological Survey to AD 1500. Chesterfield: North Derbyshire Archaeological Trust.

——1985 Gardoms Edge, Derbyshire: settlements, cairnfields and hillfort. In Upland Settlement in Britain: the second millennium BC and after. D. Spratt and C. Burgess, eds. pp. 71–75. Oxford: British Archaeological Reports.

Hawkes, C. F. C., 1939 The excavations at Quarley Hill, 1938. Proceedings of the Hampshire Field Club 14:136–194.

Herity, M., 1971 Prehistoric fields in Ireland. Irish University Review 1971:258–265.

Hirsch, E., 1995 Introduction. In The Anthropology of Landscape. E. Hirsch and M. O'Hanlon, eds. pp. 1–30. Oxford: Clarendon Press.

Homans, G. C., 1942 English Villages of the Thirteenth Century. Cambridge, MA: Harvard University Press.

Horne, P. D., and D. MacLeod, 1995 The Yorkshire Dales Mapping Project: a report for the National Mapping Programme York: RCHME.

——and —— 2001 Unravelling a Wharfdale landscape: a case study in field enhanced aerial survey. Landscapes 2:65–82.

Hunt, D., 1987 Early Farming Communities of Scotland: aspects of economy and settlement 4500–1250 BC. Oxford: British Archaeological Reports.

Ingold, T., 2000 The Perception of the Environment: essays in livelihood, dwelling and skill. London: Routledge.

Jacobi, R., 1978 Population and landscape in Mesolithic lowland Britain. *In* The Effect of Man on the Landscape: the lowland zone. S. Limbrey and J. G. Evans, eds. pp. 78–85. London: Council for British Archaeology.

——1981 The last hunters in Hampshire. *In* The Archaeology of Hampshire from the Palaeolithic to the Industrial Revolution. S. J. Shennan, and T. Shadla Hall, eds. pp. 10–25. Winchester: Hampshire Field Club Monograph.

Jobey, G., 1968 Excavations of cairns at Chatton Sandyford, Northumberland. Archaeologia Aeliana 46:5–50.

Johnson, N., and P. Rose, 1994 Bodmin Moor: an archaeological survey, vol. 1: The Human Landscape to c.1800. London: English Heritage/RCHME.

Johnston, R., 2005 Pattern without a plan: rethinking the Bronze Age coaxial field systems on Dartmoor, south-west England. Oxford Journal of Archaeology 24:1–21.

Ladle, L., 1997 Bestwall Quarry Archaeological Project, phase 6. Unpublished report for CAMAS Aggregates Wareham and District Archaeological and Local History Society.

——and A. Woodward, 2003 Middle Bronze Age house and burnt mound at Bestwall, Wareham, Dorset: an interim report. Proceedings of the Prehistoric Society 69:265–277.

Leighton, D. K., 1997 Mynydd Du and Fforest Fawr: the evolution of an upland landscape in South Wales. Aberystwyth: RCAHMW.

Macphail, R. I., M. A. Courty and A. Gebhardt, 1990 Soil micromorphological evidence of early agriculture in north west Europe. World Archaeology 22:53–69.

McOmish, D., D. Field and G. Brown, 2002 The Field Archaeology of Salisbury Plain Training Area. Swindon: English Heritage.

Megaw, J. V. S., 1976 Gwithian, Cornwall: some notes on the evidence for Neolithic and Bronze Age settlement. *In* Settlement and Economy in the Third and Second Millennia BC. C. Burgess and R. Miket, eds. pp. 51–80. Oxford: British Archaeological Reports.

Mercer, R., 1988 Hambledon Hill, Dorset, England. *In* Enclosures and Defences in the Neolithic of Western Europe. C. Burgess, P. Topping, C. Mordant and M. Maddison, eds. pp. 89–106. Oxford: British Archaeological Reports.

Moffat, A. J., 1988 The distribution of "Celtic Fields" on the East Hampshire chalklands. Proceedings of the Hampshire Field Club 44:11–23.

Palmer, R., 1984 Danebury: an Iron Age hillfort in Hampshire: an aerial photographic interpretation of its environs. London: RCHME.

Pitts, M., 2004 Heathrow today, tomorrow the world. British Archaeology 75:18–23.

Pryor, F., 1996 Sheep, stockyards and field systems: Bronze Age livestock populations in the Fenlands of eastern England. Antiquity 70:313–324.

——2001 The Flag Fen Basin: archaeology and environment of a Fenland landscape. London: English Heritage.

Rawlings, M., M. J. Allen and F. Healy, 2004 Investigation of the Whitesheet Down environs 1989–90: Neolithic causewayed enclosure and Iron Age settlement. Wiltshire Archaeological and Natural History Society Magazine 97:144–196.

Ridgeway, V., 1999 Prehistoric finds at Hopton Street in Southwark. London Archaeologist 9(3):72–76.

Ritchie, G., and A. Ritchie, 1981 Scotland: archaeology and early history London: Thames and Hudson.

Shepherd, I. A. G., 1976 Preliminary results from the Beaker settlement at Rosinish, Benbecula. *In* Settlement and Economy in the Third and Second Millennia BC. C. Burgess and R. Miket, eds. pp. 209–219. Oxford: British Archaeological Reports.

——and A. N. Tuckwell, 1977 Traces of Beaker period cultivation at Rosinish, Benbecula. Proceedings of the Society of Antiquaries of Scotland 108:108–113.

Sheppard, J. A., 1973 Field systems of Yorkshire. *In* Studies in Field Systems of the British Isles. A. R. H. Baker and R. A. Butlin, eds. pp. 145–187. Cambridge: Cambridge University Press.

Simpson, D. D. A., 1971 Beaker houses and settlements in Britain. *In* Economy and Settlement in Neolithic and Early Bronze Age Britain and Europe. D. D. A. Simpson, ed. pp. 131–152. Leicester: Leicester University Press.

Smith, N., 1999 The earthwork remains of enclosure in the New Forest. Proceedings of the Hampshire Field Club 54:1–56.

Spratt, D. A., 1989 Linear Earthworks of the Tabular Hills, North East Yorkshire Sheffield: J. R. Collis Publications.

——and C. Burgess, eds., 1985 Upland Settlement in Britain: the second millennium BC and after. Oxford: British Archaeological Reports.

Stone, J. F. S., 1931 A settlement site of the Beaker period on Easton Down, Winterslow, South Wiltshire. Wiltshire Archaeological and Natural History Society Magazine 45: 366–372.

Taylor, C., 1972 The study of settlement patterns in pre-Saxon Britain. *In* Man, Settlement and Urbanism. P. Ucko, R. Tringham and G. Dimbleby, eds. pp. 109–113. London: Duckworth.

Thompson, E. P., 1963 The Making of the English Working Class. Harmondsworth: Penguin.

Tinsley, H. M., and C. Grigson, 1981 The Bronze Age. *In* The Environment in British Prehistory, vol. 1. Simmons and M. Tooley, eds. pp. 210–249. London: Duckworth.

Trevelyan, G. M., 1942 Illustrated English Social History, vol. 3: The Eighteenth Century. Harmondsworth: Penguin.

Turner, P., trans., 1965 Thomas More: Utopia. Harmondsworth: Penguin.

Ward, C., 2002 Cotters and Squatters: housing's hidden history. Nottingham: Five Leaves.

Waton, P. V., and K. E. Barber, 1987 Rimsmoor, Dorset: biostratigraphy and chronology of an infilled doline. *In* Wessex and Isle of Wight Field Guide. K. E. Barber, ed. pp. 75–80. Cambridge: Quaternary Research Association.

Whittle, A., M. Keith-Lucas, A. Millis, B. Noddle, S. Rees and J. C. C. Romans, 1986 Scord of Brouster: an early agricultural settlement on Shetland; excavations 1977–1979. Oxford: Oxford University Committee for Archaeology.

Woodward, P. J., 1978 Flint distribution, ring ditches and Bronze Age settlement patterns in the Great Ouse Valley. Archaeological Journal 135:32–56.

Yates, D., 1999 Bronze Age field systems in the Thames Valley. Oxford Journal of Archaeology 18: 157–170.

——2001 Bronze Age agricultural intensification in the Thames Valley and Estuary. *In* Bronze Age Landscapes: tradition and transformation. J. Brück, ed. pp. 65–82. Oxford: Oxbow Books.

10

Foodways and Social Ecologies from the Middle Bronze Age to Late Iron Age

Jacqui Mulville

The second half of the second millennium B.C., while demonstrating continuity with the farming systems already in place, was a period of profound developments. As ever, food remained central to people's lives, but its production became more demanding, sophisticated and diverse. Continuing and accelerating change was seen across the face of Britain, with a move from an open landscape with few human-made boundaries to one where the ownership of land became formalised (Bradley and Yates 2007; Field, chapter 9). The division of the land was accompanied by an intensification of arable and pastoral production; significant quantities of food remains have been recovered from sites that increased in number, in size and in form with unenclosed and enclosed settlements, hill forts and non-coastal middens appearing for the first time. As for earlier prehistory, the relationship between people, plants, animals and the environment can be tracked through a consideration of foodways, encompassing not only diet but also the whole complex of food-related behaviour that includes cuisine, provisioning and acquisition, butchering and preparation methods, and disposal practices.

New Homes, New Sites, New Strategies

Across most of Britain a new range of domestic structures appeared and the round-house became ubiquitous. These sometimes substantial buildings signalled a developing concern with domestic architecture and settlements, rather than ceremonial sites, and became the main focus for the deposition of food remains. Defended hilltop settlements known as hill forts began to appear and many, such as Danebury (Cunliffe 1995) and Maiden Castle (Sharples 1991), were densely occupied by roundhouses. These sites reveal new patterns of deposition, both within houses and in associated features such as storage and rubbish pits, ditches and middens. In western and northern Scotland long-lived Atlantic roundhouses and brochs

developed, for example, Cladh Hallan, Cnip, Howe, Scatness and Dun Vulan
(Armit 2003; Parker Pearson et al. 2004). Elsewhere the occurrence of specialist
and minor sites, such as coastal salt extraction sites (salterns) or the locales associated with wetland exploitation and seasonal farmsteads, provide evidence for smaller
social units.

The increasing number of formal boundaries and field systems restricted the
movement of people and stock and limited the availability and accessibility of
resources. Also, as particular parcels of land became important, agricultural activity
would have been tethered to these areas for at least part of the year and required
new strategies for maintaining the fertility of the soil.

Evidence for the manner in which later prehistoric field systems were used is
sparse, with little cultural or biological material recovered. People removed stock
and arable products from the fields, paddocks or trackways for consumption and
so we rarely know what crops or which animals utilised these spaces. Indirect evidence for land usage, for example, by examining soil chemistry or micro-morphol-
ogy, can demonstrate the presence of stock or land enhancement (Macphail et al.
1987; Carter and Davidson 1998). Vegetable, human and animal waste were added
to the land as fertiliser, probably for cereal production, and in some cases this
resulted in deep, organic-rich, anthropogenically formed soils known as "plaggen"
(Guttmann et al. 2003).

Fields and associated trackways played a strategic role in stock control, helping
to gather herds to check on their health, select for breeding, shear or milk, trade
or remove to slaughter, and in facilitating moves to new pastures. Many of these
structures look like those still in use today (Pryor 1996). A number of waterholes
were dug across the landscape at this time, probably to provide for cattle during
the drier periods. There are few settlements closely associated with these fields,
which suggests they were visited, possibly on a daily basis, during the growing or
grazing season. In the winter animals would have been moved to sheltered locales,
possibly folded close to settlements but remaining outside, as evidence for stock
byres is rare (Guttmann et al. 2003; Mulville et al. 2005). The increasing number
of structures relating to stock management suggests a greater emphasis on large-
scale stock-keeping.

Assemblages from later prehistoric sites are often substantial and well preserved.
The sheer quantities of food and other waste produced excellent preservational
conditions. During the 1970s and 1980s, improvements in excavation and recovery
methods produced substantial, representative samples and led to the development
of new methodologies to explore arable and pastoral practices in detail. Prior to
this, the interpretation of plant and animal usage was based mainly on the presence
or absence of species, supplemented by information gleaned from artefacts or depic-
tions. The wealth of plant remains that have been preserved (mostly through charring), and the development of recovery techniques for these small and fragile items,
facilitated the careful consideration of arable management and the development of
interpretative models. Botanical information, ethnographic observation and historical accounts of cereal processing have been employed to better understand these
substantial assemblages.

Crop remains provide evidence for a whole range of processes from the timing of sowing, through harvesting, processing, cleaning to cooking and consumption (Jones 1985; Stevens 2003; van der Veen and Jones 2006). The species present inform us as to which grains were favoured, whilst the presence of a particular weed in a crop can indicate how cereals were harvested (pulled up or chopped off), when and on what sort of land they were planted. Processing has a number of stages; harvesting is followed by removal of the grain from the straw during threshing with the subsequent separation of waste and weeds from the grain sieving. Each of these stages produces one of three distinct groups of material characterised as chaff-rich (containing waste from the earlier stages of threshing and sieving), weed-rich (the waste from later fine sieving) or grain-rich (the final cleaned product). Early interpretations considered sites with cereal remains rich in chaff and/or weeds to represent producer sites and those rich in grain consumer sites, with threshing, winnowing and sieving completed elsewhere (e.g., the Upper Thames Valley Iron Age: Jones 1985).

Recent interpretations have identified new factors to be considered when interpreting cereal remains, such as the species, the size of the population involved in production, the mode of preservation and the archaeology of grain-bearing deposits. Different cereals break up to a greater or lesser degree during threshing: free-threshing wheat is easily separated from the chaff (the inedible waste) whilst glume wheat requires more intensive processing to clean (Jones 1985; van der Veen 1992). The quantities of chaff produced if these two cereal types were subject to the same processing would therefore differ and would alter the character of the products. The scale of processing, at communal or household level, can also change the characteristics of recovered grain. Crop processing must be swift to ensure dry storage of grain and the speed of processing is dependent on the available labour (Stevens 2003). Thus grain-rich deposits may indicate not a consumer site, but a greater degree of social organisation (larger households or a greater degree of cooperation) with more labour available to process grain prior to storage. Cleaner grain can also be a product of the value of the waste products themselves; chaff could be removed for use elsewhere, for example, as fodder (G. Campbell 2000).

The processes by which plant remains become preserved also need consideration (van der Veen and Jones 2006). The majority of recovered plant material is charred and derives from the by-products of grain de-husking and cleaning, with material burned either deliberately as fuel or accidentally during drying, parching or in storage. Chaff, as a waste material, is more likely to become burned during routine or "daily" processing of cereals prior to, or after, being taken from storage, whilst the accidental charring of cleaned grain is more likely to occur in places where grain is handled in bulk (for example, if a building containing stored product catches fire). An abundance of charred grain-rich material may therefore be an indicator of the *scale* of production and consumption rather than a method of distinguishing between the two.

Finally, the archaeological context of the plant material can provide important information. A burned-down granary would be expected to produce cleaned grain whilst material dumped in a ditch is likely to be the product of household activities that occurred at most sites. Only by incorporating the full range of factors into interpretive models can the complexity and organisation involved in crop production be explored. Models for the interpretation of waterlogged or dried plant material have not yet been developed as these assemblages are much rarer.

The abundance of faunal remains from later prehistoric sites led to parallel developments in the interpretation of animal husbandry; with larger and better assemblages, models based on herd structure were developed utilising ideas from both ethnography and animal husbandry. These models were first applied at Grimes Graves, Norfolk, where Neolithic flint mine shafts dug through chalk had been infilled with Bronze Age midden debris containing large quantities of bone. Preservation of the fragile bones of younger animals, as well as those of more robust adults, allowed Legge (1981a; 2005) to deduce that the cattle herd structure was made up of very young animals and older females (based on bone growth, tooth wear and eruption to age the animals, and the differences in shape and size of male and female remains to identify their sex). This age and sex profile was interpreted as a management strategy that focused on milk rather than meat or traction. If they were exploited for meat, larger, prime-age males would form the majority of the herd, or if cattle were used for traction older oxen, which once trained would have been useful for many years, would be present. Instead, this herd structure reflects the disposal of young animals excess to herd replacement requirements, leaving humans free to exploit the milk of the adult cows.

Other work based on ethnographic observation resulted in similar models for sheep (Payne 1973), and together the research facilitated the interpretation of herd structures as exploitation either for primary products (available only upon death), or for secondary products (obtained during the animal's lifetime: milk, wool, as traction or as pack animal). These models of animal production, although often critiqued, remain the predominant tools used to interpret animal husbandry (Halstead 1998). Their major drawback is that they are most effective when a single product is being emphasised, unlike subsistence farming where animals were generally managed to exploit a whole range of products.

As noted by Schulting (see chapter 4), the exploitation of animals for secondary products was one of the defining characteristics of the Neolithic (Sherratt 1981) and although these models facilitate the identification of milk production the degree of exploitation remains unclear. Recent work on residue analysis has indicated the presence of dairy fats on ceramics from the Neolithic onwards (Copley et al. 2005), but there remain few sites in Britain where a clear pattern of managing herds for *specialised* milk production in later prehistory has been identified. At only a few – Hambledon Hill, Dorset, Cladh Hallan, South Uist, and Danebury, Hampshire (Legge 1981a; 1981b; Craig et al. 2000; 2005; Copley et al. 2005; Mulville et al. 2005) – do both residue analysis and slaughter patterns (a high degree of neonatal calves) support the interpretation of a focused dairy economy. At a number of Bronze Age midden sites and at Iron Age Danebury husbandry evidence indicates that sheep also played a role in milk production (Serjeantson 2007). The dairy fats identified on pottery from Danebury (Copley et al. 2005) can only be identified as ruminant as it is not yet possible to differentiate between cattle, sheep or goat lipid residues.

It was only during the Bronze Age that sheep developed woolly, rather than hairy, coats (Ryder and Stephenson 1968). Evidence of the exploitation of this new resource is found in the large number of loom weights, spindle whorls and other wool-processing and weaving artefacts recovered. The models for sheep production predict that an abundance of older animals, particularly the finer wool-bearing castrated males (wethers), would indicate specialised wool production; with little evidence for this, it would appear that wool was only one aspect of sheep herding. The use of domestic stock as beasts of burden is indicated by ards, ard marks, chariots and horse harnesses, often of high quality, and in changes to the animals themselves – such as bit wear on the teeth of horses or pathological changes to animals as a result of traction (Bartosiewicz et al. 1997) or riding, as noted at Danebury (Brothwell 1995:217). The exploitation of cattle as pack or traction animals is unlikely to have been a primary aim, but one of the main roles of horses would have been as working animals and this is demonstrated in the number of chariot burials reported to date (e.g., at Wetwang Slack and Ferrybridge, Yorkshire). The changes wrought by the development of horse-assisted travel would have been significant and, with an increased journey range and decreased journey time, new areas opened up for exploration, exploitation and trade.

Procurement and Production

Farming

The structural characteristics of sites, the surrounding landscape and the evidence relating to agricultural production and consumption indicate that most later prehistoric settlements were farmsteads, that most people were farmers and that farming formed the basis of societies. Food resources were predominantly domestic, with cereals the principal plant foods and sheep, cattle and pig the mainstay of meat production. As noted above, the remains of cereal agriculture – cereal grains, chaff and seeds of weed species – are found at a very low density across archaeological sites, supplemented by occasional, accidental or purposeful rich deposits (Jones 1985; Stevens 2003). In southern Britain the focus of cereal production is emmer although bread wheat, barley and spelt were also grown (the latter two predominate in northern zones). Evidence from Danebury suggests that crops were sown as maslins, or mixtures of different species, in the autumn but that over time there was a switch to monocrops with, for example, wheat sown in autumn and barley in spring (G. Campbell 2000:55). Cereal harvesting methods also changed: initially crops were uprooted but with the adoption of balanced sickles stalks were severed and the roots left in the ground. New crop introductions of legumes, peas and Celtic beans supplemented the cereal crops.

The predominance of cattle in earlier prehistory suggests that they were of great social and economic significance (Ray and Thomas 2003; Pollard 2006). This changed in later prehistory. Sheep increased in importance to become the most numerous species at the majority of sites by the Late Iron Age (Albarella 2007;

Serjeantson 2007). The rise in sheep farming is related to changes in land management and environmental conditions, which increased suitable grazing; changes in
husbandry, as extensive sheep farming required less labour; and changes in the
demand for products, with wool available for the first time. Large numbers of pigs
are found at several Bronze Age midden sites (see below) but by the Iron Age their
numbers had declined (King 1978; Grant 1984; Maltby 1996; Hambleton 1999;
Albarella 2007; Serjeantson 2007). In southern Britain pigs were likely to have been
in competition with the use of land for cultivation, making the raising of pigs somewhat of a luxury, and high numbers would have reflected wealth and status (Serjeantson 1996; 2007; Parker Pearson 1999; Albarella and Serjeantson 2002).

These general patterns of stocking levels varied regionally. Sheep predominated
on the downlands of southern Britain, more cattle were farmed to the north and
east, and micro-regionally cattle were more common in the Upper Thames Valley
than in other southern areas (Hambleton 1999). The latter change in emphasis
reflected local environmental conditions: cattle were more resistant to the damper
conditions underfoot in the flood plain pasture of the valley bottom.

Domestic animal species had a diversity of uses. The numerically predominant
sheep were generally farmed for meat production and slaughtered when young
(Hambleton 1999). On some sites the slaughter of prime young cattle indicates
meat production whilst at others the emphasis on adult animals suggests their use
for traction – pulling carts and ploughs (Hambleton 1999). Elsewhere, as described
above, a specialised strategy for the exploitation of dairy products – milk, butter
and cheese – developed with the culling of excess, probably male, calves. Seasonality evidence demonstrates that many young stock animals were killed by their first
autumn for consumption, avoiding the problems of maintaining stock over the
winter.

Butchery evidence indicates the utilisation of dogs and the recently reintroduced
horse as food, but the age profiles of these species, their context of burial (often as
articulated remains) and their rarity suggest that they were not exploited intensively.
Other species were introduced at this time with domestic cat (Harcourt 1979; Grant
1984) and domestic fowl (Maltby 1997) first appearing in the Late Iron Age. Wild
and domestic cat are hard to distinguish but the presence of kitten bones on sites
suggests the presence of the latter. It is also possible that greylag geese and mallard
ducks were domesticated, although the evidence remains unclear.

Lamb, mutton or beef?

The numerical predominance of sheep in later prehistory does not reflect their
contribution to the human diet. It takes up to 13 sheep to make the equivalent of
a single cattle carcass; with unimproved carcass weights of 400 kg for cattle, 30 kg
for sheep and 130 kg for pig (Vigne 1991). The differences in carcass size would
also have shaped decisions as to which animals were slaughtered when and reflect
changes in how and when people ate. The immediate consumption of the quantity
of meat provided by cattle or pig slaughter could be achieved only by a large group

of people, thus these species were preferentially killed for communal events or when it was possible to prepare their carcasses for storage by smoking, salting or drying. The rise in the numbers of sheep could therefore reflect an increase in small-scale consumption, with household or family groups becoming the focus for food-sharing rather than the large-scale communal events indicated at sites in earlier prehistory.

Changes in consumption patterns are also reflected in the increase in the number of smaller vessels recovered from Iron Age sites. This indicates individual portions were being served rather than the communal sharing implied by large vessels (Woodward 1997; Woodward and Blinkhorn 1997).

Controlling the wild

Farming livestock is a demanding task. Even when farmed extensively, animals would have needed constant care. Herders would have been alert checking for births, sickness, injury, accidents and other threats, human or otherwise. The presence of the wild relatives of domestic livestock would have needed to be anticipated and controlled; wild cattle (aurochsen) were present up till the Late Bronze Age (J. Weinstock, pers. comm.), whilst wild boar remained at large until the Middle Ages (Yalden 1999). Both species could have been involved in local interbreeding (e.g., Bökönyi 1969), but the continuous decrease in body size observed in European populations of domestic cattle and pigs from the sixth millennium B.C. onwards (e.g., Teichert 1970; von den Driesch et al. 1992), and ancient DNA evidence, suggest that pastoralists, at least those in northern Europe, guarded against interbreeding with wild stock (Beja-Pereira et al. 2006).

Wild carnivores, such as bear and wolf, would have presented another threat to stock and their keepers. The containment of stock within the field systems may have increased their vulnerability to predators for, once corralled, they could no longer flee. There is virtually no evidence of the remains of predators being returned to sites; this is particularly true of wolves and bears (although as top predators their numbers would have been small). The enclosure of upland areas and an increasing human population would also have reduced the undisturbed habitat available for wild species, and grazers such as deer would have become a menace to arable crops. Some nuisance species appear on sites; the carcasses of a red deer and 14 fox skeletons in a single pit at Winklebury have been described as evidence of pest control (Jones 1977).

Herders would have used dogs to alert them to threats and to protect and control the herds/flocks. At this time the majority of dogs were collie-sized (Harcourt 1974; Maltby 1996:23) and their presence is attested by the numerous gnaw marks found on bones on all sites, even if their remains are sparse. Smaller rodent pests may have been kept down by domestic cats; their appearance in the Iron Age coincides with the earliest evidence for the house mouse (Corbet and Harris 1991:243).

One species whose management remains an enigma is the horse; they were probably extinct until their reintroduction in the Late Neolithic (Clutton-Brock 1987)

and became common on sites from the Middle Bronze Age onwards. These small
ponies, standing at 10–13 hands or 1.02–1.32 m, resembled the modern Exmoor
breed in terms of overall build. The absence of foals at the majority of sites suggests
that they were semi-feral, living and breeding in independent herds in a manner
similar to the British native ponies found on the moors and forests today (Harcourt
1979:158; Maltby 1996:23); however, there is some evidence of their breeding in
captivity during the Iron Age (Mulville and Levitan 2005). As noted earlier, their
main impact was to increase and assist transport.

Consuming the wild

Recovering evidence for the exploitation of wild resources on archaeological sites
is problematic due to a number of factors. The processing or consumption of wild
foods often takes place at the point of collection. Fruits and berries are rarely
exposed to the preservative effects of fire and are generally recovered only from
waterlogged or mineralised deposits. The remains of nuts are more durable, but
whilst charred nut shells are common in earlier prehistory, they become tantalisingly
rare in later deposits. Despite this paucity there is evidence for the use of wild plant
species with the collection of nuts, edible fruits of shrubs and trees (blackberries,
apples, plums, etc.) and roots and tubers.

Plants were also exploited for fuel (e.g., in cooking, industrial processes and
cremations) and to make artefacts, and played a role in construction with trees
felled, pollarded or coppiced to produce timber. Some plants, such as medicinal
species, were traded long distances for their properties (e.g., purging buckthorn at
Dun Vulan: Parker Pearson et al. 2000). The continuing impact of humans on wild
plant communities through gathering, management, habitat destruction and population pressure is visible only through the broad sweeps of the pollen record. Wild
plants were probably managed, owned and exploited by particular groups of people,
but such small-scale and local management is hard to discern.

Wild animals are also rare on later prehistoric sites (Hambleton 1999), for
example, red deer usually account for only one in every 100 specimens on sites
from the Neolithic onwards. This rarity has led various authors to suggest a proscription against the exploitation of wild animals in later prehistory (Hill 1995).
The few wild species present indicate the utilisation of the larger food animals with
occasional aurochs, wild boar or more commonly deer, recovered from sites along
with infrequent examples of other species such as badger, fox, polecat and birds.

The persistent presence of hunted animals suggests an ongoing relationship
between farmers and wild animals, although the number involved is very small.
What the nature of this relationship was is hard to define. These animal remains
may represent chance encounters, a regular minor food supply, specialised exploitation for particular products (e.g., fur, feathers or medicinal use), famine foods, a
trade in totems, social activities (e.g., hunting as a rite of passage) or pest management in an increasingly busy landscape. Hunted game may also have been consumed away from the domestic sphere, or only particular parts (e.g., prime joints)

returned to site. Small quantities of a range of body parts have been recovered from sites, with the focus for red deer being on the use of antler.

A variety of tools and techniques must have been employed in the hunting and trapping of wild animals. Whilst barbed-and-tanged arrowheads, flint knifes and blades have been recovered from Bronze Age sites, the archaeological evidence for lures, snares, traps, hides, arrows, spears and nets is almost non-existent. Many would have been made of perishable materials and we can only assume that historically or ethnographically attested methods were used.

At some, particularly wetland and coastal, sites a wider range of aerial and aquatic species are found. These are areas with a high diversity of plants and animals occurring in very large numbers, locally and seasonally. As with dryland sites, the majority of foods recovered at wetland sites derived from terrestrial activities: farming, hunting and the collecting of wild plants. Many, however, have a range of wetland or marine fauna. The fen edge site at Haddenham, Cambridgeshire, has abundant evidence for wild species, in particular beavers, swans and other wild fowl (Serjeantson 2006). Smaller wetland sites are linked with the exploitation of resources such as salt or pasture (Lane and Morris 2001). Watery places are also a focus for the deposition of metalwork and other artefacts, including human and animal remains, which are often found lying near wooden causeways or staging (Parker Pearson and Field 2004), but also from riverbeds, islands or log jams (Bradley and Gordon 1988; Knusel and Carr 1995; Garton et al. 1997).

There is little direct evidence for the exploitation of fish at the majority of inland sites, wetland or dryland, during later prehistory (Grant 1984; Serjeantson et al. 1994; Hill 1995; Dobney and Ervynck 2007). This may be a result of proscription against its consumption, possibly related to the way people viewed the aquatic environment. Any proscription against fish did not extend to coastal sites and from Atlantic Scotland down to the Isles of Scilly there is extensive evidence for the continuing utilisation of marine resources, such as fish, marine mammals, shellfish, crustacea, sea and shore birds and seaweeds (Willis 2007). These were exploited to provide meat, fat, fuel, fertiliser and fodder (Smith and Mulville 2004).

Coastal communities caught fish by line from the shore, indicated by the predominance of inshore species such as small gadids (cod species), or may have used fish traps made of wood, reed or stone (Ashbee 1974; Bell at al. 2000). Examples of fishing paraphernalia are reported, although hooks themselves are rare, with the recovery of line-sinkers (a stone with a hole attached to a line to help carry it out over the water), line-winders (waisted stones or longbones with wear marks from fine thread, possibly horsehair), bone needles used in net production and pumice fishing floats. Other marine foods were hunted or gathered. Grey seals were targeted during the autumn breeding season when the cubs were vulnerable. Whales and dolphins were recovered either by stranding, driving ashore or possibly hunting at sea (Mulville 2002). Birds were trapped or netted, eggs gathered, whilst shellfish, crustacea and seaweeds were harvested from the shoreline (e.g., Smith and Mulville 2004).

The relative contribution that marine and terrestrial resources made to the coastal human diet remains unclear; to date few sites have produced fish residues in pottery (Brown and Heron 2003), and stable isotopes do not fully reflect this diversity in human diet, with only a scattering of island/coastal individuals reported as having a weak marine signal (e.g., Barrett et al. 2001; Parker Pearson et al. 2005; Richards et al. 2006; S. Mays, pers. comm.). Stable isotopes measurements reflect only the protein content in the diet (using bone collagen as the source), and if marine foods made up less than 20 per cent of the diet, there may be little change in the isotopic signal (Fischer et al. 2007).

Island communities exploited wild terrestrial species to a greater extent than mainland sites (Smith and Mulville 2004; Mulville and Thoms 2005), and there is even evidence for the earlier importation of mammals such as red deer and the fox for specialised exploitation (Ratcliffe and Straker 1996; Fairnell and Barrett 2007). Boats were commonplace in later prehistory (Clark 1952:305), and in addition to the exchange of goods, such as bronze, across the seas and along river systems (Scarre and Healey 1993), vessels must have carried livestock (both domestic and wild).

The farming year

The detailed evidence available from later prehistory has allowed the development of sophisticated descriptions of the decisions, timings and movements embedded in the annual farming cycle. By incorporating information from historical texts on the likely dates for animal breeding and slaughtering, crop growth and ripening, nut, fruit and berry harvesting with estimates of the availability of pasture, pannage and other wild resources, Campbell and Hamilton (G. Campbell 2000:58) have produced a model for seasonal activities.

The timing of the many essential tasks for food production throughout the yearly round impacted on when communities were available for other activities such as construction or combat. It is likely that at the smaller rural settlements the majority of the population would have been part of the daily and annual agricultural round, whilst in larger or specialised settlements other tasks would have called on people's time. The increase in settlement size and number facilitated and necessitated an increasing intensification in agricultural production.

People's lives were busy fulfilling the daily rounds of preparing and cooking food, cleaning, rearing children, training and herding animals and maintaining homes and boundaries. Attempts to estimate what proportion of the population were involved on a daily basis in keeping stock, sowing and weeding crops, drying foods or hunting wild game is difficult (Fitzpatrick 1997). Some farming tasks, such as harvesting, had to be undertaken quickly in appropriate weather when the involvement of the whole community would have been welcomed. Other tasks would have been gender- or age-specific, and although we lack evidence for younger shepherds tending stock out on the hills, men milking the cattle, adults restraining stock for slaughter, women ministering to breeding or sick animals and children's nimble fingers sorting out weeds and chaff, ethnographic evidence points to all hands being put to work in appropriate tasks.

Preparation and Consumption

Harvesting and storage

The tools used to process plant and animal foods developed over this period, in particular balanced sickles, changed the way that crops were harvested, while the introduction of rotary querns simplified the processing of cereal into flour. The increasing use of metal had little effect on animal slaughter and butchery; if anything, the rarity of this material would have increased the need for careful butchery to avoid the blunting of blades. Once animals had been marked for slaughter their death was accomplished by pole-axing (hitting hard on the front of the head) and/or the cutting of their throats. Division of the carcasses was generally a skilled task, leaving few marks on the majority of bones, but the available evidence suggests the removal of the skin, careful division at joints and the filleting of meat before consumption. The only notable changes occurred late in the period when the splitting of carcasses into sides by chopping through the vertebra, possibly associated with the salting of meat, began (Maltby 2005).

Foods were kept for later use and consumption by transformation into inert forms, for example, by drying, salting, smoking to remove water, or by storage in cool places. There is evidence for "industrial ovens" (Cunliffe and Poole 1991:151) and other structures interpreted as corn dryers. Cereals, once dried, remain edible and viable for long period of time if stored appropriately. In the Bronze Age seed corn (used to sow the next crop) was probably stored in ceramic or perishable vessels with grain for consumption held in above-ground granaries protected from damp (often identified as four-post structures). Storage pests, both insect (D. Smith, pers. comm.) and rodent, were few; house mice remains are extremely rare in later prehistory and other rodent remains sparse. During the Iron Age, in parts of southern and central Britain, storage pits were cut into chalk, lined with wicker and sealed with clay. These pits may have been useful in the long-term storage of seed corn; experiments have demonstrated that, once sealed, the limited oxygen would be used up by sprouting grain, thus inhibiting the growth of the remaining grain and ensuring its viability as future crop (Reynolds 1974; 1977). Only material excess to that needed for autumnal sowing would be stored long-term so the appearance of these storage pits reflects an increase in agrarian surpluses (van der Veen and Jones 2006) up until the switch to spring sowing in the Late Iron Age.

Salt was an important preservative; its addition removes water from foods and inhibits biological action. The earliest evidence for salt-making in Britain dates to the Middle Bronze Age (Lane and Morris 2001). A bulk salt trade emerged in the early first millennium B.C. and intensified over time (Champion et al. 2001). Salt was obtained from brine-rich springs (e.g., Droitwich, Worcestershire), sea water (e.g., the saltern sites of East Anglia or the Isle of Purbeck) or salt mines (e.g., Cheshire). The curing of meat requires a cool ambient temperature and days or even weeks to complete, so is best carried out in autumn. Some meats are more suitable for preserving, and Maltby (2005) suggests that the predominance of pig at Iron Age sites is indicative of a trade in salted pork. Salt is also used in the making of dairy products and may additionally have been essential as a "lick" for stock (Clutton-Brock 1987). For many foods storage in a cool, stable environment would extend their longevity, and it has been suggested that the subterranean chambers of Iron Age western and northern Britain, known as souterrains or fogou, functioned as larders.

The processing of foods can also increase their shelf-life, for example, the transformation of liquid milk into easily storable cheeses and butters. The production of butter and cheese is demonstrated by finds of "bog butter"; more than 270 packages of fat have been discovered in Scottish and Irish peat bogs, often contained in wooden boxes, tree bark or animal skins. Many are later in date, but some were deposited in prehistory (Earwood 1997). Recent characterisation work using chemical analysis has revealed that, in addition to products derived from milk, subcutaneous fats such as lard or tallow were also represented (Berstan et al. 2004).

The preservative qualities of bogs were exploited in other ways. Evidence from microscopic patterns of bone destruction found on the human burials from Cladh Hallan, Western Isles, suggests submersion in an acidic bog environment, probably to facilitate preservation of the soft tissue (Parker Pearson et al. 2005; 2007). Once partially tanned in the acid bog environment the enfleshed and articulated corpse remained intact for hundred of years but only by keeping the body dry. This could most easily have been achieved by smoking and storage in the roof of a building. Elsewhere evidence for the drying of meat for consumption can be found in the perforated cattle scapula present on European sites (van Mensch and Ijzereef 1977), a central hole in the blade being associated with suspension of the joint over a fire.

Cooking and eating

Evidence for cookery and consumption can be found in the structures and tools used during these processes and the food remains themselves. Food preparation and cooking areas, hearths, ovens, and cooking and serving vessels have all been identified; for the latter the size and type of vessels, sooting or burning patterns and any preserved food remains therein all provide information on the type and form of food consumed. Sometimes food remains are visible as a crust of material on pottery vessels, but at other times microscopic evidence for foods can be found within tiny spaces in the ceramic walls themselves (e.g., milk proteins: Craig et al. 2000; 2005). Macroscopic food remains demonstrate that grain was ground into flour, and made into bread or griddle cakes (e.g., at Maiden Castle). The cutmarks and breakage patterns of bone indicate that animals were butchered for consumption both on and off the bone, and in general cattle were subject to a greater degree of butchery than the smaller stock such as sheep.

Domestic ovens were used for cooking or baking. These are made of stone or clay foundations, with clay walls forming a dome or supporting an oven cover. Some were single undivided chambers heated by a fire set in the base which would be raked out prior to the food being placed within it, whilst others had possible internal shelving, made of thick, flat clay plates with perforations, upon which vessels or food was placed (e.g., Cunliffe and Poole 1991:147, fig 4.94). Roasting meat on an open fire is suggested by meat hooks in the Bronze Age and by scorch marks on bone, but meat could have been cooked using low or indirect heat, and boiled, stewed or steamed on or off the bone. There is one particular type of later prehistoric site which may provide an insight into indirect heating methods. Burnt mounds litter the country in large numbers and consist of dumps of burnt stone and ash, usually near a source of fresh water. Accompanying these mounds are often wooden troughs or stone-lined pits, the joins sealed with clay, which suggests they held water. Stones were probably heated in a fire and dropped into these water-filled troughs. What the resulting steam or hot water was used for remains conjecture but one theory is that it was used for cooking. The absence of large quantities of animal remains argues against these mounds as feasting sites and other suggestions for their use has included saunas (Barfield and Hodder 1987). What-ever they were for, burnt mounds provide evidence for sophisticated indirect heating technologies that may have been applied to cooking.

Animal remains recovered from graves or special deposits as articulated limbs demonstrate that carcasses were divided into joints. For example, sheep humeri (front leg), contained within pots or by themselves, or the head (often split) and forequarters of pigs, were recovered from the square barrow burials of Yorkshire (Legge 1991; Stead 1991). At Ferry Fryston the interred pig remains – a split skull and humerus – appear to have been cooked before deposition (Bates et al., in press). There is also a bias in the elements recovered from these burials, with the left side predominating, suggesting the deliberate selection of body parts (Parker Pearson 1999). Elsewhere joints of prime beef were found accompanying the Hasleholme boat (Millett and McGrail 1987) and there are many other examples of articulating bones, representing joints, recovered from pits and ditches.

Bog bodies provide the most direct evidence for meals in the form of stomach contents. These have revealed an abundance of cereals; in the Lindow examples emmer and spelt wheat, rye bran and barley chaff predominated, and were possibly eaten as a griddle cake. Quantities of hazel nuts and weed seeds had also been consumed (Holden 1995). Meat remains have been identified in British examples but, present only as fragments of tissue, they have not been characterised. The inclusion of unusual foods, such as burnt grain, mistletoe pollen or ergot, has been interpreted variously as evidence for ritual sacrificial offerings or accidental incor-porations (Hillman 1986; Harild et al. 2007).

Later prehistoric human remains have not yet been the focus for detailed stable isotope studies, although this is changing. Few later Bronze Age remains have been analysed and the Iron Age evidence is patchy, with published examples generally made up of only small groups of individuals. The exception to this is a study of two rare cemetery sites located in Yorkshire, at Wetwang and Garton Slack (Jay and Richards 2006). Analysis of the human burials has allowed initial conclusions to be drawn about the contribution of different food sources in the Iron Age. People buried at these sites had diets relatively high in animal protein, either meat or dairy products, and although individuals were given very different burial rites, there was little variation within the population as a result of sex, age or inferred status.

Conception: Feasting and Sacrifices

In this final section the evidence for the situations and setting in which food was consumed and discarded is considered. The new predominance of domestic settlement sites marked a change in the way people interacted with one another. Although individuals congregated in large settlements, there is very little evidence for concentrated mass consumption events. There is, however, evidence for continual small-scale deposition at sites over many years, and individual acts of consumption can be identified. These provide insights into how people ate and reveal important details of the meanings ascribed to particular foods in prehistory. Food remains are found preserved within middens, in enclosure ditches and pits and strewn across floors.

Middens are large, above-ground deposits of a range of materials. In earlier prehistory they contained much shell and generally lay close to the coast but later middens began to incorporate other forms of natural and cultural debris and often developed within settlements. In the Late Bronze Age huge accumulations, over 4 ha in area and up to 2 m high developed, composed of huge collections of material: animal bones, cattle and sheep dung, ash, plant remains, fragmented potsherds and manufacturing debris as well as high-quality artefacts and disarticulated human bone. At Potterne, Wiltshire, excavation of less than 1 per cent of the midden yielded over 1 tonne of pottery and 135,000 animal bones (Lawson 2000).

Examples of middens are found in south-western Britain, at All Cannings Cross, Potterne and East Chisenbury in Wiltshire (Cunnington 1923; Brown et al. 1994; McOmish 1996; Lawson 2000), and at Runnymede Bridge in Berkshire (Needham 1991; Needham and Spence 1997), but recent work suggests that many more exist (e.g., at Llanmaes, Glamorgan, and Whitchurch, Warwickshire). Original interpretations favoured middens as sites for stabling animals, but their characteristics and the sheer quantity of material suggest more than a haphazard accumulation of rubbish. These sites provide evidence for domestic activity, manuring and crop processing, pottery manufacture, fires and feasting. That the latter played a key role in the accumulation of refuse is evidenced by large dumps of complete and near complete vessels found in association with butchered bone (Needham and Spence 1997).

The plant remains reflect arable cultivation and the collection of wild foods; middens have provided the earliest British find of the opium poppy. The presence of substantial quantities of manure and evidence for trampling demonstrates the presence of livestock at the middens, and the scale of the animal food remains represented is staggering. Estimates place the remains of close to half a million stock in the mound at East Chisenbury: during the 100-year period of occupation at least 380,000 sheep and goats, 60,000 cows and 45,000 pigs were killed and consumed (D. Serjeantson, pers. comm.). A number of the sites have a striking quantity of pig bones (up to 80 per cent at Llanmaes) and, as noted previously, these animals are often associated with high-status feasting (Serjeantson 2006). The high cull of first-year sheep at five sites (Runnymede, East Chisenbury, Grimes Graves, Potterne and Wallingford) strongly suggests that sheep flocks were kept for milking, drawing on sheep from settlements from elsewhere to replenish the flock. Ageing evidence suggests that the cull of animals was concentrated in spring or autumn, and that deposition on the site was intensified at these times.

The scale of these sites suggests the repeated gathering of large numbers of people; here they sorted and processed crops and milked, slaughtered and butchered stock, foods were eaten and the waste was discarded. As yet we do not know where supplies for the midden communities were produced. Did the fields and herds lie close to the monuments? If not, how and from what distance were these plant foods and animals transported? The large tracts of pasture that developed in the tenth to seventh centuries B.C. (McOmish et al. 2002) would have provide good grazing, and a large hinterland must have been drawn upon.

Elsewhere smaller-scale feasting events were associated with burial rites. For example, at the Ferry Fryston burial, in addition to the food remains interred in the grave, cattle skulls were deposited on the barrow mound and it is possible that pig remains were placed on the barrow at the Wetwang village chariot burial (Bates et al., in press). Examples of similar deposition of skulls are found at Irthlingborough and Gayhurst (Davis and Payne 1993; Chapman et al. 2004) during the Early Bronze Age. The side biases in the Arras square barrows have already been discussed (Parker Pearson 1999) and other examples have been found on settlement sites (e.g., there is a group of right-hand-side femurs recovered at Iron Age Yarnton) and in the middens (at Llanmaes there is an overwhelming predominance of right pig fore-limbs). This selection of one site of the animal has parallels with classical votive deposits (S. Stallibrass, pers. comm.) where the one side of the hip/thigh (i.e., the right femur) was preferentially given to the gods.

New patterns of deposition, within houses and associated features such as storage and rubbish pits and ditches, provide evidence for domestic practices. Detailed analysis of the large assemblages recovered from Wessex and Hampshire (Grant 1984; Wait 1985; Hill 1995) have revealed that many features, rather than being stuffed with random dumps of discarded material, were carefully filled in a structured manner (Hill 1995).

The presence of intentionally placed food deposits is indicated by material that has been processed in a different manner from what is expected and generally observed within the assemblages. It is assumed that that within a subsistence (i.e., self-reliant) economy stock was judiciously husbanded, food carefully stored and waste rare. Animals would be disarticulated and stripped of all meat and other useful products before their remains were discarded. Similarly for plant foods once all valuable materials had been exploited any remaining matter was utilised as fuel or composted, with little left to be discarded. In later prehistory there are groups of material that fall outside these expected discard patterns. Clean charred grain and/or complete or partial animal carcasses, skulls and composite remains (heads, joints or carcasses composed of more than one individual animal) are found in association with human bone, complete pots, metalwork or other unusual items (Grant 1984; Wait 1985; Hill 1995; Mulville and Levitan 2005). Animal species that are generally rare (e.g., horses, dogs and wild species) are also more abundant in these deposits. These accumulations are variously known as special deposits (Grant 1984), or as articulated/associated bone groups (ABGs: Hill 1995).

Archaeological investigation of these food remains rarely reveal if the deposits are the result of accidental damage, disease or other causes rendering them unfit to eat – a rotten joint of meat or spoiled grain, for example. There is very little evidence for plant foods deposited as meals – soups or stews, or as bread and cakes – in these deposits and, while a proportion of the animal remains provide evidence of butchery prior to deposition, indications of cooking methods are very rare. The complete articulated skeletons suggest that entire carcasses were deposited with minimal exploitation, although in some cases there is evidence of processing followed by the reconstitution of individual or composite animals prior to deposition. The proportion of species within these features has been used to construct a cosmology of animal significance (Hill 1995).

Food production and consumption practices are also identifiable within houses. Where floors have been preserved patterning is visible in the distribution of finds and/or structural elements, and in some cases this includes special deposits (Parker Pearson et al. 2004). Some archaeologists see the orientation and layout of houses as being influenced by cosmology, with entrances lying mainly to the east, so that the movement of the sun, clockwise, around a house would have measured the passing of time on a daily or yearly cycle (Parker Pearson 1996; Fitzpatrick 1997; Oswald 1997; Parker Pearson et al. 2005). The cycle of daily use is seen in food preparation areas being placed in the south near the door on the way in, whilst sleeping areas lie to the north. On a longer scale the house may have formed a calendar of the human life cycle, from birth to death with the doorway the point at which life began and ended. A good example of this is the series of conjoining houses at Cladh Hallan, constructed in the later Bronze Age in the Western Isles. Here the deposition of food waste in the north-east quadrant of the house is presaged by the deposition of human and animal remains as foundation burials (Parker Pearson et al. 2005; 2007). Both dogs and sheep are present as complete burials, with butchery evidence suggesting consumption of the latter, along with joints of pork, venison and beef.

This tradition of below-floor burials continues into the Early Iron Age. At Hornish Point wheelhouse a 14-year-old boy was quartered and placed in four pits, also in the north-east quadrant, accompanied by the remains of two cattle and two sheep (Barber 1997). These prime meat animals had been thoroughly processed before deposition, with evidence for skinning, filleting and marrow extraction. Considerable effort had been made to gather up even the tiniest fragments of bone, some of which had been gnawed, prior to the placement of the animals within the pits. At another wheelhouse, Sollas, over 100 individual animals were "sacrificed" on site and placed in pits as foundation burials. The presence of numerous domestic animals suggests that this was a lengthy act of consecration of a new house by a widespread community (E. Campbell 2000).

Foodways

The centrality and ubiquity of food within the human experience means that a consideration of what we eat penetrates deeply into all aspects of life. As this chapter has demonstrated, later prehistory provides an abundance of evidence: the sheer number and range of sites combined with the quality of material recovered has allowed archaeologists to construct detailed accounts of food production and consumption, to better understand human nutrition and to demonstrate the role food played in the creation of social relations and identities. Food was important in the development and organization of later prehistoric societies, for example, in the change from feasting as a method of food distribution to household-based economies. There are identifiable changes in the manner in which cereals were stored and dispersed, and in the locations where particular foods were consumed and deposited.

The advances made in understanding foodways have in turn allowed archaeologists to ask new and different questions, and research is constantly striving to further understand human life at many scales – from the effect of large environmental changes on food production techniques, to differences in particular groups' attitude to foods, to alterations in an individual diet over a lifetime. Despite these advances archaeologists remain ignorant on many aspects of the subject and often have to rely on the use of ethnographic and historical data to interpret the past, using medieval models of farming to flesh out the details of day-to-day life. We can begin to understand human diets – for example, stable isotope evidence reveals that animal products were essential to the diet, but the proportions of meat and dairy products consumed remains a matter for speculation – and we are only just beginning to be able to describe how these and other foods were cooked and eaten. Were meat and cereal stews, gruels and soups, the mainstay of the diet, or were milk, butter and cheese a regular addition? The situation is worse in relation to plant-based foods, where the bias in preservation towards particular species at particular stages in their processing leaves us at a loss to understand the role of many non-cereal plants.

REFERENCES

Albarella U., 2007 The end of the Sheep Age: people and animals in the late Iron Age. *In* The Later Iron Age in Britain and Beyond. C. Haselgrove and T. Moore, eds. pp. 393–406. Oxford: Oxbow Books.

——and D. Serjeantson, 2002 A passion for pork: butchery and cooking at the British Neolithic site of Durrington Walls. *In* Consuming Passions and Patterns of Consumption. P. Miracle and N. Milner, eds. pp. 33–49. Cambridge: McDonald Institute.

Armit, I., 2003 Towers in the North: the brochs of Scotland. Stroud: Tempus.

Ashbee, P., 1974 Ancient Scilly from the First Farmers to the Early Christians: an introduction and survey. Newton Abbot: David and Charles.

Barber, J., 1997 Bronze Age Farms and Iron Age Farm Mounds of the Outer Hebrides. Edinburgh: Scottish Trust for Archaeological Research.

Barfield, L. H., and M. A. Hodder, 1987 Burnt mounds as saunas and the prehistory of bathing? Antiquity 61:370–379.

Barrett, J. H., R. P. Beukens and R. A. Nicholson, 2001 Diet and ethnicity during the Viking colonisation of northern Scotland: evidence from fish bones and stable carbon isotopes. Antiquity 75:145–154.

Bartosiewicz, L., W. van Neer and A. Lentacker, 1997 Draught Cattle: their osteological identification and history. Tervuren: Musée Royal de l'Afrique Centrale.

Bates, A., G. G. Jones and D. C. Orton, in press Animal bone from Site D Ferry Fryston. *In* The Archaeology of the A1 (M) Darrington to Dishforth DBFO Road Scheme. F. Brown, C. Howard-Davis, M. Brennand, A. Boyle, T. Evans, S. O'Connor, A. Spence, R. Heawood and A. Lupton.

Beja-Pereira, A., D. Caramelli, C. Lalueza-Fox, C. Vernesi, N. Ferrand, A. Casoli, F. Goyache, L. J. Royo, S. Conti, M. Lari, A. Martini, L. Ouragh, A. Magid, A. Atash, A. Zsolnai, P. Boscato, C. Triantaphylidis, K. Ploumi, L. Sineo, F. Mallegni, P. Taberlet, D. Erhardt, L. Sampietro, J. Bertranpetit, G. Barbujani, G. Luikart and G. Bertorelle, 2006 The origin of European cattle: evidence from modern and ancient DNA. Proceedings of the National Academy of Sciences 103:8113–8118.

Bell, M., A. Caseldine, H. Neumann and B. Taylor, 2000 Prehistoric Intertidal Archaeology in the Welsh Severn Estuary. London: Council for British Archaeology.

Berstan R, S. N. Dudd, M. S. Copley, E. D. Morgan, A. Quye and R. P. Evershed, 2004 Characterisation of bog butter using a combination of molecular and isotopic techniques. Analyst 129:270–275.

Bökönyi, S., 1969 Archaeological problems and methods of identifying animal domestication. *In* The Domestication and Exploitation of Plants and Animals. P. J. Ucko and G. W. Dimbleby, eds. pp. 219–229. London: Duckworth.

Bradley, R., and K. Gordon, 1988 Human skulls from the river Thames, their dating and significance. Antiquity 62:503–509.

——and D. Yates, 2007 After "Celtic" fields: the social organisation of Iron Age agriculture. *In* The Earlier Iron Age in Britain and the Near Continent. C. Haselgrove and R. Pope, eds. pp. 94–102. Oxford: Oxbow Books.

Brothwell, D., 1995 The special animal pathology. *In* Danebury: An Iron Age hillfort in Hampshire, vol. 6: A Hillfort Community in Perspective. B. Cunliffe. pp. 207–233. London: Council for British Archaeology.

Brown, G., D. Field and D. McOmish, 1994 East Chisenbury midden complex, Wiltshire. *In* The Iron Age in Wessex: recent work. A. Fitzpatrick and E. Morris, eds. pp. 46–49. Salisbury: Trust for Wessex Archaeology and AFEAF.

Brown, L. D., and C. Heron, 2003 The potential role of ceramics in recognising direct evidence for the exploitation of fish. *In* Prehistoric Pottery: people, pattern and purpose. A. Gibson, ed. pp. 35–41. Oxford: British Archaeological Reports.

Campbell, E., 2000 The raw, the cooked and the burnt: interpretations of food and animals in the Hebridean Iron Age. Archaeological Dialogues 7(2):184–198.

Campbell, G., 2000 Plant utilisation: the evidence from charred plant remains. *In* The Danebury Environs Programme: the prehistory of a Wessex Landscape, vol. 1. B. Cunliffe, ed. pp. 45–59. Oxford: English Heritage and Oxford University Committee for Archaeology.

Carter, S. P., and D. A. Davidson, 1998 An evaluation of the contribution of soil micromorphology to the study of ancient arable agriculture. Geoarchaeology 15(5):499–502.

Champion, T. C., C. Haselgrove, I. Armit, J. Creighton and A. Gwilt, 2001 Understanding the British Iron Age: an agenda for action. Salisbury: Wessex Archaeology.

Chapman, A., K. Deighton and P. Halstead, 2004 Gayhurst: reconstructing the burial of an Early Bronze Age lord. Current Archaeology 195:114–118.

Clark, J. G. D., 1952 Prehistoric Europe: the economic basis. London: Methuen.

Clutton-Brock, J., 1987 A Natural History of Domesticated Mammals. Cambridge: Cambridge University Press.

Copley, M. S., R. Berstan, A. J. Mukherjee, S. N. Dudd, V. Straker, S. Payne and R. P. Evershed, 2005 Dairying in antiquity III: evidence from absorbed lipid residues dating to the British Neolithic. Journal of Archaeological Science 32:523–546.

Corbet, G. B., and S. Harris, 1991 The Handbook of British Mammals, 3rd edn. Oxford: Blackwell Scientific.

Craig O. E., J. Mulville, M. Parker Pearson, R. J. Sokol, K. Gelsthorpe, R. Stacey and M. J. Collins, 2000 Detecting milk in ancient pots. Nature 408:312.

——G. Taylor, J. Mulville, M. Parker Pearson and M. J. Collins, 2005 The identification of prehistoric dairying activities in the Scottish Atlantic margins: an integrated biomolecular approach. Journal of Archaeological Science 32:91–103.

Cunliffe, B., 1995 Danebury, vol. 6: A Hillfort Community in Perspective. London: Council for British Archaeology

——and C. Poole, 1991 Danebury: an Iron Age hillfort in Hampshire, vol. 4: The Excavations 1979–1988. London: Council for British Archaeology.

Cunnington, M. E., 1923 The Early Iron Age Inhabited Site at All Cannings Cross Farm, Wiltshire. Devizes: Simpson.

Davis, S., and S. Payne, 1993 A barrow full of cattle skulls. Antiquity 67:12–22.

Dobney, K., and A. Ervynck, 2007 To fish or not to fish? Evidence for the possible avoidance of fish consumption during the Iron Age around the North Sea. In The Later Iron Age in Britain and Beyond. C. Haselgrove and T. Moore, eds. pp. 403–418. Oxford: Oxbow Books.

Earwood, C., 1997 Bog-butter: a two thousand-year history. Journal of Irish Archaeology 8:25–42.

Fairnell, E. H., and J. H. Barrett, 2007 Fur-bearing species and Scottish islands. Journal of Archaeological Science 34(3):463–484.

Fischer, A., J. Olsen, M. P. Richards, J. Heinemeier, Á. E. Sveinbjörnsdóttir and P. Bennike, 2007 Coast–inland mobility and diet in the Danish Mesolithic and Neolithic: evidence from stable isotope values of humans and dogs. Journal of Archaeological Science 34(12):2125–2150.

Fitzpatrick, A., 1997 Everyday life in Iron Age Wessex. In Reconstructing Iron Age Societies: new approaches to the British Iron Age. A. Gwilt and C. Hazelgrove, eds. pp. 73–86. Oxford: Oxbow Books.

Garton, D., A. Howard and M. Pearce, 1997 Archaeological investigations at Langford Quarry, Nottinghamshire 1995–6. Tarmac Papers 1:29–40.

Grant, A., 1984 Animal husbandry in Wessex and the Thames Valley. In Aspects of the Iron Age in Central Southern Britain. B. W. Cunliffe and D. Miles, eds. pp. 102–119. Oxford: Oxford University Committee for Archaeology.

Guttmann, E. B. A., I. A. Simpson and S. J. Dockrill, 2003 Joined-up archaeology at Old Scatness, Shetland: thin section analysis of the site and hinterland. Environmental Archaeology 8(1):17–31.

Halstead, P., 1998 Mortality models and milking: problems of uniformitarianism, optimality, and equifinality reconsidered. Anthropozoologica 27:3–20.

Hambleton, E., 1999 Animal Husbandry Regimes in Iron Age Britain: a comparative study of faunal assemblages from British Iron Age sites. Oxford: British Archaeological Reports.

Harcourt, R., 1974 The dog in prehistoric and early historic Britain. Journal of Archaeological Science 1:151–175.

———1979. The animal bones. *In* Gussage All Saints: an Iron Age settlement in Dorset. G. J. Wainwright. pp. 150–160. London: Department of the Environment.

Harild, J. A., D. E. Robinson and J. Hudlebusch, 2007 New investigations of the Grauballe Man's gut contents. *In* Grauballe Man: an Iron Age bog body revisited. P. Asingh and N. Lynnerup, eds. pp. 154–187. Aarhus: Jutland Archaeological Society.

Hill, J. D., 1995 Ritual and Rubbish in the Iron Age of Wessex: a study on the formation of a specific archaeological record. Oxford: British Archaeological Reports.

Hillman G., 1986 Plant remains. *In* Excavations in Caernarfon 1976–7. R. B. White. pp. 101–103. Archaeologia Cambrensis 134:53–105.

Holden, T. G., 1995 The last meals of the Lindow Bog men. *In* Bog Bodies: new discoveries and new perspectives. R. C. Turner and R. G. Scaife, eds. pp. 76–82. London: British Museum.

Jay, M., and M. P. Richards, 2006 Diet in the Iron Age cemetery population at Wetwang Slack, East Yorkshire, UK: carbon and nitrogen stable isotope evidence. Journal of Archaeological Science 33(5):653–662.

Jones, G. 1985 Archaeobotany beyond subsistence reconstruction. *In* Beyond Domestication in Prehistoric Europe. G. Barker and C. Gamble, eds. pp. 107–128. London: Academic Press.

Jones, M., 1977 The animal bone. *In* The excavation of Winklebury Camp, Basingstoke, Hampshire. K. Smith. Proceedings of the Prehistoric Society 43: 31–130.

King, A. C., 1978 A comparative survey of bone assemblages from Roman sites in Britain. Bulletin of the Institute of Archaeology, University of London 15:207–232.

Knusel, C. J., and G. C. Carr, 1995 On the significance of the crania from the River Thames and its tributaries. Antiquity 69:162–169.

Lane, T., and E. Morris, eds., 2001 A Millennium of Salt-Making: prehistoric and Romano-British salt production in the Fenland. Heckington: Lincolnshire Archaeology and Heritage.

Lawson, A. J., 2000 Potterne 1982–5: animal husbandry in later prehistoric Wiltshire. Salisbury: Wessex Archaeology.

Legge, A. J., 1981a The agricultural economy. *In* Grimes Graves: excavations 1971–72. R. Mercer. pp. 79–103. London: HMSO.

———1981b Aspects of cattle husbandry. *In* Farming Practice in British Prehistory. R. Mercer, ed. pp. 169–181. Edinburgh: Edinburgh University Press.

———1991 The animal bones. *In* Iron Age Cemeteries in East Yorkshire. I. M. Stead. pp. 140–147. London: English Heritage.

———2005 Milk use in prehistory: the osteological evidence. *In* The Zooarchaeology of Fats, Oils, Milk and Dairying. J. Mulville and A. K. Outram, eds. pp. 8–13. Oxford: Oxbow Books.

Macphail, R., J. C. C. Romans and L. Robertson, 1987 The application of micromorphology to the understanding of Holocene soil development in the British Isles: with special reference to early cultivation. *In* Micromorphologie des Sols. N. Fedoroff, L. M. Bresson and M. A. Courty, eds. pp. 647–656. Plaisir: AFES.

Maltby, M. 1996 The exploitation of animals in the Iron Age: the archaeozoological evidence. *In* The Iron Age in Britain and Ireland: recent trends. T. C. Champion and J. R. Collis, eds. pp. 17–28. Sheffield: J. R. Collis.

—— 1997 Domestic fowl on Romano-British sites: inter-site comparisons of abundance. International Journal of Osteoarchaeology 7(4):402–414.

—— 2005 Salt and animal products: linking production and use in Iron Age Britain. In Integrating Zooarchaeology. M. Maltby, ed. pp. 117–122. Oxford: Oxbow Books.

McOmish, D., 1996 East Chisenbury: ritual and rubbish in the British Bronze Age–Iron Age transition. Antiquity 70:68–76.

——D. Field and G. Brown, 2002 The Field Archaeology of Salisbury Plain Training Area. Swindon: English Heritage.

Millett, M., and S. McGrail, 1987 The archaeology of the Hasholme Logboat. Archaeological Journal 144:139–144.

Mulville, J. 2002 The role of cetacea in prehistoric and historic Atlantic Scotland. International Journal of Osteoarchaeology 12(1):34–48.

——and B. Levitan, 2005 The animal bone. In Gravelly Guy, Stanton Harcourt: the development of a prehistoric and Romano-British community. G. Lambrick and T. G. Allen. pp. 263–479. Oxford: Oxford Archaeology.

——and J. Thoms, 2005 Animals and ambiguity in the Iron Age of the Western Isles. In Tall Stories? Broch studies past present and future. V. Turner, ed. pp.235–245. Oxford: Oxbow Books.

——J. Bond and O. Craig, 2005 The white stuff: milking in the North Atlantic. In The Zooarchaeology of Fats, Oils, Milk and Dairying. J. Mulville and A. Outram, eds. pp. 167–183. Oxford: Oxbow Books.

Needham, S., 1991 Excavation and Salvage at Runnymede Bridge 1978: the late Bronze Age waterfront site. London: British Museum.

——and T. Spence, 1997 Refuse and the formation of middens. Antiquity 71:77–90.

Oswald, A., 1997 A doorway on the past: practical and mystic concerns in the orientation of roundhouse doorways. In Reconstructing Iron Age Societies: new approaches to the British Iron Age. A. Gwilt and C. Hazelgrove, eds. pp. 87–95. Oxford: Oxbow Books.

Parker Pearson, M., 1996 Food, fertility and front doors in the first millennium BC. In The Iron Age in Britain and Ireland: recent trends. T. Champion and J. Collis, eds. pp. 117–132. Sheffield: Sheffield Academic Press.

—— 1999 Food, sex and death: cosmologies in the British Iron Age with particular reference to East Yorkshire. Cambridge Archaeological Journal 9:43–69.

——and N. Field, 2004 Fiskerton: an Iron Age timber causeway with Iron Age and Roman votive offerings: the 1981 excavations. Oxford: Oxbow Books.

——N. Sharples, J. Mulville and H. Smith, 2000 Between Land and Sea: excavations at Dun Vulan, South Uist. Sheffield: Sheffield University Press.

——N. Sharples, J. Symonds, with J. Mulville, J. Raven, H. Smith, H. Woolf and A. Woolf, 2004 South Uist: archaeology and history of the Dark Island. Stroud: Tempus.

——A. Chamberlain, O. Craig, P. Marshall, J. Mulville, H. Smith, C. Chenery, M. Collins, G. Cook, G. Craig, J. Evans, H. Hiller, J.-L. Schwenninger, G. Taylor and T. Wess, 2005 Evidence for mummification in Bronze Age Britain. Antiquity 79:529–546.

——A. Chamberlain, M. Collins, C. Cox, G. Craig, O. Craig, J. Hiller, P. Marshall, J. Mulville and H. Smith, 2007 Further evidence for mummification in Bronze Age Britain. Antiquity 81(312). Available at http://antiquity.ac.uk/ProjGall/parker/index.html

Payne, S., 1973 Kill off patterns in sheep and goats: the mandibles from Asvan Kale. Anatolian Studies 23:281–303.

Pollard, J., 2006. A community of beings: animals and people in the Neolithic of southern Britain. *In* Animals in the Neolithic of Britain and Europe. D. Serjeantson and D. Field, eds. pp. 135–148. Oxford: Oxbow Books.

Pryor, F., 1996 Sheep, stocklands and farm systems: Bronze Age livestock populations in the Fenlands of eastern England. Antiquity 70:313–324.

Ratcliffe, J., and V. Straker, 1996 The Early Environment of Scilly. Truro: Cornwall Archaeological Unit.

Ray, K., and J. Thomas, 2003 In the kinship of cows: the social centrality of cattle in the earlier Neolithic of southern Britain. *In* Food, Culture and Identity in the Neolithic and Early Bronze Age. M. Parker Pearson, ed. pp. 37–44. Oxford: British Archaeological Reports.

Reynolds, P. J. 1974 Experimental Iron Age storage pits: an interim report. Proceedings of the Prehistoric Society 40:118–131.

—— 1977 Experimental archaeology and the Butser Ancient Farm Project. *In* The Iron Age in Britain: a review. J. Collis, ed. pp. 32–40. Sheffield: J. R. Collis.

Richards, M. P., T. Fuller and T. I. Molleson, 2006 Stable isotope palaeodietary study of humans and fauna from the multi-period site of Newark Bay, Orkney. Journal of Archaeological Science 33(1):122–131.

Ryder, M. L., and S. K. Stephenson, 1968 Wool Growth. London: Academic Press.

Scarre, C. J., and F. Healy, eds., 1993 Trade and Exchange in Prehistoric Europe. Oxford: Oxbow Books.

Serjeantson, D., 1996 The animal bones. *In* Refuse and Disposal at Area 16 East Runnymede. Runnymede Bridge Research Excavations, vol. 2. S. R. Needham, and A. Spence, eds. pp. 194–223. London: British Museum Press

—— 2006 Animal remains. *In* Marshland Communities and Cultural Landscape: the Haddenham Project. C. Evans and I. Hodder. pp. 213–233. Cambridge: McDonald Institute.

—— 2007 Intensification of animal husbandry in the Late Bronze Age? The contribution of sheep and pigs. In The Earlier Iron Age in Britain and the Near Continent. C. Haselgrove and R. Pope, eds. pp. 80–93. Oxford: Oxbow Books.

——S. Wales and J. Evans, 1994 Fish in later prehistoric Britain: archaeo-icthyological studies. Offa 51:332–339.

Sharples, N. M., 1991 Maiden Castle: excavations and field survey 1985–6. London: English Heritage.

Sherratt, A., 1981 Plough and pastoralism: aspects of the secondary products revolution. *In* Patterns of the Past. I. Hodder, G. Isaac and N. Hammond, eds. pp. 261–306. Cambridge: Cambridge University Press.

Smith, H., and J. Mulville, 2004 Resource management in the Outer Hebrides: an assessment of the faunal and floral evidence from archaeological investigations. *In* Atlantic Connections and Adaptations: economies, environments and subsistence in lands bordering the North Atlantic. R. A. Housely and G. Coles, eds. pp. 48–64. Oxford: Oxbow Books.

Stead, I. M., 1991 Iron Age Cemeteries in East Yorkshire. London: English Heritage.

Stevens, C. J., 2003 An investigation of agricultural consumption and production models for prehistoric and Roman Britain. Environmental Archaeology 8(1):61–81.

Teichert, M., 1970 Abstammung und Morphogenese vor- und frühgeschichtlicher Hausschweine. Archiv für Tierzucht 13:507–523.

van der Veen, M., 1992 Crop Husbandry Regimes: an archaeobotanical study of farming in northern England 1000 BC–AD 500. Sheffield: Sheffield Academic Press.

——and G. Jones, 2006 The production and consumption of cereals a: implications for understanding the British Iron Age. Vegetation History and Archaeobotany 15(3): 217–228.

van Mensch, P. J. A., and G. F. Ijzereef, 1977 Smoke-dried meat in prehistoric and Roman Netherlands. *In* Ex Horreo. B. L. van Beek, R. W. Brandt and W. Groenman-van Waateringe, eds. pp. 144–150. Amsterdam: University of Amsterdam.

Vigne, J. D., 1991 The meat and offal weight (MOW) method and the relative proportion of ovicaprines in some ancient meat diets of the north-western Mediterranean. Rivista di Studi Liguri 57:21–47.

von den Driesch, A., J. Peters and M. Stork, 1992 7000 Jahre Nutztierhaltung in Bayern. Bauern in Bayern: Katalog des Gäubodenmuseums Straubing 19:157–190.

Wait, G., 1985 Ritual and Religion in Iron Age Britain. Oxford: British Archaeological Reports.

Willis, S. 2007 Sea, coast, estuary, land and culture in Iron Age Britain. *In* The Later Iron Age in Britain and Beyond. C. Haselgrove and T. Moore, eds. pp. 105–129. Oxford: Oxbow Books.

Woodward, A., 1997 Size and style: an alternative study of some Iron Age pottery in southern England. *In* Reconstructing Iron Age Societies: new approaches to the British Iron Age. A. Gwilt and C. Hazelgrove, eds. pp. 26–35. Oxford: Oxbow Books.

——and P. W. Blinkhorn, 1997 Size is important: Iron Age vessel capacities in central and southern England. *In* Not So Much a Pot, More a Way of Life. C. G. Cumberpatch and P. W. Blinkhorn, eds. pp. 153–162. Oxford: Oxbow Books.

——and J. D. Hill, eds., 2002 Prehistoric Britain: the ceramic basis. Oxford: Oxbow Books.

Yalden, D., 1999 The History of British Mammals. London: Poyser.

11

The Architecture of Routine Life

Joanna Brück

Houses are an arena in which cultural values, narratives of identity and the practicalities of daily life intersect. Perhaps because of the pivotal role of the home in the Western life course and in the construction of gender relations in our own society, it has often been easy to project an evocative – yet ultimately anachronistic – image of the house into prehistory. But what do we know about domestic architecture in the past? How easy is it to identify the remains of houses in the archaeological record? To what extent is it possible to investigate how people used and valued these buildings? Indeed, how helpful is the term "house" in examining societies so very different from our own? This chapter will review the evidence for domestic architecture in British prehistory, focusing on a selection of cross-cutting themes that have seen considerable debate in the literature in recent years. It will present a broadly chronological overview, beginning with the light shelters and the small number of more substantial structures known from the Mesolithic, and finishing with the large roundhouses and other complex domestic buildings of the Iron Age.

Mobility and Sedentism in the Mesolithic

In British prehistory, the construction of substantial, permanent domestic dwellings is considered to indicate a shift from a mobile to a sedentary way of life. For many years, archaeologists assumed that this transition coincided with the introduction of agriculture (Thomas 1999:7–11). The hunter-gatherers of the Mesolithic are thought to have practised an essentially mobile lifestyle, dependent on the seasonal availability of wild resources (e.g., Bonsall 1990; Young 1999). Certainly, few Mesolithic structures are known, and many of these are insubstantial and probably short-lived (Smith 1997; Wickham-Jones 2004). For example, at Morton in Fife, a series of light shelters associated with external hearths have been identified at what would have been a coastal site visited on a seasonal basis in the Late Mesolithic (Coles 1971; 1983). Yet, there appear to have been long-term attachments to particular locations during this period. Extensive scatters of chipped stone tools including Early and Late Mesolithic components at sites such as Nab Head in south-west Wales (David 1990) and the deep stratigraphy of midden sites such as Caisteal nan Gillean on the island of Oronsay (Mellars 1987) suggest that repeated visits to these places created histories of belonging that stretched across the generations (Pollard 1999:82). However, few of these longer-lived sites have produced structural evidence, probably because occupation was seasonal rather than continuous, and it seems that the relatively mobile habitation practices of the Mesolithic did not usually require the construction of durable domestic architecture.

This has made it all the more difficult to interpret the small number of more substantial buildings known from the period. The circular timber structure at Howick in Northumberland appears to have been particularly long-lived (Waddington et al. 2003). It produced a large assemblage of lithics (ca. 16,000 items) and was completely rebuilt at least twice. A sequence of hearths in the centre of the building indicates successive phases of occupation over a lengthy period of time. A similar structure has been found some 60 km to the north at East Barns, Dunbar, East Lothian (Gooder 2003; see fig. 11.1). It was defined by 30 post-holes,

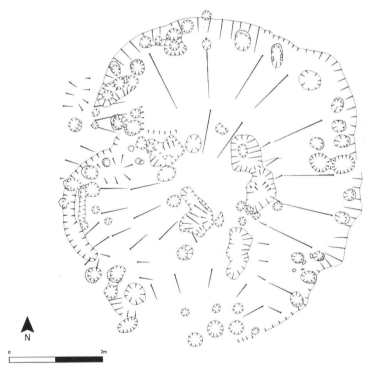

Figure 11.1   Plan of the structure at East Barns, Dunbar, East Lothian (after Gooder and Hatherley 2003:fig. 30).

most of which slope gently towards the centre of the building, suggesting that it may have had a superstructure of bent and tied wooden poles. Groups of pits and scatters of lithics were identified both inside and outside the structure. Buildings such as these challenge the usual distinction drawn between mobile hunter-gatherer and settled agricultural societies, and hint at the complexity and variability of Mesolithic occupation practices.

One interesting recent suggestion regarding Howick and similar structures is that they may have been ceremonial buildings rather than houses. Spikins (2002:50, 69) describes the sacred huts built by the Selk'nam hunter-gatherers of Tierra del Fuego in recent historic times. These were constructed for shamanic rites which were carried out when Selk'nam bands gathered at special locations for important festivals. Unlike other Selk'nam structures, these buildings were relatively permanent and substantial because of the central social and cultural roles which they played. Spikins suggests that British Mesolithic structures such as Howick may have been constructed for similar purposes. However, the problem remains that it is notoriously difficult to distinguish ritual from domestic practice archaeologically. For example, it is far from clear whether the evidence for the preparation and consumption of food from Howick and East Barns can be interpreted as the remains of ritual feasts or everyday meals.

Ritual and Secular Practice in the Neolithic

This is a particular problem when it comes to examining the evidence for houses in the Neolithic. Despite the introduction of agriculture and animal husbandry around 4000 B.C., settlement patterns appear to have remained predominantly mobile throughout the Neolithic (e.g., Barrett 1994; Whittle 1997; Thomas 1999). For most of Britain, the communities of settled farmers envisaged by many archaeologists have not materialised (Thomas 1999:7–11). The vision of a "homely rustic idyll" (Gibson 2003:136) so often projected into the Neolithic has been cogently criticised (Thomas 1996; Gibson 2003). In fact, cultivation of cereals may have been relatively small-scale at least until the Early Bronze Age (Moffett et al. 1989; Richards 1996), and wild plants and animals continued to play an important role in the diet throughout the period. Relatively little is known about Neolithic domestic architecture (for recent reviews, see Barclay 1996; 2003; Darvill 1996). Possible houses are rare in most regions, with a few notable exceptions: a small number of "villages" have been identified on the Orkney Islands (Richards 2005) and in recent excavations at Durrington Walls in Wiltshire (Parker Pearson et al. 2005; 2006).

During the earlier Neolithic, a small number of "longhouses" have been identified. The unusually large building at Balbridie, Aberdeenshire, provides an interesting example (Fairweather and Ralston 1993). This structure had apsidal ends and was defined by a wall slot containing substantial post-holes. It stood some 24 m × 12 m in size and its interior was subdivided into three different "rooms" by screens or walls set in slots. An exceptionally large assemblage of cereals was recovered from the building, which appears to have burned down at the end of its life. Other

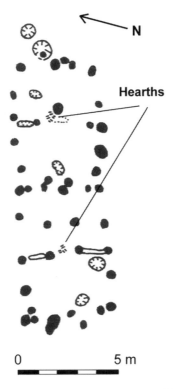

Figure 11.2   Plan of longhouse A, Lismore Fields, Derbyshire (after Garton 1987:252).

smaller longhouses have been found elsewhere, for example at Lismore Fields, Derbyshire (Garton 1987; see fig. 11.2), and White Horse Stone in Kent (Oxford Archaeological Unit 2000). By the later Neolithic, longhouses were replaced by a greater variety of structures, mostly smaller in area, and including sub-rectangular, trapezoidal, oval and circular buildings (Darvill 1996). Examples include the sub-circular stake-built structure at Gwithian in Cornwall (Megaw 1976) and the rect-angular post-built structure at Downton, Wiltshire (Rahtz 1962). Finds recovered from Neolithic houses include ceramics, flint and stone tools, animal bone and the remains of wild and domesticated plants. Possible votive deposits have also been identified. For example, a flake from a polished stone axe was recovered from one of the internal slots of house A at Lismore Fields, while a pit immediately to the west of the building produced a substantial part of a pottery bowl (Garton 1987).

The problem posed by many of these "houses" is that it is difficult to assign them an unambiguously "domestic" function. The size and rarity of the early long-houses along with associated depositional practices has meant that their interpreta-tion as domestic dwellings continues to be a matter of considerable debate. Barclay (2003:75) lists several of the suggestions that have been made regarding the possible function of the building at Balbridie. For example, it may have acted as a home for an extended family, a ceremonial structure, a house with a special function or a barn. Cross (2003), writing about Irish Neolithic longhouses, draws an analogy with early medieval halls, and suggests that these buildings' primary function was as a focus for competitive feasting, meetings and ceremonies. She argues that the substantial assemblages of cereals recovered from some of these sites indicates the consumption of alcohol on a large scale. Even the role of the smaller, less ostentatious structures of the Late Neolithic is far from clear-cut. Thomas (1996) has suggested that many of these buildings were not domestic dwellings at all, but special purpose cult houses which acted as meeting places at significant points in the annual cycle (see also Topping 1996).

The question is further complicated by the relationship between "houses" and Neolithic monuments. In Orkney and Shetland, where stone-built domestic dwellings are known in some numbers, similar materials and construction techniques were employed in both houses and tombs (Barclay 1996; Richards 2005). The cruciform layout and south-westerly orientation of Orcadian tombs and houses suggests that the same traditions of practical skill and cosmological knowledge were employed in the construction of both categories of architecture (Richards 1993). The construction of later funerary monuments on top of earlier buildings is also well documented. The site at Trelystan, Powys, is perhaps the best-known example (Gibson 1996; Pollard 1999). Here, two small rectangular structures of Late Neolithic date were overlain by two Early Bronze Age round barrows. Other examples include Chippenham in Cambridgeshire (Leaf 1936; 1940). However, the interpretation of such pre-tomb structures poses a particular challenge (Gibson 1980; 1996; Lane 1986; Thomas 1996), with some writers arguing that they were mortuary houses while others see them as domestic dwellings inhabited by significant ancestors. The discovery of at least seven houses at Durrington Walls, Wiltshire (Parker Pearson et al. 2005; 2006), raises similar questions. Durrington Walls, like other henge monuments, has long been interpreted as a focus of ceremonial activity, and while the houses predate the enclosure itself, their presence at this site creates something of an interpretative challenge: were these simply the houses of those who built the neighbouring (and contemporary) monument at Stonehenge or were they shrines, erected at a location of long-standing ritual significance?

Our ability to distinguish archaeologically between a domestic dwelling and a ceremonial building has therefore been a matter of some contention (Gibson 1982; Bradley 2005). The problem arises primarily from the distinction drawn in the modern Western world between ritual and domestic practice (Brück 1999a). In our society, the domestic domain is separated in both spatial and conceptual terms from locations where important religious rituals and public ceremonies are carried out. This is in part because of the marginalisation of domestic activities in contemporary Western society (the historical context and political significance of this will be explored further below). However, in other parts of the world, ritual and domestic practice are not usually distinguished in such categorical terms, and houses often form an important focus for ritual activities (Waterson 1990). These vary in scale from the small offerings made on a daily basis at the household altar by women in Bali to the large gatherings that take place for important ceremonies at Torajan origin-houses in Sulawesi (Waterson 1990). There is no reason why Neolithic "houses" should not have combined both a domestic/residential purpose and a ceremonial or ritual role. Indeed, this argument has been made by a number of writers in recent years. Topping (1996:163), for example, has described Neolithic houses as "domestic ritual monument[s]". Certainly, evidence for feasting activities or the votive deposition of special objects such as polished stone axes should not be taken to indicate an exclusively ritual role. In many societies, important points in the life cycle of a house such as construction and abandonment are marked out by special ceremonies which may involve feasting – particularly if the owners of the house have called on neighbours and kinsfolk to help them to build it – and the giving of offerings to particular gods, spirits or ancestors, often in the form of foundation or abandonment deposits (Brück 1999b).

The close spatial relationship between some Neolithic houses and monuments need not preclude such an argument. Houses, like tombs, are places where social relationships – and in particular the links between kinsfolk – are constructed, upheld and reconstituted (Cooney 2003). The very fact that later tombs were sometimes built on top of earlier houses suggests that they played similar roles (cf. Thomas 1996). In many societies, houses play a significant part in the construction of kinship relations and community identity (Carsten and Hugh-Jones 1995). This is particularly the case where family membership forms the basis of political allegiance or where productive activities are organised at the level of the household group, as is usual in many "pre-industrial" societies. The social, political and economic significance of houses means that they are often given elaborated if not monumentalised material forms (e.g., Waterson 1990). As a number of writers have suggested, the construction of substantial and elaborate houses in the earlier Neolithic may relate to the role of these structures in creating the new forms of family, gender and community organisation that underpinned Neolithic society, especially amongst otherwise dispersed, small-scale and relatively mobile groups (Whittle 1996a; 1996b; Last 1996). As such, houses perhaps fulfilled the roles played by long barrows, chambered tombs and causewayed enclosures in other contexts. The important question here should not be whether these buildings were domestic dwellings or shrines – they were probably both – but why the domain of the dead was monumentalised in certain communities while elsewhere it was the world of the living. This may relate to variability in kinship, inheritance and household organisation or to different ways of viewing and valuing the past.

Of course, not all Neolithic houses have provoked such interpretative conundrums. Since it was first exposed in 1850, the Neolithic "village" of Skara Brae on Orkney (Childe 1931) has captured the archaeological and public imagination. Stone furniture and fittings such as dressers, beds and hearths create an illusion of familiar domesticity. Although this has been challenged by Richards (1993; 2005), whose work on the cosmological significance of Orcadian house layout suggests that religious beliefs had a major impact on aspects of daily life, his interpretation of the organisation of domestic space reproduces in the past aspects of gender relations characteristic of British nineteenth- and twentieth-century society (Parker Pearson and Richards 1994a:41–47). He argues that the architecture of Orcadian houses creates a dualistic ordering of space. The entrance is slightly offset to the right, creating a brighter and more public area on the right-hand side of the house; he contrasts this with the darker, secluded space to the left of the doorway. Moreover, the box-bed and associated shelf on the right-hand wall is larger than that on the left, suggesting a possible difference in status. Drawing a comparison between the architecture of houses and tombs, Richards argues that the orientation of doorways to the south-east creates conceptual links between the right-hand (eastern) side of the house and ideas of life, light and fertility, while the left-hand (western) side may have been associated with concepts of death and darkness. Excavations at the nearby settlement of Barnhouse have suggested that the central hearths in Neolithic Orcadian houses were tended and cleared out from the left, with spreads of ash and charcoal and higher phosphate levels documented on this side. Richards therefore suggests that Orcadian women would have been symbolically associated with inner, private space – the part of the house associated with nature, death and lower-status activities. Although this argument is appealing for the way in which it explores the role of prehistoric architecture in the construction of social relationships, the influence of contemporary and recent historical values, expectations and social practices on Richards's interpretation has perhaps not been adequately considered.

Domesticity in Bronze Age Britain

Our tendency to assume that prehistoric houses were used and valued in similar ways to our own has had an even greater impact on our understanding of Bronze Age settlements. From the mid second millennium B.C., the number of archaeologically identifiable settlement sites increases dramatically (Barrett et al. 1991; Barrett 1994). At the same time, the dead were consigned to less substantial and less elaborate monuments. Middle Bronze Age barrows are considerably smaller than their Early Bronze Age counterparts, and by the Late Bronze Age, the normal mode of disposal of the dead is archaeologically invisible (Brück 1995). The houses of the Bronze Age pose few of the interpretative quandaries of earlier examples and present an appealing and seductive sense of familiarity (fig. 11.3). Roundhouses were now the dominant form of domestic dwelling although occasional rectangular buildings are also known. Finds recovered from Bronze Age roundhouses include ceramics employed in the preparation, consumption and storage of foodstuffs; quernstones for the grinding of grain; animal bone; objects such as loom weights, whetstones, bone awls and bronze knives suggesting small-scale productive and maintenance activities; and items relating to the care and presentation of the self, for example finger rings and bronze razors (Ellison 1981).

Bronze Age settlements usually comprise two or more roundhouses, sometimes set within an enclosure or yard bounded by banks, ditches or lengths of fence (Ellison 1981; Barrett et al. 1991). They are often accompanied by other features, for example, storage pits and ponds for the collection of rainwater. Analysis of the distribution of finds on Bronze Age settlements indicates that most of these were single household units (Ellison 1981). Each settlement comprised a major residen-

Figure 11.3 Reconstruction of the Late Bronze Age settlement at Lofts Farm, Essex. Illustration by Roger Massey-Ryan. © Essex County Council.

tial structure, in which the majority of the household's activities were carried out, plus one or more ancillary structures for special purposes such as the preparation of food, the housing of animals or particular craft activities. Careful recording of the distribution of finds on sites like Black Patch, East Sussex, has allowed the reconstruction of activity areas within individual buildings (Drewett 1982; see fig. 11.4). At this settlement, the organisation of domestic space in hut 3, the major residential structure, provides a good example. The hearth was located just inside the doorway. A scatter of flint and bronze tools in this area suggests that its occupants carried out a variety of craft activities sitting around the fire. Storage pits from which burnt barley was recovered were located towards the rear of the dwelling on the left-hand side, while a row of loom weights found along the wall on the right-hand side of the building suggests that an upright weaving loom may originally have stood in this location.

It is easy to conjure up a vision of cosy domesticity on the basis of such evidence, creating an image of the past in which the activities, values and social relationships that constituted the domestic domain in Bronze Age Britain were little different from those of the modern Western world. Drewett (1982) explicitly employed an ethnographic analogy from a very different cultural context (the Jie of Uganda) to

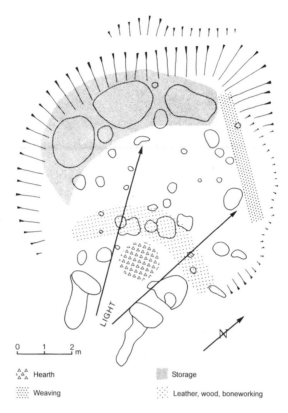

Figure 11.4 Activity areas in hut 3, Blackpatch, East Sussex (after Drewett 1982:fig. 13).

understand the use of space at this site, but until the 1990s, few other authors writing about Bronze Age settlement attempted to challenge embedded preconceptions regarding domestic organisation. The problem perhaps lies in the series of interpretative leaps which archaeologists make in studies of prehistoric houses. In particular, there is a tendency to conflate the material, behavioural, social and ideological components of ancient "houses" (Yanagisako 1979; Wilk and Netting 1984; Tringham 1995). A building identified as a "house" is assumed to have been the dwelling of a household group. In turn, the household group is usually envisaged as a nuclear family engaged in "domestic" tasks such as the preparation and consumption of food, child care and other daily maintenance activities. It is all too easy to assume that such family groups would have recognised and shared the concept of "home" familiar from our own cultural context.

Of course, a reading of the anthropological literature on houses in other societies challenges this picture of the nature and organisation of domestic practice (e.g., Bender 1967; Laslett and Wall 1972; Yanagisako 1979; Wilk and Netting 1984; Waterson 1990). Houses may be the dwellings of one or more households or family groups; in nineteenth- and early twentieth-century Borneo, for example, Iban longhouses were shared by several related families (Waterson 1990). Those who live in a house may or may not be linked by blood or marriage, as in the case of shared student households in our own society. Family organisation varies cross-culturally, and although it is extremely difficult to reconstruct forms of kinship and residence archaeologically, it is equally problematic to assume the prevalence of the patrifocal nuclear family in prehistory. The types of activities carried out by household groups differs from society to society. In the modern Western world, our houses are distinguished in both spatial and conceptual terms from the worlds of work, politics and religion, each of which is afforded its own circumscribed locale. The home is associated primarily with "natural" activities such as consumption and reproduction – a private, passive and traditionally female space contrasted with the active, cultural and public world of men (e.g., Tiffany 1978; La Fontaine 1981; Strathern 1984; Moore 1988:21–24). However, this is a product of our particular historical context. Industrialisation, the rise of the nation state, and the gender ideologies of the nineteenth and twentieth centuries have each played their role in generating the values ascribed to houses in the contemporary West. In other societies, however, production, politics and ritual are central elements of household activities (Wilk and Netting 1984; Waterson 1990). In non-industrialised societies, the organisation of agricultural and craft production is often managed by the household group, with the division of labour structured along lines of age and gender. Where rights over resources are defined in terms of household membership, the house may become a locus of political action. The English Middle Ages provide a good example: here, political affiliation was described in terms of one's membership of groups such as the House of York or the House of Lancaster. In contexts where the house plays this kind of central political and economic role, it is hardly surprising that it should become a focus for ritual activities, feasting and the like.

A critical consideration of the evidence produced by Bronze Age settlements challenges many of the assumptions outlined above. Evidence for ritual activities is well documented in the form of votive deposits in pits, ditches, post-holes and other features (Brück 1999b). For example, at Reading Business Park in Berkshire, complete fineware jars and bowls were recovered from a number of pits (Moore and Jennings 1992), while part of the body of a cow was placed on the base of a pit in roundhouse 1 at South Lodge Camp, Dorset (Barrett et al. 1991:157). Such finds allow us to challenge aspects of functionalist interpretations of settlement space such as Drewett's analysis (1982) of hut 3 at Black Patch. An awl was recovered from the left-hand post-hole of the porch at the front of this house. Drewett argues that the presence of this artefact indicates the kinds of small-scale craftwork carried out inside the building and he defines an activity area based around the hearth located just inside the doorway. However, the incorporation of this object into the entrance structure is unlikely to have been accidental. Bronze artefacts, carved chalk objects, complete quernstones and pieces of human bone, amongst other things, are often recovered from significant locations in space on Bronze Age settlements, notably boundaries and entrances (Brück 1995; 1999b). The awl from hut 3 might therefore have been deliberately placed, for example, as a foundation deposit. If so, the choice of an awl might have had more to do with the symbolic significance of this artefact – drawing an analogy between the creation of objects and the creation of the social relationships on which the household was based – than with the activities that were carried out in the building.

Political and economic practices were also often focused on the household. In certain areas of Britain, for example the Marlborough Downs (Gingell 1992), Bronze Age settlements were located within individual blocks of fields, suggesting that the household group was the primary unit of agricultural production. Elsewhere, for example on Dartmoor, inter-household cooperation appears to have been crucial to the construction and use of extensive field systems (Fleming 1988). Bronze Age houses also produce plentiful evidence for craft activities such as weaving, metalworking and pottery production. In some cases, the scale of production indicates exchange beyond the limits of the household group. For example, the marked increase in evidence for cloth production from the Middle Bronze Age onwards hints that cloth wealth may have been employed in funerary prestations, marriage transactions and other forms of intergroup exchange (Brück 2005). If the distribution, exchange and inheritance of at least certain resources was articulated through the household group, it is hardly surprising to find evidence for socio-political activities at settlement sites. For example, the burnt mound at South Lodge Camp, Dorset (Barrett et al. 1991:161), indicates the preparation and consumption of foodstuffs on a large scale, possibly indicative of feasting. The deposition of substantial numbers of fineware vessels in the upper ditch silts of Springfield Lyons and Lofts Farm in Essex suggests that feasting was one of the activities that took place during the final stages in the life of these sites (Brown 1995). The deliberate breakage and deposition of the associated ceramics can perhaps be interpreted as part of special rites of abandonment carried out to formally end the life of these settlements.

The activities carried out by Bronze Age households included tasks that, in the modern Western world, are not usually associated with the domestic domain. We might expect that the sets of cultural values ascribed to the home – if this concept existed – would likewise have been very different. This has particular significance when it comes to considering the role of women during the period (Brück 2005). In our own society, the cultural construction of the "home" as private space cut off from the active, public and highly valued world of politics, economics and religion contributes to a particular vision of what it means to be a woman (Tiffany 1978; La Fontaine 1981; Strathern 1984; Moore 1988:21–24). Clearly, it is problematic to project this into the past. As members of Bronze Age households, women are likely to have played a significant role in productive tasks, ritual activities and political processes; gender roles and relationships are therefore likely to have been quite differently constituted from those of our recent historic past.

Symbolic Spaces in the Late Bronze Age and Iron Age

Drewett's (1982) interpretation of hut 3 at Black Patch focused on the practical aspects of the use of domestic space. In recent years, however, a number of writers have explored the symbolic dimensions of spatial layout. This has been a particular interest in studies of Late Bronze Age and Iron Age roundhouses (e.g., Fitzpatrick

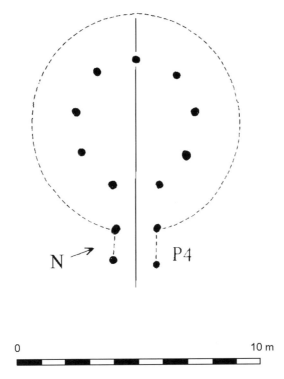

Figure 11.5 Plan of Iron Age roundhouse P4 at Moel-y-Gaer, Clwyd, with axis of symmetry (solid line) and inferred external wall line (dashed line) marked (after Guilbert 1982:fig. 3.2).

1994; Hill 1994; Parker Pearson 1996; Giles and Parker Pearson 1999). The entrances to these buildings often include substantial and elaborated porch structures, emphasising the point of transition from inside to outside; this was a way of highlighting the distinction between those who belonged to the household and those who did not. Inside these buildings, the architecture works to create ordered spaces which may have been ascribed specific meanings and values (fig. 11.5). The ring of posts which took the weight of the roof distinguished the central area from the periphery, while the symmetrical layout of many roundhouses around an imaginary axis running from the entrance to the rear divided the left-hand side from the right (Musson 1970; Guilbert 1981; 1982). In many societies, the division of space is not simply a way of creating specific areas for different activities: it is also a means of maintaining social boundaries between those associated with such tasks (Parker Pearson and Richards 1994b). The cultural values associated with spatial categories such as back and front, left and right or centre and periphery may therefore have facilitated the reproduction of social distinctions between men and women, the young and the old or guests and family.

Parker Pearson's study of Mucking North Ring, Essex (Parker Pearson and Richards 1994a), provides an interesting example of the symbolic division of settlement space. This Late Bronze Age site was surrounded by a ditch and substantial wooden palisade (fig. 11.6). The entrance faced east and was marked by a gateway.

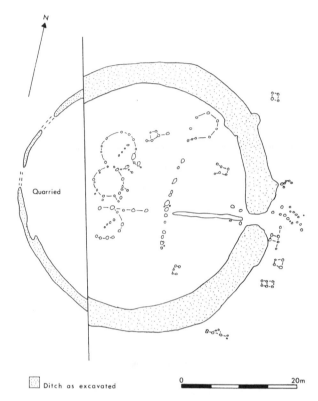

Figure 11.6 Plan of the Late Bronze Age enclosure at Mucking North Ring, Essex (after Bond 1988:fig. 3, simplified).

A fence or screen divided the back from the front of the site, blocking both visual and physical access. Roundhouses, middens and activity areas were concentrated behind the screen, while the area in front of it produced few finds or features. Parker Pearson suggests that the front and back of this settlement were ascribed distinct sets of meanings which facilitated the reproduction of gender relationships. The area behind the screen was private space, associated with domestic activities and their waste products. The area in front of the screen, on the other hand, was clean and accessible, and may have been used for the reception of guests. A series of homologous dualisms may therefore have structured Late Bronze Age people's evaluation of these spaces as follows:

front : back
east : west
clean : dirty
public : private
sacred : profane
culture : nature
high status : low status

Parker Pearson argues that men may have been associated in conceptual terms with front space and women with back space. He notes that in Iron Age burials in Wessex, men are accompanied by joints of beef and women by joints of pork. Votive deposits which include the remains of cattle tend to be found in the eastern halves of Late Bronze Age and Iron Age settlements, while those which contain pig bones are restricted to the western halves.

However, this interesting proposal remains problematic for the reasons already outlined elsewhere in this chapter. The model of gender relationships envisaged is remarkably similar to that familiar from our own recent historic past (see also Pope 2007). While it is clear that front and back space at Mucking North Ring were differentiated in both architectural and behavioural terms, the meanings and values ascribed to these categories are more difficult to access. In particular, the assumption that the "dirty", "domestic" areas behind the screen were evaluated in negative terms needs critical appraisal. There is evidence from Late Bronze Age Britain to suggest that rubbish was not viewed as it is today (Brück 1995). In many areas, domestic refuse was spread on the fields as a fertiliser (Gingell 1992). The enormous Late Bronze Age midden sites at Potterne (Lawson 2000) and East Chisenbury (McOmish 1996) in Wiltshire suggest that the accumulation of refuse may have been one way of indicating social status by providing visible evidence of large-scale craft production and the consumption of considerable quantities of food, ceramics and other goods. Certainly, the presence of buildings at these sites indicates that people were quite happy to live surrounded by rubbish. Elsewhere, the deliberate deposition of broken objects provided a means of symbolising the cyclical links between death and rebirth so that dead things may have been considered a source of new life (Brück 2001). All of this suggests that the "dirty" areas of a settlement may not have been considered profane and low-status. The implications of this for Parker Pearson's interpretation of gender relations are important.

The division of space on Iron Age settlements was not simply a means of maintaining social categories and relationships, however. It has also been argued that the roundhouse acted as a miniature model of the Iron Age cosmos (Fitzpatrick 1994; Parker Pearson 1996; Giles and Parker Pearson 1999). The concurrence between the spatial and cosmological order allowed belief systems to be given material form. This is particularly evident in the predominant orientation of dwellings. The doorways of roundhouses of this date tend to face east or south-east (Oswald 1997). This was not simply a way of ensuring maximum light penetration into the interior of the roundhouse or of avoiding prevailing south-westerly winds. Orientation towards the rising sun may also have been considered auspicious, linking the household's day-to-day tasks with concepts of light, life and fertility. It allowed the mapping onto roundhouse space of a cyclical concept of time (Fitzpatrick 1994). The diurnal and seasonal cycle of the sun as it moved clockwise around the walls of the roundhouse imparted particular symbolic meanings to household space. The southern half of the house (left of the doorway) was associated with daytime and the activities of the living, while the northern half (right of the doorway) was associated with night-time and the world of the dead. This interpretation is supported by the distribution of finds at a number of sites.

Such interpretations of roundhouse space have been particularly valuable in challenging the vision of familiar domesticity evoked in many older accounts of Iron Age settlement (for critique, see Hill 1992; Parker Pearson 1996). However, adequate attention is not always paid to the depositional processes involved in the creation of the archaeological record. For example, the finds from a roundhouse may represent objects that were used in this structure during its life, or refuse deposited in an abandoned building some time after it has fallen out of use. In either case, interesting but potentially quite different conclusions might be drawn regarding the symbolic and cultural values ascribed to domestic space. Moreover, all-embracing models of the symbolic significance of settlement space may be inappropriate (Giles and Parker Pearson 1999), and there is mounting evidence for considerable regional variability in the location of different activities in roundhouse space (Brück 1999b; cf. Webley 2003).

Nonetheless, the appearance of standardised types of roundhouse in certain parts of Britain suggests that the conventions which informed and underpinned social practice in later prehistoric houses may have become more carefully controlled and formalised. This suggests that Iron Age houses played an increasingly important role in the expression and maintenance of social power. The brochs of Atlantic Scotland provide a good example. These complex circular buildings were drystone-built and would originally have stood several stories high (Ritchie 1988; Armit 2003). The internal architecture of these structures created a series of hierarchically organised spaces, with control of access apparently a significant issue (Foster 1989). The categorisation and subdivision of space within the buildings perhaps reflects a more general concern with processes of social classification; by excluding people from certain spaces and admitting them to others, social differences were given material form through architecture. The animal remains recovered from brochs indicate that their inhabitants enjoyed a more varied diet (including exotic species) than those who lived in neighbouring non-broch settlements (Parker Pearson et al. 1996), and they can perhaps therefore be seen as high-status dwellings (but see Armit 1997). However, elsewhere in Britain it has proven difficult if not impossible to identify the houses of particularly important members of Iron Age communities. Even the interiors of hill forts – sites which on other grounds many writers have seen as the apex of a settlement hierarchy (e.g., Cunliffe 1991) – have not yielded the high-status dwellings that might be expected. Indeed, it is clear that evolutionist models of the development of social complexity do not adequately address the variability of the evidence. At Cadbury Castle in Somerset, for example (Barrett et al. 2000), the roundhouses faced a number of different directions and no overall plan for the layout of community space could be discerned. In this case, at least, there was considerable flexibility in certain aspects of spatial organisation and prescriptive models cannot be applied.

Conclusions

This chapter has attempted to argue that "houses" in the past may have been organisationally and conceptually quite different from houses in the modern Western world. In recent years, critiques of functionalist studies of domestic architecture in British prehistory have resulted in the interpretation of certain houses as shrines and others as models of the cosmos in miniature. I have suggested above that ritual and domestic practice may not have been mutually exclusive categories in the past. I have also argued that the marginalisation of domestic activities in our own society has resulted in a rather impoverished view of the role of houses in prehistoric society. This question has been addressed in recent years by the burgeoning literature on the social and symbolic significance of household space. There is a risk, however, that the baby may be thrown out with the bathwater. The post-Enlightenment distinction between ritual and secular practice tends to result in a focus on one or other element of this dichotomy. The way in which ritual practice and cosmological beliefs informed and sustained everyday "practical" activities such as grinding grain, throwing pots or weaving cloth has yet to be adequately explored (but see Giles and Parker Pearson 1996). Only when we have more fully deconstructed the concepts with which we work in our interpretations of prehistoric domestic architecture will this be possible.

ACKNOWLEDGEMENTS

Many thanks to Graeme Warren and Mel Giles for introducing me to some of the debates on Mesolithic and Iron Age "houses" respectively, and to Nigel Brown for permission to use the reconstruction drawing of Lofts Farm. Gabriel Cooney and Jessica Smyth kindly lent me relevant volumes on the Neolithic. Omissions and inaccuracies are, of course, my own.

REFERENCES

Armit, I., 1997 Architecture and the household: a response to Sharples and Parker Pearson. *In* Reconstructing Iron Age Societies: new approaches to the British Iron Age. A. Gwilt and C. Haselgrove, eds. pp. 266–269. Oxford: Oxbow Books.

——2003 Towers in the North: the brochs of Scotland. Stroud: Tempus.

Barclay, G., 1996 Neolithic buildings in Scotland. *In* Neolithic Houses in Northwest Europe and Beyond. T. Darvill and J. Thomas, eds. pp. 61–76. Oxford: Oxbow Books.

——2003 Neolithic settlement in the Lowlands of Scotland: a preliminary survey. *In* Neolithic Settlement in Ireland and Western Britain. I. Armit, E. Murphy, E. Nelis and D. Simpson, eds. pp. 71–83. Oxford: Oxbow Books.

Barrett, J., 1994 Fragments from Antiquity: an archaeology of social life in Britain, 2900–1200 BC. Oxford: Blackwell.

——R. Bradley and M. Green, 1991 Landscape, Monuments and Society: the prehistory of Cranborne Chase. Cambridge: Cambridge University Press.

——P. Freeman and A. Woodward, 2000 Cadbury Castle, Somerset: the later prehistoric and early historic archaeology. London: English Heritage.

Bender, D., 1967 A refinement of the concept of household: family, co-residence and domestic functions. American Anthropologist 69:493–504.

Bond, D., 1988 Excavation at the North Ring, Mucking, Essex: a late Bronze Age enclosure. Chelmsford: East Anglian Archaeology.

Bonsall, C., ed., 1990 The Mesolithic in Europe. Edinburgh: John Donald.

Bradley, R., 2005 Ritual and Domestic Life in Prehistoric Europe. London: Routledge.

Brown, N., 1995 Prehistoric pottery. *In* A Late Bronze Age Enclosure at Broomfield, Chelmsford. M. Atkinson. pp. 8–14. Essex Archaeology and History 26:1–24.

Brück, J., 1995 A place for the dead: the role of human remains in Late Bronze Age Britain. Proceedings of the Prehistoric Society 61:245–277.

——1999a What's in a settlement? Domestic practice and residential mobility in Early Bronze Age southern England. *In* Making Places in the Prehistoric World: themes in settlement archaeology. J. Brück and M. Goodman, eds. pp. 52–75. London: UCL Press.

——1999b Houses, lifecycles and deposition on Middle Bronze Age settlements in southern England. Proceedings of the Prehistoric Society 65:145–166.

——2001 Body metaphors and technologies of transformation in the English Middle and Late Bronze Age. *In* Bronze Age Landscapes: tradition and transformation. J. Brück, ed. pp. 65–82. Oxford: Oxbow Books.

——2005 Homing instincts: grounded identities and dividual selves in the British Bronze Age. *In* The Archaeology of Plural and Changing Identities: beyond identification. E. Casella and C. Fowler, eds. pp. 135–160. New York: Kluwer Academic/Plenum Press.

Carsten, J., and S. Hugh-Jones, 1995 About the House: Lévi-Strauss and beyond. Cambridge: Cambridge University Press.

Childe, V. G., 1931 Skara Brae: a Pictish village in Orkney. London: Kegan Paul, Trench, Trubner.

Coles, J., 1971 The early settlement of Scotland: excavations at Morton, Fife. Proceedings of the Prehistoric Society 37:28–66.

——1983 Morton revisited. *In* From the Stone Age to the "Forty Five": studies presented to R. B. K. Stevenson. A. O'Connor and D. Clarke, eds. pp. 9–18. Edinburgh: John Donald.

Cooney, G., 2003 Rooted or routed? Landscapes of Neolithic settlement in Ireland. *In* Neolithic Settlement in Ireland and Western Britain. I. Armit, E. Murphy, E. Nelis and D. Simpson, eds. pp. 47–55. Oxford: Oxbow Books.

Cross, S., 2003 Irish Neolithic settlement architecture: a reappraisal. *In* Neolithic Settlement in Ireland and Western Britain. I. Armit, E. Murphy, E. Nelis and D. Simpson, eds. pp. 195–202. Oxford: Oxbow Books.

Cunliffe, B., 1991 Iron Age Communities in Britain. London: Routledge.

Darvill, T., 1996 Neolithic buildings in England, Wales and the Isle of Man. *In* Neolithic Houses in Northwest Europe and Beyond. T. Darvill and J. Thomas, eds. pp. 77–112. Oxford: Oxbow Books.

David, A., 1990 Some aspects of the human presence in West Wales during the Mesolithic. *In* The Mesolithic in Europe. C. Bonsall, ed. pp. 241–253. Edinburgh: John Donald.

Drewett, P., 1982 Later Bronze Age downland economy and excavations at Black Patch, East Sussex. Proceedings of the Prehistoric Society 48:321–340.

Ellison, A., 1981 Towards a socioeconomic model for the Middle Bronze Age in southern England. *In* Pattern of the Past: studies in honour of David Clarke. I. Hodder, G. Isaac and N. Hammond, eds. pp. 413–438. Cambridge: Cambridge University Press.

Fairweather, A., and I. Ralston, 1993 The Neolithic timber hall at Balbridie, Grampian Region, Scotland: the building, the date, the plant macrofossils. Antiquity 67:313–323.

Fitzpatrick, A., 1994 Outside in: the structure of an Early Iron Age house at Dunstan Park, Thatcham, Berkshire. *In* The Iron Age in Wessex: recent work. A. Fitzpatrick and E. Morris, eds. pp. 68–72. Salisbury: Association Française d'Etude de l'Age du Fer/Wessex Archaeology.

Fleming, A., 1988 The Dartmoor Reaves: investigating prehistoric land divisions. London: Batsford.

Foster, S., 1989 Analysis of spatial patterns in buildings (access analysis) as an insight into social structure: examples from the Scottish Iron Age. Antiquity 63:40–50.

Garton, D., 1987 Buxton. Current Archaeology 103:250–253.

Gibson, A., 1980 A reinterpretation of Chippenham Barrow 5, with a discussion of the Beaker-associated pottery. Proceedings of the Cambridge Antiquarian Society 70:47–60.

——1982 Beaker Domestic Sites: a study of the domestic pottery of the late third and early second millennium BC in the British Isles. Oxford: British Archaeological Reports.

——1996 The Later Neolithic structures at Trelystan, Powys, Wales: ten years on. In Neolithic Houses in Northwest Europe and Beyond. T. Darvill and J. Thomas, eds. pp. 133–142. Oxford: Oxbow Books.

——2003 What do we mean by Neolithic settlement? Some approaches ten years on. In Neolithic Settlement in Ireland and Western Britain. I. Armit, E. Murphy, E. Nelis and D. Simpson, eds. pp. 136–145. Oxford: Oxbow Books.

Giles, M., and M. Parker Pearson, 1999 Learning to live in the Iron Age: dwelling and praxis. In Northern Exposure: interpretative devolution and the Iron Ages in Britain. B. Bevan, ed. pp. 217–232. Leicester: Leicester Archaeology Monograph.

Gingell, C., 1992 The Marlborough Downs: a later Bronze Age landscape. Devizes: Wiltshire Archaeological and Natural History Society.

Gooder, J., 2003 Excavating the oldest house in Scotland: East Barns, Dunbar, East Lothian. Scottish Archaeological News 42:1–2.

——and C. Hatherley, 2003 North-East Quarry, Dunbar. Discovery and Excavation in Scotland n.s. 4:56–57.

Guilbert, G., 1981 Double-ring round-houses, probable and possible in prehistoric Britain. Proceedings of the Prehistoric Society 47:299–317.

——1982 Post-ring symmetry in round-houses at Moel y Gaer and some other sites in prehistoric Britain. In Structural Reconstruction: approaches to the interpretation of the excavated remains of buildings. P. Drury, ed. pp. 67–86. Oxford: British Archaeological Reports.

Hill, J. D., 1992 Can we recognise a different European past? A contrastive archaeology of later prehistoric settlements in Southern England. Journal of European Archaeology 1: 57–75.

——1994 Why we should not take the data from Iron Age settlements for granted: recent studies of intra-settlement patterning. In The Iron Age in Wessex: recent work. A. Fitzpatrick and E. Morris, eds. pp. 4–8. Salisbury: Association Française d'Etude de l'Age du Fer/Wessex Archaeology.

La Fontaine, J., 1981 The domestication of the savage male. Man 16:333–349.

Lane, P., 1986 Past practices in the ritual present: examples from the Welsh Bronze Age. Archaeological Review from Cambridge 5(2):181–192.

Laslett, P., and R. Wall, eds., 1972 Household and Family in Past Time. Cambridge: Cambridge University Press.

Last, J., 1996 Neolithic houses: a Central European perspective. In Neolithic Houses in Northwest Europe and Beyond. T. Darvill and J. Thomas, eds. pp. 27–40. Oxford: Oxbow Books.

Lawson, A., 2000 Potterne 1982–5: Animal Husbandry in Later Prehistoric Wiltshire. Salisbury: Wessex Archaeology/English Heritage.

Leaf, C. S., 1936 Two Bronze Age barrows at Chippenham, Cambridgeshire. Proceedings of the Cambridge Antiquarian Society 36:134–155.

——1940 Further excavations in Bronze Age barrows at Chippenham, Cambridgeshire. Proceedings of the Cambridge Antiquarian Society 39:29–68.

McOmish, D., 1996 East Chisenbury: ritual and rubbish at the British Bronze Age–Iron Age transition. Antiquity 70:68–76.

Megaw, V., 1976 Gwithian, Cornwall: some notes on the evidence for Neolithic and Bronze Age settlement. *In* Settlement and Economy in the Third and Second Millennia BC. C. Burgess and R. Miket, eds. pp. 51–66. Oxford: British Archaeological Reports.

Mellars, P., 1987 Excavations on Oronsay: prehistoric human ecology on a small island. Edinburgh: Edinburgh University Press.

Moffett, L., M. Robinson and V. Straker, 1989 Cereals, fruit and nuts: charred plant remains from Neolithic sites in England and Wales and the Neolithic economy. *In* The Beginnings of Agriculture. A. Milles, D. Williams and N. Gardner, eds. pp. 243–261. Oxford: British Archaeological Reports.

Moore, H., 1988 Feminism and Anthropology. Cambridge: Polity Press.

Moore, J., and D. Jennings, 1992 Reading Business Park: a Bronze Age landscape. Oxford: Oxford Archaeological Unit.

Musson, C., 1970 House plans and prehistory. Current Archaeology 2:267–275.

Oswald, A., 1997 A doorway on the past: practical and mystic concerns in the orientation of roundhouse doorways. *In* Reconstructing Iron Age Societies: new approaches to the British Iron Age. A. Gwilt and C. Haselgrove, eds. pp. 87–95. Oxford: Oxbow Books.

Oxford Archaeological Unit, 2000 White Horse Stone: a Neolithic longhouse. Current Archaeology 168:450–453.

Parker Pearson, M., 1996 Food, fertility and front doors in the first millennium BC. *In* The Iron Age in Britain and Ireland: recent trends. T. Champion and J. Collis, eds. pp. 117–132. Sheffield: Sheffield Academic Press.

——and C. Richards, 1994a Architecture and order: spatial representation and archaeology. *In* Architecture and Order: approaches to social space. M. Parker Pearson and C. Richards, eds. pp. 38–72. London: Routledge.

——and ——1994b Ordering the world: perceptions of architecture, space and time. *In* Architecture and Order: approaches to social space. M. Parker Pearson and C. Richards, eds. pp. 1–37. London: Routledge.

——N. Sharples and J. Mulville, 1996 Brochs and Iron Age society: a reappraisal. Antiquity 60:57–67.

——J. Pollard, C. Tilley, J. Thomas, C. Richards and K. Welham, 2005 The Stonehenge Riverside Project: interim report 2005. Available at www.shef.ac.uk/content/1/c6/02/21/27/PDF-Interim-Report-2005.pdf (accessed 10 December 2007).

——C. Richards, J. Thomas, C. Tilley and K. Welham, 2006 The Stonehenge Riverside Project: summary interim report on the 2006 season. Available at www.shef.ac.uk/content/1/c6/02/21/27/summary-interim-report-2006.pdf (accessed 10 December 2007).

Piggott, S., 1954 Neolithic Cultures of the British Isles. Cambridge: Cambridge University Press.

Pollard, J., 1999 "These places have their moments": thoughts on settlement practices in the British Neolithic. *In* Making Places in the Prehistoric World: themes in settlement archaeology. J. Brück and M. Goodman, eds. pp. 76–93. London: UCL Press.

Pope, R., 2007 Ritual and the roundhouse: a critique of recent ideas on the use of domestic space. *In* The Earlier Iron Age in Britain and the Near Continent. C. Haselgrove and R. Pope, eds. pp. 204–228. Oxford: Oxbow Books.

Rahtz, P., 1962 Neolithic and Beaker sites at Downton, near Salisbury, Wiltshire. Wiltshire Archaeological and Natural History Magazine 58:115–142.

Richards, C., 1993 Monumental choreography: architecture and spatial representation in Late Neolithic Orkney. *In* Interpretative Archaeology. C. Tilley, ed. pp. 143–178. Oxford: Berg.

——2005 Dwelling among the Monuments: the Neolithic village of Barnhouse, Maeshowe passage grave and surrounding monuments at Stenness, Orkney. Cambridge: McDonald Institute for Archaeological Research.

Richards, M., 1996 "First farmers" with no taste for grain. British Archaeology 12:6.

Ritchie, J. N. G., 1988. Brochs of Scotland. Princes Risborough: Shire.

Smith, C., 1997. Late Stone Age Hunters of the British Isles. London: Routledge.

Spikins, P., 2002 Prehistoric People of the Pennines: reconstructing the lifestyles of Mesolithic hunter-gatherers on Marsden Moor. Leeds: West Yorkshire Archaeological Services.

Strathern, M., 1984 Domesticity and the denigration of women. *In* Rethinking Women's Roles: perspectives from the Pacific. D. O'Brien and S. Tiffany, eds. pp. 13–31. Berkeley: University of California Press.

Thomas, J., 1996 Neolithic houses in Mainland Britain and Ireland: a sceptical view. *In* Neolithic Houses in Northwest Europe and Beyond. T. Darvill and J. Thomas, eds. pp. 1–12. Oxford: Oxbow Books.

——1999 Understanding the Neolithic. London: Routledge.

Tiffany, S., 1978 Models and the social anthropology of women. Man 13:34–51.

Topping, P., 1996 Structure and ritual in the Neolithic house: some examples from Britain and Ireland. *In* Neolithic Houses in Northwest Europe and Beyond. T. Darvill and J. Thomas, eds. pp. 157–170. Oxford: Oxbow Books.

Tringham, R., 1995 Archaeological houses, households, homework and the home. *In* The Home: words, interpretations, meanings and environments. D. Benjamin, ed. pp. 79–107. Aldershot: Avebury.

Waddington, C., G. Bailey, I. Boomer, N. Milner, K. Pederson, R. Shiel and T. Stevenson, 2003 A Mesolithic coastal site at Howick, Northumberland. Antiquity 77. Available at http://antiquity.ac.uk/ProjGall/Waddington/waddington.html.

Waterson, R., 1990 The Living House: an anthropology of architecture in South-East Asia. Oxford: Oxford University Press.

Webley, L., 2003 Iron Age houses and social space: a case study of the three-aisled longhouses of Northern Europe during the Pre-Roman and Early Roman Iron Age. *In* Researching the Iron Age. J. Humphrey, ed. pp. 59–68. Leicester: Leicester Archaeology Monographs.

Whittle, A., 1996a Houses in context: buildings as process. *In* Neolithic Houses in Northwest Europe and Beyond. T. Darvill and J. Thomas, eds. pp. 13–26. Oxford: Oxbow Books.

——1996b Europe in the Neolithic: the creation of new worlds. Cambridge: Cambridge University Press.

——1997 Moving on and moving around: Neolithic settlement mobility. *In* Neolithic Landscapes. P. Topping, ed. pp. 15–22. Oxford: Oxbow Books.

Wickham-Jones, C., 2004 Structural evidence in the Scottish Mesolithic. *In* Mesolithic Scotland and its Neighbours: the early Holocene prehistory of Scotland, its British and Irish Context, and some northern European perspectives. A. Saville, eds. pp. 229–242. Edinburgh: Society of Antiquaries of Scotland.

Wilk, R., and R. McC. Netting, 1984 Households: changing forms and functions. *In* Households: comparative and historical studies of the domestic group. R. McC. Netting, R. Wilk and E. Arnould, eds. pp. 1–28. Berkeley: University of California Press.

Yanagisako, S., 1979 Family and household: the analysis of domestic groups. Annual Review of Anthropology 8:161–205.

Young, R., ed., 1999 Mesolithic Lifeways: current research in Britain and Ireland. Leicester: Leicester University Press.

12

Later Prehistoric Landscapes and Inhabitation

Robert Johnston

The two scenes portrayed in figure 12.1, both coastal, but from the east and west of Britain respectively, bracket the period in time covered by this contribution – ca. 2500–200 B.C. They are different landscapes. In one, the Early Bronze Age timber circle of Seahenge forms the principal archaeological trace of human activity, its form dependent upon principles of cosmology and ritual observance that were set apart from everyday life (Brennand and Taylor 2003). In the other, the Iron Age buildings on the salt marshes of the Severn Estuary are the focus for the practical and routine tasks of sheltering animals and humans, and there is no obvious manifestation of the belief systems that structured people's perceptions of their environment (Bell et al. 2000). This contrast has for a long time been evident in the ways that archaeologists study later prehistoric landscapes. The Neolithic and Early Bronze Age, up until ca. 1500 B.C., are characterized by explanations of how monuments conditioned cosmologies and social identity, and the later Bronze Age and Iron Age are interpreted through the analysis of settlement architecture, field systems and the social implications of agricultural production and consumption (e.g., Barrett et al. 1991).

There are a variety of themes that cut across this distinction and which link the examples from Holme-next-the-Sea and the Severn Estuary. In both cases the structures, places and landscapes were shaped to a significant degree by aspects of people's practical and conceptual knowledge about their environment, which comprised amongst other things skills in craftsmanship, ritual symbolism and animal husbandry. It is also possible to interpret the ways in which social identities were defined through the inhabitation of these places. Access to the interior of the timber circle, for instance, was restricted by a narrow entrance and the cramped space between the upturned tree stump and the palisade of split timbers. Social roles and the relative status of different groups might have been negotiated during the construction of the monument, but were later fixed in terms of whether or not individuals had access to the completed structure. The Iron Age buildings on the Severn

Figure 12.1 Artists' reconstructions of the landscapes of (*above*) Seahenge, an Early Bronze Age timber circle at Holme-next-the-Sea, Norfolk, and (*below*) an Iron Age building excavated on the Severn Estuary. The detail and accuracy of these illustrations was possible because of the excellent preservation of environmental remains in wetland contexts and the relative precision of the chronologies. These views show landscape at its most straightforward: an expression of how a place might have looked during a particular time in prehistory. Seahenge reconstruction drawn by Julie Curl and David Dobson. © Norfolk Archaeological Unit. Severn Estuary reconstruction drawn by S. J. Allen (Bell et al. 2000:fig. 17.7). © Martin Bell/CBA.

Estuary were occupied seasonally, and we might expect that taking on the responsibility of accompanying cattle to the salt marshes may have been dependent upon
age and gender. Finally, both examples emphasize the inseparability of social and
natural agencies, and the interconnectedness of the cultural and environmental
order. At Seahenge, the upturned tree is simultaneously both natural form and,
inverted and memorialized, a cultural place. Likewise, the ways in which people
inhabited the Severn Estuary were largely conditioned by access rights to grazing
areas, the needs of their herds and the short- and long-term rhythms of the tides
and the growth of pasture.

Landscapes, then, comprise more than can be portrayed through one image.
Landscape is a concept, as it is now applied within archaeology, that enables prehistorians to conceive of social life and environment at many different but interrelated geographic and temporal scales, from the intimacy of place and technology
to the patterning of historical and environmental processes across regions (e.g.,
Edmonds 1999). Landscapes conditioned how people lived while simultaneously
being in part a product of human activity. People defined the forms and textures
of their environments during their routine and everyday tasks, as well as through
more conscious and organized acts of reformation. Places were made and named,
pathways defined and areas of grazing and cultivation marked. Yet these actions
and the identities of individuals and groups of people were themselves conditioned
by landscapes, whether through affiliations with places and territories, the restrictions and affordances of particular types of soil and topography or the limits defined
by physical and conceptual boundaries. Social life and culture were therefore intertwined with the environment. In these ways the landscape serves to unite the study
of what might at first appear as opposed categories: place and space, ritual and
everyday, natural and social, individual and community (Tilley 1994). This is in
part possible because of the rich intellectual, cross-disciplinary traditions that an
archaeology of landscape draws upon (e.g., Wylie 2007; for recent introductions to
the archaeology of landscape see Ashmore 2004; Bender 2006).

In order to provide parameters for this contribution, the focus will be on the
concept of landscape as a means of bridging environmental and social narratives.
This is developed within three themes, each of which has been introduced above:
the practical dimensions of ecological knowledge, the ways in which space and
places were defined and controlled and the interrelationship of social and natural
agencies. These are dealt with in the context of different periods in later prehistory,
progressing from the Late Neolithic and Early Bronze Age, in the third millennium
B.C., to the middle of the Iron Age, towards the end of the first millennium B.C.

A Practical Ecology of Plants (2800–1500 B.C.)

Plants form one of the main elements that define a visual landscape, they are principal agents in many ecosystems, and they have long served to structure the lives of
human populations as dietary staple and symbolic resource. At Seahenge, the
grazed salt marshes, nearby alder carr and oak woodland formed the environment

for human inhabitation during the time when the timber circle was constructed. The vegetation was not a passive backdrop for these activities. Most obviously, 15–20 oaks from a nearby woodland were felled, trimmed of their branches and split before being placed around the central stump. They became architecture. The central stump at Seahenge was dragged to the site using a piece of "rope" formed from three stems of honeysuckle (fig. 12.2). Knowledge about the botanical world was rich and complex, and its acquisition and skilled use was an important means through which individuals' identities and roles in the project were constructed and transformed. This practical knowledge was closely related to conceptual understandings of the world. The final form of the monument demonstrated an alignment towards the midsummer rising sun, which corresponds roughly with the time of year that the posts were erected: a reference to cosmological principles that conditioned social life as much as the material qualities of wood and honeysuckle stem.

Significant and substantial changes have been recognized in the range of plants that people made use of in later prehistory, with the principal archaeological focus

Figure 12.2 An exceptionally strong and sophisticated rope made from honeysuckle stems was used to drag the central tree-stump to the timber circle at Seahenge. It was found still knotted and looped through two tow-holes. The rope had been made by first soaking the stems and then twisting them against the direction of their natural twine, to break up the fibres and make them more flexible; they were then plied back to form the rope (Taylor, in Brennand and Taylor 2003). Photo: Frances Green. © Norfolk Museums and Archaeology Service.

being on domesticated species. Cultivated plants contributed to how communities defined themselves and structured how they engaged with the landscape. This would have been apparent in how places looked, but it would have also influenced the choice of areas to cultivate, the rhythms of the agricultural cycle and the materials and technologies of everyday life. Each species of crop responded differently to soil and weather conditions, methods of cultivation, the timing of sowing, the effects of weeds and pests and methods of processing and storage (Bradley 1978; Hillman 1981). Emmer wheat, a more common cereal recovered from early assemblages, particularly in southern Britain, prefers heavier soils. Barley, which dominates the assemblages of many third- to second-millennia B.C. sites, and is particularly prevalent in northern Britain, fares better in deep loams, but is sensitive to acidity. Emmer is more likely to be sown in the autumn, while barley is better suited to a spring sowing. People's involvement in the conditions of growth of cultivated plants resulted in a developing knowledge and skill in what affected yields and the quality of the plants. Sowing barley in spring, for instance, brings lower yield, but fewer problems with frost and damp, and helps to spread the load of preparing the ground and sowing over two seasons (Hillman 1981). The diversity in crop assemblages from later prehistoric sites, the presence of different varieties of wheat and barley and variability in sub-species (McLaren 2000) might suggest that people were actively experimenting with different strategies.

The knowledge that enabled people to cultivate crops successfully was only one element in a rich understanding of the botanical world. The extent and nature of this knowledge is more difficult to reconstruct for wild varieties of plants compared to cultivars. The latter's presence in a botanical assemblage can be assumed to be the result of deliberate propagation, processing and consumption (though not necessarily at or close to the location of deposition). The remains of wild plants, on the other hand, may have been incorporated into archaeological assemblages inadvertently, for example, as weeds during harvesting. It is more difficult, therefore, to assess what role specific wild plants might have played.

The great numbers of weeds that would have grown amongst early crops provides a useful example of this uncertainty. Rye and oats, for instance, have been recovered in small quantities from a few sites dating to the second millennium B.C. While it is not possible to tell if these are cultivated or wild species, the latter is more likely, in which case they could have grown as "weeds" in the main crop of barley. Yet, the plants would have provided usable seed or fodder, and so may have been accepted and perhaps encouraged or deliberately planted. If the plants were not processed with the main crop, then they were unlikely to become incorporated into archaeological contexts. A wide range of plants that are identified by archaeologists as weeds had a range of practical uses. Fat hen, sheeps sorrel and corn spurrey, for instance, commonly listed as weeds in archaeo-botanical reports are known from historical accounts to have been used as food and fodder (Holden 1998:170). An opium poppy seed recovered from the Wilsford Shaft probably represents an arable weed, but is known to have been cultivated elsewhere in Europe; the seeds are edible and it can be used for oil or as a medicinal plant (Robinson 1989).

The categories that archaeo-botanists employ during their analyses need not, therefore, necessarily reflect how particular groups of plants were recognized in later prehistory. Species other than crops were commonplace within cultivated fields (Reynolds 1981), and their practical properties may have distinguished them from one another, and served to class them in terms other than "weeds". Nor can this practically based knowledge be restricted to parts of the landscape that were directly cultivated. Hedgerows and field edges formed important locations for a diversity of plants to grow that supplemented diets and had potential medicinal properties: blackberries, raspberries, wild strawberries, sloe, wild apple and cherry have all been found in archaeological contexts (Bradley 1978). Plants growing on wet ground, in disturbed areas or in maintained "gardens", such as reeds, rushes, sedges, flax, nettles and clematis, may well have had a role in craft-working (Hurcombe 2000). Amongst the plants recovered at Barnhouse, Orkney, heather provided bedding, fuel, fodder, dye or thatch; tormentil was a powerful astringent; and bogbean could have been used as a febrifuge (Hinton 2005). At Trethallan Farm, Cornwall, a pit within one of the later second-millennium B.C. houses contained a large number of charred hedge mustard seeds. Presumably gathered and stored, they may have been a source of oil (Straker 1991).

These examples single out a few of the many species known from later prehistoric sites, which is itself a small sample of the hundreds of species that could have served to define the botanical knowledge held by an individual or a community. The significance of particular plants depended on the contexts in which they were used. Each situation would have directed focus on different properties and values of the plants, and may have required the involvement of people with particular knowledge or status. For instance, the rough grasses that grew along field edges or on fallow pasture may not have been ordinarily valued until they were picked, dried and used as tinder in a funeral pyre, and the ashes gathered with the cremation for burial (e.g., Moffett 1999). Similarly, pignut tubers, which are edible, were found charred with a number of third-millennium B.C. burials (Robinson 1988; Moffett 1991). While we cannot demonstrate that such plants were perceived differently because they were incorporated into mortuary ceremonies, there is also good evidence from the pollen assemblages recovered from burial cists to suggest that plants such as meadowsweet and cereals were deposited (Tipping 1994a; Bunting et al. 2001). It is possible to interpret these as floral tributes or as food for the deceased in the afterlife. But plants are complex substances and so may have been chosen for their smell or colour or as metaphors for particular seasons or parts of the landscape (Fairbairn 1999; 2000).

Cultivating Identities (2500–1200 B.C.)

The control and reproduction of environmental knowledge was dependent on both people and places. Individuals might have been recognized partly through their knowledge of the names, uses and locations of particular plants, or have distinguished themselves through choosing the best times to sow or gather. Equally, access to land and soil at the correct times of year would have been vital, and would again have served as a means of structuring social relations between individuals and families and within wider communities.

In general, discussions of how places were defined in the earlier centuries of the second millennium B.C., and indeed for the third millennium, have focused on the role of monuments (Bradley 1998). Locations such as burial mounds, stone and timber circles and ceremonial enclosures served as nexus of social relations and cultural meanings. They expressed or conditioned links between people and particular places in the landscape that might have been perceived as permanent and timeless. This contrasts with the evidence for settlements from many parts of Britain. These were architecturally less permanent than monuments, and the spaces that were created within settlements both by activities and by physical structures were not respected and reproduced over long periods of time (e.g., Brück 1999).

This characterization of settlements as representing an impermanent commitment towards the landscape seems at odds with the argument put forward in the previous section. How did people develop in-depth, practical knowledge centred on experiences of cultivating and managing plant communities in the landscape when such knowledge develops as the result of spending time in particular places, and would seem to require a degree of residential permanence (e.g., Netting 1993; Head et al. 2002)? One explanation is that these scenarios are not exclusive of one another; a lack of substantive settlement architecture that characterizes many areas of Britain in the third and early second millennia is not concomitant with impermanent and fluid occupation of the landscape. Indeed, the complex and permanent settlement and agricultural structures that became widespread in the later second and first millennia would have been possible only because communities had, over successive generations, acquired the knowledge that enabled them to inhabit the same places more intensively.

Monuments may well have played a significant part in this process. Rather than being identified as places apart from everyday life – ritual landscapes – it seems apparent that in many cases they were situated in areas that formed the focus for a range of domestic activities. The small houses beneath the barrows at Trelystan (Britnell 1982) or the ring cairn at Brenig (Lynch 1993), for instance, attest to domestic occupation preceding the construction of the monuments. The Wilsford Shaft, a 30 m deep "ritual" pit beneath a barrow in Wiltshire, was situated close to arable fields (Ashbee et al. 1989). In Cranborne Chase, the third-millennium B.C. ceremonial monuments were constructed in an open, grazed landscape (French et al. 2003). While it may be the case that certain rituals served to sanctify regions of the landscape, and so excluded everyday activities, it was more common to find a variety of interrelated land use practices that contributed to the meaning of particular places.

Histories of cultivation and clearance are archaeologically visible in many parts of upland Britain where stone cleared from the soil was heaped into small cairns and low banks (fig. 12.3). These features remained as persistent markers as the fields were worked, abandoned and reoccupied over generations. The earliest of these cairn fields may have been constructed in the third millennium (e.g., Barber 1997), but they developed, expanded and were reworked throughout later prehistory. The placing of cremated human remains and material culture beneath some of the cairns in the cairn fields, and occasionally within areas of linear clearance

Figure 12.3 Aerial photographs of upland landscapes in Britain. (*Above*) Drumturn Burn, Perth-shire, east Scotland, showing the earthworks of roundhouses, field banks and small cairns under a light covering of snow. (*Below*) The earthworks visible are the remains of a coaxial field system on Horridge Common, Dartmoor, south-west England. The exceptional levels of surface preservation and visibility are characteristic of many upland areas in Britain. These regions are nonetheless not havens for conservation in perpetuity, as mineral extraction, forestation and farming regimes all continue to impact upon the survival of archaeological features (Darvill 1986; Browne and Hughes 2003). Photographs provided by the Royal Commission on the Ancient and Historical Monuments of Scotland and English Heritage. Crown Copyright.

(as at Eaglestone Flat, Derbyshire: Barnatt 1994) is further suggestive of a close link between single communities and areas of land. Such practices are reminiscent of the offerings found within burial monuments and ring cairns, and there may be a degree to which both contexts provided the means for ensuring the continuity of use rights over particular pastures or arable plots (Johnston 2001).

From the middle centuries of the second millennium, the stone cleared from the fields was less commonly piled into small cairns and was instead placed against the edges of the plots, along hedges or fences, and close up to the walls of houses. Excavated settlements such as Green Knowe, Peebleshire, and Standrop Rigg, Northumberland, are examples (Jobey 1981; 1983). At Tulloch Wood, Moray, the late third- to early second-millennium B.C. cairn fields were cleared away to form linear field banks in the middle of the second millennium (Carter 1993). As with ploughing, stone clearance structured places, qualitatively improving the soil and forming boundaries around cultivated spaces. The reconstruction of buildings on the same platforms time and again, and the aggregation of field plots one onto another, meant that these settlements became distinctive locations with long biographies. Yet, the presence of cairns, boundaries and roundhouses does not necessarily represent year-round occupation by the whole of a co-resident group (cf. Barnatt 2000). The location of many sites in high, exposed locations (e.g., Manley 1990) might be better understood as evidence that there were regions where there was a degree of seasonally organized residential mobility and a more fluid sense of tenure over places (e.g., Kitchen 2001).

Elsewhere, particularly in southern Britain, a strong case can be made for longer-term, year-round occupation of houses and settlements from the middle of the second millennium. In these contexts, the spatial divisions within settlements and between the settlement and the wider landscape were frequently more pronounced and carefully maintained. Houses were on occasions enclosed by ditches and banks, as at South Lodge and Down Farm, Dorset. In both cases there were perhaps symbolic attempts to legitimate the boundaries with deliberately placed items of metalwork at the corners and entrances of the enclosure (Barrett et al. 1991). The spaces in and around buildings were also more clearly structured both physically, with fences, and through the persistence of distinct activity areas (e.g., Blackpatch, Sussex: Drewett 1982). The contrast between this and the occupation practices of the first half of the second millennium was more pronounced here than elsewhere in Britain, and resonates more widely with changes in material culture, forms of burial and the discontinuation of rituals at major ceremonial complexes such as Stonehenge – which leads to the argument, most recently, that a process of social fragmentation was taking place in which large but relatively fluid alliances were replaced by more fixed networks of small, co-resident communities (Brück 2000).

A Divided Land (2000–1000 B.C.)

While in some regions of Britain it is possible to trace a slow accumulation of settlement and field architecture in particular places in the landscape, elsewhere a different relationship between land and social identity appears to emerge. Across Dartmoor, the Wessex downland, in the Thames Valley and on the fen edge of East Anglia, extensive areas of regular field systems have been excavated and dated to the middle and later second millennium. On Dartmoor, the boundaries took various forms, as timber fences, hedge banks and low drystone walls. They enclosed areas of grassland into large blocks, parts of which were further subdivided, often into coaxial strips. This has been explained as a system to manage increasing pressures on grazing land (Fleming 1988), although it is difficult to establish the extent to which this evolved over the longer term and consolidated existing patterns of land tenure (Johnston 2005). On the chalk downland of Wiltshire, the fields again have common alignments, but unlike Dartmoor the enclosed areas are of a more consistent shape and size (McOmish et al. 2002; McOmish 2005). The plots are defined by lynchets that formed through the accumulation of plough soil eroded from the fields during many hundreds of years of cultivation. It appears that the histories of land enclosure in each region were different. Explanations of variation therefore cannot be presented purely in terms of how systems might have functioned, but should also reflect the historical context in which they developed.

The large-scale enclosure of land has been interpreted from a variety of different perspectives. It may be seen as part of a predictable technological evolution of farming methods away from simple non-intensive horticulture. More commonly, it has been presented as a response by communities to a variety of internal and external processes, such as population increases, which made it necessary to manage access to land and to maximize productivity. A development of this is the argument that agricultural surpluses were required in order to sustain elites whose status depended on their involvement within networks of exchanging prestige goods, particularly metalwork (Rowlands 1980). Yates's research in the Thames Valley has shown a correlation between blocks of fields, high-status enclosures and metalwork finds, which he has argued demonstrates a link between strategies of agricultural intensification and the involvement of communities within long-distance exchange networks (Yates 1999; 2007).

The relationship between technological and social change is presented differently by John Barrett in his (1994) account of the second millennium B.C. He identifies a shift from long fallow to short fallow cultivation strategies, with the latter representing a managed intensification of production involving the use of ploughs and the manuring of soils. The earlier long fallow systems resulted in more generalized rights of access to the land, which were managed through cooperation amongst a wide community. These open alliances were reduced within the short fallow systems that typified the later second millennium, as individual biographies were tied more closely to portions of land and a more tightly defined community. The inheritance of land within kin groups therefore became of much greater concern, and this was expressed first through the physical expressions of genealogy typified by linear arrangements of barrows and the burials within cremation cemeteries, and then through the enclosure of land by boundaries. In support of this, there are many instances in which the boundaries are aligned upon or in some way respect the position of earlier burial monuments. The overall transformation was from a world in which people were always coming to, in or leaving places, to a world where people were place-bound and saw time from the perspective of their actions on that place.

The term "intensification" may take on different meanings in the various explanations of why land was enclosed during the second millennium. In those models where field systems sustain competitive exchange networks, intensification was primarily a process of maximizing the production of resources to meet the needs of an expanding economy. Such a perspective is open to the criticism that it interprets prehistory in terms of a modern, Western rationale derived from formalist economic models (Brück 2000). The environmental histories of many areas of southern Britain offer little support for a correspondence between the appearance of field boundaries and an aggressive over-exploitation of the landscape. Alternatively, where "intensification" is linked with the fragmentation of both communities and the landscape, it might be interpreted as a predictable corollary of "settling down". Successfully inhabiting places and land on a permanent basis required an in-depth understanding of the ecology of the land and locale, and by degrees the landscape was used more intensively. This may and indeed is likely to have led to land being perceived differently. But it does not necessitate its treatment as an alienable commodity, or its exclusive ownership by individuals or families.

Unstable Environments (1200–500 B.C.)

There is a long-held opinion among prehistorians that the period at the end of the second millennium and the beginning of the first millennium B.C. was characterized by major social changes, which are recognizable archaeologically as the appearance of defended settlements (Thomas 1997), increases in the amount of metalwork hoards and votive deposits (Bradley 1990) and the widespread reorganization of field systems (Cunliffe 2004). Amongst the explanations for what these changes represent, perhaps the most contentious is the argument that they were social and economic crises brought about, wholly or in part, by the impact of a deterioration in climate, towards cooler and wetter conditions, and the degradation of arable soils (e.g., Burgess 1985; Darvill 1987:126; Roberts 1998:200). The widespread acceptance of climatic change as a major factor in social change during this period rests partly on the apparent clarity of the association between a well-defined spell of cool wet conditions and the transformations that are interpreted as taking place in the landscape at this time. Added to this are assumptions about how communities might have responded to environmental changes that would have appeared to be beyond their control.

The prolonged spell of colder and wetter conditions attributed to the early centuries of first millennium, and known as the sub-Atlantic period, was up until relatively recently presented with some confidence by archaeologists as a 2° fall in average temperature between 1000 and 750 B.C. (Lamb 1981). Yet the basis for these reconstructions is a range of proxy signals, mainly from the pollen record and peat stratigraphy, that have since been shown to be problematic (Whittingdon and

Edwards 1997). The impact of human activity on the landscape makes it more difficult to interpret the vegetation record from the fourth millennium B.C. onwards, while the inception and development of peat may be the consequence of a variety of factors, including human degradation of soils and responses to local and short-term environmental changes.

While there is widespread support amongst environmental archaeologists for these reassessments of the data for climatic change, there is still no consensus on what should replace earlier models. Tipping (2002) identifies studies that show there was a cyclicity of between 500 and 1,500 years in climatic change, and that the consequences may have been "frequent and severe". Bell and Walker (1992) describe a dramatic fall in the tree line in Sweden at ca. 1200 B.C., a major marine incursion in the earlier first millennium (ca. 850–550 B.C.) and a recurring event identified in peat stratigraphy, allied with a change in temperature of −1 to −2°, dated to ca. 500 B.C. In his survey of the evidence, Roberts (1998) argues for a general cooling after 3500 B.C. in a series of steps, with the sub-Atlantic downturn beginning at about 500 B.C.

Given the variability in the palaeo-climatic models, it is perhaps unsurprising that it is also difficult to identify evidence for widespread and contiguous crises in patterns of settlement and subsistence. For those zones of the landscape where it would be supposed climatic change would have its most dramatic effect, the uplands and coastal wetlands, prehistorians are now more likely to interpret evidence for continuity or coping responses and a resilience to changing environmental conditions. The latter represents a positive response, perhaps typified by the small shifts in settlement location and the constructions of trackways in coastal wetlands such as the Fens, and the Gwent, Humber and Somerset Levels during major marine incursions in the earlier half of the first millennium (Bell and Walker 1992:127–128; e.g., Evans and Serjeantson 1988). For the uplands, the once ubiquitous argument for abandonment in the face of cold, wet conditions is now balanced by the case for stability in land use. In his review of the pollen data from the northern British uplands, Richard Tipping concludes that for every pollen site which shows a decline in crop growing there is another where it rises, while evidence for pasture seems to increase in intensity throughout the first millennium (Tipping 1994b; 2002; see also Young and Symonds 1995; Dark 2006).

These examples highlight the importance of situating climatic change within regional histories, and as one of a variety of material conditions that structured people's landscapes (e.g., Strauss and Orlove 2003). Long- and short-term patterns in the weather, peat formation and coastal inundation were undoubtedly of significant interest to those living in the hills or on the coast, as it placed practical constraints on how they inhabited particular places. But the nature of any constraint was dependent on the ecological knowledge, cultural understandings, personal motivations, skills and resolve that people brought to situations. It is very difficult to assess the extent to which people recognized environmental change or to reconstruct how they interpreted it, but it is still insufficient simply to argue that we expect, on the basis of ethnographic and historic studies, that the cultural perceptions of weather, place and marginality were likely to have been as important in

people's decision-making as the physical processes recognized by modern environmental science.

Communities with Animals (1000–200 B.C.)

During the second millennium B.C., the spatial dimensions of activities in the
landscape began to be defined more clearly by physical boundaries in and around
settlements or delimiting areas of land. This was significantly more pronounced in
the first millennium with the much more widespread enclosure of places and landscapes. The hill forts that dominate many accounts of Iron Age society were an
expression of this. But they were only one aspect of much wider and longer-term
process that includes early hilltop enclosures, low-lying settlements of many different forms and large- and small-scale systems of land division. The imperatives for
this enclosure have been discussed in a variety of terms, as a means of defence,
as symbolic boundaries and as expressions of social identity (e.g., Bowden and
McOmish 1987; Collis 1996; Taylor 1997). One striking aspect of these structures
of control is their association, in various ways, with the management of animals.

Animals, like plants, provided people with a range of resources, whether as food,
clothing, shelter, tools or votive offerings. At the same time, animals interact with
people: they have personable characteristics, live in social groups and, unlike fields
of crops, they are mobile. In these terms, amongst other reasons, we might expect
the interactions between people and animals to structure the landscape and places
in significant and recognizable ways.

The places where animals were kept or where people lived while looking after
their herds may be one of the more obvious examples of this. The dwellings on the
Severn Estuary were built in an area of seasonal grazing as shelters for people and
possibly also for animals. Changes in the weather and availability of grazing between
seasons meant that stock were moved between locations depending on the time of
year. The contemporary timber trackways and fish traps that have been identified
in the surrounding area would have been of use only during higher tides, and so
related to different uses and tenurial systems. While seasonality is less easily demonstrated for many upland sites, there is an argument that the commonly identified
pattern in areas of Scotland and Wales of more complex, sometimes enclosed,
settlements located in lower-lying areas and unenclosed, isolated buildings and
"paddocks" at higher altitudes reflects a form of transhumance in which animals
and their herders spend the summer months in the hills (e.g., Smith 1999; cf.
Cowley 1998).

The gathering of people and animals may have taken on a different character at
places such as Potterne, East Chisenbury and All Cannings Cross, on the edge of
the Marlborough Downs, and Salisbury Plain in Wiltshire. Here, the excavated
deposits comprised up to 3 metres of organic and cultural material that had formed
through the accumulation of "occupation soils" – principally animal bone, pottery
and manure (McOmish 1996; Lawson 2000). At Potterne (ca. 1200–550 B.C.)
and All Cannings Cross (ca. 800–600 B.C.) the excavations have been sufficiently

extensive to show that the middens extended for more than 3 hectares and included evidence for built structures, including houses. Locations such as these may have served as places for both year-round settlement and more occasional, seasonally organized, aggregations where animals (mainly sheep and cattle) were corralled, killed, butchered and consumed in vast numbers.

The times when animals and people gathered together from a wider community were evidently important social events, to judge by the quantities of butchered animal bone and broken decorated pottery found at the midden sites. Yet such occasions were as much centred on animal as on human relationships. The reproduction of the herd or flock required bulls and rams which may have been shared or whose services were exchanged amongst these large communities. With the collection of wool or the culling of young animals, a further set of resources were available to structure people's interactions with one another and to define the success of the community. On these important occasions in the year, as with more routine tasks of milking and tending stock, the rhythms of people's lives were closely structured by the biographies, reproductive cycles and daily needs of their animals. It is perhaps from this perspective that we can understand the particular emphasis that appears to be placed on domestic species in ritual observances and votive offerings. At Haddenham, Cambridgeshire, sheep burials were used as foundation deposits within the doorways of the Middle Iron Age houses, while wild animals were not treated in this way (Evans and Serjeantson 1988). At Cadbury Castle, in the later first millennium B.C. levels of the hill fort, a minimum of 34 neo-natal calves were buried close to a later "shrine", yet other animal remains on the site – sheep and pig being the main ones – were not treated so carefully (Hamilton-Dyer and Maltby 2000). These examples are representative of a widespread and recurrent pattern that is suggestive of a complex conceptual ordering of the animal world (Hill 1995; Fitzpatrick 1997; Giles and Parker Pearson 1999).

Such cosmologies as we might hope to reconstruct had wider resonances for people's perceptions of animals, beyond the ways in which burials of cattle and sheep were incorporated into rituals. However, interpretations of the organization of the first-millennium B.C. landscape have tended to focus on the increasing productive capacity of arable land and pasture, and the social power accrued and displayed through marking territories with elaborate boundaries. Land division was also structured to a significant degree by land use, and in the case of pasture by the needs of animals for particular types of grazing, for shelter and water. Across the chalk downland of Wessex, a series of long ditched boundaries were constructed mainly during the earlier part of the first millennium B.C., contemporary with the midden sites discussed above (Bradley et al. 1994; McOmish et al. 2002). Initially termed "ranch boundaries" by archaeologists, the ditches have long been associated with a model of landscape change that saw the countryside being reorganized from arable fields into much larger blocks of pasture land. The association of these ditch systems with hilltop enclosures showing little evidence for internal structures, and in some cases demonstrably functioning as locations for corralling large numbers of animals (Cunliffe 2004; e.g., Ellis and Rawlings 2001), adds significantly to this model.

Similar networks of land division are known from many areas of eastern England. In East Yorkshire, on the Wolds and the Tabular Hills, a series of dykes demarcated large blocks of land (Spratt 1989; Stoertz 1997). The interpretation of these systems of boundaries as expressions of a variety of scales of social identity (e.g., Bevan 1997) should be balanced by the evidence that land use was inherently a part of the how the landscape was structured. The close relationship between the dykes and river valleys was potentially also an expression of the needs of sheep and cattle and their instincts to stay within defined territories – hefts or stints (see discussions in Chadwick 2007; Roberts 2007).

Domesticated animals therefore played a significant part in defining how the landscape looked, the ways in which it was organized and the temporality of human inhabitation. Yet people were not unintentioned recipients of these "natural forces". They had a great deal of control over the reproductive cycles of their animals and their routine and more exceptional movements through the landscape. It remains a significant challenge for prehistorians to interpret the landscape in terms that take account of the complex duality in which human agency was conditioned by as much as it determined the shape of the non-human world.

Landscape and Inhabitation in Later Prehistory

In this chapter I have considered the ways in which people interacted with and constructed landscapes and places in later prehistory. The approach taken represents a middle ground between an emphasis upon people's adaptation to their environment and a study in which nature formed a *tabula rasa* for cultural values.

The themes forming the focus of the chapter – the practical dimensions of ecological knowledge, the ways in which space and places were defined and controlled and the interrelationship of social and natural agencies – were chosen because they reflect different facets of this theoretical perspective. They have also been chosen as representative of the broad issues that affect our understanding of landscape change during later prehistory. The role of plants, both domesticated and wild, is central to debates about whether Neolithic communities were largely sedentary or mobile. The definition of places and land through cultivation and enclosure, and the relationship of these processes to changes in how communities identified themselves, is key to any evaluation of the arguments for social transformation in the second millennium B.C., while the impact of environmental change continues to be a focus for debate regarding the interpretation of changing agricultural strategies and settlement practices during the earlier first millennium B.C.

Each theme serves to bracket a period in time and a particular aspect of people's engagement with the environment. But the result of this structure is that particular examples are not clearly situated in their historical or geographic context. It would have been possible and productive to develop these themes through the history of specific regions (e.g., Pollard and Reynolds 2002; Edmonds 2004). For instance, the changes in intensity with which areas of land, places, animals and productive technologies were defined, controlled and contested using physical boundaries are particularly well defined for the chalk downland of Wessex, and the history of the wetlands of the Severn Estuary or the Cambridgeshire Fens provides an insight into the complex relationship between a dynamic environment and the character of human occupations.

There is potentially, therefore, a tension between regional or more local histories and the broad patterns or social processes reconstructed in many archaeological accounts. It remains a challenge for archaeology to make the conceptual link between different scales of social and environmental histories. Large-scale processes can and should be identified, but they are rarely synchronous across regions, uniformly definable and geographically continuous. The creation of an archetypal landscape for Britain is not the goal of archaeology, and with a fine-grained understanding of place and landscape these models will not serve to frame our interpretations of everywhere.

REFERENCES

Ashbee, P., M. Bell and E. Proudfoot, 1989 Wilsford Shaft: excavations 1960–62. London: English Heritage.

Ashmore, W., 2004 Social archaeologies of landscape. In A Companion to Social Archaeology. L. Meskell and R. W. Preucel, eds. pp. 255–271. Oxford: Blackwell.

Barber, J., ed., 1997 The Archaeological Investigation of a Prehistoric Landscape: excavations on Arran 1978–1981. Edinburgh: Scottish Trust for Archaeological Research.

Barnatt, J., 1994 Excavation of a Bronze Age unenclosed cemetery, cairns, and field boundaries at Eaglestone Flat, Curbar, Derbyshire, 1984, 1989–1990. Proceedings of the Prehistoric Society 60:287–370.

——2000 To each their own: later prehistoric farming communities and their monuments in the Peak. Derbyshire Archaeological Journal 120:1–86.

Barrett, J. C., 1994 Fragments from Antiquity: an archaeology of social life in Britain, 2900–1200 BC. Oxford: Blackwell.

——R. Bradley and M. Green, 1991 Landscape, Monuments and Society: the prehistory of Cranborne Chase. Cambridge: Cambridge University Press.

Bell, M., and M. J. C. Walker, 1992 Late Quaternary Environmental Change: physical and human perspectives. Harlow: Longman.

——A. Caseldine and H. Neumann, 2000 Prehistoric Intertidal Archaeology in the Welsh Severn Estuary. London: Council for British Archaeology.

Bender, B., 2006 Place and landscape. In Handbook of Material Culture. C. Tilley, W. Keane, S. Küchler, M. Rowlands and P. Spyer, eds. pp. 303–314. London: Sage.

Bevan, B., 1997 Bounding the landscape: place and identity during the Yorkshire Wolds Iron Age. In Reconstructing Iron Age Societies: new approaches to the British Iron Age. A. Gwilt and C. Haselgrove, eds. pp. 181–191. Oxford: Oxbow Books.

Bowden, M., and D. McOmish, 1987 The required barrier. Scottish Archaeological Review 4:76–84.

Bradley, R., 1978 The Prehistoric Settlement of Britain. London: Routledge and Kegan Paul.

——1990 The Passage of Arms: an archaeological study of prehistoric hoards and votive deposits. Cambridge: Cambridge University Press.

——1998 The Significance of Monuments: on the shaping of human experience in Neolithic and Bronze Age Europe. London: Routledge.

——R. Entwistle and F. Raymond, 1994 Prehistoric Land Divisions on Salisbury Plain: the work of the Wessex Linear Ditches Project. London: English Heritage.

Brennand, M., and M. Taylor, 2003 The survey and excavation of a Bronze Age timber circle at Holme-next-the-Sea, Norfolk, 1998–9. Proceedings of the Prehistoric Society 69: 1–84.

Britnell, W., 1982 The excavation of two round barrows at Trelystan, Powys. Proceedings of the Prehistoric Society 48:133–201.

Browne, D., and S. Hughes, eds., 2003 The Archaeology of the Welsh Uplands. Aberystwyth: RCAHMW.

Brück, J., 1999 What's in a Settlement? Domestic practice and residential mobility in Early Bronze Age Southern England. *In* Making Places in the Prehistoric World: themes in settlement archaeology. J. Brück and M. Goodman, eds. pp. 52–75. London: UCL Press.

——2000 Settlement, landscape and social identity: the Early–Middle Bronze Age transition in Wessex, Sussex and the Thames Valley. Oxford Journal of Archaeology 19(3): 273–300.

Bunting, M. J., R. Tipping and J. Downes, 2001 "Anthropogenic" pollen assemblages from a Bronze Age cemetery at Linga Fiold, West Mainland, Orkney. Journal of Archaeological Science 28(5):487–500.

Burgess, C., 1985 Population, climate and upland settlement. *In* Upland Settlement in Britain: the second millennium BC and after. D. Spratt and C. Burgess, eds. pp. 195–230. Oxford: British Archaeological Reports.

Carter, S. T., 1993 Tulloch Wood, Forres, Moray: the survey and dating of a fragment of prehistoric landscape. Proceedings of the Society of Antiquaries of Scotland 23:215–233.

Chadwick, A., 2007 Trackways, hooves and memory-days: human and animal movements and memories around the Iron Age and Romano-British rural landscapes of the English North Midlands. *In* Prehistoric Journeys. V. Cummings and R. Johnston, eds. pp. 131–152. Oxford: Oxbow Books.

Collis, J. R., 1996 Hill-forts, enclosures and boundaries. *In* The Iron Age in Britain and Ireland: recent trends. T. C. Champion and J. R. Collis, eds. pp. 87–94. Sheffield: J. R. Collis.

Cowley, D. C., 1998 Identifying marginality in the first and second millennia BC in the Strath of Kildonan, Sutherland. *In* Life on the Edge: human settlement and marginality. C. M. Mills and G. Coles, eds. pp. 165–171. Oxford: Oxbow Books.

Cunliffe, B., 2004 Wessex cowboys? Oxford Journal of Archaeology 23(1):61–81.

Dark, P., 2006 Climate deterioration and land-use change in the first millennium BC: perspectives from the British palynological record. Journal of Archaeological Science 33:1381–1395.

Darvill, T., 1986 The Archaeology of the Uplands: a rapid assessment of archaeological knowledge and practice. London: RCHME.

——1987 Prehistoric Britain. London: Batsford.

Drewett, P., 1982 Late Bronze Age downland economy and excavations at Black Patch, East Sussex. Proceedings of the Prehistoric Society 48:321–400.

Edmonds, M., 1999 Ancestral Geographies of the Neolithic: landscapes, monuments and memory. London: Routledge.

——2004 The Langdales: landscape and prehistory in a Lakeland valley. Stroud: Tempus.

Ellis, C. J., and M. Rawlings, 2001 Excavations at Balksbury Camp, Andover 1995–97. Proceedings of the Hampshire Field Club and Archaeological Society 56:21–94.

Evans, C., and D. Serjeantson, 1988 The backwater economy of a Fen-edge community in the Iron Age: the Upper Delphs, Haddenham. Antiquity 62:360–370.

Fairbairn, A. S., 1999 Charred plant remains. *In* The Harmony of Symbols: the Windmill Hill causewayed enclosure, Wiltshire. A. Whittle, J. Pollard and C. Grigson, eds. pp. 139–161. Oxford: Oxbow Books.

——2000 On the spread of crops across Neolithic Britain. *In* Plants in Neolithic Britain and Beyond. A. S. Fairbairn, ed. pp. 107–121. Oxford: Oxbow Books.

Fitzpatrick, A. P., 1997 Everyday life in Iron Age Wessex. *In* Reconstructing Iron Age Societies: new approaches to the British Iron Age. A. Gwilt and C. Haselgrove, eds. pp. 73–86. Oxford: Oxbow Books.

Fleming, A., 1988 The Dartmoor Reaves: investigating prehistoric land divisions. London: Batsford.

French, C., H. Lewis, M. J. Allen, R. G. Scaife and M. Green, 2003 Archaeological and palaeo-environmental investigations of the Upper Allen Valley, Cranborne Chase, Dorset (1998–2000): a new model of earlier Holocene landscape development. Proceedings of the Prehistoric Society 69:201–234.

Giles, M., and M. Parker Pearson, 1999 Learning to live in the Iron Age: dwelling and praxis. *In* Northern Exposure: interpretative devolution and the Iron Ages in Britain. B. Bevan, ed. pp. 217–231. Leicester: School of Archaeological Studies.

Hamilton-Dyer, S., and M. Maltby, 2000 The animal bones from a sample of Iron Age contexts. *In* Cadbury Castle, Somerset: the later prehistoric and early historic archaeology. J. C. Barrett, P. W. M. Freeman and A. Woodward, eds. pp. 278–291. London: English Heritage.

Head, L., J. Atchison and R. Fullagar, 2002 Country and garden: ethnobotany, archaeo-botany and Aboriginal landscapes near the Keep River, Northwestern Australia. Journal of Social Archaeology 2(2):173–196.

Hill, J. D., 1995 Ritual and Rubbish in the Iron Age of Wessex: a study on the formation of a specific archaeological record. Oxford: British Archaeological Reports.

Hillman, G., 1981 Crop husbandry practices from charred remains. *In* Farming Practice in British Prehistory. R. J. Mercer, ed. pp. 123–162. Edinburgh: Edinburgh University Press.

Hinton, P., 2005 Charred plant remains from Barnhouse and Maeshowe. *In* Dwelling among the Monuments: the Neolithic village of Barnhouse, Maeshowe passage grave and sur-rounding monuments at Stenness, Orkney. C. Richards, ed. pp. 339–357. Cambridge: McDonald Institute.

Holden, T., 1998 Charred plant remains. *In* The Lairg Project 1988–1996: the evolution of an archaeological landscape in northern Scotland. R. P. J. McCullagh and R. Tipping, eds. pp. 165–170. Edinburgh: Scottish Trust for Archaeological Research.

Hurcombe, L., 2000 Plants as the raw materials for crafts. *In* Plants in Neolithic Britain and Beyond. A. S. Fairbairn, ed. pp. 155–173. Oxford: Oxbow Books.

Jobey, G., 1981 Green Knowe unenclosed platform settlement and Harehope Cairn, Peebleshire. Proceedings of the Society of Antiquaries of Scotland 110:72–113.

——1983 Excavation of an unenclosed settlement on Standrop Rigg, Northumberland, and some problems related to similar settlements between Tyne and Forth. Archaeologia Aeliana, 5th ser. 11:1–21.

Johnston, R., 2001 "Breaking new ground": land tenure and fieldstone clearance during the Bronze Age. *In* Bronze Age Landscapes: tradition and transformation. J. Brück, ed. pp. 99–109. Oxford: Oxbow Books.

——2005 Pattern without a plan: rethinking the Bronze Age coaxial field systems on Dartmoor, south-west England. Oxford Journal of Archaeology 24(1):1–21.

Kitchen, W., 2001 Tenure and territoriality in the British Bronze Age. *In* Bronze Age Landscapes: tradition and transformation. J. Brück, ed. pp. 110–120. Oxford: Oxbow Books.

Lamb, H. H., 1981 Climate from 1000 BC to 1000 AD. *In* The Environment of Man: the Iron Age to the Anglo-Saxon period. M. Jones and G. Dimbleby, eds. Oxford: British Archaeological Reports.

Lawson, A. J., 2000 Potterne 1982–5: animal husbandry in later prehistoric Wiltshire. Salisbury: Trust for Wessex Archaeology.

Lynch, F., 1993 Excavations in the Brenig Valley: a Mesolithic and Bronze Age landscape in Wales. Gwynedd: Cambrian Archaeological Association.

Manley, J., 1990 A late Bronze Age landscape on the Denbigh Moors, northeast Wales. Antiquity 64:514–526.

McLaren, F. S., 2000 Revising the wheat crops of Neolithic Britain. *In* Plants in Neolithic Britain and Beyond. A. S. Fairbairn, ed. pp. 91–100. Oxford: Oxbow Books.

McOmish, D., 1996 East Chisenbury: ritual and rubbish at the British Bronze Age–Iron Age transition. Antiquity 70:68–76.

——2005 Bronze Age land allotment on the Marlborough Downs. *In* The Avebury Landscape: aspects of the field archaeology of the Marlborough Downs. G. Brown, D. Field and D. McOmish, eds. pp. 133–136. Oxford: Oxbow Books.

——D. Field and G. Brown, 2002 The Field Archaeology of the Salisbury Plain Training Area. Swindon: English Heritage.

Moffett, L., 1991 Pignut tubers from a Bronze Age cremation at Barrow Hills, Oxfordshire, and the importance of vegetable tubers in the prehistoric period. Journal of Archaeological Science 18:187–191.

——1999 The prehistoric use of plant resources. *In* Excavations at Barrow Hills, Radley, Oxfordshire, vol. 1: The Neolithic and Bronze Age monument complex. A. Barclay and C. Halpin, eds. pp. 243–247. Oxford: Oxford Archaeology.

Netting, R. McC., 1993 Smallholders, Householders: farm families and the ecology of intensive, sustainable agriculture. Stanford: Stanford University Press.

Pollard, J., and A. Reynolds, 2002 Avebury: the biography of a landscape. Stroud: Tempus.

Reynolds, P., 1981 Deadstock and livestock. *In* Farming Practice in British Prehistory. R. J. Mercer, ed. pp. 97–122. Edinburgh: Edinburgh University Press.

Roberts, J. G., 2007 Short journeys, long distance thinking. *In* Prehistoric Journeys. V. Cummings and R. Johnston, eds. pp. 102–109. Oxford: Oxbow Books.

Roberts, N., 1998 The Holocene: an environmental history, 2nd edn. Oxford: Blackwell.

Robinson, M., 1988 The significance of the tubers of *Arrhenatherum Elatius* (L) Beauv from Site 4, Cremation 15/11. *In* The Rollright Stones: megaliths, monuments, and settlements in the prehistoric landscape. G. Lambrick, ed. London: English Heritage.

——1989 The environmental material. *In* Wilsford Shaft: excavations 1960–62. P. Ashbee, M. Bell and E. Proudfoot, eds. pp. 78–90. London: English Heritage.

Rowlands, M., 1980 Kinship, alliance and exchange in the European Bronze Age. *In* Settlement and Society in the British Later Bronze Age. J. C. Barrett and R. Bradley, eds. pp. 59–72. Oxford: British Archaeological Reports.

Smith, G., 1999 Survey of prehistoric and Romano-British settlement in north-west Wales. Archaeologia Cambrensis 148:22–53.

Spratt, D. A., 1989 Linear Earthworks of the Tabular Hills of Northeast Yorkshire. Sheffield: Department of Prehistory and Archaeology.

Stoertz, C., 1997 Ancient Landscapes of the Yorkshire Wolds. Swindon: RCHME.

Straker, V., 1991 Charred plant macrofossils. *In* Trethellan Farm, Newquay: the excavation of a lowland Bronze Age settlement and Iron Age cemetery. J. A. Nowakowski. Cornish Archaeology 30:5–242.

Strauss, S., and B. S. Orlove, eds., 2003 Weather, Climate, Culture. Oxford: Berg.

Taylor, J., 1997 Space and place: some thoughts on Iron Age and Romano-British landscapes. *In* Reconstructing Iron Age Societies: new approaches to the British Iron Age. A. Gwilt and C. Haselgrove, eds. pp. 192–204. Oxford: Oxbow Books.

Thomas, R., 1997 Land, kinship relations and the rise of enclosed settlement in first millennium B.C. Britain. Oxford Journal of Archaeology 16(2):211–218.

Tilley, C., 1994 A Phenomenology of Landscape: places, paths and monuments. Oxford: Berg.

Tipping, R., 1994a Ritual floral tributes in the Scottish Bronze Age: palynological evidence. Journal of Archaeological Science 21(1):133–139.

——1994b The form and fate of Scotland's woodlands. Proceedings of the Society of Antiquaries of Scotland 124:1–54.

——2002 Climatic variability and "marginal" settlement in upland British landscapes: a reevaluation. Landscapes 3(2):10–29.

Whittingdon, G., and K. J. Edwards, 1997 Climate change. *In* Scotland: environment, archaeology and history, 8000 BC–AD 1000. K. J. Edwards and I. B. M. Ralston, eds. pp. 11–22. Chichester: Wiley.

Wylie, J., 2007 Landscape. London: Routledge.

Yates, D. T., 1999 Bronze Age field systems in the Thames Valley. Oxford Journal of Archaeology 18(2):157–170.

——2007 Land, Power and Prestige: Bronze Age field systems in southern England. Oxford: Oxbow Books.

Young, R., and T. Symonds, 1995 Marginality and the nature of later prehistoric upland settlement. Landscape History 17:5–16.

13

Ceramic Technologies and Social Relations

Ann Woodward

This chapter will chart the dramatic changes that have occurred in the study of prehistoric ceramics in Britain over the last 40 years. During this time a fairly esoteric subject, dominated mainly by detailed analyses of decorative motifs and the construction of elaborate chronological schemes, has been transformed into a powerful source of knowledge which can inform topics as diverse as culinary habits and feasting, the symbolic power of rock inclusions contained in pottery fabrics, and ritual deposition.

Following the remarkable gathering together of Bronze Age pottery in the photographic corpus compiled by Abercromby (1912), there was a significant lull in the concerted study of Neolithic and Bronze Age pottery. Then, taking the lead from a flurry of significant work on Neolithic pottery, carried out by both Stuart Piggott and Isobel Smith in the 1950s (Smith 1965), a series of doctoral theses was instigated at the University of Cambridge. As a result, major corpora of Late Neolithic/Early Bronze Age Beakers (Clarke 1970) and Collared Urns (Longworth 1984) were published, and studies of Food Vessels, Biconical Urns and Middle Bronze Age Deverel-Rimbury pottery quickly followed. Most of the studies concentrated on vessels from graves but some, notably the Deverel-Rimbury study (Ellison 1975) and one of Beaker domestic pottery (Gibson 1982), ventured into the realms of sherd material from settlement sites.

Iron Age pottery had fared better in the early years of the twentieth century, mainly because of the sustained activities of Reginald Smith and Christopher Hawkes at the British Museum. However, by the mid 1960s Hawkes's ABC system for the development of the Iron Age and its pottery (Hawkes 1959), based as it was on a series of Continental incursions, was being questioned by Grahame Clark and F. R. Hodson, both members of the Cambridge school. At the same time, Barry Cunliffe was finalising his doctoral research on the regional groupings of Iron Age pottery in southern England, also at Cambridge. This research formed the basis for the astoundingly important series of illustrations in Cunliffe's *Iron Age Communities in Britain* (1974; latest edition 2004), which has functioned as a backbone for Iron Age studies in Britain ever since. Cumulatively these works, and myriad individual reports on prehistoric pottery from individual sites and areas, have provided a chronological and stylistic framework upon which new developments could be founded. Cunliffe's definition of regional ceramic styles, augmented by Elsdon (1989), still provide the basic key texts for any study of Iron Age pottery, while the lack of such an overview for the Neolithic and Bronze Age periods has been rectified by Gibson (2002).

No contribution of this length can encompass the entire ramifications of the study of prehistoric ceramic technologies in Britain. What follows should be accepted as a personal view of the study of ceramic technology, and how its results can be employed to answer wider archaeological questions, as experienced by one white, female archaeologist who has been studying urns, jars and inclusions for a continuous period of 37 years. At the beginning of my research into Middle Bronze Age settlements it was evident that the chronology and development of settlement sites could not be unravelled unless the pottery sequences were first documented and analysed. As a consequence, I embarked on a three-year programme of recording the details of many hundreds of Bronze Age urns. Initially seduced by the sheer variety of their forms, decoration, colour and fabrics, I soon realized that the pottery assemblages – from both settlements and urn fields – could be used to study far more than style and relative chronology. Forms and decorative schemes could be grouped regionally, at a series of nested levels; detailed coding and analysis of fabrics could lead to information concerning both manufacture and exchange; the spatial study of different vessel types across settlements could indicate a variety of different zones of activity; and the disposition of varying urn forms in settlements and funerary locations could provide important data that might inform the nature of social organisation (Ellison 1980a; 1980b). But to start at the beginning, we must consider the nuts and bolts of chronological systems.

Chronology

Although much recent research has concentrated on new themes and interpretation involving vessel shape and size, fabrics and decoration, all such studies still need to be underpinned by secure chronological frameworks. Several advances in dating techniques are aiding the construction and restructuring of such schemes, while relative chronological approaches are still important. The main relative systems of dating are stratigraphic sequences and association with other datable artefacts such as metalwork. In the early prehistoric period, long stratigraphic sequences occur rarely, but occasionally they have been excavated and they can provide significant new information, especially if the stratification can be calibrated by an absolute dating technique.

For the Iron Age, the main chronological sequences still depend greatly on the typological and stratigraphic schemes resulting from major hill fort excavations such as those undertaken at Danebury, Hampshire (Cunliffe 1984; 1991), and Cadbury

Castle, Somerset (Barrett et al. 2000). A full and thoughtful discussion of the problems of dating Late Bronze Age and Iron Age pottery has been provided by Willis (2002). As well as outlining aspects of the stratigraphic dating method, and the problem of residuality, he explains the difficulties involved in applying the absolute techniques of radiocarbon and thermoluminescence dating in these periods. The calibration curve for radiocarbon dates during the Iron Age is very flat, so precise dates cannot be achieved, and several programmes of dating using thermo-luminescence seem not to correlate well with radiocarbon dates or existing typological schemes.

For the Neolithic and Bronze Age absolute dating has taken centre stage. A good chronological scheme is now in place, and refinements are continually being attempted. Thus, it has been possible to backdate the origins of Peterborough Ware from the Late to the Middle Neolithic (Gibson and Kinnes 1997), and the problems of correlating Beaker dates with existing typological schemes are being solved by Needham through a reworking of the definitions of some of the key type descriptions (Needham 2005). Two extremely important advances have been the development of radiocarbon dating methods which can be applied first to cremated human remains, and secondly to the burnt residues of cooked food on the interior surfaces of potsherds. Early Bronze Age urns often contain, or cover, human cremations and a recent programme of dating for Scotland (Sheridan 2003) has demonstrated the high potential of this avenue of research. The dating of ceramic residues has taken off only in the last few years and many significant dating programmes are in progress. The particular importance of this technique is that the date applies to the final use of the vessel in a cooking episode, and thus the radiocarbon date applies directly to the pot itself and not, as has been usual previously, to other datable material found within the same context.

Production

Ceramics are items, usually pots, made from clay which has been heated in order to drive off the water that forms part of the chemical composition of the clay molecules. A very useful discussion of how this occurs, and of prehistoric ceramic production technology in general, is provided by Gibson (2002:ch. 2). Until the Late Iron Age all pottery was hand-built and fired on open bonfires or in pits, with the ceramic change usually occurring at a temperature of around 700°C. Sedimentary clays, with naturally occurring impurities, were usually preferred. Inclusions (the term "temper" is to be avoided) within the potting clays may have occurred naturally in the clay selected, or may have been deliberately added. The addition of inclusions aids the working of the clay during vessel-building, and helps the water between the clay particles to escape during drying. In purely technological terms, the most suitable deliberately added inclusions are grog (crushed pottery) or igneous rock fragments. Organic inclusions can also be useful but may cause problems during firing. Other commonly selected inclusions such as flint and quartz would seem less suitable, as both contain their own water of chemical composition, and may split or explode during firing. Also they have sharp edges which would have rendered vessel-forming a potentially painful process. However, such materials may have been selected for non-technological reasons, as we shall see later.

Vessels were built up by hand techniques, ranging from simple pinching, sometimes aided by the paddle and anvil technique, coil or strap building, moulding, slab construction and modular conjunction. The use of these techniques can be detected by visual inspection and by the study of wall profiles in thin section under the microscope. After forming, the vessels were left to dry, either in the open air or by the application of low heat. Firing in bonfires or pits was difficult to control, and prehistoric pots were often fired incompletely, damaged during the firing (e.g., by spalling and cracking) and characterised by variable surface colouring. Much detailed knowledge of the processes involved has been gained through experimental firings. By the Late Iron Age, pottery in certain parts of Britain was being formed using a wheel, and fired in simple kilns which employed raised pierced floors and cigar-shaped kiln bars. Potting in prehistory was a skilled process. Technological knowledge would have been passed down through the generations, and the use of fire and kilns may have linked this technology symbolically to other high temperature processes such as metalworking and indeed the drying of crops. All such processes involved irreversible transformations of materials: in the case of ceramics from plastic, damp clay to hard and fragile vessels, and these transformations may have been imbued with powerful magical significance. We do not know to what extent potters were specialists, but it is possible that such potters did exist from the Neolithic onwards, and that such people, whether women or men, may have held respected positions within society. Ethnographic data suggests that most bonfire potting in "household industries" was undertaken by women, while the more industrial production of wheel-turned pottery in kilns may have been under the control of men. The cast from one of the deep pits in the neck of a Middle Neolithic Peterborough Ware vessel from Mortlake showed that the pit had been formed by a small finger tip with a long nail. The finger used was probably the little finger of a female potter (Cotton and Johnson 2004:134, fig. 15.3).

The evidence for pottery production in prehistory has mainly been gathered from studying details of the vessels themselves. Bonfire or pit firings leave little specific evidence in the soil, but the existence of on-site pottery production can be inferred by various means: the presence of stores of raw potting clay and material for inclusions, bases of bonfires with associated sherds from wasters or spalled vessels, or tools for forming or decorating vessels. A selection of such evidence has been usefully illustrated by Hamilton (2002:figs. 5.1–5.3).

Fabric

Until the 1960s most reports on prehistoric pottery concentrated on shapes, rim forms and decoration, with scant attention paid to the clay matrix or fabric. If the clay components were considered at all, descriptions usually entailed vague references to "temper" or "grits". From the 1960s onwards the use of petrological techniques, especially thin-sectioning, in the characterisation of prehistoric pottery became more common, but it was not until the 1970s that systematic description and coding of fabric types was developed. Initially applied to the apparently uniform, but actually highly varied, flinty fabrics of Early and Middle Bronze Age urns, wide-ranging coding systems for prehistoric fabrics were rapidly developed during the early 1970s. Thus a system for the objective description and record of fabrics designed for the Wessex Archaeological Committee by Elaine Morris became the basis for *The Study of Later Prehistoric Pottery: general policies and guidelines for analysis and publication*, published and disseminated by the Prehistoric Ceramics Research Group (1997).

Although the first use of geological thin sections to study pottery from archaeological sites in the British Isles occurred before the Second World War, the technique was not widely employed until the late 1960s. Systematic research was pioneered by David Peacock and David Williams at the University of Southampton. In 1994 the United Kingdom Thin Section (UKTS) database, an initiative funded by English Heritage, was produced: it listed ca. 5,500 thin sections of prehistoric pottery. The significance of this large body of data, much of it unpublished and previously undigested, has been summarised and assessed by Morris and Woodward (2003). Prehistoric ceramics are highly suitable for investigation using thin-sectioning and ceramic petrology. Many fabrics contain distinctive coarse inclusions, often measuring more than 2 mm across, and some fabric clays contain natural inclusions which can be easily identified and assigned to specific, restricted geological deposits. A selection of fabric types seen in thin section is provided in figure 13.1. There are two principal topics which have been addressed by the use of ceramic petrology in Britain: characterization and provenancing. Characterization defines the nature of the clay matrix and the inclusions within it, and describes the appearance of those inclusions by size, shape, sorting, texture and density. Provenancing uses that information to interpret the geological sources from which the naturally occurring or deliberately added inclusions were derived, and often can suggest a likely source that is closest to the archaeological site under consideration.

Early examples of the specific identification of inclusions in prehistoric pottery include the consideration of marine shell fragments in Grooved Ware from Woodhenge, Wiltshire (Cunnington 1929), and the first record of Early Neolithic wares containing igneous inclusions at Hembury in Devon (Liddell 1935). Peacock's (1969a) analysis of these same igneous wares was a major milestone in the development of the subject. It established that the gabbroic clays employed came from the Lizard in Cornwall. In two further seminal papers, on Iron Age pottery in the south-west, and in the Welsh Marches, respectively, David Peacock demonstrated that not all coarse, Middle to Late Iron Age pottery had been locally made, but may have been manufactured for regional trade (Peacock 1968; 1969b).

A few examples of the results of petrological analysis that are of particular interest may be highlighted here. A wider-ranging study of Neolithic pottery has mapped the distribution of pottery containing soft and organic inclusions. Such inclusions, which would have rendered the vessels porous, may have been employed in order

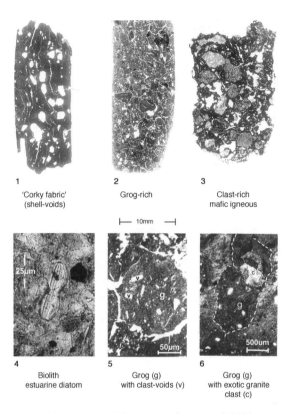

Figure 13.1 Neolithic and Bronze Age fabric types from north Wales, as seen in thin section: 1. Early Neolithic bowl from Bryn yr Hen Bobl: shell voids; 2. Early Bronze Age Collared Urn from Cefn Cwmwd: grog-rich; 3. Early Bronze Age Collared Urn from Cae Mickney: clast-rich, mafic igneous; 4. Early Neolithic vessel from Trefignath: biolith, estuarine diatom; 5. Grooved Ware from Llandygai: grog (g) with clast voids (v); 6. Grooved Ware from Trefignath: grog (g) with exotic granite clast (c). © David Jenkins.

that the pots could be used as coolers for liquids such as milk or blood (Darvill 2004). Several analysts have noticed the prominent occurrence of shiny white quartz fragments in prehistoric pottery, especially the Middle Neolithic Peterborough Ware of Wales and the Midlands. Such quartz has luminous properties and may have been regarded as a powerful magical component of these highly decorated pots. Some studies have been able to distinguish between the different sources used for the clay matrix and the inclusions contained within it. The pottery from the Trefignath Neolithic tomb on Anglesey contained inclusions from various different local outcrops of igneous rocks while the clays used derived from different marine, glacial and estuarine sources (fig. 13.1(4)).

Much of the information derived from thin-sectioning Late Bronze Age and Iron Age pottery was surveyed and interpreted by Morris (1994). She was able to define and contrast areas and periods where pottery was made locally – using clays from within a 7 km radius, and sometimes inclusions obtained from up to 10 km – with those where pottery contained inclusions from further distances. A few surprises have emerged. Petrological study of some of the pottery from the 20 years of excavation at Danebury, Hampshire, revealed that large proportions of the Early and Middle Iron Age pottery was not local. Thus the hill fort may not have been a major centre of ceramic production, although it could still have functioned as a redistribution centre for pottery and other commodities. In the Midlands some Iron Age pottery containing inclusions of igneous granodiorite from Charnwood Forest has been found widely along the Trent Valley (Knight et al. 2003). Further north, igneous and quartz inclusions from the Cleveland Dykes were used as distinctive inclusions within the Iron Age pottery at Thorpe Thewles, 8 km away (Swain 1987).

Other techniques involve the analysis of individual minerals or the chemical analysis of elements; these are usually applied in the investigation of fine and sandy fabrics. The main application of heavy mineral analysis has been in the analysis of the Durotrigian precursors of Black Burnished Ware manufactured around Poole Harbour in Dorset (see Woodward and Williams 2000). At Mucking, Essex, neutron activation analysis of pottery, briquetage and local clay samples showed that it was only the briquetage that had been made from local clays (Williams 1980), and a recent application of the technique of inductively coupled plasma spectroscopy (ICPS) has contributed to the identification of locally produced and non-local vessels on the Bronze Age site at Bestwall, Dorset.

How do fabrics change through time? An important analysis of such changes in Neolithic and earlier Bronze Age Wessex was undertaken by Cleal (1995), and consideration of Late Bronze Age and Iron Age ceramics was added by Woodward (2002a:106–109). Typical fabrics according to period were knapped flint waste in the Early Neolithic, shell (fig. 13.1(1)) or quartzite in the Middle Neolithic, grog and shell combinations in Grooved Ware, grog and sand or grog and flint in Beakers, grog in Early Bronze Age urns, and burnt flint in Middle Bronze Age vessels. Late Bronze Age fabrics also tend to have flint inclusions, but associated with much more sand. Early Iron Age fabrics include various complex recipes of calcite, shell, sand, quartzite and flint, while later in the Iron Age fabrics became much more standardised, with well-sorted inclusions, usually of fine shell or burnt flint.

Finally, we may ask, *why* do fabrics change through time? Some types of added materials perform better as opening agents, but these were not necessarily selected. Often the preferred types of inclusion were not of this type, and may have been acquired from distant sources. Research seems to indicate that inclusions added to potting clay recipes were deliberately selected for their particular colour, texture and general appearance, and that they may have possessed symbolic values. In addition to observations on the symbolic significance of the shiny and luminous quartz found in many Peterborough Ware pots, we may now also draw attention to the carefully selected hard and dark-hued rock fragments found in vessels belonging to various periods in north Wales (fig. 13.1(3)), in urns from the Lake District and from North Yorkshire, and the shells, both fossil and marine, apparent in

Grooved Ware. All of these may have derived from locations of particular ritual significance, from isolated boulders of mythical importance or from erratics forming part of stone monuments. Several researchers have noted that the rocks chosen were the same as those selected for the production of polished stone tools in the same periods, and it may be that some of the rock fragments introduced into the special pots derive from the intentional fragmentation of such artefacts: stone axe heads or battle axes in the Neolithic and Early Bronze Age periods, and querns from the later Bronze Age onwards (Woodward 2002a).

Another notable type of inclusion is bone. This has been found in Early Neolithic pottery at Hazleton, Gloucestershire, and at Briar Hill, Northamptonshire, in Beakers from Butterfield Down, Amesbury, Wiltshire, and in a Collared Urn from Balneaves, Angus (references in Morris and Woodward 2003:298; for further examples see Darvill 2004:198). At Hazleton the bone was probably non-human, but the calcined fragments at Balneaves may have been selected from a human cremation. Such inclusions may have derived from feasting debris or from the bodies of particular animals or persons. The incidence of grog in vessels (fig. 13.1(2)) has also been interpreted in symbolic terms. The grog may have been ground up from parts of known vessels which were of importance to the owner of the new vessel. Thus the new pot might contain fragments of the vessel previously belonging to a parent or ancestor. Thin-section analysis is beginning to identify many incidences of grog within grog (fig. 13.1(5) and (6)), suggesting that this process may have been sustained over several generations. Burnt (calcined) flint becomes common as inclusions from the Middle Bronze Age onwards. It may be no coincidence that this is the time when sedentary occupation and farming first developed. Burnt flint nodules would have been ubiquitous on settlement sites and may have symbolised the hearth, the home and the very essence of settled life. Flint inclusions in pottery often appear to have been sieved into size grades, and the use of sieves may again have been linked to their employment in the processing of grain.

Techniques of decoration

The incidence of decoration on pottery is not uniform through British prehistory. Some periods and areas are characterised by plain wares alone and many assemblages contain both decorated and plain wares. Furthermore some vessel types carry all-over decoration while other types have decorated zones limited to the upper parts of the pot, the shoulder or the rim only. Techniques of decoration fall into three main categories: incision, impression or applied features. Incised or grooved lines and patterns were formed using sharp or blunt instruments, probably of wood or bone, although flint tools were also employed. Linear and infilled designs often were executed using a bone comb with short or long rectangular teeth, or one with circular teeth giving a point-line effect. Especially in the earlier periods, decoration was built up using impressions from organic cords. There are three main types of cord impressions: whipped cord, in which a light thread has been wrapped more or less at right angles around a flexible cord; twisted cord, in which two strands are twisted together to form a single cord; and, less commonly, plaited cord, in which strands are plaited together to form a single cord. Also in the earlier period, impressions made with bones or shells are notable. Of particular interest are impressions made with the articular ends of the bones of birds and small mammals. Stamped impressions could be of circular or complex geometric form, and rows of regular stamped impressions were sometimes formed by the rouletting technique (in the Late Iron Age). The form of impressed decoration that occurs most widely throughout the periods is finger and thumb impressions, or patterns made with the human fingernail. Fingertip impressions usually occur in horizontal rows and sometimes were placed on cordons. The final category of decoration involves the application of extra clay embellishments, in the form of handles or lugs, vestigial handles, or cordons, which may be horizontal, vertical or curved. The different techniques of decoration are well illustrated in Gibson (2002) and Elsdon (1989).

An idea of the variation in the occurrence of these different techniques through time can be gained from figure 13.2. This table has been compiled using a variety of published assemblages, mainly from southern England; it is adapted from

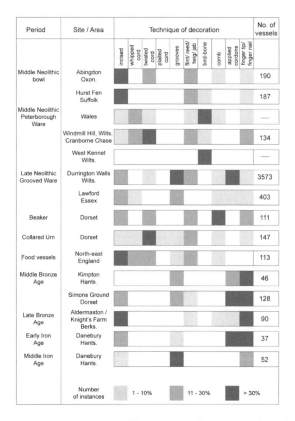

Figure 13.2   The percentage occurrence of decorative techniques in selected prehistoric pottery traditions (from Woodward 2002a). Drawing by Anne Leaver.

Woodward 2002a (fig. 11.2), where full references may be found. It is not intended to represent an exhaustive study, and the preparation of a wider-ranging analysis would no doubt reveal many further patterns. However, the preliminary study does highlight some significant trends and changes through time. Starting with two Middle Neolithic bowl assemblages, it can be seen that incised decoration was the most common, mainly forming simple linear motifs on the neck. Individual impressions formed by bones, reeds, flints or twigs were also significant. However, contemporary regional styles of pottery in the south-west were mainly plain, as in the earliest Neolithic phases. Slightly later in time, Peterborough Ware decoration is dominated by two techniques: cord impression and bird-bone designs. In the Late Neolithic, the pattern changes substantially. Grooved Ware displays no bird-bone decoration at all, and the two assemblages quantified contain low proportions of cord decoration, with the main techniques being grooving, associated at Durrington Walls with applied cordons, and at Lawford with individual circular impressions. In the Early Bronze Age, Beakers are dominated by comb-impressed designs, while incised and twisted cord patterns take second place. Twisted cord, however, is by far the most common technique used to adorn Collared Urns. In distinct contrast, Food Vessels are ornamented mainly with incised decoration and cord impressions, especially of the whipped variety.

In the Middle Bronze Age, thin-walled globular urns were decorated using incised linear and grooving techniques, while bucket urns were decorated only with cordons and rows of fingertip or fingernail impressions. In the Late Bronze Age, following the plain ware post-Deverel-Rimbury stage, pottery of the Decorated Style was dominated again by finger and thumb treatments, although some incised geometric designs occur. In the Iron Age, decoration varies greatly between regions, but the techniques seem to change through time in a fairly standard fashion. In general a high incidence of fingertip decoration and cordons in the Early Iron Age gives way to the use of grooving by the Middle Iron Age. In some regions sharply incised patterns were in vogue (e.g., Glastonbury Wares) while stamps were common in other areas (e.g., Malvernian "duck-stamped" wares and stamped designs of the East Midlands). Specific surface treatments also became more common; examples include the scored wares of the Midlands and burnishing, which tended to occur on fine bowl forms.

It seems unlikely that the different techniques of decoration were selected at random, and it may be that they also transmitted symbolic meanings or linkages. Many of the tools used to produce impressions, such as bones, twigs, reeds, straws or quills, may have been gathered in the wild, and thus symbolized particular places or ecological zones known to the users and makers, although flint and bone tools may have been made within a domestic context. The raw material for the cords used to make cord impressions may have derived from the lime tree or the hemp plant. Lime bast fibres were used particularly in the production of fish nets, and network was also used as slings for large containers (Clark 1952:44, 207, 227). Thus some cord decoration may have been skeuomorphic, mimicking slings, but it may be that the use of cord also provided a reference to other spheres of life such as the netting of fish, and boat-building. Sherratt (1987) has argued that the possible use of hemp fibres, from the *Cannabis sativa* plant, to execute the decoration on Beakers may have been a symbolic reference to the stimulating alcoholic or hallucinogenic contents of the vessels themselves.

In a similar way, consideration of bird-bone impressions invites allusion to the birds themselves. The bones of certain species were preferred – blackbird and magpie, carrion crow, rook, sparrow and jay (Liddell 1929). These birds tended to be black in colour, or displayed plumage of striking contrasts: the black-and-white magpie and the jay with its unusual flashes of pink and blue. It may be that such species were regarded as possessing magical or spiritual powers, and that such power could be transferred to pottery vessels by the use of their bones in the formation of decorative designs upon them. The use of combs may have been related symbolically to the use of similar tools in the process of weaving, or to the use of personal hair combs. Comb impressions were particularly common on Beaker pottery and may have been related, along with many of the geometric designs, to the patterns of woven cloth which are thought to have been in use at that time. A possible link to hair combs introduces a very personal and human note, which may also be connected with the growing idea of individuality. And reference to the human body brings us on to the final category of decorative techniques, the use of the human finger and thumb. This technique not only places the process within the domestic sphere but also emphasises an element of individual identification: the vessel is marked by a part of the body that made it.

Location of decoration

Studies of the location of decoration on pots, and of the structure of decorative schemes have traditionally focused on Beakers, and are neatly encapsulated in David Clarke's (1970:12, fig. II) list of zone styles for these vessels. Apart from their potential for typological and relative dating, the variety of schemes of zonation may have deeper meanings. Ian Hodder (1982:169, 175–6), in a provocative study of Neolithic pottery in the Netherlands, showed that a change from complex to more stylised decoration may have been linked to the legitimization of small social groupings in the earlier period, compared with a more unified and corporate social structure in the later period. In Britain, Richards and Thomas (1984) applied a similar type of analysis to the Late Neolithic Grooved Ware from Durrington Walls, Wiltshire. They were able to define distinctions between plain and decorated areas, and between bounded and unbounded zones of decoration (Richards and Thomas 1984:fig. 12.1). They suggested that a hierarchical system of six stages could be discerned, but the variation appeared to be spatial rather than chronological.

It is not clear why such studies of decorative schemes and complexity have not been undertaken in relation to other classes of highly decorated pottery in later periods. Two new examples may indicate the potential for these avenues of research. In the Middle Iron Age of southern England there is a particular class of decorated vessels called, by virtue of their shape, saucepan pots. Using a sample of complete or near complete vessels from Danebury, Hampshire (Cunliffe 1984:300–306;

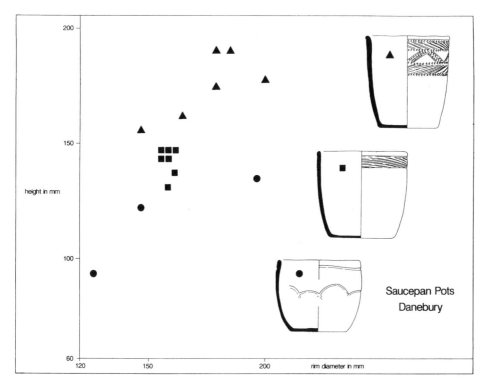

Figure 13.3 Size grouping of Middle Iron Age saucepan pot types at Danebury, Hampshire. Drawing by Nigel Dodds.

1991:298–299), a quantitative study of type and complexity of decoration showed that three main types could be discerned: a single simple geometric zone below the rim only; complex geometric zones often extending further down the pot; and a simple curvilinear arcade motif. When these three types are considered in relation to vessel size (fig. 13.3) it can be seen that the three types of decoration correlate with three size groupings: the vessels with complex geometric decoration are the largest; those with the arcade motif are the smallest; and the pots with one zone of simple geometric decoration are of medium size. The meaning of the observed variation is unclear, but it may be related to social differences on the site. It would be an interesting exercise to plot the findspots of the various saucepan pots across the excavated interior of the hill fort. Were the different types the work of individual potters? Did they occur in distinct activity areas? Do they indicate a gender division of labour? Might they represent and symbolise different kin groups occupying different zones within the hill fort?

A different kind of relationship can be deduced with the Late Bronze Age jars from All Cannings Cross, Wiltshire. The decorative motifs fall into two groups, one associated with jars of rounded profile, the other with vessels displaying sharp shoulders. Smooth-profiled jars carry floating chevrons, pendant triangles or lunate motifs, all filled with regular or random stab decoration (e.g., Cunnington 1923: pls. 29.1, 31.3). The sharp-shouldered vessels, however, are characterized by much simpler bounded linear, chevron or lozenge patterns (Cunnington 1923: pls. 31.6; 32.6; 35.6). A similar division in the types of decoration on jars can be discerned within the Late Bronze Age assemblage from Potterne, Wiltshire (Lawson 2000). Here again complex chevron patterns and strong curvilinear motifs occur on jars of rounded profile (Lawson 2000: fig. 51.42, 43; fig. 52.49), while the more sharply shouldered vessels have simpler horizontal zones of geometric decoration (Lawson 2000. fig. 53.59; fig. 54.62, 63). It is also interesting to note that jars decorated only with rows of fingertip impressions invariably have sharp shoulders. Again, the variations may signify different vessel functions, different potters or may be making reference to gender or age categories. Do the rounded jars with curvy decoration represent female characteristics? Or was it the shouldered jars with simple geometric or fingertip decoration that were connected more with food preparation and women, while the fancy rounded jars were used for ritual or feasting activities?

Shape, Size and Function

Systematic study of vessel sizes did not form part of traditional approaches to ceramic analysis. The reasons for this are difficult to assess, especially when it seems so obvious that pots were made to be used, and that vessel capacity, as well as shape, are likely to relate very closely to different potential functions. On the other hand, general functional interpretations have often been assumed, rather than dis- cussed, and have become embedded in many terminologies that are in use: e.g., Neolithic *bowls*, drinking *Beakers*, *Food* Vessels, Late Bronze Age *cups*, Iron Age *jars* and, in the Final Iron Age, *platters*. Direct evidence of vessel use can survive as external sooting on cooking vessels or as burnt food residues, and animal fats and plant waxes absorbed by the pottery can now be analysed. The potential of these sources of study is developing rapidly (e.g., Copley et al. 2005).

One pioneering attempt to consider ceramic assemblages in a systematic way was David Clarke's division of Beaker pottery into three functional categories: fine wares, everyday wares and heavy-duty wares. When researching the Middle Bronze Age pottery of southern England in the early 1970s I was able to apply this simple scheme to the globular and bucket urns for Deverel-Rimbury settlements and cem- eteries (Ellison 1981). However, the first person to consider vessel size in quan- titative terms was Julian Thomas, who charted the varying capacities of selected Neolithic and Beaker pottery in 1991 (Thomas 1999). Admittedly, the number of complete profiles available for volume measurements to be made was rather small, but some interesting patterns could be discerned.

One reason for the lack of similar studies of vessel capacity in relation to later prehistoric pottery types may be the relative absence of surviving whole pots or complete vessel profiles. Most Late Bronze Age and Iron Age pottery derives from settlement sites rather than graves, and is usually recovered as sherd material. In order to tackle this problem the author experimented with the idea of using rim

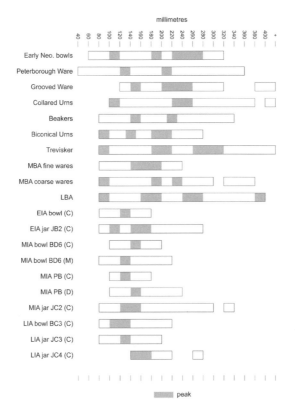

Figure 13.4   The size ranges of vessel rim diameters in selected prehistoric pottery traditions. C = Cadbury, M = Meare East, D = Danebury, BD6 = Glastonbury Ware, PB = saucepan pots. *Sources*: Biconical Urns, Trevisker and Late Bronze Age (Woodward 1990); Grooved Ware, Collared Urns, Middle Bronze Age fine and coarse wares of Avon/Stour Valleys style (Woodward 1995:fig. 17.3); Cadbury Castle, Somerset, and Iron Age fine wares (Woodward 1997:figs. 4.1 and 4.2); Neolithic bowls, Carn Brea, Cornwall (Smith 1981); Peterborough Ware (Barclay 2002:fig. 9.2); Beakers: East Anglia (Healy 1995:fig. 15.4). Drawing by Anne Leaver.

diameter as a measure of vessel size. Statistical study of a series of Iron Age pots suggested that for the relatively simple pot forms involved, such a measure could indeed provide a good indication of relative vessel size (Woodward 1997:28–29). Starting from the key ceramic sequence at Brean Down, Somerset, rim diameter ranges were measured for Biconical Urns, Trevisker pottery and Late Bronze Age jars and bowls, and later this approach was extended to detailed study of Iron Age vessel sizes too. This analysis considered the size ranges of fine and coarse wares changing through time, at Cadbury Castle, Somerset, as well as a comparison of the size ranges of different classes of fine wares across southern England. A summary of findings from these studies, augmented with data concerning earlier Neolithic bowls, Peterborough Ware and Beakers is presented in figure 13.4.

The earliest pottery assemblages of the Early and Middle Neolithic were dominated by various forms of bowl. The size peaks indicated in figure 13.4 show that most of the bowls were quite large, but smaller bowls and a series of small cups were also significant. Middle Neolithic Peterborough Ware bowls were all decorated; they show a wide diameter range but most were small or medium in size. Late Neolithic Grooved Ware pots tended to be much larger. Again most were small to medium in size but two peaks of occurrence were at larger levels than those observed for Peterborough Ware. Interestingly, although the overall range of diameter for Beakers was more restricted, the preferred diameters were similar to those within the Peterborough Ware and Grooved Ware groups. However, the capacities would have been smaller due to the greater height-to-width ratios which relate to Beaker pottery. Early Bronze Age Collared Urns show a very wide size range and, for the first time, a peak of very small vessels is present. Barclay (2002:fig. 9.3b) has shown that small Collared Urns such as these often occur with secondary cremations in round barrows. Towards the end of the Early Bronze Age, Biconical Urns and Trevisker pots were the first groups of pottery since the earlier Neolithic to show a tripartite pattern of vessel size. This is probably linked to the fact that such pottery is found on occupation sites as well as in burial contexts, although all types seem to have been found in both domestic and funerary assemblages.

Middle Bronze Age pottery also occurs in both context types: the settlements and urn cemeteries of the Deverel-Rimbury tradition. But now, for the first time, fine wares can clearly be distinguished from coarse wares, the thin-walled globular urns decorated with incised or grooved decoration contrasting markedly with bucket urns which are embellished and strengthened with fingertip-impressed cordons. Rim diameter ranges for one style of such pottery (the Avon/Stour Valley style of southern Hampshire and east Dorset) show that fine globular urns possessed a restricted range compared with coarse bucket urns. Furthermore the bucket urns fall into three main size groups, presumably related to different serving, cooking and storage functions. The far-reaching changes in ceramic associations that took place in the Late Bronze Age were first discussed in detail by Barrett (1980) and were related to developments in the serving and eating of food and drink. In terms of vessel size, this change is associated with the first occurrence of fourfold size groupings according to rim diameter, and a very large overall range of vessel sizes. As in the earlier Neolithic, small cups, probably intended for use as personal drinking vessels, form a significant component of the assemblages.

The wide-ranging variety of vessel forms – open bowls, closed bowls and many shapes of jar – continued into the Iron Age. However, the smallest form, the cup, and the very largest jar forms did not. The size ranges of Iron Age pottery are illustrated by individual plots of the ranges and peaks for various classes of Early and Middle Iron Age vessel from South Cadbury, Meare East (both Somerset) and Danebury, Hampshire. Most of the size ranges show a unimodal distribution with only one peak, and some of the ranges are quite restricted. This applies particularly to the Early and Middle Iron Age fine wares from South Cadbury: EIA bowls, MIA Glastonbury Ware bowls (BD6) and the MIA saucepan pots (PB).

Overall it is possible to define, through study of figure 13.4, several obvious trends. First, there is a very distinct tendency for vessels to become smaller in size through time. This trend develops suddenly at the beginning of the Iron Age and may signify a major change in the usage of pottery. Second, there is a strong tendency towards the development of different contemporary vessel types (defined by size, shape and decoration) within single domestic or funerary assemblages, and this trend takes off from the Middle Bronze Age. This change coincides with the first widespread establishment of settled farmsteads and field systems (at least in southern Britain), and may relate to the definition of age sets and the division of labour within the new sedentary social environment, as well as to changes in food preparation and cooking techniques associated with a greater dependence on cereals and other food crops. The final trend is the move towards marked standardization of specific vessel types, in terms of both style and size. This trend occurs strongly from the Early Iron Age onwards, as noted above.

By the Late Iron Age, the simple mathematical correlation between rim diameter and vessel size had broken down. This is because the range of vessel forms and shapes suddenly became highly diversified, due to contacts with the Continent and a significant change in culinary techniques and eating habits. This change has been dramatically demonstrated and discussed by Hill (2002:figs. 13.1, 13.2, 13.4). The new types included beakers, cups, flasks, amphorae, flagons and platters, alongside a wide range of cooking and storage jars and new forms for grinding foodstuffs (mortaria). While basic earlier Iron Age bowls and jars had been used mainly for the preparation of carbohydrate-rich stews, gruel or porridge, Late Iron Age diet was diversified by the inclusion of roast meats (pork and chicken), steamed food and fish, all displayed and consumed at table on large flat plates, and accompanied by drinks – beer or wine – served in special cups from decorative flasks and jugs (Hill 2002:148–150). The strong social significance of these table wares is confirmed by the placing of large groups of such material in the graves of prominent individuals in East Anglia. Hill argues that these changes in the preparation and consumption of food and drink predated, and provided the incentive for, the adoption of the potter's wheel, a development which may also have involved a change from the predominance of women to that of men in the production of pottery (at least in eastern England). However, the new culinary fashions were not adopted wholesale. Even in areas as close to East Anglia as the Midlands, the take-up of new vessel forms was highly selective – the simple wheel-turned cordoned bowls that do have a wide distribution are those which most closely imitate the pre-existing Iron Age bowls and jars; and it seems likely that the new bowls were used in the production of the old-style stews and porridge rather than of outlandish dishes dressed with olive oil or fish sauce (Hill 2002:155–158).

Feasting pots or everyday pots?

It has been assumed that prehistoric pots were made primarily for domestic use, as storage, cooking or serving containers, or to receive or accompany the bones or bodies of the recent dead. However, in many periods of prehistory pottery comes from contexts which are decidedly non-domestic in nature. Large assemblages tend to derive from deliberate deposits in pits, dating from the Early Neolithic right

Figure 13.5   A Late Bronze Age ceramic feasting set from Broom, Warwickshire (after Stuart Palmer). Drawing by Candida Stevens. © Birmingham and Warwickshire Archaeological Society.

through to the Late Bronze Age, or from communal monuments such as cause-wayed enclosures and henges. Many of these assemblages can be interpreted as the remains of feasting on a large scale. In an Early Neolithic pit at Coneybury, Wilt-shire, a set of vessels included one very large carinated pot with a capacity of 7 litres; this was associated with bones from animals consumed at a major summer-time feast (Cleal 1990). The Grooved Ware vessels from Durrington Walls, highly decorated and some of them immense in size, were probably designed to store large quantities of drink; and at Bestwall, Dorset, in the Middle Bronze Age, pottery from feasting episodes was associated with a burnt mound, following the closing down of a roundhouse (Ladle and Woodward 2003). The first of a series of ceramic "feasting sets" recognised from Late Bronze Age contexts was that found at Broom, Warwickshire (fig. 13.5). This was found in a pit next to a pyre and a scatter of bronze cauldron fragments.

It could be argued that much, if not all, pottery before the Iron Age was produced for special, non-domestic purposes: either for deposition in graves or as rare and exotic containers for special food and drink prepared for conspicuous consumption at feasts, festivals or other communal social events (Woodward 2000). One clue to the identification of such assemblages, as we have seen, is the presence of rare, usually open-rimmed, vessels of exceptionally large capacity. Returning to the diagram of changing vessel size ranges through time (fig. 13.4), it can readily be seen that such large vessels occur up until the Late Bronze Age. Although it can be shown that assemblages of true domestic nature first occurred in the Middle Bronze Age (coincident with the development of settled life and agriculture), and that the domestic repertoire was diversified in the Late Bronze Age (Barrett 1980), it is not until the full Iron Age that the "feasting set" ceramic mentality seems to have broken down. No doubt some Early and Middle Iron Age pots may have been used in feasts or rituals, but the techniques to recognise them have yet to be devised. Later on the Romanised wine-feasting sets from Late Iron Age Essex and Hertford-shire made a remarkable impact, but the implied changes in culinary techniques and table manners, as we have already seen, were by no means universally adopted.

The Social Dimension

How can the analysis of pottery help us to identify the actual people who made and used ceramic vessels in prehistory? As Gibson (2002:50) observed: "we are left with abundant artefacts but only the briefest glimpses of the people responsible for them." Prior to the Late Iron Age all prehistoric pottery was made at the household level, and probably by women. There is little evidence for the existence of specialist potters, and the possible products of a single hand are rare. Occasionally vessel size can be linked to age. A child buried at Doune, Perth and Kinross, was accompanied by a small Food Vessel and a miniature battle axe (McLaren 2004), and within some Middle Bronze Age urn cemeteries in the East Midlands the size of urn increased in relation to the age of the individual cremated (Allen et al. 1987). But such patterns are rarely evident elsewhere.

Another way in which pots related to individual people, or families, was through their employment as relics and heirlooms. We have already seen that the use of grog may have enabled the symbolic incorporation of ancestral pot, and the power of their owners, into the fabric of new vessels. Sherds used to make such special grog may have been obtained from funerary vessels, the existence of which can be investigated by looking for vessels in graves that were inserted in an incomplete state. I first noticed this phenomenon when studying two partial Beakers which had been placed over a hoard of gold armlets on the margin of a round barrow at Lockington, Leicestershire, and many other instances have since been noticed (Woodward 2002b). The existence of special pots that had long use lives, and eventually functioned as heirlooms, is suggested by some vessels with repairs. An excellent example is the worn Armorican vase found in a round barrow at Gallibury, Isle of Wight. The original handle had become broken off in antiquity and a pierced hole provided to support a new, presumably organic, replacement (Tomalin 1988:fig. 5).

Studies of the spatial distribution of pottery can provide clues to systems of social and economic organization and past human behaviour at several geographical scales. Some of the important results of such studies within individual sites have been summarised by Pollard (2002) and Woodward (2002c). They include the varying distribution of Grooved Ware bearing different styles of decoration at

Durrington Walls; conclusions concerning the nature of social organisation in the Middle Bronze Age derived from study of the distribution of pottery and other artefacts within pairs of roundhouses; the relation of the distribution of pottery in Iron Age roundhouses to cosmology and the daily round; and the deliberate and symbolic placing of pottery deposits within ditch terminals or other significant locations within settlement enclosures. At the regional scale, study of the distributions of different pottery styles can indicate the possible size of ethnic groupings, which appear to become more compact through time. By the Iron Age, small territories in Sussex may be signalled by the existence of different styles of decoration on saucepan pots (Hamilton 2002:fig. 5.7). Another major use of pottery distributions has been in the study and analysis of systems of trade and exchange, which has been studied extensively by Morris (1994), who has also concentrated on comparing networks of pottery exchange with the dispersal of salt contained in briquetage storage vessels.

Conclusion

In many areas of Britain a firm pattern of pottery record and associated chronology is now in place; however, it is important to attempt to fill gaps, especially in northern England. A systematic method of record is now in widespread use, but care needs to be taken not to concentrate too much on the definition of fabrics. There is a tendency to define too many fabric types per site. The approach should in fact be simple, related to the theoretical questions that are going to be posed, and the descriptions should be backed up by selective petrological analysis wherever possible. Pottery reports should concentrate on the nature of deposits and context within the site, as well as on fabric, form, decoration and dating. Pottery evidence should also be considered against other classes of artefacts. There is no room for blinkered recording by rote. The relevant questions of interpretation will never be answered unless they are framed at the outset. The major aim must be to use studies of pottery technology to further the study of prehistoric people themselves, throughout their pattern of life: everyday routine and ritual, food preparation and cooking, eating and drinking, production and exchange, feasting and death. The very close connection between people, their physical bodies and their pots is poignantly evoked by the terms used to describe such vessels: mouth, lip, lug, shoulder, waist, belly, body and foot. Such terms occur in ethnographic contexts around the world; no doubt they were current in British prehistory also.

REFERENCES

Abercromby, J., 1912 A Study of the Bronze Age Pottery of Great Britain and Ireland and its Associated Grave Goods. Oxford: Clarendon Press.
Allen, C. S. M., M. Harman and H. Wheeler, 1987 Bronze Age cremation cemeteries in the East Midlands. Proceedings of the Prehistoric Society 53:187–221.

Barclay, A., 2002 Ceramic lives. *In* Prehistoric Britain: the ceramic basis. A. Woodward and J. D. Hill, eds. pp. 85–95. Oxford: Oxbow Books.

Barrett, J. C., 1980 The pottery of the later Bronze Age in lowland England. Proceedings of the Prehistoric Society 46:297–320.

——P. W. M. Freeman and A. Woodward, 2000 Cadbury Castle, Somerset: the later prehistoric and early historic archaeology. London: English Heritage.

Clark, J. G. D., 1952 Prehistoric Europe: the economic basis. London: Methuen.

Clarke, D. L., 1970 Beaker Pottery of Great Britain and Ireland. Cambridge: Cambridge University Press.

Cleal, R. M. J., 1990 The prehistoric pottery (Coneybury Anomaly). *In* The Stonehenge Environs Project. J. Richards. pp. 45–57. London: English Heritage.

——1995 Pottery fabrics in Wessex in the fourth to second millennia BC. *In* "Unbaked Urns of Rudely Shape": essays on British and Irish pottery for Ian Longworth. I. Kinnes and G. Varndell, eds. pp. 185–194. Oxford: Oxbow Books.

Copley, M. S., R. Berstan, S. N. Dudd, S. Aillaud, A. J. Mukherjee, V. Straker, S. Payne and R. P. Evershed, 2005 Processing of milk products in pottery vessels through British prehistory. Antiquity 79:895–908.

Cotton, J., and R. Johnson, 2004 Two decorated Peterborough bowls from the Thames at Mortlake and their London context. *In* Towards a New Stone Age: aspects of the Neolithic in south-east England. J. Cotton and D. Field, eds. pp. 128–147. London: Council for British Archaeology.

Cunliffe, B. W., 1974 Iron Age Communities in Britain. London: Routledge and Kegan Paul.

——1984 Danebury: an Iron Age hillfort in Hampshire, vol. 2: The Excavations, 1969–1978: the finds. London: Council for British Archaeology.

——1991 Danebury: an Iron Age hillfort in Hampshire, vol. 5: The Excavations, 1979–1988: the finds. London: Council for British Archaeology.

Cunnington, M. E., 1923 The Early Iron Age Inhabited Site at All Cannings Cross Farm, Wiltshire. Devizes: Simpson.

——1929 Woodhenge. Devizes: Simpson.

Darvill, T., 2004 Soft-rock and organic tempering in British Neolithic pottery. *In* Monuments and Material Culture. R. Cleal and J. Pollard, eds. pp. 193–206. East Knoyle: Hobnob Press.

Ellison, A., 1975 Pottery and Settlements of the Later Bronze Age in Southern England. PhD thesis, University of Cambridge.

——1980a Deverel-Rimbury urn cemeteries: the evidence for social organisation. *In* Settlement and Society in the British Later Bronze Age. J. Barrett and R. Bradley, eds. pp. 115–126. Oxford: British Archaeological Reports.

——1980b Settlements and regional exchange: a case study. *In* Settlement and Society in the British Later Bronze Age. J. Barrett and R. Bradley, eds. pp. 127–140. Oxford: British Archaeological Reports.

——1981 Towards a socio-economic model for the Middle Bronze Age in southern England. *In* Pattern of the Past: studies in honour of David Clarke. I. Hodder, G. Isaac and N. Hammond, eds. pp. 413–438. Cambridge: Cambridge University Press.

Elsdon, S. M., 1989 Later Prehistoric Pottery in England and Wales. Princes Risborough: Shire Publications.

Gibson, A. M., 1982 British Beaker Domestic Sites: a study of the domestic pottery of the late third and early second millennia BC in the British Isles. Oxford: British Archaeological Reports.

——2002 Prehistoric Pottery in Britain and Ireland. Stroud: Tempus.

——and I. Kinnes, 1997 On the urns of a dilemma: radiocarbon and the Peterborough problem. Oxford Journal of Archaeology 16(1):65–72.

Hamilton, S., 2002 Between ritual and routine: interpreting British prehistoric pottery production and distribution. In Prehistoric Britain: the ceramic basis. A. Woodward and J. D. Hill, eds. pp. 38–53. Oxford: Oxbow Books.

Hawkes, C., 1959 The A B C of the British Iron Age. Antiquity 33:170–182.

Healy, F., 1995 Pots, pits and peat: ceramics and settlement in East Anglia. In "Unbaked Urns of Rudely Shape": essays on British and Irish pottery for Ian Longworth. I. Kinnes and G. Varndell, eds. pp. 173–184. Oxford: Oxbow Books.

Hill, J. D., 2002 Just about the potter's wheel? Using, making and depositing Middle and Later Iron Age pots in East Anglia. In Prehistoric Britain: the ceramic basis. A. Woodward and J. D. Hill, eds. pp. 143–160. Oxford: Oxbow Books.

Hodder, I., 1982 Sequences of structural change in the Dutch Neolithic. In Symbolic and Structural Archaeology. I. Hodder, ed. pp. 162–177. Cambridge: Cambridge University Press.

Kinnes, I., and G. Varndell, eds., 1995 "Unbaked Urns of Rudely Shape": essays on British and Irish Pottery for Ian Longworth. Oxford: Oxbow Books.

Knight, D., P. Marsden and J. Carney, 2003 Local or non-local? Prehistoric granodiorite-tempered pottery in the East Midlands. In Prehistoric Pottery, People, Pattern and Purpose. A. Gibson, ed. pp. 111–125. Oxford: British Archaeological Reports.

Ladle, L., and A. Woodward, 2003 A Middle Bronze Age house and burnt mound at Bestwall, Wareham, Dorset: an interim report. Proceedings of the Prehistoric Society 69:265–277.

Lawson, A. J., 2000 Potterne 1982–5: animal husbandry in later prehistoric Wiltshire. Salisbury: Wessex Archaeology.

Liddell, D., 1929 New light on an old problem. Antiquity 3:283–291.

——1935 Excavations at Hembury fort, Devon. Proceedings of the Devon Archaeological and Exploration Society 2:135.

Longworth, I. H., 1984 Collared Urns of the Bronze Age in Great Britain and Ireland. Cambridge: Cambridge University Press.

McLaren, D., 2004 An important child's burial from Doune, Perth and Kinross, Scotland. In From Sickles to Circles: Britain and Ireland at the time of Stonehenge. A. Gibson and A. Sheridan, eds. pp. 289–303. Stroud: Tempus.

Morris, E. L., 1994 Production and distribution of pottery and salt in Iron Age Britain: a review. Proceedings of the Prehistoric Society 32:336–379.

——and A. Woodward, 2003 Ceramic petrology and prehistoric pottery in the UK. Proceedings of the Prehistoric Society 69:279–303.

Needham, S., 2005 Transforming Beaker culture in north-west Europe: processes of fusion and fission. Proceedings of the Prehistoric Society 71:171–217.

Peacock, D. P. S., 1968 A petrological study of certain Iron Age pottery from western England. Proceedings of the Prehistoric Society 34:414–427.

——1969a Neolithic pottery production in Cornwall. Antiquity 49:145–149.

——1969b A contribution to the study of Glastonbury ware from south-western England. Antiquaries Journal 49:41–61.

Pollard, J., 2002 The nature of archaeological deposits and finds assemblages. In Prehistoric Britain: the ceramic basis. A. Woodward and J. D. Hill, eds. pp. 22–33. Oxford: Oxbow Books.

Prehistoric Ceramics Research Group, 1997 The Study of Later Prehistoric Pottery: general policies and guidelines for analysis and publication. Salisbury: Prehistoric Ceramics Research Group.

Richards, C., and J. Thomas, 1984 Ritual activity and structured deposition in later Neolithic Wessex. *In* Neolithic Studies: a review of some current research. R. Bradley and J. Gardiner, eds. pp. 189–218. Oxford: British Archaeological Reports.

Sheridan, A., 2003 New dates from Scottish Bronze Age cinerary urns: results from the National Museums of Scotland Dating Cremated Bones Project. *In* Prehistoric Pottery: people, pattern and purpose. A. Gibson ed. pp. 201–226. Oxford: British Archaeological Reports.

Sherratt, A. G., 1987 Cups that cheered. *In* Bell-Beakers of the Western Mediterranean. W. H. Waldren and R. C. Kennard, eds. pp. 81–114. Oxford: British Archaeological Reports.

Smith, I. F., 1965 Windmill Hill and Avebury: excavations by Alexander Keiller 1925–1939. Oxford: Clarendon Press.

——1981 Neolithic pottery. *In* Excavations at Carn Brea, Illogan, Cornwall, 1970–73. R. J. Mercer. pp. 161–185. Cornish Archaeology 20:1–204.

Swain, H. P., 1987 The Iron Age pottery. *In* The Excavation of an Iron Age Settlement at Thorpe Thewles, Cleveland, 1980–1982. D. H. Heslop. pp. 57–71. London: Council for British Archaeology.

Thomas, J., 1999 Understanding the Neolithic. London: Routledge.

Tomalin, D. J., 1988 Armorican Vases à Anse and their occurrence in southern Britain. Proceedings of the Prehistoric Society 54:203–221.

Williams, D., 1980 Petrological Examination of Late Bronze Age/Early Iron Age Pottery from Mucking, Essex. London: Ancient Monuments Laboratory Report 3077.

Willis, S., 2002 A date with the past: Late Bronze and Iron Age pottery and chronology. *In* Prehistoric Britain: the ceramic basis. A. Woodward and J. D. Hill, eds. pp. 4–21. Oxford: Oxbow Books.

Woodward, A., 1990 The Bronze Age pottery. *In* Brean Down Excavations 1983–1987. M. Bell. pp. 121–145. London: English Heritage.

——1995 Vessel size and social identity in the Bronze Age of southern Britain. *In* "Unbaked Urns of Rudely Shape": essays on British and Irish pottery for Ian Longworth. I. Kinnes and G. Varndell, eds. pp. 195–202. Oxford: Oxbow Books.

——1997 Size and style: an alternative study of some Iron Age pottery in southern England. *In* Reconstructing Iron Age Societies. C. Haselgrove and A. Gwilt, eds. pp. 26–35. Oxford: Oxbow Books.

——2000 When did pots become domestic? Special pots and everyday pots in British prehistory. Medieval Ceramics 22–23:3–10.

——2002a Inclusions, impressions and interpretation. *In* Prehistoric Britain: the ceramic basis. A. Woodward and J. D. Hill, eds. pp. 106–118. Oxford: Oxbow Books.

——2002b Beads and Beakers: heirlooms and relics in the British Early Bronze Age. Antiquity 76:1040–1047.

——2002c Sherds in space: pottery and the analysis of site organisation. *In* Prehistoric Britain: the ceramic basis. A. Woodward and J. D. Hill, eds. pp. 62–74. Oxford: Oxbow Books.

——and J. D. Hill, eds., 2002 Prehistoric Britain: the ceramic basis. Oxford: Oxbow Books.

——and D. Williams, 2000 Pottery production. *In* Cadbury Castle, Somerset: the later prehistoric and early historic archaeology. J. Barrett, P. W. M. Freeman and A. Woodward. pp. 259–261. London: English Heritage.

14

Exchange, Object Biographies and the Shaping of Identities, 10,000–1000 B.C.

Stuart Needham

Introduction

Exchange lies at the heart of human existence. In its broadest sense exchange involves the two-directional transmission of things, people, ideas or services. Transmissions (both two-way and uni-directional taken together) largely explain the development of culture and the interactions between cultures. In other words, they are key to the shaping of history. Transmissions of these kinds do not occur in the animal kingdom, where the only real forms of transmission are either genetic in the course of biological reproduction or the transfer of know-how by example. Exchange is thus an effective marker of culture in general and its particular modes are characterising features of particular cultural realms. Lévi-Strauss (1987:47) went so far as to suggest that society is founded on exchange and exists only through the existence of exchange, and Thomas's (1991:7) position is similar ("exchange relations seem to be the substance of social life"), but for Godelier (1999:35) these philosophies are too extreme.

Yet exchange is also one of the great intangibles of the archaeological record. Almost by definition, exchange functions within the systemic sphere such that readable archaeological outputs (the results of deliberate and accidental deposition) occur only secondarily as a result of subsequent actions taken for different reasons than the act of exchange itself. There can be important exceptions to this generalisation, but otherwise the form and purpose of exchange are matters for inference from archaeological by-products and plausible ethnographic analogy. Conversely, the patterns of material displacement observed in the archaeological record may be the products of many and complex mechanisms of displacement, only some of which would come under the broad heading of exchange. Thus we need the distinction between *interpreted exchange* and *observed displacement* (Needham 1993; see also the excellent critical historical review by Bradley and Edmonds 1993:5–17).

Faced with this predicament, studies of exchange can be amongst the most schizophrenic in archaeology: sometimes taking the observed archaeological fall-out all too literally without regard to systemic and in-ground formation processes or recovery biases; at other times starting from a theoretical stance drawn from external analogy without adequate consideration of the relationship to that observed fall-out. Whatever past failings there may have been, however, there can be no doubt that reconciling facts with theories in this field is one of the great challenges in archaeological interpretation.

The scope for a discussion of exchange must go beyond that of material goods (e.g., Renfrew 1993:6; Bradley and Edmonds 1993), since formal exchange can involve any combination of material (either raw or processed), people, ideas (to include associated beliefs, technical know-how, etc.) and services (particularly labour and access). We should not divorce material exchanges from the other forms simply because the former involves actual objects which often subsequently enter archaeological contexts, while the latter can be discerned only as effects on those objects. This would be an artificial division in terms of understanding human histories.

One of the big and persistent aggregate effects of multiple exchange transactions is the diffusion of elements of cultural values over large distances or throughout large areas. Diffusion is thus the grand-scale picture for a defined phenomenon and is constituted of innumerable individual interactions taking place during the lifetimes of innumerable people and material objects. Many aspects of the culture histories that archaeologists try to understand therefore depend upon an appreciation of the modes, causes and reasons for diffusions. Traditionally, such enquiry frequently sought the ultimate source of a given cultural entity, but increasingly the relevance of this has been questioned in relation to cultural contexts distanced in time and/or space from that origin, for it is now realised that specific meanings often mutate as material forms cross cultural or contextual boundaries (e.g., Appadurai 1986; Barrett 1987; Thomas 1991:21). This is where *contextual archaeology* comes to play its vital part in building from the local and regional situation an empirical understanding of the role or roles of a form irrespective of any it held earlier in the diffusion chain. For Hodder "a fully contextual approach to exchange must incorporate the symbolism of the objects exchanged" (1982:209).

Archaeology has long appreciated that valuable insights can come from studying the life histories of artefacts prior to their burial or incorporation in archaeological deposits. However, it was only from the 1980s that such pathways or *biographies* began to assume a central and indispensable place in the reconstruction of past societies. Particularly seminal was Kopytoff's 1986 article relating to individual objects, but another side to this issue was tackled by Schiffer (notably 1987) and others, who began to use gross patterns in the taphonomy of artefacts within assemblages to evaluate earlier life histories. The purpose of the latter approach was to better comprehend site formation processes, rather than document individual object histories per se. Both approaches, however, focused more attention on the systemic sphere of object circulation prior to the more limited circumstances by which material came to be finally incorporated in archaeological deposits.

The biographies of artefacts have particular poignancy when it appears that they had crossed major temporal, social or regional boundaries as a result of exchange. Glamorous though they may be in interpretative terms, however, it should not be assumed that special or exceptional cases necessarily had the greatest effect on historical sequences. The habitual, local-scale exchanges that would be endemic but generally more difficult to discern as individual events archaeologically should not be overlooked in the search for causative links. For example, economic specialisation resulting in the production of wool in one region and not a neighbouring one, as is sometimes proposed for later Bronze Age economies (Bradley et al. 1980:288), might constitute the basis of exchange between the two groups but be tangible only through different distributions of spinning equipment or exchanged objects of other kinds.

Models in Exchange and Dissemination: Historical Perspectives

The small-scale societies of prehistoric Britain existed in a pre-monetary environment and there would have been no comprehension of a profit motive in the capitalist or mercantile sense (Bradley and Edmonds 1993). For the period concerned we can safely assume a situation comparable to that summarized elegantly by Mauss (1970:69–73): the struggle for wealth had no basis in the early phases of the evolution of human societies because the "individual" accumulation of wealth was not an accepted principle of economic and social existence. This follows from an understanding that material goods and land were simply granted to people *for use* by beings of the otherworld (gods, spirits, ancestors, etc.) and, moreover, that the possession (rather than ownership) of a disproportionate share of wealth generally came with obligations to use or dispense it for the broader benefit of all the community (Godelier 1999:30, 121–122, 185–186).

Although it came to be recognised by prehistoric communities that certain materials could be stockpiled as wealth, the ability to do so would have been exploited to improve the prospect of succeeding in key ventures that were relevant to the social values of the time and the foreseeable future. A capacity to accumulate such things as gold or certain kinds of sea shells at a greater rate than one's neighbours (supposing they were universally sought after) gave one greater exchange power for other goods or marriage partners, the potential for enhanced largesse and fame through *noble expenditures* and the potential for greater spiritual elevation through gifts to the gods. The same could apply to any other valued goods, such as cattle or salt in many early societies, but different potentials and limitations arise from the accumulation of durables, perishables and livestock. For example, the conversion of plant foods into livestock can provide food over a longer time scale because of the longer life cycle of the animals (Halstead and O'Shea 1982:92).

Overall, therefore, the purpose of accumulating valuables would have been to secure an advantage in the not-distant future over one's current circumstance and over rival social groups, or at least to maintain one's existing position. Any notion of acting to secure provision for future generations would have been obstructed by the lack of fixed economic institutions and mechanisms; hence there could be no guarantee that accumulated valuables would in themselves have given long-term benefit to lineal descendants. Instead, the obvious connections would have been more immediate: that "success" in the world came from using accumulated stuff to extract obligations from competing social groups or to keep peace with the otherworld forces, and that these practices best ensured the future for descendants.

Regarding the processes of exchange responsible for observed displacement, much attention has been given to the contrasting interpretations that it resulted from one transaction by *directional trade*, or from several unconnected transactions – *down-the-line*. In reality, there is the likelihood that a much more complicated spectrum would have existed, even after discounting the complex variations in the organisation of exchange envisaged for more developed state formations (Renfrew 1975; Renfrew and Bahn 1996:335–368). Moreover, in the absence of economic motives, directional trade is likely to have related to the formation of specific elite alliances (peer–polity interaction) or cosmologically driven acquisition (see further below). Meanwhile, ethnographic examples teach us that "down-the-line" does not have to equate with an absence of connection between the individual links of the exchange chain (Godelier 1999).

A methodology once seen to be promising for archaeology involved the quantitative analysis of the spatial patterns found for a given object type of material; attempts were then made to correlate patterns with exchange models extrapolated from ethnographic evidence. This approach was highly refined in the 1970s and 1980s before its weaknesses as an explanatory mechanism (rather than just an enhanced description of occurrence) began to be appreciated (Bradley and Edmonds 1993:5–17). In fact, those authors concluded that "so many questions have arisen that we must question the assumption that the refinement of formal methods of analysis can ever provide a satisfactory 'framework for measuring exchange'" (Bradley and Edmonds 1993:10).

To aid further discussion, it is helpful to return to function and break it down into possible *elemental motives* for exchange beyond the kin group in a pre-commercial environment (note: this is quite different from Renfrew's (1993:10–11) list of reasons for why people might *travel*):

1   to obtain raw materials not available locally or within the kin group;
2   to obtain specific goods not available locally or within the kin group;
3   to subsist and survive in times of unusual need (e.g., famine);
4   to obtain marriage partners from outside the kin group;
5   to gain a competitive advantage through the materials and goods procured;
6   to gain competitive advantage by creating indebtedness;
7   to cultivate harmonious relations, create formal alliances and extend kinship ties;
8   to satisfy the curious human spirit, or engage with those beyond the familiar territory;
9   to achieve spiritual betterment through procurement of elements from the outer cosmos and sacred places;
10   to spread a particular world-view.

Motives 1–3 are economic, or might better be described as *fundamental* to avoid conjuring up modern-style economies. Elemental motive 3 not only comes into play at times of shortage per se; it may also be the basis for pre-emptive exchange strategies of the kind described by Halstead and O'Shea (1982) as *social storage*; in good years food surplus is exchanged for "tokens" (notably prestige items) that can at a later time of need be exchanged back for food. Motive 4 is also fundamental in the sense of being necessary to maintain healthy reproduction of the social group.

Motives 5–7 are what we might term the social reasons for exchange, while 8–10 relate more to the spirituality and self-belief inherent in human beings. But the main point about exchange in early and ethnographic societies is that it was rarely engaged in for just one of the above reasons; they were often intertwined in complex ways (Helms 1988).

Gift-giving (e.g., Mauss 1970; Gregory 1982; Godelier 1999) frequently embodies motives 6 and 7 simultaneously, and can readily serve others beyond, for example 2. *Commodity exchange*, on the other hand, is taken in its pure form to be more restrictive, involving just one of 1, 2 or 3, but even this may be a simplification with factors among 5–8 frequently being implicit in the transaction. Although distinguishable from much gift-giving on account of it being "balanced", that is to say the goods and services exchanged are mutually agreed at one and the same time to constitute a "fair" transaction in the current circumstances, in another respect commodity exchange need not be "balanced", for the two parties may enter into it for different reasons, for example, to acquire a staple in return for a ritually valuable item.

It is now clear that to place gift-giving and commodity exchange in diametrical opposition is a distortion of a more complex spectrum. Nicholas Thomas cautions that there is no theoretical necessity that gifts imply superiority on the part of the giver, nor should it be assumed that there was always a compulsion to reciprocate (1991:15, 17, 22). While he believes the terms "gifts" and "commodities" have some utility, he prefers not to treat "gift" as an ideal type (Thomas 1991:7–33). Similarly, it has been argued that "commoditization lies at the complex intersection of temporal, cultural, and social factors" (Appadurai 1986:15). Thomas's (1991:15–16) entreaty that "there should be a movement of perspective from economic abstractions to historical forms" mirrors the move towards contextual archaeology from processual approaches.

Although participating groups generally see clear distinctions between the different modes of exchange they themselves engage in – which may happen in different places with different exchange partners and for different reasons (Godelier 1999:165) – the goods involved are not always discrete. This means that archaeological discrimination between modes based on the exchanged object types alone is fallible. Godelier emphasises that it is the *context* of exchange which primarily defines its nature and contemporary significance (also Thomas 1991); hence, archaeological interpretation must exploit the combined evidence of an object's form, material(s) and biography, while final context of deposition may sometimes also have a bearing (Bradley and Edmonds 1993).

Another endemic exchange in prehistoric times that must be acknowledged, although rarely considered as such, is that of *otherworld exchange*. The deposition of valuables in watery or terrestrial environments for ritual purposes has received much attention over the past two decades (especially Bradley 1990) and, while one factor behind it might be the depositors' wish to impress others with their ability to dispose of riches, the underpinning rationale was probably exchange with otherworld spirits: material from this world in return for favour from the otherworld. Even if the material is, strictly speaking, always owned by the otherworld, it is overtly moving from one context of possession to another can thus be considered to be a form of exchange which is crucial to our understanding of the workings of the given society.

Typically it has been assumed that such otherworld transactions were irrevocable, but this may be a mistake (Needham 2001). Subsequent removal of a deposited offering would result in archaeological invisibility, but that should not induce us to ignore the possible rationales behind, and effects of, such a practice among prehistoric societies. So, otherworld exchange was not necessarily restricted to actions at the end of an object's life cycle. Moreover, if pre-scientific societies believed that valued and essential commodities alike were granted by gift of the gods, then we can expect exchange also to have occurred at the point of origin: the special rock source or the seed stock for the next cereal crop. Once this is accepted, it becomes possible to embrace ritual deposits at sources – as, for example, suggested by some deposits at flint mines (Barber et al. 1999:60–67) – as part of the exchange environment. Such practices could also potentially have had a role in requiring and shaping the end-of-life transactions that came much later.

Cosmologically driven exchange has also been largely overlooked in archaeology. As in many other forms of exchange, the motives of the exchange partners need not be balanced but the defining factor is that at least one party has the specific motive 9 from the above list. The spiritual betterment sought is not overtly for self-interest, but when attained will still tend to elevate the individual within his or her societal code. Helms's assumption (1993:91–92) has been that cosmological acquisition has no accompanying social contract between the parties, and hence is quite unlike other forms of prestige exchange. But it seems unlikely that there would be no reciprocation involved at all; the traveller seeking cosmological knowledge or material would, whether consciously or not, give something in return, even if just entertainment. More tangibly, the host society might well expect gifts from the traveller as a sign of good and honourable intentions.

Cosmological exchange, in terms of its ethnographic recognition, often involves long-distance exchange undertaken by specialists as an individual enterprise. With greater geographical distance comes a sense of greater exoticness which can lead to enhanced reverence for the materials/objects obtained. Similarly, in some value systems the temporal displacement that gives rise to heirlooms and relics increases their value because of reverence for ancestors and ancestral virtues. In the absence of commerce, it is elites who are instrumental in obtaining objects, materials or knowledge from afar, for it serves as a form of empowerment; the endeavour requires great skill of various kinds and it fulfils society's expectations of the individual's status (Helms 1993:4). Much of Helms's work focuses on single-expedition long-distance displacements, but down-the-line passage of cosmologically charged goods is equally attested in ethnographic case studies. In some situations the chain of exchange partners is such that the ultimate recipients are wholly unaware of the people and place in which the goods originated, despite the fact the objects concerned were considered precious and were axiomatic to that recipient group's way of life (Godelier 1999:91, 167). Such a passage through a number of intermediaries can in fact further enhance the symbolic and cosmological significance of the goods by adding richness, diversity and mystery to individual object biographies. But this element of added value is gained at the expense of real knowledge about the source.

In part related to cosmological exchange are displacements that occur in the context of *pilgrimage*. Transit can occur in either direction: in some situations it is vital that the pilgrim take something as an offering; in others, it may be just as crucial that some small element of the sacred destination (it could be nothing more than a handful of earth) is taken back home. It is this latter direction that corresponds best to cosmological acquisition, since the particular material or object is deemed to be invested with some special properties or qualities which will give certain benefits to the acquirer and his or her community.

Having set out some principles and expectations of exchange in a prehistoric context, we can move on to look at some material examples. This chapter hardly allows a complete history of exchange relations from the Mesolithic to the Middle Bronze Age; nevertheless, the case studies have been deliberately chosen to cover different periods and materials, and illustrate a range of social backgrounds to exchange.

Displacement, Exchange and Mobility Patterns

Whether or not displacement was caused by exchange is a question made even more complicated when one considers that societies in the Mesolithic and Neolithic are often interpreted as having been mobile. This applies in the cases of both wholly mobile groups and those whose annual cycle involves significant seasonal movement to a distinct habitat, as seen in transhumance. The problem is obvious: that material goods originating in one region may end up in another without having passed between hands, or at most having passed only within the kin group simply because not all members of the community were engaged in all circuits of the passage. Most seasonally mobile patterns involve the group splitting up along gender and age lines for parts of the cycle.

While in principle seasonal mobility could account for displacement over considerable distances, this is not generally thought likely for the British Mesolithic and Neolithic. However, a caveat does need to be introduced here: if expeditions to distant places for the procurement of critical resources (e.g., stone for axes) were a regular undertaking then they too must be understood in terms of a specific transregional mobility system, but they are likely also to incur exchange relations with others. For example, a local population might require payment in return for access which would be tantamount to exchange. A second possibility is that there was an expectation of payment to the otherworld for obtaining the raw materials (as raised above). In either of these cases we could find objects displaced in the opposite direction, having been carried with the travelling individuals specifically for this purpose. If both the acquired goods and those taken outward have the potential to be tangible in the archaeological record, then reciprocity may well be easily spotted, but this in itself would not isolate the particular mechanism of exchange responsible.

Recognising the displacement of durable materials in the Mesolithic is no more problematic than for later periods, but is largely confined to lithics. For example, the Wold flint from the chalklands of eastern Yorkshire and Lincolnshire is present in assemblages on the Pennines. Again, the widespread use of Arran pitchstone and Rhum bloodstone, both from island sources off the west coast of Scotland, is well documented over a long period starting in the Mesolithic, although displacement at that early date may not have been great (Wickham-Jones 1986:7). Further south, the displacement of certain objects in Mesolithic Hampshire and its surrounding regions has been discussed by Roger Jacobi (1981). He drew attention to three different lithic types – artefacts made of "Portland" chert, an unusual implement type ("blades") made of slate, and perforated quartzite pebbles – each with its own interpretative difficulties in terms of what combination of geological and human processes may have contributed to the recovered patterns. The slate blades, which have been recognised from sites between Somerset and Essex, and which are curiously not easily attributed to a function, are thought to derive from the south-west peninsula on the basis of petrological examination (Jacobi 1981 and pers. comm.). Conscious of the possibility of long-range movement and the difficulties in ascertaining the territorial range of a group, Jacobi nevertheless thought it more likely that most humanly conducted transportation would have been conducted down-the-line from region to region. What is clear, however, is that patterns of regular material movement were already (and unsurprisingly) in place.

A more recent study of Early Mesolithic material from Aveline's Hole, Somerset, has been able to show the potential for more sophisticated analysis of exchange and mobility through comparison of the results of isotopic analysis on human skeletal remains with associated artefact-based data (Schulting and Wysocki 2002; Schulting 2005). The critical point for this discussion is the relationship of the community buried at Aveline's Hole to the contemporary coast and coastal resources. At the time – around the late ninth to early eighth millennia B.C. – the closest coastline is estimated to have been 80–100 km from the site. This was the nearest source for perforated periwinkle shell beads found in the cave (Schulting 2005:223), and yet the strontium, carbon and nitrogen isotope values obtained from a number of the human bones, taken together, suggest that the population buried there were largely dependent for their food intake on the immediate environs of the Mendip Hills and lacked any observable input from marine or coastal resources (Schulting 2005). While various strands of evidence indicate that their home range may have extended 40–50 km eastwards to encompass the edge of the chalk massif, the implication is that it did not reach the coast and therefore the shell ornaments must have been obtained by exchange with other social groups. Some of the utilised flint is pebble flint which may also have come from the coast, but might have been available from river deposits closer at hand.

Stone Axes: Rite-of-Passage Acquisition

Several decades of the petrological examination of polished stone axes, plus the fact that the type is relatively abundant in the archaeological record, has led to their being foremost in considerations of distribution and exchange in the Neolithic (ca. 4000–2200 B.C.; Clough and Cummins 1979; 1988; Bradley and Edmonds 1993; Edmonds 1995). The history of this field of study has been amply covered by Bradley and Edmonds (1993:5–17), who relate it to broader changes in the inter- pretation of processes of exchange in prehistory. A number of regularly exploited rock sources have been identified to regional outcrops and for some the ancient quarries themselves have been located and explored. From these source areas, dotted through the highland zone of western and northern Britain, manufactured axes were spread far and wide across the island. The spread from individual sources, however, is very varied; some sources were evidently more "successful" than others, notably Langdale tuffs (petrological Group VI) from the Lake District, Graig Llwyd (Group VII) from north Wales and Group I greenstones from Cornwall.

This case study, however, presents a classic case of how the same pattern of aggregate displacement can be interpreted in terms of very divergent social models of distribution outwards from the relevant rock sources. It is our reconstruction of Neolithic society in toto that primarily conditions the way we see this distribu- tion working (Bradley and Edmonds 1993:16–17; Edmonds 1993). In a broad- ranging discussion about the life cycle and role of stone and flint axes, these authors argue that conceptions of "industrial production", "factories", "bulk trade" and "entrepreneurial middlemen" do not sit well with current perceptions of Neolithic society; nor are they demanded by the archaeological evidence rep- resenting different points of the *chaîne opératoire* – sites of raw material extraction, initial and secondary axe-finishing, and those showing axe consumption. However, the articulation of the exchange process (or processes) at play is still hamstrung by its invisibility; Edmonds's (1993:73) concern to shift the focus towards "rela- tions between objects and their contexts" can still only *directly* address the end- points of life cycles; these difficulties *are* acknowledged (Bradley and Edmonds 1993:43–57).

The notion that axes, or some axes, might serve to valorise a given personal classification (e.g., a social role, position or other identity) within society is attrac- tive for helping to explain why it was not always sufficient to have an axe made of *any* available and suitable stone, but rather one that conformed to certain under- standings of what that symbol should constitute materially and metaphorically. It may be that, in the few cases where given lithic sources developed extensive patterns of displacement, this was the outcome of that latter need having been propagated over a long period of time and across many social groups. As Edmonds explains (1993:77), the interrelationship between the classification of a person and the accordant material symbol could readily be reinforced by the act of procurement, perhaps involving distant travel, negotiation and cooperation with other communi- ties engaged in the venture, and later recall of the sequence of special acts and events which brought about the desired end-result. This whole process would serve to prove the worthiness of the individual (see also Field 1997:64).

If these kinds of difficulties in attainment were essential in creating the value of the object and thereby the re-classification of the person, it may not be too surprising that sometimes the rock outcrops exploited seem almost to have been chosen to be the most inaccessible possible (Bradley and Edmonds 1993; Edmonds 1995:79). Under this interpretative framework, the restricted fall-out distribution of axes from the various sources would relate not to commercial competition, but to different preferred sources of sanction for regionally based cosmological traditions. Such a tradition might be seen in the "special relationship" that Bradley and Edmonds suggest existed along an axis from the Cumbrian massif to East Yorkshire (1993:157–164). They base their argument on a range of evidence relating to artefact styles, distributions and monuments, thus helping to mitigate the difficulty arising from the fact that few findspots for axes would have resulted straightforwardly from the process of acquisition; patterns will have been blurred by many other subsequent processes. It is also worth noting that they see a significant change in the axe exchange system from the earlier to the later Neolithic: a greater concern emerging for control over access to objects – perhaps therefore finished objects – through established exchange networks, rather than control over production per se (Edmonds 1993:82; Bradley and Edmonds 1993:15–16, 54).

Inter-Elite Exchange and Prestige Goods

One much applied model for exchange in later prehistory over the past 25 years has been the *prestige goods economy*. Applications have ranged from Rowlands's (1980) seminal paper on later Bronze Age exchange systems (also Frankenstein and Rowlands 1978 in an Iron Age context) to the growth in exchangeable valuables evident during the later Neolithic to Early Bronze Age sequence (e.g., Thorpe and Richards 1984). More recently concern has grown that these are not cultural situations correctly applicable to the prestige goods model, which should strictly concern core–periphery relations (Bradley and Edmonds 1993:14–15; Preucel and Hodder 1996:103). The extent of prestige goods exchange has even been challenged for Iron Age central Europe by Gosden (1985).

If the specific dependency relationship between core and periphery necessary for the proper definition of a prestige goods system was not present through most of British prehistory, the main alternative vehicle for the circulation of prestige goods in pre-state societies would have been some kind of gift reciprocation system; but even these are found to vary enormously in ethnographic situations. Sometimes they are *non-antagonistic*, designed to enshrine long-lasting relationships which bound individuals and groups together; this serves ultimately to improve stability and security against unexpected turns of circumstance. For the Bronze Age, however, more competitive, *antagonistic* modes of exchange are believed to have been dominant. There is little evidence that these became excessively competitive, in the mode of "potlatch" (which is even rare in the ethnographic record), although the evidence for intensive feasting at the southern British midden sites at the end of the Bronze Age and into the Earliest Iron Age (850–600 B.C.) might signal something comparable (Needham 2007).

For most of the Bronze Age it is more likely that peer group competition (motives 5 and 6) was, although intense and endemic, nevertheless relatively controlled, operating within the scope of attainable resources. If inter-elite exchange is significantly associated with the creation of alliances (motive 7), and one major purpose of alliances was to facilitate the flow of certain goods and marriage partners (motives 1–4), then it follows that there is likely to be a high degree of correlation between the dominant pathways followed by gifts and exchanged commodities. This may explain why patterns of conformity in certain object types follow the patterns of raw material exchange. Hence the development of Early Bronze Age Arreton flanged axe heads from the previous Willerby low-flanged ones seems to involve some stylistic influence from the Aunjetitz world just at the time (ca. 1750 B.C.) that new metal inputs to southern Britain were probably coming from a similar direction (Needham et al. 2006).

A second issue that must be addressed here is that of archaeological discrimination between gifts and commodities. Richard Bradley's initial correlation with types of metalwork deposit that show rather different characteristics in terms of both content and context has moved the debate about hoarding practices into new and fertile terrain (Bradley 1990; see also Levy 1982 for comparison on the Danish material). But the hypothesis failed to explain *why* the different modes of exchange should show themselves so literally in the archaeological record, especially given that that record was increasingly being seen in terms of deliberate acts of votive abandonment rather than accidents of happenstance (Knapp 1988:150, 166; Needham 1990). For such a direct correlation to occur, we would need to suppose that a high proportion of deposits took the same form as they took during exchange events, thus effectively minimising communal and regional control over what was selected as offerings to the otherworld. In fact, the evidence of rich contextual differentiation from region to region and phase to phase patently tells another story – one in which choice determined by local custom was paramount in the varied expressions required of these acts of deposition (Needham 2001).

This criticism of methodology does not preclude the possibility that a distinction between gifts and commodities would have been recognised by later prehistoric communities. Instead, it reinforces the ever present difficulties we have in reconstructing systemic processes. The practice of gifting on an inter-regional scale could indeed account for far-displaced prestige goods, such as alien types of sword. But while it explains the type's presence in the given region, it does not explain its special deposition. Prestige gifts in pre-modern economies are generally "inalienable" (Weiner 1992) – that is to say, still owned by the original giver – until such time as there may be a critical change of circumstance. Such a change might be the closure of a reciprocating exchange chain, the final cancellation of a debt which thus finally allowed the received gift to become eligible for offering up (returning) to the otherworld.

Stonehenge, Pilgrimage and Exchange

Stonehenge provides us with an obvious and graphic example of a location likely to have attracted venerators from near and far. Over a period of at least 1,300 years, the monument and its environs grew in importance and stature relative to most other regional centres. From modest beginnings around 3000 B.C., the monument had been transformed by about 2200–2000 B.C. into the most sophisticated and massive of the megalithic circles (Cleal et al. 1995; Bayliss et al. 1997). From this point onwards, the monument itself became more or less fossilised *structurally*, but instead it developed a tremendous power to attract burials of influential people, which led to the development of a complex structured landscape of the dead within a radius of 4 km (Woodward and Woodward 1996; Darvill 2006:157ff.). Innumerable excavations into the barrows of this exceptionally well-preserved prehistoric landscape have yielded many grave groups with diverse materials and some of notable richness. This concentration is normally interpreted as resulting from economic power, but it is possible to explain at least part of the great diversity as resulting from pilgrims and more sedentary special incomers. In other words, some of the fine objects may not have been the products of craftsman or societies in the Stonehenge region or even inland Wessex.

A good case can be made for the slotted form of Early Bronze Age incense cup (Longworth 1983). Relative to the prolific archaeological record of Wessex, the occurrence of just two in the Stonehenge area, with two more from Berkshire and the Upper Thames, is minor by comparison with their frequency along the south coast from Dorset to Kent (Ashbee 1967; Needham et al. 2006). The slotted incense cup in the famous "rich" grave group from Wilsford G8, Wiltshire (Clarke et al. 1985:figs. 4.32, 4.56), matches the style of the coastal ones and is much more likely a displaced piece rather than a copy. As we shall see below, the person interred in G8 may have been a "foreigner" who became a resident of central Wessex, or had lineal claims to be buried in that highly sacred zone.

This same object type, the slotted incense cup, might also be invoked as an example of the drawing of an inspiration *from* Stonehenge by pilgrims from another region. Long ago it was wondered whether the cup form might actually represent a stylised model of the lintelled circle at Stonehenge (Hoare 1812:201; Thurnam 1871:367). This cannot be taken definitively as the inspiration, but the point is that it is a plausible one despite the fact that the cup is not truly a "Wessex type". Whatever opinion may be on the balance of power between inland Wessex and the south coastal communities, it is clear that these two regions had a degree of mutual interdependence (Needham et al. 2006) and in this context reverence for Stonehenge may have played a key role in the ideology of coastal groups, leading to their invention of an imitation of the monument in the form of a ritual cup.

Discussion in these terms of the extraordinary phenomenon documented around Stonehenge, and more widely in Wessex, should expose the weakness of the frequent past argument that the Wessex elite gained their power and wealth by

monopolising trade routes and thus becoming middlemen in some form of mercantile trade. Not only is it questionable that material wealth was greater or craft
expertise of higher quality in Wessex (Needham 2000a), but it is also more probable
that the real controlling agents in the flow of critical goods were surrounding
communities (Needham et al. 2006). The status of inland Wessex rested upon its
spiritual base, which itself may be assumed to have derived in some modified
form from the "ritual authority structures" (Thorpe and Richards 1984) of the Late
Neolithic.

Migration, Marriage Exchange and the Creation of Identities

The foregoing analysis has introduced spiritual reasons for the inter-regional movement of people. Also pertinent is the celebrated "Amesbury Archer", a 40- to 50-
year-old male buried in the Copper Age (ca. 2400–2200 B.C.) at the very beginning
of the burial phenomenon, on Boscombe Down just a few kilometres east of Stonehenge (Fitzpatrick 2002). His presence in that landscape may well have been due
to the spiritual draw of the monument. In death he was accompanied by an unusually rich inventory of grave goods including five fine Beaker pots, a copper dagger,
two copper knives, a pair of gold basket ornaments, a metalworking block ("cushion
stone"), a carved bone pin, 18 flint arrowheads and an array of flintknapping debris,
fire-lighting kit and specialised implements of boar's tusk and antler. Most of these
object types have far-flung parallels and the raw material for the copper and gold
must have come ultimately from a considerable distance. However, the single most
stunning piece of information from the grave stems from isotopic analysis of the
Archer's teeth. Interpretation of the strontium and oxygen isotopic measurements
combined with knowledge of the spread of the early Beaker culture favours, at the
time of writing, his childhood origin somewhere in central Europe, perhaps the
Alpine foreland or upper Danube (Andrew Fitzpatrick and Jane Evans, pers.
comm.). Regardless of whether or not he was directly involved in exchange, or
indeed whether or not he himself was the *object* of some kind of exchange, this one
compelling instance of long-distance movement within an individual's lifetime
shows graphically the potential for the rapid transfer of goods and ideas in terms
of archaeological time scales.

   In the case of the Amesbury Archer, it is easy to accept that some, if not all, of
his goods had travelled a considerable distance with him or been brought direct to
him through his distant links. More often we have little basis to evaluate the relationship in terms of displacement between goods and the person who possessed
them. Occasionally, however, when an intrusive object type is accompanied by an
unfamiliar context locally, it is possible again to argue for an association with a
foreign individual. The Early Bronze Age hoard from Lockington, Leicestershire
(ca. 2100–1900 B.C.), found on the edge of a burial mound, is a case in point
(Hughes 2000). Here, not only was the contained dagger an object ultimately displaced from Armorica, but its treatment, context and associations were also unusual,
suggesting that it was not simply an object passed down-the-line (Needham 2000b).

The long blade had been beaten, leaving its profile undulating, a feature rarely observed on contemporary British blades but found amongst Armorican parallels. It was buried in a small pit, not a grave – the near universal context for early British daggers south of the Scottish Highlands. And, thirdly, it was deposited with a pair of gold armlets and portions of two Beaker pots; the close association of dagger and armlet is extremely rare in Early Bronze Age Britain. Unusual though these other features be, none of them are readily interpreted as having been derived from the Armorican "homeland" of the dagger. Instead, it appears that the presence of a foreigner in the Trent valley, whether visitor or adopted member of the community, needed to be marked out by distinct rituals. That those rituals were not obviously related to the ultimate homeland is hardly surprising given they were presumably conducted within a local, central British cosmological framework.

The dagger at Lockington may signal that the foreigner here was male. However, in many other cases there is a stronger argument for the significant movement of women, probably as marriage partners within an elite exchange system. The powerful evidence for these practices from the central European Tumulus culture graves (especially Germany: Wels-Weyrauch 1989) is ruled out in Britain after the end of the Early Bronze Age (ca. 1550–1500 B.C.) by the demise of inhumation burials and grave goods other than pottery, but it may still be possible to identify similar processes at work in that period. The Middle Bronze Age of southern Britain, and particularly the Taunton stage within it (ca. 1400–1275 B.C.), has long been recognised to abound in ornaments, many of the types concerned being derived from Continental prototypes (Smith 1959). The Continental parallels for geometrically incised thick arm-rings, for example, spread from western France to Poland and into central Europe and comprise a number of regional variants. Smith referred to the phenomenon, as represented in Britain, as the "ornament horizon" and whatever the debates about how restricted a phase it represents (e.g., Lawson 1979) we need to explain why and how it came about. With the exception of a grave at Ramsgate on the Isle of Thanet, Kent, these foreign-inspired ornaments were deposited according to western tradition in hoards and as single finds, whereas further east many furnished graves. Yet the very adoption of this adornment suite could suggest that British and other Atlantic groups were linking in to a wider network of exchange within which elite (female) marriage partners drawn from other groups were used to cement and, moreover, proclaim the alliances necessary for the flow of bronze and other valuables.

The Taunton phase was a time of great abundance of bronze in the lands flanking both sides of the Channel and many other exchanged or imitated bronze types (such as Norman palstaves) testify to considerable interaction with the opposing coastlands (Butler 1963; Burgess 1968; O'Connor 1980). Intensive interaction was by no means peculiar to a restricted phase of the Bronze Age; it is simply that the character of the response differs from phase to phase. The slightly later seabed deposits from Langdon Bay, Dover, Kent, and Moor Sand, Salcombe, Devon – both including clear Continental types just off the British coastline – have usually been interpreted as the cargoes of wrecked vessels (of which no trace survived) and graphic evidence of "exchange in action" across the Channel (Muckelroy 1980;

1981; Needham and Dean 1987). By this phase (Penard, 1300–1150 B.C.), the transfer of novel ornament types is effectively supplanted by a new phenomenon – the transmission of a new mode of combat using a heavy slashing sword (Needham 1982). Yet again, few of the swords in question are actual imports (Colquhoun and Burgess 1988); acceptance of the new code of combat by British warriors and chieftains rapidly led to the adaptation of indigenous weapon production. Even so, it would seem that by showing allegiances through commonalities in martial equipment, it was no longer necessary to display explicit connections in elite female attire in order to maintain inter-regional relations.

This is a neat example of how both individual personas and regional cultural identities may be altered quite rapidly in accordance with more broadly adopted mores. The phenomenon is colloquially referred to as "keeping up with the Joneses" but should not be trivialised, since we know that emulation, both horizontally and vertically within society, is one of the most powerful forces behind cultural change (Miller 1982). Rather than simply deducing that the process took place in a given context, it is more important to seek an understanding of the underlying social causes for a group adopting a novel value set from outside in some cases and rejecting it in others.

Another potential case relating to the migration of individuals can be seen if we return to the Early Bronze Age "rich" graves of southern England. Just three graves belonging to the early phase (Wessex 1, ca. 1950–1750 B.C.) concern us here: Wilsford G8 and Manton in Wiltshire, and Hengistbury Head, Dorset. These three are united in including miniature halberd pendants, which have long looked exotic, not just the pendants themselves and their constituent materials (gold, copper, amber), but in terms of the object inspiring them which is believed to be the Aunjetitz metal-bound halberd of northern central Europe (Piggott 1973:361; *pace* Case 2003:183). This conclusion has been reinforced as it has become clear that the British and Irish halberd series had ceased by 2000 B.C. (Needham 2000b). Yet it seems it was not the pendants themselves that have been displaced from the east – there are no similar diminutives in the Aunjetitz region. So why would this pendant form have been designed to adorn females (as suggested by the associated grave goods) in southern Britain?

Interpreting the full array of material evidence for the early second millennium B.C., it is possible to suggest a scenario involving the emergence of specialist maritime interaction networks. One of these networks, or *maritories*, links southern England to northern France, the Low Countries and the Frisian coast (Needham et al. 2006; in press). Their emergence coincides with the appearance of boats employing a new technology of construction (Wright 1990; Clark 2004). A prime concern of the western communities within this network was the acquisition of amber, while those towards its eastern end (southern Scandinavia and northern Aunjetitz) sought decorated bronze axes and perhaps tin (Butler 1963; Jockenhövel 2004). In this context, it seems highly likely that marriage partners would be among the high-level exchanges taking place and, if so, the individuals accompanied by halberd pendants are strong candidates – the form of the pendant signifying their origins far to the east, but produced as part of a local craft repertoire obsessed with

the creation of diverse ornaments in exotic materials. Both here and at Lockington
we see the creation of very individual identities designed to accommodate and
portray two major affinities: foreign emissary meshed as one with local elite.

Another aspect of the above-described maritime network contributes a different
perspective on complex, overlapping identities. "Precious cups" (made of gold,
silver, amber and shale) are specific to a restricted zone of north-west Europe
because, it is argued, they relate closely to the water-borne contact central to this
particular network (Needham et al. 2006). The highly specialised skills of making
seaworthy vessels and of seamanship can engender certain unities between groups
separated by water and having common interests in crossing it. The unity is not
about convergence towards a common culture. The definable zone, reaching from
Armorica and Cornwall in the west to the Danish/Frisian coast and the middle
Rhine in the east, patently embraces a number of different cultural groups. Instead,
the element of unity lies in a common understanding of what is necessary both
materially and metaphysically in order to engage in such pursuits; to this end,
certain ritual acts of sanction and propitiation were, it is suggested, accepted
throughout the zone and these explain the common adoption of the precious cup,
which plays its part in servicing the rituals. This also explains why there is little to
indicate that the cups themselves were ever exchanged inter-regionally and yet at
the same time why they reflect a number of common concepts – relatively small
size, the use of a rare and/or exotic material and the adoption of an unstable form
which derived from a distant (as it happens, central European) origin.

Conclusions

It is perhaps because so much inter-regional exchange is conducted under the aus-
pices and at the instigation of the elite that the products of this exchange stand out
prominently in the archaeological record. Elite exchange can have a disproportionate effect on cultural trajectories but, even so, it is questionable whether in aggregate
this would always be the dominant force. The myriad cultural underpinning of
within-region exchanges – from systems of labour provisioning to marriage partner-
ing and basic raw material procurement – is intrinsically likely to have been a significant force acting upon the regional pattern of change in values and meanings.

One aspect of understanding the nature of prehistoric exchange, the identification of where in the landscape its respective forms took place, has been avoided in
this chapter. It is an aspect that is fraught with as many (if not more) interpretative
problems as those concerning mechanisms and participants. Likewise omitted is
any discussion about the possible emergence of weight systems which would have
obvious implications for the regularisation of (some) exchange transactions.
Although there is growing evidence for such coming into existence during the
course of the European Bronze Age, a case has yet to be made for Britain in the
period covered here.

Exchange may not underpin everything in social existence, but it is undeniably
one of the most culturally influential of human pursuits. It also, almost inevitably,

has a strong (though far from uniform) interrelationship with social structure. Archaeological evidence tends to be inherently ambiguous on many aspects of exchange. The solution to this problem, however, is not to fall back on platitudinous concepts of exchange, often still too heavily modelled on modern economic systems and concepts. Instead it must be clearly understood that it is *not* the all too visible objects of inter-regional exchange that will enlighten us on the mechanisms and rationale for exchange. Those objects may be pointers to certain factors, for example, possible axes of interaction or the level at which interaction took place, but these are not system-defining. A real understanding of the processes of exchange can be built up only from whole suites of evidence specific to the period or circumstance under consideration ranging from local subsistence economies to regimes of value, social structure and ritual practices. The challenge for British, and indeed European, studies of prehistoric exchange is not only to break free from the strictures of modern economic concepts, but also to reject the explicit (and often exceptional) ethnographic analogue and at the same time to be emboldened by the diversity of the ethnographic evidence with respect to exchange. In this way archaeological evidence, used empirically and sensitively with respect to archaeological methodologies, may unveil a rich tapestry of modes and conditions of exchange which put to rest notions of simple evolutionary schemes or straightforward correlations between exchange and social state.

REFERENCES

Appadurai, A., ed., 1986 The Social Life of Things. Cambridge: Cambridge University Press.

Ashbee, P., 1967 The Wessex grave. *In* A prehistoric and Anglo-Saxon burial ground, Ports Down, Portsmouth. A. Corney, ed. Proceedings of the Hampshire Field Club and Archaeology Society 24:20–41.

Barber, M., D. Field and P. Topping, 1999 The Neolithic Flint Mines of England. Swindon: English Heritage.

Barrett, J. C., 1985 Hoards and related metalwork. *In* Symbols of Power at the Time of Stonehenge. D. V. Clarke, T. G. Cowie and A. Foxon, eds. pp. 95–106. Edinburgh: HMSO.

——1987 Contextual archaeology. Antiquity 61:468–473.

Bayliss, A., C. Bronk Ramsey and F. G. McCormac, 1997 Dating Stonehenge. *In* Science and Stonehenge. Proceedings of the British Academy 92. B. Cunliffe and C. Renfrew, eds. pp. 39–59. Oxford: Oxford University Press.

Bradley, R., 1990 The Passage of Arms: an archaeological analysis of prehistoric hoards and votive deposits. Cambridge: Cambridge University Press.

——and M. Edmonds, 1993 Interpreting the Axe Trade. Cambridge: Cambridge University Press.

——S. Lobb, J. Richards and M. Robinson, 1980 Two Late Bronze Age settlements on the Kennet gravels: excavations at Aldermaston Wharf and Knight's Farm, Burghfield, Berkshire. *In* Proceedings of the Prehistoric Society 46:217–295.

Burgess, C. B., 1968 The later Bronze Age in the British Isles and north-western France. Archaeological Journal 125:1–45.

Butler, J. J., 1963 Bronze Age connections across the North Sea: a study in prehistoric trade and industrial relations between the British Isles, the Netherlands, north Germany and Scandinavia, c.1700–700 B.C. Palaeohistoria 9.

Case, H., 2003 Beaker presence at Wilsford 7. Wiltshire Archaeological and Natural History Magazine 96:161–194.

Clark, P., ed., 2004 The Dover Bronze Age Boat. Swindon: English Heritage.

Clarke, D. V., T. G. Cowie and A. Foxon, eds., 1985 Symbols of Power at the Time of Stonehenge. Edinburgh: HMSO.

Cleal, R. M. J., K. E. Walker and R. Montague, 1995 Stonehenge in its Landscape: twentieth century excavations. London: English Heritage.

Clough, T. H. McK., and W. A. Cummins, eds., 1979 Stone Axe Studies: archaeological, petrological, experimental and ethnographic. London: Council for British Archaeology.

——and ——eds., 1988 Stone Axe Studies, vol. 2: the petrology of prehistoric stone implements from the British Isles. London: Council for British Archaeology.

Colquhoun, I., and C. B. Burgess, 1988 The Swords of Britain. Prähistorische Bronzefunde IV.5. Munich: Beck.

Darvill, T., 2006 Stonehenge: the biography of a landscape. Stroud: Tempus.

Edmonds, M., 1993 Towards a context for production and exchange: the polished stone axe in earlier Neolithic Britain. In Trade and Exchange in European Prehistory. C. Scarre and F. Healy, eds. pp. 69–86. Oxford: Oxbow Books.

——1995 Stone Tools and Society: working stone in Neolithic and Bronze Age Britain. London: Batsford.

Field, D., 1997 The landscape of extraction: aspects of the procurement of raw material in the Neolithic. In Neolithic Landscapes. P. Topping, ed. pp. 55–67. Oxford: Oxbow Books.

Fitzpatrick, A., 2002 "The Amesbury Archer": a well-furnished Early Bronze Age burial in southern England. Antiquity 76:629–630.

Frankenstein, S., and M. J. Rowlands, 1978 The internal structure and regional context of early Iron Age society in south-western Germany. University of London Institute of Archaeology Bulletin 15:74–112.

Godelier, M., 1999 The Enigma of the Gift. Chicago: University of Chicago Press.

Gosden, C., 1985 Gifts and kin in Early Iron Age Europe. Man n.s. 20:475–493.

Gregory, C. A., 1982 Gifts and Commodities. London: Academic Press.

Halstead, P., and J. O'Shea, 1982 A friend in need is a friend indeed: social storage and the origins of social ranking. In Ranking, Resource and Exchange: aspects of the archaeology of early European society. C. Renfrew and S. Shennan, eds. pp. 92–99. Cambridge: Cambridge University Press.

Helms, M., 1988 Ulysses' Sail: an ethnographic odyssey of power, knowledge and geographical distance. Princeton: Princeton University Press.

——1993 Craft and the Kingly Ideal: art, trade and power. Austin: University of Texas.

Hoare, R. C., 1812 The Ancient History of South Wiltshire. London: William Miller.

Hodder, I., 1982 Towards a contextual approach to prehistoric exchange. In Contexts for Prehistoric Exchange. J. Ericson and T. Earle, eds. pp. 199–211. New York: Academic Press.

Hughes, G., 2000 The Lockington Gold Hoard: an Early Bronze Age barrow cemetery at Lockington, Leicestershire. Oxford: Oxbow Books.

Jacobi, R. M., 1981 The last hunters in Hampshire. In The Archaeology of Hampshire, from the Palaeolithic to the Industrial Revolution. S. J. Shennan and R. T. Schadla Hall, eds. pp. 10–25. Winchester: Hampshire Field Club and Archaeology Society.

Jockenhövel, A., 2004 Von West nach Ost? Zur Genese der Frühbronzezeit Mitteleuropas. *In* From Megaliths to Metal: essays in honour of George Eogan. H. Roche, E. Grogan, J. Bradley, J. Coles and B. Raftery, eds. pp. 155–167. Oxford: Oxbow Books.

Knapp, B., 1988 Hoards d'oeuvres: of metals and men on Bronze Age Cyprus. Oxford Journal of Archaeology 7:147–176.

Kopytoff, I., 1986 The cultural biography of things: commoditization as a process. *In* The Social Life of Things. A. Appadurai, ed. pp. 64–91. Cambridge: Cambridge University Press.

Lawson, A., 1979 A late Middle Bronze Age hoard from Hunstanton, Norfolk. *In* Bronze Age Hoards: some finds old and new. C. B. Burgess and D. Coombs, eds. pp. 42–92. Oxford: British Archaeological Reports.

Lévi-Strauss, C., 1987 Introduction to the Work of Marcel Mauss. London: Routledge and Kegan Paul.

Levy, J., 1982 Social and Religious Organisation in Bronze Age Denmark: an analysis of ritual hoard finds. Oxford: British Archaeological Reports.

Longworth, I. H., 1983 The Whinny Liggate perforated wall cup and its affinities. *In* From the Stone Age to the 'Forty-Five: studies presented to R. B. K. Stevenson. A. O'Connor and D. V. Clarke, eds. pp. 65–86. Edinburgh: John Donald.

Mauss, M., 1970 The Gift: forms and functions of exchange in archaic societies. London: Cohen and West.

Miller, D., 1982 Structures and strategies: an aspect of the relationship between social hierarchy and cultural change. *In* Symbolic and Structural Archaeology. I. Hodder, ed. pp. 89–98. Cambridge: Cambridge University Press.

Muckelroy, K., 1980 Two Bronze Age cargoes in British waters. Antiquity 54:100–109.

——1981 Middle Bronze Age trade between Britain and Europe: a maritime perspective. Proceedings of the Prehistoric Society 47:275–298.

Needham, S. P., 1982 The Ambleside Hoard: a discovery in the Royal Collections. London: British Museum.

——1990 The Petters Late Bronze Age metalwork: an analytical study of Thames valley metalworking in its settlement context. London: British Museum.

——1993 Displacement and exchange in archaeological methodology. *In* Trade and Exchange in European Prehistory. C. Scarre and F. Healy, eds. pp. 161–169. Oxford: Oxbow Books.

——2000a The development of embossed goldwork in Bronze Age Europe. Antiquaries Journal 80:27–65.

——2000b The gold and copper metalwork. *In* The Lockington Gold Hoard: an Early Bronze Age barrow cemetery at Lockington, Leicestershire. G. Hughes, ed. pp. 23–46. Oxford: Oxbow Books.

——2001 When expediency broaches ritual intention: the flow of metal between systemic and buried domains. Journal of the Royal Anthropological Institute 7:275–278.

——2007 800 BC: the Great Divide. *In* The Earlier Iron Age in Britain and the Near Continent. C. Haselgrove and R. Pope, eds. pp. 39–63. Oxfrod: Oxbow Books.

——in press Encompassing the sea: Maritories – conceptualising Bronze Age cross-sea interactions. *In* Bronze Age Connections. P. Clark, ed.

——and M. Dean, 1987 La cargaison de Langdon Bay à Douvres (Grandes Bretagne): la signification pour les échanges à travers la Manche. *In* Les Relations Entre le Continent et les Iles Britanniques à l'Age du Bronze. J.-C. Blanchet, ed. pp. 119–124. Amiens: Supplément à la Revue Archéologique de Picardie.

——K. Parfitt and G. Varndell, eds., 2006 The Ringlemere Cup: precious cups and the beginning of the Channel Bronze Age. London: British Museum.

O'Connor, B., 1980 Cross-Channel Relations in the Later Bronze Age. Oxford: British Archaeological Reports.

Piggott, S., 1973 The Wessex culture of the Early Bronze Age. *In* A History of Wiltshire, vol. 1, part 2. E. Crittall, ed. pp. 352–375. Oxford: Oxford University Press.

Polanyi, K., 1957 The economy as instituted process. *In* Trade and Market in the Early Empires: economies in history and theory. K. Polanyi, C. M. Arensberg and H. W. Pearson, eds. pp. 243–270. Glencoe, IL: Free Press.

Preucel, R., and I. Hodder, eds., 1996 Contemporary Archaeology in Theory. Oxford: Blackwell.

Renfrew, C., 1975 Trade as action at distance: questions of integration and communication. *In* Ancient Civilisation and Trade. J. A. Sabloff and C. C. Lomberg-Karlovsky, eds. pp. 3–59. Albuquerque: University of New Mexico.

——1993 Trade beyond the material. *In* Trade and Exchange in European Prehistory. C. Scarre and F. Healy, eds. pp. 5–16. Oxford: Oxbow Books.

——and P. Bahn, 1996 Archaeology: theories, methods and practice, 2nd edn. London: Thames and Hudson.

Rowlands, M. J., 1980 Kinship, alliance and exchange in the European Bronze Age. *In* Settlement and Society in the British Later Bronze Age. J. C. Barrett and R. Bradley, eds. pp. 15–55. Oxford: British Archaeological Reports.

Scarre, C., and F. Healy, eds., 1993 Trade and Exchange in European Prehistory. Oxford: Oxbow Books.

Schiffer, M. B., 1987 Formation Processes of the Archaeological Record. Albuquerque: University of New Mexico Press.

Schulting, R. J., 2005 "... Pursuing a rabbit in Burrington Combe": new research on the early Mesolithic burial cave of Aveline's Hole. Proceedings of the University of Bristol Speleological Society 23:171–265.

——and M. Wysocki, 2002 The Mesolithic human skeletal collection from Aveline's Hole: a preliminary note. Proceedings of the University of Bristol Speleological Society 22: 255–268.

Smith, M. A., 1959 Some Somerset hoards and their place in the Bronze Age of southern Britain. Proceedings of the Prehistoric Society 25:144–187.

Thomas, N., 1991 Entangled Objects: exchange, material culture and colonisation in the Pacific. Cambridge, MA: Harvard University Press.

Thorpe, I. J., and C. C. Richards, 1984 The decline of ritual authority and the introduction of Beakers into Britain. *In* Neolithic Studies: a review of some current research. R. Bradley and J. Gardiner, eds. pp. 67–84. Oxford: British Archaeological Reports.

Thurnam, J., 1871 On ancient British barrows, especially those of Wiltshire and the adjoining counties. Part II: Round barrows. Archaeologia 43:285–552.

Weiner, A., 1992 Inalienable Possessions: the paradox of keeping while giving. Berkeley: University of California Press.

Wels-Weyrauch, U., 1989 Mittelbronzezeitliche Frauentrachten in Süddeutschland (Bezeihungen zur Hagenauer Gruppierung). *In* Dynamique du Bronze Moyen en Europe Occidentale: Actes du 113e Congrès National der Sociétés Savantes, Strasbourg 1988. C. Mordant, ed. pp. 117–134. Paris: Comité des Travaux Scientifiques et Historiques.

Wickham-Jones, C. R., 1986 The procurement and use of stone for flaked tools in prehistoric Scotland. Proceedings of the Society of Antiquaries of Scotland 116:1–10.

Woodward, A. B., and P. J. Woodward, 1996 The topography of some barrow cemeteries in Bronze Age Wessex. Proceedings of the Prehistoric Society 62:275–291.

Wright, E., 1990 The Ferriby Boats: seacraft of the Bronze Age. London: Routledge.

15

Identity, Community and the Person in Later Prehistory

Melanie Giles

Introduction

This chapter reviews approaches to identity in later prehistory, focusing on the first millennium B.C., the period conventionally referred to as the Iron Age. Archaeological studies have approached identity in different ways according to the dominant paradigm of the day, moving from concepts of race and culture, to community and society, ethnicity and finally the constitution of the body and models of personhood. It seems logical to structure the discussion of these six key concepts chronologically, not to show an inevitable succession of ideas but rather to reveal their "genealogy": in Foucault's (1972) terms, to explore how the critique of concepts at the core of western European thought generated new ideas. In this way, I hope to reveal how each generation of archaeologists conceived of identity and how this was influenced by the methods and techniques they employed.

At the heart of studies on identity lies an interest in what it means to be human, both now and in the past. In the nineteenth century, this was intrinsically important because it promised to trace the origin of races through their development from prehistoric times. In this, the twenty-first century, we are perhaps more fascinated by alternative understandings of the world, which prompt us to think differently about relationships and affinities with other humans, animals, objects and landscapes. Indeed, it has been argued that archaeology's importance lies in its potential to investigate historically contingent kinds of humanity or social identity, which amount to different ways of being in the world (Barrett 1994). Since the enquiry is always carried out from our own perspective, a review of this kind brings to light broader discourses of the day, revealing how the past has been used to bolster rhetoric or underpin contentious issues surrounding origin, place and belonging. This chapter will highlight the issue of Celtic identity specifically which overshadows later prehistory, examining changes in the meaning, relevance and use of the term.

Racial and Evolutionary Approaches of the Nineteenth Century

The urge to define the attributes of different races arose from the imperialist programme of encounter, description and mapping of "new" peoples (Gosden 1999).
As an appreciation of human diversity grew alongside an understanding of geological time, models of biological evolution offered an analogy for social differentiation.
The idea of progress as a universal process of improvement was already deeply
entrenched in the Victorian imagination (Bowler 1989), but colonial encounters
suggested that not all societies had progressed as far as the "civilised" West. Two
models developed to explain different racial characteristics and social formations
(Trigger 1989). Monogenesis posited that mankind had diverged from a single
unitary origin, with subsequent divergence; polygenesis promoted multiple origins.
With racist undertones, polygenesis claimed that some races were destined to progress further than those constrained by inferior capability, who were unable to evolve
without external help. While justifying the colonial process, this theory allowed
scholars to understand some races as fossils or relics, effectively stuck in time
(Fabian 1983), incidentally providing explanatory analogies for Western prehistorians. In *Prehistoric Times, as Illustrated by Ancient Remains and the Manners and
Customs of Modern Savages*, John Lubbock made this elision of geological, archaeological and ethnographic methods clear:

> if we wish to clearly understand the antiquities of Europe, we must compare them
> with the rude implements and weapons still, or until lately, used by the savage races
> in other parts of the world. In fact, the Van Diemaner and South American are to the
> antiquary what the opossum and the sloth are to the geologist. (1865:416)

Enquiries into racial origins were integral to the growth of nationalism in the nineteenth century (Jones 1997), stimulating interest in the people behind monuments
and objects (Hides 1996). It was in this context that archaeology, with its distinctive use of philology, anatomy and historical sources, focused on the Celts.

In the early nineteenth century, there was a shift away from the generic use of
the term "Celtic" (in reference to prehistoric monuments and Druidism) towards
a specific linguistic connotation (Morse 2005). Historical syntheses of classical
texts, suggested origins, folk movements and names of later prehistoric tribes,
including a group variously referred to Keltoi (in Greek) or Galli (in Latin).
Eighteenth-century linguists such as Pezron and Lhuyd had argued that linguistic
similarities around the Atlantic seaboard derived from a common Indo-European
language group. By the early nineteenth century, ethnologists such as James Cowles
Pritchard were using the word "Celtic" to describe peoples. He regarded language
as the most reliable indicator of racial affiliation, constructing an elaborate linguistic
history of the "Celtic nations" (Augstein 1999).

The 1840s and 1850s saw new methods employed to characterise the
"Celts". Ethnologists had developed an interest in the physiognomic differences
between peoples, particularly the "ethnic attributes" of cranial features which were
believed to be "not transmutable between the races" (Davis and Thurnam 1865:2).

Craniology had been developed to study living populations, but ethnologists now turned it upon skeletal material from antiquarian "barrow openings". Using the relatively novel "Three Age System", it became possible to seriate skulls and distinguish prehistoric populations by contexts associated with stone, bronze or iron (Morse 2005). Davis and Thurnam's monumental *Crania Britannica* (1865) used craniology to explore the racial history of occupation within the British Isles. Evidence from the Iron Age cemeteries of Danes Graves and Arras was to be pivotal, but the chronology of such monuments was still poorly understood. Their analysis proved inconclusive – due to not only the small body of data but also the flawed principle that racial difference could be read from the shape and size of ancient skulls. Nevertheless, they promoted the idea of the Celts as the "truly native" populace of Britain (1865:198).

Meanwhile, museum curators and field archaeologists turned to an alternative strand of evidence to construct racial histories: the material assemblages retrieved from sites and monuments, and isolated finds from rivers and lakes. British archaeologists were influenced by Montelius's work on typology during the 1860s and 1870s, which traced the history of particular groups alongside affinities in object styles between sediment horizons. Despite exhortations from Pitt Rivers to adopt the ethnological or comparative method, curators such as A. W. Franks of the British Museum preferred to keep their material arranged regionally and nationally, so that the ethnic or racial affiliations between collections might be appreciated. In this way, early art historians such as John Kemble began to posit connections between assemblages from later prehistoric Britain, early medieval Ireland and the exotic material from the Continent using the notion of a "Celtic art style" (Kemble 1863). Building on Franks's excavations at Hallstatt, and published illustrations of objects from La Tène, the synthesis of "Celtic art" was further developed in the work of Arthur Evans, Joseph Anderson and Romilly Allen (Collis 2003; Morse 2005). By 1905, the archaeologist Mortimer could state with certainty that the

> presence of the chariot with its artistic accomplishments . . . seems to point to a somewhat sudden introduction of a higher state of civilisation, as we do not find in any of these barrows, indications of a gradual progression in the arts. (1905:lxxv)

Material culture was now studied independently of linguistics and physiognomy: both art and technology were seen not only as signatures of race but as indices of mental development and progress. However, since identity was regarded as innate, inherited by virtue of one's race, *rapid* change had to be explained through the invasion of a new racial group. For Worsaae (1867:64), the archaeological evidence did not indicate that a single, original European race "bore in themselves the germ of all future progress" but, rather, progression through the continual "addition of others, who continually supplanted the former, and laid the foundation for a more advanced civilisation". Racial conflict, migration and invasion were naturalised as primary forces of historical change in the colonial period. But, as the empire began to crumble, it was from this same work on technology, art and style that a new concept of identity developed: the notion of a "culture".

Culture-Historical Approaches of the Twentieth Century

Originally associated with cultivation, the term "culture" subsequently developed connotations of self-improvement and civilisation (Williams 1983:89). Tylor (1871) defined it as "that complex whole which includes knowledge, belief, art, morals, law, custom and any other capabilities and habits acquired by man as a member of society". Anti-colonial movements, and emergent nation states, resulted in new boundaries around groups not defined by race. "Culture" provided an alternative way of characterising group identity based on distinctive ways of life.

Cultural anthropology embraced the concept so as to avoid racist, unilinear histories of humanity. Franz Boas (1911) argued that both converging *and* diverging lines of development could be defined in history: there was no single scheme of progress, in which each race played a fixed part. He advocated close-grained, in-depth, particularist studies of different peoples, in which specific traits and traditions were understood in relation to the cultural whole or "integrated spiritual totality". Boas explained the existence of such coherent social systems of shared and stable beliefs as the result of both learned social behaviour and historical contingency (Rapport and Overing 2000:95). This view of culture as on ongoing process challenged the notion that identity was racially innate but his ideas were only selectively adopted by other anthropologists. Meanwhile, archaeologists sought the material correlates of such cultural traditions, which were assumed to be both homogeneous and conservative:

> We find certain types of remains – pots, implements, ornaments, burial rites, and house forms – constantly recurring together. Such a complex of associated traits we shall call a "cultural group" or just a "culture". We assume that such a complex is the material expression of what today would be called a people. (Childe 1929: v–vi)

Childe attributed cultural variation to ethnic rather than racial identity, following a generation of German archaeologists who claimed cultural differences observed in prehistoric remains were attributable to ethnicity (Jones 1997:15). Gustav Kossina used the notion of cultural "provinces" to chart the origin and spread of these ethnic groups. His motive was the provision of genealogical links from noble prehistoric to "superior" contemporary races, and the uses to which this explicitly nationalist work was put have been well documented (Trigger 1989). Whilst Childe distanced himself from such ends, his concept of culture remained concerned with ethnicity.

The term was embedded in the Iron Age literature at an early stage (Jones 1997:16–17). The summary of the East Yorkshire chariot and square barrow burials by John Mortimer (1905) and Canon Greenwell led the latter to describe these "habits and manners of life [which] were similar" as the result of "affinity of the blood" (1906:306). Culture history provided a useful way of classifying spatial and temporal variation (Trigger 1978:86) during a period of increased excavation (on rural settlements and hill forts), syntheses of ceramic assemblages and decorated metalwork. At this stage, archaeologists did not realise that their identification of

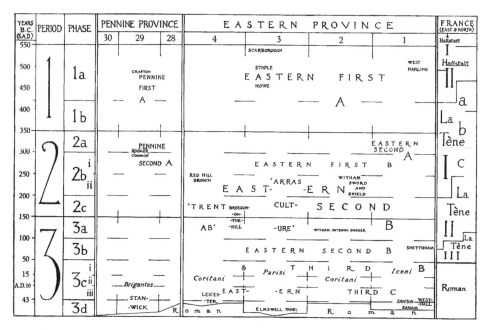

Figure 15.1 Scheme for the Pennine and Eastern Provinces (from Hawkes 1959:75, fig. 2). Reproduced by kind permission of *Antiquity*.

Iron Age cultures was tautological: based on a premise of cultural variation and diversity, reified and perpetuated through classification (Jones 1997). Following Crawford's (1921) suggestion that cultural groups could be identified through their distinctive traditions, Fox (1923:85) therefore coined the term "Hallstatt" and "La Tène cultures" to describe stylistic affinities between Cambridgeshire and the Continent. By 1931, Christopher Hawkes (1959) had proposed the "ABC" of the Iron Age: a series of successive "*cultural* entities" which were later subdivided by province and then region. By the middle of the century, Iron Age Britain was divided into a mosaic of traditions, including the "Pennine group" and "Arras culture" (fig. 15.1). These bounded, uniform archaeological entities were argued to represent distinct peoples, contiguous with territorial units whose boundaries were "physiographically clear" (Hawkes 1959:172). This angered strict culture historians such as F. R. Hodson, who argued that cultures should be defined solely on the basis of typical sites or distributions of type fossils (1960).

While Hawkes (1959:179) was careful to note the "A, B and C" resulted from a mix of both "internal development" and "influence from the Continent", Grahame Clark (1966:185) argued that Hawkes's model still rested on the notion of successive "waves" of Celtic invaders: "A . . . was in effect defined by 'Hallstatt' invasions, the B by the 'Marnian' invasions and the C by the 'Belgic' invasions". In an acrimonious exchange, Clark accused him of an "invasion neurosis" which feeds on itself and distracts attention from what is of much greater importance: when all is said, the object of British archaeology is surely to tell us about the lives of people who, generation by generation, *in unbroken succession*, occupied and shaped the culture of the British Isles. (Clark 1966:173; emphasis added)

Clark was influenced by the analysis of Iron Age material culture by Hodson (1960; 1964), based in part on Bersu's work on the Little Woodbury complex (1940). For Hodson (1964:104), the "great bulk of British Iron Age material", represented by the type fossils of the permanent roundhouse, the weaving comb and the ring-headed pin, hinted at "an archaeological entity or culture in Britain that is fundamentally apart from any Hallstatt or La Tène group on the continent . . . [which] from a purely insular point of view seem quite distinct" (fig. 15.2). In other words, the insular Iron Age could be characterised in general by continuity from the Bronze Age and notable "*cultural archaism*", especially in pottery styles and settlement forms (1964:105; emphasis original). Hodson (1964:107) attributed the unique form of these "pedestrian" remains to local "inventiveness".

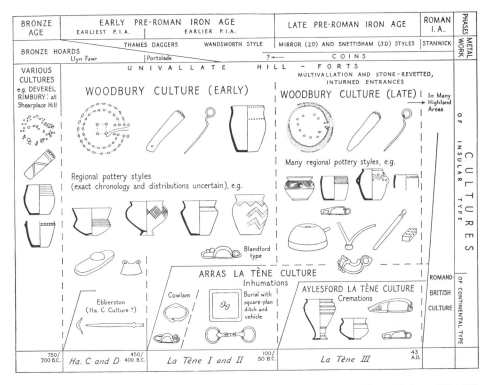

Figure 15.2 Cultural grouping within the British pre-Roman Iron Age (from Hodson 1964:108, fig. 1). Reproduced by kind permission of the Prehistoric Society.

Following the threat of Nazi invasion, it is also possible that archaeologists like Clark (1966:188) objected to a prehistory of Britain which naturalised invasion as a motor of culture change, favouring instead "minor intrusions", indigenous development or the diffusion of ideas through cultural contact and elite competition. Hawkes (1968:298) responded vigorously that "indigenous evolution" had to be clearly demonstrated but Clark (1968:299) dismissed his thinking as out of date: archaeologists should be open to "alternative explanations for the appearance of exotic traits" including a willingness to acknowledge the "inherent dynamism of economic and social life". During the 1960s, the Common Market expanded and trade was liberalised, making "commercial liaison rather than invasion" an attractive explanation for shared cultural traits (Harding 1970:236).

By the late 1960s, Hawkes's over-simplistic system could not incorporate the wealth of information derived from excavation, survey and analysis, and was being challenged by alternative models of change. Archaeologists began to reject the culture-historical paradigm and the normative conception of identity as a mind-set inherited through one's "blood and soil" (after Bauman 1992). From sociological and anthropological studies of living populations, it was increasingly evident that

> what we do *not* find are neatly bounded and mutually exclusive bodies of thought and custom, perfectly shared by all who subscribe to them, and in which their lives and works are fully encapsulated. (Ingold 1994:330).

Archaeological cultures were in fact abstractions, heuristic devices which disguised a much more messy reality: Iron Age peoples did not *live in* "cultures" but rather *acted culturally* (after Ingold 1994:330). The challenge facing archaeologists was to find new approaches to identity which dealt more explicitly with these social processes.

Community and Society

Two analytical concepts emerged as alternative objects of archaeological enquiry. They were juxtaposed in the translated work of Ferdinand Toennies (1957[1887]), who argued that "community" was characterised by small-scale groups, kinship and face-to-face interaction, compared with the larger scale of "society", which was defined by largely impersonal or contractual relations. Whilst such a simplistic division is problematic, it proved influential and reintroduced social evolutionary thought to social analysis.

The four editions of *Iron Age Communities in Britain* by Barry Cunliffe have been the main text to make use of this term, although none of them define its meaning explicitly. It is clear that Cunliffe wanted to avoid the pitfalls of culture history, and to capture the dynamic fluidity of practices between groups: "patterns of economy . . . styles of pottery and other spheres of trading [which] constitute overlapping systems" (1978:xviii). His analysis of pottery "style zones", coinage and metalwork distributions, settlement forms and funerary rituals, portrayed an Iron

Age Britain characterised by regional diversity. He argued that many of these "socio-economic systems" persisted over time and could "reasonably be identified with some of the tribal groupings" (1978:528) of the late Iron Age, recorded in classical texts (such as Ptolemy's *Geographia*) as well as material culture.

Instead, Cunliffe's language shows a debt to systems theory, particularly David Clarke's *Analytical Archaeology* (1968). Clarke envisaged social and economic organisation, material culture and religious belief as interdependent and adaptive subsystems, existing in dynamic equilibrium within a complex cultural and environmental whole. In contrast to the dendritic tree diagrams and maps employed in racial and culture-historical accounts, Clarke (1968: fig. 15) used the metaphor of electricity to capture interaction between his system's components. By the early 1970s, archaeologists possessed the technology to test systems theory models: early databases; environmental, material and landscape analysis; and absolute rather than relative dating techniques. Unfortunately, since it was argued that the system tended towards homeostasis, it became hard to explain change other than through a dominant, causal effect of the environment or other external factors. In Cunliffe's model of the Bronze Age–Iron Age transition, social transformations were initiated by climatic deterioration and soil depletion. Population and stock pressure upon land, resulted in increased competition, economic intensification, centralisation and endemic violence (Cunliffe 1995: fig. 41).

Cunliffe's characterisation of Iron Age groups and their representation as a tribal "map" proved both influential and popular, but if he had in mind the scale and character of social interaction described by Toennies when he chose the word "communities" for his book title, it is not apparent in his synthesis. The development and reproduction of identity at the level of kinship and face-to-face interaction was not an explicit issue in the models of either Clarke or Cunliffe. Like their contemporaries, the dynamics they described worked at the societal level. In this respect they were in touch with their successors whose work was influenced by the anthropologist Émile Durkheim.

Durkheim (1938:103) had proposed that society was not merely the sum of its individual members: "rather, the system formed by their association represents a specific reality which has its own characteristics." In other words, there was a collective consciousness from which individuals gained their sense of identity, role and capacity. Societies could be distinguished on the basis of differences in economics, politics, religion and kinship – the royal quartet of anthropological analysis. Anthropologists now acknowledge that, like Clarke's sub-systems, these analytical units are artificial and distinctive to the way social life is perceived in Western modernity (Rapport and Overing 2000). However, for the scholars of the 1960s, they were real and the basis for a new social typology. Marshall Sahlins and Elman Service (1960:37) replaced the old savage–barbaric–civilised schema with a new social evolutionary system of classification: band–tribe–chiefdom–state. They argued that, across time, social groups tended towards increasing complexity, characterised in terms of both their political structure and economic organisation. Archaeologists believed that such institutions should be evident in their material infrastructure. Its new role was to analyse and identify them in archaeological remains.

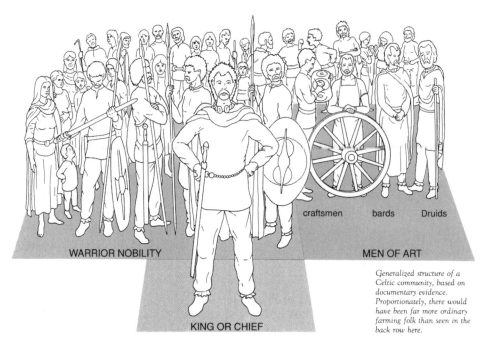

craftsmen   bards   Druids

WARRIOR NOBILITY   MEN OF ART

Generalized structure of a Celtic community, based on documentary evidence. Proportionately, there would have been far more ordinary farming folk than seen in the back row here.

KING OR CHIEF

Figure 15.3   Model of Celtic society (from James 1993:53). Reproduced by kind permission of the author and illustrator, Dr Simon James.

The later prehistoric period in Europe was universally associated with chiefdom societies, as defined by Sahlins and Service (1960), and elaborated by Fried (1967) and Earle (1978). The chiefdom was defined as a regional entity which integrated and represented the interests of local populations but which had not achieved the socio-spatial centralisation and organisational features of a state (Blair Gibson 1995:116). Within the British Iron Age, its particular complexion was derived by archaeologists from an amalgam of classical authors' accounts and analogies with early medieval Ireland; the latter supposedly untouched by Roman imperialism and therefore representative of a pristine Celtic tribal society (Jackson 1964; cited by Cunliffe 1983:166; and critiqued by Collis 1994). Visual representations powerfully capture its pyramidal or hierarchical structure (fig. 15.3).

In such models (see Cunliffe 1983; 1997; James 1993), chiefly power is usually regarded as an inherited male prerogative: authority and influence is accumulated in the hands of a particular kin group, perpetuating unequal access to resources. The chief is supported by ranked lineage groups, which include a warrior class of male adults, complemented by full-time ritual specialists (priests, bards and Druids), and skilled craftspeople who are provided with protection and patronage. The system is underpinned by labouring peasants or client farmers, and a slave class.

For these scholars, Iron Age society was held together through the central control of agricultural surplus, and authority was derived from the ability to redistribute this produce. Chiefs hosted feasts, provided support at times of crises, organised projects of public labour or commissioned the production of prestige goods for gift exchange. Frankenstein and Rowlands (1978) argued that what mattered most was the ability to control the movement of these socially valued artefacts: high status items of display, preferably exotic in character, obtained through external exchange. However, Gosden (1985) questioned the ethnographic basis for this prestige gifts model, arguing that the control of production was more important in the management of social debt and reciprocal exchange of gifts (see reply by Rowlands 1986; 1987). Iron Age archaeologists adopted the term peer polity interaction to describe the competition within networks of elites (Champion and Champion 1986). This model was used to explain the spread of Celtic artefacts and art styles between Britain and the Continent, as an alternative to invasionary models (James 1999).

The case study which epitomised this view of Iron Age society was that of the Danebury hill fort and its landscape environs (Cunliffe 1983; 1995; 2000). Using central place theory and Thiessen polygon analysis (borrowed from the New Geography), Danebury was initially identified as the residence of the chieftain and his elite, within a hierarchically organised territory of client farmsteads or small enclosures. Cunliffe sought to identify practices of production and redistribution, and long-distance exchange, at the landscape scale, but this proved more difficult than expected (see critiques summarised in Hill 1995b). Instead, it was proposed that the hill fort had changed in use and meaning over time, perhaps finally becoming the residence of the surrounding community in the Middle to Late Iron Age, when neighbouring sites were abandoned (Collis's 1981 crises model). Subsequent survey and excavation on other hill forts suggested complex histories and diverse roles (Sharples 1991; Payne 1996; Barrett et al. 2000; Lock et al. 2005; Payne et al. 2006). Archaeologists could not read social organisation from a two-dimensional view of landscape: they had to be concerned with its inhabitation, and the social practices which reproduced particular levels of identity and affiliation.

During this post-processual turn of the 1980s and 1990s, dissatisfaction grew with the traditional chiefdom model and social evolutionary approaches to complexity. Objections to the societal model also addressed its narrow view of power as hierarchical and hereditary, and its failing to question how authority was reproduced ideologically. Horizontal aspects of power in small-scale communities, those of kin, age and gender, were ignored. Women were pushed literally and figuratively to the margins and background. It also perpetuated popular Celtic stereotypes such as the Warrior and the Druid, which were in part fictions of classical, romantic and antiquarian texts (Morse 2005). Archaeologists now recognised how the colonial agendas of the classical authors homogenised and exoticised their subject (Webster 1996) and became sceptical of classical accounts of mass migration. They also rejected the notion of early medieval Ireland as a "window on the Iron Age" (Jackson 1964). That system of kingship and tribal organisation was historically contingent (Harding 2005), interpreted through the religious mores of medieval monks and influenced by contact along the Atlantic seaboard, rather than being isolated from change (Raftery 1994). The tribes of the late Iron Age were themselves a product of a century of contact with Rome, a novel scale of organisation and political affiliation within the provinces stimulated by both trade and the threat of invasion (Hill 1995c; Wells 2001).

Meanwhile, systematic aerial survey and contract archaeology revealed a British Iron Age characterised by heterogeneity and regional diversity (Gwilt and Hasel-grove 1997; Bevan 1999). Critics rejected the notion of a unified Celtic society or ethnicity as based on a spurious elision of language, social structure, technological practice and beliefs (Gwilt 1996; James 1999). La Tène art, once seen as "a 'spir-it' . . . or cultural style" – evidence of a "unity at some level" across north-western Europe (Spriggs, quoted in Megaw and Megaw 1996:177) – was also reassessed in light of inter-regional diversity and variations in use and meaning. In-depth historical studies also revealed how the meaning, use and relevance of the word "Celt" had changed over the last four centuries (Merriman 1987; Collis 2003; Morse 2005).

In order to think differently about the Iron Age itself, archaeologists turned to more subtle ethnographic analogies. Hill (1995b) proposed the Germanic mode of production to describe atomised Iron Age households in Wessex, characterised by control of their own household resources, a model recently enriched by analogies drawn with African segmentary society (Hill 2005). Hingley (1984b) proposed a contrast between the communalistic societies of the Oxford Clay Vales and the individualistic groups of the Uplands, on the basis of differences in settlement enclosure and landscape management. In the Highlands and Islands, brochs have been reinterpreted as the residences of powerful households (Hingley 1995) or elites (Sharples and Parker Pearson 1997), using monumental architecture as both a symbol of status and a setting for activities which reproduced social differentiation, such as feasting (Parker Pearson et al. 1996; Sharples 2003; but see Armit 1997).

Settlement studies have been complemented by a re-evaluation of funerary prac-tice, which acknowledges that it is the living who bury the dead. Wealth or prestige cannot be read directly from grave goods, which might be gifts from mourners re-negotiating their own status, regalia associated with particular kinds of performance or funerary paraphernalia which need to be taken out of circulation (Parker Pearson 1999). Nor can social roles be inferred from the treatment of the body (which in the Iron Age includes excarnation, cremation, inhumation and deposition in bogs), since this may vary on a regional basis and in response to different kinds of death, including human sacrifice (Aldhouse-Green 2002).

In summary, the model of the Celtic chiefdom which had characterised Iron Age community and society was based on an uncritical use of historical sources, and the reification of these analytical constructs, represented as underlying social reality. This approach to identity failed to explain how society was reproduced, since it treated cultural traditions as prior to the existence of individuals who both shaped, and were shaped by, such customs (Ingold 1996:114). Yet archaeologists do not observe society in the past: rather, they recognise regularities and differences in the patterning of material residues – over time and space – which are the historically specific conditions of different lives (Barrett 1994). The key problem with the normative accounts outlined in this section are that they tended to treat social rela-tions as extrinsic to society or community, rather than being the sinews which bound people in collective action. It was to the importance of social reproduction and the embodied constitution of identity through practice that Iron Age studies now turned.

Rethinking Identity: Symbolic Approaches

From the 1970s, social scientists began to focus on the importance of physical and symbolic boundaries in the construction of identity. Frederick Barth (1969:10) argued that ethnicity could not be mapped onto cultural similarities observed by external analysts, as its meaning derived from "categories of ascription and identification by the actors themselves". Since ethnicity had to be self-ascribed, as well as externally recognised, Barth (1969:15) argued that analysis should focus on the boundaries which defined identity rather than the "cultural stuff" which it enclosed, since it was here that the people became aware of their difference from others. Other theorists explored how symbolism enabled unity to be maintained across variations in meaning, understanding and practice (Cohen 1985), in the reproduction of "imagined communities" (Anderson 1983) bound together by social memory and ritual (Connerton 1989).

These ideas were used by archaeologists to explore and critique those who invoked common Celtic roots for present political ends, both the powerful who attempted to legitimise European unity (Megaw and Megaw 1992; James 1999) and the politically or economically marginalised who sought a sense of external difference and internal solidarity (Piccini 1999).

Coupled with sociological studies of how senses of belonging and place were generated, these approaches also encouraged an appreciation of Iron Age social space as both the medium and outcome of social relations. Richard Hingley (1984a) pointed to the "social significance" of acts of enclosure, which isolated and defined an interior, incorporated space, from an exterior "other". Building on this idea, Bowden and McOmish (1987; 1989) challenged the traditional view of hill forts as defensive monuments, arguing that their ramparts and ditches were symbols of display and prestige, used to reproduce the status and power of social groups. Shoulder-to-shoulder gang work helped constitute a sense of belonging and affiliation, monumentalised in ditch segments or episodes of rebuilding. The use of differently coloured or textured building materials from areas in the surrounding landscape symbolised families coming together in acts which constructed communities as well as places (Lock et al. 2005). Such events provided a pattern of cooperation for other practices as well as the context in which new forms of authority and leadership could arise. Whilst some hill forts were associated with seasonal or occasional aggregation, the permanent inhabitation of others meant that the sense of community was closely linked with these locales (Sharples 1991). The dependencies and obligations bound up in generations of repair to earth, timber and stone might be drawn upon in conflict mediation, but could also mask asymmetries in power (Barrett et al. 2000).

Agency and Embodiment

In the 1990s, some archaeologists moved beyond symbolic approaches to the construction of community to explore the role of human agency in social reproduction. They were influenced by Giddens's (1984) "structuration theory", which argued that history emerges in the duality which unites the actions of agents with the reproduction of structural conditions in their world. Agency (defined as the *capability* to do things) is both constrained and enabled by the conditions of everyday life. Social transformation occurs through the action of knowledgeable agents, who both make their own history and are made by those self-same historical conditions. Importantly, agency has no existence outside of the relationships into which it is thrown and emplaced (Ingold 2004). People are therefore habitually disposed towards particular ways of understanding the world and acting within it, a phenomena described by Pierre Bourdieu (1977) as *habitus* in his "theory of practice". Durable principles of practice are deeply embodied at an early age in habituated postures, gestures and ways of moving. Categories and aspects of identity such as gender materialise through people's reiterative performances (Butler 1993). However, because people bring their memories of the past to bear upon their desires for the future, change can come about either through intentional action, or the unintended consequences of their work.

Barrett et al.'s (2000:318) phenomenological analysis and interpretation of South Cadbury hill fort was informed by structuration theory and the theory of practice. It explored the inhabitation and transformation of the site over time from the scale of the human body and the perspective of its eyes. Through identifying how the hill fort constrained and enabled practices such as feeding, clothing and even wounding, they traced the emergence of historically specific social bodies, whose sense of place was learned alongside their skills, roles and capacities, their debts and obligations within the hill fort community.

Looking Ahead: Concepts of Relational Identity

How might Iron Age studies of identity develop over the next few years? Many of the above accounts present individual human beings as bounded and singular entities or universal bodies, thereby perpetuating modern, Western concepts of selfhood (see Brück 2004). In contrast, scholars of earlier prehistory now frequently draw upon models of dividual, fractal, permeable or partible personhood, based on analogies with India, Melanesia and the Classical Maya (see Fowler 2004 for summary). The anthropologist Ingold (2004) explores people as a locus of growth, development and enskillment: dynamic embodiments of a whole history of interactions, which shape their life course and inculcate them into particular "ways of being human". This notion of *relational* personhood should prove useful for Iron Age studies, since it suggests that identity is constituted in terms of people's interpersonal connections; literally, it is people's relationships which make them what they are (Brück 2004). From her analysis of Early Bronze Age mortuary rites, Brück argues that this is an appropriate way to understand the role of grave goods; not as direct possessions or status symbols, but as objects which allow mourners to comment metaphorically on their relations with the dead. Breaking down the boundaries between people, objects, animals and even places, social agents are seen as nodes in the flow of relationships, embodied in substances and gifts. For Brück, identity is not an inherited or fixed quality: personhood emerges *in* fields of relations, through properties and capacities exhibited in social engagements.

Many archaeologists have begun to approach identity as an ongoing *process*: always partial and provisional, changing hue or character according to what one was doing, where and with whom. Shifting contextually and contingently, people performed multiple roles relating to age, gender, kin, skill and status, which should challenge the "Celtic" stereotypes reviewed above. This should force us to pay closer attention to the visceral aspects of sociality: the emotional valence and micropolitics of relations (see Amit 2002). Relational approaches have also made archaeologists more cautious about the notion of the "knowledgeable agent" at the heart of Barrett's work. Knowledge, and therefore power, is unequally distributed amongst people, and can be disabled or rendered unintelligible in various ways (Berggren 2000). Within the Iron Age, evidence of both deliberate human sacrifice and the paraphernalia and representations relating to slavery remind us forcefully of this point (Aldhouse-Green 2002; 2004). More subtle studies of interpersonal violence, informed by ethnographic analogy, would therefore be welcome. Studies of power in the Iron Age might also begin to grasp that "big man" style leadership or chieftainship is not an attribute of individual authority but is socially sanctioned and reproduced (see Clay 1992). Not even death seals the picture: there is always the possibility of a "post-mortem" revision of identity (Jenkins 1996:4).

Iron Age notions of personhood may also have been grounded in broader cycles of reproduction. We therefore need to be concerned with how specific technologies might have given rise to new metaphorical understandings. Barrett (1989) suggests an increased emphasis on agriculture may have led to analogies between the life and death of things, and the fertility of people, stock and land. In Wessex, human remains are deposited amongst domestic material once dismissed as rubbish. Hingley (1990) and Hill (1995a) argue instead that these deposits were structured by cosmological principles, drawing on a symbolic universe orientated around the agricultural cycle of life and death. The bodies of people, animals and objects were transformed into new sources of fertility through their decay. Meanwhile, Richard Hingley (1997) has argued that the transformative properties of smithing were used to reinforce boundaries and thresholds, through the deliberate deposition of ironwork or its residues at places associated with transition.

Objects can also be studied as particular technologies of the self which produced certain kinds of social body (Thomas 1989; after Foucault 1984 and Mauss 1973). Several authors have suggested that by the Late Iron Age the individual was performed and displayed in ways which were different from earlier periods. Regional variations in fibulae may have been used as markers of social or political affiliation, as well as of gender and age, which could be read by people defined less by kinship and face-to-face relations during this period (Jundi and Hill 1998). Changing concepts of personal hygiene and appearance are suggested by rising numbers of toilet sets which include tweezers, ear-scoop and points, as well as razors (Hill 1997). Body painting, tattooing and scarification may have been additional ways of expressing affiliations, evidenced in awls, cosmetic pestle-and-mortar sets, botanical remains and facial designs on contemporary coinage (Carr 2005). Creighton (2000) has argued that the faces and names of tribal leaders and client kings on coins helped presence their authority in a period of social flux, extending their spatial and temporal reach and transforming people's experience of power. Other personal objects and items of dress have been reinterpreted in light of their oral and visual affect on the viewer. Head-dresses, staffs, mirrors and spoons, may have been part of a person's identity, or had identities of their own which were drawn upon in performances such as augury and rites of passage, or to intervene with powerful ancestors or spirits (Fitzpatrick 1997; Aldhouse-Green and Aldhouse-Green 2005). Imported objects or those made with exotic substances would also have evoked people's relationships with distant, powerful or even otherworldly places.

Iron Age landscapes, with their distinctive architecture of earthworks or embanked enclosures, trackways, roundhouses and monuments, were the arenas in which encounters between the local and the distant, and the present and the past, were negotiated (Barrett and Fewster 2000). Ingold's (1993) concept of the taskscape has led to a renewed interest in patterns of everyday Iron Age life which move beyond the experimental archaeology of the 1960s (e.g., Reynolds 1979). Through this approach, particular kinds of landscape can be explored as the outcome of intertwined rhythms of agriculture, human biography, stock lineage, construction histories and object lives (Barrett and Fewster 2000:31).

Different environments and patterns of subsistence gave people's relations with place a particular tenor or hue. For example, the later prehistoric "hydraulic communities" of Cambridgeshire were distinguished by their subtle water management regimes (Evans 1997). In different areas, groups were characterised by their long-term inhabitation of a specific settlement or seasonal/periodic aggregation and dispersal, leading to qualitatively different relations between people, place and cohabitants. Chadwick (2004) has suggested that analogies between cattle and people – kine and kin – may have arisen through the close bonds generated in diurnal and seasonal herding patterns, amongst the south Yorkshire and north Nottinghamshire brickwork field systems. Iron Age studies should therefore be richly placed to explore the "rollcall and rhythm of routine" through which different conceptions of personhood and scales of community were generated (Edmonds 1999).

However, some studies of identity in prehistory have recently been caught up in debates over the use of scientific techniques which focus on the identification of geographic origin (investigated through diet and physical growth, using isotope analysis) or genetic affiliation (using non-metric traits or DNA analysis). Though they have yet to be used on Iron Age assemblages, within Bronze Age studies they have suggested that we have underestimated social mobility or even migration amongst prehistoric communities (Fitzpatrick 2002). Though promising, these results are observations which require careful interpretation. Archaeologists must be wary of any universal approach to identity founded in genetic or geographic essentialism, which takes no account of inhabitation, or of the reproduction of social relationships.

Conclusion

This chapter has reviewed changes in the way in which identity was approached and understood, by archaeologists working on the Iron Age, between the nineteenth and twenty-first centuries. It has highlighted how analysis went hand in hand with methodological advances and analytical techniques, as well as conceptual developments in anthropology and sociology, which have influenced archaeological thought.

Antiquaries sought identity in the physiognomic features distinct to each race, which they believed were wedded to the stage of civilisation reached by later prehistoric populations. Culture historians preferred to find it in the stylistic traditions and traits by which groups could be identified and distinguished, in time and space. Both relied heavily on the classical historians' accounts of north-western Europe during the Late Iron Age and early Roman period, accepting invasion as a natural force of historic change. However, systematic survey and excavation in the second half of the twentieth century altered the face of later prehistoric research. Confronted with regional diversity and complexity, archaeologists made society and social organisation their focus, resurrecting evolutionary narratives, reinforced with ethnographic analogies. Augmented by systems theory, they sought to explain continuity or change in human populations through the influence of environmental and economic factors. However, towards the end of the century, post-processualists criticised the reification of society and rejected both grand narratives of progress and determinist models of change. Theoretical approaches focused instead on how the conditions of social life were reproduced through the practice of human agents, as they constructed a sense of personhood and belonging. Landscape and material culture studies have focused on relations between people, animals, places and things, inspired by radically different models of personhood drawn from ethnography. These have challenged universalist concepts of humanity. Finally, new techniques are now available to investigate aspects of geographic and biological origin, whose potential has yet to be determined in Iron Age studies.

This review reminds us that Iron Age lives are constructed through our interpretation as much as through our observations, for it is here that we conjure a sense of what it meant to be human in the past. At the very least, we should be capable of exploring later prehistoric people as "living, experiencing, thinking, affectively engaged human beings who follow . . . (in varying degrees and a myriad of manners) particular lifeways" (Rapport and Overing 2000:96). However, as the discussion of Celtic identity has shown, we should also be able to explore how *we* are constituted in part through this engagement with the past, and how it challenges and transforms our own sense of identity and place in the world.

REFERENCES

Aldhouse-Green, M., 2002 Dying for the Gods: human sacrifice in Iron Age and Roman Europe. Stroud: Tempus.

——2004 Chaining and shaming: images of defeat, from Lyn Cerrig Bach to Sarmitzegetusa. Oxford Journal of Archaeology 23(3):319–340.

——and S. Aldhouse-Green, 2005 The Quest for the Shaman. London: Thames and Hudson.

Amit, V., 2002 Reconceptualizing community. In Realizing Community. V. Amit, ed. pp. 1–20. London: Routledge.

Anderson, B. 1983 Imagined Communities: reflections on the origin and spread of nationalism. London and New York: Verso.

Armit, I., 1997 Architecture and the household: a response to Sharples and Parker Pearson. In Reconstructing Iron Age Societies. A. Gwilt and C. Haselgrove, eds. pp. 266–269. Oxford: Oxbow Books.

Augstein, H. F., 1999 James Cowles Pritchard's Anthropology: remaking the science of man in early nineteenth century Britain. Amsterdam: Rodopi.

Barrett, J. C., 1989 Food, gender and metal: questions of social reproduction. In The Bronze Age–Iron Age Transitions in Europe: aspects of continuity and change in European societies c.1200 to 500 B.C. M. L. Sørensen and R. Thomas, eds. pp. 304–320. Oxford: British Archaeological Reports.

——1994 Fragments from Antiquity. Oxford: Blackwell.

——and K. Fewster, 2000 Intimacy and structural transformation (with a comment by L. McFadyen). In Philosophy and Archaeological Practice. C. Holtorf and H. Karlsson, eds. pp. 25–38. Göteborg: Bricoleur Press.

——P. W. M. Freeman and A. Woodward, 2000 Cadbury Castle, Somerset: the later prehistoric and early historic archaeology. London: English Heritage

Barth, F., ed. 1969 Ethnic Groups and Boundaries: the social organisation of cultural difference. London: Allen and Unwin.

Bauman, Z., 1992 Soil, blood and identity. Sociological Review 40(4):675–701.

Berggren, K., 2000 The Knowledge-Able Agent? On the paradoxes of power. In Philosophy and Archaeological Practice. C. Holtorf and H. Karlsson, eds. pp. 39–51. Gothenburg: Bricoleur Press.

Bersu, G., 1940 Excavations at Little Woodbury, Wiltshire. Part 1: The settlement as revealed by excavation. Proceedings of the Prehistoric Society 6:30–111.

Bevan, Bill, ed., 1999 Northern Exposure: interpretive devolution and the Iron Ages in Britain. Leicester: University of Leicester School of Archaeological Studies.

Blair Gibson, D., 1995 Chiefdoms, confederacies, and statehood in early Ireland. In Celtic Chiefdom, Celtic State. B. Arnold and D. Blair Gibson, eds. pp. 116–128. Cambridge: Cambridge University Press.

Boas, F., 1911 The Mind of Primitive Man. New York: Macmillan.

Bourdieu, Pierre, 1977 Outline for a Theory of Practice. Cambridge: Cambridge University Press.

Bowden, M., and D. McOmish, 1987 The required barrier. Scottish Archaeological Review 4:76–84.

——and——1989 Little Boxes: more about hillforts. Scottish Archaeological Review 6: 12–16.

Bowler, P., 1989 The Invention of Progress: the Victorians and their past. Oxford: Blackwell.

Brück, J., 2004 Material metaphors: the relational construction of identity in Early Bronze Age burials in Ireland and Britain. Journal of Social Archaeology 4(3):307–333.

Butler, J., 1993 Bodies that Matter: on the discursive limits of sex. New York and London: Routledge.

Carr, G., 2005 Woad, tattooing and identity in later Iron Age and early Roman Britain. Oxford Journal of Archaeology 24(3):273–292.

Chadwick, A., 2004 Trackways, Hooves and Memory-Days: human and animal memories and movements around the Iron Age and Romano-British rural landscapes of the English north midlands. Paper delivered at TAG 2004, Glasgow.

Champion, T., and S. Champion, 1986 Peer polity interaction in the European Iron Age. In Peer Polity Interaction and Socio-Political Change. C. Renfrew and J. Cherry, eds. pp. 59–68. Cambridge: Cambridge University Press.

Childe, V. G., 1929 The Danube in Prehistory. Oxford: Clarendon Press.

Clark, J. G. D., 1966 The invasion hypothesis in British archaeology. Antiquity 40:172–189.

——1968 Response to C. F. C. Hawkes. Notes and News: response to "British Prehistory: the invasion hypothesis". Antiquity 40:298–299.

Clarke, D. L., 1968 Analytical Archaeology. Methuen: London.

Clay, B., 1992 Other times, other places: agency and the Big Man in Central New Ireland. Man n.s. 27:719–733.

Cohen, A., 1985 The Symbolic Construction of Community. London: Routledge.

Collis, J. R., 1981 A theoretical study of hill-forts. In Hill-Fort Studies: papers presented to A. H. A. Hogg. G. Guilbert, ed. pp. 66–76. Leicester: Leicester University Press.

——1994 Reconstructing Iron Age Society. In Europe in the First Millennium B.C. K. Kristiansen and J. Jensen, eds. pp. 31–39. Sheffield: J. R. Collis.

——2003 The Celts: origins, myths and inventions. Stroud: Tempus.

Connerton, P., 1989 How Societies Remember. Cambridge: Cambridge University Press.

Crawford, O. G. S. 1921 Man and his Past. London: Oxford University Press.

Creighton, J., 2000 Coins and Power in Late Iron Age Britain. Cambridge: Cambridge University Press.

Cunliffe, B., 1978 Iron Age Communities in Britain, 1st edn. London: Routledge.

——1983 Danebury: anatomy of an Iron Age hillfort. London: Batsford.

——1995 Danebury, vol. 6: a hillfort community in perspective. London: Council for British Archaeology.

——1997 The Ancient Celts. Oxford: Oxford University Press.

——2000 The Danebury Environs Programme: the prehistory of a Wessex landscape, vol. 1: Introduction. Oxford: English Heritage and Oxford University Committee for Archaeology.

Davis, J. B., and J. Thurnam, 1865 Crania Britannica: delineations and descriptions of the skulls of the aboriginal and early inhabitants of the British Islands. London: printed for the subscribers.

Durkheim, E., 1938 The Rules of Sociological Method. New York: Free Press.

Earle, T., 1978 Economic and Social Organisation of a Complex Chiefdom: the Halelea District, Kaua'I, Hawaii. Ann Arbor: Department of Anthropology, University of Michigan.

Edmonds, M., 1999 Ancestral Geographies of the Neolithic. London: Routledge.

Evans, C., 1997 Hydraulic communities: Iron Age enclosure in the East Anglia fenlands. In Reconstructing Iron Age Societies. A. Gwilt and C. Haselgrove, eds. pp. 216–227. Oxford: Oxbow Books.

Fabian, J., 1983 Time and the Other: how anthropology makes its object. New York: Columbia University Press.

Fitzpatrick, A., 1997 Who were the Druids? London: Weidenfeld and Nicholson.

——2002 "The Amesbury Archer": a well-furnished early Bronze Age burial in southern England. Antiquity 76:629–630.

Foucault, M., 1972 The Archaeology of Knowledge. London: Routledge.

——1984 The Care of the Self: the history of sexuality, vol. 3. London: Penguin.

Fowler, C., 2004 The Archaeology of Personhood. London: Routledge.

Fox, C., 1923 The Archaeology of the Cambridge Region. Cambridge: Cambridge University Press.

Frankenstein, S., and M. J. Rowlands, 1978 Early Iron Age society in southwest Germany. Bulletin of the Institute of Archaeology 15:73–112.

Fried, M. H. 1967 The Evolution of Political Society: an essay in political economy. New York: Random House.

Giddens, A., 1984 The Constitution of Society: outline of the theory of Structuration. Cambridge: Polity Press.

Gosden, C., 1985 Gifts and kin in Early Iron Age Europe. Man n.s. 20:475–493.

——1999 Archaeology and Anthropology: a changing relationship. London: Routledge.

Greenwell, W., 1906 Early Iron Age burials in Yorkshire. Archaeologia 60:251–324.

Gwilt, A., 1996 Ageing structures and shifting ideologies. Antiquity 70:699–702.

——and C. Haselgrove, eds. 1997. Reconstructing Iron Age Societies. Oxford: Oxbow Books.

Harding, D. W., 1970 The "New" Iron Age. Current Archaeology 20:235–240.

——2005 The Iron Age in Northern Britain: Celts and Romans, natives and invaders. London: Routledge.

Hawkes, C., 1931 Hill-forts. Antiquity 5:60–97.

——1959 The ABC of the British Iron Age. Antiquity 33:170–182.

——1968 Notes and news: response to "British Prehistory: the invasion hypothesis". Antiquity 40:297–298.

Hides, S., 1996 The genealogy of material culture and cultural identity. In Cultural Identity and Archaeology: the construction of European communities. P. Graves-Brown, S. Jones and C. Gamble, eds. pp. 25–47. London: Routledge.

Hill, J. D., 1995a Ritual and Rubbish in the Iron Age of Wessex. Oxford: British Archaeological Reports.

——1995b How should we understand Iron Age societies and hillforts? A contextual study from southern Britain. In Different Iron Ages: studies on the Iron Age in temperate Europe. J. D. Hill and C. Cumberpatch, eds. pp. 45–66. Oxford: British Archaeological Reports.

——1995c The pre-Roman Iron Age in Britain and Ireland (ca. 800 BC to AD 100): an overview. Journal of World Prehistory 9(1):47–98.

——1997 "The end of one kind of body and the beginning of another kind of body"? Toilet instruments and "Romanization" in southern England during the first century. In Reconstructing Iron Age Societies. A. Gwilt and C. Haselgrove, eds. pp. 96–107. Oxford: Oxbow Books.

——2005 Are we any closer to understanding how later Iron Age Societies worked? Paper delivered to the Iron Age Research Workshop Round Table, Cambridge University, June 2005.

Hingley, R., 1984a The archaeology of settlement and the social significance of space. Scottish Archaeological Review 3:22–27.

——1984b Towards social analysis in archaeology: Celtic society in the Iron Age of the Upper Thames Valley (400–0 BC). In Aspects of the Iron Age in Southern Britain.

B. Cunliffe and D. Miles, eds. pp. 72–88. Oxford: University of Oxford Committee for Archaeology.

—— 1990 Iron Age "Currency Bars": the archaeological and social context. Archaeological Journal 147:91–117.

—— 1995 The Iron Age in Atlantic Scotland: searching for the meaning of the substantial house. *In* Different Iron Ages: studies on the Iron Age in temperate Europe. J. D. Hill and C. Cumberpatch, eds. pp. 185–194. Oxford: British Archaeological Reports.

—— 1997 Iron, ironworking and regeneration: a study of the symbolic meaning of metalworking in Iron Age Britain. *In* Reconstructing Iron Age Societies. A. Gwilt and C. Haselgrove, eds. pp. 9–18. Oxford: Oxbow Books.

Hodson, F. R., 1960 Reflections on "The ABC of the British Iron Age". Antiquity 34: 138–140.

—— 1964 Cultural grouping within the British pre-Roman Iron Age. Proceedings of the Prehistoric Society 30:99–110.

Ingold, T., 1993 The temporality of landscape. World Archaeology 25(2):152–174.

—— 1994 Introduction to culture. *In* Companion Encyclopaedia of Anthropology: humanity, culture and social life. T. Ingold, ed. pp. 329–349. London and New York: Routledge.

—— ed., 1996, 1990 debate: human worlds are culturally constructed. *In* Key Debates in Anthropology. T. Ingold, ed. pp. 99–146. London: Routledge.

—— 2004 Beyond biology and culture: the meaning of evolution in a relational world. Social Anthropology 12(2):209–226.

Jackson, K. H., 1964 The Oldest Irish Tradition: a window onto the Iron Age. Cambridge: Cambridge University Press.

James, S., 1993 Exploring the World of the Celts. London: Thames and Hudson.

—— 1999 The Atlantic Celts: ancient people or modern invention? London: British Museum Press.

Jenkins, R., 1996 Social Identity. London: Routledge.

Jones, S., 1997 The Archaeology of Ethnicity. London: Routledge.

Jundi, S., and J. D. Hill, 1998 Brooches and identities in first century AD Britain: more than meets the eye? *In* TRAC97: Proceedings of the Seventh Annual Theoretical Roman Conference, Nottingham 1997. C. Forcey, J. Hawthorne and R. Witcher, eds. pp. 125–137. Oxford: Oxbow Books.

Kemble, J., 1863 Horae Ferales; or, Studies in the Archaeology of the Northern Nations. R. G. Latham and A. W. Franks, eds. London: Lowell Read.

Lock, G., C. Gosden and P. Daly, 2005 Segsbury Camp: excavations in 1996 and 1997 at an Iron Age hillfort on the Oxfordshire Ridgeway. Oxford: Oxford University School of Archaeology.

Lubbock, J., 1865 Prehistoric Times, as Illustrated by Ancient Remains, and the Manners and Customs of Modern Savages. London: Williams and Norgate.

Mauss, M., 1973 Techniques of the body. Economy and Society 2:70–88.

Megaw, R., and V. Megaw, 1992 The Celts: the first Europeans? Antiquity 66:254–260.

—— and —— 1996 Ancient Celts and modern ethnicity. Antiquity 70:175–181.

Merriman, N. J., 1987 Value and motivation in pre-history: the evidence for "Celtic spirit". *In* The Archaeology of Contextual Meanings. I. Hodder, ed. pp. 111–116. Cambridge: Cambridge University Press.

Morse, M., 2005 How the Celts Came to Britain: druids, skulls and the birth of archaeology. Stroud: Tempus.

Mortimer, J. R., 1905 Forty Years' Researches in British and Saxon burial mounds of East Yorkshire. London: Dent.

Moscati, S., O. H. Frey, V. Kruta, B. Raftery and M. Szabó, eds., 1991 The Celts. London: Rizzoli.

Parker Pearson, M., 1999 The Archaeology of Death and Burial. Stroud: Sutton.

——J. Mulville and N. Sharples, 1996 Brochs and Iron Age society: a reappraisal. Antiquity 70:57–67.

Payne, A., 1996 The use of magnetic prospection in the exploration of Iron Age hillfort interiors in southern England. Archaeological Prospection 3:163–184.

——M. Corney and B. Cunliffe, 2006 The Wessex Hillforts Project. London: English Heritage.

Piccini, A., 1999 "Good to think": social constructions of Celtic heritage in Wales. Environment and Planning D: Society and Space 17:705–721.

Raftery, B., 1994 Pagan Celtic Ireland: the enigma of the Irish Iron Age. London: Thames and Hudson.

Rapport, N., and J. Overing, 2000 Social and Cultural Anthropology: the key concepts. London: Routledge.

Reynolds, P., 1979 Iron Age Farm: the Butser experiment. London: British Museum.

Rowlands, M., 1986 Modernist fantasises in prehistory? Man n.s. 21:745–746.

——1987 The concept of Europe in prehistory. Man n.s. 22:558–559.

Sahlins, M., and E. E. Service, 1960 Evolution and Culture. Ann Arbor: University of Michigan Press.

Sharples, N., 1991 Maiden Castle. London: English Heritage.

——2003 From monuments to artefacts: changing social relationships in the later Iron Age. In Sea Change: Orkney and northern Europe in the later Iron Age AD 300–800. J. Downes and A. Ritchie, eds. pp. 151–165. Balgavies, Angus: Pinkfoot Press.

——and M. Parker Pearson, 1997 Why were brochs built? Recent studies in the Iron Age of Atlantic Scotland. In Reconstructing Iron Age Societies. A. Gwilt and C. Haselgrove, eds. pp. 254–265. Oxford: Oxbow Books.

Thomas, J., 1989 The technologies of the self and the constitution of the subject. Archaeological Review from Cambridge 8:101–107.

Toennies, F., 1957 [1887] Community and Society. New York: Harper.

Trigger, B., 1978 Time and Tradition: essays in archaeological interpretation. Edinburgh: Edinburgh University Press.

——1989 A History of Archaeological Thought. Cambridge: Cambridge University Press.

Tylor, E. B., 1871 Primitive Culture: researches into the development of mythology, philosophy, religion, art, and custom. London: John Murray.

Webster, J., 1996 Ethnographic barbarity: imperialist discourse and the archaeology of "Celtic" society'. In Roman Imperialism: post-colonial perspectives. J. Webster and N. Cooper, eds. pp. 111–123. Leicester: Leicester University Press.

Wells, P., 2001 Beyond Celts, Germans and Scythians. London: Duckworth.

Williams, R., 1983 Keywords: a vocabulary of culture and society. London: Flamingo.

Worsaae, J. J. A., 1847 An account of the formation of the Museum at Copenhagen, and general remarks on the classification of antiquities found in the north and west of Europe. Proceedings of the Royal Irish Academy 3:310–315, 327–344.

Index

Page numbers in *italic* denote illustrations and tables.

Cadbury Castle, 11, 262, 281, 289, 301, 302, 342
Cae Gwyn, *23*
Cairnderry, 154
Cairnholy, 78, 154
Cairnpapple, *141*
cairns, 184, 188, 189
  Bronze Age, 153
  cairnfields, 204, 274–6
  clearance, 204, 274–6
  ring, 188, 276
  round, 136, 184
Caisteal nan Gillean, 249
Caldey Island, 93
Callanish, 5
Callis Wold, 79
Callow Hill, *24*
Cambridgeshire, 334
Camden, William, 3
Campbell, G., 234
Campbell, John, 18
Cannabis sativa, 298
Cannon Hill, 80
Carding Mill Bay, 66
Carn Ban, 138, *138*
Carrowmore, 78
Case, Humphrey, 63, 205
Casterley, 217
Castle Menzies, 79
Castlerigg, *141*, 151
Cat Hole, *23*, 30, *43*
cats, 230, 231
cattle, 59, 63, 67, 70–1, 74, 95, 97, 98, 99, 105, 108, 109, 110, 226, 229, 230, 236, 238–9, 261, 270, 312, 344
  Anatolian origin, 70
  bones, 64, 101
  burial, 257, 281
  head and hooves deposits, 110–11
  herd structure, 228
  herding, 168
  skulls, *101*, 108, 110–11, 195, 239
  special treatment, 110–11
Caulfield, Seamus, 98
Cavalli-Sforza, Luca, 59–60
caves, 18
Céide Fields (Behy/Glenulra), 70, 98, 207, 210, 212
Celtic society, 338–40, *338*
Celts, 331–2
central place theory, 122, 123–4, 339
ceramic (*see also* pottery),
  characterization, 292
  petrology, 291–4, *293*
  provenancing, 292
  research, 288–9
  technology, 59, 76–7, 288–306
cereals, 58, 59, 63, 71–2, 94–5, 203, 205, 210, 229, 250
  barley, 94, 229
  chaff, 226
  oats, 272

processing, 226
rye, 272
sowing, 226
wheat, 94, 229
Chadwick, Adrian, 344
chaîne opératoire, 162–6, 172, 318
  techno-psychological, 163
  techno-sociological, 163–4
chalkland, *206*, 214, 283
chariots, 229
  burials, 239
Charlton Down, 208
Charmy Down, 211
Charnwood Forest, 294
Chasséen, 76
Chasséo-Michelsberg, 76
Chatterton, R., 171
Cheddar Gorge (*see also* Gough's Cave and Sun Hole), 37, 40–1, 42
cheese, 105
Chelm's Coombe, *24*, 49
chiefdoms, 146, 179
  Celtic, 338–40
  Scottish, 5
Childe, Gordon, 59, 333
children, 164, 166, 305
  burials, 182
Chippenham, 252
Christianity, 8
chronologies, 14
Church Hole (Creswell Crags), 19, *23*, 37–8, *41*, 42, *43*, 44, 47
  engraved images, 38, *39*, *40*
Cirque de la Patrie, 30
cists, 188
Clactonian, 161
Cladh Hallan, 226, 228, 240
Claish, 79, 94
Clandon Barrow, 142
Clark, Grahame, 62, 122, 125, 170, 288, 334–6
Clarke, David, 123, 124, 298, 300, 337
Classical texts, 11, 337, 338
Clava cairns, 11
Cleal, Rosamund, 75, 294
Cleveland Dykes, 294
climate, 203, 278–80
climatic change, 21–2, 218
cloth, 258, 298
  production, 258
clothing, 31–2, 38, 41
Clwyd, 207
Cnip, 226
Cnoc Coig, 66, 91, 93, 103
Co. Mayo, 215
coffins, 179, 188
cognition, 13, 163–4
coinage, 8
Coldrum, 78
Coles, Bryony, 6
colonial processes, 331